Judgment under uncertainty:
Heuristics and biases

Judgment under uncertainty: Heuristics and biases

Edited by

Daniel Kahneman
University of British Columbia

Paul Slovic
Decision Research
A Branch of Perceptronics, Inc.
Eugene, Oregon

Amos Tversky
Stanford University

Cambridge University Press

Cambridge
London   New York   New Rochelle
Melbourne   Sydney

Published by the Press Syndicate of the University of Cambridge
The Pitt Building, Trumpington Street, Cambridge CB2 1RP
32 East 57th Street, New York, NY 10022, USA
296 Beaconsfield Parade, Middle Park, Melbourne 3206, Australia

First published 1982
Reprinted 1982, 1983 (Twice)

Printed in the United States of America

Library of Congress Cataloging in Publication Data
Main entry under title:
Judgment under uncertainty.
Bibliography: p.
Includes index.
1. Judgment. I. Kahneman, Daniel, 1934–
II. Slovic, Paul, 1938–   III. Tversky,
Amos.
BF441.J8   153.4'6   81-10042
ISBN 0 521 24064 6 hard covers   AACR2
ISBN 0 521 28414 7 paperback

Contents

Contributors

*Marc Alpert   *Graduate School of Business Administration, Harvard University*
Teresa M. Amabile   *Department of Psychology, Brandeis University*
Craig A. Anderson   *Department of Psychology, Stanford University*
Maya Bar-Hillel   *Department of Psychology, The Hebrew University, Jerusalem*
Eugene Borgida   *Department of Psychology, University of Minnesota*
Jean Chapman   *Department of Psychology, University of Wisconsin*
Loren J. Chapman   *Department of Psychology, University of Wisconsin*
*E. I. Chesnick   *Department of Psychology, University of Manchester, England*
John Cohen   *Department of Psychology, University of Manchester, England*
Rick Crandall   *University of Illinois, Champaign-Urbana*
Robyn M. Dawes   *Department of Psychology, University of Oregon*
David M. Eddy   *Center for the Study of Health and Clinical Policy, Duke University*
Ward Edwards   *Social Science Research Institute, University of Southern California*
Hillel J. Einhorn   *Center for Decision Research, University of Chicago*
Baruch Fischhoff   *Decision Research, A Branch of Perceptronics, Inc., Eugene, Oregon*
Geoffrey T. Fong   *Institute for Social Research, University of Michigan*
Charles F. Gettys   *Department of Psychology, University of Oklahoma*
*D. Haran   *Department of Psychology, University of Manchester, England*
Dennis L. Jennings   *Department of Psychology, New York University*
Christopher Jepson   *Institute for Social Research, University of Michigan*
Daniel Kahneman   *Department of Psychology, University of British Columbia*
Clinton Kelly III   *Advanced Research Projects Agency, Arlington, Virginia*
David H. Krantz   *Bell Laboratories, Murray Hill, New Jersey*
Ellen J. Langer   *Department of Psychology, Harvard University*

*Asterisk indicates affiliation when article was originally published.

Sarah Lichtenstein   *Decision Research, A Branch of Perceptronics, Inc., Eugene, Oregon*

Richard E. Nisbett   *Institute for Social Research, University of Michigan*

Stuart Oskamp   *Department of Psychology, Claremont Graduate School*

Cameron R. Peterson   *Decisions & Designs, Inc., McLean, Virginia*

Lawrence D. Phillips   *Decision Analysis Unit, Brunel University*

Howard Raiffa   *Graduate School of Business Administration, Harvard University*

Harvey Reed   *Department of Psychology, University of Michigan at Dearborn*

Lee Ross   *Department of Psychology, Stanford University*

Michael Ross   *Department of Psychology, University of Waterloo, Ontario*

Fiore Sicoly   *Department of Psychology, University of Waterloo, Ontario*

Max Singer   *Hudson Institute, Arlington, Virginia*

Paul Slovic   *Decision Research, A Branch of Perceptronics, Inc., Eugene, Oregon*

Shelley E. Taylor   *Department of Psychology, University of California, Los Angeles*

Yaacov Trope   *Department of Psychology, The Hebrew University, Jerusalem*

Amos Tversky   *Department of Psychology, Stanford University*

Preface

The approach to the study of judgment that this book represents had origins in three lines of research that developed in the 1950s and 1960s: the comparison of clinical and statistical prediction, initiated by Paul Meehl; the study of subjective probability in the Bayesian paradigm, introduced to psychology by Ward Edwards; and the investigation of heuristics and strategies of reasoning, for which Herbert Simon offered a program and Jerome Bruner an example. Our collection also represents the recent convergence of the study of judgment with another strand of psychological research: the study of causal attribution and lay psychological interpretation, pioneered by Fritz Heider.

Meehl's classic book, published in 1954, summarized evidence for the conclusion that simple linear combinations of cues outdo the intuitive judgments of experts in predicting significant behavioral criteria. The lasting intellectual legacy of this work, and of the furious controversy that followed it, was probably not the demonstration that clinicians performed poorly in tasks that, as Meehl noted, they should not have undertaken. Rather, it was the demonstration of a substantial discrepancy between the objective record of people's success in prediction tasks and the sincere beliefs of these people about the quality of their performance. This conclusion was not restricted to clinicians or to clinical prediction: People's impressions of how they reason, and of how well they reason, could not be taken at face value. Perhaps because students of clinical judgment often used themselves and their friends as subjects, the interpretation of errors and biases tended to be cognitive, rather than psychodynamic: Illusions, not delusions, were the model.

With the introduction of Bayesian ideas into psychological research by Edwards and his associates, psychologists were offered for the first time a fully articulated model of optimal performance under uncertainty, with which human judgments could be compared. The matching of human judgments to normative models was to become one of the major paradigms of research on judgment under uncertainty. Inevitably, it led to concerns with the biases to which inductive inferences are prone and the methods that could be used to correct them. These concerns are reflected in most of the selections in the present volume. However, much of the early work used the normative model to explain human performance and introduced separate processes to explain departures from optimality. In contrast, research on judgmental heuristics seeks to explain both correct and erroneous judgments in terms of the same psychological processes.

The emergence of the new paradigm of cognitive psychology had a profound influence on judgment research. Cognitive psychology is concerned with internal processes, mental limitations, and the way in which the processes are shaped by the limitations. Early examples of conceptual and empirical work in this vein were the study of strategies of thinking by Bruner and his associates, and Simon's treatment of heuristics of reasoning and of bounded rationality. Bruner and Simon were both concerned with strategies of simplification that reduce the complexity of judgment tasks, to make them tractable for the kind of mind that people happen to have. Much of the work that we have included in this book was motivated by the same concerns.

In recent years, a large body of research has been devoted to uncovering judgmental heuristics and exploring their effects. The present volume provides a comprehensive sample of this approach. It assembles new reviews, written especially for this collection, and previously published articles on judgment and inference. Although the boundary between judgment and decision making is not always clear, we have focused here on judgment rather than on choice. The topic of decision making is important enough to be the subject of a separate volume.

The book is organized in ten parts. The first part contains an early review of heuristics and biases of intuitive judgments. Part II deals specifically with the representativeness heuristic, which is extended, in Part III, to problems of causal attribution. Part IV describes the availability heuristic and its role in social judgment. Part V covers the perception and learning of covariation and illustrates the presence of illusory correlations in the judgments of lay people and experts. Part VI discusses the calibration of probability assessors and documents the prevalent phenomenon of overconfidence in prediction and explanation. Biases associated with multistage inference are covered in Part VII. Part VIII reviews formal and informal procedures for correcting and improving intuitive judgments. Part IX summarizes work on the effects of judgmental biases in a specific area of concern, the perception of risk. The final part includes some current thoughts on several conceptual and methodological issues that pertain to the study of heuristics and biases.

For convenience, all references are assembled in a single list at the end of the book. Numbers in boldface refer to material included in the book, identifying the chapter in which that material appears. We have used ellipses (. . .) to indicate where we have deleted material from previously published articles.

Our work in preparing this book was supported by Office of Naval Research Grant N00014-79-C-0077 to Stanford University and by Office of Naval Research Contract N0014-80-C-0150 to Decision Research.

We wish to thank Peggy Roecker, Nancy Collins, Gerry Hanson, and Don MacGregor for their help in the preparation of this book.

Daniel Kahneman
Paul Slovic
Amos Tversky

Part I

Introduction

1.   Judgment under uncertainty: Heuristics and biases

Amos Tversky and Daniel Kahneman

Many decisions are based on beliefs concerning the likelihood of uncertain events such as the outcome of an election, the guilt of a defendant, or the future value of the dollar. These beliefs are usually expressed in statements such as "I think that . . . ," "chances are . . . ," "it is unlikely that . . . ," and so forth. Occasionally, beliefs concerning uncertain events are expressed in numerical form as odds or subjective probabilities. What determines such beliefs? How do people assess the probability of an uncertain event or the value of an uncertain quantity? This article shows that people rely on a limited number of heuristic principles which reduce the complex tasks of assessing probabilities and predicting values to simpler judgmental operations. In general, these heuristics are quite useful, but sometimes they lead to severe and systematic errors.

The subjective assessment of probability resembles the subjective assessment of physical quantities such as distance or size. These judgments are all based on data of limited validity, which are processed according to heuristic rules. For example, the apparent distance of an object is determined in part by its clarity. The more sharply the object is seen, the closer it appears to be. This rule has some validity, because in any given scene the more distant objects are seen less sharply than nearer objects. However, the reliance on this rule leads to systematic errors in the estimation of distance. Specifically, distances are often overestimated when visibility is poor because the contours of objects are blurred. On the other hand, distances are often underestimated when visibility is good because the objects are seen sharply. Thus, the reliance on clarity as an indication of distance leads to common biases. Such biases are also found in the intuitive judgment of probability. This article describes three heuristics

This chapter originally appeared in *Science*, 1974, *185*, 1124–1131. Copyright © 1974 by the American Association for the Advancement of Science. Reprinted by permission.

that are employed to assess probabilities and to predict values. Biases to which these heuristics lead are enumerated, and the applied and theoretical implications of these observations are discussed.

Representativeness

Many of the probabilistic questions with which people are concerned belong to one of the following types: What is the probability that object A belongs to class B? What is the probability that event A originates from process B? What is the probability that process B will generate event A? In answering such questions, people typically rely on the representativeness heuristic, in which probabilities are evaluated by the degree to which A is representative of B, that is, by the degree to which A resembles B. For example, when A is highly representative of B, the probability that A originates from B is judged to be high. On the other hand, if A is not similar to B, the probability that A originates from B is judged to be low.

For an illustration of judgment by representativeness, consider an individual who has been described by a former neighbor as follows: "Steve is very shy and withdrawn, invariably helpful, but with little interest in people, or in the world of reality. A meek and tidy soul, he has a need for order and structure, and a passion for detail." How do people assess the probability that Steve is engaged in a particular occupation from a list of possibilities (for example, farmer, salesman, airline pilot, librarian, or physician)? How do people order these occupations from most to least likely? In the representativeness heuristic, the probability that Steve is a librarian, for example, is assessed by the degree to which he is representative of, or similar to, the stereotype of a librarian. Indeed, research with problems of this type has shown that people order the occupations by probability and by similarity in exactly the same way (Kahneman & Tversky, 1973, 4). This approach to the judgment of probability leads to serious errors, because similarity, or representativeness, is not influenced by several factors that should affect judgments of probability.

Insensitivity to prior probability of outcomes

One of the factors that have no effect on representativeness but should have a major effect on probability is the prior probability, or base-rate frequency, of the outcomes. In the case of Steve, for example, the fact that there are many more farmers than librarians in the population should enter into any reasonable estimate of the probability that Steve is a librarian rather than a farmer. Considerations of base-rate frequency, however, do not affect the similarity of Steve to the stereotypes of librarians and farmers. If people evaluate probability by representativeness, therefore, prior probabilities will be neglected. This hypothesis was tested in an experiment where prior probabilities were manipulated

(Kahneman & Tversky, 1973, 4). Subjects were shown brief personality descriptions of several individuals, allegedly sampled at random from a group of 100 professionals – engineers and lawyers. The subjects were asked to assess, for each description, the probability that it belonged to an engineer rather than to a lawyer. In one experimental condition, subjects were told that the group from which the descriptions had been drawn consisted of 70 engineers and 30 lawyers. In another condition, subjects were told that the group consisted of 30 engineers and 70 lawyers. The odds that any particular description belongs to an engineer rather than to a lawyer should be higher in the first condition, where there is a majority of engineers, than in the second condition, where there is a majority of lawyers. Specifically, it can be shown by applying Bayes' rule that the ratio of these odds should be $(.7/.3)^2$, or 5.44, for each description. In a sharp violation of Bayes' rule, the subjects in the two conditions produced essentially the same probability judgments. Apparently, subjects evaluated the likelihood that a particular description belonged to an engineer rather than to a lawyer by the degree to which this description was representative of the two stereotypes, with little or no regard for the prior probabilities of the categories.

The subjects used prior probabilities correctly when they had no other information. In the absence of a personality sketch, they judged the probability that an unknown individual is an engineer to be .7 and .3, respectively, in the two base-rate conditions. However, prior probabilities were effectively ignored when a description was introduced, even when this description was totally uninformative. The responses to the following description illustrate this phenomenon:

Dick is a 30 year old man. He is married with no children. A man of high ability and high motivation, he promises to be quite successful in his field. He is well liked by his colleagues.

This description was intended to convey no information relevant to the question of whether Dick is an engineer or a lawyer. Consequently, the probability that Dick is an engineer should equal the proportion of engineers in the group, as if no description had been given. The subjects, however, judged the probability of Dick being an engineer to be˙.5 regardless of whether the stated proportion of engineers in the group was .7 or .3. Evidently, people respond differently when given no evidence and when given worthless evidence. When no specific evidence is given, prior probabilities are properly utilized; when worthless evidence is given, prior probabilities are ignored (Kahneman & Tversky, 1973, 4).

Insensitivity to sample size

To evaluate the probability of obtaining a particular result in a sample drawn from a specified population, people typically apply the representativeness heuristic. That is, they assess the likelihood of a sample result, for example, that the average height in a random sample of ten men will be 6 feet (180 centimeters), by the similarity of this result to the corresponding parameter (that is, to the average height in the population of men). The similarity of a sample statistic to a population parameter does not depend on the size of the sample. Consequently, if probabilities are assessed by representativeness, then the judged probability of a sample statistic will be essentially independent of sample size. Indeed, when subjects assessed the distributions of average height for samples of various sizes, they produced identical distributions. For example, the probability of obtaining an average height greater than 6 feet was assigned the same value for samples of 1000, 100, and 10 men (Kahneman & Tversky, 1972b, 3). Moreover, subjects failed to appreciate the role of sample size even when it was emphasized in the formulation of the problem. Consider the following question:

A certain town is served by two hospitals. In the larger hospital about 45 babies are born each day, and in the smaller hospital about 15 babies are born each day. As you know, about 50 percent of all babies are boys. However, the exact percentage varies from day to day. Sometimes it may be higher than 50 percent, sometimes lower.

For a period of 1 year, each hospital recorded the days on which more than 60 percent of the babies born were boys. Which hospital do you think recorded more such days?

The larger hospital (21)
The smaller hospital (21)
About the same (that is, within 5 percent of each other) (53)

The values in parentheses are the number of undergraduate students who chose each answer.

Most subjects judged the probability of obtaining more than 60 percent boys to be the same in the small and in the large hospital, presumably because these events are described by the same statistic and are therefore equally representative of the general population. In contrast, sampling theory entails that the expected number of days on which more than 60 percent of the babies are boys is much greater in the small hospital than in the large one, because a large sample is less likely to stray from 50 percent. This fundamental notion of statistics is evidently not part of people's repertoire of intuitions.

A similar insensitivity to sample size has been reported in judgments of posterior probability, that is, of the probability that a sample has been drawn from one population rather than from another. Consider the following example:

Imagine an urn filled with balls, of which ⅔ are of one color and ⅓ of another. One individual has drawn 5 balls from the urn, and found that 4 were red and 1 was white. Another individual has drawn 20 balls and found that 12 were red and 8 were white. Which of the two individuals should feel more confident that the urn contains ⅔ red balls and ⅓ white balls, rather than the opposite? What odds should each individual give?

In this problem, the correct posterior odds are 8 to 1 for the 4:1 sample and 16 to 1 for the 12:8 sample, assuming equal prior probabilities. However, most people feel that the first sample provides much stronger evidence for the hypothesis that the urn is predominantly red, because the proportion of red balls is larger in the first than in the second sample. Here again, intuitive judgments are dominated by the sample proportion and are essentially unaffected by the size of the sample, which plays a crucial role in the determination of the actual posterior odds (Kahneman & Tversky, 1972b). In addition, intuitive estimates of posterior odds are far less extreme than the correct values. The underestimation of the impact of evidence has been observed repeatedly in problems of this type (W. Edwards, 1968, 25; Slovic & Lichtenstein, 1971). It has been labeled "conservatism."

Misconceptions of chance

People expect that a sequence of events generated by a random process will represent the essential characteristics of that process even when the sequence is short. In considering tosses of a coin for heads or tails, for example, people regard the sequence H-T-H-T-T-H to be more likely than the sequence H-H-H-T-T-T, which does not appear random, and also more likely than the sequence H-H-H-H-T-H, which does not represent the fairness of the coin (Kahneman & Tversky, 1972b, 3). Thus, people expect that the essential characteristics of the process will be represented, not only globally in the entire sequence, but also locally in each of its parts. A locally representative sequence, however, deviates systematically from chance expectation: it contains too many alternations and too few runs. Another consequence of the belief in local representativeness is the well-known gambler's fallacy. After observing a long run of red on the roulette wheel, for example, most people erroneously believe that black is now due, presumably because the occurence of black will result in a more representative sequence than the occurrence of an additional red. Chance is commonly viewed as a self-correcting process in which a deviation in one direction induces a deviation in the opposite direction to restore the equilibrium. In fact, deviations are not "corrected" as a chance process unfolds, they are merely diluted.

Misconceptions of chance are not limited to naive subjects. A study of the statistical intuitions of experienced research psychologists (Tversky & Kahneman, 1971, 2) revealed a lingering belief in what may be called the "law of small numbers," according to which even small samples are highly representative of the populations from which they are drawn. The responses of these investigators reflected the expectation that a valid hypothesis about a population will be represented by a statistically significant result in a sample – with little regard for its size. As a consequence, the researchers put too much faith in the results of small samples and grossly overestimated the replicability of such results. In the actual conduct of research, this bias leads to the selection of samples of inadequate size and to overinterpretation of findings.

Insensitivity to predictability

People are sometimes called upon to make such numerical predictions as the future value of a stock, the demand for a commodity, or the outcome of a football game. Such predictions are often made by representativeness. For example, suppose one is given a description of a company and is asked to predict its future profit. If the description of the company is very favorable, a very high profit will appear most representative of that description; if the description is mediocre, a mediocre performance will appear most representative. The degree to which the description is favorable is unaffected by the reliability of that description or by the degree to which it permits accurate prediction. Hence, if people predict solely in terms of the favorableness of the description, their predictions will be insensitive to the reliability of the evidence and to the expected accuracy of the prediction.

This mode of judgment violates the normative statistical theory in which the extremeness and the range of predictions are controlled by considerations of predictability. When predictability is nil, the same prediction should be made in all cases. For example, if the descriptions of companies provide no information relevant to profit, then the same value (such as average profit) should be predicted for all companies. If predictability is perfect, of course, the values predicted will match the actual values and the range of predictions will equal the range of outcomes. In general, the higher the predictability, the wider the range of predicted values.

Several studies of numerical prediction have demonstrated that intuitive predictions violate this rule, and that subjects show little or no regard for considerations of predictability (Kahneman & Tversky, 1973, 4). In one of these studies, subjects were presented with several paragraphs, each describing the performance of a student teacher during a particular practice lesson. Some subjects were asked to *evaluate* the quality of the lesson described in the paragraph in percentile scores, relative to a specified population. Other subjects were asked to *predict*, also in percentile scores, the standing of each student teacher 5 years after the practice lesson. The judgments made under the two conditions were identical. That is, the prediction of a remote criterion (success of a teacher after 5 years) was identical to the evaluation of the information on which the prediction was based (the quality of the practice lesson). The students who made these predictions were undoubtedly aware of the limited predictability of teaching competence on the basis of a single trial lesson 5 years earlier; nevertheless, their predictions were as extreme as their evaluations.

The illusion of validity

As we have seen, people often predict by selecting the outcome (for example, an occupation) that is most representative of the input (for example, the description of a person). The confidence they have in their prediction depends primarily on the degree of representativeness (that is, on the quality of the match between the selected outcome and the input) with little or no regard for the factors that limit predictive accuracy. Thus, people express great confidence in the prediction that a person is a librarian when given a description of his personality which matches the stereotype of librarians, even if the description is scanty, unreliable, or outdated. The unwarranted confidence which is produced by a good fit between the predicted outcome and the input information may be called the illusion of validity. This illusion persists even when the judge is aware of the factors that limit the accuracy of his predictions. It is a common observation that psychologists who conduct selection interviews often experience considerable confidence in their predictions, even when they know of the vast literature that shows selection interviews to be highly fallible. The continued reliance on the clinical interview for selection, despite repeated demonstrations of its inadequacy, amply attests to the strength of this effect.

The internal consistency of a pattern of inputs is a major determinant of one's confidence in predictions based on these inputs. For example, people express more confidence in predicting the final grade-point average of a student whose first-year record consists entirely of B's than in predicting the grade-point average of a student whose first-year record includes many A's and C's. Highly consistent patterns are most often observed when the input variables are highly redundant or correlated. Hence, people tend to have great confidence in predictions based on redundant input variables. However, an elementary result in the statistics of correlation asserts that, given input variables of stated validity, a prediction based on several such inputs can achieve higher accuracy when they are independent of each other than when they are redundant or correlated. Thus, redundancy among inputs decreases accuracy even as it increases confidence, and people are often confident in predictions that are quite likely to be off the mark (Kahneman & Tversky, 1973, 4).

Misconceptions of regression

Suppose a large group of children has been examined on two equivalent versions of an aptitude test. If one selects ten children from among those who did best on one of the two versions, he will usually find their performance on the second version to be somewhat disappointing. Conversely, if one selects ten children from among those who did worst on one version, they will be found, on the average, to do somewhat better on the other version. More generally, consider two variables X and Y which have the same distribution. If one selects individuals whose average X score deviates from the mean of X by k units, then the average of their Y scores will usually deviate from the mean of Y by less than k units. These observations illustrate a general phenomenon known as regression toward the mean, which was first documented by Galton more than 100 years ago.

In the normal course of life, one encounters many instances of regression toward the mean, in the comparison of the height of fathers and sons, of the intelligence of husbands and wives, or of the performance of individuals on consecutive examinations. Nevertheless, people do not develop correct intuitions about this phenomenon. First, they do not expect regression in many contexts where it is bound to occur. Second, when they recognize the occurrence of regression, they often invent spurious causal explanations for it (Kahneman & Tversky, 1973, 4). We suggest that the phenomenon of regression remains elusive because it is incompatible with the belief that the predicted outcome should be maximally representative of the input, and, hence, that the value of the outcome variable should be as extreme as the value of the input variable.

The failure to recognize the import of regression can have pernicious consequences, as illustrated by the following observation (Kahneman & Tversky, 1973, 4). In a discussion of flight training, experienced instructors noted that praise for an exceptionally smooth landing is typically followed by a poorer landing on the next try, while harsh criticism after a rough landing is usually followed by an improvement on the next try. The instructors concluded that verbal rewards are detrimental to learning, while verbal punishments are beneficial, contrary to accepted psychological doctrine. This conclusion is unwarranted because of the presence of regression toward the mean. As in other cases of repeated examination, an improvement will usually follow a poor performance and a deterioration will usually follow an outstanding performance, even if the instructor does not respond to the trainee's achievement on the first attempt. Because the instructors had praised their trainees after good landings and admonished them after poor ones, they reached the erroneous and potentially harmful conclusion that punishment is more effective than reward.

Thus, the failure to understand the effect of regression leads one to overestimate the effectiveness of punishment and to underestimate the effectiveness of reward. In social interaction, as well as in training, rewards are typically administered when performance is good, and punishments are typically administered when performance is poor. By regression alone, therefore, behavior is most likely to improve after punishment and most likely to deteriorate after reward. Consequently, the human condition is such that, by chance alone, one is most often rewarded for punishing others and most often punished for rewarding them. People are generally not aware of this contingency. In fact, the elusive role of regression in determining the apparent consequences of reward and punishment seems to have escaped the notice of students of this area.

Availability

There are situations in which people assess the frequency of a class or the probability of an event by the ease with which instances or occurrences can be brought to mind. For example, one may assess the risk of heart attack among middle-aged people by recalling such occurrences among one's acquaintances. Similarly, one may evaluate the probability that a given business venture will fail by imagining various difficulties it could encounter. This judgmental heuristic is called availability. Availability is a useful clue for assessing frequency or probability, because instances of large classes are usually reached better and faster than instances of less frequent classes. However, availability is affected by factors other than frequency and probability. Consequently, the reliance on availability leads to predictable biases, some of which are illustrated below.

Biases due to the retrievability of instances

When the size of a class is judged by the availability of its instances, a class whose instances are easily retrieved will appear more numerous than a class of equal frequency whose instances are less retrievable. In an elementary demonstration of this effect, subjects heard a list of well-known personalities of both sexes and were subsequently asked to judge whether the list contained more names of men than of women. Different lists were presented to different groups of subjects. In some of the lists the men were relatively more famous than the women, and in others the women were relatively more famous than the men. In each of the lists, the subjects erroneously judged that the class (sex) that had the more famous personalities was the more numerous (Tversky & Kahneman, 1973, 11).

In addition to familiarity, there are other factors, such as salience, which affect the retrievability of instances. For example, the impact of seeing a house burning on the subjective probability of such accidents is probably greater than the impact of reading about a fire in the local paper. Furthermore, recent occurrences are likely to be relatively more available than earlier occurrences. It is a common experience that the subjective probability of traffic accidents rises temporarily when one sees a car overturned by the side of the road.

Biases due to the effectiveness of a search set

Suppose one samples a word (of three letters or more) at random from an English text. Is it more likely that the word starts with *r* or that *r* is the third letter? People approach this problem by recalling words that begin with *r* (road) and words that have *r* in the third position (car) and assess the relative frequency by the ease with which words of the two types come to mind. Because it is much easier to search for words by their first letter than by their third letter, most people judge words that begin with a given consonant to be more numerous than words in which the same consonant appears in the third position. They do so even for consonants, such as *r* or *k*, that are more frequent in the third position than in the first (Tversky & Kahneman, 1973, **11**).

Different tasks elicit different search sets. For example, suppose you are asked to rate the frequency with which abstract words (*thought, love*) and concrete words (*door, water*) appear in written English. A natural way to answer this question is to search for contexts in which the word could appear. It seems easier to think of contexts in which an abstract concept is mentioned (*love* in love stories) than to think of contexts in which a concrete word (such as *door*) is mentioned. If the frequency of words is judged by the availability of the contexts in which they appear, abstract words will be judged as relatively more numerous than concrete words. This bias has been observed in a recent study (Galbraith & Underwood, 1973) which showed that the judged frequency of occurrence of abstract words was much higher than that of concrete words, equated in objective frequency. Abstract words were also judged to appear in a much greater variety of contexts than concrete words.

Biases of imaginability

Sometimes one has to assess the frequency of a class whose instances are not stored in memory but can be generated according to a given rule. In such situations, one typically generates several instances and evaluates frequency or probability by the ease with which the relevant instances can be constructed. However, the ease of constructing instances does not always reflect their actual frequency, and this mode of evaluation is prone to biases. To illustrate, consider a group of 10 people who form committees of k members, $2 \le k \le 8$. How many different committees of k members can be formed? The correct answer to this problem is given by the binomial coefficient $\binom{10}{k}$ which reaches a maximum of 252 for $k = 5$. Clearly, the number of committees of k members equals the number of committees of $(10 - k)$ members, because any committee of k members defines a unique group of $(10 - k)$ nonmembers.

One way to answer this question without computation is to mentally construct committees of k members and to evaluate their number by the ease with which they come to mind. Committees of few members, say 2, are more available than committees of many members, say 8. The simplest scheme for the construction of committees is a partition of the group into disjoint sets. One readily sees that it is easy to construct five disjoint committees of 2 members, while it is impossible to generate even two disjoint committees of 8 members. Consequently, if frequency is assessed by imaginability, or by availability for construction, the small committees will appear more numerous than larger committees, in contrast to the correct bell-shaped function. Indeed, when naive subjects were asked to estimate the number of distinct committees of various sizes, their estimates were a decreasing monotonic function of committee size (Tversky & Kahneman, 1973, 11). For example, the median estimate of the number of committees of 2 members was 70, while the estimate for committees of 8 members was 20 (the correct answer is 45 in both cases).

Imaginability plays an important role in the evaluation of probabilities in real-life situations. The risk involved in an adventurous expedition, for example, is evaluated by imagining contingencies with which the expedition is not equipped to cope. If many such difficulties are vividly portrayed, the expedition can be made to appear exceedingly dangerous, although the ease with which disasters are imagined need not reflect their actual likelihood. Conversely, the risk involved in an undertaking may be grossly underestimated if some possible dangers are either difficult to conceive of, or simply do not come to mind.

Illusory correlation

Chapman and Chapman (1969) have described an interesting bias in the judgment of the frequency with which two events co-occur. They presented naive judges with information concerning several hypothetical mental patients. The data for each patient consisted of a clinical diagnosis and a drawing of a person made by the patient. Later the judges estimated the frequency with which each diagnosis (such as paranoia or suspiciousness) had been accompanied by various features of the drawing (such as peculiar eyes). The subjects markedly overestimated the frequency of co-occurrence of natural associates, such as suspiciousness and peculiar eyes. This effect was labeled illusory correlation. In their erroneous judgments of the data to which they had been exposed, naive subjects "rediscovered" much of the common, but unfounded, clinical lore concerning the interpretation of the draw-a-person test. The illusory correlation effect was extremely resistant to contradictory data. It persisted even when the correlation between symptom and diagnosis was actually negative, and it prevented the judges from detecting relationships that were in fact present.

Availability provides a natural account for the illusory-correlation effect. The judgment of how frequently two events co-occur could be based on the strength of the associative bond between them. When the association is strong, one is likely to conclude that the events have been frequently paired. Consequently, strong associates will be judged to have occurred together frequently. According to this view, the illusory correlation between suspiciousness and peculiar drawing of the eyes, for example, is due to the fact that suspiciousness is more readily associated with the eyes than with any other part of the body.

Lifelong experience has taught us that, in general, instances of large classes are recalled better and faster than instances of less frequent classes; that likely occurrences are easier to imagine than unlikely ones; and that the associative connections between events are strengthened when the events frequently co-occur. As a result, man has at his disposal a procedure (the availability heuristic) for estimating the numerosity of a class, the likelihood of an event, or the frequency of co-occurrences, by the ease with which the relevant mental operations of retrieval, construction, or association can be performed. However, as the preceding examples have demonstrated, this valuable estimation procedure results in systematic errors.

Adjustment and anchoring

In many situations, people make estimates by starting from an initial value that is adjusted to yield the final answer. The initial value, or starting point, may be suggested by the formulation of the problem, or it may be the result of a partial computation. In either case, adjustments are typically insufficient (Slovic & Lichtenstein, 1971). That is, different starting points yield different estimates, which are biased toward the initial values. We call this phenomenon anchoring.

Insufficient adjustment

In a demonstration of the anchoring effect, subjects were asked to estimate various quantities, stated in percentages (for example, the percentage of African countries in the United Nations). For each quantity, a number between 0 and 100 was determined by spinning a wheel of fortune in the subjects' presence. The subjects were instructed to indicate first whether that number was higher or lower than the value of the quantity, and then to estimate the value of the quantity by moving upward or downward from the given number. Different groups were given different numbers for each quantity, and these arbitrary numbers had a marked effect on estimates. For example, the median estimates of the percentage of African countries in the United Nations were 25 and 45 for groups that received 10 and 65, respectively, as starting points. Payoffs for accuracy did not reduce the anchoring effect.

Anchoring occurs not only when the starting point is given to the subject, but also when the subject bases his estimate on the result of some incomplete computation. A study of intuitive numerical estimation illustrates this effect. Two groups of high school students estimated, within 5 seconds, a numerical expression that was written on the blackboard. One group estimated the product

$$8 \times 7 \times 6 \times 5 \times 4 \times 3 \times 2 \times 1$$

while another group estimated the product

$$1 \times 2 \times 3 \times 4 \times 5 \times 6 \times 7 \times 8$$

To rapidly answer such questions, people may perform a few steps of computation and estimate the product by extrapolation or adjustment. Because adjustments are typically insufficient, this procedure should lead to underestimation. Furthermore, because the result of the first few steps of multiplication (performed from left to right) is higher in the descending sequence than in the ascending sequence, the former expression should be judged larger than the latter. Both predictions were confirmed. The median estimate for the ascending sequence was 512, while the median estimate for the descending sequence was 2,250. The correct answer is 40,320.

Biases in the evaluation of conjunctive and disjunctive events

In a recent study by Bar-Hillel (1973) subjects were given the opportunity to bet on one of two events. Three types of events were used: (i) simple events, such as drawing a red marble from a bag containing 50 percent red marbles and 50 percent white marbles; (ii) conjunctive events, such as drawing a red marble seven times in succession, with replacement, from a bag containing 90 percent red marbles and 10 percent white marbles; and (iii) disjunctive events, such as drawing a red marble at least once in seven successive tries, with replacement, from a bag containing 10 percent red marbles and 90 percent white marbles. In this problem, a significant majority of subjects preferred to bet on the conjunctive event (the probability of which is .48) rather than on the simple event (the probability of which is .50). Subjects also preferred to bet on the simple event rather than on the disjunctive event, which has a probability of .52. Thus, most subjects bet on the less likely event in both comparisons. This pattern of choices illustrates a general finding. Studies of choice among gambles and of judgments of probability indicate that people tend to overestimate the probability of conjunctive events (Cohen, Chesnick, & Haran, 1972, 24) and to underestimate the probability of disjunctive events. These biases are readily explained as effects of anchoring. The stated probability of the elementary event (success at any one stage) provides a natural starting point for the estimation of the probabilities of both conjunctive and disjunctive events. Since adjustment from the starting point is typically insufficient, the final estimates remain too close to the probabilities of the elementary events in both cases. Note that the overall probability of a conjunctive event is lower than the probability of each elementary event, whereas the overall probability of a disjunctive event is higher than the probability of each elementary event. As a consequence of anchoring, the overall probability will be overestimated in conjunctive problems and underestimated in disjunctive problems.

Biases in the evaluation of compound events are particularly significant in the context of planning. The successful completion of an undertaking, such as the development of a new product, typically has a conjunctive character: for the undertaking to succeed, each of a series of events must occur. Even when each of these events is very likely, the overall probability of success can be quite low if the number of events is large. The general tendency to overestimate the probability of conjunctive events leads to unwarranted optimism in the evaluation of the likelihood that a plan will succeed or that a project will be completed on time. Conversely, disjunctive structures are typically encountered in the evaluation of risks. A complex system, such as a nuclear reactor or a human body, will malfunction if any of its essential components fails. Even when the likelihood of failure in each component is slight, the probability of an overall failure can be high if many components are involved. Because of anchoring, people will tend to underestimate the probabilities of failure in complex systems. Thus, the direction of the anchoring bias can sometimes be inferred from the structure of the event. The chain-like structure of conjunctions leads to overestimation, the funnel-like structure of disjunctions leads to underestimation.

Anchoring in the assessment of subjective probability distributions

In decision analysis, experts are often required to express their beliefs about a quantity, such as the value of the Dow-Jones average on a particular day, in the form of a probability distribution. Such a distribution is usually constructed by asking the person to select values of the quantity that correspond to specified percentiles of his subjective probability distribution. For example, the judge may be asked to select a number, X_{90}, such that his subjective probability that this number will be higher than the value of the Dow-Jones average is .90. That is, he should select the value X_{90} so that he is just willing to accept 9 to 1 odds that the Dow-Jones average will not exceed it. A subjective probability distribution for the value of the Dow-Jones average can be constructed from several such judgments corresponding to different percentiles.

By collecting subjective probability distributions for many different quantities, it is possible to test the judge for proper calibration. A judge is properly (or externally) calibrated in a set of problems if exactly Π percent of the true values of the assessed quantities falls below his stated values of

X_{II}. For example, the true values should fall below X_{01} for 1 percent of the quantities and above X_{99} for 1 percent of the quantities. Thus, the true values should fall in the confidence interval between X_{01} and X_{99} on 98 percent of the problems.

Several investigators (Alpert & Raiffa, 1969, 21; Staël von Holstein, 1971b; Winkler, 1967) have obtained probability disruptions for many quantities from a large number of judges. These distributions indicated large and systematic departures from proper calibration. In most studies, the actual values of the assessed quantities are either smaller than X_{01} or greater than X_{99} for about 30 percent of the problems. That is, the subjects state overly narrow confidence intervals which reflect more certainty than is justified by their knowledge about the assessed quantities. This bias is common to naive and to sophisticated subjects, and it is not eliminated by introducing proper scoring rules, which provide incentives for external calibration. This effect is attributable, in part at least, to anchoring.

To select X_{90} for the value of the Dow-Jones average, for example, it is natural to begin by thinking about one's best estimate of the Dow-Jones and to adjust this value upward. If this adjustment – like most others – is insufficient, then X_{90} will not be sufficiently extreme. A similar anchoring effect will occur in the selection of X_{10}, which is presumably obtained by adjusting one's best estimate downward. Consequently, the confidence interval between X_{10} and X_{90} will be too narrow, and the assessed probability distribution will be too tight. In support of this interpretation it can be shown that subjective probabilities are systematically altered by a procedure in which one's best estimate does not serve as an anchor.

Subjective probability distributions for a given quantity (the Dow-Jones average) can be obtained in two different ways: (i) by asking the subject to select values of the Dow-Jones that correspond to specified percentiles of his probability distribution and (ii) by asking the subject to assess the probabilities that the true value of the Dow-Jones will exceed some specified values. The two procedures are formally equivalent and should yield identical distributions. However, they suggest different modes of adjustment from different anchors. In procedure (i), the natural starting point is one's best estimate of the quality. In procedure (ii), on the other hand, the subject may be anchored on the value stated in the question. Alternatively, he may be anchored on even odds, or 50–50 chances, which is a natural starting point in the estimation of likelihood. In either case, procedure (ii) should yield less extreme odds than procedure (i).

To contrast the two procedures, a set of 24 quantities (such as the air distance from New Delhi to Peking) was presented to a group of subjects who assessed either X_{10} or X_{90} for each problem. Another group of subjects received the median judgment of the first group for each of the 24 quantities. They were asked to assess the odds that each of the given values exceeded the true value of the relevant quantity. In the absence of any bias, the second group should retrieve the odds specified to the first group, that is, 9:1. However, if even odds or the stated value serve as anchors, the odds of the second group should be less extreme, that is, closer to 1:1. Indeed, the median odds stated by this group, across all problems, were 3:1. When the judgments of the two groups were tested for external calibration, it was found that subjects in the first group were too extreme, in accord with earlier studies. The events that they defined as having a probability of .10 actually obtained in 24 percent of the cases. In contrast, subjects in the second group were too conservative. Events to which they assigned an average probability of .34 actually obtained in 26 percent of the cases. These results illustrate the manner in which the degree of calibration depends on the procedure of elicitation.

Discussion

This article has been concerned with cognitive biases that stem from the reliance on judgmental heuristics. These biases are not attributable to motivational effects such as wishful thinking or the distortion of judgments by payoffs and penalties. Indeed, several of the severe errors of judgment reported earlier occurred despite the fact that subjects were encouraged to be accurate and were rewarded for the correct answers (Kahneman & Tversky, 1972b, 3; Tversky & Kahneman, 1973, 11).

The reliance on heuristics and the prevalence of biases are not restricted to laymen. Experienced researchers are also prone to the same biases – when they think intuitively. For example, the tendency to predict the outcome that best represents the data, with insufficient regard for prior probability, has been observed in the intuitive judgments of individuals who have had extensive training in statistics (Kahneman & Tversky, 1973, 4; Tversky & Kahneman, 1971, 2). Although the statistically sophisticated avoid elementary errors, such as the gambler's fallacy, their intuitive judgments are liable to similar fallacies in more intricate and less transparent problems.

It is not surprising that useful heuristics such as representativeness and availability are retained, even though they occasionally lead to errors in prediction or estimation. What is perhaps surprising is the failure of people to infer from lifelong experience such fundamental statistical rules as regression toward the mean, or the effect of sample size on sampling variability. Although everyone is exposed, in the normal course of life, to numerous examples from which these rules could have been induced, very few people discover the principles of sampling and regression on their own. Statistical principles are not learned from everyday experience because the relevant instances are not coded appropriately. For example, people do not discover that successive lines in a text differ more in average word length than do successive pages, because they simply do not attend to the average word length of individual lines or pages. Thus, people do not learn the relation between sample size and sampling variability, although the data for such learning are abundant.

The lack of an appropriate code also explains why people usually do not detect the biases in their judgments of probability. A person could conceivably learn whether his judgments are externally calibrated by keeping a tally of the proportion of events that actually occur among those to which he assigns the same probability. However, it is not natural to group events by their judged probability. In the absence of such grouping it is impossible for an individual to discover, for example, that only 50 percent of the predictions to which he has assigned a probability of .9 or higher actually come true.

The empirical analysis of cognitive biases has implications for the theoretical and applied role of judged probabilities. Modern decision theory (de Finetti, 1968; Savage, 1954) regards subjective probability as the quantified opinion of an idealized person. Specifically, the subjective probability of a given event is defined by the set of bets about this event that such a person is willing to accept. An internally consistent, or coherent, subjective probability measure can be derived for an individual if his choices among bets satisfy certain principles, that is, the axioms of the theory. The derived probability is subjective in the sense that different individuals are allowed to have different probabilities for the same event. The major contribution of this approach is that it provides a rigorous subjective interpretation of probability that is applicable to unique events and is embedded in a general theory of rational decision.

It should perhaps be noted that, while subjective probabilities can sometimes be inferred from preferences among bets, they are normally not formed in this fashion. A person bets on team A rather than on team B because he believes that team A is more likely to win; he does not infer this belief from his betting preferences. Thus, in reality, subjective probabilities determine preferences among bets and are not derived from them, as in the axiomatic theory of rational decision (Savage, 1954).

The inherently subjective nature of probability has led many students to the belief that coherence, or internal consistency, is the only valid criterion by which judged probabilities should be evaluated. From the standpoint of the formal theory of subjective probability, any set of internally consistent probability judgments is as good as any other. This criterion is not entirely satisfactory, because an internally consistent set of subjective probabilities can be incompatible with other beliefs held by the individual. Consider a person whose subjective probabilities for all possible outcomes of a coin-tossing game reflect the gambler's fallacy. That is, his estimate of the probability of tails on a particular toss increases with the number of consecutive heads that preceded that toss. The judgments of such a person could be internally consistent and therefore acceptable as adequate subjective probabilities according to the criterion of the formal theory. These probabilities, however, are incompatible with the generally held belief that a coin has no memory and is therefore incapable of generating sequential dependencies. For judged probabilities to be considered adequate, or rational, internal consistency is not enough. The judgments must be compatible with the entire web of beliefs held by the individual. Unfortunately, there can be no simple formal procedure for assessing the compatibility of a set of probability judgments with the judge's total system of beliefs. The rational judge will nevertheless strive for compatibility, even though internal consistency is more easily achieved and assessed. In particular, he will attempt to make his probability judgments compatible with his knowledge about the subject matter, the laws of probability, and his own judgmental heuristics and biases.

Summary

This article described three heuristics that are employed in making judgments under uncertainty: (i) representativeness, which is usually employed when people are asked to judge the probability that an object or event A belongs to class or process B; (ii) availability of instances or scenarios, which is often employed when people are asked to assess the frequency of a class or the plausibility of a particular development; and (iii) adjustment from an anchor, which is usually employed in numerical prediction when a relevant value is available. These heuristics are highly economical and usually effective, but they lead to systematic and predictable errors. A better understanding of these heuristics and of the biases to which they lead could improve judgments and decisions in situations of uncertainty.

Part II

Representativeness

2.   Belief in the law of small numbers

Amos Tversky and Daniel Kahneman

"Suppose you have run an experiment on 20 subjects, and have obtained a significant result which confirms your theory ($z = 2.23$, $p < .05$, two-tailed). You now have cause to run an additional group of 10 subjects. What do you think the probability is that the results will be significant, by a one-tailed test, separately for this group?"

If you feel that the probability is somewhere around .85, you may be pleased to know that you belong to a majority group. Indeed, that was the median answer of two small groups who were kind enough to respond to a questionnaire distributed at meetings of the Mathematical Psychology Group and of the American Psychological Association.

On the other hand, if you feel that the probability is around .48, you belong to a minority. Only 9 of our 84 respondents gave answers between .40 and .60. However, .48 happens to be a much more reasonable estimate than .85.[1]

Apparently, most psychologists have an exaggerated belief in the likelihood of successfully replicating an obtained finding. The sources of such

[1] The required estimate can be interpreted in several ways. One possible approach is to follow common research practice, where a value obtained in one study is taken to define a plausible alternative to the null hypothesis. The probability requested in the question can then be interpreted as the power of the second test (i.e., the probability of obtaining a significant result in the second sample) against the alternative hypothesis defined by the result of the first sample. In the special case of a test of a mean with known variance, one would compute the power of the test against the hypothesis that the population mean equals the mean of the first sample. Since the size of the second sample is half that of the first, the computed probability of obtaining $z \geq 1.645$ is only .473. A theoretically more justifiable approach is to interpret the requested probability within a Bayesian framework and compute it relative to some appropriately selected prior distribution. Assuming a uniform prior, the desired posterior probability is .478. Clearly, if the prior distribution favors the null hypothesis, as is often the case, the posterior probability will be even smaller.

This chapter originally appeared in *Psychological Bulletin*, 1971, 2, 105–10. Copyright © 1971 by the American Psychological Association. Reprinted by permission.

beliefs, and their consequences for the conduct of scientific inquiry, are what this paper is about. Our thesis is that people have strong intuitions about random sampling; that these intuitions are wrong in fundamental respects; that these intuitions are shared by naive subjects and by trained scientists; and that they are applied with unfortunate consequences in the course of scientific inquiry.

We submit that people view a sample randomly drawn from a population as highly representative, that is, similar to the population in all essential characteristics. Consequently, they expect any two samples drawn from a particular population to be more similar to one another and to the population than sampling theory predicts, at least for small samples.

The tendency to regard a sample as a representation is manifest in a wide variety of situations. When subjects are instructed to generate a random sequence of hypothetical tosses of a fair coin, for example, they produce sequences where the proportion of heads in any short segment stays far closer to .50 than the laws of chance would predict (Tune, 1964). Thus, each segment of the response sequence is highly representative of the "fairness" of the coin. Similar effects are observed when subjects successively predict events in a randomly generated series, as in probability learning experiments (Estes, 1964) or in other sequential games of chance. Subjects act as if *every* segment of the random sequence must reflect the true proportion: if the sequence has strayed from the population proportion, a corrective bias in the other direction is expected. This has been called the gambler's fallacy.

The heart of the gambler's fallacy is a misconception of the fairness of the laws of chance. The gambler feels that the fairness of the coin entitles him to expect that any deviation in one direction will soon be cancelled by a corresponding deviation in the other. Even the fairest of coins, however, given the limitations of its memory and moral sense, cannot be as fair as the gambler expects it to be. This fallacy is not unique to gamblers. Consider the following example:

The mean IQ of the population of eighth graders in a city is *known* to be 100. You have selected a random sample of 50 children for a study of educational achievements. The first child tested has an IQ of 150. What do you expect the mean IQ to be for the whole sample?

The correct answer is 101. A surprisingly large number of people believe that the expected IQ for the sample is still 100. This expectation can be justified only by the belief that a random process is self-correcting. Idioms such as "errors cancel each other out" reflect the image of an active self-correcting process. Some familiar processes in nature obey such laws: a deviation from a stable equilibrium produces a force that restores the equilibrium. The laws of chance, in contrast, do not work that way: deviations are not canceled as sampling proceeds, they are merely diluted.

Thus far, we have attempted to describe two related intuitions about chance. We proposed a representation hypothesis according to which people believe samples to be very similar to one another and to the population from which they are drawn. We also suggested that people believe sampling to be a self-correcting process. The two beliefs lead to the same consequences. Both generate expectations about characteristics of samples, and the variability of these expectations is less than the true variability, at least for small samples.

The law of large numbers guarantees that very large samples will indeed be highly representative of the population from which they are drawn. If, in addition, a self-corrective tendency is at work, then small samples should also be highly representative and similar to one another. People's intuitions about random sampling appear to satisfy the law of small numbers, which asserts that the law of large numbers applies to small numbers as well.

Consider a hypothetical scientist who lives by the law of small numbers. How would his belief affect his scientific work? Assume our scientist studies phenomena whose magnitude is small relative to uncontrolled variability, that is, the signal-to-noise ratio in the messages he receives from nature is low. Our scientist could be a meteorologist, a pharmacologist, or perhaps a psychologist.

If he believes in the law of small numbers, the scientist will have exaggerated confidence in the validity of conclusions based on small samples. To illustrate, suppose he is engaged in studying which of two toys infants will prefer to play with. Of the first five infants studied, four have shown a preference for the same toy. Many a psychologist will feel some confidence at this point, that the null hypothesis of no preference is false. Fortunately, such a conviction is not a sufficient condition for journal publication, although it may do for a book. By a quick computation, our psychologist will discover that the probability of a result as extreme as the one obtained is as high as $\frac{3}{8}$ under the null hypothesis.

To be sure, the application of statistical hypothesis testing to scientific inference is beset with serious difficulties. Nevertheless, the computation of significance levels (or likelihood ratios, as a Bayesian might prefer) forces the scientist to evaluate the obtained effect in terms of a *valid* estimate of sampling variance rather than in terms of his subjective biased estimate. Statistical tests, therefore, protect the scientific community against overly hasty rejections of the null hypothesis (i.e., Type I error) by policing its many members who would rather live by the law of small numbers. On the other hand, there are no comparable safeguards against the risk of failing to confirm a valid research hypothesis (i.e., Type II error).

Imagine a psychologist who studies the correlation between need for achievement and grades. When deciding on sample size, he may reason as follows: "What correlation do I expect? $r = .35$. What N do I need to make the result significant? (Looks at table.) $N = 33$. Fine, that's my sample."

The only flaw in this reasoning is that our psychologist has forgotten about sampling variation, possibly because he believes that any sample must be highly representative of its population. However, if his guess about the correlation in the population is correct, the correlation in the sample is about as likely to lie below or above .35. Hence, the likelihood of obtaining a significant result (i.e., the power of the test) for $N = 33$ is about .50.

In a detailed investigation of statistical power, J. Cohen (1962, 1969) has provided plausible definitions of large, medium, and small effects and an extensive set of computational aids to the estimation of power for a variety of statistical tests. In the normal test for a difference between two means, for example, a difference of $.25\sigma$ is small, a difference of $.50\sigma$ is medium, and a difference of 1σ is large, according to the proposed definitions. The mean IQ difference between clerical and semiskilled workers is a medium effect. In an ingenious study of research practice, J. Cohen (1962) reviewed all the statistical analyses published in one volume of the *Journal of Abnormal and Social Psychology*, and computed the likelihood of detecting each of the three sizes of effect. The average power was .18 for the detection of small effects, .48 for medium effects, and .83 for large effects. If psychologists typically expect medium effects and select sample size as in the above example, the power of their studies should indeed be about .50.

Cohen's analysis shows that the statistical power of many psychological studies is ridiculously low. This is a self-defeating practice: it makes for frustrated scientists and inefficient research. The investigator who tests a valid hypothesis but fails to obtain significant results cannot help but regard nature as untrustworthy or even hostile. Furthermore, as Overall (1969) has shown, the prevalence of studies deficient in statistical power is not only wasteful but actually pernicious: it results in a large proportion of invalid rejections of the null hypothesis among published results.

Because considerations of statistical power are of particular importance in the design of replication studies, we probed attitudes concerning replication in our questionnaire.

Suppose one of your doctoral students has completed a difficult and time-consuming experiment on 40 animals. He has scored and analyzed a large number of variables. His results are generally inconclusive, but one before-after comparison yields a highly significant $t = 2.70$, which is surprising and could be of major theoretical significance.

Considering the importance of the result, its surprisal value, and the number of analyses that your student has performed, would you recommend that he replicate the study before publishing? If you recommend replication, how many animals would you urge him to run?

Among the psychologists to whom we put these questions there was overwhelming sentiment favoring replication: it was recommended by 66 out of 75 respondents, probably because they suspected that the single significant result was due to chance. The median recommendation was for the doctoral student to run 20 subjects in a replication study. It is instructive to consider the likely consequences of this advice. If the mean and the variance in the second sample are actually identical to those in the first sample, then the resulting value of t will be 1.88. Following the reasoning of Footnote 1, the student's chance of obtaining a significant result in the replication is only slightly above one-half (for $p = .05$, one-tail test). Since we had anticipated that a replication sample of 20 would appear reasonable to our respondents, we added the following question:

Assume that your unhappy student has in fact repeated the initial study with 20 additional animals, and has obtained an insignificant result in the same direction, $t = 1.24$. What would you recommend now? Check one: [the numbers in parentheses refer to the number of respondents who checked each answer]

    (a) He should pool the results and publish his conclusion as fact. (0)

    (b) He should report the results as a tentative finding. (26)

    (c) He should run another group of [median 20] animals. (21)

    (d) He should try to find an explanation for the difference between the two groups. (30)

Note that regardless of one's confidence in the original finding, its credibility is surely enhanced by the replication. Not only is the experimental effect in the same direction in the two samples but the magnitude of the effect in the replication is fully two-thirds of that in the original study. In view of the sample size (20), which our respondents recommended, the replication was about as successful as one is entitled to expect. The distribution of responses, however, reflects continued skepticism concerning the student's finding following the recommended replication. This unhappy state of affairs is a typical consequence of insufficient statistical power.

In contrast to Responses b and c, which can be justified on some grounds, the most popular response, Response d, is indefensible. We doubt that the same answer would have been obtained if the respondents had realized that the difference between the two studies does not even approach significance. (If the variances of the two samples are equal, t for the difference is .53.) In the absence of a statistical test, our respondents followed the representation hypothesis: as the difference between the two samples was larger than they expected, they viewed it as worthy of explanation. However, the attempt to "find an explanation for the difference between the two groups" is in all probability an exercise in explaining noise.

Altogether our respondents evaluated the replication rather harshly. This follows from the representation hypothesis: if we expect all samples to be very similar to one another, then almost all replications of a valid hypothesis should be statistically significant. The harshness of the criterion for successful replication is manifest in the responses to the following question:

An investigator has reported a result that you consider implausible. He ran 15 subjects, and reported a significant value, $t = 2.46$. Another investigator has attempted to duplicate his procedure, and he obtained a nonsignificant value of t with the same number of subjects. The direction was the same in both sets of data.

You are reviewing the literature. What is the highest value of t in the second set of data that you would describe as a failure to replicate?

The majority of our respondents regarded $t = 1.70$ as a failure to replicate. If the data of two such studies ($t = 2.46$ and $t = 1.70$) are pooled, the value of t for the combined data is about 3.00 (assuming equal variances). Thus, we are faced with a paradoxical state of affairs, in which the same data that would increase our confidence in the finding when viewed as part of the original study, shake our confidence when viewed as an independent study. This double standard is particularly disturbing since, for many reasons, replications are usually considered as independent studies, and hypotheses are often evaluated by listing confirming and disconfirming reports.

Contrary to a widespread belief, a case can be made that a replication sample should often be larger than the original. The decision to replicate a once obtained finding often expresses a great fondness for that finding and a desire to see it accepted by a skeptical community. Since that community unreasonably demands that the replication be independently significant, or at least that it approach significance, one must run a large sample. To illustrate, if the unfortunate doctoral student whose thesis was discussed earlier assumes the validity of his initial result ($t = 2.70$, $N = 40$), and if he is willing to accept a risk of only .10 of obtaining a t lower than 1.70, he should run approximately 50 animals in his replication study. With a somewhat weaker initial result ($t = 2.20$, $N = 40$), the size of the replication sample required for the same power rises to about 75.

That the effects discussed thus far are not limited to hypotheses about means and variances is demonstrated by the responses to the following question:

You have run a correlational study, scoring 20 variables on 100 subjects. Twenty-seven of the 190 correlation coefficients are significant at the .05 level; and 9 of these are significant beyond the .01 level. The mean absolute level of the significant correlations is .31, and the pattern of results is very reasonable on theoretical grounds. How many of the 27 significant correlations would you expect to be significant again, in an exact replication of the study, with $N = 40$?

With $N = 40$, a correlation of about .31 is required for significance at the .05 level. This is the mean of the significant correlations in the original study. Thus, only about half of the originally significant correlations (i.e., 13 or 14) would remain significant with $N = 40$. In addition, of course, the correlations in the replication are bound to differ from those in the original study. Hence, by regression effects, the initially significant coefficients are most likely to be reduced. Thus, 8 to 10 repeated significant correlations from the original 27 is probably a generous estimate of what one is entitled to expect. The median estimate of our respondents is 18. This is more than the number of repeated significant correlations that will be found if the correlations are recomputed for 40 subjects randomly selected from the original 100! Apparently, people expect more than a mere duplication of the original statistics in the replication sample; they expect a duplication of the significance of results, with little regard for sample size. This expectation requires a ludicrous extension of the representation hypothesis; even the law of small numbers is incapable of generating such a result.

The expectation that patterns of results are replicable almost in their entirety provides the rationale for a common, though much deplored practice. The investigator who computes all correlations between three indexes of anxiety and three indexes of dependency will often report and interpret with great confidence the single significant correlation obtained. His confidence in the shaky finding stems from his belief that the obtained correlation matrix is highly representative and readily replicable.

In review, we have seen that the believer in the law of small numbers practices science as follows:

1. He gambles his research hypotheses on small samples without realizing that the odds against him are unreasonably high. He overestimates power.

2. He has undue confidence in early trends (e.g., the data of the first few subjects) and in the stability of observed patterns (e.g., the number and identity of significant results). He overestimates significance.

3. In evaluating replications, his or others', he has unreasonably high expectations about the replicability of significant results. He underestimates the breadth of confidence intervals.

4. He rarely attributes a deviation of results from expectations to sampling variability, because he finds a causal "explanation" for any discrepancy. Thus, he has little opportunity to recognize sampling variation in action. His belief in the law of small numbers, therefore, will forever remain intact.

Our questionnaire elicited considerable evidence for the prevalence of the belief in the law of small numbers.[2] Our typical respondent is a believer, regardless of the group to which he belongs. There were practically no differences between the median responses of audiences at a

---

[2] W. Edwards (1968, 25) has argued that people fail to extract sufficient information or certainty from probabilistic data; he called this failure conservatism. Our respondents can hardly be described as conservative. Rather, in accord with the representation hypothesis, they tend to extract more certainty from the data than the data, in fact, contain.

mathematical psychology meeting and at a general session of the American Psychological Association convention, although we make no claims for the representativeness of either sample. Apparently, acquaintance with formal logic and with probability theory does not extinguish erroneous intuitions. What, then, can be done? Can the belief in the law of small numbers be abolished or at least controlled?

Research experience is unlikely to help much, because sampling variation is all too easily "explained." Corrective experiences are those that provide neither motive nor opportunity for spurious explanation. Thus, a student in a statistics course may draw repeated samples of given size from a population, and learn the effect of sample size on sampling variability from personal observation. We are far from certain, however, that expectations can be corrected in this manner, since related biases, such as the gambler's fallacy, survive considerable contradictory evidence.

Even if the bias cannot be unlearned, students can learn to recognize its existence and take the necessary precautions. Since the teaching of statistics is not short on admonitions, a warning about biased statistical intuitions may not be out of place. The obvious precaution is computation. The believer in the law of small numbers has incorrect intuitions about significance level, power, and confidence intervals. Significance levels are usually computed and reported, but power and confidence limits are not. Perhaps they should be.

Explicit computation of power, relative to some reasonable hypothesis, for instance, J. Cohen's (1962, 1969) small, large, and medium effects, should surely be carried out before any study is done. Such computations will often lead to the realization that there is simply no point in running the study unless, for example, sample size is multiplied by four. We refuse to believe that a serious investigator will knowingly accept a .50 risk of failing to confirm a valid research hypothesis. In addition, computations of power are essential to the interpretation of negative results, that is, failures to reject the null hypothesis. Because readers' intuitive estimates of power are likely to be wrong, the publication of computed values does not appear to be a waste of either readers' time or journal space.

In the early psychological literature, the convention prevailed of reporting, for example, a sample mean as $M \pm PE$, where PE is the probable error (i.e., the 50% confidence interval around the mean). This convention was later abandoned in favor of the hypothesis-testing formulation. A confidence interval, however, provides a useful index of sampling variability, and it is precisely this variability that we tend to underestimate. The emphasis on significance levels tends to obscure a fundamental distinction between the size of an effect and its statistical significance. Regardless of sample size, the size of an effect in one study is a reasonable estimate of the size of the effect in replication. In contrast, the estimated significance level in a replication depends critically on sample size. Unrealistic expectations concerning the replicability of significance levels may be corrected if the distinction between size and significance is clarified, and if the computed size of observed effects is routinely reported. From this point of view, at least, the acceptance of the hypothesis-testing model has not been an unmixed blessing for psychology.

The true believer in the law of small numbers commits his multitude of sins against the logic of statistical inference in good faith. The representation hypothesis describes a cognitive or perceptual bias, which operates regardless of motivational factors. Thus, while the hasty rejection of the null hypothesis is gratifying, the rejection of a cherished hypothesis is aggravating, yet the true believer is subject to both. His intuitive expectations are governed by a consistent misperception of the world rather than by opportunistic wishful thinking. Given some editorial prodding, he may be willing to regard his statistical intuitions with proper suspicion and replace impression formation by computation whenever possible.

3. Subjective probability:
A judgment of representativeness

Daniel Kahneman and Amos Tversky

Subjective probabilities play an important role in our lives. The decisions we make, the conclusions we reach, and the explanations we offer are usually based on our judgments of the likelihood of uncertain events such as success in a new job, the outcome of an election, or the state of the market. Indeed an extensive experimental literature has been devoted to the question of how people perceive, process, and evaluate the probabilities of uncertain events in the contexts of probability learning, intuitive statistics, and decision making under risk. Although no systematic theory about the psychology of uncertainty has emerged from this literature, several empirical generalizations have been established. Perhaps the most general conclusion, obtained from numerous investigations, is that people do not follow the principles of probability theory in judging the likelihood of uncertain events. This conclusion is hardly surprising because many of the laws of chance are neither intuitively apparent, nor easy to apply. Less obvious, however, is the fact that the deviations of subjective from objective probability[1] seem reliable, systematic, and difficult to eliminate. Apparently, people replace the laws of chance by heuristics, which sometimes yield reasonable estimates and quite often do not.

---

[1] We use the term "subjective probability" to denote any estimate of the probability of an event, which is given by a subject, or inferred from his behavior. These estimates are not assumed to satisfy any axioms or consistency requirements. We use the term "objective probability" to denote values calculated, on the basis of stated assumptions, according to the laws of the probability calculus. It should be evident that this terminology is noncommittal with respect to any philosophical view of probability.

This chapter is an abbreviated version of a paper that appeared in *Cognitive Psychology*, 1972, 3, 430-454. Copyright © 1972 by Academic Press, Inc. Reprinted by permission.

In the present paper, we investigate in detail one such heuristic called representativeness. A person who follows this heuristic evaluates the probability of an uncertain event, or a sample, by the degree to which it is: (*i*) similar in essential properties to its parent population; and (*ii*) reflects the salient features of the process by which it is generated. Our thesis is that, in many situations, an event A is judged more probable than an event B whenever A appears more representative than B. In other words, the ordering of events by their subjective probabilities coincides with their ordering by representativeness.

Representativeness, like perceptual similarity, is easier to assess than to characterize. In both cases, no general definition is available, yet there are many situations where people agree which of two stimuli is more similar to a standard, or which of two events is more representative of a given process. In this paper we do not scale representativeness, although this is a feasible approach. Instead, we consider cases where the ordering of events according to representativeness appears obvious, and show that people consistently judge the more representative event to be the more likely, whether it is or not. Although representativeness may play an important role in many varieties of probability judgments, e.g., political forecasting and clinical judgment, the present treatment is restricted to essentially repetitive situations where objective probabilities are readily computable.

Most data reported in this paper were collected in questionnaire form from a total of approximately 1500 respondents in Israel. The respondents were students in grades 10, 11, and 12 of college-preparatory high schools (ages 15–18). Special efforts were made to maintain the attention and the motivation of the subjects (Ss). The questionnaires were administered in quiz-like fashion in a natural classroom situation, and the respondents' names were recorded on the answer sheets. Each respondent answered a small number (typically 2–4) of questions each of which required, at most, 2 min. The questions were introduced as a study of people's intuitions about chance. They were preceded by standard oral instructions which explained the appropriate question in detail. The experimental design was counterbalanced to prevent confounding with school or age. Most questions were pretested on university undergraduates (ages 20–25) and the results of the two populations were indistinguishable.

Determinants of representativeness

In this section we discuss the characteristics of samples, or events, that make them representative, and demonstrate their effects on subjective probability. First, we describe some of the features that determine the similarity of a sample to its parent population. Then, we turn to the analysis of the determinants of apparent randomness.

Similarity of sample to population

The notion of representativeness is best explicated by specific examples. Consider the following question:

All families of six children in a city were surveyed. In 72 families the *exact order* of births of boys and girls was G B G B B G.
    What is your estimate of the number of families surveyed in which the *exact order* of births was B G B B B B?

The two birth sequences are about equally likely, but most people will surely agree that they are not equally representative. The sequence with five boys and one girl fails to reflect the proportion of boys and girls in the population. Indeed, 75 of 92 Ss judged this sequence to be less likely than the standard sequence ($p < .01$ by a sign test). The median estimate was 30. Similar results have been reported by Cohen and Hansel (1956), and by Alberoni (1962).

One may wonder whether Ss do not simply ignore order information, and answer the question by evaluating the frequency of families of five boys and one girl relative to that of families of three boys and three girls. However, when we asked the same Ss to estimate the frequency of the sequence B B B G G G, they viewed it as significantly less likely than G B B G B G ($p < .01$), presumably because the former appears less random. Order information, therefore, is not simply ignored.

A related determinant of representativeness is whether the sample preserves the majority–minority relation in the population. We expect a sample that preserves this relation to be judged more probable than an (objectively) equally likely sample where this relation is violated. This effect is illustrated in the following problem:

There are two programs in a high school. Boys are a majority (65%) in program A, and a minority (45%) in program B. There is an equal number of classes in each of the two programs.
    You enter a class at random, and observe that 55% of the students are boys. What is your best guess – does the class belong to program A or to program B?

Since the majority of students in the class are boys, the class is more representative of program A than of program B. Accordingly, 67 of 89 Ss guessed that the class belongs to program A ($p < .01$ by sign test). In fact, it is slightly more likely that the class belongs to program B (since the variance for $p = .45$ exceeds that for $p = .65$).

A sample in which the various possible outcomes are present is, in general, more representative than a comparable sample in which some of the outcomes are not included. For example, given a binomial process with $p = \frac{4}{5}$, a significant majority of Ss judge a sample of 10 successes and 0 failures to be less likely than a sample of 6 successes and 4 failures, although the former sample is, in fact, more likely.

The biasing effects of representativeness are not limited to naive subjects. They are also found (Tversky & Kahneman, 1971, 2) in the intuitive judgments of sophisticated psychologists. Statistical significance is commonly viewed as the representation of scientific truth. Hence, a real effect (in the population) is expected to be represented by a significant result (in the sample) with insufficient regard for the size of the sample. As a consequence, researchers are prone to overestimate the likelihood of a significant result whenever they believe the null hypothesis to be false.

For example, the following question was posed to the participants of a meeting of the Mathematical Psychology Group and of the American Psychological Association:

Suppose you have run an experiment on 20 Ss, and have obtained a significant result which confirms your theory ($z = 2.23$, $p < .05$, two-tailed). You now have cause to run an additional group of 10 Ss. What do you think the probability is that the results will be significant, by a one-tailed test, separately for this group?

A realistic estimate of the desired probability is somewhat lower than .50. The median estimate of the respondents was as high as .85. This unjustified confidence in the replicability of significance has severe consequences for the conduct of research: It leads to unrealistic expectations concerning significance, and results in the planning of studies which are deficient in statistical power, see J. Cohen (1962).

Reflection of randomness

To be representative, it is not sufficient that an uncertain event be similar to its parent population. The event should also reflect the properties of the uncertain process by which it is generated, that is, it should appear random. As is true of the similarity of sample to population, the specific features that determine apparent randomness differ depending on context. Nevertheless, two general properties, irregularity and local representativeness, seem to capture the intuitive notion of randomness. These properties are now discussed in turn.

A major characteristic of apparent randomness is the absence of systematic patterns. A sequence of coin[2] tosses, for example, which contains an obvious regularity is not representative. Thus, alternating sequences of heads and tails, such as H T H T H T H T or T T H H T T H H, fail to reflect the randomness of the process. Indeed, Ss judge such sequences as relatively unlikely and avoid them in producing simulated random sequences (Tune, 1964; Wagenaar, 1970).

Some irregularity is expected, not only in the order of outcomes, but also in their distribution, as shown in the following problem:

On each round of a game, 20 marbles are distributed at random among five

---

[2] In this paper we deal with fair coins only.

children: Alan, Ben, Carl, Dan, and Ed. Consider the following distributions:

	I		II
Alan	4	Alan	4
Ben	4	Ben	4
Carl	5	Carl	4
Dan	4	Dan	4
Ed	3	Ed	4

In many rounds of the game, will there be more results of type I or of type II?

The uniform distribution of marbles (II) is, objectively, more probable than the nonuniform distribution (I), yet it appears too lawful to be the result of a random process. Distribution I, which departs slightly from an equitable partition, is more representative of random allocation. A significant majority of Ss (36 of 52, $p < .01$ by a sign test) viewed distribution I as more probable than distribution II. The presence of some perturbation contributes to the representativeness and hence to the apparent likelihood of uncertain events.

Ss answer the above problem as if they ignored the individual nature of the two distributions and compared, instead, the two respective classes of distributions, disregarding the particular assignment of marbles to children. This does not mean that Ss do not appreciate the distinction between a class and its instances. What they do not appreciate is the proper impact of this distinction on judgments of relative frequency.

People view chance as unpredictable but essentially fair. Thus, they expect that in a purely random allocation of marbles each child will get approximately (though not exactly) the same number of marbles. Similarly, they expect even short sequences of coin tosses to include about the same number of heads and tails. More generally, a representative sample is one in which the essential characteristics of the parent population are represented not only globally in the entire sample, but also locally in each of its parts. A sample that is locally representative, however, deviates systematically from chance expectations: it contains too many alternations and too few clusters.

The law of large numbers ensures that very large samples are highly representative of the populations from which they are drawn. Elsewhere (Tversky & Kahneman, 1971, 2), we have characterized the expectancy of local representativeness as a belief in the law of small numbers, according to which "the law of large numbers applies to small numbers as well." This belief, we suggest, underlies the erroneous intuitions about randomness, which are manifest in a wide variety of contexts.

Research on the perception of randomness (e.g., Tune, 1964; Wagenaar, 1970) shows that when people are asked to simulate a random process, such as a series of coin tosses, they produce sequences which are locally representative, with far too many short runs. Moreover, people tend to regard as unlikely, or reject as nonrandom, sequences which have the correct distribution of run lengths, presumably because long runs are not locally representative.

Similar findings have also been obtained in the hundreds of studies on probability learning and binary prediction (Estes, 1964; M. R. Jones, 1971). The gambler's fallacy, or the negative-recency effect, is a manifestation of the belief in local representativeness. For if the proportions of the two outcomes are to be preserved in short segments, then a long sequence of one outcome must be followed by the other outcome in order to restore the balance. In a locally representative world, in fact, the gambler's fallacy is no longer fallacious.

In his *Introduction to Probability Theory*, Feller (1968, p. 160) describes an example which illustrates the erroneous belief in local representativeness. During the intensive bombing of London in the Second World War, it was generally believed that the bombing pattern could not be random, because a few sections of town were hit several times while many others were not hit at all. Thus, the pattern of hits violated local representativeness, and the randomness hypothesis seemed unacceptable. To test this hypothesis, the entire area of South London was divided into small sections of equal area, and the actual distribution of hits per section was compared to the expected (Poisson) distribution under the assumption of random bombing. Contrary to the general belief, the correspondence between the distributions was remarkably good. "To the untrained eye," Feller remarks, "randomness appears as regularity or tendency to cluster."

Most students are surprised to learn that in a group of as few as 23 people, the probability that at least two of them have the same birthday (i.e., same day and month) exceeds .5. Clearly, with 23 people the expected number of birthdays per day is less than than $1/15$. Thus a day with two birthdays, in the presence of 343 "empty" days, is highly nonrepresentative, and the event in question, therefore, appears unlikely. More generally, we conjecture that the counterintuitive nature of many results in probability theory is attributable to violations of representativeness. (For a striking example from the theory of random walks, see Feller, 1968, pp. 84–88.)

A representative sample, then, is similar to the population in essential characteristics, and reflects randomness as people see it; that is, all its parts are representative and none is too regular. Only a few of all possible samples meet all these constraints. Most samples do not, and therefore do not appear random. Among the 20 possible sequences (disregarding direction and label) of six tosses of a coin, for example, we venture that only H T T H T H appears really random. For four tosses, there may not be any.

The tendency to regard some binary sequences as more random than others had dramatic consequences in the Zenith radio experiments[3] in

---

[3] We thank R. P. Abelson for calling this study to our attention.

which the audience was challenged to send in guesses of the identity of five binary symbols that were "telepathed" by a panel. The analysis of over a million responses (Goodfellow, 1938) revealed that the number of hits was far in excess of chance for some sequences and far below chance for others, depending largely on the apparent randomness of the target sequences. The implications of this finding for ESP research are obvious.

Random-appearing sequences are those whose verbal description is longest. Imagine yourself dictating a long sequence of binary symbols, say heads and tails. You will undoubtedly use shortcut expressions such as "four Ts," or "H–T, three times." A sequence with many long runs allows shortcuts of the first type. A sequence with numerous short runs calls for shortcuts of the second type. The run structure of a random-appearing sequence minimizes the availability of these shortcuts, and hence defies economical descriptions. Apparent randomness, therefore, is a form of complexity of structure. Determinants of structural complexity, such as codability (Garner, 1970; Glanzer & Clark, 1963; Vitz & Todd, 1969) affect apparent randomness as well.

Sampling distributions

We have proposed that Ss assign probabilities to events so that the more representative events are assigned higher probabilities, and equally representative events are assigned equal probabilities. In this section, we investigate the implication of this hypothesis for the study of subjective sampling distributions, i.e., the probabilities that Ss assign to samples of a given size from a specified population.

When the sample is described in terms of a single statistic, e.g., proportion or mean, the degree to which it represents the population is determined by the similarity of that statistic to the corresponding parameter of the population. Since the size of the sample does not reflect any property of the parent population, it does not affect representativeness. Thus, the event of finding more than 600 boys in a sample of 1000 babies, for example, is as representative as the event of finding more than 60 boys in a sample of 100 babies. The two events, therefore, would be judged equally probable, although the latter, in fact, is vastly more likely. Similarly, according to the present analysis, the subjective probabilities that the average height in a sample of men lies between 6 ft 0 in. and 6 ft 2 in. would be independent of the size of the sample.

To test these predictions, nine different groups of Ss produced subjective sampling distributions for three sample sizes ($N = 10, 100, 1000$) and for each of the following three populations.

Distribution of sexes. (Binomial, $p = .50$) Ss were told that approximately N babies are born every day in a certain region. For $N = 1000$, for instance,

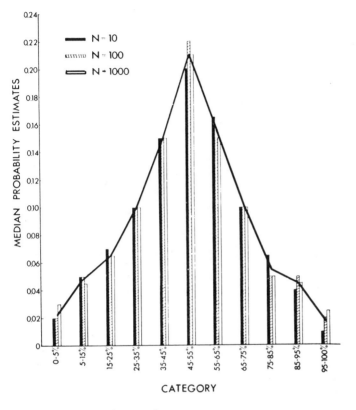

Figure 1. Distribution of sexes.

the question read as follows:

On what percentage of days will the number of boys among 1000 babies be as follows:
> *Up to 50 boys*
> *50 to 150 boys*
> *150 to 250 boys*
> . . . .
> *850 to 950 boys*
> *More than 950 boys*
> *Note that the categories include all possibilities, so your answers should add up to about 100%.*

For $N = 100$, the 11 categories were: up to 5, 5–15, etc. For $N = 10$, each category contained a single outcome, e.g., 6 boys.

Distribution of heartbeat type. (Binomial, $p = .80$) Here, Ss were told that approximately N babies are born every day in a certain region, and that 80% of all newborns have a heartbeat of type α and the remaining 20%

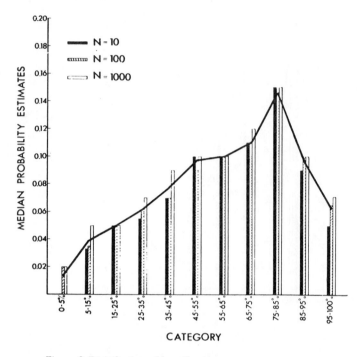

Figure 2. Distribution of heartbeat types.

have a heartbeat of type β. For each sample size, Ss produced sampling distributions for the number of babies born every day with heartbeat of type α using the same 11 categories as above.

Distribution of height. Ss were told that a regional induction center records the average height of the N men who are examined every day. They were also told that the average height of the male population lies between 170–175 cm (in Israel height is measured in centimeters), and that the frequency of heights decreases with the distance from the mean. For each sample size, Ss produced a sampling distribution of average height, in the following seven categories: up to 160, 160–165, . . . , more than 185.

Median estimates for the three populations, respectively, are shown in Figures 1, 2 and 3 for all three values of N. (Size of group varied from 45 to 84 with an average of 62.) It is apparent that sample size has no effect whatsoever on the subjective sampling distributions. Independent groups, faced with problems that differ only in sample size, produce indistinguishable distributions. This result holds for populations that are defined abstractly, e.g., the binomial, as well as for populations that are known to Ss through daily experience, e.g., the height of men.

Since subjective sampling distributions are independent of N, the solid lines in each figure, which connect the means of the median estimates, can

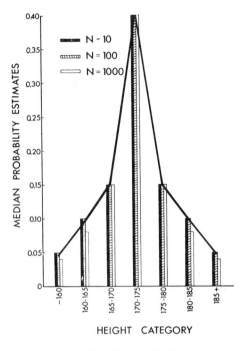

Figure 3. Distribution of height.

be regarded as "universal" sampling distributions for the respective population. To depict the magnitude of the true effect of sample size, which Ss completely ignore, the correct sampling distributions for $p = .50$ and $p = .80$ are shown, together with the corresponding "universal" sampling distribution, in Figures 4 and 5, respectively.

It can be seen that the "universal" curves are even flatter than the correct curves for $N = 10$. For $p = .50$, the "universal" variance (.048) is roughly equal to the correct sampling variance for $N = 5$ (.05). For $p = .80$, the variance of the "universal" curve (.068) lies between the correct sampling variance for $N = 2$ and that for $N = 3$.

In binomial distributions, the mean generally coincides with the mode. Consequently, when $p \neq .50$, the short tail must be higher than the long tail; see, for example, the correct distribution for $N = 10$ in Figure 4. Figure 4 also shows that this property is violated by the "universal" curve for $p = .80$ whose mean is only .63. Thus, although the mode of the subjective sampling distribution is properly located at the most representative value, the mean is displaced towards the long tail. The same result has been obtained in other studies, e.g., Cohen and Hansel (1956), Peterson, DuCharme, and Edwards (1968). Thus, for $p = .80$ the "universal" sampling distribution of the proportion is not a binomial at all!

The present experiment differs from previous studies of the subjective

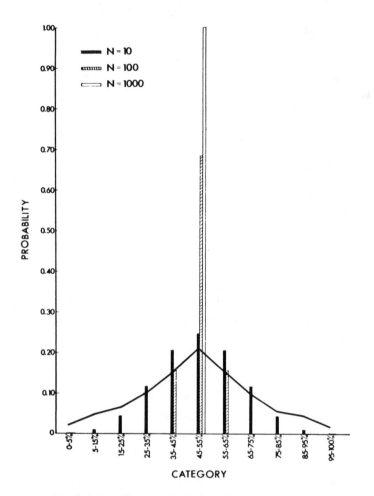

Figure 4. Sampling distribution $p = .50$.

binomial (Peterson, DuCharme, & Edwards, 1968; Wheeler & Beach, 1968) in two respects. First, the earlier work was concerned with sample sizes much smaller than those of the present study. Second, and more important, the number of events among which probabilities were distributed was not the same for different sample sizes: for a sample of size N, Ss evaluated $N + 1$ outcomes. In the present study, in contrast, Ss evaluate the *same* number of categories for all sample sizes. The invariance of the subjective sampling distribution with respect to N, which is demonstrated in Figures 1, 2 and 3, may not hold exactly when the number of categories varies, or when the sample is small enough to permit enumeration of possibilities. For larger samples, enumeration is impossible, and the natural recourse is to a direct appreciation of representativeness, which is dominated by sample mean, or sample proportion.

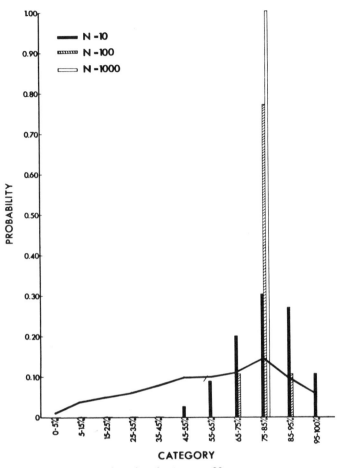

Figure 5. Sampling distribution p = .80.

To further explore the representativeness prediction concerning sample size, an additional experiment was conducted. Ss were 97 Stanford under-graduates with no background in probability or statistics, run in small groups of 5 to 12 members each. Ss were presented, in a fixed order, with three problems each defining a sampling process with a specified mean and a critical value above that mean, and asked to judge whether a particular sampling outcome is more likely to occur in a small or in a large sample. Each S was paid $1 for participation in the experiment and an additional $1 if his answer to one of the problems (randomly selected after completion of the task) was correct.

To control for response bias, each problem was presented in two forms. Half the Ss judged, for all three problems, whether an outcome that is *more* extreme than the specified critical value is more likely to occur in a small or in a large sample. The correct answer, of course, is that an extreme outcome is more likely to occur in a small sample. The remaining Ss judged whether an outcome that is *less* extreme than the specified critical value is more likely to occur in a small or in a large sample. The correct answer here is that such an outcome is more likely to occur in a large sample. The three problems are presented below. The values shown are the numbers of Ss who chose each response category, for each of the two forms. The correct answers are starred.

1. A certain town is served by two hospitals. In the larger hospital about 45 babies are born each day, and in the smaller hospital about 15 babies are born each day. As you know, about 50% of all babies are boys. The exact percentage of baby boys, however, varies from day to day. Sometimes it may be higher than 50%, sometimes lower.

For a period of 1 year, each hospital recorded the days on which (more/less) than 60% of the babies born were boys. Which hospital do you think recorded more such days?

	More than 60%	Less than 60%
The larger hospital	12	9*
The smaller hospital	10*	11
About the same (i.e., within 5% of each other)	28	25

2. An investigator studying some properties of language selected a paperback and computed the average word-length in every page of the book (i.e., the number of letters in that page divided by the number of words). Another investigator took the first line in each page and computed the line's average word-length. The average word-length in the entire book is four. However, not every line or page has exactly that average. Some may have a higher average word-length, some lower.

The first investigator counted the number of pages that had an average word-length of 6 or (more/less) and the second investigator counted the number of lines that had an average word-length of 6 or (more/less). Which investigator do you think recorded a larger number of such units (pages for one, lines for the other)?

	More than 6	Less than 6
The page investigator	8	10*
The line investigator	21*	15
About the same (i.e., within 5% of each other)	20	23

3. A medical survey is being held to study some factors pertaining to coronary diseases. Two teams are collecting data. One checks three men a day, and the other checks one man a day. These men are chosen randomly from the population. Each man's height is measured during the checkup. The average height of adult males is

5 ft 10 in., and there are as many men whose height is above average as there are men whose height is below average.

The team checking three men a day ranks them with respect to their height, and counts the days on which the height of the middle man is (more/less) than 5 ft 11 in. The other team merely counts the days on which the man they checked was (taller/shorter) than 5 ft 11 in. Which team do you think counted more such days?

	More than 5 ft 11 in.	Less than 5 ft 11 in.
The team checking 3	7	14*
The team checking 1	18*	17
About the same (i.e., within 5% of each other)	23	17

If Ss have any insight into the role of sample size, they should find it easy to select the correct answers to these simple ordinal questions. On the other hand, if they judge equally representative outcomes to be equally likely, they should show no systematic preference for the correct answer. This is clearly the case. The modal answer is "same" in almost all comparisons; moreover, there is no significant preference for the correct answer in any of the problems.

This experiment confirms the conclusions of the initial study in spite of several procedural differences. Here, each S makes a direct ordinal judgment of the likelihood of an outcome with two sample sizes under conditions designed to motivate accuracy. This procedure should enhance the salience of sample size. Furthermore, the last problem compares a single observation to the median of a sample of three observations. Apparently, Ss fail to notice even the obvious fact that medians must be less variable than single observations.

The notion that sampling variance decreases in proportion to sample size is apparently not part of man's repertoire of intuitions. Indeed, misconceptions of the role of sample size occur frequently in everyday life. On the one hand, people are often willing to take seriously a result stated in percentages, with no concern for the number of observations, which may be ridiculously small. On the other hand, people often remain skeptical in the face of solid evidence from a large sample, as in the case of the well-known politician who complained bitterly that the cost of living index is not based on the whole population, but only on a large sample, and added, "Worse yet – a *random* sample."

We surely do not mean to imply that man is incapable of appreciating the impact of sample size on sampling variance. People can be taught the correct rule, perhaps even with little difficulty. The point remains that people do not follow the correct rule, when left to their own devices. Furthermore, the study of the conduct of research psychologist (J. Cohen, 1962; Tversky & Kahneman, 1971, 2) reveals that a strong tendency to underestimate the impact of sample size lingers on despite knowledge of the correct rule and extensive statistical training. For anyone who would wish to view man as a reasonable intuitive statistician, such results are discouraging. . . .

Normative models and descriptive heuristics

The view has been expressed (see, e.g., W. Edwards, 1968, 25) that man, by and large, follows the correct Bayesian rule, but fails to appreciate the full impact of evidence, and is therefore conservative. Peterson and Beach (1967), for example, concluded that the normative model provides a good first approximation to the behavior of the Ss who are "influenced by appropriate variables and in appropriate directions" (p. 43). This view has not been shared by all. In a more recent review of the literature, Slovic and Lichtenstein (1971) argued that the above evaluation of man's performance as an intuitive statistician is far "too generous," while Pitz, Downing, and Reinhold (1967) concluded, on the basis of their data, that human performance in Bayesian tasks is "nonoptimal in a more fundamental way than is implied by discussions of conservatism" (p. 392).

The usefulness of the normative Bayesian approach to the analysis and the modeling of subjective probability depends primarily not on the accuracy of the subjective estimates, but rather on whether the model captures the essential determinants of the judgment process. The research discussed in this paper suggests that it does not. In particular, we have seen that sample size has no effect on subjective sampling distributions, that posterior binomial estimates are determined (in the aggregate case, at least) by sample proportion rather than by sample difference, and that they do not depend on the population proportion. In his evaluation of evidence, man is apparently not a conservative Bayesian: he is not Bayesian at all.

It could be argued that the failure of the normative model to describe human behavior is limited to naive Ss faced with unfamiliar random processes, and that the normative model could provide an adequate account of the evaluation of the more familiar random processes that people encounter in everyday life. There is very little evidence, however, to support this view. First, it has been shown (Tversky & Kahneman, 1971, 2) that the same type of systematic errors that are suggested by considerations of representativeness can be found in the intuitive judgments of sophisticated scientists. Apparently, acquaintance with the theory of probability does not eliminate all erroneous intuitions concerning the laws of chance. Second, in our daily life we encounter numerous random processes (e.g., the birth of a boy or a girl, hitting a red light at a given intersection, getting a hand with no hearts in a card game) which obey the binomial law, for example, to a high degree of approximation. People, however, fail to extract from these experiences an adequate conception of the binomial process. Apparently, extensive exposure to numerous examples alone does not produce optimal behavior.

In their daily lives, people ask themselves and others questions such as: What are the chances that this 12-year-old boy will grow up to be a scientist? What is the probability that this candidate will be elected to office? What is the likelihood that this company will go out of business? These problems differ from those discussed earlier in the paper in that, due to their unique character, they cannot be readily answered either in terms of frequency of occurrence in the past, or in terms of some well-defined sampling process.

In this paper, we investigated in some detail one heuristic according to which the likelihood of an event is evaluated by the degree to which it is representative of the major characteristics of the process or population from which it originated. Although our experimental examples were confined to well-defined sampling processes (where objective probability is readily computable), we conjecture that the same heuristic plays an important role in the evaluation of uncertainty in essentially unique situations where no "correct" answer is available. The likelihood that a particular 12-year-old boy will become a scientist, for example, may be evaluated by the degree to which the role of a scientist is representative of our image of the boy. Similarly, in thinking about the chances that a company will go out of business, or that a politician will be elected for office, we have in mind a model of the company, or of the political situation, and we evaluate as most likely those outcomes which best represent the essential features of the corresponding model. . . .

4.   On the psychology of prediction

Daniel Kahneman and Amos Tversky

In this paper, we explore the rules that determine intuitive predictions and judgments of confidence and contrast these rules to the normative principles of statistical prediction. Two classes of prediction are discussed: category prediction and numerical prediction. In a categorical case, the prediction is given in nominal form, for example, the winner in an election, the diagnosis of a patient, or a person's future occupation. In a numerical case, the prediction is given in numerical form, for example, the future value of a particular stock or of a student's grade point average.

In making predictions and judgments under uncertainty, people do not appear to follow the calculus of chance or the statistical theory of prediction. Instead, they rely on a limited number of heuristics which sometimes yield reasonable judgments and sometimes lead to severe and systematic errors (Kahneman & Tversky, 1972b, 3; Tversky & Kahneman, 1971, 2; 1973, 11). The present paper is concerned with the role of one of these heuristics – representativeness – in intuitive predictions.

Given specific evidence (e.g., a personality sketch), the outcomes under consideration (e.g., occupations or levels of achievement) can be ordered by the degree to which they are representative of that evidence. The thesis of this paper is that people predict by representativeness, that is, they select or order outcomes by the degree to which the outcomes represent the essential features of the evidence. In many situations, representative outcomes are indeed more likely than others. However, this is not always the case, because there are factors (e.g., the prior probabilities of outcomes and the reliability of the evidence) which affect the likelihood of outcomes but not their representativeness. Because these factors are ignored, intuitive predictions violate the statistical rules of prediction in systematic and fundamental ways. To confirm this hypothesis, we show that the ordering of outcomes by perceived likelihood coincides with their ordering by representativeness and that intuitive predictions are essentially unaffected by considerations of prior probability and expected predictive accuracy.

In the first section, we investigate category predictions and show that they conform to an independent assessment of representativeness and that they are essentially independent of the prior probabilities of outcomes. In the next section, we investigate numerical predictions and show that they are not properly regressive and are essentially unaffected by considerations of reliability. The following three sections discuss, in turn, methodological issues in the study of prediction, the sources of unjustified confidence in predictions, and some fallacious intuitions concerning regression effects.

Categorical prediction

Base rate, similarity, and likelihood

The following experimental example illustrates prediction by representativeness and the fallacies associated with this mode of intuitive prediction. A group of 69 subjects[1] (the *base-rate* group) was asked the following question: "Consider all first-year graduate students in the U.S. today. Please write down your best guesses about the percentage of these students who are now enrolled in each of the following nine fields of specialization." The nine fields are listed in Table 1. The first column of this table presents the mean estimates of base rate for the various fields.

A second group of 65 subjects (the *similarity* group) was presented with the following personality sketch:

Tom W. is of high intelligence, although lacking in true creativity. He has a need for order and clarity, and for neat and tidy systems in which every detail finds its appropriate place. His writing is rather dull and mechanical, occasionally enlivened by somewhat corny puns and by flashes of imagination of the sci-fi type. He has a strong drive for competence. He seems to have little feel and little sympathy for other people and does not enjoy interacting with others. Self-centered, he nonetheless has a deep moral sense.

The subjects were asked to rank the nine areas in terms of "how similar is Tom W. to the typical graduate student in each of the following nine fields of graduate specialization?" The second column in Table 1 presents the mean similarity ranks assigned to the various fields.

Finally, a *prediction* group, consisting of 114 graduate students in

---

[1] Unless otherwise specified, the subjects in the studies reported in this paper were paid volunteers recruited through a student paper at the University of Oregon. Data were collected in group settings.

Table 1. *Estimated base rates of the nine areas of graduate specialization and summary of similarity and prediction data for Tom W.*

Graduate specialization area	Mean judged base rate (in %)	Mean similarity rank	Mean likelihood rank
Business Administration	15	3.9	4.3
Computer Science	7	2.1	2.5
Engineering	9	2.9	2.6
Humanities and Education	20	7.2	7.6
Law	9	5.9	5.2
Library Science	3	4.2	4.7
Medicine	8	5.9	5.8
Physical and Life Sciences	12	4.5	4.3
Social Science and Social Work	17	8.2	8.0

psychology at three major universities in the United States, was given the personality sketch of Tom W., with the following additional information:

The preceding personality sketch of Tom W. was written during Tom's senior year in high school by a psychologist, on the basis of projective tests. Tom W. is currently a graduate student. Please rank the following nine fields of graduate specialization in order of the likelihood that Tom W. is now a graduate student in each of these fields.

The third column in Table 1 presents the means of the ranks assigned to the outcomes by the subjects in the prediction group.

The product–moment correlations between the columns of Table 1 were computed. The correlation between judged likelihood and similarity is .97, while the correlation between judged likelihood and estimated base rate[2] is −.65. Evidently, judgments of likelihood essentially coincide with judgments of similarity and are quite unlike the estimates of base rates. This result provides a direct confirmation of the hypothesis that people predict by representativeness, or similarity.

The judgments of likelihood by the psychology graduate students drastically violate the normative rules of prediction. More than 95% of those respondents judged that Tom W. is more likely to study computer science than humanities or education, although they were surely aware of the fact that there are many more graduate students in the latter field. According to the base-rate estimates shown in Table 1, the prior odds for

[2] In computing this correlation, the ranks were inverted so that a high judged likelihood was assigned a high value.

humanities or education against computer science are about 3 to 1. (The actual odds are considerably higher.)

According to Bayes' rule, it is possible to overcome the prior odds against Tom W. being in computer science rather than in humanities or education, if the description of his personality is both accurate and diagnostic. The graduate students in our study, however, did not believe that these conditions were met. Following the prediction task, the respondents were asked to estimate the percentage of hits (i.e., correct first choices among the nine areas) which could be achieved with several types of information. The median estimate of hits was 23% for predictions based on projective tests, which compares to 53%, for example, for predictions based on high school seniors' reports of their interests and plans. Evidently, projective tests were held in low esteem. Nevertheless, the graduate students relied on a description derived from such tests and ignored the base rates.

In general, three types of information are relevant to statistical prediction: (a) prior or background information (e.g., base rates of fields of graduate specialization); (b) specific evidence concerning the individual case (e.g., the description of Tom W.); (c) the expected accuracy of prediction (e.g., the estimated probability of hits). A fundamental rule of statistical prediction is that expected accuracy controls the relative weights assigned to specific evidence and to prior information. When expected accuracy decreases, predictions should become more regressive, that is, closer to the expectations based on prior information. In the case of Tom W., expected accuracy was low, and prior probabilities should have been weighted heavily. Instead, our subjects predicted by representativeness, that is, they ordered outcomes by their similarity to the specific evidence, with no regard for prior probabilities.

In their exclusive reliance on the personality sketch, the subjects in the prediction group apparently ignored the following considerations. First, given the notorious invalidity of projective personality tests, it is very likely that Tom W. was never in fact as compulsive and as aloof as his description suggests. Second, even if the description was valid when Tom W. was in high school, it may no longer be valid now that he is in graduate school. Finally, even if the description is still valid, there are probably more people who fit that description among students of humanities and education than among students of computer science, simply because there are so many more students in the former than in the latter field.

Manipulation of expected accuracy

An additional study tests the hypothesis that, contrary to the statistical model, a manipulation of expected accuracy does not affect the pattern of predictions. The experimental material consisted of five thumbnail personality sketches of ninth-grade boys, allegedly written by a counselor on the basis of an interview in the context of a longitudinal study. The design was the same as in the Tom W. study. For each description, subjects in one group (N = 69) ranked the nine fields of graduate specialization (see Table 1) in terms of the similarity of the boy described to their "image of the typical first-year graduate student in that field." Following the similarity judgments, they estimated the base-rate frequency of the nine areas of graduate specialization. These estimates were shown in Table 1. The remaining subjects were told that the five cases had been randomly selected from among the participants in the original study who are now first-year graduate students. One group, the high-accuracy group (N = 55), was told that "on the basis of such descriptions, students like yourself make correct predictions in about 55% of the cases." The low-accuracy group (N = 50) was told that students' predictions in this task are correct in about 27% of the cases. For each description, the subjects ranked the nine fields according to "the likelihood that the person described is now a graduate student in that field." For each description, they also estimated the probability that their first choice was correct.

The manipulation of expected accuracy had a significant effect on these probability judgments. The mean estimates were .70 and .56, respectively for the high- and low-accuracy group (t = 3.72, $p < .001$). However, the orderings of the nine outcomes produced under the low-accuracy instructions were not significantly closer to the base-rate distribution than the orderings produced under the high-accuracy instructions. A product-moment correlation was computed for each judge, between the average rank he had assigned to each of the nine outcomes (over the five descriptions) and the base rate. This correlation is an overall measure of the degree to which the subject's predictions conform to the base-rate distribution. The averages of these individual correlations were .13 for subjects in the high-accuracy group and .16 for subjects in the low-accuracy group. The difference does not approach significance (t = .42, df = 103). This pattern of judgments violates the normative theory of prediction, according to which any decrease in expected accuracy should be accompanied by a shift of predictions toward the base rate.

Since the manipulation of expected accuracy had no effect on predictions, the two prediction groups were pooled. Subsequent analyses were the same as in the Tom W. study. For each description, two correlations were computed: (a) between mean likelihood rank and mean similarity rank and (b) between mean likelihood rank and mean base rate. These correlations are shown in Table 2, with the outcome judged most likely for each description. The correlations between prediction and similarity are consistently high. In contrast, there is no systematic relation between prediction and base rate: the correlations vary widely depending on whether the most representative outcomes for each description happen to be frequent or rare.

Table 2. *Product–moment correlations of mean likelihood rank with mean similarity rank and with base rate*

	Modal first prediction				
	Law	Computer science	Medicine	Library science	Business administration
With mean similarity rank	.93	.96	.92	.88	.88
With base rate	.33	−.35	.27	−.03	.62

Here again, considerations of base rate were neglected. In the statistical theory, one is allowed to ignore the base rate only when one expects to be infallible. In all other cases, an appropriate compromise must be found between the ordering suggested by the description and the ordering of the base rates. It is hardly believable that a cursory description of a fourteen-year-old child based on a single interview could justify the degree of infallibility implied by the predictions of our subjects.

Following the five personality descriptions, the subjects were given an additional problem:

About Don you will be told nothing except that he participated in the original study and is now a first-year graduate student. Please indicate your ordering and report your confidence for this case as well.

For Don the correlation between mean likelihood rank and estimated base rate was .74. Thus, the knowledge of base rates, which was not applied when a description was given, was utilized when no specific evidence was available.

Prior versus individuating evidence

The next study provides a more stringent test of the hypothesis that intuitive predictions are dominated by representativeness and are relatively insensitive to prior probabilities. In this study, the prior probabilities were made exceptionally salient and compatible with the response mode. Subjects were presented with the following cover story:

A panel of psychologists have interviewed and administered personality tests to 30 engineers and 70 lawyers, all successful in their respective fields. On the basis of this information, thumbnail descriptions of the 30 engineers and 70 lawyers have been written. You will find on your forms five descriptions, chosen at random from the 100 available descriptions. For each description, please indicate your probability that the person described is an engineer, on a scale from 0 to 100.

The same task has been performed by a panel of experts, who were highly accurate in assigning probabilities to the various descriptions. You will be paid a bonus to the extent that your estimates come close to those of the expert panel.

These instructions were given to a group of 85 subjects (the low-engineer, or L group). Subjects in another group (the high-engineer, H group; $N = 86$) were given identical instructions except for the prior probabilities: they were told that the set from which the descriptions had been drawn consisted of 70 engineers and 30 lawyers. All subjects were presented with the same five descriptions. One of the descriptions follows:

Jack is a 45-year-old man. He is married and has four children. He is generally conservative, careful, and ambitious. He shows no interest in political and social issues and spends most of his free time on his many hobbies which include home carpentry, sailing, and mathematical puzzles.
The probability that Jack is one of the 30 engineers in the sample of 100 is ———%.

Following the five descriptions, the subjects encountered the *null* description:

Suppose now that you are given no information whatsoever about an individual chosen at random from the sample.
The probability that this man is one of the 30 engineers in the sample of 100 is ———%.

In both the high-engineer and low-engineer groups, half of the subjects were asked to evaluate, for each description, the probability that the person described was an engineer (as in the example above), while the other subjects evaluated, for each description, the probability that the person described was a lawyer. This manipulation had no effect. The median probabilities assigned to the outcomes *engineer* and *lawyer* in the two different forms added to about 100% for each description. Consequently, the data for the two forms were pooled, and the results are presented in terms of the outcome *engineer*.

The design of this experiment permits the calculation of the normatively appropriate pattern of judgments. The derivation relies on Bayes' formula, in odds form. Let O denote the odds that a particular description belongs to an engineer rather than to a lawyer. According to Bayes' rule, $O = Q \cdot R$, where Q denotes the prior odds that a randomly selected description belongs to an engineer rather than to a lawyer; and R is the likelihood ratio for a particular description, that is, the ratio of the probability that a person randomly drawn from a population of engineers will be so described to the probability that a person randomly drawn from a population of lawyers will be so described.

For the high-engineer group, who were told that the sample consists of 70 engineers and 30 lawyers, the prior odds Q_H equal 70/30. For the low-engineer group, the prior odds Q_L equal 30/70. Thus, for each description, the ratio of the posterior odds for the two groups is

$$\frac{O_H}{O_L} = \frac{Q_H \cdot R}{Q_L \cdot R} = \frac{Q_H}{Q_L} = \frac{7/3}{3/7} = 5.44$$

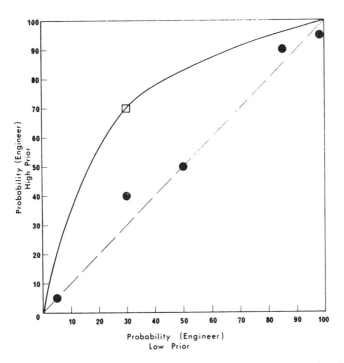

Figure 1. Median judged probability (engineer) for five descriptions and for the null description (square symbol) under high and low prior probabilities. (The curved line displays the correct relation according to Bayes's rule.)

Since the likelihood ratio is cancelled in this formula, the same value of O_H/O_L should obtain for all descriptions. In the present design, therefore, the correct effect of the manipulation of prior odds can be computed without knowledge of the likelihood ratio.

Figure 1 presents the median probability estimates for each description, under the two conditions of prior odds. For each description, the median estimate of probability when the prior is high ($Q_H = 70/30$) is plotted against the median estimate when the prior is low ($Q_L = 30/70$). According to the normative equation developed in the preceding paragraph, all points should lie on the curved (Bayesian) line. In fact, only the empty square which corresponds to the null description falls on this line: when given no description, subjects judged the probability to be 70% under Q_H and 30% under Q_L. In the other five cases, the points fall close to the identity line.

The effect of prior probability, although slight, is statistically significant. For each subject the mean probability estimate was computed over all cases except the null. The average of these values was 50% for the low-engineer group and 55% for the high-engineer group ($t = 3.23$, $df = 169$, $p < .01$). Nevertheless, as can be seen from Figure 1, every point is closer to the identity line than to the Bayesian line. It is fair to conclude that explicit manipulation of the prior distribution had a minimal effect on subjective probability. As in the preceding experiment, subjects applied their knowledge of the prior only when they were given no specific evidence. As entailed by the representativeness hypothesis, prior probabilities were largely ignored when individuating information was made available.

The strength of this effect is demonstrated by the responses to the following description:

Dick is a 30-year-old man. He is married with no children. A man of high ability and high motivation, he promises to be quite successful in his field. He is well liked by his colleagues.

This description was constructed to be totally uninformative with regard to Dick's profession. Our subjects agreed: median estimates were 50% in both the low- and high-engineer groups (see Figure 1). The contrast between the responses to this description and to the null description is illuminating. Evidently, people respond differently when given no specific evidence and when given worthless evidence. When no specific evidence is given, the prior probabilities are properly utilized; when worthless specific evidence is given, prior probabilities are ignored.[3]

There are situations in which prior probabilities are likely to play a more substantial role. In all the examples discussed so far, distinct stereotypes were associated with the alternative outcomes, and judgments were controlled, we suggest, by the degree to which the descriptions appeared representative of these stereotypes. In other problems, the outcomes are more naturally viewed as segments of a dimension. Suppose, for example, that one is asked to judge the probability that each of several students will receive a fellowship. In this problem, there are no well-delineated stereotypes of recipients and nonrecipients of fellowships. Rather, it is natural to regard the outcome (i.e., obtaining a fellowship) as determined by a cutoff point along the dimension of academic achievement or ability. Prior probabilities, that is, the percentage of fellowships in the relevant group, could be used to define the outcomes by locating the cutoff point. Consequently, they are not likely to be ignored. In addition, we would expect extreme prior probabilities to have some effect even in the presence of clear stereotypes of the outcomes. A precise delineation of the conditions under which prior information is used or discarded awaits further investigation.

One of the basic principles of statistical prediction is that prior probability, which summarizes what we knew about the problem before receiving independent specific evidence, remains relevant even after such evidence is obtained. Bayes' rule translates this qualitative principle into a multiplicative relation between prior odds and the likelihood ratio. Our subjects,

---

[3] But see p. 159.

however, failed to integrate prior probability with specific evidence. When exposed to a description, however scanty or suspect, of Tom W. or of Dick (the engineer/lawyer), they apparently felt that the distribution of occupations in his group was no longer relevant. The failure to appreciate the relevance of prior probability in the presence of specific evidence is perhaps one of the most significant departures of intuition from the normative theory of prediction.

Numerical prediction

A fundamental rule of the normative theory of prediction is that the variability of predictions, over a set of cases, should reflect predictive accuracy. When predictive accuracy is perfect, one predicts the criterion value that will actually occur. When uncertainty is maximal, a fixed value is predicted in all cases. (In category prediction, one predicts the most frequent category. In numerical prediction, one predicts the mean, the mode, the median, or some other value depending on the loss function.) Thus, the variability of predictions is equal to the variability of the criterion when predictive accuracy is perfect, and the variability of predictions is zero when predictive accuracy is zero. With intermediate predictive accuracy, the variability of predictions takes an intermediate value, that is, predictions are regressive with respect to the criterion. Thus, the greater the uncertainty, the smaller the variability of predictions. Predictions by representativeness do not follow this rule. It was shown in the previous section that people did not regress toward more frequent categories when expected accuracy of predictions was reduced. The present section demonstrates an analogous failure in the context of numerical prediction.

Prediction of outcomes versus evaluation of inputs

Suppose one is told that a college freshman has been described by a counselor as intelligent, self-confident, well-read, hard working, and inquisitive. Consider two types of questions that might be asked about this description:

(a) *Evaluation:* How does this description impress you with respect to academic ability? What percentage of descriptions of freshmen do you believe would impress you more? (b) *Prediction:* What is your estimate of the grade point average that this student will obtain? What is the percentage of freshmen who obtain a higher grade point average?

There is an important difference between the two questions. In the first, you evaluate the input; in the second, you predict an outcome. Since there is surely greater uncertainty about the second question than about the first, your prediction should be more regressive than your evaluation. That is, the percentage you give as a prediction should be closer to 50% than the percentage you give as an evaluation. To highlight the difference between the two questions, consider the possibility that the description is inaccurate. This should have no effect on your evaluation: the ordering of descriptions with respect to the impressions they make on you is independent of their accuracy. In predicting, on the other hand, you should be regressive to the extent that you suspect the description to be inaccurate or your prediction to be invalid.

The representativeness hypothesis, however, entails that prediction and evaluation should coincide. In evaluating a given description, people select a score which, presumably, is most representative of the description. If people predict by representativeness, they will also select the most representative score as their prediction. Consequently, the evaluation and the prediction will be essentially identical. Several studies were conducted to test this hypothesis. In each of these studies the subjects were given descriptive information concerning a set of cases. An *evaluation* group evaluated the quality of each description relative to a stated population, and a *prediction* group predicted future performance. The judgments of the two groups were compared to test whether predictions are more regressive than evaluations.

In two studies, subjects were given descriptions of college freshmen, allegedly written by a counselor on the basis of an interview administered to the entering class. In the first study, each description consisted of five adjectives, referring to intellectual qualities and to character, as in the example cited. In the second study, the descriptions were paragraph-length reports, including details of the student's background and of his current adjustment to college. In both studies the evaluation groups were asked to evaluate each one of the descriptions by estimating "the percentage of students in the entire class whose descriptions indicate a higher academic ability." The prediction groups were given the same descriptions and were asked to predict the grade point average achieved by each student at the end of his freshman year and his class standing in percentiles.

The results of both studies are shown in Figure 2, which plots, for each description, the mean prediction of percentile grade point average against the mean evaluation. The only systematic discrepancy between predictions and evaluations is observed in the adjectives study where predictions were consistently higher than the corresponding evaluations. The standard deviation of predictions or evaluations was computed within the data of each subject. A comparison of these values indicated no significant differences in variability between the evaluation and the prediction groups, within the range of values under study. In the adjectives study, the average standard deviation was 25.7 for the evaluation group ($N = 38$) and 24.0 for the prediction group ($N = 36$) ($t = 1.25$, $df = 72$, ns). In the reports study, the average standard deviation was 22.2 for the evaluation group ($N = 37$) and 21.4 for the prediction group ($N = 63$) ($t = .75$, $df = 98$, ns). In both studies the prediction and the evaluation groups produced equally extreme judgments, although the former predicted a remote objective criterion on the basis of sketchy interview information, while the latter

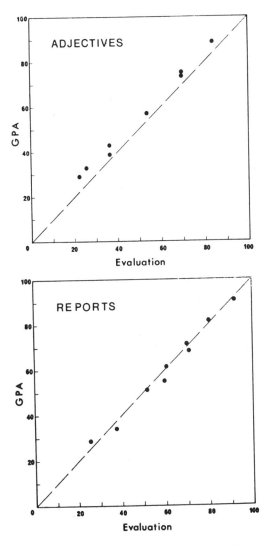

Figure 2. Predicted percentile grade point average as a function of percentile evaluation for adjectives and reports.

merely evaluated the impression obtained from each description. In the statistical theory of prediction, the observed equivalence between prediction and evaluation would be justified only if predictive accuracy were perfect, a condition which could not conceivably be met in these studies.

Further evidence for the equivalence of evaluation and prediction was obtained in a master's thesis by Beyth (1972). She presented three groups of subjects with seven paragraphs, each describing the performance of a student-teacher during a particular practice lesson. The subjects were students in a statistics course at the Hebrew University. They were told that the descriptions had been drawn from among the files of 100 elementary school teachers who, five years earlier, had completed their teacher training program. Subjects in an evaluation group were asked to evaluate the quality of the lesson described in the paragraph, in percentile scores relative to the stated population. Subjects in a prediction group were asked to predict in percentile scores the current standing of each teacher, that is, his overall competence five years after the description was written. An evaluation–prediction group performed both tasks. As in the studies described above, the differences between evaluation and prediction were not significant. This result held in both the between-subjects and within-subject comparisons. Although the judges were undoubtedly aware of the multitude of factors that intervene between a single trial lesson and teaching competence five years later, this knowledge did not cause their predictions to be more regressive than their evaluations.

Prediction versus translation

The previous studies showed that predictions of a variable are not regressive when compared to evaluations of the inputs in terms of that variable. In the following study, we show that there are situations in which predictions of a variable (academic achievement) are no more regressive than a mere translation of that variable from one scale to another. The grade point average was chosen as the outcome variable, because it correlates and distributional properties are well known to the subject population.

Three groups of subjects participated in the experiment. Subjects in all groups predicted the grade point average of 10 hypothetical students on the basic of a single percentile score obtained by each of these students. The same set of percentile scores was presented to all groups, but the three groups received different interpretations of the input variable as follows.

1. *Percentile grade point average.* The subjects in Group 1 ($N = 32$) were told that "for each of several students you will be given a percentile score representing his academic achievements in the freshman year, and you will be asked to give your best guess about his grade point average for that year." It was explained to the subjects that "a percentile score of 65, for example, means that the grade point average achieved by this student is better than that achieved by 65% of his class, etc."

2. *Mental concentration.* The subjects in Group 2 ($N = 37$) were told that "the test of mental concentration measures one's ability to concentrate and to extract all the information conveyed by complex messages. It was found that students with high grade point averages tend to score high on the mental concentration test and vice versa. However, performance on the mental concentration test was found to depend on the mood and mental state of the person at the time he took the test. Thus, when tested repeatedly, the same person could obtain quite different scores, depend-

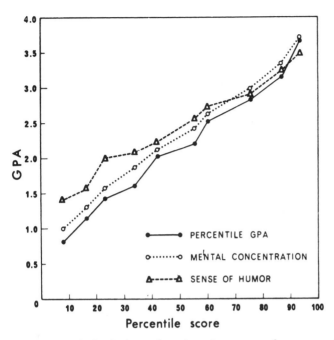

Figure 3. Predictions of grade point average from percentile scores on three variables.

ing on the amount of sleep he had the night before or how well he felt that day."

3. *Sense of humor.* The subjects in Group 3 ($N = 35$) were told that "the test of sense of humor measures the ability of people to invent witty captions for cartoons and to appreciate humor in various forms. It was found that students who score high on this test tend, by and large, to obtain a higher grade point average than students who score low. However, it is not possible to predict grade point average from sense of humor with high accuracy."

In the present design, all subjects predicted grade point average on the basis of the same set of percentile scores. Group 1 merely translated values of percentile grade point average onto the grade point average scale. Groups 2 and 3, on the other hand, predicted grade point average from more remote inputs. Normative considerations therefore dictate that the predictions of these groups should be more regressive, that is, less variable, than the judgments of Group 1. The representativeness hypothesis, however, suggests a different pattern of results.

Group 2 predicted from a potentially valid but unreliable test of mental concentration which was presented as a measure of academic ability. We hypothesized that the predictions of this group would be nonregressive when compared to the predictions of Group 1. In general, we conjecture that the achievement score (e.g., grade point average) which best repre-

Table 3. *Averages of individual prediction statistics for the three groups and results of planned comparisons between groups 1 and 2, and between groups 2 and 3*

	Group				
Statistic	1. Percentile grade point average	1 vs. 2	2. Mental concentration	2 vs. 3	3. Sense of humor
Mean predicted grade point average	2.27	*ns*	2.35	.05	2.46
SD of predictions	.91	*ns*	.87	.01	.69
Slope of regression	.030	*ns*	.029	.01	.022
r	.97	*ns*	.95	*ns*	.94

sents a percentile value on a measure of ability (e.g., mental concentration) is that which corresponds to the same precentile on the scale of achievement. Since representativeness is not affected by unreliability, we expected the predictions of grade point average from the unreliable test of mental concentration to be essentially identical to the predictions of grade point average from percentile grade point average. The predictions of Group 3, on the other hand, were expected to be regressive because sense of humor is not commonly viewed as a measure of academic ability.

The mean predictions assigned to the 10 percentile scores by the three groups are shown in Figure 3. It is evident in the figure that the predictions of Group 2 are no more regressive than the predictions of Group 1, while the predictions of Group 3 appear more regressive.

Four indices were computed within the data of each individual subject: the mean of his predictions, the standard deviation of his predictions, the slope of the regression of predicted grade point average on the input scores, and the product–moment correlation between them. The means of these values for the three groups are shown in Table 3.

It is apparent in the table that the subjects in all three groups produced orderly data, as evinced by the high correlations between inputs and predictions (the average correlations were obtained by transforming individual values to Fisher's z). The results of planned comparisons between Groups 1 and 2 and between Groups 2 and 3 confirm the pattern observed in Figure 3. There are no significant differences between the predictions from percentile grade point average and from mental concentration. Thus, people fail to regress when predicting a measure of achievement from a measure of ability, however unreliable.

The predictions from sense of humor, on the other hand, are regressive, although not enough. The correlation between grade point average and sense of humor inferred from a comparison of the regression lines is about .70. In addition, the predictions from sense of humor are significantly higher than the predictions from mental concentration. There is also a tendency for predictions from mental concentration to be higher than predictions based on percentile grade point average. We have observed this finding in many studies. When predicting the academic achievement of an individual on the basis of imperfect information, subjects exhibit leniency (Guilford, 1954). They respond to a reduction of validity by raising the predicted level of performance.

Predictions are expected to be essentially nonregressive whenever the input and outcome variables are viewed as manifestations of the same trait. An example of such predictions has been observed in a real-life setting, the Officer Selection Board of the Israeli Army. The highly experienced officers who participate in the assessment team normally evaluate candidates on a 7-point scale at the completion of several days of testing and observation. For the purposes of the study, they were required in addition to predict, for each successful candidate, the final grade that he would obtain in officer training school. In over 200 cases, assessed by a substantial number of different judges, the distribution of predicted grades was found to be virtually identical to the actual distribution of final grades in officer training school, with one obvious exception: predictions of failure were less frequent than actual failures. In particular, the frequencies of predictions in the two highest categories precisely matched the actual frequencies. All judges were keenly aware of research indicating that their predictive validity was only moderate (on the order of .20 to .40). Nevertheless, their predictions were nonregressive.

Methodological considerations

The representativeness hypothesis states that predictions do not differ from evaluations or assessments of similarity, although the normative statistical theory entails that predictions should be less extreme than these judgments. The test of the representativeness hypothesis therefore requires a design in which predictions are compared to another type of judgment. Variants of two comparative designs were used in the studies reported in this paper.

In one design, labeled A-XY, different groups of subjects judged two variables (X and Y) on the basis of the same input information (A). In the case of Tom W., for example, two different groups were given the same input information (A), that is, a personality description. One group ranked the outcomes in terms of similarity (X), while the other ranked the outcomes in terms of likelihood (Y). Similarly, in several studies of numerical prediction, different groups were given the same information (A), for example, a list of five adjectives describing a student. One group provided an evaluation (X) and the other a prediction (Y).

In another design, labeled AB-X, two different groups of subjects judged the same outcome variable (X) on the basis of different information inputs

(A and B). In the engineer/lawyer study, for example, two different groups made the same judgment (X) of the likelihood that a particular individual is an engineer. They were given a brief description of his personality and different information (A and B) concerning the base-rate frequencies of engineers and lawyers. In the context of numerical prediction, different groups predicted grade point average (X) from scores on different variables, percentile grade point average (A) and mental concentration (B).

The representativeness hypothesis was supported in these comparative designs by showing that contrary to the normative model, predictions are no more regressive than evaluations or judgments of similarity. It is also possible to ask whether intuitive predictions are regressive when compared to the actual outcomes, or to the inputs when the inputs and outcomes are measured on the same scale. Even when predictions are no more regressive than translations, we expect them to be slightly regressive when compared to the outcomes, because of the well-known central-tendency error (Johnson, 1972; Woodworth, 1938). In a wide variety of judgment tasks, including the mere translation of inputs from one scale to another, subjects tend to avoid extreme responses and to constrict the variability of their judgments (Stevens & Greenbaum, 1966). Because of this response bias, judgments will be regressive, when compared to inputs or to outcomes. The designs employed in the present paper neutralize this effect by comparing two judgments, both of which are subject to the same bias.

The present set of studies was concerned with situations in which people make predictions on the basis of information that is available to them prior to the experiment, in the form of stereotypes (e.g., of an engineer) and expectations concerning relationships between variables. Outcome feedback was not provided, and the number of judgments required of each subject was small. In contrast, most previous studies of prediction have dealt with the learning of functional or statistical relations among variables with which the subjects had no prior acquaintance. These studies typically involve a large number of trials and various forms of outcome feedback. (Some of this literature has been reviewed in Slovic and Lichtenstein, 1971.) In studies of repetitive predictions with feedback, subjects generally predict by selecting outcomes so that the entire sequence or pattern of predictions is highly representative of the distribution of outcomes. For example, subjects in probability-learning studies generate sequences of predictions which roughly match the statistical characteristics of the sequence of outcomes. Similarly, subjects in numerical prediction tasks approximately reproduce the scatterplot, that is, the joint distribution of inputs and outcomes (see, e.g., Gray, 1968). To do so, subjects resort to a mixed strategy: for any given input they generate a distribution of different predictions. These predictions reflect the fact that any one input is followed by different outcomes on different trials. Evidently, the rules of prediction are different in the two paradigms,

although representativeness is involved in both. In the feedback paradigm, subjects produce response sequences representing the entire pattern of
association between inputs and outcomes. In the situations explored in the
present paper, subjects select the prediction which best represents their
impressions of each individual case. The two approaches lead to different
violations of the normative rule: the representation of uncertainty through a
mixed strategy in the feedback paradigm and the discarding of uncertainty
through prediction by evaluation in the present paradigm.

Confidence and the illusion of validity

As demonstrated in the preceding sections, one predicts by selecting the
outcome that is most representative of the input. We propose that the
degree of confidence one has in a prediction reflects the degree to which
the selected outcome is more representative of the input than are other
outcomes. A major determinant of representativeness in the context of
numerical prediction with multiattribute inputs (e.g., score profiles) is the
consistency, or coherence, of the input. The more consistent the input, the
more representative the predicted score will appear and the greater the
confidence in that prediction. For example, people predict an overall B
average with more confidence on the basis of B grades in two separate
introductory courses than on the basis of an A and a C. Indeed, internal
variability or inconsistency of the input has been found to decrease
confidence in predictions (Slovic, 1966).

The intuition that consistent profiles allow greater predictability than
inconsistent profiles is compelling. It is worth noting, however, that this
belief is incompatible with the commonly applied multivariate model of
prediction (i.e., the normal linear model) in which expected predictive
accuracy is independent of within-profile variability.

Consistent profiles will typically be encountered when the judge
predicts from highly correlated scores. Inconsistent profiles, on the other
hand, are more frequent when the intercorrelations are low. Because
confidence increases with consistency, confidence will generally be high
when the input variables are highly correlated. However, given input
variables of stated validity, the multiple correlation with the criterion is
inversely related to the correlations among the inputs. Thus, a paradoxical
situation arises where high intercorrelations among inputs increase confidence and decrease validity.

To demonstrate this effect, we required subjects to predict grade point
average on the basis of two pairs of aptitude tests. Subjects were told that
one pair of tests (creative thinking and symbolic ability) was highly
correlated, while the other pair of tests (mental flexibility and systematic
reasoning) was not correlated. The scores they encountered conformed to
these expectations. (For half of the subjects the labels of the correlated and
the uncorrelated pairs of tests were reversed.) Subjects were told that "all
tests were found equally successful in predicting college performance." In

this situation, of course, a higher predictive accuracy can be achieved with the uncorrelated than with the correlated pair of tests. As expected, however, subjects were more confident in predicting from the correlated tests, over the entire range of predicted scores ($t = 4.80$, $df = 129$, $p < .001$). That is, they were more confident in a context of inferior predictive validity.

Another finding observed in many prediction studies, including our own, is that confidence is a J-shaped function of the predicted level of performance (see Johnson, 1972). Subjects predict outstandingly high achievement with very high confidence, and they have more confidence in the prediction of utter failure than of mediocre performance. As we saw earlier, intuitive predictions are often insufficiently regressive. The discrepancies between predictions and outcomes, therefore, are largest at the extremes. The J-shaped confidence function entails that subjects are most confident in predictions that are most likely to be off the mark.

The foregoing analysis shows that the factors which enhance confidence, for example, consistency and extremity, are often negatively correlated with predictive accuracy. Thus, people are prone to experience much confidence in highly fallible judgments, a phenomenon that may be termed the *illusion of validity*. Like other perceptual and judgmental errors, the illusion of validity often persists even when its illusory character is recognized. When interviewing a candidate, for example, many of us have experienced great confidence in our prediction of his future performance, despite our knowledge that interviews are notoriously fallible.

Intuitions about regression

Regression effects are all about us. In our experience, most outstanding fathers have somewhat disappointing sons, brilliant wives have duller husbands, the ill-adjusted tend to adjust and the fortunate are eventually stricken by ill luck. In spite of these encounters, people do not acquire a proper notion of regression. First, they do not expect regression in many situations where it is bound to occur. Second, as any teacher of statistics will attest, a proper notion of regression is extremely difficult to acquire. Third, when people observe regression, they typically invent spurious dynamic explanations for it.

What is it that makes the concept of regression counterintuitive and difficult to acquire and apply? We suggest that a major source of difficulty is that regression effects typically violate the intuition that the predicted outcome should be maximally representative of the input information.[4]

To illustrate the persistence of nonregressive intuitions despite consid-

---

[4] The expectation that every significant particle of behavior is highly representative of the actor's personality may explain why laymen and psychologists alike are perennially surprised by the negligible correlations among seemingly interchangeable measures of honesty, of risk taking, of aggression, and of dependency (Mischel, 1968).

erable exposure to statistics, we presented the following problem to our sample of graduate students in psychology:

A problem of testing. A randomly selected individual has obtained a score of 140 on a standard IQ test. Suppose than an IQ score is the sum of a "true" score and a random error of measurement which is normally distributed.
Please give your best guess about the 95% upper and lower confidence bounds for the true IQ of this person. That is, give a high estimate such that you are 95% sure that the true IQ score is, in fact, lower than that estimate, and a low estimate such that you are 95% sure that the true score is in fact higher.

In this problem, the respondents were told to regard the observed score as the sum of a "true" score and an error component. Since the observed score is considerably higher than the population mean, it is more likely than not that the error component is positive and that this individual will obtain a somewhat lower score on subsequent tests. The majority of subjects (73 of 108), however, stated confidence intervals that were symmetric around 140, failing to express any expectation of regression. Of the remaining 35 subjects, 24 stated regressive confidence intervals and 11 stated counterregressive intervals. Thus, most subjects ignored the effects of unreliability in the input and predicted as if the value of 140 was a true score. The tendency to predict as if the input information were error free has been observed repeatedly in this paper.

The occurrence of regression is sometimes recognized, either because we discover regression effects in our own observations or because we are explicitly told that regression has occurred. When recognized, a regression effect is typically regarded as a systematic change that requires substantive explanation. Indeed, many spurious explanations of regression effects have been offered in the social sciences.[5] Dynamic principles have been invoked to explain why businesses which did exceptionally well at one point in time tend to deteriorate subsequently and why training in interpreting facial expressions is beneficial to trainees who scored poorly on a pretest and detrimental to those who did best. Some of these explanations might not have been offered, had the authors realized that given two variables of equal variances, the following two statements are logically equivalent: (a) Y is regressive with respect to X; (b) the correlation between Y and X is less than unity. Explaining regression, therefore, is tantamount to explaining why a correlation is less than unity.

As a final illustration of how difficult it is to recognize and properly interpret regression, consider the following question which was put to our sample of graduate students. The problem described actually arose in the experience of one of the authors.

A problem of training. The instructors in a flight school adopted a policy of consistent positive reinforcement recommended by psychologists. They verbally

---

[5] For enlightening discussions of regression fallacies in research, see, for example, Campbell (1969) and Wallis and Roberts (1956).

reinforced each successful execution of a flight maneuver. After some experience with this training approach, the instructors claimed that contrary to psychological doctrine, high praise for good execution of complex maneuvers typically results in a decrement of performance on the next try. What should the psychologist say in response?

Regression is inevitable in flight maneuvers because performance is not perfectly reliable and progress between successive maneuvers is slow. Hence, pilots who did exceptionally well on one trial are likely to deteriorate on the next, regardless of the instructors' reaction to the initial success. The experienced flight instructors actually discovered the regression but attributed it to the detrimental effect of positive reinforcement. This true story illustrates a saddening aspect of the human condition. We normally reinforce others when their behavior is good and punish them when their behavior is bad. By regression alone, therefore, they are most likely to improve after being punished and most likely to deteriorate after being rewarded. Consequently, we are exposed to a lifetime schedule in which we are most often rewarded for punishing others, and punished for rewarding.

Not one of the graduate students who answered this question suggested that regression could cause the problem. Instead, they proposed that verbal reinforcements might be ineffective for pilots or that they could lead to overconfidence. Some students even doubted the validity of the instructors' impressions and discussed possible sources of bias in their perception of the situation. These respondents had undoubtedly been exposed to a thorough treatment of statistical regression. Nevertheless, they failed to recognize an instance of regression when it was not couched in the familiar terms of the height of fathers and sons. Evidently, statistical training alone does not change fundamental intuitions about uncertainty.

5.   Studies of representativeness

Maya Bar-Hillel

Daniel Kahneman and Amos Tversky have proposed that when judging the probability of some uncertain event people often resort to heuristics, or rules of thumb, which are less than perfectly correlated (if, indeed, at all) with the variables that actually determine the event's probability. One such heuristic is *representativeness*, defined as a subjective judgment of the extent to which the event in question "is similar in essential properties to its parent population" or "reflects the salient features of the process by which it is generated" (Kahneman & Tversky, 1972b, p. 431, 3). Although in some cases more probable events also appear more representative, and vice versa, reliance on the representativeness of an event as an indicator of its probability may introduce two kinds of systematic error into the judgment. First, it may give undue influence to variables that affect the representativeness of an event but not its probability. Second, it may reduce the importance of variables that are crucial to determining the event's probability but are unrelated to the event's representativeness.

The representativeness concept has occasionally been criticized as too vague and elusive, presumably because it lacks a general operational definition. This is not to say, however, that it is impossible to assess representativeness independently of probability judgments, a conclusion which has often been implied by the critics. In the "Tom W." study, for example, Kahneman and Tversky (1973, 4) defined representativeness as the similarity of some individual, Tom W., to "the typical graduate student in . . . [some] fields of graduate specialization" (1973, p. 238) and ranked it independently of the likelihood that Tom W. was enrolled in those fields. In other studies, the independent ranking by representativeness was sidestepped only because readers could so readily supply it themselves via thought experiments.

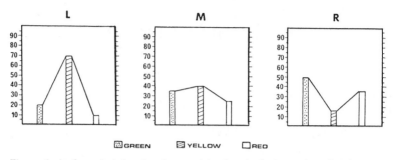

Figure 1. A characteristic stimulus used in the similarity and probability study. (*Source:* Bar-Hillel, 1974).

Similarity and probability

Shortly after the representativeness notion was introduced, I carried out a small study in which representativeness was ranked both by a priori criteria (to be spelled out later in this chapter) and experimentally, by subjects' judgments. These rankings were then compared with independently gathered probability judgments (Bar-Hillel, 1974). The tasks studied enjoyed the advantage of having unique, well-defined probabilities associated with them, along with a simple visual representation that lent itself easily to judgments of perceptual similarity.

The stimuli in this study were triples of bar graphs, denoted L, M, and R for left graph, middle graph, and right graph, respectively. One example is shown in Figure 1. Each graph consisted of three bars that were colored, from left to right, green, yellow, and red. The length of each bar was a multiple of 5 units, and the lengths of the three bars within each graph summed to 100.

All the triples (L, M, R) of bar graphs used in this experiment shared the following properties:

1. Every bar in the middle graph was midway in length between the corresponding bars in the graphs on the left and on the right. (If, however, the average length of the left and right bars did not yield a multiple of five, the middle bar was rounded to the nearest multiple of five.) For example, in Figure 1, the length of the green bar in the M graph is 35, which is midway between 20 and 50, the respective lengths of the bars in the L and R graphs. The same holds for the yellow and red bars. (Note, however, that the lengths of these bars have been rounded off: 42.5 to 40 and 22.5 to 25.)

2. The rank order of the lengths of the bars in the M graph coincided with the rank order of either those in the L graph or those in the R graph, but not both, since the L graph and the R graph were always rank ordered differently. For example, in Figure 1 the rank order of M and L is the same, red being shortest and yellow tallest in both, but is different in R, where yellow is the shortest bar. This was accentuated by a thin line sequentially

connecting the top of all the bars in a graph, although the X-axis was a nominal variable.

3. Suppose the M graph is interpreted as describing a trinomial population, and the L and R graphs are interpreted as samples of size 20 that might be drawn from this population. Then the sample whose rank order matched that of the M graph was always the less probable sample. For example, in Figure 1, M describes a trinomial population with parameters .35, .40, and .25. The odds in favor of drawing sample R (i.e., 10 green, 3 yellow, and 7 red beads) rather than sample L (i.e., 4 green, 14 yellow, and 2 red beads) are about 8 to 5, since

$$\frac{P(L|M)}{P(R|M)} = \frac{(20!/4!14!2!)}{(20!/10!3!7!)} \times \frac{(.35)^4(.40)^{14}(.25)^2}{(.35)^{10}(.40)^3(.25)^7} = .6127$$

Thus R is the more likely sample.

4. Suppose, alternatively, that L and R are interpreted as populations and M as a sample. Then the sample M was always less likely to emerge from the population whose rank order it matched. For example, in Figure 1, M describes a sample of 7 green, 8 yellow, and 5 red beads. The odds in favor of drawing M from population R (i.e., parameters .50, .15, and .35) rather than from population L (i.e., parameters .20, .70, and .10) are about 7 to 5, since

$$\frac{P(M|L)}{P(M|R)} = \frac{(20!/7!8!5!)}{(20!/7!8!5!)} \times \frac{(.20)^7(.70)^8(.10)^5}{(.50)^7(.15)^8(.35)^5} = .7017$$

Thus R is the likelier population.

Twenty-eight such triples were shown to three different groups of subjects, operating under three different sets of instructions. One group was told that each graph described a trinomial distribution, where L and R describe two populations and M describes a sample drawn from one of those populations. The 25 subjects in this group judged whether the sample depicted in M is more likely to be drawn from the L population or from the R population. Another group was told that M described a trinomial population, whereas L and R were two trinomial samples. The 26 subjects in this group judged which of the two samples was more likely to be drawn from the given population. These groups were first presented with a large glass jar filled with green, yellow, and red beads. They were shown how the jar (i.e., population) composition can be described by an appropriate bar graph. A sample of 20 beads was randomly drawn in their presence, and its bar graph representation was also demonstrated. The subjects were then instructed to think of L and R as representations of jar populations, with M representing a sample of 20 beads, or of L and R as samples, with M representing a population, according to the group they were in.

The third and last group, consisting of 25 subjects, was given no

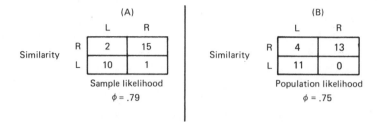

Figure 2. The joint distribution of subjects' rankings of L and R by similarity versus likelihood as samples (A) or populations (B). (*Source:* Bar-Hillel, 1974.)

interpretation for the graphs and was merely asked to judge which of the two graphs, L or R, more closely resembled the middle one, M.

For each of the three criteria separately ([1] more likely to yield sample M; [2] more likely to emerge from population M; [3] more similar to M), a stimulus was classified as L or R according to the graph selected by a majority of the subjects.

The two major findings of this study were:

1. The empirical similarity rankings given by subjects coincided perfectly with the a priori similarity criterion embodied in property 2 above. In other words, on all 28 stimuli, over 80% of the subjects judged M to be more similar to the graph in which the heights of the colored bars were ordered in the same way.

2. The rankings of L and R by likelihood, whether as samples or as populations, were highly correlated with their ranking by similarity. Of 17 triples in which R was judged more similar to M, only 2 were judged less likely as samples, and 4 were judged less likely as populations. Of the 11 samples in which L was judged more similar to M, only 1 was ranked lower than R, and that was as a sample. Thus, the similarity rankings disagreed with the probability rankings for less than 13% of the stimuli. The joint classification of the similarity judgments with the likelihood judgments is given in Figure 2; in A, L and R were samples, in B, they were populations.

The ϕ coefficient of correlation between the likelihood rankings as samples and the likelihood rankings as populations was .75, about as high as the ϕ correlations between each of the likelihood rankings and the similarity rankings. This supports the position that subjects in both the probability-judgment groups were basing their orderings largely on similarity, the judgment performed by the third group.

What features make samples seem representative?

Olson (1976) pointed out that although "the notion of judgment based on an assessment of representativeness enjoys considerable support, both experimental and introspective, in a wide range of judgmental situations," it is not complete until we can determine "the factors that make particular task and problem characteristics the salient ones with respect to which representativeness is judged" (p. 608). In some contexts, such as the similarity and probability study, these have been identified. To give another example, the cue that determines sample representativeness for unordered samples of varying size drawn from some Bernoulli distribution appears to be the disparity between the proportion of "successes" in the sample and the corresponding population parameter (Kahneman & Tversky, 1972b, 3). The study I shall now describe (Bar-Hillel, 1980b) suggests a general methodology for identifying the representativeness-controlling features for samples from any population. It is exemplified by an attempt to identify the cues that determine representativeness for samples (of three observations) taken from bell-shaped (e.g., normal) distributions.

The basic tenet is simple: If we assume that judgments of representativeness and of likelihood are determined by the same essential characteristics, then these characteristics can be discovered by asking people to render probability judgments for a suitably selected set of samples. This procedure reverses the roles of probability and representativeness. In other words, probability judgments are used not to confirm representativeness but to infer representativeness. Asking subjects, however, to rank samples by representativeness directly may well be begging the question. They might retort: "Well, what do you *mean* by representativeness?" Instead, the proposed strategy substitutes a clear, unambiguous question ("Which of these samples is more likely to be drawn at random from this population?") that under standard assumptions has a normative answer.

Subjects were given a problem such as the following:

The average height of American college men is 175 cm. Three files were randomly drawn from a college registrar's office, belonging to John, Mike, and Bob. Which outcome is more likely with respect to the heights of these three men?

John – 178 cm		John – 177 cm
Mike – 170 cm	or	Mike – 177 cm
Bob – 176 cm		Bob – 177cm

The actual numbers given differed on different forms and can be found in the stimuli columns of Table 1 (the previous example corresponds to row 1). By systematically varying the numbers used, it was possible to check just which sample features, and in what order, were determining the subjects' responses. Before I offer a summation of the emergent picture, a few explanatory comments are in order, to help the reader come to grips with the table.

1. The sample labeled *A* is always the one that was perceived as more likely than the sample with which it was paired. In the original questionnaire forms, the *A* samples appeared as often on the right as on the left. The exact proportion of subjects that chose *A* over *B* is listed in the responses columns.

Table 1. *Judgments and statistical measures of the relative likelihood of pairs of samples in Bar-Hillel (1980b)*

	Stimuli for sample A			Stimuli for sample B			Responses		n	$\frac{P(B)}{P(A)}$	True answer	KS statistic	
	John	Mike	Bob	John	Mike	Bob	A(%)	B(%)				A	B
Three different vs. three identical observations													
1.	178	170	176	177	177	177	95	5	188	1.39	B	.31	.63
2.	181	165	177	175	175	175	93	7	29	6.42	B	.30	.50
3.	178	170	176	175	175	175	97	3	30	1.59	B	.31	.50
4.	178	180	176	175	175	175	85	15	26	1.59	B	.57	.50#
5.	178	180	176	177	177	177	80	20	25	1.39	B	.57	.63
6.	191	183	189	175	175	175	72	28	25	1300	B	.91	.50#
Three different vs. two identical observations													
7.	178	170	176	176	170	176	72	28	25	1.12	B	.31	.43
8.	178	170	176	178	170	178	76	24	25	.68	A	.31	.36
9.	176	174	175	178	170	178	57	43	29	.56	A	.43	.36#
Larger range preferred													
10.	178	170	176	176	174	175	62	38	29	1.58	B	.31	.43
11.	178	170	176	177	173	176	71	29	31	1.43	B	.31	.37
12.	178	170	176	178	172	177	54	46	28	1.14	B	.31	.31
13.	178	170	176	177	171	175	54	46	28	1.14	B	.31	.37
Smaller range preferred													
14.	178	170	176	179	169	177	54	46	26	.75	A	.31	.30#
15.	178	170	176	181	165	177	77	23	30	.23	A	.31	.30#
16.	178	170	176	180	170	175	64	36	25	.81	A	.31	.20#
17.	178	170	176	181	169	175	59	41	27	.60	A	.31	.17#
Two-sided vs. one-sided samples													
18.	178	170	176	172	170	174	78	22	27	1.00	either	.31	.57
19.	178	170	176	178	180	176	64	36	25	1.00	either	.31	.57
20.	178	170	176	184	176	182	76	24	25	.26	A	.31	.57
21.	181	165	177	178	180	176	63	37	32	4.29	B	.57	.57

22.	176	174	175	184	176	182	73	27	30	.87	A	.37	.57
23.	177	171	175	178	180	176	93	7	28	.17	A	.43	.57
24.	176	174	175	178	180	176	79	21	37	1.58	B	.43	.57
25.	183	175	177	184	176	182	87	13	30	.42	A	.50	.57
26.	185	175	177	184	176	182	85	15	27	.68	A	.50	.57
27.	178	180	176	184	176	182	91	9	34	.26	A	.57	.57
28.	178	180	176	181	179	183	81	19	26	.32	A	.57	.75

Both samples one-sided

Source: Bar-Hillel (1980b).

2. The sample that is more likely from a normative standpoint can be seen in the statistical measures column. Sample A is more likely than sample B if and only if $P(A)/P(B) > 1$, that is, iff

$$\frac{f(X_1) \cdot f(X_2) \cdot f(X_3)}{f(Y_1) \cdot f(Y_2) \cdot f(Y_3)} > 1$$

where $A = [X_1, X_2, X_3]$, $B = [Y_1, Y_2, Y_3]$. This ratio was computed for the normal density function with $\mu = 175$ cm, $\sigma = 6$ cm. Since the statistically correct answer appears in the A and B columns about equally often, subjects' responses are clearly related to it at no better than chance level.

Perhaps the most striking feature of the results tabulated in Table 1 is that there is no single cue on which subjects rely in ordering the samples. For example, sometimes they choose the sample whose mean is closer to the population mean (e.g., row 1), and sometimes they choose the opposite (e.g., row 2). Sometimes they choose the sample containing the more extreme observations (e.g., row 13), and sometimes the opposite (e.g., row 14). Indeed, it seems as if a host of cues are relevant – number of identical observations, whether both sides of the population mean are represented, sample mean and range – and are considered in some kind of sequential fashion, as depicted in Figure 3. This strengthens the view that whatever determines the judged likelihood of a sample constitutes a concept unto itself. Had subjects been using a single cue, it would not have been necessary to label it *representativeness*. It is the fact that the subjects' judgments seem to be based on complex configural considerations of the gestalt of samples that lends force to terming – nay, conceptualizing – their heuristic *judgment by representativeness*.

Can the flow chart in Figure 3 be viewed as more than a merely convenient and compact summary of the results in Table 1? How seriously can we take it to be a process model of the subjects' actual reasoning in a task of the kind described? On the one hand, obviously not all features of the model can be expected to generalize – to other samples, to other sample sizes, to other distributions. I would not, for example, bet that any sample with variance would always be judged more likely than any sample without variance – although this does hold for the samples employed in my experiment. The sequential model is, thus, only an approximation of people's actual cognitive strategy. As such, however, it enjoys the attractive psychological advantage of being believable, since it incorporates but a small number of computationally simple cues.

An interesting observation suggests itself at this point and ties the previously described study to the present one. In the bar graphs study, two kinds of probability rankings were compared with similarity rankings: (a) the ranking of two samples as more or less likely outcomes from some population, denoted $P(s/p)$; (b) the ranking of two populations as more or less likely sources of some sample, denoted $P(p/s)$ (sometimes called inverse probabilities). The two tasks yielded very close results, suggesting

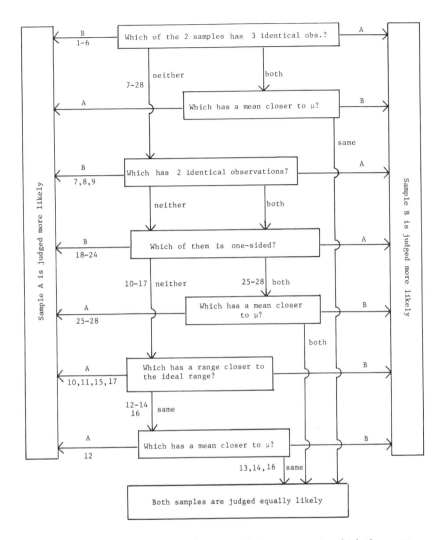

Figure 3. Flow chart summarizing the cues and the sequence in which they were used for ranking samples by likelihood. (*Source:* Bar-Hillel, 1980b.)

that they were both done in a closely related way – indeed, by hypothesis, that they were both done by representativeness (i.e., here, visual similarity). There is a statistical concept that is somewhat analogous to the psychological concept of representativeness – that of goodness of fit. Measures of goodness of fit are typically used in hypothesis testing when the population that yielded some known sample is sought, in the absence of any prior probability. Thus when evaluating populations, representativeness seems to correspond more closely to the concept of goodness of fit between a sample and a population than to the concept of the probability of a population conditional on some sample, $P(p/s)$.

In the heights-distribution study, however, the population that was the source of the samples was given. Therefore, subjects had no business assessing either inverse probabilities or goodness of fit. Nevertheless, it is interesting to see whether their judgments can, somehow, be reconstructed as an intuitive attempt to assess the latter.

One possible measure of goodness of fit between samples of size three and a normal distribution is the one-sample, two-sided Kolmogorov-Smirnov (KS) statistic (see, e.g., Siegel, 1956, pp. 47–52). This statistic is interpreted so that the larger its value (which is the maximal distance between the distribution functions of the sample and the population), the less likely it is that the sample was drawn randomly from the population. The last two columns of Table 1 list the KS statistic for each of the studied samples. In 18 pairs, the ordering of the samples by the KS statistic agreed with their ordering by most subjects; in 3 pairs the KS statistic was tied (in 1 of which, row 12, the subjects were practically tied, too), and in 7 pairs (marked in Table 1 by asterisks) the orderings conflict.

It is of little consequence to compare the extent of the agreement between the KS ordering and the subjects' ordering with that between the normative ordering and the subjects' ordering (the latter agreed on 13 of the 28 stimuli), since the latter figures are just by-products of the particular stimuli employed, which were not randomly *sampled* in any way from all possible stimuli or what not. It is much more instructive to consider where the hierarchical-features model differs from the goodness-of-fit model. The cases where the KS ordering was tied but the subjects' ordering was not (rows 21, 27, and to a small extent 12) can be attributed to the KS values, having been computed with a standard deviation of 6 cm. This resulted in the sample [181, 169, 175] (sample *B*, row 17), which has a range of 12 cm, having the smallest KS value, when the "ideal" (i.e., most representative) range in the subjects' judgments was somewhat smaller – 8 to 10 cm. Since we have no way, on the basis of the present data, to ascertain the standard deviation of people's subjective distribution of heights, it is hard to know what to make of this discrepancy.

A second kind of discrepancy, which accounts for rows 4, 6, 9, and 14–17, occurs because the KS model, but not the hierarchical model, allows for compensation. In other words, if some sample has a major "flaw" (such as consisting of three identical observations, or representing only one-half of the population bell), subjects judge it less representative than just about any sample without that flaw, but the KS model considers factors that are further down in the hierarchical model, too. Since, as I said before, the hierarchical nature of the proposed process model should be regarded as an approximation, this discrepancy is more one of degree than one of kind.

Other goodness-of-fit measures are computed by statisticians. That they do not all agree indicates that the property they purport to measure is not clear and uniquely defined. Although the trained statistician has a more sophisticated intuition than the lay subject, both may well be trying to get at the same underlying notion. To date, even the statisticians' efforts in this direction fall short of being completely satisfactory.

The role of sample size in sample evaluation

Some sample characteristics correspond to certain population parameters; these characteristics are called sample statistics. The representativeness heuristic has typically been applied to them, in which case representativeness is equivalent to *similarity*, or *closeness*, of the sample statistics to the corresponding population parameters. I shall call this the primary sense of representativeness. But samples can be described by reference to the procedure whereby they were drawn as well. For example, a sample can be drawn with replacement or without; drawn from a known population or an unknown one; etc. Presumably, the notion of representativeness could also be applied to these. Thus, people might (and there is anecdotal evidence that they do) judge a sample drawn at random to be less representative than a stratified sample, or a large sample to be more representative than a small one (Bar-Hillel, 1980b). I shall call this the secondary sense of representativeness. Since it concerns sampling methods, and not post hoc sample statistics, representativeness in this secondary sense reflects expectations about representativeness in the primary sense. In other words, to judge a large sample more representative than a small one is to expect that its "salient features" or "essential properties" will better reflect those of the population, in advance of being told what they actually are.

The experimental problems that I shall describe in this last section studied this secondary sense of representativeness, as applied to the feature of sample size.

Problem 1: Two pollsters are conducting a survey to estimate the proportion of voters who intend to vote YES on a certain referendum. Firm A is surveying a sample of 400 individuals. Firm B is surveying a sample of 1,000 individuals. Whose estimate would you be more confident in accepting?

   Firm A's____   Firm B's____   About the same____

This problem, and two variants thereof (which, respectively, added the information that the total size of the community surveyed was 8,000 and 50,000), were given to 72 subjects. Over 80% of them had more confidence in the large sample, compared with only 4% favoring the smaller sample.

Had we concluded from this merely that the larger a sample is, the more representative it is judged (i.e., the more accurate or reliable it is expected to be), these results would be almost too trivial to warrant reporting. It is not sample size per se that determines a sample's representativeness, however, but rather something more akin to the ratio between the sample size and the population size. Where the samples considered are taken from the same population, the two are linearly related, so they give the same ordering. Where population size is varied as well as sample size, however, the difference becomes apparent. Consider the following problem:

Problem 2: Two pollsters are conducting surveys to estimate the proportion of voters in their respective cities who intend to vote YES on a certain referendum.
   Firm A operates in a city of 1 million voters
   Firm B operates in a city of 50,000 voters
Both firms are sampling one out of every 1,000 voters.
Whose estimate would you be more confident in accepting? ____

Here, although Firm A has a sample of 1,000 and Firm B of only 50, the percentage of Ss who expressed more confidence in the larger sample dropped to 50%, whereas 29% indicated equal confidence in both samples. In another group of subjects who were told that both firms sampled 1,000 people (rather than 1 in every 1,000), 9% indicated equal confidence in the samples, compared with 62% who were more confident in the sample polled in the smaller city. The explanatory comments that subjects were asked to supply confirmed the notion that they were considering the *proportionate* sample sizes, as well as the absolute sizes.

Sometimes sample-to-population ratio is indeed important for evaluating a sample – for example, when sampling is done without replacement and especially when a reasonably large proportion of it is being sampled. If, however, sampling is done with replacement (i.e., population size is infinite), or if only a small proportion of a large population is being sampled (which renders the population, for all pragmatical purposes, infinite), then considerations of relative size pale beside those of absolute size.

Problem 3: You are presented with two covered urns. Both of them contain a mixture of red and green beads. The number of beads is different in the two urns: the small one contains 10 beads, and the large one contains 100 beads. However, the percentage of red and green beads is the same in both urns. The sampling will proceed as follows: You draw a bead blindly from the urn, note its color, and replace it. You mix, draw blindly again, and note down the color again. This goes on to a total of 9 draws from the small urn, or 15 draws from the large urn. In which case do you think your chances for guessing the majority color are better?

Since the sampling procedure described in problem 3 is with replacement, the number of beads in the two urns is completely unimportant from a normative standpoint. Subjects' choices should have overwhelmingly favored the larger sample of 15 beads. Instead, 72 of 110 subjects chose the smaller sample of 9 beads. This can be explained only by noting that the ratio of sample size to population size is 90% in the latter case and only 15% in the former. Other results reported in Bar-Hillel (1979) support the same conclusion.

Thus, if sample statistics, the prime candidates for the role of "essential properties," are not known, sample size may assume that role. People clearly perceive that size is an advantageous property of samples. Why does this awareness fail to carry over to the primary sense of representativeness? In other words, given that people believe larger samples are more likely than smaller ones to be good representatives of their parent population, why do they fail to judge certain deviant results (e.g., a sample proportion of 60% drawn from a population characterized by a 50% proportion) as less likely in larger than in smaller samples?

Possibly the judgment that a certain sample result is less likely in larger samples depends on its being perceived as nonrepresentative. From a normative standpoint, only a sample whose mean is identical to the population mean is "accurate." All others are inaccurate, albeit some more so than others. From a psychological standpoint, sample results may be judged as representative even if they deviate somewhat from the population parameters. Perhaps 60% is not perceived as nonrepresentative and therefore does not evoke subjects' second-order sense of representativeness.

To test this possibility, I gave subjects several variations of Kahneman and Tversky's (1972b, 3) maternity-ward problem:

A certain town is served by two hospitals. In the larger hospital about 45 babies are born each day, and in the smaller hospital about 15 babies are born each day. As you know, about 50% of all babies are boys. The exact percentage of baby boys, however, varies from day to day. Sometimes it may be higher than 50%, sometimes lower.

For a period of 1 year, each hospital recorded the days on which (more/less) than 60% of the babies born were boys. Which hospital do you think recorded more such days? (1972b, p. 443)

In separate problems given to separate groups, the proportion of boys was varied from 60% to 70%, 80%, and 100%. Table 2 shows the effect of this change on subjects' response distribution.

The second column replicates, both in the problem and in the results, Kahneman and Tversky's version. But note that once the proportion of boys exceeds 70%, the modal response becomes "the smaller hospital," which is the correct answer. By the time all babies are said to be boys, "the smaller hospital" is even the majority response. Another set of problems stated the proportion as less than 60%, 70%, or 80%. For these, "the same" was the modal response throughout.

These results suggest that once a sample result is perceived as nonrepresentative, sample size is more likely to play a proper role in people's evaluation of the sample, presumably because a smaller size is more compatible with nonrepresentative results than a larger one. If, however, the stated sample result does not trigger the label "nonrepresentative," people by and large ignore sample size. Proportions higher than 70% seem to be coded as nonrepresentative. Proportions that include 50% do not.

Table 2. *Proportion of subjects responding to the maternity-ward problem, with variations*

	Over 60%[a]	Over 60%[b]	Over 70%[b]	Over 80%[b]	100%[c]
Larger	24%	20%	25%	26%	19%
Smaller	20%	20%	43%	42%	54%
Same	56%	60%	32%	32%	27%
N	50	40	28	27	41

	Under 60%[a]		Under 70%[b]	Under 80%[b]	
Larger	20%		31%	29%	
Smaller	24%		28%	25%	
Same	56%		41%	46%	
N	45		29	28	

[a]From Kahneman and Tversky (1972b, 3).
[b]Previously unpublished data, Bar-Hillel.
[c]From Bar-Hillel (1979). Here, the larger and smaller hospitals average 15 and 5 babies a day, respectively.

Discussion

This chapter presents a summary of three studies of subjective probability judgments that relate to the notion of representativeness. Each of them, however, does so in a different way.

The first study is a straightforward demonstration that similarity judgments and likelihood judgments are correlated. Unlike many of the other tasks that tested the same hypotheses (see, e.g., Kahneman & Tversky, 1972b, 3; 1973, 4), subjects here can be faulted neither for failing to take other considerations (or, at least, other obvious or simple considerations) into account nor for giving undue weight to erroneous or irrelevant considerations. As a matter of fact, short of actually computing the probabilities that they were asked to compare, there is little the subjects could have done other than using the strategy they used. This somewhat diminishes the power of the demonstration. Taken together with other results, however, it points out how compelling similarity considerations – even of the simple visual kind that this study evoked – can be when judging what are often complex events, computationally or conceptually.

Prior to the sample-features study, the tests of representativeness had typically concentrated on single-parameter populations, or on one-dimensional cues. This allowed an immediate and a priori ranking of stimuli by similarity, making it unnecessary to obtain independent experimentally derived rankings. (Nevertheless, even some of these "obvious" cues were later doubted [see, e.g., Olson, 1976].) But when stimuli grow more complex, the similarity relationships among them become less obvious, since many cues affect the overall judgment. This study exploited the by then established correlation between probability and representativeness to shed some light on how the latter is determined in samples characterized by more than a single cue.

Often, the best way to find out how similar two stimuli are is to inquire directly about similarity. This is somewhat more problematic when one wants to find out how well sample S represents population P. It is useful, therefore, to be able to assess that indirectly, for example, by asking how likely sample S is to be drawn from population P. The second study in this chapter shows the viability of this approach while giving a description of what sample features make samples appear representative in one particular context.

Finally, the third study points out an important distinction, that between the representativeness of a sample and the representativeness of the sample results. In its primary sense, representativeness is a judgment that applies to sample results. In other words, in order to assess how representative some sample is of some population in this sense, the essential characteristics of both have to be known. Thus, it is meaningful to rate, say, the representativeness of a sample of 15 newborns, 9 of whom are boys, vis-à-vis the general newborn sex distribution (with its known proportion of boys). It is meaningless to rate the representativeness of this sample if the proportion of boys either in the sample or in the population is unknown. But there is another, secondary sense of representativeness that would render the second rating meaningful, too. In this other sense, samples are more representative if they are judged to be more likely to be representative in the primary sense. In other words, regardless of the population mean, and before the sample mean is divulged, a sample of 45 newborns is more representative (in the secondary sense) than one of 15 newborns, because it is more likely to resemble the population once its proportion of boys is divulged. Post hoc, of course, the sample of 45 may prove to have 60% boys, as compared with 53% boys in the smaller sample. But if the two senses are kept distinct, this should cause no confusion.

The third study demonstrated that people respond to sample size when making secondary judgments of representativeness, even though they often fail to realize the implications this necessarily has for the primary, and standard, judgment of representativeness.

6.   Judgments of and by representativeness

Amos Tversky and Daniel Kahneman

Several years ago, we presented an analysis of judgment under uncertainty that related subjective probabilities and intuitive predictions to expectations and impressions about representativeness. Two distinct hypotheses incorporated this concept: (i) people expect samples to be highly similar to their parent population and also to represent the randomness of the sampling process (Tversky & Kahneman, 1971, 2; 1974, 1); (ii) people often rely on representativeness as a heuristic for judgment and prediction (Kahneman & Tversky, 1972b, 3; 1973, 4).

The first hypothesis was advanced to explain the common belief that chance processes are self-correcting, the exaggerated faith in the stability of results observed in small samples, the gambler's fallacy, and related biases in judgments of randomness. We proposed that the lay conception of chance incorporates a belief in the law of small numbers, according to which even small samples are highly representative of their parent populations (Tversky & Kahneman, 1971, 2). A similar hypothesis could also explain the common tendency to exaggerate the consistency and the predictive value of personality traits (Mischel, 1979) and to overestimate the correlations between similar variables (see Chap. 15) and behaviors (Shweder & D'Andrade, 1980). People appear to believe in a hologram-like model of personality in which any fragment of behavior represents the actor's true character (Kahneman & Tversky, 1973, 4).

The hypothesis that people expect samples to be highly representative of their parent populations is conceptually independent of the second hypothesis, that people often use the representativeness heuristic to make predictions and judge probabilities. That is, people often evaluate the probability of an uncertain event or a sample "by the degree to which it is

This work was supported by the Office of Naval Research under Contract N00014-79-C-0077 to Stanford University.

(i) similar in essential properties to its parent population and (ii) reflects the salient features of the process by which it is generated" (Kahneman & Tversky, 1972b, p. 431, **3**). This hypothesis was studied in several contexts, including intuitive statistical judgments and the prediction of professional choice (Kahneman & Tversky, 1972b, **3**; 1973, **4**).

The two representativeness hypotheses have been used to explain a variety of observations, such as the relative ineffectiveness of consensus information and the use of similarity in the interpretation of projective tests (Nisbett & Ross, 1980). These hypotheses have also provided direction to a well-rewarded search for significant violations of normative rules in intuitive judgments. Most of this research has been concerned with judgments *by* representativeness, that is, with the role of representativeness in prediction and inference. Relatively little work has been devoted to judgments *of* representativeness, that is, to the nature of this relation and its determinants, outside the context of random sampling (Bar-Hillel, 1980b). The first part of this chapter is concerned with the nature of the representativeness relation and also with the conditions in which the concept of representativeness is usefully invoked to explain intuitive predictions and judgments of probability. In the second part of the chapter we illustrate the contrast between the logic of representativeness and the logic of probability in judgments of the likelihood of compound events.

The representativeness relation

Representativeness is a relation between a process or a model, M, and some instance or event, X, associated with that model. Representativeness, like similarity, can be assessed empirically, for example, by asking people to judge which of two events, X_1 or X_2, is more representative of some model, M, or whether an event, X, is more representative of M_1 or of M_2. The model in question could be of a person, a fair coin, or the world economy, and the respective outcomes might be a comment, a sequence of heads and tails, or the present price of gold.

Representativeness is a directional relation: We say that a sample is more or less representative of a particular population and that an act is representative of a person. We do not normally say that the population is representative of the sample or that the person is representative of the act. In some problems, however, it is possible to reverse the roles of model and outcome. For example, one may evaluate whether a person is representative of the stereotype of librarians or whether the occupation of librarian is representative of that person.

We distinguish four basic cases in which the concept of representativeness is commonly invoked.

1. *M is a class and X is a value of a variable defined in this class.* It is in this sense that we speak of (more or less) representative values of the income of

college professors, or of marriage age in a culture. Naturally, the most representative value will be close to the mean, median, or mode of the distribution of the relevant variable in the class M. The relation of representativeness is mainly determined in this case by what the judge knows about the frequency distribution of the relevant variable.

2. *M is a class and X is an instance of that class.* Most readers will probably agree that John Updike is a more representative American writer than Norman Mailer. Clearly, such a judgment does not have a basis in frequency; it reflects the degree to which the styles, themes, and ideas of these authors are central to contemporary American writings. Similar considerations determine the representativeness of instances that are themselves classes rather than individuals. For example, a robin is judged to be a more typical bird than a chicken, although it is less frequent (Rosch, 1978; Smith, Shoben, & Rips, 1974). Thus, an instance is representative of a category if it has the essential features that are shared by members of that category and does not have many distinctive features that are not shared by category members (Rosch, 1975; Tversky, 1977).

Contemporary work on concept formation (Rosch & Mervis, 1975; Mervis & Rosch, 1981), semantic memory (Bransford & Franks, 1971), and pattern recognition (Posner & Keele, 1968) has shown that the most representative, or prototypical, elements of a category are better learned, recalled, and recognized than elements that are more frequent but less representative. Moreover, people often err by "recognizing" a prototypical stimulus that has never been shown. Representativeness, therefore, can bias recognition memory as well as judgments of frequency.

It should perhaps be noted that there are two ways in which an element can be highly representative of a class. The two senses of representativeness correspond closely to the relations of typicality and prototypicality. An element is highly representative of a category if it is typical or modal; it can also be representative if it is an ideal type that embodies the essence of the category. New York, for example, is the prototype of an American city, but Cincinnati is more likely to be selected as a typical city. Similarly, our notions of the prototypical and of the typical Frenchwoman may be quite different. The former is probably a young, elegant Parisian, while the latter is more likely to be a chubby middle-aged woman from the provinces.

3. *M is a class and X is a subset of M.* Most people will probably agree that the population of Florida is less representative of the U.S. population than is the population of Illinois and that students of astronomy are less representative of the entire student body than are students of psychology. The criteria of representativeness are not the same for a subset and for a single instance, because an instance can only represent the central tendency of attributes, whereas a subset can also represent range and variability. A man whose height, weight, age, and income match the average values for the U.S. population is, clearly, representative of that

population. A group of 100 men with the same characteristics would fail to represent the variability of the attributes.

If the class M consists of distinct clusters such that the variability within each cluster is very small relative to the variability between the clusters, we tend to treat each cluster as an instance of the category rather than as a subset. Thus, it is natural to regard "robin" as a kind of bird, or as an instance of the category "bird," although the set of robins is a subset of the class of birds. More generally, (2) can be regarded as a special case of (3) where the subset X consists of a single member. Similarly, (1) can be regarded as a unidimensional version of (2). The three types of representativeness are distinguished by the complexity of X, where (1) is the single-element, single-attribute case, (2) is the single-element, multiattribute case, and (3) is the multiple element case – with one or more attributes.

A particularly important example of the representativeness of a subset is the case in which X is a random sample from a specified population. A random sample is expected to represent the randomness of the selection process, not only the essential features of the population from which it is drawn. When 100 people are selected at random, for example, a sample of 53 men and 47 women may appear more representative than a sample of 50 men and 50 women, because the former represents the irregularity of random sampling while the latter does not (Kahneman & Tversky, 1972b, 3). The statistical concept of a representative sample is discussed by Kruskal and Mosteller (1979a, 1979b).

4. *M is a (causal) system and X is a (possible) consequence.* This case differs from the preceding ones in that M is no longer a class of objects or instances but rather a system that produces various effects. For example, M can be the U.S. economy and X the rate of inflation, or M can be a person and X an act performed by M, for example, divorce, suicide, professional choice. Here, X is representative of M either because it is frequently associated with M (e.g., high fever commonly accompanies pneumonia) or because people believe, correctly or incorrectly, that M causes X (e.g., capital punishment prevents kidnappings). Intrusions of causal schemas in judgments of conditional probabilities are illustrated and discussed in Tversky and Kahneman (1980, 8).

In summary, a relation of representativeness can be defined for (1) a value and a distribution, (2) an instance and a category, (3) a sample and a population, (4) an effect and a cause. In all four cases, representativeness expresses the degree of correspondence between X and M, but its determinants are not the same in the four cases. In case (1), representativeness is dominated by perceived relative frequency or statistical association. In cases (2) and (3), representativeness is determined primarily by similarity, for example, of an instance to other instances, or of sample statistics to the corresponding parameters of a population. Finally, in case (4), representativeness is controlled largely by (valid or invalid) causal beliefs.

Representativeness and probability

The use of representativeness to explain probability judgments and intuitive predictions rests on the assumptions that:

1. The relation "X is (very, . . . , not at all) representative of M" can be meaningfully assessed by judges.
2. These assessments should not be based on impressions of probability or frequency, which are to be explained by representativeness.
3. The relation of representativeness has a logic of its own, which departs systematically from the logic of probability.

When these assumptions are satisfied, it is of interest to test whether judgments of probability are mediated by assessments of representativeness.

The evaluation of the probability of an uncertain event or the prediction of an unknown quantity is a complex process, which comprises an interpretation of the problem, a search for relevant information, and the choice of an appropriate response. It can be compared with the operation of a flexible computer program that incorporates a variety of potentially useful subroutines. In the terms of this analogy, the representativeness heuristic is one of the procedures that may be used to retrieve, interpret, and evaluate information. The use of this heuristic, of course, does not preclude the use of other procedures, much as the use of imagery as a heuristic for recall does not preclude the use of other strategies. However, the reliance on heuristics leads to characteristic biases. When imagery is used to recall the people who were present at a particular meeting, for example, participants who were clearly visible are expected to be remembered better than those who were not. Similarly, the use of representativeness to assess subjective probability produces overestimation of some probabilities and underestimation of others.

Early studies gave rise to the extreme hypothesis that some probability judgments are based exclusively on representativeness. For example, the observation that subjective sampling distributions are essentially independent of sample size (Kahneman & Tversky, 1972b, 3) suggested that people evaluate the probability of a sample by the similarity of its statistics to the corresponding parameters of the population. Most of the available data, however, support a more moderate hypothesis that intuitive predictions and probability judgments are highly sensitive to representativeness although they are not completely dominated by it. Thus, subjective probabilities are strongly influenced by (normatively) irrelevant factors that affect representativeness and are relatively insensitive to (normatively) relevant variables that do not affect representativeness. The magnitude of representativeness biases and the impact of variables such as sample size, reliability, and base rate depend on the nature of the problem, the characteristics of the design, the sophistication of the respondents, and the presence of suggestive clues or other demand characteristics. The role of these factors in judgment research is discussed in Chapter 34.

If the reliance on representativeness leads to systematic errors, why do people use this relation as a basis for prediction and judgment? The answer to this question has three parts. First, representativeness appears readily accessible and easy to evaluate. Modern research on categorization (Mervis & Rosch, 1981; Rosch, 1978) suggests that conceptual knowledge is often organized and processed in terms of prototypes or representative examples. Consequently, we find it easier to evaluate the representativeness of an instance to a class than to assess its conditional probability. Second, probable events are usually more representative than less probable events. For example, a sample that resembles the population is generally more likely than a highly atypical sample of the same size. Third, the belief that samples are generally representative of their parent populations leads people to overestimate the correlation between frequency and representativeness or between statistical association and connotative similarity. Thus, representativeness is used because (i) it is accessible, (ii) it often correlates with probability, and (iii) people overestimate this correlation. The reliance on representativeness, however, leads to predictable errors of judgment because representativeness has a logic of its own, which differs from the logic of probability.

The contrast between representativeness and probability is most pronounced (i) when the evidence is fallible or (ii) when the target event is highly specific. In case (i), an outcome that is highly representative of our model may nevertheless be improbable – if our mental model is based on evidence of limited validity. Consider, for example, the probability that a candidate who made an excellent impression during an interview will succeed in a very difficult task. Because impressions based on interviews are notoriously fallible and success or failure on the job is controlled by numerous factors that are not predictable from a brief conversation, success may be very unlikely even when it is highly representative of our impression of the candidate.

In case (ii), a representative outcome may be very improbable because it is highly specific or detailed. In general, an event can be improbable either because it is atypical or because it is highly specific. A weight under 135 lbs. is atypical for a middle-aged man; a weight of 157.625 lbs. is typical but highly specific. Indeed, the latter is more representative for a middle-aged man, although the former is much more probable. As this example illustrates, an increase in specificity does not generally lead to diminished representativeness. Consequently, the comparison of events that differ in specificity often creates a conflict between representativeness and probability. For example, a random sample of four cards consisting of the king of hearts, ace of spades, nine of diamonds, and four of clubs, appears more representative than a sample consisting of four cards of the same suit, although the latter is far more probable. Thus, representativeness biases in probability judgments should be most pronounced in the assessment of events that are representative but highly specific. Such biases are demonstrated in studies of probability judgments of compound events described in the next section.

On the evaluation of compound events

The sharpest contrast between probability and representativeness arises in the evaluation of compound events. Suppose that we are given some information about an individual (e.g., a personality sketch) and that we speculate about various attributes or combinations of attributes that this individual may possess, such as occupation, avocation, or political affinity. One of the basic laws of probability is that specification can only reduce probability. Thus, the probability that a given person is both a Republican and an artist must be smaller than the probability that the person is an artist. This condition holds not only in the standard probability calculus but also in non-standard models (e.g., Shafer, 1976; Zadeh, 1978).

However, the requirement that $P(A \& B) \leq P(B)$, which may be called the conjunction rule, does not apply to similarity or representativeness. A blue square, for example, can be more similar to a blue circle than to a circle, and an individual may resemble our image of a Republican artist more than our image of a Republican. Because the similarity of an object to a target can be increased by adding to the target features that are shared by the object (see Tversky, 1977), similarity or representativeness can be increased by specification of the target. If probability judgments are mediated by representativeness or similarity it should be possible to construct problems where a conjunction of outcomes appears more representative and hence more probable than one of its components.

The conjunction effect: Study 1

This prediction was first tested in an experiment conducted in Jerusalem in 1974. We presented 184 subjects with four personality sketches. Each sketch matched the stereotype of a particular occupation (e.g., a cab driver) and differed sharply from the stereotype of a particular political party (e.g., labor), or vice versa. Hence, each description (X) was representative of one target, denoted A, and unrepresentative of another target, denoted B. Every sketch was followed by a list of five or six target events described by an occupation, a political affiliation, or a conjunction, for example, a cab driver who is a member of the labor party. For each description, half the subjects received a list including both target A and target B while the other half received a list including the compound target ($A \& B$). The remaining four targets were identical in the two lists. Half the subjects were asked to rank the targets according to "the degree to which X is representative of that class," and the other half ranked them according to "the probability that X is a member of that class."

The design of the study permitted an indirect comparison of representativeness and probability for the event B and the compound (A & B) in relation to the four constant alternatives. The results may be summarized as follows. First, all four descriptions were judged to be more representative of the compound target (A & B) than of target B alone. Second, the representativeness ordering and the likelihood ordering of each set of targets were almost identical in all cases; the average product–moment correlation between mean ranks was .96. In particular, the compound target (A & B) was assigned a significantly higher mean rank in the probability ordering than the simple target B. Evidently, the reliance on the representativeness heuristic led the respondents to regard a conjunctive event as more probable than one of its components, contrary to the conjunction rule of probability theory. This pattern of judgments will be called the conjunction effect.

Study 2: Bill and Linda

Because the stimulus material used in the early study was highly specific to Israeli culture, we constructed an English version of the problems and replicated the study with several significant variations. First, we compared the results of a between-subject design, in which each respondent compared either the compound target (A & B) or the simple target, B, to the same set of alternatives, to a within-subjects design in which each respondent compared the two critical targets directly. We hypothesized that the conjunction rule would fail in the former design, as in our previous study, but we expected that the frequency of violations would be greatly reduced in the latter design where the participants were asked, in effect, to compare $P(A)$ with $P(A \& B)$. Second, we expected that even limited statistical sophistication would eliminate most violations of the conjunction rule, at least in a within-subjects design.

To investigate these hypotheses, we conducted both a within-subjects (direct) and a between-subjects (indirect) study, with the same stimulus material. The study was replicated in three groups of respondents that differed in statistical sophistication. The statistically naive group consisted of undergraduate students from the University of British Columbia and Stanford University who had no background in probability or statistics. The intermediate group consisted of graduate students in psychology and education and of medical students from Stanford University who had taken several courses in statistics and were all familiar with the basic concepts of probability. The statistically sophisticated group consisted of graduate students in the decision science program of the Stanford Business School who had all taken several advanced courses in probability and statistics.

Two brief personality sketches were constructed. Each participant encountered one of these sketches in the within-subjects treatment and the other in a between-subjects treatment. In the former, the personality sketch was followed by eight possible outcomes, including a representative outcome, an unrepresentative outcome, and the conjunction of the two. In the between-subjects treatment the list of outcomes included either the two critical single outcomes or their conjunction. The within-subjects forms of the two problems are shown here. The numbers in parentheses are the mean ranks assigned to the various outcomes by the subjects who received this form.

Bill is 34 years old. He is intelligent, but unimaginative, compulsive, and generally lifeless. In school, he was strong in mathematics but weak in social studies and humanities.

Please rank order the following statements by their probability, using 1 for the *most* probable and 8 for the least probable.
  (4.1) Bill is a physician who plays poker for a hobby.
  (4.8) Bill is an architect.
  (1.1) Bill is an accountant.   (A)
  (6.2) Bill plays jazz for a hobby.   (J)
  (5.7) Bill surfs for a hobby.
  (5.3) Bill is a reporter.
  (3.6) Bill is an accountant who plays jazz for a hobby.   ($A \& J$)
  (5.4) Bill climbs mountains for a hobby.

Linda is 31 years old, single, outspoken, and very bright. She majored in philosophy. As a student, she was deeply concerned with issues of discrimination and social justice, and also participated in anti-nuclear demonstrations.

Please rank the following statements by their probability, using 1 for the most probable and 8 for the least probable.
  (5.2) Linda is a teacher in elementary school.
  (3.3) Linda works in a bookstore and takes Yoga classes.
  (2.1) Linda is active in the feminist movement.   (F)
  (3.1) Linda is a psychiatric social worker.
  (5.4) Linda is a member of the League of Women Voters.
  (6.2) Linda is a bank teller.   (T)
  (6.4) Linda is an insurance salesperson.
  (4.1) Linda is a bank teller and is active in the feminist movement.   ($T \& F$)

As the reader has probably guessed, the description of Bill was constructed to be representative of an accountant (A) and unrepresentative of a person who plays jazz for a hobby (J). The description of Linda was constructed to be representative of an active feminist (F) and unrepresentative of a bank teller (T). In accord with psychological principles of similarity (Tversky, 1977) we expected that the compound targets, an accountant who plays jazz for a hobby ($A \& J$) and a bank teller who is active in the feminist movement ($T \& F$), would fall between the respective simple targets. To test this prediction, we asked a group of 88

Table 1. *The conjunction effect*

	Naive		Intermediate		Sophisticated	
	Linda	Bill	Linda	Bill	Linda	Bill
Within-subjects design						
Conjunction effect (%)	89	92	90	86	85	83
M rank: *A* & *B*	4.2	3.6	3.9	3.5	4.0	3.4
M rank: *B*	6.3	6.4	6.2	6.4	6.1	5.6
N	88	94	53	56	32	32
Between-subjects design						
M rank: *A* & *B*	3.3	2.3	2.9	2.4	3.1	2.5
M rank: *B*	4.4	4.5	3.9	4.2	4.3	4.6
N	86	88	55	56	32	32

statistically naive subjects to rank the eight targets "by the degree to which Bill (Linda) resembles the typical member of that class." The similarity rankings validated our hypotheses about the descriptions. The proportion of respondents who displayed the predicted order for Bill ($A > A$ & $J > J$) was 87%; the percentage of subjects who displayed the predicted order for Linda ($F > T$ & $F > T$) was 85%.

All participants received either the description of Bill or the description of Linda in the within-subjects form and rank ordered the eight targets according to their probabilities. These data are summarized in the upper part of Table 1, where the row labeled "conjunction effect (%)" presents the percentage of subjects in each group that ranked the compound target above the less representative simple target. The rows labeled "*A* & *B*" and "*B*" at present, respectively, the mean ranks assigned to the compound and to the less representative simple target. The mean rank of similarity is plotted in Figure 1 against the overall mean rank of probability in the within-subjects design.

In the between-subjects condition, two versions of each problem were constructed by deleting from the target list either the compound target or the two simple targets. The personality sketch, the instructions, and the remaining five targets were the same as in the within-subjects version. The results of the between-subjects design for all groups of respondents are presented in the lower part of Table 1.

The results summarized in Table 1 show that the compound target was ranked as more probable than the critical simple target in both within-subjects and between-subjects designs. This result held for both descriptions and for all groups. Much to our surprise, statistical sophistication had a negligible effect on the conjunction effect, which was exhibited by more than 80% of the subjects in all three groups.

In the preceding studies, the critical targets were embedded in a larger set of possible outcomes, which could have masked the relation of inclusion between them. It is of interest, therefore, to investigate whether

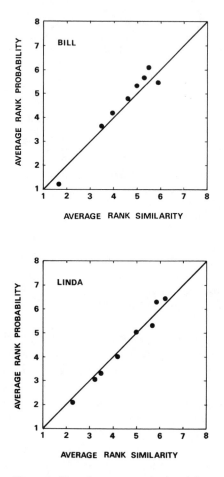

Figure 1. Plot of average ranks for eight outcomes, ranked by probability and by similarity for two descriptions.

people violate the conjunction rule even when the logical relation between the targets is highly transparent. To test this hypothesis, we presented a new group of (statistically naive) subjects with the descriptions of Bill and Linda. Each subject was presented with one of the two descriptions, and was asked which of the two critical targets [i.e., *J* and (*A* & *J*), or *T* and (*T* & *F*)] was more probable. This procedure did not reduce the conjunction effect: The compound target was selected by 92% of the subjects (*N* = 88) in the case of Bill and by 87% of the subjects (*N* = 86) in the case of Linda.

The massive failure of the conjunction rule raises intriguing questions concerning its normative appeal. To examine this question, we interviewed 36 graduate students, from the intermediate group, who had participated in the experiment. They were asked (1) how they had ordered the two critical categories, (2) why they had done so, and (3) to consider the argument that "the probability that Bill is both an accountant and a jazz player cannot exceed the probability that he is a jazz player, because every member of the former category is also a member of the latter." More than two-thirds of the subjects (1) said that they had selected the compound target, (2) gave some version of a similarity or a typicality argument as a reason, and (3) agreed, after some reflection, that their answer was wrong, because it was at variance with the conjunction rule. Only two of the subjects maintained that the probability order need not agree with class inclusion, and only one claimed that he had misinterpreted the question. Although the interview might have biased the respondents in favor of the conjunction rule, the results suggest that statistically informed subjects, at least, are willing to regard a violation of this rule as a regrettable error. For further discussion of this issue, see Chapter 34.

In interpreting the failure of the conjunction rule, it is important to consider whether the effect is attributable, in whole or in part, to linguistic conventions or conversational rules. For example, in an early study we presented people with the following description, "John is 27 years old, with an outgoing personality. At college he was an outstanding athlete but did not show much ability or interest in intellectual matters." We found that John was judged more likely to be a "gym teacher" than merely a "teacher." Although every gym teacher is, in a sense, a teacher, it could be argued that the term *teacher* is understood here in a sense that excludes a gym teacher or a driving-school instructor. This problem is avoided in the present design by defining the critical outcome extensionally as an intersection of two sets, for example, accountants and amateur jazz players.

Violations of the conjunction rule have also been observed in sequential problems, where the target consists of a sequence of events. Slovic, Fischhoff, and Lichtenstein (1976) presented subjects with a personality sketch of a person who resembled the stereotype of an engineer but not of a journalist. Their subjects assigned a lower probability to the event "Tom W. will select journalism as his college major" than to the event "Tom W. will select journalism as his college major but quickly become unhappy with his choice and switch to engineering." Strictly speaking, the former event includes the latter, and the above judgment violates the conjunction rule. This example, however, is open to the objection that, according to normal rules of conversation, the statement that Tom W. chose journalism as his college major implies that he also remained a journalism major. Otherwise, the statement would be misleading.

Similar objections can also be raised regarding the examples of Bill and Linda. Thus, it may be argued that subjects read, for example, the category "a bank teller" as "a bank teller who is *not* active in the feminist movement" in contrast to the given category "a bank teller who is active in the feminist movement." However, the presence of the conjunction effect in a between-subjects design, in which the critical targets are not compared directly, indicates that the effect cannot be adequately explained in terms of a reformulation of the target categories according to standard conversational implicatures. Rather, the observed judgments reveal a common tendency to evaluate the probabilities of the relevant events by the degree to which Linda is representative of the typical or the prototypical members of the respective categories.

Furthermore, we have observed the conjunction effect in several tasks that appear free of conversational implications. The following problems, for example, concern the prediction of future events where the interpretation of B as $(B \ \& \ \text{not-}A)$ seems implausible.

Study 3: Predictions for 1981

The problems described here were designed to test the conjunction rule in predictions of real-world events where subjects rely on their general knowledge. These problems were answered by a group of 93 statistically naive subjects in December 1980. The following instructions were given:

In this questionnaire you are asked to evaluate the probability of various events that may occur during 1981. Each problem includes four possible events. Your task is to rank order these events by probability, using 1 for the most probable event, 2 for the second, 3 for the third and 4 for the least probable event.

The questionnaire included six questions. Two of the questions are shown here. The results for other questions were very similar. The numbers in parentheses are the average ranks for each event; we also show the percentage of subjects who ranked the compound target as more probable than the simple target.

Tennis 1981 (Conjunction effect: 72%)
Suppose Bjorn Borg reaches the Wimbledon finals in 1981. Please rank order the following outcomes from most to least likely.
(1.7) Borg will win the match.
(2.7) Borg will lose the first set.
(3.5) Borg will win the first set but lose the match.
(2.2) Borg will lose the first set but win the match.

U.S. Politics, 1981 (Conjunction effect: 68%)
Please rank order the following events by their probability of occurrence in 1981.
(1.5) Reagan will cut federal support to local government.
(3.3) Reagan will provide federal support for unwed mothers.
(2.7) Reagan will increase the defense budget by less than 5%.
(2.9) Reagan will provide federal support for unwed mothers and cut federal support to local governments.

As in the preceding studies, the compound category was judged more probable than one of its components. The result is compatible with a notion of representativeness, which refers in this case to the relation between a causal system and its outcomes rather than to the similarity of a description to a stereotype. In the second problem, for example, it appears unrepresentative for President Reagan to provide federal support for unwed mothers and quite representative for him to cut federal support for local governments. The conjunction of these acts appears intermediate in representativeness, and the assessments of probability evidently follow the same pattern.

In the first problem, most respondents evaluated Borg's winning the title as the most probable event and regarded the possibility of Borg losing the first set as less likely. The conjunction of the two, namely Borg losing the first set but winning the match, was again judged as less likely than the first possibility but more likely than the second. Evidently, the subjects combined events according to principles of representativeness, or causal impact, rather than according to the laws of probability.

Discussion

The results reported in the preceding studies provide direct support for the hypothesis that people evaluate the probability of events by the degree to which these events are representative of a relevant model or process. Because the representativeness of an event can be increased by specificity, a compound target can be judged more probable than one of its components. This prediction was supported by studies using both within-subjects and between-subjects designs in subject populations that cover a broad range of statistical sophistication.

Unlike other probabilistic rules, such as regression toward the mean, which naive subjects find difficult to understand and accept, the conjunction rule is both simple and compelling. The majority of the subjects were willing to endorse it in an abstract form, although almost all of them violated it in practice when it conflicted with the intuition of representativeness. The present results contrast with the findings of Johnson-Laird and Wason (1977) about the verification of "if-then" statements (see also Johnson-Laird, Legrenzi, & Sonino-Legrenzi, 1972). These investigators found that most subjects failed the verification task with abstract material but not in a concrete example. Our respondents, on the other hand, endorsed the conjunction rule in an abstract form but violated it in concrete examples (see Chap. 34).

The finding that a conjunction often appears more likely than one of its components could have far-reaching implications. We find no good reason to believe that the judgments of political analysts, jurors, judges, and physicians are free of the conjunction effect. This effect is likely to be particularly pernicious in the attempts to predict the future by evaluating the perceived likelihood of particular scenarios. As they stare into the crystal ball, politicians, futurologists, and laypersons alike seek an image of the future that best represents their model of the dynamics of the present. This search leads to the construction of detailed scenarios, which are internally coherent and highly representative of our model of the world. Such scenarios often appear more likely than less detailed forecasts, which are in fact more probable. As the amount of detail in a scenario increases, its probability can only decrease steadily, but its representativeness and hence its apparent likelihood may increase. The reliance on representativeness, we believe, is a primary reason for the unwarranted appeal of detailed scenarios and the illusory sense of insight that such constructions often provide.

The confusion between considerations of probability and of similarity applies not only to the prediction of an uncertain future but also to the reconstruction of an uncertain past, for example in history and criminal law. Here too, an account of past events is often incorporated into a representative scenario, which includes plausible guesses about unknown events. The inclusion of such guesses can only decrease the probability that the entire account is true, but it provides a sense of representativeness and coherence that may increase the perceived likelihood of the scenario. For example, the hypothesis "the defendant left the scene of the crime" may appear less plausible than the hypothesis "the defendant left the scene of the crime for fear of being accused of murder," although the latter account is less probable than the former. A good story is often less probable than a less satisfactory one.

Finally, it is important to realize that the conjunction effect is the symptom of a more fundamental problem. It merely reveals the inconsistency between the logic of probability and the logic of representativeness, which often governs people's beliefs about uncertain events. Since human judgment is indispensable for many problems of interest in our lives, the conflict between the intuitive concept of probability and the logical structure of this concept is troublesome. On the one hand, we cannot readily abandon the heuristics we use to assess uncertainty, because much of our world knowledge is tied to their operation. On the other hand, we cannot defy the laws of probability, because they capture important truths about the world. Like it or not, A cannot be less probable than (A & B), and a belief to the contrary is fallacious. Our problem is to retain what is useful and valid in intuitive judgment while correcting the errors and biases to which it is prone.

Part III
Causality and attribution

7. Popular induction: Information is not necessarily informative

Richard E. Nisbett, Eugene Borgida, Rick Crandall, and Harvey Reed

The cognitive theory that currently exerts the greatest influence on social psychologists is attribution theory, the formalized version of which was introduced by Harold Kelley in 1967. The theory poses a view of man as lay scientist, attempting to infer causes for the effects he observes. The causes he attributes determine his view of his social world, and this view may determine his behavior. An extremely broad range of phenomena, from Asch's conformity research to Schachter's emotion work, may be usefully described as instances of the causal attribution process at work. In fact, it seems quite possible that Kelley's most important contribution may ultimately be seen to have been his creation of a language, or roadmap, with which to describe and interrelate diverse social psychological phenomena.

In addition to his organizational contribution, Kelley posited three formal sources of influence on the causal attribution process. In attempting to attribute causes for events of the form "Actor responds in X fashion to situation A," the lay attributor responds to three sources of information: distinctiveness information (Does the actor respond in X fashion in all situations of the general type, or only in situation A?); consistency information (Does the actor respond in X fashion at all times, under a broad variety of circumstances, or does he respond in X fashion only occasionally?); and consensus information (Do most other actors respond in X fashion, or is the response relatively rare?). Attribution of cause will depend on the answers to each of these questions. The actor is thus seen as the primary cause of his response to the extent that he responds in that way in all situations of the general type and to the extent that his responses are not exhibited by others. The situation is seen as causal to the

This is an abbreviated version of a paper that appeared in J. S. Carroll and J. W. Payne (Eds.), *Cognition and Social Behavior*. Hillsdale, N.J.: Lawrence Erlbaum Assoc., Inc., 1976. Reprinted by permission.

extent that the actor's response is unique to situation A and to the extent that his response is widely shared.

Kelley's analysis of the attribution process has been acclaimed as well as criticized on the grounds that it is commonsensical in the extreme. Whether one likes or dislikes the theory for this quality, it comes as a surprise to discover that one of its fundamental axioms has found virtually no support in subsequent research. This is the notion that people respond to consensus information in allocating cause. Theory and common sense notwithstanding, there is mounting evidence that people are largely uninfluenced in their causal attributions by knowledge of the behavior of others. Knowledge that the actor's response is widely shared seems not to prompt the inference that the situation rather than the actor is the chief causal agent. Conversely, knowledge that the actor's response is unique seems not to prompt the inference that the actor rather than the situation is the chief causal agent.

In the pages that follow we review the evidence showing that there is little support for the view that people utilize consensus information in making attributions. This evidence concerns both instances where the actor is another person and instances, drawn primarily from our own research, where the actor is the self. We then show the similarity between the failure of consensus information to affect attributions and the demonstration by Kahneman and Tversky (1973, 4) that base-rate information fails to affect predictions. We propose explanations for both failures in terms of the relative impact of abstract (consensus, base-rate) information versus concrete (actor- or target-related) information. Finally, we apply the distinction between abstract and concrete information to questions of communication and persuasion.

Consensus information and the perception of others

There are two studies that examine the effects of consensus information on attributions about the behavior of others. Both studies show a remarkable weakness of consensus information. The first of these is by L. Z. McArthur (1972). Her study was a direct test of Kelley's propositions about the effects of distinctiveness, consistency, and consensus on causal attributions. Subjects were given one-line descriptions of the form "actor responds to stimulus in X fashion" and were additionally given information on the Kelley dimensions of distinctiveness, consistency, and consensus. For example, subjects might be told that, "While dancing, Ralph trips over Joan's feet," and told additionally that Ralph trips over almost all girls' feet (or over almost no other girl's feet), that Ralph almost always (or almost never) trips over Joan's feet, and that almost everyone else (or almost no one else) trips over Joan's feet. Subjects were then asked whether the tripping incident was Ralph's fault, Joan's fault, or just the fault of circumstances. Subjects were also asked about their predictions for response generalization (How likely would Ralph be to advise Joan to enroll in a social dancing course?) and stimulus generalization (How likely would Ralph be to trip on an icy sidewalk?).

Distinctiveness information accounted for 10% of the variance in causal attribution (summing over all causes) and 63% of the variance in stimulus generalization expectancies. Consistency information accounted for 20% of the variance in causal attributions and 14% of the variance in response generalization expectancies. In contrast, consensus information accounted for less than 3% of the variance in any of the three sorts of inference. These results appear to violate not only the common sense of attribution theory, but any kind of common sense at all. Although subjects appear to believe that it is important to know whether Ralph trips over most girls' feet and whether he usually trips over Joan's feet, it is of no concern to them whether other people trip over Joan's feet!

Common sense – attributional or any other variety – is also violated in the other study concerning the perceptions of others. Miller, Gillen, Schenker, and Radlove (1973) asked college students to read the procedure section of the classic Milgram (1963) study of obedience. Half of their subjects were given the actual data of the Milgram study, showing that virtually all subjects administered a very substantial amount of shock to the confederate and that a majority went all the way to the top of the shock scale. The other subjects were left with their naive expectations that such behavior would be rare. Then all subjects were requested to rate two individuals, both of whom had gone all the way, on 11 trait dimensions heavily laden with an evaluative component, for example, attractiveness, warmth, likeability, aggressiveness. For only one of the 11 ratings did the consensus information have a significant effect. The knowledge that maximum shock administration was modal behavior was therefore virtually without effect on evaluations of individuals who had given the maximum amount of shock.

Consensus information and self-perception

Consensus information also appears to have little impact on attributions made about the self. Bem (1967) proposed and Kelley (1967) incorporated into attribution theory the notion that people perform cause–effect analyses of their own behavior in a manner entirely similar to their attributions about the behavior of others. They observe their responses, taking note of the situations in which they occur, and make inferences about their feelings and motive states. For example, the subject in the classic Schachter and Singer (1962) experiment who knows that he has been injected with a drug that produces autonomic arousal, and who is then placed in a situation designed to elicit strong emotions, performs a kind of cause–effect analysis. He feels the symptoms of arousal, which ordinarily he may attribute to the emotional impact of the situation, but instead attributes them to the drug he has taken. The result is that he reports and manifests behaviorally fewer of the symptoms of emotion than subjects who do not know that they have been injected with an arousal agent and fewer emotional symptoms even than control subjects who have not been injected with the arousal agent at all. The subject therefore perceives the cause of his autonomic responses as "external" to himself and feels and behaves accordingly.

Several years ago, we began a program of therapeutic interventions based on this notion that people can be led to externalize the cause of their own reactions. It seemed that whenever an individual has responses that are maladaptive, disruptive, or pathological, there may be something to be gained by persuading the person to attribute his responses to something external to himself. The first study, and the only successful one, was by Storms and Nisbett (1970). The pathological state studied was insomnia. We asked college students who had trouble getting to sleep to take a pill (actually a placebo) 15 minutes before retiring, which they were told would cause increased heart rate, rapid, irregular breathing, a feeling of bodily warmth, and a general state of alertness. These are of course the symptoms of insomnia. Subjects who took these pills reported getting to sleep more quickly on the nights they took them than they had on nights without the pills and more quickly than control subjects who took no pills. Storms and Nisbett reasoned that one or both of two different attribution processes could have accounted for the results. Insomnia is probably caused in large part by arousal at bedtime produced by any number of causes, including anxiety about personal problems, an inconvenient diurnal rhythm, or chronic neurosis. As the individual lies in bed in a state of arousal, his revery includes thoughts with emotional content. The arousal can become associated with, and can amplify, the emotional cognitions. The resulting heightened emotional state intensifies the arousal, and so on, in a vicious cycle. This cycle could be broken, however, by the knowledge that the arousal is exogenous in nature. The person would then infer nothing about how worried he was about his exam, or how angry he was about his roommate, from observation of his arousal state. On the nights with the pills, arousal would be seen as inevitable and thus as dissociated from any thoughts in his head. The cycle of heightened arousal thus broken, sleep could ensue.

Alternatively, or additionally, a somewhat different process with more general applicability might have been at work. Our insomniac subjects reported that they were quite concerned about the fact that they were insomniacs. They took it as evidence of more general pathology and as reflecting badly on their state of psychological adjustment. For a subject with such worries, the knowledge of inevitable, extrinsically produced arousal should be reassuring. At least tonight, the subject might reason, the insomnia could not be taken as evidence of general psychopathology. To the extent that such a concern was itself partially responsible for the insomnia, sleep should have occurred more quickly on the nights with the pills.

Attempts to manipulate depression

Armed with this successful intervention with insomniacs, we began a series of attempts to modify states of depression. The technique in all studies was a consensus manipulation, designed to externalize the cause of the depressive affect by convincing the subject that it was widely shared. To the extent that the state is shared by similar others, its existence reflects less negatively on the self. It should seem less rooted in the subject's own unique, possibly pathological reactions to his particular circumstances and environment. With worry and concern about one's ability to deal with one's life situation reduced, the depression might be partially abated.

Study I: The Sunday blues. Many college students experience a general letdown feeling on Sundays. Although the day may begin well enough with brunch, coffee, and the Sunday papers, a sense of ennui often begins in the afternoon. There is much to be done for the week ahead, too much to seriously consider a Sunday outing, although perhaps not enough to begin work just this minute. By late afternoon, no excursion and no work have taken place, the Sunday papers, including perhaps even financial and travel sections, have been rather too thoroughly absorbed, and a long evening of tedious study looms ahead. By evening, if all has gone as badly as it often does, work is proceeding painfully, or not at all, and a gray mood of malaise and self-doubt has settled in.

It occurred to us that if the phenomenon were general, and if people knew this, the Sunday blues could be lessened in intensity. If the individual student knows that the dormitories around him are full of people in the same stale state, then his own negative emotions should be somewhat mitigated. Instead of deciding he is not cut out for the academic life or brooding on the possibility that he may never have a fulfilling relationship with a woman, he may simply acknowledge that people tend to be low on Sunday and let it go at that.

In order to test this notion, we requested a large number of male undergraduates at Yale University to fill out a number of mood scales at 4:00 P.M. and 10:00 P.M. on Sunday. The mood scales were several Wessman and Ricks (1966) scales loading highly on their euphoria–disphoria factor. In addition, subjects were requested to fill out a questionnaire at 10:00 P.M., reporting on their academic and social activities for the day and on the number of instances in which they gave vent to some disphoric affect, for example, by shouting or weeping. Finally, subjects took a packet of cartoons out of a folder and rated them for funniness.

After this initial Sunday premeasure, subjects were sorted into three groups, each with 18 subjects. One, a control group, was simply told that the investigators were studying mood patterns on Sunday and participants were asked to fill out on the following Sunday the same package of materials they had filled out the previous Sunday. For a second group, the Sunday blues syndrome was described in detail and subjects were given (false) statistics to indicate its widespread occurrence in the college population. Subjects were told that 92% of Yale students reported having experienced the phenomenon at least occasionally, whereas 65% experienced it on most Sundays. A third group was given the same consensus information as the second group and, in addition, was given a theory to account for the phenomenon. Subjects were told that it is caused by an "arousal crash" on Sundays: The normal weekday arousal is typically followed by even higher arousal on Saturday; then on Sunday, there is an arousal trough. This lack of arousal is often interpreted as, or converted into, depression.

The anticipation was that subjects in the latter two experimental groups would reinterpret their sour experiences on Sunday, personalizing them less and becoming, as it were, less depressed about their depression. If so, they should have shown a decrease in disphoric affect on the mood scales from the premanipulation Sunday to the postmanipulation Sunday; a decrease in disphoric behavior, such as blowing up or weeping; an increase in both academic and social activity; and a higher average rating of the funniness of the cartoons in the package for the second Sunday. They did none of these things. Not by a single indicator did the mood of experimental subjects improve as compared with control subjects.

Study II: Chronic depression. Insufficiently daunted, we attempted a similar intervention with male undergraduates who described themselves as chronically depressed. Twenty subjects were recruited by means of an advertisement in the University of Michigan's student newspaper that called for "depressed male upperclassmen to participate in a study by the Institute for Social Research on depression."

On arrival at the laboratory, subjects were randomly assigned to one of two groups. Control subjects were told that a new mood scale had been developed and that it was important to obtain daily mood reports, using the scales, from people who described themselves as being depressed. This would help to assess the validity of the scale and its ability to detect mood changes.

Experimental subjects were given the same story and in addition were told that the experimenters were in the final stages of testing a theory of depression in young male adults. The theory, based on fact at least in its particulars, went as follows. Subjects were told that it had been known for some time that mood maintenance in adults depended in part on the presence of gonadal hormones – in the male, on testosterone. There had been until recently a paradox, however, in that children almost never become depressed. Because children have extremely low levels of all gonadal hormones, this seemed a contradiction of the general rule that hormones are promotive of good moods. The paradox had recently been solved by the discovery that the limbic lobe, the emotional center of the brain, switches over in adolescence to a dependence on gonadal hormone for mood maintenance. In most males, the switchover is timed fairly well to correspond to the rise in testosterone level, which reaches a peak at about age 25. In many young men, however, the switchover is completed before the "fuel," so to speak, is available in sufficient quantities to maintain mood.

The strong implication to the subject was that he was such a young man. It was anticipated that the manipulation would cause an improvement in mood for three confounded reasons:

1. A time limit was implied for the depression.
2. The negative affect was "externalized" in the sense that it could now be attributed to an unfortunate biological incident rather than to the web of the subject's own life and any pathological inability to come to grips with it.
3. The negative affect, and the reasons for it, were shared by many others in a way suggesting nonuniqueness of the subject's problems and his response to them.

All subjects were requested to fill out the Wessman and Ricks mood forms at the end of each day for a 2-week period. The questionnaire also included a report on how the subject had slept the night before, because sleep disturbances are frequent symptoms of depression. Finally, subjects' grade point averages were obtained at the end of the semester in which the study took place.

There were no differences in the mood reports of experimental and control subjects at any point in the 2-week period, nor were there any differences in report of the quality of sleep. There were, in fact, no hints of any trend in the direction of the hypothesis on these variables. There was a tendency for experimental subjects to get somewhat higher grade point averages, as predicted, but this fell short of statistical significance $(.05 < p < .10)$. . . .

Attribution and the psychology of prediction

Kahneman and Tversky have demonstrated an inferential failure that seems highly pertinent to the inferential failure observed in studies of the effects of consensus information. These investigators, in a paper titled "The Psychology of Prediction" (1973, 4), have shown that people ignore population base rates when making predictions about the category membership of a target member of the population. . . .

If subjects are not influenced by base-rate information in their predictions about the category membership of a target case, then their attributions seem scarcely likely to be much influenced by consensus information. Consensus information is precisely base-rate information. It is base-rate information about behavioral responses rather than about category membership. An attribution, moreover, is a more complicated and indirect inference than a prediction. Kahneman and Tversky ask their subjects to produce a rather direct and uncomplicated chain of inference: "If the majority of the members of the population belong to a particular category, then odds are the target case does also." Their subjects fail to make such an inference. In the attribution research we have been discussing, a still more elaborate chain of inference is requested: "If the majority of the members of the population behave in a particular way, then the situation must exert strong pressures toward that behavior, and therefore it is unparsimonious to invoke personal idiosyncracies to account for the behavior of the target case if his behavior is modal."

It remains to be tested, of course, whether subjects are unwilling to apply behavioral base rates to predictions about target cases. If they are, then the question we have been pursuing must be shifted from "Why do people fail to alter their attributions in response to consensus information?" to the more fundamental "Why do people treat base-rate information as if it were uninformative?"

Study V: Behavioral base rates, prediction, and attribution. In order to examine the question of people's willingness to alter their predictions in the face of behavioral base-rate information, two psychology experiments were described to subjects (Nisbett & Borgida, 1975). University of Michigan students read detailed descriptions of (a) an experiment by Nisbett and Schachter (1966) in which subjects were asked to take as much electric shock as they could bear, and (b) an experiment on helping behavior of Darley and Latané (1968) in which, as several students discussed problems of college adjustment over earphones from separate cubicles, one of the "subjects" began to have what sounded like a seizure. The two experiments were chosen because in our teaching experience, college students' guesses about behavioral base rate were wide of the mark. Whereas students tend to assume that few subjects take much electric shock, the modal behavior is actually to tolerate the highest intensity the apparatus can deliver, enough amperage to cause the subject's entire arm to jerk involuntarily. And whereas students tend to assume most people would quickly leave their cubicles to help the seizure victim, the typical subject never does anything to help the victim in the six-person condition of the Darley and Latané experiment.

Because subjects were ignorant of the true behavioral base rates, it was possible to give some of the subjects the actual base rate from the two experiments and thereby create differential base-rate information conditions. Subjects with knowledge of the base rate (consensus information condition) were shown brief videotaped interviews with students described as subjects in the original experiments (or, in one variation of the consensus information condition, shown brief written descriptions of the backgrounds and personalities of the students). Consensus information subjects then were asked to predict how the target cases they viewed or read about would have behaved. It is therefore possible to compare the predictions of consensus information subjects with both the actual base-rate information they possessed and with the guesses about base rate made by subjects lacking consensus information.

Figure 1 shows the results for the shock experiment. The top bar graph shows the actual base-rate data given to consensus information subjects. The second row shows the estimates about base rate made by subjects lacking knowledge of the base rate. It may be seen that estimates by these no-consensus information subjects are quite different from the actual data. They assume taking a moderate amount of shock to have been modal behavior. The third row presents consensus information subjects' guesses about the behavior of the target cases they have viewed or read about. Although these subjects were fully cognizant of the base rate, it may be seen that the distribution does not resemble even remotely the actual base rate. Instead, the distribution is highly similar to the guesses about base rate made by subjects lacking knowledge of the base rate. Results were entirely similar for the helping experiment.

The experiment allowed an opportunity to test another hypothesis, this one suggested by Tversky and Kahneman (1971, 2) in an article entitled "Belief in the Law of Small Numbers." These authors argued that even scientists are rather insensitive to sample size and are willing to draw recklessly strong inferences about populations from knowledge about even a very small number of cases. In order to test this notion in the present context, some subjects were left ignorant of the base rates in both experiments and were shown brief videotaped interviews with two subjects from each experiment. Subjects in this target information condition were told that both subjects in both experiments had behaved in the most extreme possible way, i.e., that the two subjects in the shock experiment had both taken the maximum possible shock, and the two subjects in the helping experiment had never helped the victim. Subjects in the target information condition were then asked to indicate what they thought the distribution of the entire subject population of the experiments would have been. For both experiments, subjects were willing to infer that the population mode was identical to the behavior of the two subjects whom they had observed. It may be seen in the bottom row of Figure 1 that estimates for base rate in the shock experiment were remarkably similar to the true base rate. Estimates were not so similar for the helping experiment but were nevertheless rather close to the J curve form of the actual base rate. Subjects were as willing to infer that the population mode was similar to the behavior of the two cases they viewed when sample selection procedure was unspecified as when it was repeat-

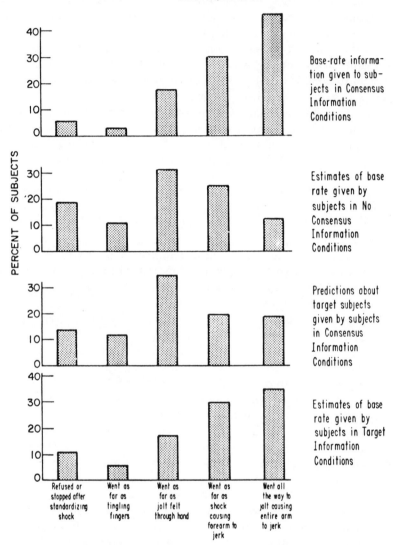

Figure 1. Base rate, estimates of base rate, and predictions about target subjects in the shock experiment.

edly and vividly brought to their attention that the two cases had been selected at random from a hat containing the names of all original subjects.

In summary, subjects did not employ base-rate information when called on to make predictions about the behavior of target cases. It is important to note that, in addition to the prediction questions, several atrribution questions were asked, e.g., whether situational forces or personal inclina-tions were responsible for the behavior of a target person. There was no substantial effect of consensus information for any of these attribution questions. The latter failure seems virtually inevitable given the former failure. Therefore, the question as to why people should ignore consensus information in making attributions should be reduced to the more funda-mental question as to why base-rate information should be disregarded for even such a simple inference as prediction. Any answer to this more fundamental question about people's failure to be informed by base-rate information ideally should account simultaneously for the other major finding in the present study. This is the finding that subjects are, in effect, "overly" informed by target case information, being willing to assume that extreme behavior is modal when told that as few as two subjects have behaved in the most extreme possible way.

Abstract versus concrete information

Kahneman and Tversky (1973, 4) themselves have not speculated at length on the reasons for people's failure to be influenced by base-rate informa-tion. Their basic explanation appears to center on the idea that people are simply not very good at dealing with probabilistic data. Even in the sphere of gambling, where people know that the laws of chance are operative and have at least some rudimentary schemata for dealing with likelihoods, people can show remarkable blindness and biases. Outside of such situa-tions people may utterly fail to see the relevance of such "merely" probabilistic information as base rate. Or, lacking any notion of how to properly combine base-rate information with target case information, they may opt for simply ignoring base-rate information altogether.

There is surely considerable truth to this notion that people lack good schemata for working with probabilistic information. In fact, it has the virtue of accounting for the single exception in the attribution literature to the rule that people ignore consensus information. This is the clear evidence of utilization of success and failure base rates when making attributions about the ability of a particular individual (Weiner et al., 1971). If most people fail at a particular task, then the target is perceived as having high ability; if they succeed, the target is seen as having lower ability. Of course, we have all had a lifetime of experience in estimating ability in relation to the performance of others. Ability, in fact, is by definition a base-rate derived inference.

It seems to us, however, that another principle may be at work as well. Almost by its very nature, base-rate or consensus information is remote, pallid, and abstract. In contrast, target case information is vivid, salient, and concrete. In the depression studies, we were attempting to pit the memory of rather dry, statistical information against vivid, pressing reactions to stimuli in an all too real world. In the cracker-tasting study, consensus information abstracted from evidence concerning the level of liquid in bottles was pitted against sense impressions. In the study describing the shock and helping experiments, tabular frequency data were pitted against a videotape or a written description of a real human being with parents, career plans, hobbies, and personal quirks. The logical pertinence of the base-rate information notwithstanding, such information may simply lack the clout to trigger further cognitive work.

This hypothesis, as it happens, is not original. In 1927, Bertrand Russell proposed that "popular induction depends upon the emotional interest of the instances, not upon their number" (p. 269). In the experiments by Kahneman and Tversky, and in those by ourselves and others on the effects of consensus information, sheer number of instances has been pitted against instances of some emotional interest. Consistent with Russell's hypothesis, emotional interest has in every case carried the day.

We may speculate that concrete, emotionally interesting information has greater power to generate inferences because of the likelihood of such information's calling up "scripts" or schemas involving similar information. The inference then proceeds along the well-worn lines of the previously existing script. Abstract information is probably less rich in potential connections to the associative network by which scripts can be reached. Consistent with this speculation, Nisbett and Borgida (1975) found that consensus information concerning the behavior of others in the shock experiment and the helping experiment not only failed to affect subjects' predictions about how they would have behaved had they been in the experiments but was never mentioned by a single subject in the postexperimental interview concerning why they had made their predictions. Instead, subjects seized on particular concrete details of the experimental situation and related them to similar situations in their own histories. "I'm sure I would have helped the guy because I had a friend who had an epileptic sister."

Russell's hypothesis has some important implications for action in everyday life. A homely example will serve as an illustration. Let us suppose that you wish to buy a new car and have decided that on grounds of economy and longevity you want to purchase one of those solid, stalwart, middle class Swedish cars – either a Volvo or a Saab. As a prudent and sensible buyer, you go to *Consumer Reports*, which informs you that the consensus of their experts is that the Volvo is mechanically superior, and the consensus of the readership is that the Volvo has the better repair record. Armed with this information, you decide to go and strike a bargain with the Volvo dealer before the week is out. In the interim, however, you go to a cocktail party where you announce this intention to an acquaintance. He reacts with disbelief and alarm: "A Volvo! You've got to be kidding. My brother-in-law had a Volvo. First, that fancy fuel injection computer thing went out. 250 bucks. Next he started having trouble with the rear end. Had to replace it. Then the transmission and the clutch. Finally sold it in three years for junk." The logical status of this information is that the N of several hundred Volvo-owning *Consumer Reports* readers has been increased by one, and the mean frequency of repair record shifted up by an iota on three or four dimensions. However, anyone who maintains that he would reduce the encounter to such a net informational effect is either disingenuous or lacking in the most elemental self-knowledge.

Study VI: Influenceability by abstract versus concrete information. It seemed worthwhile to operationalize the *Consumer Reports* thought–experiment (Borgida & Nisbett, 1977). Because our most readily available subject population consisted of psychology students at The University of Michigan, we chose psychology courses at The University of Michigan as our consumer goods. Ten upper level lecture courses in psychology, differing in their reported quality, were singled out. Groups of underclasspersons planning to become psychology majors were greeted in a classroom by a faculty member experimenter. The experimenter told the students that he was on a faculty committee concerned with long-range planning for the department. One of the problems with planning concerned determining how many students would be taking which courses in the future. Subjects were told that in order to get some indications of projected enrollment, they were being asked to fill out a tentative course schedule for their undergraduate careers in psychology.

Control subjects then were asked to look over a catalog (actually a mockup consisting of 27 courses and excluding labs, statistics, and cross-listed courses) and put a check next to the 5–10 courses they expected to take and to circle their check marks for any courses they felt certain they would take.

The two experimental groups were told that in order to help them in making their decisions, they would be given extra information on the high-enrollment lecture courses. For both groups, this extra information consisted in part of a detailed description, more comprehensive than the catalog blurb, of the content and format of each of the 10 courses. Then for one experimental group (face-to-face condition), subjects were introduced to a panel of upper level psychology students. These students then proceeded to make brief comments about each of the courses on the list of 10 that they had taken. Between one and four students, usually two or three, commented on each course. Each comment began with an evaluation of the course employing one of the following five terms: "excellent," "very good," "good," "fair," "poor." The student then made a few remarks about the course. An example, in its entirety, is below:

While there's a lot of material to cover, it's all very clearly laid out for you. You know where you are at all times, which is very helpful in trying to get through the

Table 1. *Mean number of courses chosen and weighted choice tendency*

	Recommended courses		Nonrecommended courses		Unmentioned courses	
Condition	Number chosen	Weighted choice tendency	Number chosen	Weighted choice tendency	Number chosen	Weighted choice tendency
Face to face						
(N = 22)	4.73^a	$8.31^{a,b}$	$.50^a$	$.77^{a,b}$	$3.09^{a,b}$	$4.32^{a,b}$
Base rate						
(N = 18)	4.11	6.33^b	.94	1.56^b	4.17^b	5.89^b
Control						
(N = 18)	3.33^a	5.22^a	1.39^a	2.17^a	$5.39^{a,b}$	7.17^a
F (2, 55)	6.14*	10.34**	6.59*	6.65*	13.24**	8.19**

[a]Column means sharing this superscript differ from each other at the .01 level by the Newman-Keuls test.
[b]Column means sharing this superscript differ from each other at the .05 level by the Newman-Keuls test.
*$p < .005$; **$p < .001$.

course. It's a very wide and important field of psychology to become introduced to. But the reason I rated it very good instead of excellent is that the material isn't particularly thought-provoking.

In the other experimental condition (base-rate condition), subjects were told that they would read mean evaluations of the course based on the scales filled out by all students in the course at the end of the preceding term. Beneath the description of each course was a five-point scale, labeled from excellent to poor. A mark was placed on each scale to indicate the mean evaluation, and the number of students on which the mean was based was indicated. These Ns ranged from 26 to 142. The mean evaluation of each particular course was rigged so as to be identical with the average of the evaluations given by the confederates in the face-to-face condition.

The design therefore makes it possible to compare the effectiveness of recommendations based on first-hand hearsay, that is, the brief comments of two or three students who have taken the course, with the effectiveness of much more stable, broadly based information. Table 1 presents the mean number of recommended (mean evaluations 2.50 or better), nonrecommended (mean evaluations 3.75 or poorer), and unmentioned courses chosen by the three groups. Beside each category is the weighted choice tendency, an index that gives a weighting of 0 to a course if it has not been chosen, 1 if it has been chosen, and 2 if it has been circled as a definite choice.

It may be seen that the face-to-face method had a much larger impact on course choice. Subjects in that group were much more inclined to take recommended courses and much less inclined to take nonrecommended or unmentioned courses than control subjects. In contrast, the base-rate method affected only the taking of unmentioned courses.

It might be argued that the face-to-face group had more information than the base-rate group. One version of this argument is precisely the point we wish to make. Our students behaved as if they had extracted more information from the *in vivo* comments of a couple of people than from the dry, statistical summaries of entire populations. A different version of this argument, however, is that the comments made by students in the face-to-face condition contained genuinely valuable information not available in the base-rate condition, concerning, for example, course organization, grading procedures, or teacher accessibility.

In order to deal with the latter objection, we replicated the study with one important variation. The base-rate group was given a verbatim written transcript of the comments made by face-to-face confederates. Moreover, those comments were explicitly described as *representative* views of the students taking the course, culled from the entire stack of evaluations at the end of the term. Subjects in this condition, with access to stable mean evaluations based on large and complete populations, with the verbatim comments of confederates, and with the "knowledge" that these were representative comments, were less affected in their choices than subjects who simply heard the confederates verbalize their comments in the face-to-face condition.

Communicating with creatures of concreteness

It is not hard to see the implications of Bertrand Russell's dictum about popular induction, and the above illustration of it, to general questions of communication and persuasion. If people are unmoved by the sorts of dry, stastistical data that are dear to the hearts of scientists and policy planners, then social and technological progress must be impeded unless effective, concrete, emotionally interesting ways of communicating conclusions are developed. We have collected several "case studies" of persuasion that we believe are well understood in terms of the distinction between abstract and concrete information. We present them below in the hope that they may serve as a source of real-world inspiration and guidance for research on questions concerning the nature of information and its persuasive impact.

1. An early version of the Green Revolution was made possible in the early 1930s by advances in agricultural technique. The government duly proceeded to inform the nation's farmers of these techniques by means of county agricultural agents spouting statistics and government pamphlets and sat back to await the glowing reports of increased crop production. No such reports followed and it soon became clear that farmers were not converting to the new techniques. Some clever government official then set up a program whereby government agricultural agents moved in on

selected farms and cultivated the crops along with the farmers, using the new techniques. Neighboring farmers watched the crop results and immediately converted to the techniques.

2. The waiting lists at cancer detection clinics, as of this writing, are months long and have been since the fall of 1974. This was not because of the issuance of new statistics by the Surgeon General, AMA, or any other organization. The long waiting lists date from the time of the mastectomies performed on Mrs. Ford and Mrs. Rockefeller.

3. Timothy Crouse, in his book on the press coverage of the 1972 Presidential campaign titled *The Boys on the Bus* (1974), reported that on election eve a large group of the reporters following the McGovern campaign sagely agreed that McGovern could not lose by more than 10 points. These people were wire service reporters, network television reporters, and major newspaper and newsmagazine reporters. They knew that all the major polls had McGovern trailing by 20 points, and they knew that in 24 years not a single major poll had been wrong by more than 3%. However, they had seen with their own eyes wildly enthusiastic crowds of tens of thousands of people acclaim McGovern.

4. *The New York Times* (Kaufman, 1973) recently carried an interview with a New York subway graffitist who had been badly burned in an electrical fire started by a spark that ignited his cans of spray paint. The boy, whose *nom de plume* was "Ali," admitted that 2 weeks before his accident he had read of a boy named Bernard Brown who was crushed to death while painting graffiti on trains. "Maybe if we knew the name he used, say 'Joe 146' it would have made an impression," he said, "but I remember laughing about it thinking he must be some kind of dude who didn't know what he was doing. . . ."

We believe that the present research and examples drawn from everyday life show that some kinds of information that the scientist regards as highly pertinent and logically compelling are habitually ignored by people. Other kinds of information, logically much weaker, trigger strong inferences and action tendencies. We can think of no more useful activity for psychologists who study information processing than to discover what their subjects regard as information worthy of processing.

8.   Causal schemas in judgments under uncertainty

Amos Tversky and Daniel Kahneman

Many of the decisions we make, in trivial as well as in crucial matters, depend on the apparent likelihood of events such as the keeping of a promise, the success of an enterprise, or the response to an action. Since we generally do not have adequate formal models to compute the probabilities of such events, their assessment is necessarily subjective and intuitive. The manner in which people evaluate evidence to assess probabilities has aroused much research interest in recent years, e.g., W. Edwards (1968, 25); Kahneman and Tversky (1979a, **30**); Slovic (1972a); Slovic, Fischhoff, and Lichtenstein (1977); Tversky and Kahneman (1974, **1**). This research has identified several judgmental heuristics which are associated with characteristic errors and biases. The present paper is concerned with the role of causal reasoning in judgments under uncertainty and with some biases that are associated with this mode of thinking.

It is a psychological commonplace that people strive to achieve a coherent interpretation of the events that surround them, and that the organization of events by schemas of cause–effect relations serves to achieve this goal. The classic work of Michotte (1963) provided a compelling demonstration of the irresistible tendency to perceive sequences of events in terms of causal relations, even when the perceiver is fully aware that the relation between the events is incidental and that the imputed causality is illusory. The prevalence of causal schemas in the perception of elementary social relations was highlighted in Heider's (1958) seminal work, and the study of causal attribution is one of the foci of contemporary social psychology (Jones et al., 1971; Ross, 1977).

The present chapter is concerned with the role of causal schemas in

This chapter is the first part of a paper that appeared in M. Fishbein (Ed.), *Progress in Social Psychology*. Hillsdale, N.J.: Lawrence Erlbaum Assoc., Inc., 1980. Reprinted by permission.

judgment under uncertainty. In particular, we investigate judgments of the conditional probability $P(X/D)$ of some target event X, on the basis of some evidence or data D. For a psychological analysis of the impact of evidence, it is useful to distinguish between different types of relations that the judge may perceive between D and X. If D is perceived as a cause of the occurrence or nonoccurrence of X, we refer to D as a *causal* datum. On the other hand, if X is treated as a possible cause of D, we refer to D as a *diagnostic* datum. For example, a description of A's personality is commonly viewed as providing causal data for the prediction of his behavior, while the description of A's behavior provides diagnostic information about his personality. If D is neither the cause nor the effect of X, but they are both perceived as consequences of another factor, we refer to D as *indicational.* Thus, behavior in one situation provides indicational data for behavior in another, if both behaviors are regarded as manifestations of the same trait. Finally, if D and X do not appear to be related by either a direct or an indirect causal link, we refer to D as *incidental.*

In a normative treatment of conditional probability, the distinctions between the various types of relation of D to X are immaterial, and the impact of data depends solely on their informativeness. In contrast, we propose that the psychological impact of data depends critically on their role in a causal schema. In particular, we hypothesize that causal data have greater impact than other data of equal informativeness; and that in the presence of data that evoke a causal schema, incidental data which do not fit that schema are given little or no weight.

In the first part of the paper, we compare the effects of causal and diagnostic data, and show that people assign greater impact to causal than to diagnostic data of equal informativeness. We also explore a class of problems where a particular datum has both causal and diagnostic significance, and demonstrate that intuitive assessments of $P(X/D)$ are dominated by the direct causal impact of D on X, with insufficient regard for diagnostic considerations . . . .

Causal and diagnostic reasoning

Inferential asymmetries

A causal schema has a natural course; it evolves from causes to consequences. Hence we suggest that it is more natural and easier to follow the normal sequence and reason from causes to consequences than to invert this sequence and reason from consequences to causes. If causal inferences are indeed easier and more natural than diagnostic inferences, then one would expect people to infer effects from causes with greater confidence than causes from effects – even when the effect and the cause actually provide the same amount of information about each other. We tested this hypothesis using two different measures: judgments of conditional probabilities and confidence in the accuracy of predictions.

In one set of questions, we asked subjects to compare the two conditional probabilities $P(Y/X)$ and $P(X/Y)$ for a pair of events X and Y such that (1) X is naturally viewed as a cause of Y; and (2) $P(X) = P(Y)$, that is, the marginal probabilities of the two events are equal. The latter condition implies that $P(Y/X) = P(X/Y)$. Our prediction was that most subjects would view the causal relation as stronger than the diagnostic relation, and would erroneously assert that $P(Y/X) > P(X/Y)$.

In another set of questions, we asked subjects to compare their confidence in predictions involving two continuous variables, depending on which of these variables was given and which was to be predicted. Here again, the problems are constructed so that one of the variables is naturally viewed as causal with respect to the other. If the two variables have similar marginal distributions, there is no valid statistical reason to expect a difference in the accuracy with which one variable can be predicted from the other. Nevertheless, we hypothesized that many subjects would state that a prediction from cause to effect can be made with greater confidence than a prediction from effect to cause.

The predicted asymmetry between causal and diagnostic inferences was observed with both types of questions. The effect is illustrated by the following problems, where the values in parentheses indicate the number of college students (of the University of Oregon) who chose each answer.[1]

Problem 1: Which of the following events is more probable?
  (a) That a girl has blue eyes if her mother has blue eyes. ($N = 69$)
  (b) That the mother has blue eyes, if her daughter has blue eyes. ($N = 21$)
  (−) The two events are equally probable. ($N = 75$)

Problem 2: In a survey of high-school seniors in a city, the height of boys was compared to the height of their fathers. In which prediction would you have greater confidence?
  (a) The prediction of the father's height from the son's height. ($N = 23$)
  (b) The prediction of the son's height from the father's height. ($N = 68$)
  (−) Equal confidence. ($N = 76$)

Clearly, the distribution of height or eye-color is essentially the same in successive generations. To verify subjects' perception of this fact, we asked another group of 91 subjects whether the proportion of blue-eyed mothers in a large sample of mothers and daughters is greater ($N = 15$), equal ($N = 64$), or smaller ($N = 12$), than the proportion of blue-eyed daughters. Thus, although the subjects regarded the two prior probabilities as equal, they

---

[1] An earlier draft of this paper reported a spuriously low proportion of "Equal" responses based on an Israeli sample. We are indebted to Anna M. B. Gonzalez and Michael Kubovy, for this observation. The present data, collected at the University of Oregon, agree with results obtained by Gonzalez at Yale.

nevertheless judged the "causal" conditional probability to be higher than the "diagnostic" one.

Strictly speaking, of course, the father's height is not a cause of his son's height. In common usage, however, it is quite acceptable to say that a boy is tall because his father is 6'4", while the statement that the father is 6'4" because his son is tall is clearly anomalous. More generally, we expect an asymmetry of inference regarding two variables whenever the first appears to explain the second better than the second explains the first. To illustrate, consider the following problems that were presented to two different groups of subjects:

Problem 3: Which of the following statements makes more sense?
  (a) Tom is heavy because he is tall. (*N* = 63)
  (b) Tom is tall because he is heavy. (*N* = 7)

Problem 4: In which prediction would you have greater confidence?
  (a) The prediction of a man's height from his weight. (*N* = 16)
  (b) The prediction of a man's weight from his height. (*N* = 78)

Although height and weight are not regarded as causes for each other, the majority of respondents felt that being tall is a better explanation for being heavy than vice versa, perhaps because the prototypical tall man is quite heavy, while the prototypical heavy man is not tall. Accordingly, the majority of subjects expressed greater confidence in predicting a man's weight from his height than in predicting a man's height from his weight. Such an asymmetry, of course, could not be justified on statistical grounds.

Problems 3 and 4 suggest that an asymmetry of inference occurs even in the absence of a direct causal link between the two variables – provided one of them (e.g., height) is more naturally viewed as an explanation of the other (e.g., weight). The following two problems are concerned with the case where two variables are viewed as indications, or manifestations, of some underlying trait. One of the variables, however, provides a more direct manifestation or a more valid measure of the underlying trait. We expect that inferences from the stronger to the weaker indication will be made with greater confidence than inferences in the inverse direction.

Problem 5: Which of the following events is more probable?
  (a) That an athlete won the decathlon, if he won the first event in the decathlon. (*N* = 21)
  (b) That an athlete won the first event in the decathlon, if he won the decathlon. (*N* = 75)
  (−) The two events are equally probable. (*N* = 70)

Problem 6: Two tests of intelligence were administered to a large group of students: a one-hour comprehensive test, and a 10-minute abbreviated version. In which prediction would you have greater confidence?
  (a) The prediction of a student's score on the short test from his score on the comprehensive test. (*N* = 80)

(b) The prediction of a student's score on the comprehensive test from his score on the short test. ($N = 47$)

($-$) Equal confidence. ($N = 39$)

Here again, the correct answer is 'equal' in both problems. In Problem 5, the prior probability that an (unspecified) athlete will win the decathlon is $1/N$, where N is the number of competitors. This is also the prior probability that an unspecified athlete will win the first event. Consequently, the two conditional probabilities must be equal. In Problem 6, the standard assumption of linear regressions entails accuracy in the prediction of one test from another. The responses to both problems, however, exhibit a marked preference for one direction of prediction over the other.

Problems 5 and 6 both involve two indications of the same underlying trait, which differ in strength. Victory in the decathlon and victory in a single event are both manifestations of athletic excellence, but the former provides a stronger indication of excellence than the latter. Similarly, performance in intelligence tests reflects an underlying trait of intelligence, and the more comprehensive test provides a better measure of this trait than does the abbreviated version. The results confirm the hypothesis that the prediction from the stronger indication to the weaker is associated with greater confidence than the inverse prediction.

The asymmetries of inference observed in the preceding problems are related to the asymmetries of proximity relations, investigated by Tversky (1977). Empirical studies show that the judged similarity of a prominent object or prototype to a less prominent object or variant is smaller than the similarity of the variant to the prototype. For example, a focal red is less similar to an off-red than vice versa (Rosch, 1975), "a good" form is less similar to a "bad" form than vice versa, and the similarity of a prominent country (e.g., Red China) to a less prominent country (e.g., North Korea) is smaller than the converse similarity (Tversky, 1977). The asymmetries of prediction appear to follow the same rule. Thus, we generally perceive the son as more similar to his father than vice versa, and we also attribute properties of the father to the son with greater confidence than vice versa. The same process, therefore, may underly both asymmetries of similarity and asymmetries of inference.

Causal and diagnostic significance of evidence

The previous section showed that the impact of causal data on the judged probability of a consequence is greater than the impact of diagnostic data on the judged probability of a cause. The present section investigates questions in which the evidence has both causal and diagnostic significance with respect to the target event. We study the hypothesis that people tend to focus on the causal impact of the data for the future, and tend to neglect their diagnostic implications about the past. We first discuss a class of problems in which the dominance of causal over diagnostic considerations produces inconsistent and paradoxical probability assessments. The following pair of problems was introduced by Turoff (1972) in a discussion of the cross-impact method of forecasting.

Problem 7a: Which of the following two probabilities is higher?

(*i*) The probability that, within the next five years, Congress will pass a law to curb mercury pollution, if the number of deaths attributed to mercury poisoning during the next five years exceeds 500.

(*ii*) The probability that, within the next five years, Congress will pass a law to curb mercury pollution, if the number of deaths attributed to mercury poisoning during the next five years does not exceed 500.

Problem 7b: Which of the following two probabilities is higher?

(*i*) The probability that the number of deaths attributed to mercury poisoning during the next five years will exceed 500, if Congress passes a law within the next five years to curb mercury pollution.

(*ii*) The probability that the number of deaths attributed to mercury poisoning during the next five years will exceed 500, if Congress does not pass a law within the next five years to curb mercury pollution.

Let C be the event that within the next 5 years Congress will have passed a law to curb mercury pollution, and let D be the event that within the next 5 years, the number of deaths attributed to mercury poisoning will exceed 500. Let $\overline{C}$ and $\overline{D}$ denote the negations of C and D, respectively.

A large majority of respondents state that Congress is more likely to pass a law restricting mercury pollution if the death toll exceeds 500 than if it does not, that is, $P(C/D) > P(C/\overline{D})$. Most people also state that the death toll is less likely to reach 500 if a law is enacted within the next five years than if it is not, that is, $P(D/C) < P(D/\overline{C})$. These judgments reflect the causal beliefs that a high death toll would increase the pressure to pass an antipollution measure, and that such a measure would be effective in the prevention of mercury poisoning. In a sample of 166 students, 140 chose the modal answer to both questions. This seemingly plausible pattern of judgments violates the most elementary rules of conditional probability.

Clearly, $P(C/D) > P(C/\overline{D})$ implies $P(C/D) > P(C)$. Furthermore, the inequality

$$P(C/D) = \frac{P(C \& D)}{P(D)} > P(C)$$

holds if and only if $P(C \& D) > P(C)\, P(D)$ which holds if and only if

$$P(D) < \frac{P(C \& D)}{P(C)} = P(D/C)$$

which in turn implies $P(D/C) > P(D/\overline{C})$, provided $P(C)$ and $P(D)$ are nonzero. Hence, $P(C/D) > P(C/\overline{D})$ implies $P(D/C) > P(D/\overline{C})$, contrary to the prevailing pattern of judgment.

It is easy to construct additional examples of the same type, in which people's intuitions violate the probability calculus. Such examples consist of a pair of events, A and B, such that the occurrence of B increases the likelihood of the subsequent occurrence of A, while the occurrence of A decreases the likelihood of the subsequent occurrence of B. For example, consider the following problem.

Problem 8: Let A be the event that before the end of next year, Peter will have installed a burglar alarm system in his home. Let B denote the event that Peter's home will be burglarized before the end of next year. Let $\overline{A}$ and $\overline{B}$ denote the negations of A and B, respectively.[2]

Question: Which of the two conditional probabilities, $P(A/B)$ or $P(A/\overline{B})$, is higher?

Question: Which of the two conditional probabilities, $P(B/A)$ or $P(B/\overline{A})$, is higher?

A large majority of subjects (132 of 161) stated that $P(A/B) > P(A/\overline{B})$ and that $P(B/A) < P(B/\overline{A})$, contrary to the laws of probability. We interpret this pattern of judgments as another indication of the dominance of causal over diagnostic considerations. To appreciate the nature of the effect, let us analyze the structure of Problem 8.

First, consider $P(A/B)$, the conditional probability that Peter will install an alarm system in his home before the end of next year, assuming that his home will be burglarized sometime during this period. The alarm system could be installed either before or after the burglary. The information conveyed by the condition, that is, the assumption of a burglary, has causal significance with respect to the future and diagnostic significance with respect to the past. Specifically, the occurrence of a burglary provides a cause for the subsequent installation of an alarm system, and it provides a diagnostic indication that the house had not been equipped with an alarm system at the time of the burglary. Thus, the causal impact of the burglary increases the likelihood of the alarm system while the diagnostic impact of the burglary decreases this likelihood. The nearly unanimous judgments that $P(A/B) > P(A/\overline{B})$ indicates that the causal impact of B dominates its diagnostic impact.

Precisely the same analysis applies to $P(B/A)$: the probability that Peter's house will be burglarized before the end of next year, given that he will have installed an alarm system sometime during this period. The presence of an alarm system is causally effective in reducing the likelihood of a subsequent burglary; it also provides a diagnostic indication that the occurrence of a burglary could have prompted Peter to install the

---

[2] The symbols A, B, etc., are introduced here to facilitate the exposition. The subjects were given verbal descriptions of the events.

alarm system. The causal impact of the alarm system reduces the likelihood of a burglary; the diagnostic impact of the alarm system increases this likelihood. Here again, the prevalence of the judgment that $P(B/A) < P(B/\overline{A})$ indicates that the causal impact of A dominates its diagnostic impact. Instead of weighing the causal and the diagnostic impacts of the evidence, people apparently assess the conditional probabilities $P(A/B)$ and $P(B/A)$ primarily in terms of the direct causal effect of the condition, which leads to contradictions in problems of this type.

A salient feature of Turoff's problems is the uncertain temporal relation between the conditioning event and the target event. Even in the absence of temporal uncertainty, however, it is often the case that the conditioning event has both causal and diagnostic significance. The present analysis leads to the hypothesis that assessments of conditional probabilities are dominated by causal considerations, even when the temporal relation between the events is fully specified.

Problem 9: Which of the following two probabilities is higher?

$P(R/H)$ The probability that there will be rationing of fuel for individual consumers in the U.S. during the 1990s, if you assume that a marked increase in the use of solar energy for home heating will occur during the 1980s.

$P(R/\overline{H})$ The probability that there will be rationing of fuel for individual consumers in the U.S. during the 1990s, if you assume that no marked increase in the use of solar energy for home heating will occur during the 1980s.

It is perhaps instructive to consider the normative (Bayesian) approach to this problem, in the light of the distinction we have drawn between causal and diagnostic considerations. The event H that there will be a marked increase in the use of solar energy for home heating during the 1980s has both causal and diagnostic significance. The direct causal impact of H on R is clearly negative. Others things being equal, a marked increase in the use of solar energy can only alleviate a fuel crisis in later years. However, a marked increase in the use of solar energy during the '80s also provides a strong indication of an impending energy crisis. In particular, it suggests that fuel prices in the '80s are sufficiently high to make the investment in solar energy for home heating economical for a large number of consumers. High fuel prices in the '80s, in turn, suggest a state of shortage of fossil fuel, which increases the likelihood of fuel rationing in the subsequent decade. Thus, the direct casual impact of H on R reduces the likelihood of R, whereas the diagnostic implications of H indirectly increase the likelihood of R.

Although the question of the relative strength of these factors cannot be settled formally, we contend that the diagnostic implications of H could outweigh its causal impact. The amount of fuel that may be saved by the increased use of solar energy for home heating is unlikely to be large enough to avert an impending crisis. On the other hand, the scarcity of fuel which is implied by H is highly indicative of a forthcoming energy crisis. According to this line of reasoning, $P(R/H) > P(R/\overline{H})$, where $\overline{H}$ is the negation of H.

The hypothesis of this section, however, was that people generally overweigh the direct causal contribution of the conditioning event in assessments of conditional probabilities, and do not give sufficient weight to its diagnostic significance. This hypothesis entails, in Problem 9, that the stipulation of an increase in the use of solar energy for heating in the 1980s should reduce the judged probability of fuel rationing in the 1990s. Indeed, 68 of 83 respondents stated that $P(R/H) < P(R/\overline{H})$. The same pattern of judgments is observed in other problems of this type, where the indirect diagnostic implications of the condition are in conflict with its direct causal implications. Although this pattern of judgments does not violate the rules of probability, as was the case in Turoff's problems, it reflects, we believe, a common tendency to neglect the diagnostic significance of the conditioning event in judgments of conditional probability.

Prediction, explanation, and revision

In the preceding sections we presented some evidence in support of the hypothesis that causal inferences have greater efficacy than diagnostic inferences. First we showed that inferences from causes to consequences are made with greater confidence than inferences from consequences to causes. Second, we showed that when the same data have both causal and diagnostic significance, the former is generally given more weight than the latter in judgments of conditional probability.

We turn now to the more general question of the relation between an image, model, or schema of a system, for example, the energy situation or the personality of an individual, and some outcome or manifestation of that system, for example, an increased use of solar energy or a display of hostility. Models or schemas are commonly employed to predict and explain outcomes, which in turn are used to revise or update the models. Thus, a person may apply the model to predict the outcome or to assess its probability; he may also use the model to explain the occurrence of a particular event or consequence. Finally, he may employ the information provided by the occurrence of a particular event to correct or revise his model.

Prediction and explanation represent two different types of causal inference, while model-revision is an example of diagnostic inference. In prediction, the judge selects that outcome which is most congruent with his model of the system. In explanation, the judge identifies those features of the model that are most likely to give rise to the specified outcome. In revision, on the other hand, the judge corrects or completes the elements of the model that are least congruent with the data.

Most inferences in everyday life rely on models or schemas which are imprecise, incomplete and occasionally incorrect. People recognize this, however, and are often willing to acknowledge that their models of systems such as the intentions of a person or the energy situation could be in error. The presence of uncertainty regarding the accuracy of a model has implications for the proper conduct of prediction, explanation and revision. If a model is subject to error, predictions from that model should be moderate or regressive, that is, they should not greatly depart from base-rate predictions. For instance, one should be more reluctant to predict that a person will engage in a rare or unusual behavior when one's information about the person comes from an unreliable source than when the same information comes from a more believable source.

Explanations that are based on uncertain models should also be tempered with caution, since the causal factors that are used in the explanation may not exist in reality. Furthermore, explanation in the presence of uncertainty should always be combined with model-revision. For example, if a person engages in an activity that appears incompatible with our impression of his personality, we should seriously consider the possibility that our impression was incorrect, and that it should be revised in the direction suggested by the new data. The greater the uncertainty about the model and the more surprising the behavior, the greater should the revision be. An adequate explanation should take into account the changes in the model that are implied or suggested by the event that is to be explained. From a normative point of view, therefore, explanation in the presence of uncertainty about the model involves both diagnostic and causal inferences.

Previous research has shown that people commonly over-predict from highly uncertain models. For example, subjects confidently predict the professional choice or academic performance of an individual on the basis of a brief personality sketch, even when this sketch is attributed to an unreliable source (Kahneman & Tversky, 1973, 4). The intentions and traits that are inferred from a personality sketch are naturally viewed as causes of such outcomes as professional choice or success in school. The over-prediction that is observed in such problems is therefore compatible with the high impact of causal data that was illustrated in the preceding sections.

In the context of explanation and revision, the strength of causal reasoning and the weakness of diagnostic reasoning are manifest in the great ease with which people construct causal accounts for outcomes which they could not predict, and in the difficulty that they have in revising uncertain models to accommodate new data. It appears easier to assimilate a new fact within an existing causal model than to revise the model in the light of this fact. Moreover, the revisions that are made to accommodate new facts are often minimal in scope and local in character.

To illustrate this notion, we turn to previously unreported observations from an earlier study of intuitive prediction (Kahneman & Tversky, 1973, 4). In that study, 114 graduate students in psychology were presented with a paragraph-length description of a graduate student, Tom W., which had allegedly been written during his senior year in high school by a clinical psychologist, on the basis of projective tests. The following description was given:

Tom W. is of high intelligence, although lacking in true creativity. He has a need for order and clarity, and for neat and tidy systems in which every detail finds its appropriate place. His writing is rather dull and mechanical, occasionally enlivened by somewhat corny puns and by flashes of imagination of the sci-fi type. He has a strong drive for competence. He seems to have little feel and little sympathy for other people and does not enjoy interacting with others. Self-centered, he nonetheless has a deep moral sense.

The subjects were first asked to predict Tom W.'s field of graduate specialization by ranking nine possibilities in terms of their likelihood. There was a strong consensus among the respondents that Tom W. is most likely to be in computer science or engineering, and least likely to be in social sciences and social work or in the humanities and education. Response to an additional question also exhibited general agreement that projective tests do not provide a valid source of information for the prediction of professional choice. After completing the prediction task, the subjects were asked the following question.

In fact, Tom W. is a graduate student in the School of Education and he is enrolled in a special program of training for the education of handicapped children. Please outline very briefly the theory which you consider most likely to explain the relation between Tom W.'s personality and his choice of career.

What is the proper approach to this question? The respondents were faced with an apparent conflict between a hard fact, Tom W.'s choice of career, and a detailed but unreliable description of his personality. The high confidence with which people predict professional choice from personality descriptions implies a belief in a high correlation between personality and vocational choice. This belief, in turn, entails that professional choice is highly diagnostic with respect to personality. In the above example, Tom W.'s vocational choice is unlikely in view of his personality description, and that description is attributed to a source of low credibility. A reasonable diagnostic inference should therefore lead to a substantial revision of one's image of Tom W.'s character, to make it more compatible with the stereotype of his chosen profession. If one believes that students of special education are generally compassionate, then Tom W.'s professional choice should raise doubts about his having "little feel and little sympathy for other people," as stated in the psychologist's report. An adequate response to the problem should at least raise the possibility that Tom W.'s personality is not as described, and that he is in fact kinder and more humane than his description suggests.

Our subjects did not follow this approach. Only a small minority (21%)

even mentioned any reservations about the validity of the description. The overwhelming majority of respondents, including the skeptics, resolved the conflict either by reference to suitably chosen aspects of Tom W.'s description (e.g., his deep moral sense) or by a reinterpretation of the psychological significance of his choice (e.g., as an expression of a need for dominance).

It could be argued that our subjects' failure to revise their image of Tom W. merely reflects the demand characteristics of the task which they had been assigned, namely to "explain the relation between Tom W.'s personality and his choice of career." According to this account, the task is naturally interpreted as calling for an attempt to relate Tom W.'s professional choice to the *description* of his personality without questioning its validity. We believe, however, that the prevalent tendency to treat the image of Tom W. as if it were perfectly valid, in spite of severe doubts, exemplifies a much broader phenomenon: the tendency to explain without revising, even when the model that is used in the explanation is highly uncertain.

In our view, the subjects' responses illustrate both the reluctance to revise a rich and coherent model, however uncertain, and the ease with which such a model can be used to explain new facts, however unexpected. We were impressed by the fluency which our respondents displayed in developing causal accounts of Tom W.'s unexpected choice of vocation, and have no reason to believe that they would have been less facile in explaining other unexpected behaviors on his part.

Highly developed explanatory skills probably contribute to the proverbial robustness and stability of impressions, models, conceptions, and paradigms in the face of incompatible evidence (Abelson, 1959; Hovland, 1959; Janis, 1972; Jervis, 1975; Kuhn, 1962). The impetus for revising a model can only come from the recognition of an incongruence between that model and some new evidence. If people can explain most occurrences to their own satisfaction with minimal and local changes in their existing conceptions, they will rarely feel the need for drastic revision of these conceptions. In this manner, the fluency of causal thinking inhibits the process of diagnostic revision. . . .

9. Shortcomings in the attribution process: On the origins and maintenance of erroneous social assessments

Lee Ross and Craig A. Anderson

Introduction to attribution theory and attributional errors

Attribution theory and intuitive psychology

Attribution theory, in its broadest sense, is concerned with the attempts of ordinary people to understand the causes and implications of the events they witness. It deals with the "naive psychology" of people as they interpret their own behavior and the actions of others. The current ascendancy of attribution theory in social psychology thus culminates a long struggle to upgrade that discipline's conception of man. No longer the stimulus–reponse (S–R) automaton of radical behaviorism, promoted beyond the rank of information processor and cognitive consistency seeker, psychological man has at last been awarded a status equal to that of the scientist who investigates him. For in the perspective of attribution theory, people are intuitive psychologists who seek to explain behavior and to draw inferences about actors and about their social environments.

To better understand the perceptions and actions of this intuitive scientist we must explore his methods. First, like the academic psychologist, he is guided by a number of implicit assumptions about human nature and human behavior – for example, that the pursuit of pleasure and the avoidance of pain are ubiquitous and powerful human motives, or that conformity to the wishes and expectations of one's peers is less exceptional and less demanding of further interpretation than non-conformity. The lay psychologist, like the professional one, also relies heavily upon data, albeit data that rarely satisfy formal requirements regarding randomness

This chapter draws heavily, both in content and organization, from a contribution by the first author to *Advances in Experimental Social Psychology* (1977). Permission for use of these materials is gratefully acknowledged.

or representativeness. Sometimes these data result from first-hand experiences; more often, they are the product of informal social communication, mass media, or other indirect sources. The intuitive psychologist must further adopt or develop techniques for coding, storing, and retrieving the data. Finally, he must employ various strategies for summarizing, analyzing, and interpreting the data – that is, he must employ rules, heuristics, or schemas that permit him to form new inferences. The intuitive scientist's ability to master his social environment, accordingly, will depend upon the accuracy and adequacy of his hypotheses, evidence, and analyses. Conversely, any systematic errors in existing theories, biases in available data, or inadequacies in methods of analysis, yield serious consequences – both for the lay psychologist and for the society that he builds and perpetuates. These shortcomings, explored from the vantage point of contemporary attribution theory, provide the focus of this chapter.[1]

The broad outlines of attribution theory were first sketched by Heider (1944, 1958) and developed in greater detail by Jones and Davis (1965), Kelley (1967, 1971, 1973), and their associates (see Jones et al., 1971; Weiner, 1974). These theorists dealt with two closely related tasks confronting the social observer. The first task is that of causal judgment: The observer seeks to identify the cause, or set of causes, to which some particular effect (i.e., some action or outcome) may most reasonably be *attributed*. The second task is that of social inference: The observer of an episode forms inferences about the *attributes* or dispositions of the relevant actors and about the attributes or properties of the situations to which they have responded.

Causal judgment and social inference tasks have both been the subject of intensive theoretical and empirical inquiry and, until recently, had constituted virtually the entire domain of attribution theory. Lately, however, a third task of the intuitive psychologist has begun to receive some attention; that task is the *prediction* or *estimation* of outcomes and behavior. The intuitive psychologist not only must seek explanations and make dispositional inferences; he must also form expectations and make guesses about actions and outcomes that are currently unknown or that will occur in the future. For instance, when a presidential candidate promises to "ease the burden of the average taxpayer," we consider possible causes for the statement and implications about the candidate's personal dispositions. (Did the promise simply reflect the demands of political expediency? Can we conclude anything about the candidate's true convictions?) But we are also likely to speculate about his subsequent behavior and his views on related issues that have not yet been explored. (If elected, will he slash property taxes? Does he favor curtailment of social welfare programs?) The

[1] For a more thorough and systematic explanation of the layman/scientist parallel, the reader is referred to Nisbett and Ross, 1980.

psychology of intuitive prediction, in short, is a natural extension of attribution theory's domain.

Logically and psychologically, of course, the three attribution tasks are interdependent. Explanations for an event, and inferences about the actors and entities that figure in that event, are intimately related. And together they provide the basis for speculation about the nature of events that are currently unknown or are likely to unfold in the future. Each task, however, offers unique possibilities (and unique problems of interpretation and methodology; see Ross, 1977, pp. 175–179) for revealing the assumptions and strategies that underlie the intuitive scientist's performance. It is worth noting that in recent years the use of estimations and predictions as dependent variables in studies of lay inference has become increasingly popular. One reason for this increased popularity is particularly important. Unlike the causal judgments of dispositional inferences that follow from a perceiver's analysis of an event, estimations or predictions about new or unknown events can often be evaluated with respect to their *accuracy*. That is, one can compare predictions and estimates about events with actual observations or measurements. This permits assessment both of the relative adequacy of the intuitive scientist's attributional strategy and of the direction of specific errors or biases.

Logical attributional principles vs. self-serving biases

Contemporary attribution theory has pursued two distinct but complementary goals. One goal has been to demonstrate that social perceivers' assessments and inferences generally follow the dictates of some logical or rational model. The other goal has been to illustrate and explicate the sources of bias or error that distort those generally veridical assessments and inferences. We shall consider briefly the so-called logical, or rational, schemata employed by the intuitive psychologist and then devote the remainder of the chapter to the sources of error in his attempts at understanding, predicting, and controlling the events that unfold around him.

The "covariation" and "discounting" principles. Individuals must, for the most part, share a common understanding of the social actions and outcomes that affect them, for without such consensus, social interaction would be chaotic, unpredictable, and beyond the control of the participants. Introspection by attribution theorists, buttressed by some laboratory evidence, has led to the postulation of a set of "rules" that may generally be employed in the interpretation of behaviors and outcomes. These "common sense" rules or schemata are analogous, in some respects, to the more formal rules and procedures that social scientists and statisticians follow in their analysis and interpretation of data.

H. H. Kelley, E. E. Jones, and their associates have distinguished two cases in which logical rules, or schemata, may be applied. In the *multiple* observation case the attributer has access to behavioral data that might be represented as rows or columns of an Actor × Object × Situation (or Instance) response matrix. Typically, in this domain of research summary statements are provided to the participants rather than actual responses. Thus the potential attributer learns that "Most theatergoers like the new Pinter play," or "Mary can't resist stray animals," or "The only television program that Ann watches is Masterpiece Theatre." In the *single* observation case the attributer must deal with the behavior of a single actor on a single occasion. For instance, he may see Sam comply with an experimenter's request to deliver a painful shock to a peer, or he may learn that "Louie bet all his money on a long shot at Pimlico."

The logical rules or principles governing attributions in these two cases are rather different (Kelley, 1967, 1971, 1973). In the multiple observation case the attributer applies the "covariance principle"; that is, he assesses the degree to which observed behaviors or outcomes occur in the presence, but fail to occur in the absence, of each causal candidate under consideration. Accordingly, the attributer concludes that the new Pinter play is a good one to the extent that it is liked by a wide variety of playgoers, that it is liked by individuals who praise few plays (e.g., "critics"), and that it is applauded as vigorously on the ninetieth day of its run as on the ninth.

In the single observation case the attributer's assessment strategy involves the application of the "discounting principle," by which the social observer "discounts" the role of any causal candidate in explaining an event to the extent that the other plausible causes or determinants can be identified. This attributional principle can be restated in terms of social inferences rather than causal attributions: To the extent that situational or external factors constitute a "sufficient" explanation for an event, that event is attributed to the situation and no inference logically can be made (and, presumably, no inference empirically is made) about the dispositions of the actor. Conversely, to the extent that an act or outcome seems to occur in spite of and not because of attendant situational forces, the relevant event is attributed to the actor and a "correspondent inference" (Jones & Davis, 1965) is made – that is, the attributer infers the existence and influence of some trait, ability, intention, feeling, or other disposition that could account for the actor's action or outcome. Thus, we resist the conclusion that Louie's long-shot plunge at Pimlico was reflective of his stable personal attributes to the extent that such factors as a hot tip, a desperate financial crisis, or seven pre-wager martinis could be cited. On the other hand, we judge Louie to be an inveterate long-shot player if we learn that his wager occurred in the face of his wife's threat to leave him if he ever lost his paycheck at the track again, his knowledge that he would not be able to pay the rent if he lost, and a track expert's overheard remark that the favorite in the race is "even better than the track odds suggest."

It is worth noting that the application of these two different principles places rather different demands upon the intuitive scientist. The covariance principle requires the attributer to apply rules that are essentially logical or statistical in nature and demands no further insight about the characteristics of the entities in question. Application of the discounting principle, by contrast, demands considerable insight about the nature of man and the impact of such situational forces as financial need, alcohol consumption, and a spouse's threat of abandonment. In a sense, the covariance principle can be applied by a mere "statistician," whereas the discounting principle requires a "psychologist" able to assess the role of various social pressures and situational forces and even to distinguish intended acts and outcomes from unintended ones (cf. Jones & Davis, 1965).

Evidence concerning the systematic use of common-sense attributional principles comes primarily from questionnaire studies in which subjects read and interpret brief anecdotes about the responses of one or more actors to specified objects or "entities" under specified circumstances (e.g., L. Z. McArthur, 1972, 1976). Occasional studies of narrower scope have exposed the attributer to seemingly authentic responses, encounters, and outcomes (e.g., Jones, Davis, & Gergen, 1961; Jones & DeCharms, 1957; Jones & Harris, 1967; Strickland, 1958; Thibaut & Riecken, 1955). Such research has demonstrated that attributers can, and generally do, make at least some use of the hypothesized principles or rules of thumb. What the methodologies employed to date have left ambiguous is the *degree* of the layperson's accuracy and the magnitude and direction of his errors.

Self-serving motivational biases in attribution. In speculating about possible distortions in an otherwise logical attribution system, theorists were quick to postulate "ego-defensive" biases through which attributors maintained or enhanced their general self-esteem or positive opinion of their specific dispositions and abilities (Heider, 1958; Jones & Davis, 1965; Kelley, 1967). Attempts to prove the existence of such a motivational bias have generally involved demonstrations of asymmetry in the attribution of positive and negative outcomes – specifically, a tendency for actors to attribute "successes" to their own efforts, abilities, or dispositions while attributing "failure" to luck, task difficulty, or other external factors. Achievement tasks (e.g., Davis & Davis, 1972; Feather, 1969; Fitch, 1970; Wolosin, Sherman, & Till, 1973) and teaching performances (e.g., Beckman, 1970; Freize & Weiner, 1971; Johnson, Feigenbaum, & Weiby, 1964) have provided most of the evidence for this asymmetry. It has also been shown that actors may give themselves more credit for success and less blame for failure than do observers evaluating the same outcomes (Beckman, 1970; Gross, 1966; Polefka, 1965).

Critics skeptical of broad motivational biases, however, have experienced little difficulty in mounting challenges to such research (see Miller

& Ross, 1975, also Nisbett & Ross, 1980, Chap. 10, for detailed discussions). The most telling argument against research purporting to show motivational biases is the obvious distinction between subjects' private perceptions and their public judgments. One can easily create situations where a person will publicly deny (or claim) responsibility for an event that he privately accepts (or does not accept) as his responsibility. While these public judgments may be self-serving in the sense of preserving one's public image, they do not imply the operation of ego-defensive biases in the sense of preserving one's private image (Miller, 1978).

Furthermore, asymmetries in the private attributions (were they available to researchers) of success and failure, and differences in the judgments of actors and observers may reflect other non-motivational sources of bias. As several researchers have noted, success, at least in test situations, is likely to be anticipated and congruent with the actor's past experience, whereas failure may be unanticipated and unusual. Similarly, successful outcomes are intended and are the object of plans and actions by the actor, whereas failures are unintended events that occur in spite of the actor's plans and efforts. Observers, furthermore, rarely are fully aware of the past experiences or present expectations and intentions of the actors whose outcomes they witness.

Challenges to the existence of pervasive ego-defensive biases have been empirical as well as conceptual. Thus, in some studies subjects seem to show "counterdefensive," or esteem-attenuating, biases. For example, Ross, Bierbrauer, and Polly (1974), using an unusually authentic instructor–learner paradigm, found that instructors rated their own performances and abilities as more important determinants of failure than of success. Conversely, the instructors rated their learner's efforts and abilities as more critical determinants of success than failure. In the same study these seemingly counterdefensive attributional tendencies proved to be even more pronounced among professional teachers than among inexperienced undergraduates, a result that contradicted the obvious derivation from ego-defensiveness theory that those most directly threatened by the failure experience would be most defensive.

Researchers who insist that self-serving motivational biases exist can, of course, provide alternative interpretations of studies that seem to show no motivational biases or counterdefensive biases (cf. Bradley, 1978). Indeed, in many respects the debate between proponents and skeptics has become reminiscent of earlier and broader debates in learning theory and basic perception in which the fruitlessness of the search for a "decisive" experiment on the issue of motivational influences (i.e., one that could not be interpreted by the "other side") became ever more apparent as data multiplied and conceptual analysis sharpened.

One response to this state of affairs has been to abandon motivational constructs temporarily and to concentrate upon those non-motivational factors (i.e., informational, perceptual, and cognitive factors) that influence and potentially distort attributional judgments. Beyond the existing conceptual difficulties, empirically mixed results, and historical lessons that discourage the investigators who would search for encompassing motivational biases, there are two additional reasons for the contemporary shift. First, there is a growing conviction that a fuller appreciation of non-motivational influences might lead us to understand and anticipate those circumstances in which attributions of responsibility are likely to enhance the attributer's self-esteem and those in which such attributions are likely to attentuate his self-esteem (cf. Miller & Ross, 1975). Second, there is the increasing recognition that accurate attributions generally are apt to be more "self-serving" than inaccurate ones – that is, that distortions of causal judgment are apt to leave the organism *badly* prepared for the task of long-term survival, however pleasant the immediate consequences of certain inaccurate perceptions and influences.

The rest of this chapter deals with a limited number of such non-motivational biases (see Nisbett & Ross, 1980, for a more thorough review). It also discusses a general phenomenon that increases the "costs" of such biases – the tendency for erroneous impressions, judgments, and even broader theories to survive in the face of logically powerful data that contradict these beliefs. Let us recognize from the outset, however, that the errors and biases dealt with are not inexplicable perversities on the intuitive scientist's part. Typically, they reflect the operation of mechanisms and strategies that serve the organism reasonably well in many circumstances; otherwise they surely would not survive the learning history of the individual or the evolutionary history of the species. These errors and biases can fairly be regarded as "domain specific" failings of inferential strategies and tactics that are at least cost efficient (and probably generally quite accurate as well) in the organism's overall experience.

Non-motivational attribution biases

The fundamental attribution error

The first identified (Heider, 1958) and most frequently cited non-motivation bias, one that we shall term the *fundamental attribution error*, is the tendency for attributers to underestimate the impact of situational factors and to overestimate the role of dispositional factors in controlling behavior. As "intuitive" psychologists, we seem too often to be nativists, or proponents of individual differences, and too seldom S – R behaviorists. We too readily infer broad personal dispositions and expect consistency in behavior or outcomes across widely disparate situations and contexts. We jump to hasty conclusions upon witnessing the behavior of our peers, overlooking the impact of relevant environmental forces and constraints.

General evidence for the fundamental attribution error. Beyond anecdotes and appeals to experience, the evidence most frequently cited for this general bias (e.g., Jones & Nisbett, 1971; Kelley, 1971) involves the attributer's apparent willingness to draw "correspondent" personal inferences about actors who have responded to very obvious situational pressures. For instance, Jones and Harris (1967) found that listeners assumed some correspondence between communicators' pro-Castro remarks and their private opinions even when these listeners *knew* that the communicators were obeying the experimenter's explicit request under no-choice conditions.

A more direct type of evidence that observers may ignore or underestimate situational forces has been provided by Bierbrauer (1973), who studied subjects' impressions of the forces operating in the classic Milgram (1963) situation. In Bierbrauer's study, participants witnessed a verbatim reenactment of one subject's "obedience" to the point of delivering the maximum shock to the supposed victim. Regardless of the type and amount of delay before judging, regardless of whether they actually played the role of a subject in the reenactment or merely observed, Bierbrauer's participants showed the fundamental attribution error; that is, they consistently and dramatically underestimated the degree to which subjects in general would yield to those situational forces that compelled obedience in Milgram's situation (see Figure 1). In other words, they assumed that the particular subject's obedience reflected his distinguishing personal dispositions rather than the potency of situational pressures and constraints acting upon all subjects.

The special case of role-conferred advantages in self-presentation. The tendency of social observers to underestimate the potency of situational forces and constraints and to overestimate the role of individual dispositions has figured heavily in the strategy, conceptual analyses, and even in the professional debates of contemporary social psychology (see Nisbett & Ross, 1980; Ross, 1977). Certain special cases of this fundamental attribution error help to focus our attention on mediating processes and more specific failures of the intuitive psychologist. An experiment by Ross, Amabile, and Steinmetz (1977), dealing with evaluations made about actors who were role-advantaged or role-disadvantaged (by random assignment), is a case in point. The particular roles dealt with by Ross et al. were those of questioner and contestant in a general-knowledge quiz game. The questioner's role obliged the subject to compose a set of challenging general-knowledge questions, to pose these questions to the contestant, and to provide accurate feedback after each response by the contestant. The contestant's role was restricted to answering, or attempting to answer, the relevant questions. Both of these participants (and, in a subsequent reenactment, observers as well) were then required to rate the questioner's and the contestant's general knowledge.

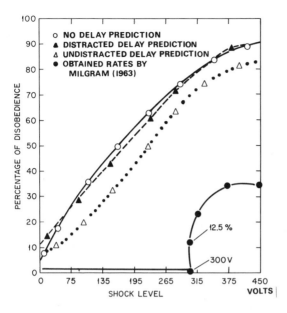

Figure 1. Comparison of predicted and actual disobedience rates.

The arbitrary assignment and fulfillment of these roles, it should be apparent, forced the participants and observers to deal with blatantly non-representative or biased "samples" of the questioners' and contestants' knowledge. The questioners' role encouraged them to display esoteric knowledge and guaranteed that they would avoid areas of ignorance; the contestants were denied such advantages in self-presentation. Indeed, there was virtually no ambiguity about the arbitrariness of the role assignment or about the differing prerogatives associated with each role, unlike many real-world situations in which social roles similarly confer advantages and disadvantages in self-display. Nevertheless, the unequal contest between questioners and contestants led to consistently biased and erroneous impressions. The participants, in a sense, simply failed to make adequate allowance for the situationally conferred advantages and disadvantages of the relevant roles. Thus, contestants rated their questioners as far superior to themselves, and uninvolved observers clearly agreed (see Figure 2). The observers, armed with the knowledge that they could no more answer the esoteric questions posed than could the contestants, recognized that the contestants were not deficient in their general knowledge. What the observers concluded, instead, was that the questioners were truly outstanding in their general knowledge. Interestingly, the questioners themselves were not misled by their encounter. An appreciation of this fact shifts our focus from the general existence of the fundamental attribution error, and the specific impact of social roles, to

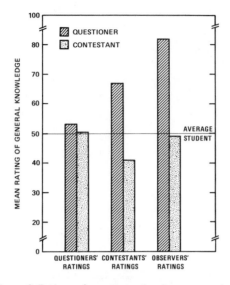

Figure 2. Ratings of questioners' and contestants' general knowledge.

the particular "data samples" upon which the various participants relied for their inferences. Unlike the contestants and the observers, the questioners were in no case forced to rely exclusively upon "biased" samples of general knowledge. Presumably, they had a great deal of additional evidence about the extent and limitations of their own general knowledge and about the unrepresentativeness of the esoteric items of information they displayed in their questions; consequently, they rated both themselves and the contestants as "average."

Both the social and theoretical implications of the Ross, Amabile, and Steinmetz demonstration should be clear. It prompts us to consider the countless social contexts in which formal or informal roles constrain interpersonal encounters and, in so doing, bias the impressions of the participants – even to the point of seeming to justify the prerogatives and limitations that are imposed by the advantaged and disadvantaged roles. It also prompts us to sharpen our focus on one of the specific failings of the intuitive scientist – his seeming insensitivity to the limited inferential value of biased data samples (see also Hamill, Wilson, & Nisbett, 1980; Nisbett & Ross, 1980, Chap. 4).

Salience or availability biases

Perhaps the most energetically researched area of attributional bias has been that involving the effects of attention and of the perceptual and cognitive factors that mediate attention. Briefly stated, it appears that whenever some aspect of the environment is made disproportionately salient or "available" to the perceiver (cf. Tversky & Kahneman, 1973, **11**) that aspect is given more weight in causal attribution. Thus, when an actor is made visually salient because of a unique racial or sexual status within a larger group (Taylor et al., 1976), because of some striking feature of appearance or dress (McArthur & Post, 1977; McArthur & Soloman, 1978), because of an instructional set (Regan & Totten, 1975), or even because of seating arrangements or other determinants of visual perspective (e.g., Storms, 1973; Taylor & Fiske, 1975), that actor is assigned disproportionate responsibility for any outcome to which she or he contributes. (See Taylor & Fiske, 1978, for a more complete review.) Indeed, a number of studies derived from "objective self-awareness" theory (Duval & Wicklund, 1972; Wicklund, 1975) have shown that actors' perceptions of their own causal roles can similarly be influenced by simple manipulations that direct their attention toward or away from the self as a social object (e.g., Duval & Hensley, 1976; Ellis & Holmes, 1979).

Recognition and understanding of how salience or availability factors affect the attributional process may help us better to understand the bases of many familiar attributional and inferential biases, perhaps even subsuming them as special cases. The fundamental attribution error, for instance, may importantly reflect the fact that actors are simply more salient than environmental features and therefore are more likely to be noticed in the attributer's initial search for causal candidates. Indeed, when situational factors and constraints are made disproportionately salient to the attributer, we might expect attributional errors that seem to be opposite to the so-called fundamental error. Thus, a supervisor can be led to incorrectly attribute a worker's trustworthy performance to an external factor – that is, the supervisor's surveillance – when that external factor is made highly salient (see Strickland, 1958). By the same token, an actor's intrinsic interest in a given task can be undermined (e.g., Deci, 1971; Lepper & Greene, 1975, 1978; Lepper, Greene, & Nisbett, 1973) if that actor is led to focus attention on an external incentive or constraint that seemingly encourages, but is in fact not necessary to encourage, performance in that task.

Consider also Jones and Nisbett's (1971) empirical generalization that actors, in accounting for their behavior, are relatively more inclined to cite situational factors and less inclined to cite dispositional factors than are observers of such behavior. To the extent that actors and observers show corresponding differences in their focus of attention – that is, actors attend to relevant features of their environment while observers focus their attention on the actors themselves – the Jones and Nisbett generalization becomes a special case of the attention/attribution generalization. Indeed, experimental evidence suggests that by manipulating actors' and observers' focus of attention, or perspective, their tendencies to cite situational versus dispositional causes can likewise be manipulated (e.g., Storms, 1973; Taylor & Fiske, 1975).

Finally, let us consider an inferential shortcoming noted by that astute fictional detective/psychologist Sherlock Holmes – the tendency to over-look the inferential value of non-occurrences. Such informative non-occurrences are events or actions that have *not* occurred in some context, which by not occurring thereby contain potentially important information (cf. Ross, 1977). The special relevance of the relatively low cognitive availability of non–occurrences should be clear. When one searches for or considers causal candidates, non-occurrences are unlikely to be highly salient or appropriately attended to; accordingly, one is not apt to give them sufficient weight in accounting for observed actions and outcomes. Jill is more likely to attribute Jack's anger to something she has "done" than to something she has failed to do, simply because the former is apt to be more salient to her than the latter. Indeed, assuming that the sins of omission are apt to be less salient than the sins of commission, Jack is apt to make the same error in accounting for his own anger.

The false consensus or egocentric attribution bias

The final non-motivational, or "informational," bias to be considered in this chapter relates to people's estimates of social consensus – the perceived commonness or oddity of the various responses they witness. Unlike the professional psychologist, who relies upon well-defined sampling techniques and statistical procedures for making such estimates, the layperson must rely upon intuitions and subjective impressions based on limited access to relevant data. The possibilities for bias in such estimates, and in the various social inferences or attributions that reflect such estimates, are thus legion. The specific attributional bias that we shall consider here concerns people's tendency to perceive a "false consensus" – that is, to see their own behavioral choices and judgments as relatively common and appropriate to existing circumstances while viewing alternative responses as uncommon, deviant, and inappropriate.

References to "egocentric attribution" (Heider, 1958; Jones & Nisbett, 1971), to "attributive projection" (Holmes, 1968), and to specific findings and phenomena related to false consensus biases have appeared sporadically in the social perception and attribution literatures (cf. Katz & Allport, 1931; Kelley & Stahelski, 1970). Perhaps the most compelling evidence, however, has been provided in a series of studies by Ross, Greene, and House (1977).

In the first study reported, subjects read descriptions of hypothetical conflict situations of the sort they might personally face and were to (a) estimate the commonness of the two possible response alternatives; (b) indicate the alternative they, personally, would follow; (c) assess the traits of the "typical" individual who would follow each of the two specified alternatives.

The estimates and ratings demonstrated the "false consensus" effect; subjects estimated that the alternative they chose would be relatively more common than the unchosen alternative. An obvious corollary to the false consensus proposition is that the intuitive psychologist judges those responses that differ from his own to be more revealing of the actor's stable dispositions than those responses that are similar to his own. The Ross, Greene, and House (1977) data support this prediction; subjects made relatively more confident and extreme predictions about the typical person who would perform the subject's unchosen alternative than about the typical person who would perform the subject's chosen alternative.

The term *relative* is critical in this formulation of the false consensus bias and it requires some clarification. Obviously, the man who would walk a tightrope between two skyscrapers, launch a revolution, or choose a life of clerical celibacy recognizes that his choices would be shared by few of his peers. The false consensus bias would, however, lead him to see his personal choices as less deviant than they would seem to us who would not walk tightropes, launch revolutions, or become celibate clerics. Similarly, the present thesis concedes that for some response categories virtually all raters' estimates may be biased in the same direction. The incidence of infant abuse, for instance, might be underestimated by abusing and non-abusing parents alike. The relative terms of the false consensus hypothesis lead only to the prediction that abusing parents will estimate child abuse to be more common and less revealing of personal dispositions than will non-abusing parents.

In a final demonstration by Ross, Greene, and House (1977) the hypothetical questionnaire methodology was abandoned and subjects were confronted with a real and consequential conflict situation. Subjects were asked to walk around campus for 30 minutes wearing a large sandwich-board sign bearing the message "EAT AT JOE'S." The experimenter made it clear to subjects that they could easily refuse to participate in the sandwich-board study but that he would prefer them to participate and thereby "learn something interesting while helping the research project." Subjects were subsequently asked to make their own decision about taking part in the study, to estimate the probable decisions of others, and to make trait inferences about particular peers who agreed or refused to participate.

The results using this "real" conflict situation (Table 1) confirmed the findings of earlier questionnaire studies dealing with hypothetical responses. Overall, subjects who agreed to wear the sandwich-board sign estimated that 62% of their peers would make the same choice. Subjects who refused to wear the sign estimated that only 33% of their peers would comply with the experimenter's request. Furthermore, as predicted, compliant and non-compliant subjects disagreed sharply in the relative strength of inferences they were willing to make about one peer who agreed and one who refused to wear the sandwich board. Compliant subjects made more confident and more extreme inferences about the personal characteristics of the non-compliant peer; non-compliant subjects made stronger inferences about the compliant peer.

Table 1. *The false consensus effect: Raters' estimates of commonness and trait inferences regarding two behavioral alternatives*

	Estimated commonness of agreement (%)	Estimated commonness of refusal (%)	Strength of trait inferences[a]	
			About subject who agrees to wear sign	About subject who refuses to wear sign
Subjects who agree to wear sign ($n = 48$)	62	38	120.1	125.3
Subjects who refuse to wear sign ($n = 32$)	33	67	139.7	106.8

[a]Sum of ratings for four traits; higher number indicates more confident and more extreme inferences by rater.
Source: Summarized from Ross, Greene, & House (1977).

Some broad implications of the Ross, Greene, and House (1977) demonstrations for our conception of the intuitive psychologist should be clear. Lay estimates of deviance and normalcy, and the host of social inferences and interpersonal responses that accompany such estimates, are systematically and egocentrically biased in accord with the layperson's own behavioral choices. More generally, it is apparent that attributional analyses may be distorted not only by errors in the intuitive psychologist's eventual analysis of social data but also by earlier biases in sampling or estimating such data.

Several non-motivational factors appear to play a role in producing false consensus phenomena. Principal among these are (a) selective-exposure and availability factors, and (b) factors pertaining to the resolution of situational ambiguity.

Selective-exposure factors underlying false consensus are fairly straightforward. Obviously, we know and associate with people who share our background, experiences, interests, values, and outlook. Such people *do*, in disproportionate numbers, respond as we would in a wide variety of circumstances. Indeed, our close association is determined, in part, by feelings of general consensus, and we may be inclined to avoid those whom we believe unlikely to share our judgments and responses. This exposure to a biased sample of people and behavior does not demand that we err in our estimates concerning the relevant populations, but it does make such errors likely. More subtle and more cognitive in character are the factors that increase our ability to recall, visualize, or imagine paradigmatic instances of behavior. In a given situation the specific behaviors we have chosen or would choose are likely to be more readily retrievable from memory and more easily imagined than opposite behaviors. In Kahneman and Tversky's (1973, 4) terms, the behavioral choices we favor may be more cognitively "available," and we are apt to be misled by this ease or difficulty of access in estimating the likelihood of relevant behavioral options.

A second non-motivational source of the false consensus effect arises from the intuitive psychologist's response to ambiguity – both about the nature and magnitude of situational forces and about the meaning and implications of various response alternatives. Attempts to resolve such ambiguity involve interpretation, estimation, and guesswork, all of which can exert a parallel effect on the attributor's own behavior choices and upon his predictions and inferences about the choices of others. Thus, subjects who anticipated and feared the ridicule of peers for wearing the "EAT AT JOE'S" sign and who regarded the experimenter's wishes and expectations as trivial were likely to refuse to wear the sign, to assume similar refusals by their peers, and to draw strong inferences about the traits of any subject who chose to wear the sign. Opposite priorities, of course, would have produced opposite personal choices and opposite social estimates and inferences.

In summary, the false consensus bias both reflects and creates distortions in the attribution process. It results from non-random sampling and retrieval of evidence and from idiosyncratic resolution of ambiguous situational factors and forces. In turn, it biases judgments about deviance and deviates, and, more generally, promotes variance and error in the interpretation of social phenomena.

Belief perseverance in the face of empirical challenges

The intuitive psychologist's various shortcomings – those described in this chapter and elsewhere (see Nisbett & Ross, 1980) – can lead him to hold beliefs about himself, about other people, or even about the nature of the social world, that are premature and in many cases erroneous. As long as they remain private and are not acted upon, such beliefs may seem inconsequential – merely tentative in nature and adjustable to new input. A gradually increasing body of theory and research, however, can now be marshaled to suggest the contrary.

It appears that beliefs – from relatively narrow personal impressions to broader social theories – are remarkably resilient in the face of empirical challenges that seem logically devastating. Two paradigms illustrate this resilience. The first involves the capacity of belief to survive and even be strengthened by new data, which, from a normative standpoint, should lead to the moderation of such beliefs. The second involves the survival of beliefs after their original evidential bases have been negated.

Belief perseverance and polarization in the face of new data

Individuals, social factions, interest groups, and even nations often hold differing beliefs about pressing social or political issues. Such divergences in opinion are hardly surprising. Given the informal and often purely intuitive basis on which such opinions are formulated, and given the role that social communications (often highly biased ones) play in shaping our beliefs, honest disagreements are inevitable. But what happens when the holders of divergent viewpoints are allowed to examine relevant evidence – especially when that evidence is relatively formal in nature and is identical for all concerned parties?

An optimistic expectation is that the contending factions would narrow the gap between their beliefs. This narrowing might consist of change toward the position justified by the relevant evidence, if such evidence were consistent and compelling; alternatively, it might consist of change toward greater moderation or mutual tolerance, if the relevant evidence were mixed or inconclusive. A less optimistic expectation is that the contending factions would remain unmoved; that is, they would disregard the new evidence and hold fast to their original positions. A recent experiment by Lord, Lepper, and Ross (1979) suggests an even more disheartening result (disheartening, at least, for those who hope or expect the objective data of the social scientist to dampen the fires of social dispute).

Lord et al. (1979) first selected subjects who either supported capital punishment and believed it to be an effective deterrent (proponents) or opposed capital punishment and believed it not to be a deterrent (opponents). The subjects were presented, in a counterbalanced design, with two purportedly authentic empirical studies. One seemingly provided empirical support for their position; the other seemingly opposed that position. At strategic points in the reading of these two studies, the two groups completed ratings dealing both with their evaluations of the two studies and with their own changes in attitudes and beliefs. These ratings dramatically revealed the capacity of theory-holders to interpret new evidence in a manner that strengthens and sustains their theories. First, both proponents and opponents of capital punishment consistently rated the study that supported their beliefs as "more convincing" and "better conducted" than the study that opposed those beliefs. Second, and in contrast to any normative strategy imaginable for incorporating new evidence relevant to one's beliefs, the net effect of reading the two studies was to polarize further the beliefs of the death penalty opponents and proponents. The manner in which this polarization occurred was particularly illuminating (see Figure 3). Upon reading a brief statement of a result that supported their own viewpoint, subjects' beliefs became considerably more extreme; these changes were maintained or enhanced when the subjects considered details about the procedure and data. By contrast, upon reading a brief result statement that opposed their own viewpoint, subjects became only slightly less extreme; and upon reading the relevant details concerning procedures and data the subjects tended to revert to the beliefs they had held before ever learning of the study's existence. In fact, many individual subjects who had read both the results summary and the procedural details of a study that opposed their belief ultimately became more convinced of the correctness of that belief! No such effects occurred when the same results and procedures were read by subjects whose initial views were supported.

Obviously, professional scientists frequently are guilty of the same offense as intuitive ones. Again and again one sees contending factions that are involved in scholarly disputes – whether they involve the origins of the universe, the line of hominid ascent, or the existence of ego-defensive attribution biases – draw support for their divergent views from the same corpus of findings. Later in this chapter we shall consider the processes underlying such phenomena in more detail and comment more specifically on the normative status of the scientist's willingness to process evidence in the light of his existing theories and expectations. First it is necessary to consider a second general class of perseverance phenomena.

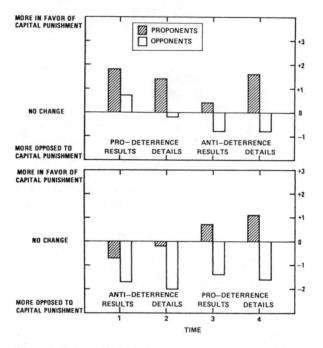

Figure 3. Top panel: Attitude changes on capital punishment relative to start of experiment as reported across time by subjects who received pro-deterrence study first. Bottom panel: Attitude changes on capital punishment relative to start of experiment as reported across time by subjects who received anti-deterrence study first.

Belief perseverance after evidential discrediting

Sometimes, one's beliefs are threatened not by new data but rather by challenges to the "formative" evidence for such beliefs – that is, to the information or analysis that led one to form the belief in the first place. At an anecdotal level it is easy to cite such instances. Sally fails miserably in her first attempts to learn how to skate and then finds out that her borrowed skates were much too large to give her the needed ankle support. Mary assumes that John's bouquet of flowers reflects thoughtfulness, a romantic nature, and a certain conventionalism, only to learn subsequently that John's father owns a flower shop. Broader theories or beliefs about the world similarly can be challenged. A baby-sitter decides, on the basis of his experience with a single infant who cried all night, that bottle feeding produces colicky babies, only to discover that the infant in question was suffering from a high fever. Or a scientist discovers that a classic experiment that figured in the emergence of a particular theory was tainted with some severe artifact or by outright fraud.

The perseverance hypothesis, in its general formulation, suggests that the social perceivers identified above would persist in their initial assessments to an unwarranted and inappropriate degree. But the terms of such a contention are obviously too general and too vague to be testable. When, precisely, can we infer that a social perceiver is "inappropriately" persisting in an impression or belief whose basis has been undermined? To explore the perseverance hypothesis experimentally, what clearly is required is a paradigm that permits us to specify precisely how much perseverance and how much change might be warranted.

One such paradigm is suggested by the dilemma of the social psychologist who has made use of deception in the course of an experiment and then seeks to debrief the subjects who had been the target of such deception. The psychologist reveals the totally contrived and inauthentic nature of the information presented presuming that this debriefing will thereby eliminate any effects such information might have exerted upon the subjects' feelings or beliefs. Many professionals, however, have expressed public concern that such experimental deceptions may do great harm that is not fully undone by conventional debriefing procedures (e.g., Kelman, 1972; A.G. Miller, 1972; Orne, 1972; Silverman, 1965).

A series of experiments by Lepper, Ross, and their colleagues (see also earlier studies by Walster et al., 1967; Valins, 1974) have used the total discounting, or debriefing, paradigm to explore the phenomenon of belief perseverance in the face of evidential discrediting. We may begin discussing this work by outlining a pair of experiments by Ross, Lepper, and Hubbard (1975) that dealt with subjects' postdebriefing impressions about their own abilities at a particular task or about the abilities of a peer.

Postdebriefing perseverance of personal impressions. The procedure employed by Ross et al. (1975) was quite straightforward. Subjects first received continuous false feedback as they performed a novel discrimination task (i.e., distinguishing authentic suicide notes from fictitious ones). In the first experiment reported this procedure was used to manipulate the subjects' perceptions of their own performance and ability. A second experiment introduced observers, who formed social impressions as they witnessed the false feedback manipulation. In both experiments after this manipulation of first impressions had been completed, the experimenter totally discredited the "evidence" upon which the actors' and/or observers' impressions had been based. Specifically, the actor (overheard in Experiment 2 by the observer) received a standard debriefing session in which he learned that his putative outcome had been predetermined and that his feedback had been totally unrelated to actual performance. Before dependent variable measures were introduced, in fact, every subject was led to explicitly acknowledge his understanding of the nature and purpose of the experimental deception.

Following this total discrediting of the original information, the subjects completed a dependent variable questionnaire dealing with the actors' performances and abilities. The evidence for postdebriefing

Table 2. *Postdebriefing perceptions of the actor's performance and ability*

	Actor's own perceptions			Observer's perceptions of actors		
	Success	Failure	t	Success	Failure	t
Estimated initial number correct	18.33	12.83	5.91***	19.00	12.42	4.43***
Predicted future number correct	18.33	14.25	4.23***	19.08	14.50	2.68*
Rated ability at task	5.00	3.83	2.65*	5.33	4.00	3.36**

*p < .05. **p < .01. ***p < .001.
Source: Summarized from Experiment 2 of Ross, Lepper, & Hubbard (1975).

impression perseverance was unmistakable for actors and observers alike. On virtually every measure (i.e., objective estimates of the actor's just-completed performance, estimates for performance on a future set of discrimination problems, and subjective estimates of the actor's abilities) the totally discredited initial outcome manipulation produced significant "residual" effects upon actors' and observers' assessments (see Table 2).

Follow-up experiments have since shown that a variety of unfounded personal impressions, once induced by experimental procedures, can survive a variety of total discrediting procedures. For example, Jennings, Lepper, and Ross (1980) have demonstrated that subjects' impressions of their ability at interpersonal persuasion (having them succeed or fail to convince a confederate to donate blood) can persist after they have learned that the initial outcome was totally inauthentic. Similarly, in two related experiments Lepper, Ross, and Lau (1979) have shown that students' erroneous impressions of their "logical problem solving abilities" (and their academic choices in a follow-up measure two months later) persevered even after they had learned that good or poor teaching procedures provided a totally sufficient explanation for the successes or failures that were the basis for such impressions.

Postdebriefing perseverance of discredited theories. A recent series of experiments by Anderson, Lepper, and Ross (1980) have extended the domain of perseverance demonstrations from personal impressions to broader beliefs about the world. Anderson et al.'s studies first manipulated and then attempted to undermine subjects' theories about the functional relationship between two measured variables: the adequacy of firefighters' professional performances and their prior scores on a paper and pencil test of risk preference. In one particularly pertinent variation, the formative evidence consisted of only one pair of specific cases – i.e., one successful and one unsuccessful firefighter with appropriately discrepant scores in their respective tests of risk-taking preferences. Interestingly, such minimal data did suffice to produce strong theories, on the subjects' part, about the probable relationship between the relevant measures. More important, however, was the finding that such theories survived the revelations that the cases in question had been totally fictitious and the different subjects had, in fact, received opposite pairings of riskiness scores and job outcomes. Indeed, when comparisons were made between subjects who had been debriefed and those who had not been, it appeared that over 50% of the initial effect of the "case history" information remained after debriefing.

In summary, it is clear that beliefs can survive potent logical or empirical challenges. They can survive and even be bolstered by evidence that most uncommitted observers would agree logically demands some weakening of such beliefs. They can even survive the total destruction of their original evidential bases. While much work remains to be done in specifying the precise limits and exploring inevitable exceptions to such phenomena, it is clear that the costs of the layperson's attributional biases and other inferential shortcomings are apt not to be corrected but instead to be compounded by subsequent experience and deliberations. The question that must at last be addressed, therefore, is *how* and *why* does such perseverance occur? That is, what cognitive mechanisms underlie the unwarranted persistence of our impressions, beliefs, and broader social theories?

Possible mechanisms underlying belief perseverance

Biased search, recollection, and assimilation of information. There can be little doubt that our beliefs influence the processes by which we seek out, store, and interpret relevant information. Indeed, without prior knowledge and corresponding preconceptions, our understanding of everyday experience would demand considerably more time and effort, and in all likelihood that understanding would be greatly diminished. But an inevitable consequence of our willingness to process evidence in the light of our prior beliefs is the tendency to perceive more support for those beliefs than actually exists in the evidence at hand.

Such "confirmation biases" (see Einhorn & Hogarth, 1978; Hamilton, 1979; Hastie & Kumar, 1979; Wason & Johnson-Laird, 1972) have long been noted by philosophers of science (e.g., Bacon, 1620/1960). Perhaps most noteworthy is the theory holder's response to equivocal or ambiguous data. As Lord et al. (1979) have documented, potentially confirmatory evidence is apt to be taken at face value while potentially disconfirmatory evidence is subjected to highly critical and skeptical scrutiny. Thus, two consequences follow: First, any pattern of evidence processed in this fashion, even evidence that is essentially random, will tend to *bolster* the initial belief. Second, once evidence has been processed in this fashion it gains the capacity to *sustain* the prior belief when that belief is subjected to new empirical disconfirmation or to attacks on its original evidential basis.

The role of biased assimilation has been shown fairly convincingly, we think, for the case where the theory holder is confronted with new data (i.e., Lord et al., 1979). But the role of this mechanism in the discounting or debriefing paradigm is perhaps less obvious, and we are forced to rely on speculation rather than hard data. We suggest that the subject who forms an initial impression about himself, about another person, or about some functional relationship is apt to search his memory and the immediate situation for additional data relevant to that impression. Such data, then, are apt to be recalled and regarded as pertinent or probative only to the extent that they confirm the impression at hand. Thus a subject who has succeeded or failed at a given task recalls similar successes or failures at related tasks – and decides upon their relevance to the present case – on the basis of the congruency of the relevant outcomes. Similarly, a subject who has come to believe that variables X and Y are functionally related will recall, and give credence to, cases that confirm rather than challenge that presumed relationship. Once again, such biased searching, recollection, and assimilation not only bolster one's initial belief, they also produce a pattern of biased evidence that remains highly available to sustain the belief in question when its *initial* basis is attacked or even destroyed. The critical assumption here is that people do not constantly update or reevaluate the evidence relevant to their beliefs. They do not commonly decide "now that my prior hypothesis has been undermined somewhat I must go back and reassess all of the evidence that I ever considered in the light of that hypothesis."

The formation of causal explanations. People do more than merely note evidence relevant to their impressions or beliefs. They also engage in causal analysis or explanation (Heider, 1958). That is, they try to *account for* the characteristics of self or others, or for the functional relationships that they have come to believe exist. Thus, the subject who believes herself a superior or inferior discriminator of suicide notes in the Ross et al. (1975) study might search for some aspect of her background that would account for such a talent or deficiency. Similarly, the subject who is induced to believe in a positive or negative relationship between firefighting ability and risk preference will have little difficulty in postulating a logical basis for either relationship. Once again, this process not only buttresses an initial impression or belief, it is apt to sustain that impression or belief in the face of subsequent challenges or attacks.

Evidence for the operation of this perseverance mechanism comes primarily from two debriefing studies demonstrating that when subjects are explicitly required to formulate such explanations, prior to debriefing, the magnitude of the perseverance effect is increased. In the Anderson et al. (1980) study one group of subjects was explicitly instructed to explain the positive or negative relationship suggested by the two firefighter cases. As predicted, this manipulation greatly enhanced the relevant perseverance effect. In fact, subjects who explained the basis for a positive or for a negative relationship before being debriefed were only trivially less certain of that relationship than subjects who received no debriefing. Similar results were obtained by Ross, Lepper, Strack, and Steinmetz (1977), who found that subjects induced to explain outcomes in the lives of clinical patients (whose earlier case histories they had read) continued to regard such outcomes as relatively likely even when they learned that the explained events were inauthentic and had been contrived by the experimenter.

Behavioral confirmation or "self-fulfilling" hypotheses. The two research paradigms used by Ross, Lepper, and their colleagues to investigate perseverance phenomena lack one element that may be critical to many everyday situations. Specifically, subjects in those studies lacked the opportunity to act upon their beliefs. Such actions are important partially because they can increase the psychological costs or "dissonance" (Festinger, 1957) involved in changing one's beliefs (cf. Ashmore & Collins, 1968; Collins & Hoyt, 1972; Hovland, Campbell, & Brock, 1957). Furthermore, such actions create new data relevant to those beliefs. Not only may this new data be processed in a biased manner, but the data themselves may also be biased in a direction that tends to confirm the relevant hypothesis.

The idea of self-confirming, or self-fulfilling, hypotheses is not a new one to social scientists. The famous but controversial "Pygmalion" studies by Rosenthal and Jacobson (1968), which dealt with the impact of teachers' expectations upon the "blooming" of their students' abilities and performances, is a case in point. However, a recent series of studies by Snyder and his colleagues have considerably advanced our appreciation and understanding of such phenomena by demonstrating the manner in which subjects' expectations, or the hypotheses they are led to test, can generate "objective support" for those expectations or hypotheses (e.g., Snyder & Swann, 1978a, 1978b; Snyder, Tanke, & Berscheid, 1977).

Concluding remarks: Beliefs do change!

Our foregoing discussion of phenomena and mechanisms should not make the reader lose sight of the fact that beliefs about ourselves, our political leaders, and even our scientific theories *do* change. In part such change may simply be the result of brute force. Even if logical or empirical challenges have less impact than might be warranted by normative standards (see Ross & Lepper, 1980) they may still get the job done. In part, such change may reflect the fact that formal methods of hypothesis testing sometimes are deliberately employed to protect us from the dangers of informal ones. But we suspect there is more to the story, for there is evidence that prior theories can sometimes be overcome without massive amounts of disconfirming evidence or decisive well-controlled experiments. Thus, the changes in outlook and belief that can be wrought by vivid, concrete, first-hand experience (see Nisbett & Ross, 1980) and the effectiveness of groups and leaders that accomplish dramatic political or religious conversions offer inviting targets for future research.

10. Evidential impact of base rates

Amos Tversky and Daniel Kahneman

In many contexts people are required to assess the probability of some target event (e.g., the diagnosis of a patient or the sales of a textbook) on the basis of (a) the base-rate frequency of the target outcome in some relevant reference population (e.g., the frequency of different diagnoses or the distribution of textbook sales), (b) some specific evidence about the case at hand (e.g., the patient's response to a diagnostic test or the table of contents of the text in question).

Concern with the role of base-rate data in intuitive predictions about individual cases was expressed by Meehl & Rosen (1955), who argued, using Bayes' rule, that predictions of rare outcome (e.g., suicide) on the basis of fallible data is a major source of error in clinical prediction. Meehl & Rosen did not conduct experimental studies but they cited examples from the literature on clinical diagnosis, in which base-rate information was not taken into account.

To obtain an experimental test of the impact of base-rate data, we presented subjects with a description of a graduate student, or a professional, and asked them to predict his field of study or his profession, respectively (Kahneman & Tversky, 1973, 4). These studies showed that posterior probability judgments were determined primarily by the degree to which the description was similar to or representative of the respective professional stereotype (e.g., of librarians or lawyers). The base-rate frequencies of these categories, which were either known to the subjects from their daily experience or stated explicitly in the question, were largely neglected. (We use the term *neglect* to describe situations in which the base rate is either ignored or grossly underweighted.)

Predictions by representativeness or similarity are generally insensitive

This work was supported by the Office of Naval Research under Contract N00014–79–C–0077 to Stanford University.

to base-rate frequencies. However, the phenomenon of base-rate neglect is far more general, since it also occurs in judgments that cannot be readily interpreted in terms of representativeness (Hammerton, 1973). For example, Casscells, Schoenberger, and Grayboys (1978) presented 60 students and staff at Harvard Medical School with the following question:

If a test to detect a disease whose prevalence is 1/1000 has a false positive rate of 5%, what is the chance that a person found to have a positive result actually has the disease, assuming you know nothing about the person's symptoms or signs? (p. 999)

The most common response, given by almost half of the participants, was 95%. The average answer was 56%, and only 11 participants gave the appropriate response of 2%, assuming the test correctly diagnoses every person who has the disease. Evidently, even highly educated respondents often fail to appreciate the significance of outcome base rate in relatively simple formal problems (see, e.g., Bar-Hillel, 1980a; Lyon & Slovic, 1976). The strictures of Meehl & Rosen (1955) regarding the failure to appreciate base rates are not limited to clinical psychologists; they apply to physicians and other people as well.

The conditions under which base-rate data are used or neglected have been studied extensively by students of judgment and social psychology [see Borgida & Brekke (1981) and Kassin (1979b) for reviews of the literature]. The independent variables investigated in these studies may be divided into two types: procedural and evidential. Procedural variables refer to properties of the design, the task, and the display, while evidential variables refer to the nature of the source and the interpretation of the evidence.

For example, a procedural variable of considerable importance is whether the judge treats each problem as a special case or engages in a task of multiple predictions. Considerable evidence from studies of probability learning and related tasks indicates that people tend to match the distribution of the criterion in making multiple predictions, particularly in the presence of outcome feedback. Because people attempt to generate a pattern of predictions that is representative of the outcome distribution, experiments using repeated judgments with the same base rate produce larger base-rate effects than experiments in which each judgment is treated as a special problem. (See Bar-Hillel & Fischhoff, 1981; Manis et al., 1980).

Another procedural variable of interest is the difference between a within-subjects and a between-subjects design. For example, Fischhoff, Slovic, & Lichtenstein (1979) showed that base-rate data have more impact when the base rates vary in the problems presented to each subject than when different base rates are presented to different subjects. The within-subjects procedure, however, induces a general tendency to assign a higher weight to the varied attribute, even when it is normatively irrelevant (Fischhoff & Bar-Hillel, 1980). For further discussion of the contrast between comparative (within-subjects) and non-comparative (between-subjects) designs and their implications for the testing of lay statistical intuitions, see Chapter 34.

Although procedural variables have a considerable effect, the present chapter is confined to the discussion of evidential variables that control the interpretation and the impact of the base-rate data. Specifically, we focus on the distinction between two types of base rates, which we label causal and incidental.

Causal and incidental base rates

A base rate is called causal if it suggests the existence of a causal factor that explains why any particular instance is more likely to yield one outcome rather than another. A base rate is called incidental if it does not lead to such an inference.

A compelling demonstration of the contrast between causal and incidental base rates was presented by Ajzen (1977). In one experiment, the respondents assessed the probability that a student, whose academic ability was briefly described, had passed a particular examination. The causal base rate was presented as follows:

Two years ago, a final exam was given in a course at Yale University. About 75% of the students failed (passed) the exam.

This base rate is causal because it implies that the exam was exceptionally difficult (if 75% of the students failed) or relatively easy (if 75% of the students passed). The inferred cause (i.e., the difficulty of the exam) "explains" the base rate and makes every individual student less (or more) likely to pass the exam.

The incidental base rate was presented as follows:

Two years ago, a final exam was given in a course at Yale University. An educational psychologist interested in scholastic achievement interviewed a large number of students who had taken the course. Since he was primarily concerned with reactions to success (failure), he selected mostly students who had passed (failed) the exam. Specifically, about 75% of the students in his sample had passed (failed) the exam.

This base rate is incidental, or non-causal, because the proportion of successful and unsuccessful students in the sample was selected arbitrarily by the investigator. Unlike the causal base rate, it does not permit any inference regarding the difficulty of the exam.

Ajzen's (1977) study showed that the causal base rate was much more potent than the incidental, although variations of both types of base rate produced significant effects. For the causal base rate, the judged probability of success (averaged across descriptions) was higher by .34 when the base rate of success was high than when it was low. For the incidental base rate, the corresponding difference was only .12. In the terms of the present analysis, the ease or difficulty of an examination is one of the contributing causes that affect the student's performance, and it is therefore integrated with other contributing causes, such as the intelligence and the motivation of the student in question.

The base rate of success was used in the preceding study to define an examination as easy or hard. In a second study, the base rate of preferences was used to define options as more or less attractive (Ajzen, 1977). Subjects were required to assess the probability that students for whom a personality sketch was provided would choose either history or economics as an elective general-interest course. The causal base rate, which served to define the relative attractiveness of the two options, consisted of the proportions of students enrolled in the two courses (.70 and .30). The incidental base rate was introduced as follows:

To obtain student reaction, the history (economics) professor recently interviewed 70 students who had taken his general interest course in history (economics). In order to enable comparisons, he also interviewed 30 students who had taken the course in economics (history).

Note that, unlike the causal base rate, the incidental version provides no information about the popularity of the two courses. The effect of the incidental base rate was not significant in this study, although there was a probability difference of .025 in the expected direction. In contrast, the causal base rate had a strong effect: The mean judged probability of choice was .65 for a popular course (high base rate) and .36 for an unpopular course (low base rate). Evidently, the attractiveness of courses is inferred from the base rate of choices and is integrated with personal characteristics in assessing the probability that a particular student will select one course rather than the other. From a normative standpoint, however, the causal and the incidental base rates in these examples should have roughly comparable effects.

Our next example illustrates a different type of causal base rate; it also permits the calculation of the correct posterior probability under some reasonable assumptions. Consider the following modified version of the cab problem, originally introduced by Kahneman and Tversky (1972a) and later investigated by Bar-Hillel (1980a), and Tversky and Kahneman (1980, 8).

A cab was involved in a hit and run accident at night. Two cab companies, the Green and the Blue, operate in the city. You are given the following data:

   (a) 85% of the cabs in the city are Green and 15% are Blue.

   (b) a witness identified the cab as Blue. The court tested the reliability of the witness under the same circumstances that existed on the night of the accident and concluded that the witness correctly identified each one of the two colors 80% of the time and failed 20% of the time.

What is the probability that the cab involved in the accident was Blue rather than Green?

To obtain the correct answer, let B and G denote respectively the hypotheses that the cab involved in the accident was Blue or Green, and let W be the witness's report. By Bayes' rule in odds form, with prior odds of 15/85 and a likelihood ratio of 80/20,

$$P(B/W)/P(G/W) = P(W/B)P(B)/P(W/G)P(G)$$
$$= (.8)(.15)/(.2)(.85) = 12/17$$

and hence

$$P(B/W) = 12/(12 + 17) = .41$$

In spite of the witness's report, therefore, the hit-and-run cab is more likely to be Green than Blue, because the base rate is more extreme than the witness is credible.

A large number of subjects have been presented with slightly different versions of this problem, with very consistent results. The median and modal answer is typically .80, a value which coincides with the credibility of the witness and is apparently unaffected by the relative frequency of Blue and Green cabs.

Base-rate information, however, was utilized in the absence of case data. When item (b) was omitted from the question, almost all subjects gave the base rate (.15) as their answer. Furthermore, the base rate controlled the subjects' expectation about the evidence. A different group of subjects was presented with the above problem except that the sentence "a witness identified the cab as Blue" was replaced by "a witness identified the color of the cab." These respondents were then asked, "What is the probability that the witness identified the cab as Blue?" The median and modal response to this question was .15. Note that the correct answer is $.2 \times .85 + .8 \times .15 = .29$. In the absence of other data, therefore, the base rate was used properly to predict the target outcome and improperly to predict the witness's report.

A different pattern of judgments was observed when the incidental base rate (of cabs) was replaced by a causal base rate (of accidents). This was accomplished by replacing item (a) with

(a′) Although the two companies are roughly equal in size, 85% of cab accidents in the city involve Green cabs and 15% involve Blue cabs.

The answers to this problem were highly variable, but the base rate was no longer ignored. The median answer was .60, which lies between the reliability of the witness (.80) and the correct answer (.41). The base rate in (a′) is causal because the difference in rates of accidents between companies of equal size readily elicits the inference that the drivers of the Green cabs are more reckless and/or less competent than the drivers of the Blue cabs. This inference accounts for the differential base rates of accidents and implies that any Green cab is more likely to be involved in an accident than any Blue cab. In contrast, the base rate in (a) is incidental because the difference between the number of Blue and Green cabs in the city does not justify a causal inference that makes any particular Green cab more likely to be involved in an accident than any particular Blue cab.

Note that according to the present analysis the posterior probability that the errant cab is Blue rather than Green is the same under both (a) and (a'). Nevertheless, the correlation between cab color and involvement in accidents is 0 for the incidental base rate and .7 for the causal! This statistical fact reflects the difference between the two base rates and helps explain why the causal base rate is utilized while the incidental base rate is ignored.

Other evidential variables

The causal or incidental nature of base-rate data is not the only evidential variable that affects their impact on intuitive judgments. Even in the absence of a causal interpretation, base-rate data are not superseded by non-specific, impoverished, or incoherent case data. For example, Bar-Hillel (1980a) studied a version of the original cab problem in which the information about the witness (item b) was replaced by a report that the hit-and-run cab was equipped with an intercom and that intercoms are installed in 80% of Green cabs and in 20% of Blue cabs. In this problem, the (incidental) base rate was not discarded, and the median response was .48. Bar-Hillel suggested that the evidence regarding the intercom did not replace the base rate because it is less specific than an identification by a witness. Thus, base-rate data are combined with other evidence either when the former have a causal interpretation or when the latter are no more specific than the base rate (Bar-Hillel, 1980a).

Both specificity and causality may help explain the difference between the results of Kahneman and Tversky (1973, 4), who found an essential neglect of base rate in predicting a student's field of study on the basis of a personality sketch, and the results of McCauley and Stitt (1978), who found a substantial correlation between the judged base rates of traits and the judged probabilities of these traits given a particular nationality, for example, the probability that a person is efficient if he is German. Aside from several procedural differences, the latter study differs from the former in three important aspects. First, subjects were asked to predict relative frequency (e.g., the proportion of Germans who are efficient) rather than the probability for an individual case. Second, the evidence consisted of class membership, for example, German, rather than detailed descriptions of a specific individual. Third, the base-rate frequency of traits may be easier to interpret causally than that of professions. Lay personality theories suggest reasons why most people are fun loving and only a few are masochistic. These reasons apply to people in general and to Germans in particular, thereby providing a causal interpretation of the base rate of traits.

A situation of special interest concerns specific but non-diagnostic evidence (e.g., a description of a person that is equally similar to an engineer and a lawyer). The experimental findings here are not entirely consistent. Kahneman & Tversky (1973, 4) found base-rate neglect, while Ginosar and Trope (1980) found exclusive reliance on base rate under apparently similar experimental conditions. Most studies, however, obtained intermediate results where the base rate was not discarded but rather diluted by nondiagnostic evidence about the case at hand (see e.g., Manis et al., 1980; Wells & Harvey, 1977).

Internal versus external attributions

A class of base-rate problems of particular interest to social psychologists arises when the evidence and the base rate refer respectively to internal–dispositional and to external–situational factors that affect an outcome. A student's success in an examination, for example, is determined jointly by the difficulty of the exam and by the student's talent. Similarly, one's response to a request to donate money to a particular cause depends on one's generosity and on the nature of the request. External factors, such as the difficulty of an exam or the effectiveness of the request, are naturally expressed by the relevant base rates (e.g., 75% of students failed the exam; most people contributed to the cause). The question regarding the relative impact of situational and dispositional factors in social attribution can thus be reformulated in terms of the weight that is assigned to the corresponding base rates.

Nisbett & Borgida were the first to explore the link between the use of base-rate information in judgment research and the relative weight of situational factors in the study of attribution of behavior. They showed that knowledge of the low frequency of helping behavior in the Darley-Latané (1968) study did not affect subjects' predictions of the behavior of an individual participant in the study, who was observed in a brief filmed interview. The study of Nisbett and Borgida (1975) contributed to the convergence of cognitive and social-psychological approaches to the study of judgment. It also provoked controversy (Borgida, 1978; Wells & Harvey, 1977, 1978) and stimulated a flurry of research on the role of consensus information in the prediction of behavior (Borgida & Brekke, 1981; Kassin, 1979b; Nisbett & Ross, 1980; Ross, 1977).

In contrast to the examples of the exam and the cabs, in which causal and incidental base rates are clearly distinguished, the base rates in many consensus studies are subject to alternative interpretations. To illustrate the point, let us compare the study of Nisbett and Borgida (1975) with the causal base-rate condition in Ajzen's (1977) experiment, where the subjects evaluated the probability that a particular student passed an exam that 75% of the class had failed. The formal structure of the two problems is precisely the same, but the base rate was largely neglected in the former study and used in the latter. It appears that the surprising base rate was given a situational interpretation in Ajzen's study but was interpreted as an accident of sampling in the Nisbett-Borgida study.

The judgments of Ajzen's subjects indicate that they inferred from the low base rate of success that the exam had been difficult, although they could have used the same evidence to conclude that the students who took the test were inept. In contrast, the subjects of Nisbett and Borgida apparently inferred that the participants in the helping study were mostly unfeeling brutes (Wells & Harvey, 1977). They did not draw the correct conclusion that the situation of the Darley-Latané study is not conducive to helping behavior.

Whether an extreme base rate is attributed to an accident of sampling or to situational factors depends on the context of the problem: It is more plausible that an unusual distribution of test results is due to the difficulty (or ease) of an exam than to the exceptional composition of the class. On the other hand it is harder to revise one's conception about the conditions under which people help a stricken stranger than to assume that the participants in the helping study were exceptionally unhelpful.

The apparent neglect of base-rate data in predictions about individual cases is associated with an inference about unusual characteristics of the members of the group. A causal interpretation of the base rate becomes more likely if this inference is blocked. This hypothesis has been supported by several studies, which restored a base-rate effect by stressing the representativeness of a sample in which surprising behaviors had been observed (Hansen & Donoghue, 1977; Hansen & Lowe, 1976; Wells & Harvey, 1978). The impact of base-rate data was even enhanced in one study by informing the subjects that the sample for which base rates were provided was large and therefore reliable (Kassin, 1979a). The major conclusion of this research is that the use or neglect of consensus information in individual prediction depends critically on the interpretation of that information.

Part IV
Availability

11. Availability: A heuristic for judging frequency and probability

Amos Tversky and Daniel Kahneman

Introduction

Much recent research has been concerned with the validity and consistency of frequency and probability judgments. Little is known, however, about the psychological mechanisms by which people evaluate the frequency of classes or the likelihood of events.

We propose that when faced with the difficult task of judging probability or frequency, people employ a limited number of heuristics which reduce these judgments to simpler ones. Elsewhere we have analyzed in detail one such heuristic – representativeness. By this heuristic, an event is judged probable to the extent that it represents the essential features of its parent population or generating process. . . .

When judging the probability of an event by representativeness, one compares the essential features of the event to those of the structure from which it originates. In this manner, one estimates probability by assessing similarity or connotative distance. Alternatively, one may estimate probability by assessing availability, or associative distance. Life-long experience has taught us that instances of large classes are recalled better and faster than instances of less frequent classes, that likely occurrences are easier to imagine than unlikely ones, and that associative connections are strengthened when two events frequently co-occur. Thus, a person could estimate the numerosity of a class, the likelihood of an event, or the

This chapter is an abbreviated version of a paper that appeared in *Cognitive Psychology*, 1973, 4, 207–232. Copyright © 1972 by Academic Press, Inc. Reprinted by permission.

frequency of co-occurrences by assessing the ease with which the relevant mental operation of retrieval, construction, or association can be carried out.

For example, one may assess the divorce rate in a given community by recalling divorces among one's acquaintances; one may evaluate the probability that a politician will lose an election by considering various ways in which he may lose support; and one may estimate the probability that a violent person will "see" beasts of prey in a Rorschach card by assessing the strength of association between violence and beasts of prey. In all these cases, the estimation of the frequency of a class or the probability of an event is mediated by an assessment of availability.[1] A person is said to employ the availability heuristic whenever he estimates frequency or probability by the ease with which instances or associations could be brought to mind. To assess availability it is not necessary to perform the actual operations of retrieval or construction. It suffices to assess the ease with which these operations could be performed, much as the difficulty of a puzzle or mathematical problem can be assessed without considering specific solutions.

That associative bonds are strengthened by repetition is perhaps the oldest law of memory known to man. The availability heuristic exploits the inverse form of this law, that is, it uses strength of association as a basis for the judgment of frequency. In this theory, availability is a mediating variable, rather than a dependent variable as is typically the case in the study of memory. Availability is an ecologically valid clue for the judgment of frequency because, in general, frequent events are easier to recall or imagine than infrequent ones. However, availability is also affected by various factors which are unrelated to actual frequency. If the availability heuristic is applied, then such factors will affect the perceived frequency of classes and the subjective probability of events. Consequently, the use of the availability heuristic leads to systematic biases.

This paper explores the availability heuristic in a series of ten studies.[2] We first demonstrate that people can assess availability with reasonable speed and accuracy. Next, we show that the judged frequency of classes is biased by the availability of their instances for construction, and retrieval. The experimental studies of this paper are concerned with judgments of frequencies, or of probabilities that can be readily reduced to relative

---

[1] The present use of the term "availability" does not coincide with some usages of this term in the verbal learning literature (see, e.g., Horowitz, Norman, & Day, 1966; Tulving & Pearlstone, 1966).

[2] Approximately 1500 subjects participated in these studies. Unless otherwise specified, the studies were conducted in groups of 20–40 subjects. Subjects in Studies 1, 2, 3, 9 and 10 were recruited by advertisements in the student newspaper at the University of Oregon. Subjects in Study 8 were similarly recruited at Stanford University. Subjects in Studies 5, 6 and 7 were students in the 10th and 11th grades of several college-preparatory high schools in Israel.

frequencies. The effects of availability on the judged probabilities of essentially unique events (which cannot be reduced to relative frequencies) are discussed in the fifth and final section.

Assessments of availability

Study 1: Construction

The subjects ($N = 42$) were presented with a series of word-construction problems. Each problem consisted of a 3×3 matrix containing nine letters from which words of three letters or more were to be constructed. In the training phase of the study, six problems were presented to all subjects. For each problem, they were given 7 sec to estimate the number of words which they believed they could produce in 2 min. Following each estimate, they were given two minutes to write down (on numbered lines) as many words as they could construct from the letters in the matrix. Data from the training phase were discarded. In the test phase, the construction and estimation tasks were separated. Each subject estimated for eight problems the number of words which he believed he could produce in 2 min. For eight other problems, he constructed words without prior estimation. Estimation and construction problems were alternated. Two parallel booklets were used, so that for each problem half the subjects estimated and half the subjects constructed words.

Results. The mean number of words produced varied from 1.3 (for XUZONLCJM) to 22.4 (for TAPCERHOB), with a grand mean of 11.9. The mean number estimated varied from 4.9 to 16.0 (for the same two problems), with a grand mean of 10.3. The product–moment correlation between estimation and production, over the sixteen problems, was 0.96.

Study 2: Retrieval

The design and procedure were identical to Study 1, except for the nature of the task. Here, each problem consisted of a category, e.g., *flowers* or *Russian novelists*, whose instances were to be recalled. The subjects ($N = 28$) were given 7 sec to estimate the number of instances they could retrieve in 2 min, or 2 min to actually retrieve the instances. As in Study 1, the production and estimation tasks were combined in the training phase and alternated in the test phase.

Results. The mean number of instances produced varied from 4.1 (city names beginning with F) to 23.7 (four-legged animals), with a grand mean of 11.7. The mean number estimated varied from 6.7 to 18.7 (for the same two categories), with a grand mean of 10.8. The product–moment correlation between production and estimation over the 16 categories was 0.93.

Discussion

In the above studies, the availability of instances could be measured by the total number of instances retrieved or constructed in any given problem.[3] The studies show that people can assess availability quickly and accurately. How are such assessments carried out? One plausible mechanism is suggested by the work of Bousfield and Sedgewick (1944), who showed that cumulative retrieval of instances is a negatively accelerated exponential function of time. The subject could, therefore, use the number of instances retrieved in a short period to estimate the number of instances that could be retrieved in a much longer period of time. Alternatively, the subject may assess availability without explicitly retrieving or constructing any instances at all. Hart (1967), for example, has shown that people can accurately assess their ability to recognize items that they cannot recall in a test of paired-associate memory.

Availability for construction

We turn now to a series of problems in which the subject is given a rule for the construction of instances and is asked to estimate their total (or relative) frequency. In these problems – as in most estimation problems – the subject cannot construct and enumerate all instances. Instead, we propose, he attempts to construct some instances and judges overall frequency by availability, that is, by an assessment of the ease with which instances could be brought to mind. As a consequence, classes whose instances are easy to construct or imagine will be perceived as more frequent than classes of the same size whose instances are less available. This prediction is tested in the judgment of word frequency, and in the estimation of several combinatorial expressions.

Study 3: Judgment of word frequency

Suppose you sample a word at random from an English text. Is it more likely that the word starts with a *K*, or that *K* is its third letter? According to our thesis, people answer such a question by comparing the availability of the two categories, i.e., by assessing the ease with which instances of the two categories come to mind. It is certainly easier to think of words that start with a *K* than of words where *K* is in the third position. If the judgment of frequency is mediated by assessed availability, then words

---

[3] Word-construction problems can also be viewed as retrieval problems because the response-words are stored in memory. In the present paper we speak of retrieval when the subject recalls instances from a natural category, as in Studies 2 and 8. We speak of construction when the subject generates exemplars according to a specified rule, as in Studies 1 and 4.

that start with K should be judged more frequent. In fact, a typical text contains twice as many words in which K is in the third position than words that start with K.

According to the extensive word-count of Mayzner and Tresselt (1965), there are altogether eight consonants that appear more frequently in the third than in the first position. Of these, two consonants (X and Z) are relatively rare, and another (D) is more frequent in the third position only in three-letter words. The remaining five consonants (K,L,N,R,V) were selected for investigation.

The subjects were given the following instructions:

The frequency of appearance of letters in the English language was studied. A typical text was selected, and the relative frequency with which various letters of the alphabet appeared in the first and third positions in words was recorded. Words of less than three letters were excluded from the count.

You will be given several letters of the alphabet, and you will be asked to judge whether these letters appear more often in the first or in the third position, and to estimate the ratio of the frequency with which they appear in these positions.

A typical problem read as follows:

Consider the letter R.
Is R more likely to appear in
_ the first position?
_ the third position? (check one)
My estimate for the ratio of these two values is ___: 1.

Subjects were instructed to estimate the ratio of the larger to the smaller class. For half the subjects, the ordering of the two positions in the question was reversed. In addition, three different orderings of the five letters were employed.

Results. Among the 152 subjects, 105 judged the first position to be more likely for a majority of the letters, and 47 judged the third position to be more likely for a majority of the letters. The bias favoring the first position is highly significant ($p < .001$, by sign test). Moreover, each of the five letters was judged by a majority of subjects to be more frequent in the first than in the third position. The median estimated ratio was 2:1 for each of the five letters. These results were obtained despite the fact that all letters were more frequent in the third position.

In other studies we found the same bias favoring the first position in a within-subject design where each subject judged a single letter, and in a between-subjects design, where the frequencies of letters in the first and in the third positions were evaluated by different subjects. We also observed that the introduction of payoffs for accuracy in the within-subject design had no effect whatsoever. Since the same general pattern of results was obtained in all these methods, only the findings obtained by the simplest procedure are reported here.

A similar result was reported by Phillips (1966) in a study of Bayesian inference. Six editors of a student publication estimated the probabilities that various bigrams, sampled from their own writings, were drawn from the beginning or from the end of words. An incidental effect observed in that study was that all the editors shared a common bias to favor the hypothesis that the bigrams had been drawn from the beginning of words. For example, the editors erroneously judged words beginning with *re* to be more frequent than words ending with *re*. The former, of course, are more available than the latter.

Study 4: Permutations

Consider the two structures, A and B, which are displayed below.

```
(A)                                                      (B)
x x x x x x x x                                          x x
x x x x x x x x                                          x x
x x x x x x x x                                          x x
                                                         x x
                                                         x x
                                                         x x
                                                         x x
                                                         x x
                                                         x x
```

A path in a structure is a line that connects an element in the top row to an element in the bottom row, and passes through one and only one element in each row.

In which of the two structures are there more paths?
How many paths do you think there are in each structure?

Most readers will probably share with us the immediate impression that there are more paths in A than in B. Our subjects agreed: 46 of 54 respondents saw more paths in A than in B ($p < .001$, by sign test). The median estimates were 40 paths in A and 18 in B. In fact, the number of paths is the same in both structures, for $8^3 = 2^9 = 512$.

Why do people see more paths in A than in B? We suggest that this result reflects the differential availability of paths in the two structures. There are several factors that make the paths in A more available than those in B. First, the most immediately available paths are the columns of the structures. There are 8 columns in A and only 2 in B. Second, among the paths that cross columns, those of A are generally more distinctive and less confusable than those in B. Two paths in A share, on the average, about 1/8 of their elements, whereas two paths in B share, on the average, half of their elements. Finally, the paths in A are shorter and hence easier to visualize than those in B.

Study 5: Combinations

Consider a group of ten people who have to form committees of r members, where r is some number between 2 and 8. How many different committees of r members can they form? The correct answer to this problem is given by the binomial coefficient $\binom{10}{r}$, which reaches a maximum of 252 for $r = 5$. Clearly, the number of committees of r members equals the number of committees of $10 - r$ members because any elected group of, say, two members defines a unique nonelected group of eight members.

According to our analysis of intuitive estimation, however, committees of two members are more available than committees of eight. First, the simplest scheme for constructing committees is a partition of the group into disjoint subsets. Thus, one readily sees that there are as many as five disjoint committees of two members, but not even two disjoint committes of eight. Second, committees of eight members are much less distinct, because of their overlapping membership; any two committees of eight share at least six members. This analysis suggests that small committees are more available than large committees. By the availability hypothesis, therefore, the small committees should appear more numerous.

Four groups of subjects (total $N = 118$) estimated the number of possible committees of r members that can be formed from a set of ten people. The different groups, respectively, evaluated the following values of r: 2 and 6; 3 and 8; 4 and 7; 5.

Median estimates of the number of committees are shown in Figure 1, with the correct values. As predicted, the judged numerosity of committees decreases with their size.

The following alternative formulation of the same problem was devised in order to test the generality of the findings:

In the drawing below, there are ten stations along a route between Start and Finish. Consider a bus that travels, stopping at exactly r stations along this route.

START ⎸　⎸　⎸　⎸　⎸　⎸　⎸　⎸　⎸　⎸ FINISH

What is the number of different patterns of r stops that the bus can make?

The number of different patterns of r stops is again given by $\binom{10}{r}$. Here too, of course, the number of patterns of two stops is the same as the number of patterns of eight stops, because for any pattern of stops there is a unique complementary pattern of non-stops. Yet, it appears as though one has more degrees of freedom in constructing patterns of two stops where "one has many stations to choose from" than in constructing patterns of eight stops where "one must stop at almost every station." Our previous analysis suggests that the former patterns are more available: more such patterns are seen at first glance, they are more distinctive, and they are easier to visualize.

Four new groups of subjects (total $N = 178$) answered this question, for

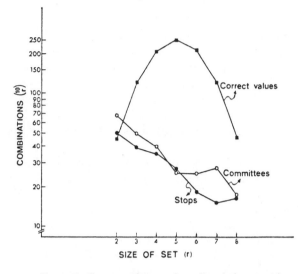

Figure 1. Correct values and median judgments (on a logarithmic scale) for the Committees problem and for the Stops problem.

$r = 2, \ldots, 8$, following the same design as above. Median estimates of the number of stops are shown in Figure 1. As in the committee problem, the apparent number of combinations generally decreases with r, in accordance with the prediction from the availability hypothesis, and in marked contrast to the correct values. Further, the estimates of the number of combinations are very similar in the two problems. As in other combinatorial problems, there is marked underestimation of all correct values, with a single exception in the most available case, where $r = 2$.

The underestimation observed in Experiments 4 and 5 occurs, we suggest, because people estimate combinatorial values by extrapolating from an initial impression. What a person sees at a glance or in a few steps of computation gives him an inadequate idea of the explosive rate of growth of many combinatorial expressions. In such situations, extrapolating from an initial impression leads to pronounced underestimation. This is the case whether the basis for extrapolation is the initial availability of instances, as in the preceding two studies, or the output of an initial computation, as in the following study.

Study 6: Extrapolation

We asked subjects to estimate, within 5 sec, a numerical expression that was written on the blackboard. One group of subjects ($N = 87$) estimated the product $8 \times 7 \times 6 \times 5 \times 4 \times 3 \times 2 \times 1$, while another group ($N = 114$) estimated the product $1 \times 2 \times 3 \times 4 \times 5 \times 6 \times 7 \times 8$. The median estimate for the descending sequence was 2,250. The median estimate for the ascending sequence was 512. The difference between the estimates is highly significant ($p < .001$, by median test). Both estimates fall very short of the correct answer, which is 40,320.

Both the underestimation of the correct value and the difference between the two estimates support the hypothesis that people estimate 8! by extrapolating from a partial computation. The factorial, like other combinatorial expressions, is characterized by an ever-increasing rate of growth. Consequently, a person who extrapolates from a partial computation will grossly underestimate factorials. Because the results of the first few steps of multiplication (performed from left to right) are larger in the descending sequence than in the ascending sequence, the former expression is judged larger than the latter. The evaluation of the descending sequence may proceed as follows: "8 times 7 is 56 times 6 is already above 300, so we are dealing with a reasonably large number." In evaluating the ascending sequence, on the other hand, one may reason: "1 times 2 is 2 times 3 is 6 times 4 is 24, and this expression is clearly not going very far. . . ."

Study 7: Binomial – availability vs. representativeness

The final study of this section explores the role of availability in the evaluation of binomial distributions and illustrates how the formulation of a problem controls the choice of the heuristic that people adopt in intuitive estimation.

The subjects ($N = 73$) were presented with these instructions:

Consider the following diagram:

```
X  X  O  X  X  X
X  X  X  X  O  X
X  O  X  X  X  X
X  X  X  O  X  X
X  X  X  X  X  O
O  X  X  X  X  X
```

A path in this diagram is any descending line which starts at the top row, ends at the bottom row, and passes through exactly one symbol (X or O) in each row.

What do you think is the percentage of paths which contain

      6 – X and no – O   ____ %
      5 – X and   1 – O   ____ %
            •
            •
            •

      No – X and 6 – O   ____ %

Note that these include all possible path-types and hence your estimates should add to 100%.

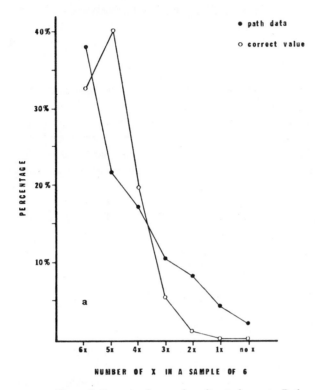

Figure 2. Correct values and median judgments: Path problem.

The actual distribution of path-type is binomial with $p = 5/6$ and $n = 6$. People, of course, can neither intuit the correct answers nor enumerate all relevant instances. Instead, we propose, they glance at the diagram and estimate the relative frequency of each path-type by the ease with which individual paths of this type could be constructed. Since, at every stage in the construction of a path (i.e., in each row of the diagram) there are many more Xs than Os, it is easier to construct paths consisting of six Xs than paths consisting of, say, five Xs and one O, although the latter are, in fact, more numerous. Accordingly, we predicted that subjects would erroneously judge paths of 6 Xs and no O to be the most numerous.

Median estimates of the relative frequency of all path-types are presented in Figure 2, along with the correct binomial values. The results confirm the hypothesis. Of the 73 subjects, 54 erroneously judged that there are more paths consisting of six Xs and no O than paths consisting of five Xs and one O, and only 13 regarded the latter as more numerous than the former ($p < .001$, by sign test). The monotonicity of the subjective distribution of path-types is apparently a general phenomenon. We have obtained the same result with different values of p (4/5 and 5/6) and n (5, 6 and 10), and different representations of the population proportions (e.g., four Xs and one O or eight Xs and two Os in each row of the path diagram).

To investigate further the robustness of this effect, the following additional test was conducted. Fifty combinatorially naive undergraduates from Stanford University were presented with the path problem. Here, the subjects were not asked to estimate relative frequency but merely to judge "whether there are more paths containing six Xs and no O, or more paths containing five Xs and one O." The subjects were run individually, and they were promised a $1 bonus for a correct judgment. The significant majority of subjects (38 of 50, $p < .001$, by sign test) again selected the former outcome as more frequent. Erroneous intuitions, apparently, are not easily rectified by the introduction of monetary payoffs.

We have proposed that when the binomial distribution is represented as a path diagram, people judge the relative frequency of the various outcomes by assessing the availability of individual paths of each type. This mode of evaluation is suggested by the sequential character of the definition of a path and by the pictorial representation of the problem. Consider next an alternative formulation of the same problem.

Six players participate in a card game. On each round of the game, each player receives a single card drawn blindly from a well-shuffled deck. In the deck, 5/6 of the cards are marked X and the remaining 1/6 are marked O. In many rounds of the game, what is the percentage of rounds in which

    6 players receive X and no player receives O   ___%

    5 players receive X and 1 player receives O   ___%

                    .

                    .

                    .

    No player receives X and 6 players receive O   ___%

Note that these include all the possible outcomes and hence your estimates should add to 100%.

This card problem is formally identical to the path problem, but it is intended to elicit a different mode of evaluation. In the path problem, individual instances were emphasized by the display, and the population proportion (i.e., the proportion of Xs in each row) was not made explicit. In the card problem, on the other hand, the population proportion is explicitly stated and no mention is made of individual instances. Consequently, we hypothesize that the outcomes in the card problem will be evaluated by the degree to which they are representative of the composition of the deck rather than by the availability of individual instances. In the card problem, the outcome "five Xs and one O" is the most representative, because it matches the population proportion (see Kahneman & Tversky, 1972b, **3**). Hence, by the representativeness heuristic, this outcome should be judged more frequent than the outcome "six Xs and no O," contrary to the observed pattern of judgments in the path problem.

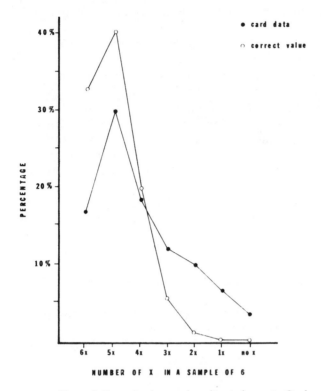

Figure 3. Correct values and median judgments: Card problem.

The judgments of 71 of 82 subjects who answered the card problem conformed to this prediction. In the path problem, only 13 of 73 subjects had judged these outcomes in the same way; the difference between the two versions is highly significant ($p < .001$, by a χ^2 test).

Median estimates for the card problem are presented in Figure 3. The contrast between Figures 2 and 3 supports the hypothesis that different representations of the same problem elicit different heuristics. Specifically, the frequency of a class is likely to be judged by availability if the individual instances are emphasized and by representativeness if generic features are made salient.

Availability for retrieval

In this section we discuss several studies in which the subject is first exposed to a message (e.g., a list of names) and is later asked to judge the frequency of items of a given type that were included in the message. As in the problems studied in the previous section, the subject cannot recall and count all instances. Instead, we propose, he attempts to recall some instances and judges overall frequency by availability, i.e., by the ease with which instances come to mind. As a consequence, classes whose instances are readily recalled will be judged more numerous than classes of the same size whose instances are less available. This prediction is first tested in a study of the judged frequency of categories. . . .

Study 8: Fame, frequency, and recall

The subjects were presented with a recorded list consisting of names of known personalities of both sexes. After listening to the list, some subjects judged whether it contained more names of men or of women, others attempted to recall the names in the list. Some of the names in the list were very famous (e.g., Richard Nixon, Elizabeth Taylor), others were less famous (e.g., William Fulbright, Lana Turner). Famous names are generally easier to recall. Hence, if frequency judgments are mediated by assessed availability, then a class consisting of famous names should be judged more numerous than a comparable class consisting of less famous names.

Four lists of names were prepared, two lists of entertainers and two lists of other public figures. Each list included 39 names recorded at a rate of one name every 2 sec. Two of the lists (one of public figures and one of entertainers) included 19 names of famous women and 20 names of less famous men. The two other lists consisted of 19 names of famous men and 20 names of less famous women. Hence, fame and frequency were inversely related in all lists. The first names of all personalities always permitted an unambiguous identification of sex.

The subjects were instructed to listen attentively to a recorded message. Each of the four lists was presented to two groups. After listening to the recording, subjects in one group were asked to write down as many names as they could recall from the list. The subjects in the other group were asked to judge whether the list contained more names of men or of women.

Results. (a) Recall. On the average, subjects recalled 12.3 of the 19 famous names and 8.4 of the 20 less famous names. Of the 86 subjects in the four recall groups, 57 recalled more famous than nonfamous names, and only 13 recalled fewer famous than less famous names ($p < .001$, by sign test).

(b) Frequency. Among the 99 subjects who compared the frequency of men and women in the lists, 80 erroneously judged the class consisting of the more famous names to be more frequent ($p < .001$, by sign test). . . .

Retrieval of occurrences and construction of scenarios

In all the empirical studies that were discussed in this paper, there existed an objective procedure for enumerating instances (e.g., words that begin with K or paths in a diagram), and hence each of the problems had an objectively correct answer. This is not the case in many real-life situations where probabilities are judged. Each occurrence of an economic recession, a successful medical operation, or a divorce, is essentially unique, and its probability cannot be evaluated by a simple tally of instances. Nevertheless, the availability heuristic may be applied to evaluate the likelihood of such events.

In judging the likelihood that a particular couple will be divorced, for example, one may scan one's memory for similar couples which this question brings to mind. Divorce will appear probable if divorces are prevalent among the instances that are retrieved in this manner. Alternatively, one may evaluate likelihood by attempting to construct stories, or scenarios, that lead to a divorce. The plausibility of such scenarios, or the ease with which they come to mind, can provide a basis for the judgment of likelihood. In the present section, we discuss the role of availability in such judgments, speculate about expected sources of bias, and sketch some directions that further inquiry might follow.

We illustrate availability biases by considering an imaginary clinical situation.[4] A clinician who has heard a patient complain that he is tired of life, and wonders whether that patient is likely to commit suicide may well recall similar patients he has known. Sometimes only one relevant instance comes to mind, perhaps because it is most memorable. Here, subjective probability may depend primarily on the similarity between that instance and the case under consideration. If the two are very similar, then one expects that what has happened in the past will recur. When several instances come to mind, they are probably weighted by the degree to which they are similar, in essential features, to the problem at hand.

How are relevant instances selected? In scanning his past experience does the clinician recall patients who resemble the present case, patients who attempted suicide, or patients who resemble the present case *and* attempted suicide? From an actuarial point of view, of course, the relevant class is that of patients who are similar, in some respects, to the present case, and the relevant statistic is the frequency of attempted suicide in this class.

Memory search may follow other rules. Since attempted suicide is a dramatic and salient event, suicidal patients are likely to be more memorable and easier to recall than depressive patients who did not attempt suicide. As a consequence, the clinician may recall suicidal patients he has encountered and judge the likelihood of an attempted suicide by the degree of resemblance between these cases and the present patient. This approach leads to serious biases. The clinician who notes that nearly all suicidal patients he can think of were severely depressed may conclude

---

[4] This example was chosen because of its availability. We know of no reason to believe that intuitive predictions of stockbrokers, sportscasters, political analysts or research psychologists are less susceptible to biases.

that a patient is likely to commit suicide if he shows signs of severe depression. Alternatively, the clinician may conclude that suicide is unlikely if "this patient does not look like any suicide case I have met." Such reasoning ignores the fact that only a minority of depressed patients attempt suicide and the possibility that the present patient may be quite unlike any that the therapist has ever encountered.

Finally, a clinician might think only of patients who were both depressed and suicidal. He would then evaluate the likelihood of suicide by the ease with which such cases come to mind or by the degree to which the present patient is representative of this class. This reasoning, too, is subject to a serious flaw. The fact that there are many depressed patients who attempted suicide does not say much about the probability that a depressed patient will attempt suicide, yet this mode of evaluation is not uncommon. Several studies (Jenkins & Ward, 1963; Smedslund, 1963; Ward & Jenkins, 1965) showed that contingency between two binary variables such as a symptom and a disease is judged by the frequency with which they co-occur, with little or no regard for cases where either the symptom or the disease was not present.

Some events are perceived as so unique that past history does not seem relevant to the evaluation of their likelihood. In thinking of such events we often construct *scenarios*, i.e., stories that lead from the present situation to the target event. The plausibility of the scenarios that come to mind, or the difficulty of producing them, then serve as a clue to the likelihood of the event. If no reasonable scenario comes to mind, the event is deemed impossible or highly unlikely. If many scenarios come to mind, or if the one scenario that is constructed is particularly compelling, the event in question appears probable.

Many of the events whose likelihood people wish to evaluate depend on several interrelated factors. Yet it is exceedingly difficult for the human mind to apprehend sequences of variations of several interacting factors. We suggest that in evaluating the probability of complex events only the simplest and most available scenarios are likely to be considered. In particular, people will tend to produce scenarios in which many factors do not vary at all, only the most obvious variations take place, and interacting changes are rare. Because of the simplified nature of imagined scenarios, the outcomes of computer simulations of interacting processes are often counter-intuitive (Forrester, 1971). The tendency to consider only relatively simple scenarios may have particularly salient effects in situations of conflict. There, one's own moods and plans are more available to one than those of the opponent. It is not easy to adopt the opponent's view of the chessboard or of the battlefield, which may be why the mediocre player discovers so many new possibilities when he switches sides in a game. Consequently, the player may tend to regard his opponent's strategy as relatively constant and independent of his own moves. These considerations suggest that a player is susceptible to the *fallacy of initiative*

– a tendency to attribute less initiative and less imagination to the opponent than to himself. This hypothesis is consistent with a finding of attribution-research (Jones & Nisbett, 1971) that people tend to view their own behavior as reflecting the changing demands of their environment and others' behavior as trait-dominated.

The production of a compelling scenario is likely to constrain future thinking. There is much evidence showing that, once an uncertain situation has been perceived or interpreted in a particular fashion, it is quite difficult to view it in any other way (see, e.g., Bruner & Potter, 1969). Thus, the generation of a specific scenario may inhibit the emergence of other scenarios, particularly those that lead to different outcomes. . . .

Perhaps the most obvious demonstration of availability in real life is the impact of the fortuitous availability of incidents or scenarios. Many readers must have experienced the temporary rise in the subjective probability of an accident after seeing a car overturned by the side of the road. Similarly, many must have noticed an increase in the subjective probability that an accident or malfunction will start a thermonuclear war after seeing a movie in which such an occurrence was vividly portrayed. Continued preoccupation with an outcome may increase its availability, and hence its perceived likelihood. People are preoccupied with highly desirable outcomes, such as winning the sweepstakes, or with highly undesirable outcomes, such as an airplane crash. Consequently, availability provides a mechanism by which occurrences of extreme utility (or disutility) may appear more likely than they actually are. . . .

12. Egocentric biases in availability and attribution

Michael Ross and Fiore Sicoly

One instance of a phenomenon examined in the present experiments is familiar to almost anyone who has conducted joint research. Consider the following: You have worked on a research project with another person, and the question arises as to who should be "first author" (i.e., who contributed more to the final product?). Often, it seems that both of you feel entirely justified in claiming that honor. Moreover, since you are convinced that your view of reality must be shared by your colleague (there being only one reality), you assume that the other person is attempting to take advantage of you. Sometimes such concerns are settled or prevented by the use of arbitrary decision rules, for example, the rule of "alphabetical priority" – a favorite gambit of those whose surnames begin with letters in the first part of the alphabet.

We suggest, then, that individuals tend to accept more responsibility for a joint product than other contributors attribute to them. It is further proposed that this is a pervasive phenomenon when responsibility for a joint venture is allocated by the participants. In many common endeavors, however, the participants are unaware of their divergent views, since there is no need to assign "authorship"; consequently, the ubiquity of the phenomenon is not readily apparent. The purpose of the current research was to assess whether these egocentric perceptions do occur in a variety of settings and to examine associated psychological processes.

In exploring the bases of such differential perceptions, we are not so naive as to suggest that intentional self-aggrandizement never occurs. Nonetheless, it is likely that perceptions can be at variance in the absence of deliberate deceit; it is from this perspective that we approach the issue.

Excerpts from a paper that appeared in *The Journal of Personality and Social Psychology*, 1979, 37, 322–336. Copyright © 1979 by the American Psychological Association. Reprinted by permission.

To allocate responsibility for a joint endeavor, well-intentioned participants presumably attempt to recall the contributions each made to the
final product. Some aspects of the interaction may be recalled more
readily, or be more available, than others, however. In addition, the
features that are recalled easily may not be a random subset of the whole.
Specifically, a person may recall a greater proportion of his or her own
contributions than would other participants.

An egocentric bias in availability of information in memory, in turn,
could produce biased attributions of responsibility for a joint product. As
Tversky and Kahneman (1973, 11) have demonstrated, people use availability, that is, "the ease with which relevant instances come to mind"
(1973, p. 209), as a basis for estimating frequency. Thus, if self-generated
inputs were indeed more available, individuals would be more likely to
claim more responsibility for a joint product than other participants would
attribute to them.

There are at least four processes that may be operating to increase the
availability of one's own contributions: (a) selective encoding and storage
of information, (b) differential retrieval, (c) informational disparities, and
(d) motivational influences.

Selective encoding and storage

For a number of reasons, the availability of the person's own inputs may
be facilitated by differential encoding and storage of self-generated
responses. First, individuals' own thoughts (about what they are going to
say next, daydreams, etc.) or actions may distract their attention from the
contributions of others. Second, individuals may rehearse or repeat their
own ideas or actions; for example, they might think out their position
before verbalizing and defending it. Consequently, their own inputs may
receive more "study time," and degree of retention is strongly related to
study time (Carver, 1972). Third, individuals' contributions are likely to fit
more readily into their own cognitive schema, that is, their unique
conception of the problem based on past experience, values, and so forth.
Contributions that fit into such preexisting schemata are more likely to be
retained (Bartlett, 1932; Bruner, 1961).

Differential retrieval

The availability bias could also be produced by the selective retrieval of
information from memory. In allocating responsibility for a joint outcome,
the essential question from each participant's point of view may be, "How
much did *I* contribute?" Participants may, therefore, attempt to recall
principally their own contributions and inappropriately use the information so retrieved to estimate their *relative* contributions, a judgment that

cannot properly be made without a consideration of the inputs of others as well.

Informational disparities

There are likely to be differences in the information available to the contributors that could promote egocentric recall. Individuals have greater access to their own internal states, thoughts, and strategies than do observers. Moreover, participants in a common endeavor may differ in their knowledge of the frequency and significance of each other's independent contributions. For example, faculty supervisors may be less aware than their student colleagues of the amount of time, effort, or ingenuity that students invest in running subjects, performing data analyses, and writing preliminary drafts of a paper. On the other hand, supervisors are more cognizant of the amount and of the importance of the thought, reading, and so on that they put into the study before the students' involvement begins.

Motivational influences

Motivational factors may also mediate an egocentric bias in availability. One's sense of self-esteem may be enhanced by focusing on, or weighting more heavily, one's own inputs. Similarly, a concern for personal efficacy or control (see deCharms, 1968; White, 1959) could lead individuals to dwell on their own contributions to a joint product.

The preceding discussion outlines a number of processes that may be operating to render one's own inputs more available (and more likely to be recalled) than the contributions of others. Consequently, it may be difficult to imagine a disconfirmation of the hypothesis that memories and attributions are egocentric. As Greenwald (1978) has observed, however, the egocentric character of memory "is not a necessary truth. It is possible, for example, to conceive of an organization of past experience that is more like that of some reference work, such as a history text, or the index of a thesaurus" (p. 4). In addition, we were unable to find published data directly supportive of the hypothesized bias in availability. Finally, recent developments in the actor–observer literature seem inconsistent with the hypothesis that memories and attributions are egocentric. Jones and Nisbett (1971) speculated that actors are disposed to locate the cause of their behavior in the environment, whereas observers attribute the same behavior to stable traits possessed by the actors. Though a variety of explanations were advanced to account for this effect (Jones & Nisbett, 1971), the recent emphasis has been on perceptual information processing (Storms, 1973; Taylor & Fiske, 1975). The actor's visual receptors are aimed toward the environment; an observer may focus directly on the actor.

Thus, divergent aspects of the situation are salient to actors and observers, a disparity that is reflected in their causal attributions. This proposal seems to contradict the thesis that actors in an interaction are largely self-absorbed.

Two studies offer suggestive evidence for the present hypothesis. Rogers, Kuiper, and Kirker (1977) showed that trait adjectives were recalled more readily when subjects had been required to make a judgment about self-relevance (to decide whether each trait was descriptive of them) rather than about a number of other dimensions (e.g., synonymity judgments). These data imply that self-relevance increases availability; however, Rogers et al. did not contrast recall of adjectives relevant to the self with recall of adjectives relevant to other people – a comparison that would be more pertinent to the current discussion. Greenwald and Albert (1968) found that individuals recalled their own arguments on an attitude issue more accurately than the written arguments of other subjects. Since the arguments of self and other were always on opposite sides of the issue, the Greenwald and Albert finding could conceivably reflect increased familiarity with, and memory for, arguments consistent with one's own attitude position rather than enhanced memory for self-generated statements (although the evidence for attitude-biased learning is equivocal, e.g., Greenwald & Sakumura, 1967; Malpass, 1969).

We conducted a pilot study to determine whether we could obtain support for the hypothesized bias in availability. Students in an undergraduate seminar were asked to estimate the number of minutes each member of the seminar had spoken during the immediately preceding class period. An additional 26 subjects were obtained from naturally occurring two-person groups approached in cafeterias and lounges. The participants in these groups were asked to estimate the percentage of the total time each person had spoken during the current interaction.

It was assumed that subjects would base their time estimates on those portions of the conversation they could recall readily. Thus, if there is a bias in the direction of better recall of one's own statements, individuals' estimates of the amount of time they themselves spoke should exceed the average speaking time attributed to them by the other member(s) of the group.

The results were consistent with this reasoning. For seven of the eight students in the undergraduate seminar, assessments of their own discussion time exceeded the average time estimate attributed to them by the other participants ($p < .05$, sign test). Similarly, in 10 of the 13 dyads, estimates of one's own discussion time exceeded that provided by the other participant ($p < .05$, sign test). The magnitude of the bias was highly significant over the 13 dyads, $F(1, 12) = 14.85$, $p < .005$; on the average, participants estimated that they spoke 59% of the time. These data provide preliminary, albeit indirect, evidence for the hypothesized availability bias in everyday situations. . . .

Experiment 1

In this experiment, we wished to examine egocentric biases in naturally occurring, continuing relationships. Married couples appeared to represent an ideal target group. Spouses engage in many joint endeavors of varying importance. This circumstance would appear to be rife with possibilities for egocentric biases.

Accordingly, the first experiment was conducted (a) to determine if egocentric biases in allocations of responsibility occur in marital relationships; (b) to replicate, using a different dependent measure, the egocentric bias in availability obtained in the pretest; and (c) to correlate the bias in availability with the bias in responsibility. If the bias in responsibility is caused by a bias in availability, the two sets of data should be related.

Method

Subjects: The subjects were 37 married couples living in student residences. Twenty of the couples had children. The subjects were recruited by two female research assistants who knocked on doors in the residences and briefly described the experiment. If the couple were willing to participate, an appointment was made. The study was conducted in the couple's apartment; each couple was paid $5 for participating.

Procedure. A questionnaire was developed on the basis of extensive preliminary interviews with six married couples. In the experiment proper, the questionnaire was completed individually by the husband and wife; their anonymity was assured. The first pages of the questionnaire required subjects to estimate the extent of their responsibility for each of 20 activities relevant to married couples by putting a slash through a 150-mm straight line, the endpoints of which were labeled "primarily wife" and "primarily husband."[1] The twenty activities were making breakfast, cleaning dishes, cleaning house, shopping for groceries, caring for your children, planning joint leisure activities, deciding how money should be spent, deciding where to live, choosing friends, making important decisions that affect the two of you, causing arguments that occur between the two of you, resolving conflicts that occur between the two of you, making the house messy, washing the clothes, keeping in touch with relatives, demonstrating affection for spouse, taking out the garbage, irritating spouse, waiting for spouse, deciding whether to have children.

Subjects were next asked to record briefly examples of the contributions they or their spouses made to each activity. Their written records were subsequently examined to assess if the person's own inputs were generally more "available." That is, did the examples reported by subjects tend to focus more on their own behaviors than on their spouses'? A rater, blind to the experimental hypothesis,

---

[1] In the preliminary interviews, we used percentage estimates. We found that subjects were able to remember the percentages they recorded and that postquestionnaire comparisons of percentages provided a strong source of conflict between the spouses. The use of the 150-mm scales circumvented these difficulties; subjects were not inclined to convert their slashes into exact percentages that could then be disputed.

recorded the number of discrete examples subjects provided of their own and of their spouses' contributions. A second rater coded one third of the data; the reliability (Pearson product–moment correlation) was .81.

Results

The responses of both spouses to each of the responsibility questions were summed, so that the total included the amount that the wife viewed as her contribution and the amount that the husband viewed as his contribution. Since the response scale was 150 mm long, there were 150 "units of responsibility" to be allocated. A sum of greater than 150 would indicate an egocentric bias in perceived contribution, in that at least one of the spouses was overestimating his or her responsibility for that activity. To assess the degree of over- or underestimation that spouses revealed for each activity, 150 was subtracted from each couple's total. A composite score was derived for the couple, averaging over the 20 activities (or 19, when the couple had no children).

An analysis of variance, using the couple as the unit of analysis, revealed that the composite scores were significantly greater than zero, $M = 4.67$, $F(1, 35) = 12.89$, $p < .001$, indicating an egocentric bias in perceived contributions. Twenty-seven of the 37 couples showed some degree of overestimation ($p < .025$, sign test). Moreover, on the average, overestimation occurred on 16 of the 20 items on the questionnaire, including negative items – for example, causing arguments that occur between the two of you, $F(1, 32) = 20.38$, $p < .001$. Although the magnitude of the overestimation was relatively small, on the average, note that subjects tended to use a restricted range of the scale. Most responses were slightly above or slightly below the halfway mark on the scale. None of the items showed a significant underestimation effect.

The second set of items on the questionnaire required subjects to record examples of their own and of their spouses' contributions to each activity. A mean difference score was obtained over the 20 activities (averaging over husband and wife), with the number of examples of spouses' contributions subtracted from the number of examples of own contributions. A test of the grand mean was highly significant, $F(1, 35) = 36.0$, $p < .001$; as expected, subjects provided more examples of their own ($M = 10.9$) than of their spouses' ($M = 8.1$) inputs. The correlation between this self–other difference score and the initial measure of perceived responsibility was determined. As hypothesized, the greater the tendency to recall self-relevant behaviors, the greater was the overestimation in perceived responsibility, $r(35) = .50$, $p < .01$.

The number of words contained in each behavioral example reported by the subjects was also assessed to provide a measure of elaboration or richness of recall. The mean number of words per example did not differ as a function of whether the behavior was reported to be emitted by self

(M = 10.0) or spouse (M = 10.1), $F < 1$. Further, this measure was uncorrelated with the measure of perceived responsibility, $r(35) = -.15$, ns.

In summary, both the measure of responsibility and the measure reflecting the availability of relevant behaviors showed the hypothesized egocentric biases. Moreover, there was a significant correlation between the magnitude of the bias in availability and the magnitude of the bias in responsibility. This finding is consistent with the hypothesis that egocentric biases in attributions of responsibility are mediated by biases in availability. Finally, the amount of behavior recalled seemed to be the important factor, rather than the richness of the recall. . . .

Experiment 2

In Experiment 2, we had the players on 12 intercollegiate basketball teams individually complete a questionnaire in which they were asked to recall an important turning point in their last game and to assess why their team had won or lost.

It is a leap to go from the self–other comparisons that we have considered in the previous studies to own team–other team comparisons. There are, however, a number of reasons to expect that the actions of one's own team should be more available to the attributor than the actions of the other team: I know the names of my teammates, and therefore, I have a ready means of organizing the storage and retrieval of data relevant to them; our success in future games against other opponents depends more on our own offensive and defensive abilities than on the abilities of the opposing team. Consequently, I may attend more closely to the actions of my teammates, which would enhance encoding and storage. Also, there are informational disparities: The strategies of my own team are more salient than are the strategies of the opposing team (Tversky & Kahneman, 1973, 11). If the initiatives of one's own team are differentially available, players should recall a turning point in terms of the actions of their team and attribute responsibility for the game outcome to their team. . . .

Method

Subjects. Seventy-four female and 84 male intercollegiate basketball players participated in the study. The team managers were contacted by telephone; all agreed, following discussions with their players, to have their teams participate in the study.

Procedure. The questionnaires were administered after six games in which the teams participating in the study played each other. Thus, for the three male games chosen, three of the six male teams in the study were competing against the other three male teams. Similarly, the three female games selected included all six of the female teams. The questionnaires were administered at the first team practice following the target game (1 or 2 days after the game), except in one case where, because of the team's schedules of play, it was necessary to collect data immediately after the game (two female teams). The questionnaires were completed individually, and the respondents' anonymity was assured. The relevant questions, from the current perspective, were the following:

1. Please describe briefly one important turning point in the last game and indicate in which period it occurred.

2. Our team won/lost our last game because. . . .

The responses to the first question were examined to determine if the turning point was described as precipitated by one's own team, both teams, or the other team. Responses to the second question were examined to assess the number of reasons for the win or loss that related to the actions of either one's own or the opposing team. The data were coded by a person who was unaware of the experimental hypotheses. A second observer independently coded the responses from 50% of the subjects. There was 100% agreement for both questions.

Results

There were no significant sex differences on the two dependent measures; the results are, therefore, reported collapsed across gender. Since team members' responses cannot be viewed as independent, responses were averaged, and the team served as the unit of analysis.

A preliminary examination of the "turning point" data revealed that even within a team, the players were recalling quite different events. Nevertheless, 119 players recalled a turning point that they described as precipitated by the actions of their own team; 13 players recalled a turning point that they viewed as caused by both teams; 16 players recalled a turning point seen to be initiated by the actions of the opposing team (the remaining 10 players did not answer the question). Subjects described such events as a strong defense during the last 2 minutes of the game, a defensive steal, a shift in offensive strategies, and so on.

The percentage of players who recalled a turning point caused by their teammates was derived for each team. These 12 scores were submitted to an analysis that compared them to a chance expectancy of 50%. The obtained distribution was significantly different from chance, $F(1, 11) = 30.25$, $p < .001$, with a mean of 80.25%. As hypothesized, most reports emphasized the actions of the players' own team.

The percentage of players who recalled a turning point caused by their teammates was examined in relation to the team's performance. The average percentage was higher on the losing team than on the winning team in five of the six games ($p < .11$, sign test). The mean difference between the percentages on losing ($M = 88.5$) and winning ($M = 72.$) teams was nonsignificant ($F < 1$).

The players' explanations for their team's win or loss were also examined. Of the 158 participants, only 14 provided any reasons that involved the actions of the opposing team. On the average, subjects reported 1.79 reasons for the win or loss that involved their own team and .09 reasons that involved the opposing team, $F(1, 11) = 272.91$, $p < .001$. Finally, the tendency to ascribe more reasons to one's own team was nonsignificantly greater after a loss ($M = 1.73$) than after a win ($M = 1.65$), $F < 1$.

Discussion

The responses to the turning point question indicate that the performances of subjects' teammates were more available than those of opposing team members. Further, subjects ascribed responsibility for the game outcome to the actions or inactions of their teammates rather than to those of members of the opposing team. Thus, biases in availability and judgments of responsibility can occur at the group level. Rather and Heskowitz (1977) provide another example of group egocentrism: "CBS [news] became a solid Number One after the Apollo moonshot in 1968. If you are a CBS person, you tend to say our coverage of the lunar landing tipped us over. If you are a NBC person, you tend to cite the break-up of the Huntley–Brinkley team as the key factor" (p. 307). . . .

Experiment 3

In Experiment 3, we attempted to vary the individual's focus of attention so as to affect availability. We employed a manipulation designed to promote selective retrieval of information directly relevant to attributions of responsibility.

In our initial analysis, we suggested that egocentric attributions of responsibility could be produced by the selective retrieval of information from memory and that retrieval might be guided by the kinds of questions that individuals ask themselves. Experiment 3 was conducted to test this hypothesis. Subjects were induced to engage in differing retrieval by variations in the form in which questions were posed. Graduate students were stimulated to think about either their own contributions to their BA theses or the contributions of their supervisors. The amount of responsibility for the thesis that subjects allocated to either self or supervisor was then assessed. It was hypothesized that subjects would accept less responsibility for the research effort in the supervisor-focus than in the self-focus condition.

Method

Subjects. The subjects were 17 female and 12 male psychology graduate students. Most had completed either 1 or 2 years of graduate school. All of these students had conducted experiments that served as their BA theses in their final undergraduate year.

Procedure. The subjects were approached individually in their offices and asked to complete a brief questionnaire on supervisor–student relations. None refused to participate. The two forms of the questionnaire were randomly distributed to the subjects; they were assured that their responses would be anonymous and confidential.

One form of the questionnaire asked the subjects to indicate their own contribution to each of a number of activities related to their BA theses. The questions were as follows: (a) "I suggested ___ percent of the methodology that was finally employed in the study." (b) "I provided ___ percent of the interpretation of results." (c) "I initiated ___ percent of the thesis-relevant discussions with my supervisor." (d) "During thesis-related discussions I tended to control the course and content of the discussion ___ percent of the time." (e) "All things considered, I was responsible for ___ percent of the entire research effort." (f) "How would you evaluate your thesis relative to others done in the department?"

The second form of the questionnaire was identical to the above, except that the word *I* (self-focus condition) was replaced with *my supervisor* (supervisor-focus condition) on Questions 1–5. Subjects were asked to fill in the blanks in response to the first five questions and to put a slash through a 150-mm line, with endpoints labeled "inferior" and "superior," in response to Question 6.

Results and discussion

For purposes of the analyses, it was assumed that the supervisor's and the student's contribution to each item would add up to 100%. Though the experiment was introduced as a study of supervisor–student relations, it is possible that the students may have considered in their estimates the inputs of other individuals (e.g., fellow students). Nevertheless, the current procedure provides a conservative test of the experimental hypothesis. For example, if a subject responded 20% to an item in the "I" version of the questionnaire, it was assumed that his or her supervisor contributed 80%. Yet the supervisor may have contributed only 60%, with an unspecified person providing the remainder. By possibly overestimating the supervisor's contribution, however, we are biasing the data against the experimental hypothesis: The "I" version was expected to reduce the percentage of responsibility allocated to the supervisor.

Subjects' responses to the first five questions on the "I" form of the questionnaire were subtracted from 100, so that higher numbers would reflect greater contributions by the supervisor in both conditions. Question 5 dealt with overall responsibility for the research effort. As anticipated, subjects allocated more responsibility to the supervisor in the supervisor-focus ($M = 33.3\%$) than in the self-focus ($M = 16.5\%$) condition, $F(1, 27) = 9.05$, $p < .01$. The first four questions were concerned with different aspects of the thesis, and the average response revealed a similar result: supervisor-focus $M = 33.34$; self-focus $M = 21.82$; $F(1, 27) = 5.34$, $p < .05$. Finally, subjects tended to evaluate their thesis more positively in the self-focus condition than in the supervisor-focus condition: 112.6 versus 94.6, $F(1, 27) = 3.59, p < .10$.

The contrasting wording of the questions had the anticipated impact on subjects' allocations of responsibility. The supervisor version of the questionnaire presumably caused subjects to recall a greater proportion of their supervisors' contributions than did the "I" form of the questionnaire. This differential availability was then reflected in the allocations of responsibility. Note, however, that the questions were not entirely successful in controlling subjects' retrieval. The supervisor was allocated only one-third of the responsibility for the thesis in the supervisor-focus condition.

In light of the present data, the basketball players' attributions of responsibility for the game outcome in Experiment 2 need to be reexamined. Recall that the players were asked to complete the sentence, "Our team won/lost our last game because. . . ." This question yielded a highly significant egocentric bias. With hindsight, it is evident that the form of the question — "*Our* team . . . *our* last game" — may have prompted subjects to focus on the actions of their own teams, even though the wording does not preclude references to the opposing team. The "turning point" question in Experiment 2 was more neutrally worded and is not susceptible to this alternative interpretation.

The leading questions in these studies emanate from an external source; many of our retrieval queries are self-initiated, however, and our recall may well be biased by the form in which we pose retrieval questions to ourselves. For example, basketball players are probably more likely to think in terms of "Why did *we* win or lose?" than in terms of a neutrally phrased "Which team was responsible for the game outcome?". . .

The present research demonstrates the prevalence of self-centered biases in availability and judgments of responsibility. In everyday life, these egocentric tendencies may be overlooked when joint endeavors do not require explicit allocations of responsibility. If allocations are stated distinctly, however, there is a potential for dissension, and individuals are unlikely to realize that their differences in judgment could arise from honest evaluations of information that is differentially available.

13. The availability bias in social perception and interaction

Shelley E. Taylor

Every day the social perceiver makes numerous, apparently complex social judgments – Predicting another's behavior, attributing responsibility, categorizing an individual, evaluating anothers, estimating the power or influence of a person, or attributing causality. A central task of social psychology has been to determine how the social perceiver makes these judgments. Until recently, research on this topic was marked by a rationalistic bias, the assumption that judgments are made using thorough, optimal strategies (see, for example, Fischhoff, 1976, for discussion of this point). Errors in judgment were attributed to two sources: (a) accidental errors due to problems with information of which the perceiver was presumably unaware; and (b) errors which resulted from the irrational motives and needs of the perceiver.

Within social psychology this perspective is represented by research on causal attribution. In early attribution formulations (e.g., Jones & Davis, 1965; Kelley, 1967) the social perceiver was characterized as a naive scientist who gathered information from multiple sources in the environment to make attributions regarding cause–effect relations. When departures from these normative models were observed, they were believed to stem from biases such as hedonic relevance (Jones & Davis, 1965) or other egocentric needs (see Miller & Ross, 1975).

However, over a period of years, a growing body of evidence suggested not only that people's judgments and decisions are less complete and rational than was thought but that not all errors can be traced to motivational factors. Even in the absence of motives, judgments are often made on the basis of scant data, which are seemingly haphazardly combined and influenced by preconceptions (see, e.g., Dawes, 1976). These findings led to a revised view of the cognitive system. People came to be seen as

Preparation of this paper was supported by NSF Research Grant No. BNS 77–09922.

capacity-limited, capable of dealing with only a small amount of data at a time. Rather than being viewed as a naive scientist who optimizes, the person was said to "satisfice" (Simon, 1957) and use shortcuts that would produce decisions and judgments efficiently and accurately.

One of the most provocative and influential contributions to this revised view of the judgment process is the work by Kahneman and Tversky on cognitive heuristics (Kahneman & Tversky, 1973, 4; Tversky & Kahneman, 1974, 1). According to Tversky and Kahneman (1974, 1), heuristics are used under conditions of uncertainty, or the unavailability or indeterminacy of important information. In non-social judgments, uncertainty derives primarily from the fact that information relevant to a particular judgment is almost always incomplete. The appropriate factual material may be inaccessible, it may not be gathered together in time to bear on the decision, or it may be too voluminous to be properly organized and utilized in a judgment task.

Heuristics are likely strategies for making social judgments as well as non-social ones for several reasons. First, the distinction between social and non-social judgments is an arbitrary one, in that virtually any signifi-cant judgment has social consequences. Second, social judgments involve the same kinds of uncertainty that characterize non-social judgments. Third, social judgments include new sources of uncertainty. Information about people is more ambiguous, less reliable, and more unstable than is information about objects or non-social events, since people do not wear their personal attributes on their faces the way objects wear their color, shape, or size. Thus, personal attributes must be inferred rather than observed directly. People have intentions, not all of which are directly stated. Given that most significant social actions can be committed for a variety of reasons and will produce a variety of consequences, the mean-ing of social action is fundamentally ambiguous. Although objects main-tain their attributes cross-situationally and over time, people's motives change from situation to situation, and goals change from minute to minute as well as over the lifetime; thus, even an accurate inference in one situation may have little predictive utility. The impossibility of having complete, reliable, predictive information about people and social interac-tions suggests that people adopt heuristics that enable them to make inferences and predictions from what scanty and unrealiable data are available.

The availability heuristic

One such heuristic is availability. "A person is said to employ the availability heuristic whenever he estimates frequency or probability by the ease with which instances or associations come to mind" (Tversky & Kahneman, 1973, p. 208, 11). One assumes that if examples are brought to mind quickly, then there must be a lot of them, or that if an association is easily made, then it must be accurate, since associative bonds are built with experience. Furthermore, it is *ease* of retrieval, construction, and association that provides the estimate of frequency or probability, not the sum total of examples or associations that come to mind. Thus, one important difference between the use of the availability heuristic and the use of some more elaborate inferential process is that little actual retrieval or construction need be completed; an estimate of the ease with which this process would be performed is sufficient as a basis for inference.

Tversky and Kahneman (1973, 11) suggest two general classes of tasks in which an availability bias might figure prominently: the construction of instances and associations and the retrieval of associations and instances. These two general tasks are also tasks of the social perceiver. Under many circumstances, we may be asked to construct social behavior, as in trying to guess how some friend is going to behave when he learns his wife is leaving him. In such cases one is constructing a social reality against which the actual social event can be compared. In other cases, one may draw on past examples of an individual's behavior to make inferences, as in recalling instances of how this same friend coped with crisis in the past as a basis for inferring how he will cope now.

To some extent the assumptions regarding the relationship between ease of construction or retrieval and numbers of examples or associations are accurate, and to the extent that they are, an individual using the availability heuristic will reach correct inferences or at least inferences that match those reached by using more exhaustive and exhausting procedures. Under other circumstances, however, those inferences may not be accurate because there are biases in the available data that are brought to bear on the problem. There are at least three ways in which a bias in the available data might bias subsequent social processes. First, highly salient data may be more available and hence exert a disproportionate influence on the judgment process. Second, biases in the retrieval process itself may yield an unrepresentative data base. Third, the perceiver's enduring cognitive structures such as beliefs and values foster preconceptions that heighten the availability of certain evidence, thus biasing the judgment process. The presence of any of these evidentiary or processing biases may lead to biased inferences.

Availability and salience biases: An example

Salience biases refer to the fact that colorful, dynamic, or other distinctive stimuli disproportionately engage attention and accordingly disproportionately affect judgments. One example of such a bias has been termed the *fundamental attribution error* (see Ross, 1977), and it refers to a pervasive bias to see people as causal agents in the environment. That is, in a social setting in which either a person or some situational variable is a plausible causal candidate for an outcome, there exists a general bias to see people as causal agents, particularly their enduring dispositional attributes.

Some people are more salient than others, and this differential salience within the social environment can also bias the judgment process. Studies that have applied gestalt principles of figural emphasis to the social world (see, e.g., McArthur & Post, 1977; Taylor & Fiske, 1975; Fiske et al., 1979) reveal that an individual who is brightly lit, moving (as in a rocking chair), highly contrasting (through such seemingly trivial manipulations as shirt color), or novel will draw off a disproportionate amount of attention.

Social consequences of the salience bias are illustrated by studies examining the impact of solo status or token integration on people's impressions of individuals. When a company is about to desegregate and include members of a minority group, such as blacks, women, or the handicapped, often an intermediate step occurs prior to full integration. In this step, one or two members of this previously excluded group may be brought into what has otherwise been a white male work group, thus creating instances of solo status. Solo status may come about for any of several reasons. There may be an absence of qualified applicants from the particular minority group; the organization may wish to avoid the threat suggested by a larger influx of minority group members; or a solo may be used to ward off affirmative action forces. Regardless of the reasons for token integration, the token or solo individual is often treated as a representative of his or her social group. Accordingly, the evaluations that are made of his or her performance are often used to predict how well other members of that group would do if they were to come into the organization as well. The significance of solo status is its novelty. In an otherwise male environment, a woman stands out, as does a black, in an otherwise white environment. Such distinctiveness fosters a salience bias.

In an experimental analog to this situation, subjects observed an audio-visual portrayal of a small group (six persons) having an informal discussion. Some subjects saw a group that included one black, one male, or one female in an otherwise white, female, or male group, respectively (Taylor et al., 1976; Taylor, Fiske, Etcoff, & Ruderman, 1978). Others observed comparison groups in which the content of the group discussion was identical to that of the solo conditions, but the sex or race composition of the group was equalized (e.g., three men, three women). Subjects observed the group discussion and then recorded their impressions of the individuals in the groups.

Consistent with the argument that there is a salience bias created by solo or token status, a solo black's behavior was recalled somewhat better than the behavior of that same individual in a comparable equally mixed group, and the solo was also judged as doing more of the talking compared with a comparable individual in the mixed group.[1] This salience bias, in turn, leads to evaluative extremity. When an individual was a solo in a group, that person's behavior was evaluated more extremely in either a positive or negative direction, compared with the same behavior in a mixed group. An obnoxious person was perceived as even more so when a solo; a nice person was perceived as even nicer when a solo.

Using the availability heuristic as an explanatory framework, one may infer that when subjects were asked to evaluate an individual in the group, they tried to access examples of relevant behaviors or associations to the stimulus persons, and the ease with which such instances or associations came to mind led them to make evaluatively extreme judgments. In the case of the solo, more examples of relevant behaviors are available because there is a larger data base, leading to evaluative extremity. These results suggest quite strongly that a distinctive individual who is a solo, who is handicapped, or who is otherwise different from other individuals with whom he interacts, will evoke evaluatively extreme judgments in those around him. The implications of these findings for the social world are, of course, profound. For example, if solos are used as a basis for making desegregation decisions and perceptions of a solo are inherently biased, then wrong decisions may be made. Exaggeratedly negative evaluations of a solo may lead to unwarranted termination of a desegregation program. Exaggeratedly positive evaluations can set up false expectations for the behavior of other members of the minority group, expectations which may not be met.

Motivation clearly cannot account for these biases in the perceptions of salient others. Although some motivational processes may be engaged in reactions to the handicapped or to a solo, it is difficult to find them in evaluations of a person who is salient by virtue of shirt color or motion. Accordingly, one must look to cognitive factors, and the availability heuristic provides one possible explanation for these effects.

Availability and retrieval biases: Two examples

A second source of availability biases derives from how information is stored or retrieved. That is, memory is organized in particular ways that may facilitate the retrieval or construction of certain kinds of examples or inferences and interfere with others. One source of interference is simple limitation on the amount of information that can be held in memory, which can lead to confusion in the associative traces or examples that are stored.

Rothbart and his colleagues (Rothbart et al., 1978) demonstrated this problem in a study of the attributes of social groups. Subjects were given trait information about hypothetical group members (e.g., Phil is lazy)

---

[1] No recall measures were collected in the studies on the solo male and solo female.

under one of two conditions. Subjects either saw the names of several different group members (Ed, Phil, Fred, Joe) paired with a particular trait (lazy) or they saw the same name–trait pairing (Phil is lazy) an equivalent number of times. Subjects were later asked to characterize the group as a whole. If subjects are able to remember accurately which names were paired with which traits, then inferences about the group as a whole should be stronger if several group members have a particular trait than if only one member has the trait. When the total number of name–trait pairings that subjects were exposed to was low, subjects showed this caution in their inferences about the group. However, when the total number of name–trait pairings was high, it was apparently difficult for subjects to keep straight how many individuals had which traits, and they began to behave as if multiple instances of the same name–trait pairing was as informative as several different names paired with that trait. The group came to be characterized as lazy even when only a few of its members actually were lazy.

The social world is active and often overwhelmingly informative, and as such it usually mirrors Rothbart et al.'s (1978) high memory-load condition more than the low memory-load condition. These conditions would, then, facilitate the information of group stereotypes from the behavior of just a few individuals whose behavior shows up a large number of times. As Rothbart et al. note, media are more taken with negative than positive events, and accordingly all of these biases could favor the formation of negative group stereotypes, particularly if group membership is salient when mentioned in media coverage.

A second example of the impact of retrieval biases on social judgments is egocentric attributions (Ross & Sicoly, 1979, 12). In many contexts an individual must make judgments regarding who is responsible for what has transpired. Authorship of a paper must be decided, a consulting fee must be divided up among co-workers, or credit for a group win or loss must be split up. Short of each person's keeping a list of his own and the other person's contributions (a strategy some desperate sufferers have been forced to adopt), all parties must make some approximation of who did what on the joint endeavor. The availability heuristic provides a potential strategy for so doing. One may think over examples of one's own and the other persons' contributions and on the basis of how many examples come to mind decide who did more. Biases may be present, however, that interfere with an accurate assessment. One hypothesized bias is egocentric recall, the ability to bring to mind one's own contributions somewhat better than those of another person. This bias in recall may, in turn, produce biases in perceived responsibility. For example, if I can remember six times that I took the trash out and only three times that my husband did so, I may conclude that I have responsibility for taking out the trash. In a recent investigation, marital chores proved to be a particularly useful as well as electric context in which to examine the availability bias (Ross & Socoly, 1979, **12**). Thirty-seven married couples were interviewed regarding their contributions to the various activities married people must perform, such as making breakfast or cleaning dishes. Each member of the couple was asked to indicate whether each activity was performed primarily by the husband or primarily by the wife. Each person then also recalled specific examples of what that person or the spouse had contributed to the activity, a measure designed to tap the relative availability of one's own versus the spouse's contributions.

The results clearly indicated that each spouse thought she or he had contributed more to the joint activities than the other spouse. When the responsibility scores of the two partners were added together, they exceeded the total possible responsibility that could be taken. The number of specific examples of contributions that each spouse had made was also calculated, and results indicated that the number of contributions credited to the self far exceeded the number of contributions credited to the spouse. The correlation between remembered examples and attribution of responsibility was high ($+.51$), suggesting that the bias in recall may have produced the bias in responsibility.

One possible explanation for these effects relies on motivational principles and maintains that people take more than their fair share of credit to preserve or enhance a positive self-image. If this is true, then we should find that when a joint project fails, people will deny personal credit for the failure and attribute responsibility to the other. For example, if a couple makes a purchase that turns out to be a lemon, each may credit the other for the decision. Ross and Sicoly (1979, **12**) examined this possibility and found that it contributed only weakly to egocentric attributions. People were nearly as likely to take disproportionate credit for a bad joint project as a good one.

A cognitive explanation for these effects draws on how retrieval or storage of information produces biases in perceived responsibility. An exposure bias may be present such that one observes one's own contributions more closely than those of another, and so when reconstructing who is responsible for what, more of one's own contributions come to mind. For example, if both spouses are working at the same time, one may be distracted from the other's contributions and observe his or her own contributions more closely. Alternatively, one may be less aware of the other's contributions because one is not physically present when one's spouse is doing his or her share of the work; accordingly, one may underestimate the amount of time and effort the spouse has actually put in. Additionally, bias may be present if one has mulled over one's own contributions more than the other's contributions. This is especially likely to be true when the joint project involves a lot of thinking, writing, or other kind of extended work as in planning a major household repair or organizing a party. A third possibility is that one's own contributions fit one's personal constructs or schemata, that is, ways of carving up or encoding information. Information that fits a pre-existing schema seems to be recalled more easily, and thus the heightened availability of one's own contributions may reflect a retrieval bias (see Taylor & Crocker, 1979b). To summarize, biases in how information is stored or retrieved can lead to biased social judgments. One possible mediator is use of the availability heuristic.

Availability and biases due to cognitive structures

A third way in which availability can bias social judgments is through the social perceiver's use of well-practiced rules, schemas, or other cognitive structures. People have enduring structures for processing incoming information that they employ frequently and hence come to utilize as cognitive habits. We know, for example, that people are more likely to use some traits as ways of organizing information about people over other traits. For example, academicians often discriminate among people on the trait of intelligence, whereas for sports enthusiasts, athletic skill rather than intelligence is a discriminating factor. This kind of bias in the tendency to use particular schemas or constructs can also bias judgments. For example, if one is asked one's impressions of a particular individual, one may employ one's favored traits (e.g., intelligence) as a way of searching memory and describe the individual less in terms of his actual behavior than in terms of one's own preferred traits (see, e.g., D'Andrade, 1965). A similar bias can occur in the construction of social behavior, since people also employ their personal constructs and schemas when confronted with new situations or when asked to make predictions about the future. For example, an academician may predict a friend's ability to get out of a bad situation on the basis of how smart the friend is, whereas the sports enthusiast may predict the same friend's ability to get out of the situation on the basis of how fast the friend can run. Accordingly, use of rules, schemas, and personal constructs may lead one to make inferences that an individual who does not share the same cognitive structures would not make.

Perhaps the most intriguing example of the effects of enduring schematic structures on the perception of data is provided by the phenomenon of stereotyping. Expecting that a person will engage in a particular behavior can lead to inferences that a person has engaged in the behavior. Stereotypes are particular kinds of expectations that can function to guide and shape reality, and they may do so, at least in part, through an availability bias. Hamilton and Rose (1978) explored this possibility in their stereotyping research. In one study, subjects were given lists of sentences of the form, "Carol, a librarian, is attractive and serious." In each of the sentences, a member of an occupation was described as possessing two traits. Some of the traits bore a stereotypic association to the occupation as, for example, in the case of the trait "serious," with the occupation "librarian"; in other cases the traits were non-stereotypic for that occupation (such as "attractive" for a librarian) but were stereotypic for another occupation (such as "attractive" for a stewardess). In all the sentences, every trait was paired with every occupation an equal number of times. Each trait was paired with a stereotyped occupation one-third of the time and with non-stereotyped occupations two-thirds of the time. However, when subjects were asked to estimate the number of times each trait had described a member of each occupation, they misremembered the trait–occupation pairings to favor stereotypic associations. For example, they were more likely to remember that librarians has been serious than that waitresses had been serious.

Although motivational factors may provide an explanation for these states, they are unlikely to do so. Some stereotypes may figure prominently in an individual's needs and goals, but stereotypes for occupations such as waitress or librarian are fairly banal and probably do not. Accordingly, these results are better understood as a cognitive phenomenon. The availability heuristic provides one possible explanation by assuming that when subjects are asked how often the trait and the occupation are paired, they estimate frequency using the strength of the association between the occupation and the trait; under most circumstances associations are stronger after many pairings. However, in this case, there is a bias in the strength of the associated connection by virtue of the stereotypic association between some of the trait–occupation pairs. Accordingly, since those associations are stronger, the perceiver estimates that those traits and occupations had been more frequently paired than had the non-stereotypic trait–occupation pairs. Again, the social implications of this kind of bias are great. Stereotypes, once formed, can bias the gathering and storage of information and subsequent impressions. A consequence is that unjustified inferences about social groups or individuals may be perpetuated in the absence of any empirical basis.

Conclusions

The past few decades have witnessed a shift away from a view of judgments as the products of rational, logical decision making marred by the occasional presence of irrational needs and motives toward a view of the person as heuristic user. Empirical work on non-social judgments indicates that the perceiver employs shortcuts or heuristics to free capacity and transmit information as quickly as possible, and recent research in social psychology suggests that these processes also apply to the formation and use of social judgments. The ease with which examples or associations are brought to mind provides an estimate of likelihood (i.e., frequency or probability), which in turn provides a basis for making other social judgments such as evaluating another, imputing causality or responsibility, describing another's attributes, categorizing others, or describing oneself.

An observant critic will note that in the studies presented, the evidence for use of the availability heuristic is inferential rather than direct, and one may reasonably demand more clear evidence that it is the ease with which examples or associations can be brought to mind that is actually mediating judgments. There are several reasons for the vagueness. First, unlike the cognitive research on availability, none of these social investigations was designed to examine availability per se; rather each was designed to elucidate some intrinsically interesting social phenomenon, and the availability heuristic was raised as one of several possible explanations for the phenomenon. Second, there has been as yet no agreed-upon measure of availability. Some studies have used the speed with which information is retrieved as a measure of availability (see Pryor & Kriss, 1977), whereas other investigations have looked at volume of information recalled as an index of availability of information (see Ross and Sicoly, 1979, **12**). Since the two measures do not always correlate well (see Pryor & Kriss, 1977), measurement ambiguity has hindered empirical progress.

Some of this measurement problem, however, is moot because of a third problem, namely, conceptual ambiguity surrounding the use of the term *availability*. There is a trivial sense in which all social inference is mediated by availability; one's judgments are always based on what comes to mind. This use of the term *availability* must be distinguished more carefully from use of the availability heuristic through clear criteria for determining whether or not and how the availability heuristic has been engaged and whether or not the availability of examples or associations is mediating subsequent judgments. Social psychologists have tended to focus on *what* information is available and *why*; to advance the caliber of social explanation requires redirecting efforts to *how* the availability heuristic ties the content of what is available to cognitive processing.

The impact of the concept of availability on social psychology has nonetheless been great for several reasons. First, it highlights errors in processing that can be understood without recourse to motivational constructs. This is not to say that the impact of motives on judgments is unimportant but merely to point out that major errors in cognition exist as well. Second, though rational theories have provided useful normative models against which actual judgments can be compared, departures from these models are so common and blatant that descriptive models are needed. In the examples provided here as well as in many others, the availability heuristic has provided one possible description. Under some circumstances, use of the availability heuristic leads to perfectly appropriate conclusions; however, under those circumstances where there is a bias in what information is available, faulty inferences follow. Specifically, biases in salience, biases in retrieval, and biases due to cognitive structures such as schemas, beliefs, and values can lead to the heightened availability of incorrect or misleading information in social judgment tasks.

Given that biases in availability may be quite prevalent, why does use of the availability heuristic persist? One obvious reason is that it produces more right than wrong answers, and in a cost/benefit sense, it pays off in time and energy saved. A second answer is that many errors in the conclusions produced by the availability heuristic will not matter. For example, if one's biased impressions will not affect one's future functioning, as in forming an incorrect impression of a person one meets only once, then the bias will matter little. An availability bias may also matter little if it is constant over time. For example, if one regards one's boss as gruff, it may not matter that he is gruff only when he is in the boss role, if that is the only circumstance under which one interacts with him. A third answer is that many errors will be corrected. Whenever biases in availability are uncorrelated over time, the process will begin to correct itself with repeated encounters. For example, if several of one's friends have recently divorced, one's estimate of the divorce rate may be temporarily exaggerated, but assuming that one's friends do not continue to divorce indefinitely, one's estimated divorce rate should eventually come into line with objective data. Finally, in some cases, error will be detected through communication. For example, if the assertion that one is picking up one's share of the housework meets with apoplectic objections from one's spouse, that position is likely to be modified. In short, normal social intercourse provides a basis for really testing one's inferences, and blatantly false conclusions with far-reaching implications are likely to be corrected.

But erroneous perceptions with severe consequences may, under some circumstances, persist. For example, as the stereotyping studies illustrate, if there is a bias in the formation of a judgment, it may in turn lead to a bias in maintaining that judgment via the cognitive structure (in this case, a stereotype) that is formed. These hand-in-glove or complimentary biases can, as a consequence, be highly resistant to counterevidence. To the extent that they exist, they may have a damaging effect on both individual perceptions and social policy. In short, one cannot trust availability biases to be inconsequential, and accordingly, strategies for the detection and correction of biased inferences are needed.

14. The simulation heuristic

Daniel Kahneman and Amos Tversky

Our original treatment of the availability heuristic (Tversky & Kahneman, 1973, **11**) discussed two classes of mental operations that "bring things to mind": the retrieval of instances and the construction of examples or scenarios. *Recall* and *construction* are quite different ways of bringing things to mind; they are used to answer different questions, and they follow different rules. Past research has dealt mainly with the retrieval of instances from memory, and the process of mental construction has been relatively neglected.

To advance the study of availability for construction, we now sketch a mental operation that we label the simulation heuristic. Our starting point is a common introspection: There appear to be many situations in which questions about events are answered by an operation that resembles the running of a simulation model. The simulation can be constrained and controlled in several ways: The starting conditions for a "run" can be left at their realistic default values or modified to assume some special contingency; the outcomes can be left unspecified, or else a target state may be set, with the task of finding a path to that state from the initial conditions. A simulation does not necessarily produce a single story, which starts at the beginning and ends with a definite outcome. Rather, we construe the output of simulation as an assessment of the ease with which the model could produce different outcomes, given its initial conditions and operating parameters. Thus, we suggest that mental simulation yields a measure of the propensity of one's model of the situation to generate various outcomes, much as the propensities of a statistical model can be assessed by Monte Carlo techniques. The ease with which the

This chapter is drawn from the Katz-Newcomb Lecture in Social Psychology "On the Psychology of Possible Worlds," Ann Arbor, Michigan, April, 1979. The work was supported by the Office of Naval Research under Contract N00014-79-C-0077 to Stanford University.

simulation of a system reaches a particular state is eventually used to judge the propensity of the (real) system to produce that state.

We shall argue that assessments of propensity and probability derived from mental simulations are used in several tasks of judgment and also that they play a significant role in several affective states. We first list some judgmental activities in which mental simulation appears to be involved. We then describe a study of the cognitive rules that govern the mental undoing of past events, and we briefly discuss the implications of these rules for emotions that arise when reality is compared with a favored alternative, which one had failed to reach but could easily imagine reaching. We conclude this brief sketch of the simulation heuristic by some remarks on scenarios, and on the biases that are likely to arise when this heuristic is used.

1. *Prediction.* Imagine the first meeting between two persons that you know well, who have never met before. How do you generate predictions such as "They will get on famously" or "They will grate on one another"?

2. *Assessing the probability of a specified event.* How do you assess the likelihood of American armed intervention to secure the oilfields of Saudi Arabia in the next decade? Note the difference between this task and the preceding one. The simulation in the present case has a specified target-state, and its object is to obtain some measure of the "ease" with which this target state can be produced, within the constraints of a realistic model of the international system.

3. *Assessing conditioned probabilities.* If civil war breaks out in Saudi Arabia, what are the likely consequences? Note that this simulation exercise differs from mere prediction, because it involves a specified initial state, which may diverge more or less from current reality. The assessment of remote contingencies, in particular, involves an interesting ambiguity: What changes should be made in one's current model *before* the "run" of the simulation? Should one make only the minimal changes that incorporate the specified contingency (e.g., civil war in Saudi Arabia), subject to elementary requirements of consistency? Or should one introduce all the changes that are made probable by the stipulation of the condition? In that case, for example, one's model of the political system would first be adjusted to make the civil war in Saudi Arabia as unsurprising as possible, and the simulation would employ the parameters of the revised model.

4. *Counterfactual assessments.* How close did Hitler's scientists come to developing the atom bomb in World War II? If they had developed it in February 1945, would the outcome of the war have been different? Counterfactual assessments are also used in many mundane settings, as when we judge that "she could have coped with the job situation if her child had not been ill."

5. *Assessments of causality.* To test whether event A caused event B, we may undo A in our mind, and observe whether B still occurs in the simulation. Simulation can also be used to test whether A markedly

increased the propensity of B, perhaps even made B inevitable. We suggest that a test of causality by simulation is involved in examples such as "You know very well that they would have quarreled even if she had not mentioned his mother."

Studies of undoing

Our initial investigations of the simulation heuristic have focused on counterfactual judgments. In particular, we have been concerned with the process by which people judge that an event "was close to happening" or "nearly occurred." The spatial metaphor is compelling and has been adopted in many philosophical investigations: It appears reasonable to speak of the distance between reality and some once-possible but unrealized world. The psychological significance of this assessment of distance between what happened and what could have happened is illustrated in the following example:

Mr. Crane and Mr. Tees were scheduled to leave the airport on different flights, at the same time. They traveled from town in the same limousine, were caught in a traffic jam, and arrived at the airport 30 minutes after the scheduled departure time of their flights.
 Mr. Crane is told that his flight left on time.
 Mr. Tees is told that his flight was delayed, and just left five minutes ago.
 Who is more upset?
 Mr. Crane   Mr. Tees

It will come as no surprise that 96% of a sample of students who answered this question stated that Mr. Tees would be more upset. What is it that makes the stereotype so obvious? Note that the objective situation of the two gentlemen is precisely identical, as both have missed their planes. Furthermore, since both had expected to miss their planes, the difference between them cannot be attributed to disappointment. In every sense of the word, the difference between Tees and Crane is immaterial. The only reason for Mr. Tees to be more upset is that it was more "possible" for him to reach his flight. We suggest that the standard emotional script for this situation calls for both travelers to engage in a simulation exercise, in which they test how close they came to reaching their flight in time. The counterfactual construction functions as would an expectation. Although the story makes it clear that the expectations of Mr. Tees and Mr. Crane could not be different, Mr. Tees is now more disappointed because it is easier for him to imagine how he could have arrived 5 minutes earlier than it is for Mr. Crane to imagine how the 30 minutes delay could have been avoided.

There is an Alice-in-Wonderland quality to such examples, with their odd mixture of fantasy and reality. If Mr. Crane is capable of imagining unicorns – and we expect he is – why does he find it relatively difficult to imagine himself avoiding a 30-minute delay, as we suggest he does? Evidently, there are constraints on the freedom of fantasy, and the psychological analysis of mental simulation consists primarily of an investigation of these constraints.

Our understanding of the rules of mental simulations is still rudimentary and we can present only early results and tentative speculations in a domain that appears exceptionally rich and promising. We have obtained preliminary observations on the rules that govern a special class of simulation activity – undoing the past. Our studies of undoing have focused on a situation in which this activity is especially common – the response of surviving relatives to a fatal accident. Here again, as in the case of Mr. Tees and Mr. Crane, we chose to study what we call the emotional script for a situation. For an example, consider the following story:

Mr. Jones was 47 years old, the father of three and a successful banking executive. His wife has been ill at home for several months.

On the day of the accident, Mr. Jones left his office at the regular time. He sometimes left early to take care of home chores at his wife's request, but this was not necessary on that day. Mr. Jones did not drive home by his regular route. The day was exceptionally clear and Mr. Jones told his friends at the office that he would drive along the shore to enjoy the view.

The accident occurred at a major intersection. The light turned amber as Mr. Jones approached. Witnesses noted that he braked hard to stop at the crossing, although he could easily have gone through. His family recognized this as a common occurrence in Mr. Jones' driving. As he began to cross after the light changed, a light truck charged into the intersection at top speed, and rammed Mr. Jones' car from the left. Mr. Jones was killed instantly.

It was later ascertained that the truck was driven by a teenage boy, who was under the influence of drugs.

As commonly happens in such situations, the Jones family and their friends often thought and often said, "If only . . .", during the days that followed the accident. How did they continue this thought? Please write one or more likely completions.

This version (labeled the "route" version) was given to 62 students at the University of British Columbia. Another group of 61 students received a "time" version, in which the second paragraph read as follows:

On the day of the accident, Mr. Jones left the office earlier than usual, to attend to some household chores at his wife's request. He drove home along his regular route. Mr. Jones occasionally chose to drive along the shore, to enjoy the view on exceptionally clear days, but that day was just average.

The analysis of the first completion of the "If only" stem is given in Table 1. Four categories of response were found: (i) Undoing of route; (ii) Undoing of time of departure from the office; (iii) Mr. Jones crossing at the amber light; (iv) Removing the drugged boy from the scene.

A particularly impressive aspect of the results shown in Table 1 is an

Table 1. *Analysis of first completion of the "if only" stem*

Response categories	Time version	Route version
(i) Route	8	33
(ii) Time	16	2
(iii) Crossing	19	14
(iv) Boy	18	13
(v) Other	1	3

event that fails to occur: Not a single subject mentioned that if Mr. Jones had come to the intersection two or three seconds earlier he would have gone through safely. The finding is typical: Events are not mentally undone by arbitrary alterations in the values of continuous variables. Evidently, subjects do not perform the undoing task by eliminating that necessary condition of the critical event that has the lowest prior probability – a procedure that would surely lead them to focus on the extraordinary coincidence of the two cars meeting at the intersection. Whatever it is that people do, then, is not perfectly correlated with prior probability.

The alterations that people introduce in stories can be classified as downhill, uphill, or horizontal changes. A downhill change is one that removes a surprising or unexpected aspect of the story, or otherwise increases its internal coherence. An uphill change is one that introduces unlikely occurrences. A horizontal change is one in which an arbitrary value of a variable is replaced by another arbitrary value, which is neither more nor less likely than the first. The experimental manipulation caused a change of route to be downhill in one version, uphill in the other, with a corresponding variation in the character of changes of the timing of Mr. Jones's fatal trip. The manipulation was clearly successful: Subjects were more likely to undo the accident by restoring a normal value of a variable than by introducing an exception. In general, uphill changes are relatively rare in the subjects' responses, and horizontal changes are non-existent.

The notion of downhill and uphill changes is borrowed from the experience of the cross-country skier, and it is intended to illustrate the special nature of the distance relation that can be defined for possible states of a system. The essential property of that relation is that it is not symmetric. For the cross-country skier, a brief downhill run from A to B is often paired with a long and laborious climb from B to A. In this metaphor, exceptional states or events are peaks, normal states or events are valleys. Thus, we propose that the psychological distance from an exception to the norm that it violates is smaller than the distance from the norm to the same exception. The preference for downhill changes is perhaps the major rule that mental simulations obey; it embodies the essential constraints that lend realism to counterfactual fantasies.

A notable aspect of the results shown in Table 1 is the relatively low proportion of responses in which the accident is undone by eliminating the event that is naturally viewed as its cause: The insane behavior of the drugged boy at the intersection. This finding illustrates another property of mental simulation, which we label the focus rule: Stories are commonly altered by changing some property of the main object of concern and attention. In the present case, of course, the focus of attention was Mr. Jones, since the subjects had been instructed to empathize with his family. To test the focus rule, a new version of the accident story was constructed, in which the last paragraph was replaced by the following information:

It was later ascertained that the truck was driven by a teenage boy, named Tom Searler. Tom's father had just found him at home under the influence of drugs. This was a common occurrence, as Tom used drugs heavily. There had been a quarrel, during which Tom grabbed the keys that were lying on the living room table and drove off blindly. He was severely injured in the accident.

Subjects given this version of the story were asked to complete the stem "If only . . .," either on behalf of Mr. Jones's relatives or on behalf of Tom's relatives. Here again, we consider the first response made by the subjects. The majority of subjects who took the role of Tom's relatives (68%) modified the story by removing him from the scene of the accident – most often by not allowing the fatal keys on the table. In contrast, only a minority (28%) of the subjects identifying with Mr. Jones's relatives mentioned Tom in their responses.

We have described this study of undoing in some detail, in spite of its preliminary character, to illustrate the surprising tidiness of the rules that govern mental simulation and to demonstrate the existence of widely shared norms concerning the counterfactual fantasies that are appropriate in certain situations. We believe that the cognitive rules that govern the ease of mental undoing will be helpful in the study of a cluster of emotions that could be called counterfactual emotions, because of their dependence on a comparison of reality with what might or should have been: Frustration, regret, and some cases of indignation, grief, and envy are all examples. The common feature of these aversive emotional states is that one's hedonic adaptation level is higher than one's current reality, as if the unrealized possibilities were weighted into the adaptation level, by weights that correspond to the ease with which these possibilities are reached in mental simulation.

Remarks on scenarios

In the context of prediction and planning under uncertainty, the deliberate manipulation of mental models appears to be sufficiently important to deserve the label of a distinctive simulation heuristic. The clearest example of such activities is the explicit construction of scenarios as a procedure for the estimation of probabilities.

What makes a good scenario? In the terms already introduced, a good scenario is one that bridges the gap between the initial state and the target event by a series of intermediate events, with a general downhill trend and no significant uphill move along the way. Informal observations suggest that the plausibility of a scenario depends much more on the plausibility of its weakest link than on the number of links. A scenario is especially satisfying when the path that leads from the initial to the terminal state is not immediately apparent, so that the introduction of intermediate stages actually raises the subjective probability of the target event.

Any scenario is necessarily schematic and incomplete. It is therefore of interest to discover the rules that govern the selection of the events that are explicitly specified in the scenario. We hypothesize that the "joints" of a scenario are events that are low in redundancy and high in causal significance. A non-redundant event represents a local minimum in the predictability of the sequence, a point at which significant alternatives might arise. A causally significant event is one whose occurrence alters the values that are considered normal for other events in the chain that eventually leads to the target of the scenario.

The elaboration of a single plausible scenario that leads from realistic initial conditions to a specified end state is often used to support the judgment that the probability of the end state is high. On the other hand, we tend to conclude that an outcome is improbable if it can be reached only be invoking uphill assumptions of rare events and strange coincidences. Thus, an assessment of the "goodness" of scenarios can serve as a heuristic to judge the probability of events. In the context of planning, in particular, scenarios are often used to assess the probability that the plan will succeed and to evaluate the risk of various causes of failure.

We have suggested that the construction of scenarios is used as a heuristic to assess the probability of events by a mediating assessment of the propensity of some causal system to produce these events. Like any other heuristic, the simulation heuristic should be subject to characteristic errors and biases. Research is lacking in this area, but the following hypotheses appear promising: (i) The search for non-redundant and causally significant "joints" in scenario construction is expected to lead to a bias for scenarios (and end-states) in which dramatic events mark causal transitions. There will be a corresponding tendency to underestimate the likelihood of events that are produced by slow and incremental changes. (ii) The use of scenarios to assess probability is associated with a bias in favor of events for which one plausible scenario can be found, with a corresponding bias against events that can be produced in a multitude of unlikely ways. Such a bias could have especially pernicious consequences in a planning context, because it produces overly optimistic estimates of the probability that the plan will succeed. By its very nature, a plan consists of a chain of plausible links. At any point in the chain, it is sensible to expect that events will unfold as planned. However, the cumulative probability of at least one fatal failure could be overwhelmingly high even when the probability of each individual cause of failure is negligible. Plans fail because of surprises, occasions on which the unexpected uphill change occurs. The simulation heuristic, which is biased in favor of downhill changes, is therefore associated with a risk of large and systematic errors.

Part V
Covariation and control

15. Informal covariation assessment: Data-based versus theory-based judgments

Dennis L. Jennings, Teresa M. Amabile, and Lee Ross

The flow of social experience frequently challenges us to recognize empirical covariations. Sometimes, these covariations are merely another test of our powers of observation and are of no immediate practical concern to us. At other times – for example, when those covariations involve early symptoms of problems and later manifestations, or behavioral strategies employed and outcomes obtained, or relatively overt characteristics of people or situations and relatively covert ones – such detection abilities may help to determine our success in adapting to the demands of everyday social life. More generally, covariation detection will play a large role in our continuing struggle as "intuitive scientists" (see Nisbett & Ross, 1980; Ross, 1977, 1978) to evaluate and update the hypotheses we hold about ourselves, our peers, and our society. An obvious question therefore presents itself: How proficient are we, as laypeople, at assessing the empirical covariations presented by experiential evidence?

Before proceeding to discuss past or present research, we should note that everyday observation provides a great deal of relevant evidence; and it hints that the answer to the proficiency question is apt to be far from a simple one. On the one hand, both the generally adaptive nature of social behavior and the generally harmonious quality of social interaction leave little doubt that the participants in our culture possess many profound

We wish to thank Professors Daniel Kahneman, Amos Tversky, and Paul Slovic for their helpful comments and suggestions. We also wish to acknowledge the stalwart efforts of Rita French and Julia Steinmetz who were co-investigators for some of the research reported herein. The research was supported in part by a National Science Foundation Graduate Fellowship to the first author and by National Institute of Mental Health Grant MH–26736 and National Science Foundation Grant BNS–78–01211 to Lee Ross and Mark Lepper.

The organization and content of this chapter owe an obvious debt to an earlier treatment of the same topic by L. Ross and R. E. Nisbett in *Human Inference: Strategies and Shortcomings of Social Judgment*, Prentice-Hall, Inc., 1980.

insights about behavioral causes and consequences. In fact, contemporary attribution theorists (e.g., Jones et al., 1971; Kelley, 1967, 1971, 1973; Weiner, 1974), who have been uniquely concerned with the basis for such insights, generally seem to have treated the ability to detect covariation as a "given" and proceeded to the inferential use that is made of such perceived covariations. On the other hand, everyday experience also offers eloquent testimony to the existence of ill-founded prejudices, ruinous behavioral strategies, and other manifestations of erroneous causal or correlational theories. It should be apparent, therefore, that any adequate portrait of informal covariation assessment must address the unevenness of the layperson's performance. It must somehow reconcile subtle insights about some functional relationships with ignorance or illusions about other relationships.

Prior investigation of covariation assessment

It is noteworthy, perhaps, that even the staunchest defenders of the layperson's capacities as an intuitive scientist (e.g., Peterson & Beach, 1967) have had little that was flattering to say about the layperson's handling of bivariate observations. We shall review two lines of research that support this unflattering portrait, focusing in each case on procedural aspects and results that will prove pertinent to the subsequent report of our own research on lay covariation assessment.

Reading contingency tables: The "ecological validity" issue

One important line of prior research has dealt with people's ability to recognize functional relationships presented in simple 2 × 2 contingency tables. Typically, these tables summarized the number of instances of the presence and absence of variable X (for example, a particular disease) purportedly associated with the presence and absence of variable Y (for example, a particular symptom). With bivariate data so neatly assembled and "packaged," the subjects' task seemingly was an unusually simple and straightforward one. Nevertheless, the evidence (e.g., Jenkins & Ward, 1965; Smedslund, 1963; Ward & Jenkins, 1965), shows that laypeople generally have fared quite poorly at such tasks.

Judgmental strategies that ignore one or more of the four cells proved to be at the root of most subjects' difficulties. One common failing, for instance, involves the virtually exclusive reliance upon the size of the "present-present" cell relative to the entire population. Thus many subjects may say that symptom X is associated with disease A simply because the contingency table reports a relatively large number of cases in which people do, in fact, have both the disease and the symptom. Subjects paying attention to only two of the four cells may similarly be misled. Noting, for instance, that more people with the disease lack symptom A

than possess it, they may therefore conclude that the relevant relationship is a negative one; or noting that more people with the symptom have the disease than are free of it, they may conclude that the relationship is a positive one.

Without formal statistical training, however, very few people appreciate the fact that valid inferences in such cases can be made only by considering *all* of the four cells. One satisfactory method, for example, might involve comparing *proportions* (i.e., comparing the proportion of diseased people manifesting the particular symptom with the proportion of non-diseased people manifesting that symptom). The formal strategy dictated by contemporary texts on statistical inference, of course, would similarly involve attending to all four cells. Specifically, one would be required to note discrepancies between observed cell frequencies and those frequencies to be "expected" on the basis of the relevant marginal frequencies or probabilities (thereby providing the information required for calculation of a chi-square statistic).

Skeptics inclined to champion the layperson's cause might be tempted to dismiss such demonstrations as evidence only that people are poor at "reading" contingency tables and to contend that the subjects' errors in such tasks primarily are products of the task's novelty and artificiality. The relationship between laboratory performances and everyday real-world performance – that is, the issue of "ecological validity" – is an important problem and one that cannot be evaded in the research reported in this chapter. Let us, accordingly, begin to address the issue here in the hopes that the reader will be forewarned and forearmed.

First, while the table-reading task is undeniably unusual and ecologically unrepresentative, let us note that the logic (and the various logical shortcomings) displayed by subjects in those laboratory tasks is quite consistent with that displayed in a variety of everyday inferences. Consider, for example, the perplexing question, "Does God answer prayers?" "Yes," the layperson who consults only the present-present cell may answer, "because many times I've asked God for something, and He's given it to me." His more sophisticated and skeptical peer is apt to ask, "But how often have you asked God for something and *not* gotten it?" Comparison of two cells, however, still is utterly inadequate for the inferential task at hand. Even the addition of a third cell – favorable outcomes that occurred in the absence of prayer – would leave the issue in doubt, for all four cells are required before any solid inference can be made. And even the most sophisticated of intuitive psychologists would probably balk at the suggestion that data from the "absent-absent" cell (i.e., favorable outcomes that were not prayed for and that did not occur) are indispensable for assessing the impact of prayers on worldly outcomes.

The charge of non-representativeness can be answered even more forcefully, however. If the fourfold-table task creates some unique problems the same task also *spares* subjects most of the demands that contribute to the difficulty of everyday covariation assessments. These demands include initially sampling, coding, storing, and retrieving the relevant data and then arranging them in a form that permits covariation assessment. Consider, for instance, the man who undertakes to test the stereotyped notion that red-haired people are hot-tempered (or, more precisely, that the presence of red hair is positively correlated with the presence of a hot temper). First, he must decide which data are to be considered. Shall he attempt to sample or recall instances of hot-headed red-haired people? Or shall he consider some red-haired people and note how many are hot-tempered, or some hot-tempered people and note how many have red hair? Very likely he will adopt some such strategy or combination of strategies without ever entertaining the possibility that the relative frequency of even-tempered brunettes might be relevant to the inferential task at hand. This state of affairs contrasts with the fourfold-table task that makes all of the relevant data equally available to the subject, even if it does not demand that they all be given proper subsequent consideration.

Let us suppose that the individual in question somehow does recognize that testing his stereotype demands that he consider the data in all four cells. How shall he draw an appropriate data sample from which to generate the relevant cell frequencies? Should he simply consider the first set of people who happen to come to mind? Should he consider all of the people in some restricted class (for instance, his family members, his circle of friends, or the tenants in his apartment building)? Or should he attempt to adopt some "random" method for generating cases from the overall population? The potential sources of bias in most informal sampling methods are obvious. Samples of the people who first come to mind are apt to show serious "availability" biases (Tversky & Kahneman, 1973, 11). And samples of friends or family members or neighbors are likely to show the same bias, as well as violating the independence requirement (not a trivial problem, since one's family, one's friends, or even one's neighbors may tend to share behavioral tendencies, physical characteristics, and even correspondences between them). The "novel" fourfold-table procedure, of course, spares the covariation assessor the task of confronting these perplexing and potentially crippling problems.

The tasks of data coding, storage, and retrieval bring a host of additional factors and problems into play in everyday covariation assessment. Most importantly, the implicit hypothesis that redheads are hot-tempered may bias decisions about who is or is not hot-tempered and whose hair is or is not red. This issue receives further attention later in this chapter. For now let us merely note that one's prior expectations or hypotheses constitute a potentially biasing influence on every stage of information processing, an influence that is precluded when one is presented with data for which all of the processing involved in coding, storing, and retrieving have already been completed. More generally, let us simply reiterate that such real-world impediments to accurate covariation assessment are apt to prove far more forbidding then any arising from the artificiality or unfamiliarity of the contingency-table methodology.

Illusory correlation: The impact of preconceptions on perceptions

How successful are people at dealing with bivariate distributions when the relevant observations are presented individually rather than prepackaged in the form of contingency tables? Much of the existing evidence derives from the Chapmans' seminal work on illusory correlation. For a detailed account of this research see Chapman & Chapman, 1967, 1969; also see chapter 17, this volume. Our brief review here focuses on the particular issues and findings that set the stage for our own, more recent, efforts.

Perhaps the simplest summary of the Chapmans' findings and conclusions about subjects' ability to detect covariations between clinical signs and symptoms is that reported covariations seem to reflect true covariations far less than theory-based or semantically based preconceptions about the nature of the relationships that "ought" to exist. While these findings were dramatic, controversial, and of considerable immediate relevance to the practitioner, the general point they made about the effects of preconceptions upon observed associations was essentially a familiar one.

As L.J. Chapman himself noted in his initial (1967) paper, illusory correlations are not restricted to the domain of clinical judgment. Most superstitions essentially are empirically groundless beliefs about the association between particular actions or events and subsequent positive or negative outcomes. Racial, ethnic, regional, religious, or occupational stereotypes similarly are beliefs about covariations, beliefs that are strongly held and remarkably resistant to the impact of non-supporting data (cf. Adorno et al., 1950; Allport, 1954; P. Goldberg, 1968; J.M. Jones, 1972; Taynor & Deaux, 1973). Research on "implicit personality theory" can also be cited in this context. Over half a century ago Thorndike described the so-called halo effect, whereby perceivers expect and report the association of all positive personality characteristics. Subsequent researchers (e.g., Koltuv, 1962; Norman & Goldberg, 1966; Passini & Norman, 1966) have greatly extended this work and explored the conceptual schemas and beliefs about personality that dispose perceivers to report consistent relationships among different traits or different indicators of the same trait whose empirical linkages are very weak or even non-existent.

There is thus a wealth of empirical and anecdotal evidence that, in the realm of covariation assessment, the contest between expectations and evidence is apt to be an unequal one. Just as in other types of perceptual and cognitive judgments (cf. Bruner, 1957a, 1957b; Bruner, Postman, & Rodrigues, 1951), the intuitive scientist's preconceptions about empirical relationships are apt to determine what he detects, what he fails to detect, and what he sees that is not really there to be seen. Such facile generalizations about the supremacy of theory over data, however, can lead us to overlook an important ambiguity – or at least an important unresolved question – in the Chapmans' studies. Specifically, we can identify two separate issues of interest about intuitive covariation assessment that are, in a sense, confounded in those studies and in subsequent follow-ups (e.g., Golding & Rorer, 1972; Starr & Katkin, 1969). The first issue involves people's difficulties in detecting covariations presented in immediately available data – that is, their capacity to recognize and assess covariations when they are "unencumbered" by any specific theories or expectations about the empirical relationship in question. The second issue involves the tendency for the subjects' intuitions or theories to lead them to assume the existence of strong correlations where such assumptions are belied by the best "objective" evidence.

The separation of these issues suggests the need to investigate subjects' covariations assessment performances in two very different tasks. The first task is essentially a "psychophysical" one yielding evidence about the relationship between subjective judgments and objective measurements. In this task subjects are simply to be presented with sets of bivariate observations about which they can hold no preconceived theories and then to be asked to assess the strength of relationship in each set. The investigator can then attempt to measure the difficulty of the subjects' task (primarily by noting the degree of variability associated with particular judgments) and to determine the nature of the "psychometric" function relating the subjective estimates to the objective measurements.

The second task deals with the opposite extreme to such purely "data-based" assessments; it concerns assessments that are exclusively, or almost exclusively, "theory-based." Thus pairs of variables or measurements that can be linked by the subjects' intuitions or theories are to be specified, but no relevant bivariate data are to be furnished by the investigator. If any data are brought to bear by subjects in such assessments, therefore, they must be supplied from the subjects' everyday experiences and recollections; and as such they are susceptible to the host of "processing" errors and biases alluded to earlier in our discussion. For purposes of evaluation and comparison, the experimenter also must have some means of assessing the accuracy, or the nature of the errors, associated with such intuitive assessments. That is, he must possess some "objective" measure of correlation for each pair of variables specified to the subjects.

Experimental comparison of data-based and theory-based covariation assessment

Recently we conducted a study pursuing the issues and employing the basic strategy just outlined. For the data-based task, three different types of bivariate distributions, described in more detail in the next section, were employed. For the theory-based assessments, pairs of associated variables were specified but no actual data were presented by the experimenter. To facilitate comparisons between data-based and theory-based assessment, a within-subjects design was used in which subjects employed the same subjective rating scale for both tasks (with counterbalancing for order of presentation).

In each case, continuous variables rather than dichotomous ones (in contrast to the work of Chapman & Chapman, 1967, 1969, and Jenkins & Ward, 1965) were used in the relevant covariation assessment tasks. This feature was designed to capture more faithfully the nature of most everyday assessment tasks.[1]

Subjects and rating tasks

A total of 64 Stanford undergraduates, none of whom had completed a college-level course in statistics, participated in this experiment designed to compare data-based and theory-based assessments of covariation. For both types of assessments, subjects used a simple rating scale to describe their subjective impression of the direction and strength of relationships between pairs of variables. In using this scale, subjects first estimated whether the relationship in question was positive or negative. They then estimated how strong the relationship was by placing an "X" on a 100-point rating scale with end points anchored with "perfect relationship" and "no relationship."

Data-based covariation estimates. One part of the experiment dealt with covariation estimates based on sets of bivariate observations provided by the experimenter. Three sets of stimulus materials were employed to create the relevant bivariate distributions. For each type of stimulus material, a set of bivariate distributions was created to represent different objective covariations between two variables. Subjects were asked to study each distribution and estimate the relationship it portrayed using the 100-point subjective rating scale.

We anticipated that the accuracy of subjects' estimates in this task would depend in part on the difficulties they had in coding, processing, and remembering the data. To test this assumption, the three types of stimulus materials differed markedly in the information-processing demands they placed upon subjects prior to covariation estimation, particularly with respect to the demand for estimation of stimulus magnitudes and for

---

[1] Our literature search revealed that covariation estimation tasks featuring continuous variables have very rarely been employed by previous investigators. The exception uncovered in that search was one rarely cited study (reported by Erlick, 1966; Erlick & Mills, 1967) that dealt primarily with the effects of variance on perceived relatedness and yielded very little data relevant to present concerns.

Table 1. *Pairs of variables described to raters and their objective correlations*

	Variables specified	Objective correlation
A	Students' self-ratings of liberalism	−.28[a]
	Students' ratings of the performance of business leaders in the past decade	
B	Students' self-ratings of intellectualism	−.19[a]
	Students' ratings of the performance of U.S. presidents in the past decade	
C	Students' self-ratings of shyness	−.12[a]
	Number of U.S. states visited by students	
D	Students' self-ratings of ambitiousness	.01[a]
	Students' heights	
E	Students' ratings of the performance of university presidents in the past decade	.08[a]
	Time spent per week by students on recreational athletics	
F	Students' self-ratings of intellectualism	.17[a]
	Students' family incomes	
G	Children's dishonesty as measured by false report of athletic performance	.18[b]
	Children's dishonesty as measured by amount of cheating in solving a puzzle	
H	Students' family incomes	.28[a]
	Students' ratings of the performance of business leaders in the past decade	
I	Sixth graders' ability to "delay gratification"	.31[c]
	Sixth graders' ability to resist temptation to cheat	
J	Students' self-ratings of conscientiousness	.35[d]
	Ratings of those students' conscientiousness by roommate	
K	Students' self-ratings of intellectualism	.37[a]
	Students' self-ratings of ambitiousness	
L	Students' ratings of Congress's performance in the past decade	.40[a]
	Students' ratings of labor leaders' performance in the past decade	
M	Time spent per week by students on recreational athletics	.52[a]
	Students' self-ratings of physical fitness	
N	Students' ratings of U.S. presidents' performance in the past decade	.55[a]
	Students' ratings of business leaders' performance in the past decade	
O	Self-ratings of political conservatism	.57[e]
	A composite of self-rating items from the Ethnocentricity scale	
P	Students' height	.79[a]
	Students' weight	

[a] Correlation obtained from a survey (N = 295) of Stanford University students.
[b] Correlation obtained from Hartshorne & May (1928).
[c] Correlation obtained from Mischel & Gilligan (1964).
[d] Correlation obtained from Bem & Allen (1974).
[e] Correlation obtained from Adorno et al. (1950).

storing and retrieving information from memory. Thus, the first type presented sets of 10 simple number pairs. The second type presented drawings, each portraying a set of 10 men of varying heights holding walking sticks of varying heights. The final type of distribution was presented in the form of audiotapes on which a set of 10 individuals were each heard first to say some letter occupying a particular ordinal position in the alphabet (purportedly the initial letter of their surname) and then immediately to sing a musical note of varying duration.

Theory-based covariation estimates. The other part of the experiment (order of presentation of the two parts was counterbalanced) dealt with covariation estimates based on subjects' a priori expectations or theories rather than any immediately available bivariate data.

Pairs of measurements or variables were specified, and subjects were required to estimate first the direction and then the strength of the relationship for each pair, always employing the same simple 100-point subjective rating scale as that employed for the data-based assessments. Some of these pairs in this part of the experiment dealt with divergent behavioral measures of personal dispositions, for example, two measures of honesty used in Hartshorne and May's (1928) classic study of cross-situational consistency in moral behavior; others dealt with personal attitudes, habits, or preferences. In each case, however, the subjective covariation estimates we obtained could be compared with "objective" correlations culled from previous empirical studies. (A complete list of these variables pairs and pertinent correlations is presented in Table 1.)

Results

Data-based covariation estimates

Our first concern involves the estimates of covariation that subjects made in response to immediately available bivariate data. Two specific questions can be addressed: First, how readily could individuals detect covariations of various magnitude in the absence of any "theory" about the relevant data distributions? Second, what was the nature of the "psychophysical function" relating the mean of the raters' subjective estimates to an objective measure of covariation?

Examination of the data suggested that the estimation task was very difficult. The standard deviations and interquartile ranges associated with the overall group estimates for each data set were extremely high (see Figure 1). What is particularly notable is the difficulty many subjects experienced in simply recognizing the existence of positive relationships, even those of respectable magnitude. In fact it is only when objective correlations reach the level of $+.6$ to $+.7$ that the interquartile interval consistently excludes negative estimates of the relationship. The instabil-

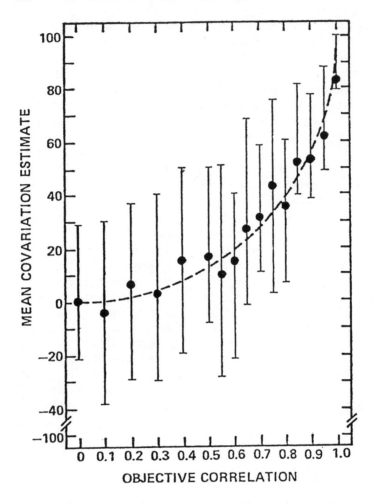

Figure 1. Means and interquartile ranges for "data-based" covariation estimates, pooling results for the three types of distribution. The "psychophysical function," $100\,(1 - \sqrt{1 - r^2}$, is shown as a dashed line.

ity of covariation estimates, incidentally, did not seem to differ systematically for the three types of bivariate data distributions, despite the apparent differences in the amount of information processing (and hence the possibilities for random or systematic error) associated with these three types. This apparent insensitivity to increased information-processing demands may offer some clues about the nature of the subjects' assessment "strategy" – a possibility that we pursue somewhat later in this chapter.

Also presented in Figure 1 are data relevant to the second question about data-based assessment, the question of the "functional relationship" between objective and subjective indicators of covariation. (The reader will note that means for the three stimulus domains are pooled in this presentation of results. Neither inspection nor significance tests revealed any significant or consistent trends distinguishing the results for the three stimulus domains, and the result of such pooling is a smoother and more comprehensible function than that obtained for any of the three individual domains.) For the reader's convenience we have fit a curve to the points in our graph. This curve, we should emphasize, was drawn post hoc; it was not derived from any "psychophysical theory."

It is clear by inspection that, despite the within-group variability for individual estimates, the function relating mean subjective estimates to objective correlations (Pearson r's) was a rather smooth one. More specifically, there seems to be a sharply accelerating function relating the two variables. Thus, relationships in the range commonly dealt with by psychologists concerned with measuring personality traits or other cross-situational consistencies in social behavior (i.e., $r = .2$ to $.4$) are barely detectable, yielding mean estimates in the range of 4 to 8 on the 100-point scale. Even relationships considered very strong by such psychologists (i.e., $r = .6$ to $.8$) result in rather modest subjective estimates of covariation. Objective correlations of $.7$, for instance, produced a mean subjective estimate of 34 – a rating midway between the points labeled "rather weak" and "moderate" on the 100-point subjective scale. Only when the objective correlations approached the $.85$ level did the group mean reach the midpoint of the subjective scale, and only beyond that point did subjects consistently rate the relationships as strongly positive.

A closer look at the estimates suggests that subjective ratings of relatedness or covariation are not a linear function of r or even r squared. Rather, the pattern of the pooled mean estimates seems well-captured by the expression, $1 - \sqrt{1-r^2}$. (The reader may recognize this expression as the "coefficient of alienation," a measure of the reduction in the standard error associated with prediction of variable Y based on knowledge both of variable X and the correlation between X and Y [Huntsberger, 1967].) Indeed, the similarity between the actual mean estimates and those described by this expression was quite striking – to be precise, 95% of the between-means variation is accounted for by the function based on the coefficient of alienation. We hasten to remind our readers, however, that they should not misinterpret the meaning of this neat fit. The goodness of fit portrayed in Figure 1 applies only to group estimates; individual estimates attested to the subjects' difficulties in distinguishing different levels of covariation.

It obviously is premature to conclude anything about the precise nature of the "psychophysical" function relating subjective responses to objective measures of covariation. Details of the task, context, and perhaps even the population of raters would undoubtedly produce differences in the function, differences that could be captured only through the inclusion of appropriate parameters. Nevertheless, the present results do probably suffice to suggest that modest correlations of the sort so often reported by the cadre of personality assessors (cf. Mischel, 1968, 1969) are likely to go largely undetected or to make only the weakest of impressions on the layperson who encounters such covariations in the absence of theory-based preconceptions.

It is further worth reemphasizing that the three different data-based covariation estimation tasks produced remarkably similar results despite the greatly differing information-processing demands they placed upon subjects. Thus, the psychophysical function, illustrated in Figure 1, accurately reflects the relationship between subjective estimates and objective measures for *each* of the three tasks undertaken by subjects. The correlations between the means of subjects' actual estimates and the estimates predicted by the function range from $r = .91$ for the tone/letter pairs to $r = .98$ for the number pairs.

Theory-based estimates

Thus far we have presented evidence that relatively strong objective correlations (in terms of Pearson's r) are required to prompt subjective assessments even modestly different from zero. Considered in isolation, the psychophysical function for data-based assessments could simply be evidence that the layperson's subjective metric is a cautious or conservative one relative to that employed by most formal statisticians. (Certainly few would dispute that r^2 is a more appropriate index of relatedness than r, since it can so much more readily be related to predictive utility or reduction in uncertainty about the value of one variable based on knowledge of the other, associated, variable.) In short, the obtained data-based estimates do not suggest any systematic shortcoming on the part of the intuitive psychologist, although the variability associated with such estimates leaves little doubt about the difficulties and uncertainties of the estimation task.

With these findings and possible interpretations in mind, we can now turn to the results for subjective covariation estimates about the relationships listed in Table 1. These estimates, we should recall, were made in the absence of immediately available data; presumably, they were made only on the basis of the raters' informal theories or intuitions, with no data save that highly "processed" data noted and recalled from everyday experience. Figure 2 provides a first view of these results. It is clear, immediately, that no single function – linear or otherwise – captures the relationship between subjective estimates and objective measures. Nevertheless, there is an undeniable tendency for subjects' theory-based estimates to show a rough correspondence with the objective evidence. That is, positive empirical relationships were estimated to be positive; negative relationships were estimated to be negative; relatively strong empirical relation-

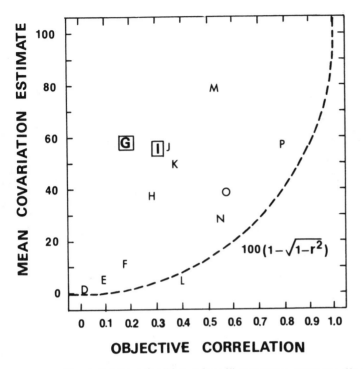

Figure 2. Means for "theory-based" covariation estimates. (See Table 1 for key to specified variables.)

ships generally were estimated to be stronger than relatively weak ones; and so forth.

Perhaps the most striking feature of these theory-based estimates, however, is that once freed from the constraints imposed by immediately available data subjects ceased to be cautious or conservative. They willingly ventured into the middle and even upper regions of the subjective 100-point scale even when dealing with variable pairs that objectively were only modestly correlated. The illustration provided in Figure 2 drives this point home. Several pairs of variables correlated at levels that, in the case of data-based assessments, had yielded mean subjective estimates quite close to 0 (e.g., $r = .3$) now produced estimates of 30, 40, or more, on the subjective 100-point scale.

Variable pairs G and I merit special emphasis, since they deal with theory-based estimates of cross-situational behavioral consistency and thereby speak to an issue of particularly active theoretical interest at the present time (cf. Alker, 1972; Allport, 1966; Bem & Allen, 1974; Bem & Funder, 1978; Bem & Lord, 1979; Mischel, 1968, 1969). The message conveyed by the subjective estimates for these two relationships is clear and dramatic. When faced with immediately available objective data presenting correlations in the range $r = .2$ to $r = .3$, subjects had provided mean estimates averaging between 0 and 10 on the 100-point rating scale. Now, in the absence of immediately available data, but dealing with bivariate domains featuring the same $r = .2$ to $r = .3$ range, subjects' implicit personality theories led them to offer covariation estimates that averaged in the 50 to 60 range. What degree of covariation in immediately available bivariate data would have been required to prompt similar estimates in the absence of "theories" or preconceptions? The answer, as we can see in Figure 2, is that only empirical correlations in the range of $r = .90$ could have prompted such estimates.

The results of our own research thus can be summarized with a pair of empirical generalizations.

1. When immediately available bivariate data are examined in the absence of any theories or preconceptions about their relatedness, the intuitive psychologist has great difficulty in detecting covariations of the magnitudes that are apt to characterize a wide range of functional relationships presented by everyday social experience. In particular, covariations in the range of magnitudes commonly dealt with by psychometricians seeking cross-situational behavioral consistencies are most likely to go undetected or be perceived as close to zero.

2. When no objective, immediately available, bivariate data can be examined, but prior theories or preconceptions can be brought to bear, the intuitive psychologist is apt to expect and predict covariations of considerable magnitude – often of far greater magnitude than are likely to have been presented by past experience or to be borne out by future experience.

Taken together, these generalizations help to sharpen the focus of the present contrast between data-based and theory-based assessments. The theories we hold apparently lead us to expect and predict stronger empirical relationships than actually exist; and many of the empirical relationships that do exist, even ones of consequential magnitude, are apt to go undetected unless we already expected to find them.

On the origin and survival of theories

Covariation assessment strategies

Beyond offering generalizations about the outcomes of various assessment tasks, it is important to begin considering the judgmental processes and strategies that might underlie such outcomes. Once again the distinction between data-based and theory-based assessment proves a critical one, and once again the Chapmans' seminal findings provide a convenient point of departure.

Data versus theories. It was clear from the Chapmans' studies that preconceptions overcame the information provided by immediately available data. Less clear, however, was the manner in which this occurred. Did the subjects actually "see" the relationships that they reported? Or did they merely report the relationships that they expected to be present in the data, without any corresponding subjective impression? Or did the subjects "compromise" between their subjective perceptions and expectations, giving some weight to each? It is impossible to give a definitive answer on the basis of the reported results, although there is clear evidence both that subjects did give at least some weight to their immediate perceptions of the data and that their perceptions were not totally determined by their expectations. Specifically, we note the Chapmans' report that repeated exposure to non-relationships did ultimately reduce reports of illusory correlation. However, it was also clear that the data could never totally triumph over the subjects' preconceptions, for even extended exposure to *negative* relationships could not completely eliminate reports of illusory positive correlations.

The questions concerning intuitive strategies for covariation assessment thus come sharply into focus. How do subjects decide what degree of relationship is present in the data at hand? How do they decide what degree of relationship "ought" to be present in a representative set of bivariate observations that are addressed by their intuitive theories or preconceptions? When, and how, do preconceptions transform one's subjective experiences of covariation? In beginning to speculate about the answers to such questions it is once again helpful to focus initially on purely data-based and purely (or at least largely) theory-based assessments, and only then return to the case when immediately available data and theory-based expectations clash.

Strategies for data-based assessment. Perhaps our most striking finding regarding data-based assessment involved the subjects' responses to bivariate distributions offering covariations of magnitudes that are likely to be encountered in everyday experience and are relevant to informal social theories – specifically, subjects found it very difficult to detect such relationships and, on the average, they rated the relevant covariations to be quite close to zero. What implications do such results have concerning the informal covariation assessment strategies that might have been employed by our subjects?

In speculating about this issue, it is important to remember that individual raters did not generally estimate objectively weak correlations to be close to zero. Instead, they offered a fairly broad range of estimates for which only the relevant means were close to the zero point. Once again, it is difficult to discern exactly what the subjects actually "saw" and what they estimated in spite of what they saw. The strikingly smooth and consistent "psychometric" function relating mean estimates to actual correlations leaves little doubt that the subjects did make use of data characteristics that were consistently related to the objective correlation.

The amount of variability in their estimates, however, indicates that the data characteristics utilized were only very roughly related to objective measures of covariation.

Our suspicion, buttressed by the introspections of some naive raters who have undertaken the task, is that subjects' impressions of "relatedness" do not reflect any attempt to consider the total sample of relevant bivariate observations. Rather, subjects may rely upon a few special cases, probably the extreme cases of variable X or variable Y. Thus, they may simply observe the direction and extremity of the value of Ys associated with the extreme values of X, and vice versa. Factors influencing attention and memory might also play a role; thus vividness and concreteness, as well as primacy and recency of presentation, might influence which data points are relied upon.

Reliance upon a limited number of special or "test" cases in this fashion, particularly reliance upon extreme scores, would produce certain consequences that seem highly consistent with our own findings: First, manipulations of stimulus domain (i.e., numbers vs. pictures vs. audiotapes) that were designed to vary the necessity for magnitude estimation and memory prior to covariation assessment should have exerted little impact, since these additional demands were rendered trivial if the raters merely relied upon a very limited number of special cases. Second, depending upon which particular cases they happened to take note of, subjects dealing with weak relationships could be expected to estimate the relationships to be moderately positive or moderately negative rather than zero. By contrast, subjects dealing with strong relationships should have shown quite consistent and extreme estimates, since highly positive relationships permit little variability in the values of one variable that can be associated with extreme values of the other variable. The shape of our psychometric function, and the reduced variability associated with estimates of the strongest empirical relationship presented, are consistent with these postulated consequences of relying upon extreme cases, although such evidence is far from conclusive. Clearly, more definitive answers could come only from research designs that deliberately manipulated the value of extreme, or otherwise disproportionately available, cases.

Strategies for theory-based assessment. When we turn our attention to theory-based assessments, the obvious question to be posed involves the extent to which any data may have been utilized in addition to pure theory. In some cases, of course, it is probable that no data are consulted at all. Raters, for instance, may have relied solely upon semantically based or theory-based intuitions and expectations; that is, applied "representativeness" criteria (cf. Kahneman & Tversky, 1973, 4) in considering the relationships between the two variables in each pair. Few readers are likely to dispute the contention that people hold - or at least can readily generate - social theories that have such origins. Indeed, any layperson can generate new theories or predictions about functional relationships far too rapidly for those theories to depend upon the generation and analysis of actual cases.

Nevertheless, we do not question the possibility that *some* theory-based covariation estimates may involve resort to actual evidence. Once again, however, we suspect that the layperson is far more likely to rely upon particular test cases – subject to many sources of significant biases in coding, storage, and recall – than to generate and informally analyze some overall sample of bivariate data.

Some theories or beliefs about particular relationships may thus be based at least partially on data. Others may be based on deductions from broader beliefs about the world, conventional folk wisdom, semantic associations, or persuasive communications by family, friends, or the mass media. Regardless of their origins, however, it is clear that many such beliefs are both erroneous and able to survive and perhaps even flourish in the face of evidence that would create grave doubts in any unbiased observer – certainly in any unbiased observer who owned a calculator, an introductory statistics text, and some conventional knowledge about how to use them. We shall, therefore, conclude this chapter by briefly addressing a pair of related questions about the clash between intuitive theories and everyday experiences with the empirical covariations that "test" those theories: First, what are the mechanisms by which erroneous or highly exaggerated beliefs about functional relationships can survive in the face of seemingly compelling logical or evidential challenges? Second, how can our emerging portrait of the layperson's deficiencies be reconciled with the obvious capacity of organisms to show learning (in particular, operant and respondent conditioning) and with the obvious accuracy and adequacy of so many of our everyday beliefs and social strategies?

These questions can only be touched upon here, and we refer the interested reader to more comprehensive discussions in Chapter 9 of this volume and in other publications (e.g., Nisbett & Ross, 1980).

Mechanisms of theory perseverance

Theories about empirical relationships, like impressions about particular individuals, often show an amazing capacity to survive in the face of empirical challenges. One set of mechanisms that accounts for such perseverance has its origin in the simple fact that people characteristically act upon their beliefs; these actions may range from simple public advocacy to the investment of one's time, energies, wealth, or reputation. Such behavioral commitment makes it highly "dissonant" (Abelson et al., 1968; Festinger, 1957, 1964) for the actor simply to update his beliefs in the light of new evidence. Indeed, an actor's beliefs or expectations can constitute a self-fulfilling prophecy, whereby initially groundless beliefs cause the actor to behave in a manner that produces outcomes or data that ultimately validate his beliefs (Merton, 1948; Rosenhan, 1973; Rosenthal & Jacobsen, 1968; Snyder & Swann, 1976; Snyder, Tanke, & Berscheid, 1977).

Recent research by Lepper, Ross, and their colleagues has illustrated additional mechanisms or processes that may underlie belief perseverance. These mechanisms involve the lay scientist's propensities both to assimilate newly considered items of information as a function of their consistency with prior beliefs and to go beyond the assimilation of data to the development of causal explanations capable of explaining *why* the hypothesized state of affairs would hold (see Chapter 9 of this volume and Anderson, Lepper, & Ross, 1980; Jennings, Lepper, & Ross, 1980; Lord, Ross, & Lepper, 1979; Nisbett & Ross, 1980; Ross, 1977; Ross, Lepper, & Hubbard, 1975; Ross, Lepper, Strack, & Steinmetz, 1977).

Covariation detection, conditioning, and other real-world successes

Our bleak portrait of the layperson's capacities to detect and assess covariation may seem at first blush to be incongruent with an enormous body of laboratory evidence, and an even broader base of everyday experience, illustrating classical and operant conditioning. Every rat who has ever learned to escape in a shuttle box, every child who has ever discerned the advantages of adding sugar to her breakfast cereal, every lover who has discovered that honesty is not always the best policy, every mother who has ever shown a lactation reflex in response to a child's cry, proves that organisms do recognize covariations among environmental stimuli. Does the work of the Chapmans and that of the present investigators therefore deal with some very narrow and aberrant class of covariation assessment problems at which the layperson is uniquely deficient? Nisbett and Ross (1980) have discussed this issue and contended that the answer is no. Instead, they claim, it is the conditioning phenomena that constitute the "exception," and it is the limited capacity to detect and assess covariation described throughout this chapter that illustrates the "rule."

We cannot review the relevant arguments in detail, but the gist of Nisbett and Ross's thesis is that classical and operant conditioning generally are obtained under sharply constrained circumstances involving stimulus salience and distinctiveness, optimal interstimulus and intertrial intervals, and an absence of irrelevant or distracting stimulus events. Two additional factors they cite, however, merit special emphasis. First, it is noteworthy that while conditioning can be maintained with relatively low covariation between conditioned stimulus (CS) and unconditioned stimulus (UCS) or response and reinforcement, it almost invariably is initially *obtained* with conditions of perfect covariation – that is, the CS or response is invariably followed by an UCS or reinforcement, and the latter is never presented in the absence of the former. The asymmetry between necessary conditions for acquisition of a conditioned response and the maintenance or "perseverance" of such a response thus may illustrate, to some extent, the same asymmetry between data-based and theory-based covariation assessment that has been explored in the present chapter. That is, during maintenance the organism may continue to expect, and perhaps even to perceive, a greater covariation between CS and UCS or between response and reinforcement than objectively is justified. It may accept reinforced trials at face value while attributing non-reinforced trials to extenuating circumstances, third variable influences, or even chance.

Finally, and perhaps most important, is the mounting evidence that both operant and classical conditioning benefit from, and in some cases may even demand, a reasonably good fit between the contingencies to be learned and the prior theories or expectations that the organism brings to the laboratory. At the very least, it is clear that not all CS–UCS or response–reinforcement contingencies are equally learnable. Perhaps the most impressive demonstrations of this point have been provided by Garcia and his coworkers (e.g., Garcia, McGowan, & Greene, 1972). These investigators have reported that rats can learn, on a single trial, to avoid a novel-tasting food that is followed by gastrointestinal illness, even if the interval between eating and sickness is as much as 12 hours; by contrast, the animal that becomes ill several hours after consuming a food of familiar taste but novel shape shows no such avoidance learning. On the other hand, when immediate pain replaces delayed sickness as the UCS, an opposite pattern of results is obtained; that is, the rat readily learns to avoid novel shapes but not novel tastes when such stimuli are immediately followed by electric shock. As Nisbett and Ross (1980) summarize, the rat may be characterized as possessing two "theories," both of which are well suited to the actual contingencies of its ecology: (a) Distinctive gustatory cues, when followed by later (even much later) gastric distress, should be considered suspect; (b) Distinctive tactile or spatial cues, when followed by immediate somatic pain should be considered suspect.

The argument, in more general terms (cf. Testa, 1974) is thus that organisms – people as well as rats – are likely to see those covariations, and only those covariations, that their own history or the history of their species disposes them to see. When not guided by "theories," covariation detection becomes very difficult and is likely to occur only when the relevant correlations approach unity, and/or when the conditions for learning are optimal in terms of the very factors that have been explicated in the laboratories of a long and distinguished line of Hullians and Skinnerians.

Sometimes, of course, everyday circumstances *are* optimal for learning. Thus, in our everyday experience we learn what countless switches, levers, buttons, and other manipulanda do, and what a bewildering variety of signs, symbols, and signals mean, because the relevant covariations are so close to perfect. Equally important, perhaps, is the fact that the layperson, like the formal scientist, often can "test" new hypotheses that he has come to entertain. Sample data can deliberately be generated that are far better suited for the inferential task at hand than the samples offered by accidental experience and haphazard recollection.

Indeed, our mastery of our environment has increasingly depended upon our capacity to substitute relatively formal tools of inference for informal ones. Our success reflects the legacy of generations of ordinary men and women who have carefully noted and recorded their findings and, more recently, that of countless scientists trained in the arts of formal experimentation and statistical analysis.

16. The illusion of control

Ellen J. Langer

While most people will agree that there is much overlap between skill and luck, a full understanding of how inextricably bound the two are has yet to be attained. In principle the distinction seems clear. In skill situations there is a causal link between behavior and outcome. Thus, success in skill tasks is controllable. Luck, on the other hand, is a fortuitous happening. Success in luck or chance activities is apparently uncontrollable. The issue of present concern is whether or not this distinction is generally recognized. The position taken here is that it is not. While people may pay lip service to the concept of chance, they behave as though chance events are subject to control. If this is correct, it is of interest to determine the variables responsible for this confusion. . . .

Some observational support for the assertion that people treat chance events as controllable comes from sociologists Goffman (1967) and Henslin (1967). While studying gambling practices in Las Vegas, Goffman noted that dealers who experienced runs of bad luck ran the risk of losing their jobs. Henslin studied dice playing and noted that dice players clearly behave as if they were controlling the outcome of the toss. They are careful to throw the dice softly if they want low numbers or to throw hard for high numbers. They believe that effort and concentration will pay off. Control can also be exerted when betting; for example, always bet with the person who looks like he has the most control. These behaviors are all quite rational if one believes that the game is a game of skill.

If one were going to try to exert control over a chance event, one would exert influence before the outcome of the event was determined. Strickland, Lewicki, and Katz (1966) tested this notion. Subjects were involved in a dice-throwing game in which they selected from a number of

Excerpts from a paper that appeared in *The Journal of Personality and Social Psychology*, 1975, 32, 311–328. Copyright © 1975 by American Psychological Association. Reprinted by permission.

alternative wagers either before the dice were tossed or just after the toss but before the outcome was disclosed. They found that subjects took greater risks, that is, placed larger bets, when betting before rather than after the toss.

The previous research shows that people often fail to respond differentially to controllable and uncontrollable events. However, the factors that govern this illusory control behavior have not been studied systematically. One way to identify these factors is to explore characteristics of skill situations. In skill situations people engage in various overt and covert behaviors designed to maximize the probability of success: choosing which materials are appropriate for the situation and which responses to make, familiarizing oneself with these materials and responses, spending some time thinking about the task to arrive at possible strategies that may be employed, and exerting effort while actively engaged in the task to increase the chance of success. In addition, skill situations have certain characteristics not necessarily instigated by the individual in order to maximize the likelihood of success. Competition is one such factor.

These skill-related factors may be responsible for inducing an illusion of control. An illusion of control is defined as an expectancy of a personal success probability inappropriately higher than the objective probability would warrant. The following studies were designed to assess the effectiveness of these skill-related factors in occasioning an illusion of control. Specifically, the research to be described was designed to test the following hypothesis: By encouraging or allowing participants in a chance event to engage in behaviors that they would engage in were they participating in a skill event, one increases the likelihood of inducing a skill orientation; that is, one induces an illusion of control. Thus, one should be able to introduce any of the previously mentioned aspects of a skill situation – *choice, stimulus* or *response familiarity, passive* or *active involvement, competition* – into a chance situation where the participants no longer influence the outcome and occasion behavior more appropriate to a skill event.

A strong test of this hypothesis is the introduction of these factors into situations such as lotteries, where the outcomes are completely chance determined. If these factors are successful in inducing an illusion of control in these mechanical situations, then the effects should be far greater when they are introduced into situations where there is already an element of control. . . .

Experiment 1: Effects of competition on the illusion of control

Since people often engage in competition when they are assessing their skills, it is hypothesized that the introduction of this skill-related factor into a chance setting induces an illusion of controllability. The amount of control one actually has in producing a successful outcome in skilled competition varies as a function of the ability of one's opponent. If people respond to chance events in which there is competition as if these events were skill determined, then the illusion of control should also vary as a function of characteristics of one's opponent.

In the following study subjects compete in a chance task against either an attractive, confident confederate or an awkward and nervous confederate. If the task is responded to as if the outcome is uncontrollable, then factors other than the likelihood of winning play a larger role in influencing subjects' bets. Under these circumstances, subjects are likely to bet a lot when competing against the confident confederate either because the confederate is expected to bet a lot and subjects want to appear similar to him or because risk is a value in our society (Wallach & Wing, 1968). Subjects may also bet a lot when playing against the awkward confederate in order to appear different from him or, again, because risk is a value. However, they may also bet less when betting against the awkward confederate because he is expected to bet less, so subjects can take less risk and still appear to be risky. In either case, subjects should not bet more against the awkward confederate than against the confident confederate. On the other hand, if, as predicted, competition induces a skill orientation, then subjects will bet on the basis of the likelihood of winning. Since the less competent one's opponent is, the more likely one is to win, subjects should wager more when competing against the awkward confederate than when competing against the confident confederate.

Method

Subjects: Subjects were 36 male undergraduates enrolled in the introductory psychology course at Yale University. They were recruited by an advertisement that offered course credit and a chance to win money for participation in a study on the relationship between cognitive and physiological responses. They were randomly assigned to one of two experimental conditions, with 18 subjects in each.

Procedure. When each subject entered the room in which the experiment was to take place, he found waiting a confederate posing as another subject. The confederate, a male undergraduate blind to the experimental hypothesis, played the role of either a confident or an unconfident person (dapper or schnook condition).

Dapper condition. In this condition the confederate appeared confident and outgoing and was dressed in a well-fitting sports coat. He introduced himself to the subject and pointed out a sign posted in the room. The sign said that the experimenter would be right back and asked subjects to fill out a brief questionnaire while waiting. To make the study appear to be concerned with physiological matters, the questionnaire asked about diet, family diseases, and the like. The subject and the confederate completed the form and interacted during this time for approximately 10 minutes. The conversation was unstructured but focused mainly on sports events. After this interaction the confederate nonchalantly knocked on the wall that separated himself and the subject from the experimenter to signal her to return to the room.

Schnook condition. In this condition the confederate appeared rather shy, behaved awkwardly, had a nervous twitch, and was dressed in a sports coat that was too small for him. In all other respects this condition was identical to the dapper condition.

In both conditions the confederate removed his coat before the experimenter entered the room. After she apologized for being late, the experimenter instructed the subjects to sit down and not talk while she prepared the materials for the study. By employing these measures, it was possible to keep the experimenter blind to the preceding experimental manipulation. The subject and the confederate sat at a table facing each other. After the experimenter placed a televolter, alcohol, gauze sponges, electrodes, electrode gel, and tape on the table, she recited the following instructions:

> We're interested in the effects of certain motoric and cognitive responses on physiological responses. Specifically, we're interested in changes in skin resistance as a function of pressured and nonpressured tasks. The study was designed so that, hopefully, you will enjoy the tasks while I get the information I need. You'll have the chance to either win or lose money so it should be fun — but there's no guarantee that you'll walk out of here with any extra money. Okay, now the first thing I want you to do is tape these electrodes to your hands. I want to put it on the hand that you don't write with. Are you right or left handed? Don't worry, none of this will hurt. [The experimenter tapes electrodes, plugs in the televolter, and brings out a deck of playing cards.]
>
> The first task is a card game. The rules are that you'll each choose a card from the deck, and whoever selects the higher card wins that round. There will be four rounds, and before each you'll write down how much you want to bet. You can wager anywhere from 0 to 25¢ on each round. You'll then show your bets to me but not to each other. Don't look at the card you choose. This way your bets and the outcomes won't influence your physiological responses on the next task. I'll turn the cards over for you and figure out how much was won or lost later with each of you individually. The betting is just between each of you and myself, so if you win I'll pay you and if you lose you'll pay me either in money or subject time. Are you willing to participate? [Confederate quickly answers, "Sure."] Good, now we can begin. Don't write down your bet until I say ready so that I can get a baseline reading.

The experimenter then instructed subjects to record their bets and show them to her. The bets were recorded, and then subjects alternately drew a card and, on request, simultaneously showed them to the experimenter, who recorded the outcome and then placed the cards face down on a nearby table. Before each step the experimenter appeared to be recording skin resistance fluctuations. This procedure was repeated for four trials.

Dependent measure and manipulation check. The dependent measure was the amount of money subjects wagered on each round.

After the card game was over, subjects were told that the next task would be run individually, so that one of the subjects would have to go to another room where another experimenter would give him instructions. They were also told that once this experiment was over, this experimenter would tell the other experimenter the outcome of the card game so that the debts could be settled. The experimenter asked the confederate to leave and told him and the subject to say goodbye to each other, since their joint participation was over. Each subject was then given an interpolated task so that he won approximately $2 regardless of his previous bets. The subject examined a jar of jelly beans and estimated the number present while the experimenter recorded skin resistance fluctuations. Then the subject was given another questionnaire that was physiological in nature. After he was asked whether he thought the other subject's presence had any effect on his physiological responses, he was asked to rate the other subject on a 6-point scale ranging from 1 (not very competent interpersonally) to 6 (very competent interpersonally). The remaining questions were filler items that related to physiological matters. After these measures were obtained, all subjects were thanked and told to call the author next month if they wanted to know the purpose and results of the study.

Results

Before examining whether or not the amounts of money wagered varied as a function of the competence of the confederate, it is important to make sure that the confederate was indeed perceived differentially in the two conditions. The mean rating of the confederate's competence was 4.8 when he was supposed to be dapper and 3.17 when he was playing a schnook. There was almost no overlap between the two conditions. The difference between the two means is highly significant ($t = 5.46, p < .005$). Therefore, it is safe to say that subjects in the dapper condition saw themselves as competing against a more competent individual than subjects in the schnook condition.

It will be recalled that subjects could wager anywhere from nothing to 25¢ on each of four rounds of betting. These four bets were averaged to give a single score for each subject. The mean bet for subjects in the dapper condition was 11.04¢ as compared with 16.25¢ for subjects in the schnook condition ($t = 2.39, p < .025$). The difference between the two groups should be even more apparent when we examine the first bets made, since the first round of betting most closely followed the experimental manipulation. The mean first bet for the dapper condition was 9.28¢, while the mean first bet for the schnook condition was 16.72¢ ($t = 3.16, p < .005$).

Conceptual test of the manipulation. In order to make sure that the assumption that Yale subjects expect the attractive confederate to bet more than the unattractive confederate was true, two questionnaires were administered to random samples of Yale undergraduates. On the first questionnaire, the task and the participants were described and subjects were asked whom they thought would bet more. Twelve of the 16 subjects expected the attractive person to bet more ($x^2 = 4, p < .05$). The second questionnaire described the task and asked people how much they thought they would wager on each trial. All of the 15 subjects asked responded with the maximum wager (25¢).

Experiment 2: Effects of choice on the illusion of control

Once again, it was hypothesized that when a chance situation mimics a skill situation, people behave as if they have control over the uncontrollable event even when the fact that success or failure depends on chance is salient. A lottery provides a vehicle for studying this illusion of control because, apart from the decision of whether or not to buy a ticket, the outcome is entirely governed by chance. If one *could* exert control over the outcome of a lottery, one would increase the likelihood of having one's ticket selected. This ticket would then be of greater value than a ticket belonging to someone without this control. And if it were of greater value, it then follows that one would require a higher price from a potential buyer.

In the following study a lottery was conducted to assess the effects of choice, an important factor in a skill situation, on the illusion of control. It was predicted that subjects who were given their choice of lottery ticket would require a higher price for it.

Method

Subjects. The lottery tickets were made available to adult male and female office workers employed by one of two firms located in Long Island, an insurance agency and a manufacturing company.[1] Since various drawings and sports pools were not uncommon to these offices, an elaborate justification for running the present lottery was unnecessary. With the exception of four females, all people approached by the alleged ticket agent purchased lottery tickets. Subjects were randomly assigned to conditions with the result that there were 24 males and 3 females in the choice condition and 23 males and 3 females in the no-choice condition.

Materials. The lottery tickets were standard 4 × 2 inch (10.16 × 5.08 cm) football cards. On each card appeared a famous football player, his name, and his team. The cards were alphabetically arranged first by team name and then by the individual player's name. There were two matched sets of tickets, each comprising 227 football cards. Each subject kept the ticket from one set while the same ticket from the other set was deposited in a cardboard carton from which the winning ticket would later be selected.

Procedure. The lottery was conducted by a male employee of the insurance agency and a female employee of the manufacturing firm 1 week prior to the 1973 Superbowl game. Both experimenters were blind to the hypotheses of the study. They each approached the members of their respective offices and asked them if they wished to purchase a lottery ticket costing $1. Subjects were told that the tickets were being sold in both their office and in another office (the other office was named) and that the entire pot, approximately $50, would go to the winner. Subjects were also informed of the date of the drawing. After having agreed to enter the lottery, the first subject approached was given the box of cards and told to

---

[1] The firms wish to remain anonymous.

select the ticket(s) he wanted. The subject named the card so that the experimenter could select the same card from the second set and deposit it in the closed carton. At this time the experimenter also recorded the subject's name and the card selected. The second subject approached was treated in the same manner except that after agreeing to enter the lottery, he or she was handed a card which matched the choice of the preceding subject. Subjects were thus alternately placed in the choice or no-choice condition. The day after the tickets were sold in one office, the same procedure was carried out in the second office.

Dependent measure. All subjects were individually approached by the experimenter from whom they purchased their ticket the morning of the lottery drawing. They were each told: "Someone in the other office wanted to get into the lottery, but since I'm not selling tickets any more, he asked me if I'd find out how much you'd sell your ticket for. It makes no difference to me, but how much should I tell him?" The amount quoted constituted the dependent measure. In the event that a subject said that he would not sell his ticket, the experimenter was instructed to prod him until he gave a figure and then to record the response "won't sell" alongside of the amount he finally offered.

Results

As predicted, the choice manipulation had a considerable effect on the value of the lottery ticket. The mean amount of money required for the subject to sell his ticket was $8.67 in the choice condition and only $1.96 in the no-choice condition ($t = 4.33$, $p < .005$). Although they were asked how much they would sell their ticket for rather than if they would sell, 15 subjects initially responded that they would not sell. Of these, 10 subjects were in the choice condition and 5 in the no-choice condition ($p < .10$). The difference previously cited, however, was not simply a function of the amounts quoted by these subjects after prodding, since their responses ranged from $3 to the entire pot of $53, with only 3 subjects in the last category.

While not specifically tested until the following study, one of the results obtained in this study concerns the effect of familiarity on the illusion of control. Females are not as likely as males to be familiar with the game of football. Hence, they should be less likely to enter the lottery in the first place, and if they do enter, they should require less money to sell their ticket. It should be recalled that only four persons refused to participate in the lottery and that each of them was female. Of the six females that did enter, four asked $1 and two asked $2 for their tickets. Thus the mean amount for females was $1.33 as compared with $5.89 for males ($t = 2.14$, $p < .05$). . . .

Implications and applications

On the basis of the evidence just presented, it seems that subjects do not distinguish chance- from skill-determined events in the way that is suggested by their definitions. The objective contingency does not appear to be the crucial variable governing subjects' behavior. Instead, whether or not an event is reacted to as if it is controllable largely depends on factors like competition, choice, familiarity, and involvement, which may be orthogonal to the actual contingency. This has been shown to be the case even in situations that are as clearly governed by chance as a lottery. . . .

Why does this occur? People are motivated to control their environment. The importance of control in this context has been widely discussed by both therapists and social science researchers. Whether it is seen as a need for competence (White, 1959), an instinct to master (Hendrick, 1943), a striving for superiority (Adler, 1930), or a striving for personal causation (deCharms, 1968), most social scientists agree that there is a motivation to master one's environment, and a complete mastery would include the ability to "beat the odds," that is, to control chance events. The more difficult a problem is, the more competent one feels in being able to solve it. The greatest satisfaction or feeling of competence would therefore result from being able to control the seemingly uncontrollable. . . .

In addition to the motivation to control, there is another reason for the lack of discrimination between controllable and uncontrollable events. This is the fact that skill and chance factors are so closely associated in people's experience. That is, there is not only a motivation not to discriminate, but there is often a true difficulty in making the discrimination, since there is an element of chance in every skill situation and an element of skill in almost every chance situation. The former is obvious and needs no further explication here. Examples of the latter are knowing what a good bet is in a game of dice (i.e., knowing the odds) or knowing which slot machines are rigged to give the highest payoffs. . . .

17. Test results are what you think they are

Loren J. Chapman and Jean Chapman

Every day psychiatrists and clinical psychologists must make vital decisions:

*What is his problem? Should he be committed to a mental hospital? Is he a
suicide-risk or a homicide-risk? Is this patient well enough to be discharged from
the hospital, or should he stay?*

For help with their decisions the clinicians almost always use psychological tests.

According to a survey by Norman Sundberg, the two most widely used
tests of any kind are the Rorschach inkblot test and the Draw-a-Person test
(DAP). Both are projective tests, based on the premise that a person
projects part of his personality when he responds to an ambiguous,
unstructured situation. For example, since there are no objective shapes in
an inkblot, anything a person sees in one presumably reflects his own
drives, conflicts and personality. Similarly, when one draws a picture of a
person on a blank sheet of paper, he is thought to project a bit of himself
into his creation.

Self

Our recent research suggests that the Rorschach and DAP may be projective tests in more ways than one. In interpreting the results of these tests,
the average clinician may project his own preconceptions and assumptions
into his description of the patient.

Our first studies in this area were with the Draw-a-Person test, in which
a clinician gives the subject a pencil and a blank sheet of paper and asks
him to draw a person. Karen Machover published the test in 1949. She

This paper originally appeared in *Psychology Today*, November 1971, pp. 18–22, 106–110.

described the pictures typically drawn by persons with various emotional problems and explained how to interpret several picture characteristics as keys to personality. She said, for example, that "the paranoid individual gives much graphic emphasis to the eyes," and "the sex given the proportionately larger head is the sex that is accorded more intellectual and social authority."

Machover's test manual is filled with far-reaching generalizations about what kinds of persons draw what kinds of pictures, but she presents very little supporting data.

Parts

Some clinicians have been unwilling to take Machover's word for it; they have tested her assertions experimentally. Jules Holzberg and Murray Wexler, for example, tried to determine whether paranoid persons really do draw elaborate eyes. They compared the drawings of 18 paranoid schizophrenic patients and 76 student nurses, but they found no difference in the way the two groups drew eyes.

Dozens of similar studies have tested Machover's predictions about other picture characteristics – head, ears, lips, hair, clothing, mouths, etc. – but again and again the DAP signs have failed to hold up. A few experimenters have found that better-adjusted subjects tend to produce better overall drawings, but the overwhelming conclusion from the research evidence is that the specific content of a drawing is not a valid indicator of personality characteristics.

Sign

It should be pointed out that this type of research does not demand perfect discrimination. If 50 per cent of homosexual persons draw figures in a certain way, and only 25 per cent of other persons draw figures that way, the drawing characteristic may still be considered a valid diagnostic sign, since in the long run it may contribute information toward a diagnosis of homosexuality.

Most clinicians know about the research showing that the DAP signs are invalid, yet many thousands continue to use the test regularly because they claim they have seen the signs work in their own clinical practice. "I'll trust my own senses before I trust some journal article," said one clinical psychologist. "I know that paranoids don't seem to draw big eyes in the research labs," said another, "but they sure do in my office."

Illusion

Some critics say that clinicians are so wrapped up in their theories and traditions that they are not influenced by the facts. We think there is another explanation, however. The clinician who continues to trust DAP signs in the face of negative evidence may be experiencing an *illusory correlation*, a phenomenon we discovered several years ago in research on word associations.

We found that words that are highly associated with each other tend to be seen as occurring together more often than they really do. In these experiments a subject sat in a comfortable chair as we projected various word-pairs (e.g., *bacon–tiger*) onto a large screen in front of him. The word-pairs changed every two seconds. The word on the left side of a pair was always one of four possible words: *bacon*, *lion*, *blossoms*, or *boat*. Each word appeared as often as any other (25 per cent of the time), but it appeared always on the left side of the screen. The word on the right side of a pair was either *eggs*, *tiger*, or *notebook*, with equal probabilities.

We arranged the word-pairs systematically so that each left-side word appeared an equal number of times with each right-side word. For example, when *bacon* appeared on the left side, *eggs* was paired with it on a third of the trials, *tiger* on another third of the trials, and *notebook* on the remaining third. But when we asked the subjects later about the word-pairs, they said that when *bacon* appeared on the left, *eggs* was paired with it 47 per cent of the time, and that when *lion* was on the left, *tiger* was the word that most often appeared on the right. Even though every word-pair appeared as often as every other, the subjects claimed that the pairs with strong verbal association occurred more often than the others.

The tendency to see two things as occurring together more often than they actually do we called illusory correlation.

There seemed to be an essential similarity between students who claim that certain words occur together more often than they actually do and clinical psychologists who claim to see validity in the DAP test signs when the research says there is none.

Tell

The DAP signs and interpretations may be different today from what they were when Machover introduced the test over 20 years ago, of course, so we asked modern professionals how they used the test. We sent question-naires to 110 clinicians who were active in diagnostic testing. We wrote brief descriptions of six types of patients and asked each clinician to tell us what characteristics he had seen in the drawings of each. The six descrip-tions were (1) "He is worried about how manly he is," (2) "He is suspicious of other people," (3) "He is worried about how intelligent he is," (4) "He is concerned with being fed and taken care of by other people," (5) "He has had problems of sexual impotence," and (6) "He is very worried that people are saying bad things about him." We told the clinicians to assume in each case that the patient was a man who drew a picture of a man.

We received 44 completed questionnaires, and it was clear that the clinicians generally agreed with each other as to the drawing characteristics they had seen in each case. For example, most clinicians (91 per cent) said that the suspicious patient would draw large or atypical eyes. Eighty-two per cent said that a person worried about his intelligence would tend to draw a large or emphasized head (see Table 1).

The agreement was not perfect, but it was impressive. In general, the clinicians agreed on two or three drawing characteristics that they would expect from each type of patient.

Pairs

Most of the clinicians had Ph.D.s and they averaged 8.4 years' experience in psychodiagnostics. We wondered what sort of DAP signs observers would find when they had almost no experience at all.

To find out, we gathered 45 drawings of male figures – 35 by psychotic patients at a nearby state hospital and 10 by graduate students in clinical psychology. We measured each picture for head size, eye size, etc., and had independent judges rate the drawings on the more subjective characteristics, such as muscularity and femininity.

To each picture we attached two of the six diagnostic statements we had sent out to clinicians – for example, "The man who drew this (1) is suspicious of other people, and (2) has had problems of sexual impotence." There were 15 distinct pairs that could be made from the six statements, so we used each pair on three different pictures.

We assigned the statements systematically to all types of pictures. For example, "He is worried about how intelligent he is" appeared just as often on pictures with small heads as on pictures with large heads.

We then screened a group of college students and selected 108 who claimed they had never heard of the Draw-a-Person test and knew nothing about how it was interpreted.

We tested the students in groups. Before each testing we briefly explained the rationale of the DAP test. We said the student would see a series of drawings, along with brief statements about the men who drew them. We said that many of the men had the same problems, and that the students should examine the pictures carefully and look for common characteristics in the drawings by men with each type of problem. The students then looked at the pictures in a prearranged random order, with 30 seconds allowed for each picture.

Proof

Though we had carefully counterbalanced the pictures and the statements so that there were no objective relationships between them, nearly every subject reported that he *saw* relationships. And the relationships that students found were remarkably similar to the relationships that clinicians

Table 1. Percentage of clinicians and naive students reporting various drawing characteristics as accompanying the six symptom statements

Characteristics of drawings	Worried about manliness		Suspicious of others		Worried about intelligence		Concerned with being fed & cared for		Has problems of sexual impotence		Worried about people saying bad things	
	C	S	C	S	C	S	C	S	C	S	C	S
1 Broad shoulders, muscular	80	76	0	6	0	8	0	12	25	31	0	6
2 Eyes atypical	0	0	91	58	0	6	0	3	2	2	43	26
3 Head large or emphasized	0	5	0	13	82	55	2	7	0	3	9	10
4 Mouth emphasized	0	0	7	5	0	1	68	8	2	1	5	5
5 Sexual area elaborated	14	5	0	0	0	0	0	0	55	8	0	0
6 Ears atypical	0	0	55	6	0	3	0	0	2	0	64	7
7 Facial expression atypical	0	17	18	44	2	21	2	21	2	14	18	52
8 Feminine, childlike	23	22	7	12	2	11	32	39	23	25	11	13
9 Hair distinctive	23	13	2	2	2	8	0	1	11	6	0	3
10 Detailed drawing	20	8	2	6	34	13	0	3	7	3	2	6
11 Passive posture	5	4	2	8	0	2	36	21	2	2	0	8
12 Buttons on clothes	0	0	0	0	0	0	23	1	0	0	0	0
13 Sexual area deemphasized	0	0	0	0	0	0	0	0	18	27	0	0
14 Phallic nose, limbs	9	0	0	0	0	0	0	0	23	2	0	0
15 Fat	0	2	0	1	0	0	7	16	0	4	0	1

Note: C = clinician. S = student. The characteristics listed are those mentioned by at least 15 percent of the clinicians or the students for at least one symptom. For nearly every drawing characteristic, the symptom most often associated with it by the clinicians is the same symptom associated with it by the students.

reported seeing in everyday practice. There were some differences, of course, but the students tended to describe the typical drawing of each type of patient in the same terms that the clinicians had used. And in the students' case, we know the signs were illusions, because they were not in the data.

Our previous research on word-pairs suggests an explanation: recall that we found that words with strong associative connections tend to be seen as occurring together. Perhaps the same mechanism was behind the DAP signs. We made a word-association questionnaire to determine how closely the symptom areas (suspiciousness, intelligence, impotence, etc.) are associated with various parts of the body (eyes, head, sexual organs, muscles, etc.). Questions took the following form: "The tendency for SUSPICIOUSNESS to call to mind HEAD is (1) very strong, (2) strong, (3) moderate, (4) slight, (5) very slight, (6) no tendency at all."

We gave the questionnaire to 45 students who had not participated in the other parts of the experiment. The verbal associations they reported neatly paralleled the illusory correlations that naive students had seen between symptoms and drawing characteristics. And the verbal associations were an even closer match with the correlations reported by practicing clinicians.

Pay

In our next experiment we tested 56 subjects on three successive days to see whether they would realize that there was no true correlation between symptoms and pictures if they had a chance to look at the test materials more than once. The correlations were seen as strongly on the third day as on the first. We began to realize how strong an illusory correlation can be and we wondered what conditions, if any, would allow one to overcome it.

We tested a series of 41 new subjects individually and let each look at each picture as long as he wanted to. To encourage them to study the pictures carefully, we offered $20 to the student whose judgments were most accurate.

It didn't work. The students saw the illusory correlations just as strongly as ever.

Finally we pulled all the stops and gave the subjects every opportunity we could think of to check their own perceptions. We gave each subject the full stack of drawings to study by himself; we told him he could look at them in any order for as long as he wanted. He could sort the pictures into piles and make direct comparisons. He could put all the drawings by suspicious men in one pile and study them for similarities. We gave every subject scratch paper, a pencil and a ruler; we again offered $20 to the person whose judgments were most accurate, and we gave each subject a copy of the final questionnaire so he could see what questions he would have to answer.

Manly

In these generous conditions the illusory correlation did drop significantly for most of the symptoms, but it didn't disappear. For example, in
normal conditions 76 per cent of students saw a relationship between
worrying about one's manliness and the tendency to draw muscular
figures; in the new conditions, 45 per cent still claimed to see the
relationship that wasn't there. The illusory correlation is powerful, and
remarkably resistant to any attempts to change it.

Students even claim to see the typical correlations when the cards are
stacked in the opposite direction. In one study, for example, we placed the
statement, "He is worried about his intelligence" only on pictures with
small heads; the statement about suspiciousness appeared exclusively on
drawings with *small* eyes, etc. This reduced the illusory correlation somewhat, but didn't eliminate it. Sixteen per cent still said that patients who
worried about intelligence drew big-headed figures and 50 per cent still
saw a relationship between worrying about one's manliness and the
tendency to draw muscular figures – even though the true relationships
were in the opposite direction.

It is clear from our research that clinical interpretations of the DAP test
likely have a strong component of illusory correlation. And the decisions
that clinicians make about their patients may be projections of the
clinicians' own preconceptions.

Blots

We wondered whether there were illusory correlations in the most
popular test of all – the Rorschach inkblots – and if so, whether they
would be seen as clearly as real correlations, the few Rorschach signs that
have been found to be valid indicators of certain personality characteristics.

In the Rorschach's 50-year history, many clinicians have reported, for
example, that certain responses are given more often by homosexuals than
by others. In 1949, William Wheeler summarized 20 Rorschach signs of
homosexuality. Other researchers have tested the Wheeler signs, but only
2 of the 20 signs have been found valid by more than one investigator.
One of these (number seven) is a response to the fourth inkblot of "a
human or animal–contorted, monstrous, or threatening." The other valid
sign is Wheeler's number eight, the report of an ambiguous animal –
human figure on the fifth card.

Signs

To find how clinicians actually use the Rorschach to diagnose homosexuality, we sent questionnaires to 76 clinicians, asking them to describe two
percepts that homosexual patients typically see in the 10 Rorschach
inkblots. Of the clinicians who returned completed questionnaires, 32 said

they had seen the Rorschach protocols of a number of homosexuals. These 32 clinicians described several Rorschach signs, but the ones they mentioned most often were (1) buttocks or anus, (2) genitals, (3) feminine clothing, (4) human figures of indeterminate sex, with no clear male or female features, and (5) human figures with both male and female features. All of these are Wheeler signs that have not been supported by research. On the other hand, only two clinicians mentioned valid sign number seven – a contorted, monstrous figure, and none mentioned the other valid sign, number eight – a part-human–part-animal figure.

Some clinicians, it would appear, see signs in the Rorschach that aren't there, and fail to see the signs that are there. Again our work with word-associations suggests a reason. The two valid signs are not intuitive: homosexuality does not easily bring to mind either snarling beasts or human–animal crossbreeds. But homosexuality does have a high verbal association with the five signs clinicians reported most often. Somehow it is intuitively reasonable to expect that homosexuals might tend to see buttocks, feminine clothing, or mixed-sex figures in inkblots.

Ideas

We tested these notions objectively by asking 34 independent student judges to rate how strongly the word "homosexuality" tended to call to mind various ideas. Their ratings agreed – the popular but invalid signs have a stronger verbal association with homosexuality than do the two unpopular but valid signs. This suggests that the signs of homosexuality that clinicians claim to see in the Rorschach may simply reflect their own assumptions and expectations.

We tested this contention with a design similar to the one we used to study the Draw-a-Person test. We obtained several Rorschach cards, and on each we attached a response – some perception that a person had supposedly seen on the card. There was a circle around the area of the card that the response referred to.

On some inkblots the response was a valid homosexuality sign (e.g., "a giant with shrunken arms"), on others the response was a nonvalid sign (e.g., "a woman's laced corset"), and on others it was a neutral sign (e.g., "a map of Spain"). Below the response were two descriptions of the person who had made the response. We selected these descriptions in all possible pairs from a group of four: (1) "He has sexual feelings toward other men," (2) "He believes other people are plotting against him," (3) "He feels sad and depressed much of the time," and (4) "He has strong feelings of inferiority." We, of course, were most interested in the first statement.

Mix

As in the DAP studies, we systematically assigned the symptom statements to the cards so that there was no consistent relationship between any of the statements and any of the signs.

After the students looked at a series of cards, we asked them what kind of Rorschach images had been reported by patients with each of the four types of symptoms. The homosexual men, the students reported more often saw buttocks, genitals, etc. – in short, the same five nonvalid signs that clinicians had reported. None of the students saw a relationship between homosexuality and the two valid signs.

In a later variation we purposely introduced a negative correlation into the test materials, so that the statement "He has sexual feelings toward other men" *never* appeared on a card that had been perceived as feminine clothing, buttocks, etc. This did not reduce the illusory correlation – the students saw it just as strongly as before.

Tie

These studies show how easy it is to believe that two independent events are connected, especially when there is some subjective verbal association between the events. Our subjects saw massive illusory correlations between symptoms and projective test signs on a brief, structured task. The clinician's task is much more complex, of course. A real patient's problems are numerous and vague – rarely does a patient have only two clearly defined symptoms. And real patients make many different responses on projective tests, not just one. It also seems likely that in actual practice the illusory correlations that a clinician observes are reinforced by the reports of his fellow clinicians who themselves are subject to the same illusions. The consensus would make everyone's illusions stronger. Our students, on the other hand, were not allowed to speak to one another during the test, so each had to find the illusory correlations on his own. For all of these reasons it seems likely that practicing clinicians deal with illusory correlations that are even stronger than the ones our subjects reported.

Hard

We do not mean to imply that clinical psychologists are incompetent or unresponsive to the facts, as some might be quick to conclude. Our data point not to the incompetence of the clinician, but to the extreme difficulty of his task. Clinicians are subject to the same illusions as everyone else. By analogy, nearly everyone says that two horizontal lines have different lengths when they appear in the Müller-Lyer illusion:

but no one would call a carpenter an incompetent judge of distances simply because he too sees the illusion.

Clinicians must be made aware of illusory correlations if they are to compensate for them. Ideally, the clinician should experience such illusions firsthand. It may be sound training policy to require each graduate student in clinical psychology to serve as an observer in tasks like the ones we have described. He could then examine closely the size and source of the illusory correlations he experiences and thereby, one hopes, learn to guard against such errors in his clinical practice.

The experience would also remind him that his senses are fallible, that his clinical judgments must be checked continually against objective measures, and that his professional task is one of the most difficult and complex in all of psychology.

18. Probabilistic reasoning in clinical medicine: Problems and opportunities

David M. Eddy

To a great extent, the quality and cost of health care are determined by the decisions made by physicians whose ultimate objective is to design and administer a treatment program to improve a patient's condition. Most of the decisions involve many factors, great uncertainty, and difficult value questions.

This chapter examines one aspect of how these decisions are made, studying the use of probabilistic reasoning to analyze a particular problem: whether to perform a biopsy on a woman who has a breast mass that might be malignant. Specifically, we shall study how physicians process information about the results of a mammogram, an X-ray test used to diagnose breast cancer. The evidence presented shows that physicians do not manage uncertainty very well, that many physicians make major errors in probabilistic reasoning, and that these errors threaten the quality of medical care.

The problem

A breast biopsy is not a trivial procedure. The most common type (around 80%) is the excisional biopsy, in which the suspicious mass is removed surgically for microscopic examination and histological diagnosis by a pathologist. Usually the patient is admitted to a hospital and given a full set of preoperative diagnostic tests. The biopsy is almost always done under general anesthesia (with a probability of approximately 2 out of 10,000 of an anesthetic death). A small (1- to 2-in.) incision is made, and tissue the size of a pecan to a plum is removed. In many cases (perhaps 1 in

The preparation of this paper was supported by a grant from The Henry J. Kaiser Family Foundation.

2) the loss of tissue is barely noticeable; in others there is an indentation remaining. In an occasional case (perhaps 1 in 200) there is an infection or drainage that can persist for several weeks. The charge is approximately $700. This procedure can be done on an outpatient basis and under local anesthesia. As an alternative to the excisional biopsy, some surgeons prefer in some cases to obtain tissue by using a needle. This can be done on an outpatient basis, leaves no scar or other residual effects, and is far less expensive. However, it is thought by many physicians to be less reliable in that an existing malignant lesion may be missed.

An important factor that affects the need for biopsy is the possibility that the breast mass is a cancer. To estimate this possibility, a physician can list the possible diseases, assess the frequencies with which various signs and symptoms occur with each disease, compare this information with the findings in the patient, estimate the chance that she has each of the diseases on the list, and perform a biopsy if the probability of cancer or another treatable lesion is high enough. To help the physician, many textbooks describe how non-malignant diseases can be differentiated from cancer. For example, the following passage describes one such benign disease – chronic cystic disease.

Chronic cystic disease is often confused with carcinoma of the breast. It *usually* occurs in parous women with small breasts. It is present *most commonly* in the upper outer quadrant but *may* occur in other parts and eventually involve the entire breast. It is *often* painful, particularly in the premenstrual period, and accompanying menstrual disturbances are *common*. Nipple discharge, *usually* serous, occurs in *approximately* 15% of the cases, but there are no changes in the nipple itself. The lesion *is* diffuse without sharp demarcation and without fixation to the overlying skin. Multiple cysts are firm, round, and fluctuant and *may* transilluminate *if* they contain clear fluid. A large cyst in an area of chronic cystic disease *feels* like a tumor, but it is *usually* smoother and well delimited. The axillary lymph nodes are *usually* not enlarged. Chronic cystic disease *infrequently* shows large bluish cysts. More often, the cysts are multiple and small.[1] (del Regato, 1970, pp. 860–861)

Similar descriptions are available for fibroadenomas, fat necrosis, trauma, and a half dozen other breast conditions, as well as for cancer.

This type of probabilistic information can be used to help a physician analyze the possible causes of a patient's breast mass. With assessments of the values of the possible outcomes (e.g., properly diagnosing a cancer, doing an unnecessary biopsy of a non-malignant lesion, not biopsying and missing a malignant lesion, and properly deciding not to biopsy a benign lesion), the physician can assess the chance that the patient, with her particular signs and symptoms, has cancer, and the physician can select an action.

---

[1] In this and all subsequent quotations, the italics are added.

The case of mammography

Other diagnostic tests are available to help the physician estimate the chance that a particular woman's breast lesion is malignant. Perhaps the most important and commonly used is mammography. The value of this test rests on the fact that the components of malignant cells absorb X rays differently from the components of non-malignant cells. By studying the mammograms, a radiologist may be able to see certain signs that occur with different frequencies in different lesions, and from this information a judgment can be made about the nature of the lesion in question. Typically, mammograms are classified as positive or negative for cancer. Occasionally an expanded classification scheme is used, such as one containing the three classes: malignant, suspicious, and benign.

The test is not perfect, in that some malignant lesions are incorrectly classified as benign and some benign lesions are called malignant. Thus, one factor that is very important to the clinician is the accuracy of the test.

Probabilistic reasoning

Let us develop this notion more precisely. The purpose of a diagnostic test is to provide information to a clinician about the condition of a patient. The physician uses this information to revise the estimate of the patient's condition and to select an action based on that new estimate. The action may be an order for further diagnostic tests, or if the physician is sufficiently confident of the patient's condition, a therapeutic action may be taken. The essential point is that the physician can have degrees of certainty about the patient's condition. The physician will gather evidence to refine this certainty that the patient does or does not have cancer, and when that certainty becomes sufficiently strong (in the context of the severity of the disease and the change in prognosis with treatment), action will be taken.

We can associate a probability, the physician's subjective probability that the patient has cancer, with this degree of certainty. The impact on patient care of a diagnostic test such as mammography, therefore, lies in its power to change the physician's certainty or subjective probability that the patient has cancer.

The notion of a subjective probability or degree of certainty appears in many different forms in the medical vernacular. For example, one author writes that "because the older age group has the greatest proportion of malignant lesions, there is heightened *index of suspicion* of cancer in the mind of a clinician who faces an older patient" (Gold, 1969, p. 162). Another author states that the mammogram can reduce the number of breast biopsies "in many instances when the examining physician's *rather firm opinion* of benign disease is supported by a *firm mammographic diagnosis* of benignancy" (Wolfe, 1964, p. 253). A third describes it this way: "If the *subjective impression* of the clinician gives enough reason for suspicion of carcinoma, the clinician will be compelled to biopsy despite a negative mammogram" (Clark, et al., 1965, p. 133). Other expressions that reflect this notion include, "*confidence level*" (Byrne, 1974, p. 37). "*impression of malignancy*" (Wolfe, 1967, p. 138), "a *more positive diagnosis*" (Egan, 1972, p. 392), and so forth. These statements are not precise because few physicians are formally acquainted with the concepts of subjective probability and decision analysis. Nonetheless, there is ample evidence that the notions of degrees of certainty are natural to physicians and are used by them to help select a course of action.

Interpreting the accuracy of mammography

Now consider a patient with a breast mass that the physician thinks is probably benign. Let this probability be 99 out of 100. You can interpret the phrase "that the physician thinks is probably [99 out of 100] benign" as follows. Suppose the physician has had experience with a number of women who, in all important aspects such as age, symptoms, family history, and physical findings are similar to this particular patient. And suppose the physician knows from this experience that the frequency of cancer in this group is, say, 1 out of 100. Lacking any other information, the physician will therefore assign (perhaps subconsciously) a subjective probability of 1% to the event that this patient has cancer.

Now let the physician order a mammogram and receive a report that in the radiologist's opinion the lesion is malignant. This is new information and the actions taken will obviously depend on the physician's new estimate of the probability that the patient has cancer. A physician who turns to the literature can find innumerable helpful statements, such as the following: "The accuracy of mammography is approximately 90 percent" (Wolfe, 1966, p. 214); "In [a patient with a breast mass] a positive [mammogram] report of carcinoma is highly accurate" (Rosato, Thomas, & Rosato, 1973, p. 491); and "The accuracy of mammography in correctly diagnosing malignant lesions of the breast averages 80 to 85 percent" (Cohn, 1972, p. 98). If more detail is desired, the physician can find many statements like "The results showed 79.2 per cent of 475 malignant lesions were correctly diagnosed and 90.4 per cent of 1,105 benign lesions were correctly diagnosed, for an overall accuracy of 87 per cent" (Snyder, 1966, p. 217).

At this point you can increase your appreciation of the physician's problem by estimating for yourself the new probability that this patient has cancer: The physician thinks the lump is probably (99%) *benign*, but the radiologist has produced a *positive* X-ray report with the accuracy just given.

Table 1. *Accuracy of mammography in diagnosing benign and malignant lesions*

Results of X ray	Malignant lesion (cancer)	Benign lesion (no cancer)
Positive	.792	.096
Negative	.208	.904

Source: The numbers are from Snyder (1966).

Bayes' formula can be applied to assess the probability. This formula tells us that

$$P(\text{ca}\,|\,\text{pos}) = \frac{P(\text{pos}\,|\,\text{ca})\,P(\text{ca})}{P(\text{pos}\,|\,\text{ca})\,P(\text{ca}) + P(\text{pos}\,|\,\text{benign})\,P(\text{benign})}$$

where

   $P(\text{ca}\,|\,\text{pos})$ is the probability that the patient has cancer, given that she has a positive X-ray report (the posterior probability)

   $P(\text{pos}\,|\,\text{ca})$ is the probability that, if the patient has cancer, the radiologist will correctly diagnose it (the true-positive rate, or sensitivity)

   $P(\text{ca})$ is the probability that the patient has cancer (prior probability)

   $P(\text{benign})$ is the prior probability that the patient has benign disease $[P(\text{benign}) = 1 - P(\text{ca})]$

   $P(\text{pos}\,|\,\text{benign})$ is the probability that, if the patient has a benign lesion, the radiologist will incorrectly diagnose it as cancer (the false-positive rate)

Table 1 summarizes the numbers given by Snyder. The entries in the cells are the appropriate probabilities (e.g., $P(\text{pos}\,|\,\text{ca}) = .792$).

Using 1% as the physician's estimate of the prior probability that the mass is malignant and taking into account the new information provided by the test, we obtain

$$P(\text{ca}\,|\,\text{pos}) = \frac{(0.792)\,(0.01)}{(0.792)\,(0.01) + (0.096)\,(0.99)} = 0.077$$

Thus, the physician should estimate that there is approximately an 8% chance that the patient has cancer.

Incorrect probabilistic reasoning

Unfortunately, most physicians (approximately 95 out of 100 in an informal sample taken by the author) misinterpret the statements about the accuracy of the test and estimate $P(\text{ca}\,|\,\text{pos})$ to be about 75%. Other investigators have observed similar results (Casscells, Schoenberger, & Grayboys, 1978). When asked about this, the erring physicians usually report that they assumed that the probability of cancer given that the patient has a positive X ray [$P(\text{ca}|\text{pos})$] was approximately equal to the probability of a positive X ray in a patient with cancer [$P(\text{pos}|\text{ca})$]. The latter probability is the one measured in clinical research programs and is very familiar, but it is the former probability that is needed for clinical decision making. It seems that many if not most physicians confuse the two.

There are really two types of accuracy for any test designed to determine whether or not a specific disease is present. The *retrospective accuracy* concerns $P(\text{pos}|\text{ca})$ and $P(\text{neg}|\text{no ca})$. (The abbreviation "no ca" refers to the event the patient does not have cancer. This can occur because she either has a benign disease or she has no disease at all.) This accuracy, the one usually referred to in the literature on mammography, is determined by looking back at the X-ray diagnosis after the true (histological) diagnosis is known. Let us use the term *predictive accuracy* to describe $P(\text{ca}|\text{pos})$ and $P(\text{benign}|\text{neg})$, the accuracy important to the clinician who has an X-ray report of an as yet undiagnosed patient and who wants to predict that patient's disease state.

Confusing retrospective accuracy versus predictive accuracy. A review of the medical literature on mammography reveals a strong tendency to equate the predictive accuracy of a positive report with the retrospective accuracy of an X-ray report; that is, to equate $P(\text{ca}|\text{pos}) = P(\text{pos}|\text{ca})$. There are many reasons to suspect that this error is being made. First, the wordings of many of the statements in the literature strongly suggest that the authors believe that the predictive accuracy [$P(\text{ca}|\text{pos})$] equals the retrospective accuracy [$P(\text{pos}|\text{ca})$] that they report in their studies. For example, a 1964 article in *Radiology* stated, "*the total correctness* of the X-ray diagnosis was 674 out of 759, or 89 percent" (vol. 84, p. 254). A contributor to *Clinical Obstetrics and Gynecology* in 1966 said, "Asch found a 90 percent *correlation* of mammography with the pathologic findings in 500 patients" (vol. 9, p. 217). "The *agreement* in radiologic and pathologic diagnosis was 91.6 percent" (Egan, 1972, p. 379). All of these statements imply that if the patient has a positive test the test will be correct and the patient will have cancer 90% of the time. This is not true.

Second, some authors make the error explicitly. The following appeared in a 1972 issue of *Surgery, Gynecology and Obstetrics* in an article entitled "Mammography in its Proper Perspective" and was intended to rectify some confusion that existed in the literature: "In women with proved carcinoma of the breast, in whom mammograms are performed, there is no X-ray evidence of malignant disease in approximately one out of five patients examined. If then on the basis of a negative mammogram, we are to defer biopsy of a solid lesion of the breast, then there is a one in five chance that we are deferring biopsy of a malignant lesion" (vol. 134, p. 98). The author has incorrectly stated that $P(\text{neg}\,|\,\text{ca}) = .2$ implies $P(\text{ca}\,|\,\text{neg}) = .2$. His error becomes very serious when he concludes that "to defer biopsy of a *clinically benign* solid lesion of the breast that has been called *benign* on mammography is to take a step backward in the eradication of carcinoma of the breast in our female population." The chance that such a patient has cancer depends on the prior probability, but is less than 1 in 100. His analysis is in error by more than a factor of 20.

Surgery, Gynecology and Obstetrics published in 1970 (vol. 131, pp. 93–98) the findings of another research group, who computed the "correlation of radiographic diagnosis with pathologic diagnosis" as follows. They took all the patients with histologically proven diagnoses and separated them into three groups on the basis of the X-ray diagnosis – "benign," "carcinoma," and "suspected carcinoma." In the "X-ray benign" ("negative" in our terminology) group, the tally showed that 84% in fact had benign lesions. It was also noted that 87.5% of the "X-ray carcinoma" (or "positive") group had biopsy-proven malignant lesions. Thus, $P(\text{ca}\,|\,\text{pos}) = 87.5\%$ and $P(\text{benign}\,|\,\text{neg}) = 84\%$. But the authors mistook this predictive accuracy for the retrospective accuracy. They stated that "A correct mammographic diagnosis was made in 84 percent *of those with benign lesions* and in 87.5 percent *of those with carcinoma.*" In fact, the true-positive rate $[P(\text{pos}\,|\,\text{ca})]$ in this study was actually 66% and the true-negative rate $[P(\text{neg}\,|\,\text{benign})]$ was 54%.

In a letter to the editor in the September 11, 1976, issue of the *National Observer*, a physician presented five "observations and facts" to support his opinion that "routine [i.e., screening] mammography is not in the best interest of the population at large at any age." Here is the first set of observations.

(1) The accuracy of the examination of mammography is reported to be between 80 percent and 90 percent, depending on such factors as the age of the patient, whether or not she has fibrocystic disease, the type of radiographic equipment, the experience of the radiologist, and what our definition of "accurate" is. . . . Even if we conclude that accuracy is 85 percent generally (and I am sure that not every radiologist in the nation can approach that figure in his own practice), then that means that *15 percent of the women X-rayed will wind up with incorrect interpretations of the findings, or more likely, their mammograms will simply fail to demonstrate the disease. This means that 15 percent of the women will be given a false sense of security if they are told their X-rays are normal, if indeed they already have cancer.* It is difficult to assess the harm done to this group, for they would obviously be better off with no information rather than with incorrect information. Told that her mammogram is normal and she need not come back for one more year, a woman with breast cancer may well ignore a lump in her breast which might otherwise send her to the doctor immediately.

There are several errors in this author's reasoning. First, the "accuracy" of mammography cannot be expressed as a single number. Assume the author means that the true-positive and true-negative rates both equal 85%.

Second, these rates (of 85%) are observed when mammography is used to make a differential diagnosis of known signs and symptoms. Such lesions are generally more advanced than the lesions being sought in a screening examination, which is the situation the author is addressing. More reasonable estimates for the true-positive and true-negative rates in screening programs are 60% and 98%, respectively.

Third, even using 85%, we find several inaccuracies in the reasoning. Consider the second sentence. There are two ways an incorrect interpretation can occur: (a) the patient can have cancer and a negative examination, $P(\text{ca,neg})$; or (b) she can have a positive examination but not have cancer, $P(\text{no ca,pos})$.[2] From elementary probability theory we know that

$$P(\text{ca,neg}) = P(\text{neg} \mid \text{ca}) \, P(\text{ca})$$

$P(\text{neg} \mid \text{ca})$ is the complement of $P(\text{pos} \mid \text{ca})$ and therefore equals .15 in this case. We do not know $P(\text{ca})$ precisely, but for a screening population we are reasonably certain that it is less than .005. That is, fewer than 5 out of 1,000 women harbor an asymptomatic but mammogram-detectable cancer of the breast.

Thus,

$$P(\text{ca,neg}) \leq (.15)\,(.005) = .00075$$

Also,

$$P(\text{no ca,pos}) = P(\text{pos} \mid \text{no ca}) \, P(\text{no ca}) \geq (.15)\,(.995) = .14925$$

The total probability of an incorrect interpretation [i.e., $P(\text{ca,neg}) + P(\text{no ca,pos})$] is the sum of these two numbers, which is 15%, as the author states. However, this does not mean that "more likely, their mammograms will simply fail to demonstrate the disease." $P(\text{ca,neg}) = .00075$ is *not* more likely than $P(\text{no ca,pos}) = .14925$. It is about 200 times *less* likely.

Another problem is that 85% "accurate" does not mean that "15 percent of the women will be given a false sense of security if they are told their X-rays are normal." The author appears to be trying to estimate $P(\text{ca} \mid \text{neg})$. Now by Bayes' formula,

$$P(\text{ca} \mid \text{neg}) = \frac{P(\text{neg} \mid \text{ca}) \, P(\text{ca})}{P(\text{neg} \mid \text{ca}) \, P(\text{ca}) + P(\text{neg} \mid \text{no ca}) \, P(\text{no ca})}$$

$$= \frac{(.15)(.005)}{(.15)(.005) + (.85)(.995)} = .00089$$

That is, if 10,000 asymptomatic women are screened, and if we use the author's misestimate of the accuracy, 8,458 of them will leave with a

[2] $P(A,B)$ is the joint probability that both events A and B occur.

Table 2. *Presence of cancer and results of X rays in 1000 women who have abnormal physical examinations*

	Women with cancer	Women with no cancer	Total
Women with positive X rays	74	110	184
Women with negative X rays	6	810	816
Total	80	920	1,000

Note: A true-positive rate of .92 (P(pos|ca) = 0.92) implies that of 80 women who have cancer, 74 will have positive X rays and 6 will have negative X rays. Of all the women with positive X rays, 74/184 have cancer, or P(ca|pos) = 74/184 = 40%.
Source: The numbers are from Wolfe (1964).

negative examination. The author thinks that about 1,269 of them will have a false sense of security. In fact, only about 9 will. This number has been overestimated by a factor of about 150.

Finally, adding the phrase, "if indeed they already have cancer" further confuses the meaning of the sentence. The phrases "a false sense of security," "if [given] they are told their X-rays are normal," and "if they already have cancer" translate symbolically into $P(ca \mid neg,ca)$. This probability is 1, not .15.

The importance of P(ca). In addition to confusing the two accuracies, many authors do not seem to understand that, for a test of constant retrospective accuracy, the meaning to the physician of the test results (the predictive accuracy) depends on the initial risk of cancer in the patient being mammogrammed. Even if it is assumed that the true-positive and true-negative rates are constant for all studies, the proper interpretation of the test results – the chance that a patient with a positive (or negative) mammogram has cancer – will depend on the prevalence of cancer in the population from which the patient was selected, on the pretest probability that a patient has cancer. This can be extremely important when one compares the use of the test in a diagnostic clinic (where women have signs and symptoms of breast disease) with its use in a screening clinic for asymptomatic women.

The importance of this is shown by an example. Suppose a clinician's practice is to mammogram women who have an abnormal physical examination. The frequency of cancer in such women has been found in one study to be approximately 8% (Wolfe, 1964). In one series of mammograms in this population, a true-positive rate of 92% and a true-negative rate of 88% was obtained (Wolfe, 1964). Let the physician now face a patient who he feels is representative of this sample population (i.e., let $P(\text{ca}) = 8\%$). Suppose he orders a mammogram and receives a positive result from the radiologist. His decision to order a biopsy should be based on the new probability that the patient has cancer. That probability can be calculated to be 40% (see Table 2). Would a negative report have ruled out cancer? The probability that this woman, given a negative report, still has cancer is slightly less than 1%. The logic for this estimate is shown in Table 2.

Now, suppose the clinician orders the test to screen for cancer in a woman who has no symptoms and a negative physical examination. The prevalence of mammography-detectable cancer in such women is about .10% (e.g., Shapiro, Strax, & Venet, 1967). For the purposes of this example, let the retrospective accuracy of the radiologist be unchanged – that is, in this population of patients let him again have a true-positive rate of 92% and a true-negative rate (for the diagnosis of benign lesions) of 88%.[3] The literature provides data only on the retrospective accuracy of the test in women who have cancer and benign diseases. In one study about 60% of these women had no disease at all (Wolfe, 1965). Thus, in this case,

$$P(\text{ca} \mid \text{pos}) = [P(\text{pos} \mid \text{ca})P(\text{ca})] \div$$
$$[P(\text{pos} \mid \text{ca})P(\text{ca}) + P(\text{pos} \mid \text{benign})P(\text{benign})$$
$$+ P(\text{pos} \mid \text{no disease})P(\text{no disease})]$$

$P(\text{benign})$, $P(\text{no disease})$, and $P(\text{pos} \mid \text{no disease})$ are not discussed explicitly in the literature. This is instructive and it leads us to suspect that their importance in the analysis of these problems is not understood. For this example, we shall use the data presented by Wolfe (1965) and assume that $P(\text{no disease})$ is about 60% and $P(\text{benign})$ is about 40%. We shall also make an assumption favorable to mammography and let $P(\text{pos} \mid \text{no disease})$ be 0%.

To continue with this example, say the radiologist reports that the mammogram in this asymptomatic woman is positive. Given the positive mammography report, the probability that the patient has cancer ($P(\text{ca} \mid \text{pos})$) is about 1 out of 49, or about 2.0% (Table 3). In the previous example that involved women with symptoms, $P(\text{ca} \mid \text{pos})$ was 40%. Thus, depending on who is being examined, there can be about a *twentyfold difference* in the chance that a woman with a positive mammogram has cancer.

This raises a major question about medical reasoning – when trying to evaluate a patient's signs and symptoms, how should a physician use information about the basic frequency of the possible diseases in the

---

[3] This is not a good assumption, since the "accuracy" changes as the population being examined changes. For example, the true-positive rate is lower when one is using the test in an asymptomatic population because the cancers tend to be much smaller and harder to detect. The assumption is made only to demonstrate the importance of $P(\text{ca})$.

Table 3. *Presence of cancer and results of X ray in 1,000 women who have no symptoms*

	Women with cancer	Women with benign lesions	Women with no cancer	Total
Women with positive X rays	1	48	0	49
Women with negative X rays	0	352	599	951
Total	1	400	599	1,000

Note: A true-positive rate of 0.92 implies that the X ray will detect cancer in the one woman who has the disease. A true-negative rate of 0.88 for benign disease implies that of 400 women with benign disease, 352 will have negative X rays, whereas in 48 the X ray will be positive. Thus, 49 women will have positive X rays, but only one has cancer, or $P(ca|pos) = 1/49 = 2\%$.

population at large? The profession appears to be confused about this issue. On the one hand, physicians make statements that the relative commonness of a disease should *not* affect the estimate of the probability that a particular patient has the disease. This notion appears in several maxims, such as, "The patient is a case of one" and, "Statistics are for dead men." In discussions of specific problems, the idea is sometimes expressed subtly as in the statement, "The younger women obviously have a fewer number of the malignancies which, however, should exert very little influence on the individual case" (Wolfe, 1967, p. 138). It can also be stated explicitly and presented as a rule to be obeyed. For example, the following appeared in a textbook on clinical diagnosis: "When a patient consults his physician with an undiagnosed disease, neither he nor the doctor knows whether it is rare until the diagnosis is finally made. Statistical methods can only be applied to a population of thousands. The individual either has a rare disease or doesn't have it; the relative incidence of two diseases is completely irrelevant to the problem of making his diagnosis" (DeGowin & DeGowin, 1969, p. 6).

On the other hand, these statements are often inconsistent with the behavior of physicians who try, however imperfectly, to use this diagnostic information. Witness the following maxims that are passed on in medical schools: "When you hear hoofbeats, think of horses not of zebras," "Common things occur most commonly," "Follow Sutton's law: go where the money is," and so forth. It appears that many physicians sense the value of information on the prior probability of a disease but that the formal lessons of probability theory are not at all well understood. Without a formal theory, physicians tend to make the same kinds of errors in probabilistic reasoning that have been observed in other contexts (Kahneman & Tversky, 1973, 4; Lyon & Slovic, 1976).

Implications: Mammograms and biopsies

These problems can have important practical implications. For instance, in the examples just cited two authors based their conclusions on incorrect probabilistic reasoning. One incorrectly argued that a woman with a breast mass that appears benign on physical examination and benign on the X ray still has a 20% chance of having cancer and recommended that she be biopsied. Another author based a recommendation against screening on a gross misestimate of the frequency with which women would have a false sense of security (i.e., have a cancer missed by the mammogram). Both authors may have come to the same conclusion with correct reasoning, but they may not have.

The value of diagnostic information. The value of mammography in women who have symptoms and signs of breast disease lies in its ability to provide diagnostic information that will affect the clinician's decision to biopsy. More precisely, the outcome of the test should change a clinician's estimate of the probability that the patient has cancer. As one author puts it:

Mammography can assist the clinician in differentiating between benign and malignant lesions.... Some lesions, especially the small ones, may lack the characteristics that give the clinician an index of suspicion high enough to justify biopsy. It is here that the ... mammogram may provide additional objective evidence. Thus, in the case of an indeterminate lesion of the breast, mammography can aid the physician in deciding whether to perform a biopsy study (Clark & Robbins, 1965, p. 125).

For any diagnostic test to be useful it must provide information that can potentially change a decision about how the patient should be managed – to call for a biopsy in some patients who would otherwise not be biopsied, and, we should hope, to obviate biopsies in some women who would otherwise receive them. This notion is developed formally in statistical decision theory and has been used to analyze some medical problems in a research setting (e.g., Lusted et al., 1977).

Many physicians recognize that the X-ray report carries useful information that should help in patient management, but precisely how the information should be used is ordinarily not stated. The explanations given by most authors contain few specific directions. "Mammography is not designed to dictate treatment procedures but may provide, in certain cases, just that bit of more precise information, so that undesirable sequelae are avoided" (Egan, 1972, p. 392). "Mammography is a valuable adjunctive to the surgeon in the diagnosis and treatment of breast lesions" (Lyons, 1975, p. 231). "Mammography may assist in clarifying confusing palpable findings" (Egan, 1969, p. 146). It "plays a supportive or auxiliary role ..." (Block & Reynolds, 1974, p. 589). The precise nature and degree of the support is usually left to the clinician's judgment.

Mammograms and biopsies: The practice. It seems that the role of mammography in such cases is only partially understood. To understand this, let us examine the impact that clinical investigators predict mammography will have on the need to biopsy diseased breasts. While the statements quoted above imply that the use of X rays should help select patients for biopsy, an equal number of statements suggest that mammography cannot, indeed should not, perform this function. "Any palpable lesion requires verification by excision and biopsy regardless of the X-ray findings" (Lesnick, 1966, p. 2007). "While mammography is usually definitive it is not a substitute for biopsy" (Egan, 1969, p. 148). "In no way would this procedure detract from the importance of biopsy. As a matter of fact, the use of routine mammography will reaffirm the importance of biopsy, since X-ray evidence of a malignant lesion requires biopsy for confirmation. . . . It in no way detracts from the importance of the biopsy. . . . [B]iopsy is as much a necessity for the confirmation of X-ray findings as it is for the confirmation of physical signs" (Gershon-Cohen, & Borden, 1964, pp. 2753, 2754). "It is apparent that mammography is not a substitute for surgery" (DeLuca, 1974, p. 318). "Let us state emphatically that mammography is not a substitute for biopsy" (McClow & Williams, 1973, p. 618).

One of the most precise policy statements on how mammography should be used to help select patients for biopsy appeared in *Archives of Surgery* in 1966 (vol. 93, pp. 853–856). A careful examination of the directions reveals that only half of the test's potential is used. The scheme for using mammography "to determine the treatment or disposition of each patient" involves three categories of patients:

Category A: "The patients with a 'lump' or 'dominant lesion' in the breast are primarily surgical problems and there should be no delay in obtaining a biopsy. Mammography, in this instance, is strictly *complementary. . . .* It may disclose occult tumors" (p. 854).

Category B: "The patients have symptoms referable to the breast but no discrete mass or 'dominant lesion'. . . . In this category, the surgeon and clinician will find the greatest yield from mammography because here the modality is *confirmatory.*" Here the mammogram will give confirmation and encouragement, "if the clinical impression is benign. It should not, however, dissuade him from a prior opinion to biopsy" (p. 855).

Category C: These patients have no signs or symptoms, there are no clinical indications for biopsy, and a mammogram can only increase the number of biopsies.

Thus, the author has outlined a plan that nullifies the value of mammographic information in selecting patients in whom a biopsy can be avoided. Only the added bit of information that implies biopsy is used. The information that might eliminate a biopsy is ignored.

Mammograms and biopsies: The potential. To appreciate how problems in probabilistic reasoning can affect the actual delivery of medical care, let us now examine the role that mammography might play in differential diagnosis and in the selection of patients for biopsy. As described above, the purpose of the test is to change the decision maker's subjective estimate of the chance that a patient has cancer. If that probability is high enough (as determined by the physician and patient), biopsy is recommended. Call this probability the *biopsy threshold*.[4] Now consider the impact of the test on the management of two groups of patients.

The first group consists of those patients who, on the basis of a history and physical examination, are thought by the clinician to have clinically obvious cancer. Using data published by Friedman et al. (1966), let the prior probability (the frequency) of cancer in this group be 90%. If a mammogram were performed on such a patient, a positive result would increase the probability of cancer [$P(\text{ca}\,|\,\text{pos})$] to perhaps 95%. A negative mammogram would still leave the patient with a 71% chance of having cancer. This high probability is the motivation of such statements as: "If the subjective impression of the clinician gives enough reason for suspicion of cancer, the clinician will be compelled to biopsy" (Clark et al. 1965, p. 133). A 71% chance of malignancy is still high enough that almost anyone would want to be biopsied.

Now consider a second group of patients who have a dominant mass that is not obviously carcinoma. In one study the probability that such a mass is malignant was 14% (Friedman et al., 1966). In the absence of further information, the clinical policy in such cases is to biopsy the lesion: "If a dominant lump develops, it should be removed and examined microscopically" (del Regato, 1970, p. 861). Using this as a guideline, let us suppose that the patient's biopsy threshold is 10%. That is, if, to the best of the physician's knowledge, the probability that his patient has cancer is above 10% then the patient and physician agree that a biopsy should be done.[5] Using a biopsy threshold of 10%, we can determine the

---

[4] Anyone needing to be convinced of the existence of a biopsy threshold can reason as follows. Can we agree that no one is willing to be biopsied if the chance of cancer is 1 in 30 trillion? And can we agree that virtually everyone wants to confirm the diagnosis and be treated if that chance is 98 in 100? If so, then somewhere between 1 in 30 trillion and 98 in 100 everyone has a biopsy threshold. Of course if a woman refuses biopsy and treatment even when the chance of cancer is certain, then she has no threshold.

[5] The biopsy threshold is a very fascinating and important number. Shifting it exerts great leverage on the number of women biopsied, the frequency of unproductive biopsies, the cost of managing a patient, as well as a patient's prognosis. Because of risk aversion and the fact that they are making the decision for someone else, physicians generally set the biopsy threshold quite low. The statement "if there is *any* chance that the lesion is malignant, a biopsy should be done" is typical. "If the physician is not completely satisfied that the lesion is benign, it should be biopsied without delay" (Allen, 1965, p. 640). There is evidence that women themselves generally set the threshold higher than do physicians – although there is wide variation.

For example, we can examine data from a large clinical trial in which mammography and a breast physical examination were used to screen asymptomatic women for breast cancer (Shapiro, Strax, & Venet, 1971). Depending on how the breast lesion was detected (i.e., by which test or combination of tests), the probability that a woman's breast disease was cancer

impact of a mammogram on the management of 1,000 such patients. Without the test, all patients would have to be biopsied, 860 of them unproductively. The approximate fate of the original 1,000 patients with a dominant lesion when mammography is used is presented in Figure 1.[6]

Patients with positive mammograms have a 53% chance of having cancer and, since we have assumed they have a biopsy threshold of 10% they should be biopsied. Because the probability is 34% that a patient with an uncertain mammogram has cancer, these patients should also be biopsied. Patients with a negative mammogram have a 4% chance of having cancer, and, since this is below their assumed biopsy threshold (10%), they would not want to be biopsied but would prefer to be followed closely. The total number of immediate biopsies has been reduced from 1,000 to 240. At least 30 more biopsies will have to be done eventually because 30 of the 760 remaining patients have cancer.

In this way, the expected benefits from having a mammogram (such as a reduction of the chance of an unnecessary biopsy from approximately 86% to a little over 13%) can be compared with the costs (e.g., a radiation hazard and about $75), and the slight decrease in expected survival (there is a 3%

varied from 15% to 54%. On the basis of a positive physical examination, physicians recommended that 545 women who had negative mammograms be biopsied. Despite the fact that the frequency of cancer in this group was 15%, 31% of the women declined the recommended biopsy. The frequency of cancer in women who had a positive mammogram and a negative breast physical examination was 20%, but 29% of the women in this group declined a recommended biopsy. In women who had positive results on both tests, the frequency of cancer was 54% and only 5% of these women preferred not to be biopsied at the recommended time. Thus, from this crude information it appears that about 31% of women had a biopsy threshold greater than 15%, 29% of women had a biopsy threshold greater than 20%, and in 5% of women the threshold exceeded 54%.

[6] To sketch the impact of mammography on these patients (and the patients with other signs and symptoms) much information is needed that is not directly available in the literature. It is fortunate that in one study (Friedman et al., 1966) the data on the frequency of cancer and the retrospective accuracy of mammography are presented separately for three groups of patients – those with obvious carcinoma, those with a dominant mass, and patients with other signs and/or symptoms of breast disease. The published data are incomplete, however, and the data on the frequency of an uncertain X-ray diagnosis in benign and malignant lesions are not included. The data available in the Friedman study were used, and for this example the following assumptions were made: (1) Lesions not biopsied were in fact benign, (2) lesions not biopsied were coded negative, (3) half of the benign lesions that were not coded negative were coded positive (the other half being coded uncertain), and (4) half of the malignant lesions that were not coded positive were coded negative. The first two assumptions are the most optimistic interpretation of mammography's accuracy. The third and fourth assumptions are very important and as the false-positive (or false-negative) rate tends toward zero, the power of a positive (negative) X-ray report to rule cancer in (out) increases. Likewise, as the false-positive or false-negative rates increase, the test loses its predictive power. Interpretation of Friedman's data is made even more difficult by its presentation in terms of breasts rather than patients. Nonetheless, there is much information in this report and it is reasonable to use it in this example provided the reader understands that this is an illustration, not a formal analysis. A formal analysis of these questions would require better data. The figures for the accuracy used in the text for the evaluation of the patients in group 2 are as follows: $P(\text{pos}|\text{ca}) = .52$, $P(\text{uncertain}|\text{ca}) = .24$, $P(\text{neg}|\text{ca}) = .24$, $P(\text{pos}|\text{benign}) = .075$, $P(\text{uncertain}|\text{benign}) = .075$, and $P(\text{neg}|\text{benign}) = .85$.

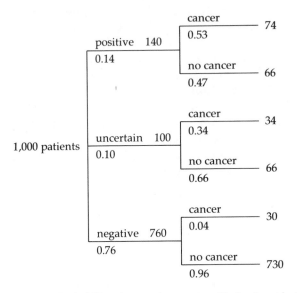

Figure 1. Probability of cancer in women with dominant lesions.

chance that diagnosis of a malignant lesion will be postponed a month or so). If the notion of a biopsy threshold and some simple probability theory were used, many patients in this group who had negative mammograms would be spared a biopsy. In the absence of this type of analysis "the surgical consensus here is that all patients [in this group] should have a biopsy, *regardless of mammographic findings*" (Friedman et al., 1966, p. 889).

The importance of the biopsy threshold in this example should be stressed. If the physician and his patient had set the threshold at 1% – that is, if the patient felt that a 1 in 100 chance of having cancer was sufficient to warrant a biopsy – then a negative mammogram report would not have eliminated the need for the biopsy (a 4% chance of cancer would exceed this threshold). The mammogram may have given the clinician some information but this information would not have contributed to the decision to biopsy. Use of mammography in this case would have to be justified on other grounds.

The practice revisited. This type of analysis helps make clear the potential usefulness of mammography in the differential diagnosis of various lesions. It also helps us evaluate the following policy statements:

1. "Mammography adds little to the management of the clinically [i.e., physically] palpable breast nodule that, on the basis of its own characteristics, requires biopsy" (from *Archives of Surgery*, 1974, vol. 108, p. 589). In the study of the patients with a dominant mass, biopsy was required on

clinical grounds alone. The use of mammography split the group into subgroups with frequencies of cancer ranging from 53% to 4%. Biopsy might be avoided in the latter group and the number of biopsies might be reduced 73% (from 1,000 per 1,000 to 270 per 1,000).

2. "For clinical purposes mammography must provide accuracy at approximately the 100 percent level before it alone can direct management" (from *Archives of Surgery*, 1974, vol. 108, p. 589). In a population like the second group discussed above, it might be quite rational to let mammography select patients for biopsy. Recall that the true-positive rate used in that example was 52% and that a more accurate test would be even more valuable.

3. "Mammography is not a substitute for biopsy" (from *Oncology*, 1969, vol. 23, p. 148). The purpose of both mammography and biopsy is to provide information about the state of the patient. Some patients, in the absence of mammography, require biopsy. In some of these patients a negative mammogram would obviate the biopsy, and in these cases the mammogram would replace the biopsy.

4. "Every decision to biopsy should be preceded by a mammogram" (from *Oncology*, 1969, vol. 23, p. 146). Consider clinically obvious carcinoma. The probability of cancer will be above almost anyone's biopsy threshold no matter what the outcome of the mammogram. The primary justification for this policy in such a case must lie in the chance that the clinically obvious is benign (otherwise the patient would have to have a mastectomy [breast removal] anyway) *and* that there is a hidden, non-palpable, malignant lesion. The probability of this compound event is the product of the probabilities of the two events, which is extremely small (on the order of 1 out of 5,000).

5. "To defer biopsy of a *clinically benign* lesion of the breast which has been called *benign on mammography* is to take a step backward in the eradication of carcinoma of the breast" (from *Surgery, Gynecology and Obstetrics*, 1972, vol. 134, p. 98). Let "clinically benign" be represented by a P(ca) of 5%. After a negative mammogram, the probability that such a patient has cancer is approximately 1%. Out of 100 biopsies, 99 would be unproductive. Is the deferral of biopsy here a step backward or forward? The other point is that if the policy were followed, all lesions from "clinically benign" through clinically obvious carcinoma would require a biopsy no matter what the outcome of the test was. This seems to contradict the author's statement that "when used in its proper perspective, mammography is an excellent adjunct to the physician in the management of carcinoma of the breast" (from *Surgery, Gynecology and Obstetrics*, 1972, vol. 134, p. 98).

6. "Mammography must never be used instead of biopsy when dealing with a 'dominant lesion' of the breast and should never change the basic surgical approach in breast diseases, i.e., a 'lump is a lump' and must be

biopsied either by incision or aspiration" (from *Archives of Surgery*, 1966, vol. 93, p. 854). Patients with dominant lesions and biopsy thresholds over 5% would disagree with this statement.

7. "The fallacy comes in relying on [mammography] in doubtful cases. It is essential after examining and palpating the breast to decide whether you would or would not do a biopsy if X-ray were not available. If you would do a biopsy, then do it. If you are sure there is no indication for surgery or physical examination, then order a mammogram. As soon as one says to himself, and particularly if he says to a patient, 'I am not quite sure about this – let's get an X-ray,' one unconsciously has committed himself to reliance on the negativity of the mammogram, when one should only rely on positivity. This is a psychological trap into which we all tend to fall and is much more serious than a certain number of false-positive diagnoses reached with mammography" (Rhoads, 1969, p. 1182). Not a single biopsy will be avoided by this policy. This is a shame because, as the author of the above statement himself puts it, "there are few areas in which so much surgery is necessitated which could be avoided by better methods of diagnosis than the breast."

We are now in a position to appreciate the following story that appeared in the San Francisco *Chronicle* (Kushner, 1976). A woman reporter had just discovered a mass in her breast and described a consultation with her physician.

"I'd like you to get a xeromammogram. It's a new way to make mammograms – pictures of the breasts."

"Is it accurate?"

He shrugged, "Probably about as accurate as any picture can be. You know," he warned, "even if the reading is negative – which means the lump isn't malignant – the only way to be certain is to cut the thing out and look at it under a microscope."

The woman then discussed the problem with her husband.

"What did the doctor say?"

"He wants to do a xeromammogram. Then, whatever the result is the lump will have to come out."

"So why get the X-ray taken in the first place?"

"It's something to go on, I guess. And our doctor says it's right about 85 percent of the time. . . . So, first I've scheduled an appointment to have a thermogram. If that's either positive or negative, and if it agrees with the Xerox pictures from the mammogram, the statistics say the diagnosis would be 95 percent reliable."

In summary, it would seem reasonable to ask that if the purpose of mammography is to help physicians distinguish benign from malignant breast disease, thereby sparing some patients a more extensive and traumatic procedure such as a biopsy, then we ought to let the test perform that function. If on the other hand the physician should always adhere to a prior biopsy decision and be unmoved by the mammogram outcome, then we ought not to claim that the purpose of the test is to help distinguish benign from malignant disease, since that distinction will be made definitively from a biopsy. Finally, if the purpose of the test is to search for hidden and clinically unsuspected cancer in a different area of the breast (away from a palpable mass that needs biopsy anyway), we ought to recognize explicity that the chances of such an event are extremely small and that the use of the test amounts to screening.

My purpose is not to argue for a specific mammography or biopsy policy – to do so would require better data and a better assessment of patient values. It is to suggest that we have not developed a formal way of reasoning probabilistically about this type of problem, that clinical judgment may be faulty, and that current clinical policies may be inconsistent or incorrect.

Discussion

These examples have been presented to illustrate the complexity of medical decision-making and to demonstrate how some physicians manage one aspect of this complexity – the manipulation of probabilities. The case we have studied is a relatively simple one, the use of a single diagnostic test to sort lesions into two groups, benign and malignant. The data base for this problem is relatively good. The accuracy and diagnostic value of the test has been studied and analyzed in many institutions for many years. As one investigator put it, "I know of no medical procedure that has been more tested and retested than mammography" (Egan, 1971, p. 1555).

The probabilistic tools discussed in this chapter have been available for centuries. In the last two decades they have been applied increasingly to medical problems (e.g., Lusted, 1968), and the use of systematic methods for managing uncertainty has been growing in medical school curricula, journal articles, and postgraduate education programs. At present, however, the application of these techniques has been sporadic and has not yet filtered down to affect the thinking of most practitioners. As illustrated in this case study, medical problems are complex, and the power of formal probabilistic reasoning provides great opportunities for improving the quality and effectiveness of medical care.

19. Learning from experience and suboptimal rules in decision making

Hillel J. Einhorn

Current work in decision-making research has clearly shifted from representing choice processes via normative models (and modifications thereof) to an emphasis on heuristic processes developed within the general framework of cognitive psychology and theories of information processing (Payne, 1980; Russo, 1977; Simon, 1978; Slovic, Fischhoff, & Lichtenstein, 1977; Tversky & Kahneman 1974, 1, 1980). The shift in emphasis from questions about how well people perform to how they perform is certainly important (e.g., Hogarth, 1975). However, the usefulness of studying both questions together is nowhere more evident than in the study of heuristic rules and strategies. The reason for this is that the comparison of heuristic and normative rules allows one to examine discrepancies between actual and optimal behavior, which then raises questions regarding why such discrepancies exist. In this chapter, I focus on how one learns both types of rules from experience. The concern with learning from experience raises a number of issues that have not been adequately addressed; for example, Under what conditions are heuristics learned? How are they tested and maintained in the face of experience? Under what conditions do we fail to learn about the biases and mistakes that can result from their use?

The importance of learning for understanding heuristics and choice behavior can be seen by considering the following:

1. The ability to predict when a particular rule will be employed is currently inadequate (Wallsten, 1980). However, concern for how and under what conditions a rule is learned should increase one's ability to

This is an abbreviated version of a paper that appeared in T. S. Wallsten (Ed.), *Cognitive Processes in Choice and Decision Behavior*. Hillsdale, N.J.: Lawrence Erlbaum Assoc., Inc., 1980. Reprinted by permission.

This research was supported by a grant from the Illinois Department of Mental Health and Developmental Disabilities, Research and Development No. 740–02. I would like to thank Robin Hogarth for his comments on an earlier version of this paper.

predict when it is likely to be used. For example, if a rule is learned in situations where there is little time to make a choice, prediction of the use of such a rule is enhanced by knowing the time pressure involved in the task.

2. A concomitant of (1) is that it should be possible to influence how people judge and decide by designing situations in which tasks incorporate or mimic initial learning conditions. The implications of this for both helping *and* manipulating people are enormous (Fischhoff, Slovic, & Lichtenstein, 1978; 1980).

3. Consideration of learning focuses attention on environmental variables and task structure. Therefore, variables such as amount of reinforcement, schedules of reinforcement, number of trials (= amount of experience), etc., should be considered in understanding judgment and decision behavior (cf. Estes, 1976). Although the importance of the task for understanding behavior has been continually stressed (Brunswik, 1943; Castellan, 1977; Cronbach, 1975; Dawes, 1975b; W. Edwards, 1971; Einhorn & Hogarth, 1978; Simon & Newell, 1971), psychologists seem as prone to what Ross (1977) calls the fundamental attribution error (underweighting environmental factors in attributing causes) as anyone else.

4. A major variable in understanding heuristics is outcome feedback. Since outcome feedback is the main source of information for evaluating the quality of our decision/judgment rules, knowledge of how task variables both affect outcomes and influence the way outcomes are coded and stored in memory becomes critical in explaining how heuristics are learned and used.

5. The area of learning is the focal point for considering the relative merits of psychological versus economic explanations of choice behavior. Some economists have argued that although one does not act "rationally" all the time, one will learn the optimal rule through interaction with the environment. Vague assertions about equilibrium, efficiency, and evolutionary concepts are advanced to bolster this argument. Therefore, study of how (and how well) people learn from experience is important in casting light on the relative merits of psychological and economic theories of choice.

Learning from experience: How?

It is obvious that decision making is action oriented; one has to choose what action to take in order to satisfy basic needs and wants. Therefore, it is important for any organism to learn the degree to which actions will lead to desirable or undesirable outcomes. This means that a great deal of learning from experience must involve the learning of action–outcome linkages. Furthermore, since actions and outcomes are contiguous, people are prone to see the links between them as representing cause-and-effect relationships (Michotte, 1963). Therefore, the strong tendency to see causal relations can be seen as an outgrowth of the need to take action to satisfy basic needs. Moreover, as pointed out by Kahneman and Tversky (1979b), the learning of causal relationships and the organizing of events into causal "schemata" allow people to achieve a coherent interpretation of their experience. Finally, the learning of action–outcome links is important for understanding how people learn their own tastes or utilities. For example, consider a child who chooses a particular vegetable to eat, experiences an unpleasant taste, and thereby learns to associate a negative utility with that food. Note that it is typically by choosing that consequences can be experienced and utility learned. Therefore, the learning of action–outcome links and the learning of utility are closely tied together.

Although we learn from experience by taking action, how does one initially learn which alternative to choose? Undoubtedly, much initial learning occurs by trial and error; that is, people randomly choose an option and observe the outcome (cf. Campbell, 1960). The process by which trial-and-error learning gives way to the development of strategies or rules is not well known (cf. Siegler, 1979). However, one can speculate that both reinforcement from trial-and-error learning and generalization (both stimulus and response) play an important role (Staddon & Simmelhag, 1971). In any event, the rules we develop seem directly tied to learning what outcomes will follow from particular actions. As described above, learning from experience is basically inductive in nature, that is, one experiences specific instances or cases and heuristics are developed to provide some general way to deal with them. The inductive nature of learning from experience has several implications regarding heuristics:

1. *Specificity of rules.* If learning occurs inductively via specific cases, then heuristic rules should be extremely context dependent. Much evidence now suggests that this is indeed the case (Grether & Plott, 1979; Lichtenstein & Slovic, 1971; Simon & Hayes, 1976; Tversky & Kahneman, 1980). The way in which a problem is worded or displayed or a particular response is asked for all seem to make an important difference in the way information is processed and responses generated. A dramatic example of this specificity can be seen in the work of Simon and Hayes (1976) on "problem isomorphs." They have shown that different surface wordings of structurally identical problems (i.e., problems that can be solved using identical principles) greatly change how people represent the problem in memory and consequently solve it. An important implication of this result is that in order to make heuristic models more predictive, one must contend with the task as represented and not necessarily with the task structure as seen by an experimenter. A particularly timely example of the importance of this phenomenon in predicting behavior is provided by observing that behavior depends on whether a tax cut is represented as a gain or a smaller loss (Kahneman & Tversky, 1979b).

2. *Generality of rules.* If heuristics are rules learned through induction, it

is necessary to group tasks by similarity or else there would be as many rules as situations. Since this latter possibility is unacceptable, heuristics must have some generality over tasks. However, this conclusion contradicts what was said above about context dependence and specificity of rules. This paradox can be resolved if one considers the range of tasks to which a rule can be applied. For example, consider the rule "Never order fish in a meat restaurant." While such a rule is general with respect to a certain type of restaurant, it is certainly more specific than the rule "Judge the probability with which event B comes from process A by their degree of similarity" (Tversky & Kahneman, 1974, 1). The latter heuristic is clearly at a much higher level of generality. In fact, it may be that heuristics like representativeness, availability, anchoring, and adjusting are "metaheuristics," that is, they are rules on how to generate rules. Therefore, when confronted by problems that one has not encountered before (like judging probabilities of events), or problems whose specificity makes them seem novel, metaheuristics direct the way in which specific rules can be formed to solve the problem. The idea of a metaheuristic allows one to retain the generality that any rule necessarily implies, yet at the same time allows for the important effects of context, wording, response mode, and so on. In order to illustrate, consider the study by Slovic, Fischhoff, and Lichtenstein (1976; see also Chapter 33) in which people were asked to judge the relative probabilities of death from unusual causes. For example, which has a higher probability: being killed by lightening or dying from emphysema? When confronted with such a question, there are many ways to attempt an answer. One rule that could be used would be: "Think of all the people I know that have died from the two causes and pick the event which caused more deaths." In my own case, I would choose emphysema (which does have a higher probability, although most people pick being killed by lightning). However, I could have just as easily developed a rule that would lead to the opposite answer; for example, "Think of all of the cases of being killed by lightning and of death from emphysema that I have ever *heard about* (newspapers, television, etc.)." If this were my rule, I would choose being killed by lightning as being more probable. Note that in both cases I have used an availability heuristic. Clearly, the way in which a question is phrased could induce specific rules that lead to different results, yet these specific rules could be classified under a single, more general strategy, or metaheuristic (also see, Einhorn, Kleinmuntz, & Kleinmuntz, 1979).

   3. *Strength of heuristics.* If heuristics are learned inductively, then learning occurs over many trials with many reinforcements. As will be discussed, because of the way feedback occurs and because of the methods that we use to test rules via experience, positive reinforcement can occur even for incorrect rules (Wason, 1960). Moreover, in addition to the large number of reinforcements that we experience, the size or intensity of reinforcement can be large. For example, gaining a sizable amount of

money following the use of some rule for picking stocks should have a considerable reinforcement effect. Therefore, unlike laboratory studies of human learning, where ethical considerations prevent large positive and negative reinforcements, our own experience poses no such constraints.

Learning from experience: How well?

The question of how well we learn from experience focuses attention on comparing heuristic rules with optimal rules. Therefore, it must be asked how the latter are learned and what the implications are for applying them in our own experience? Optimal rules, such as Bayes' theorem, optimization, etc., are learned *deductively*. In fact, much of what can be called formal learning is of a deductive character, that is, we are taught scientific laws, logical principles, mathematical and statistical rules, etc. Such rules are by their very nature abstract and context independent. Furthermore, when context can influence the form of a rule, one is frequently told that the rule holds, "other things being equal." Of course, in our own experience other things are rarely equal, which makes the learning of optimal rules via induction so difficult. (The original discoverers or inventors of optimal rules overcame these difficulties; however, this distinguishes them from the rest of us.)

The abstract nature of deductive rules has important implications regarding the difficulty people have of applying optimal methods in specific situations. This difficulty centers around the ability to discern the structure of tasks that are embedded in a rich variety of detail. Therefore, when one is faced with a specific problem that is rich in detail and in which details may be irrelevant or redundant, one's attention to specifics is likely to divert attention from the general structure of the problem. In fact, the very abstractness of deductively learned optimal rules may prevent them from being retrieved from memory (cf. Nisbett et al. 1976, chap ref. 7). Abstract rules, therefore, may not be very "available" in specific cases. However, this begs the question since it is important to know *why* these rules are not available.

Consider the way action–outcome combinations are likely to be organized and stored in memory. In particular, consider whether such information is more likely to be organized and stored by content or task structure. It would seem easier and more "natural" to organize action–outcome combinations by subject matter rather than by structure; for example, experiences with schools, parents, members of the opposite sex, etc., rather than Bayesian problems, selection situations, optimization problems, and so on. The fact that content can differ while structure remains the same is quite difficult to see (Einhorn et al., 1979; Kahneman & Tversky, 1979b; Simon & Hayes, 1976). Therefore, I think it unlikely that most people organize their experiences by task structure. This is not to say that one could not be trained to do so. In fact, much of professional training is exactly this; for example, one is taught to recognize problems as belonging to a class of problems having a given structure and (sometimes) known solution. Optimal rules can thus be "available" through extensive training. Of course, there is the danger of such rules being *too* readily available; that is, problems are forced into a structure that is not appropriate because a solution within that structure exists. It is a truism that when presented with a problem, professionals view the problem within the structures they have been trained to see. Therefore, although professional training does involve a concern for structure, such training is generally within a narrowly defined content area.

Further evidence illustrating the need to group problems by content rather than structure is provided by considering the way public knowledge about the world is organized and taught. For example, departmentalized education, professional training, cataloging of information in libraries and encyclopedias, and so on, illustrate the organizing of information by content rather than structure. While there are great advantages in organizing knowledge in this way, there are also costs. The difficulty of applying optimal rules developed in one content area to structurally similar problems in other content areas may be one such cost. However, at the level of the individual learner other difficulties are now considered which may be even more costly.

Although task structure is difficult to discern, outcomes are not; they are highly visible, available, and often unambiguous. Consideration of reinforcement via outcome feedback is essential in understanding how heuristics are maintained in the face of experience. Furthermore, if outcomes are a function of task structure to a considerable degree and the decision maker's knowledge of such structure is lacking, then rules that are irrelevant or even poor may still be reinforced by positive outcome feedback. (E.g., "superstitious" behavior in animal learning; see Staddon & Simmelhag, 1971.)

Two examples are now presented where normatively poor heuristics can lead to good outcomes and where awareness of the poor quality of the rule may be lacking. Consider shopping in the supermarket and coming to cans of juice with the following prices and overall quality (adapted from Tversky, 1969):

Brand	Price	Quality
X	60¢	High
Y	55¢	Medium
Z	50¢	Low

Assume that I use the following rule to choose among the three brands: If the price difference is five cents or less, choose the brand with the higher quality; if the price difference is greater than five cents, choose according to price. Such a simple rule (which is a lexicographic semiorder) leads to: $X > Y$, $Y > Z$, but $Z > X$. Therefore, this rule leads to intransitive choices, which are clearly irrational. However, note that after I choose X over Y, I may then eliminate Y from the remaining set and compare X with Z. Therefore, I end up with Z, which may be quite acceptable after I taste it. I then congratulate myself on what a good shopper I am – I saved money and I got a reasonable product. The important point to note here is that by not making the Y versus Z comparison, I remain unaware that my rule leads to an intransitive choice. All I *am* aware of is that I made a choice with minimal fuss and strain, and the outcome was satisfactory. Positive outcome feedback thus reinforces a normatively poor rule, and awareness that something is wrong is missing.

The second example is a probabilistic one (cf. Schum, 1980). Imagine that you are a military general in a politically tense area and you are concerned that your enemies will invade your country. Furthermore, from past experience it is known that when enemy troops mass at the border, the probability of invasion is .75. However, you don't have direct access to information about enemy troops but must rely on a report of such activity by your intelligence sources. As it turns out, every time your intelligence sources report that troops are massing, they are really there. Consider that you now receive a report from your sources that enemy troops are at the border. What is the probability of invasion? More formally, let

H = hypothesis of being invaded
D = troops massing at the border
D^* = report of troops massing at the border

The problem states that $p(H|D) = .75$ and $p(D|D^*) = 1.0$ and asks you for $p(H|D^*)$. If you are like most people, you probably answered .75. However, the information given is not sufficient to answer the question in the normatively correct way. In fact, it is possible that in the above problem $p(H|D^*) = 0$! Since most people find this very difficult to believe, consider Figure 1, which illustrates the problem by means of a Venn diagram. Note that the intersection of H with D^* is null, so that the conditional probability, $p(H|D^*)$, is zero. The reason that people find this result so surprising is that they have made a logical fallacy of the form: if $D^* \Rightarrow D$, then $D \Rightarrow D^*$. Although D occurs whenever D^* is given, the reverse is not necessarily the case. In fact, an intuitive way to see the issue is to think that the enemy is particularly cunning so that your intelligence sources see their troops only when there is no invasion planned. However, when an invasion is planned and troops are at a border, they are hidden so that your sources do not report them.

This example illustrates the difficulty of applying optimal rules (in this case the rules of formal logic) to a specific task. While very few people would make the logical error when it is presented in a recognizable form, the importance of the example lies in showing how the specifics of the problem hide its real structure so that optimal rules are easily violated (cf. Tversky & Kahneman, 1980). A second point can be made with respect to

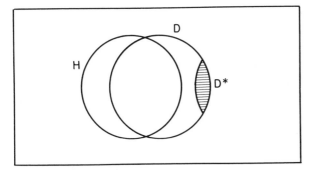

Figure 1. Venn diagram showing the relationship between the hypothesis (H), datum (D), and report of datum (D^*).

this example. Consider that the general makes the logical error and estimates the chance of war at .75. He then sends *his* troops to the border thereby causing an invasion by the enemy. Therefore, the faulty reasoning of the general is reinforced by outcome feedback: "After all," he might say, "those SOB's did invade us, which is what we thought they'd do."

The two examples illustrate the basic point of this chapter: Without knowledge of task structure, outcome feedback can be irrelevant or even harmful for correcting poor heuristics. Moreover, positive outcome feedback without task knowledge tends to keep us unaware that our rules are poor, since there is very little motivation to question how successes were achieved. The conditions under which outcome feedback does not play a correcting role vis-à-vis heuristics and strategies are denoted outcome-irrelevant learning structures (OILS). Such structures may be much more common than we think. Before examining one such structure in detail, consider probabilistic judgments within the framework of OILS, since much of the work on heuristics is directly concerned with this type of judgment. Consider that you judge the probability of some event to be .70. Let us say that the event doesn't happen. What does this outcome tell you about the quality of the rules used to generate the judgment? One might argue that any *single* outcome is irrelevant in assessing the "goodness" (i.e., degree of calibration) of probabilistic judgments. Therefore, in an important sense, immediate outcome information is irrelevant for correcting poor heuristics. It is only if one keeps a "box score" of the relative frequency of outcomes when one judges events with a given probability that one can get useful feedback from outcomes. However, this is likely to be a necessary but not sufficient condition for making well-calibrated judgments. First, over what time period does one keep the box score before deciding that the judgment is or isn't calibrated? Furthermore, how close is "close enough" in order to say that the judgment is accurate (in the sense of being well calibrated)? Note that this whole mode of evaluating outcomes involves reinforcement that is delayed for long time periods.

Thus it is not clear that such feedback will have much of a self-correcting effect. Second, in order to learn about the goodness of rules for estimating probability, one's box score must include not only one's estimates and the resulting outcomes but also one's rules for deriving those estimates. For example, if I kept a record of outcomes for 100 cases in which I gave estimates of .7, what would the information that 53 of those times the event happened tell me about the quality of the rules I used? Since it is likely that many different rules could have been used to estimate probabilities in the 100 different situations, the outcome information is irrelevant and outcome feedback is not useful unless one is aware of one's rules and a record is kept of their use (cf. Nisbett & Wilson, 1977, on whether we are aware of our own cognitive processes).

I do not mean to imply that it is impossible to learn to make well-calibrated probability judgments. If one makes *many* probability judgments in the *same situation*, such as weather forecasters and horse-racing handicappers do, and outcome feedback is quickly received, such conditions may not be outcome irrelevant, and feedback can be self-correcting. However, such conditions would seem to be the exception rather than the rule for most of us.

Although probabilistic judgments typically occur in OILS, what about non-probabilistic judgments? Surely, if one makes a prediction about something one can check to see if the prediction is correct or not. Therefore, it would seem that outcomes should be relevant for providing self-correcting feedback. The remainder of this chapter discusses this issue within the context of one general and prevalent task structure, although the specific content of such tasks may be quite different.

Selection task[1]

A very general task involving non-probabilistic judgments is now examined, since outcome information seems both available and relevant for providing self-correcting feedback. The task to be considered is one in which judgments are made for the purpose of choosing between alternative actions. For example, consider a situation with two possible actions, A and B. Denote by x an overall, evaluative judgment, which may itself be a function of various types and amounts of information. Furthermore, let x_c be a cutoff point such that

$$\begin{aligned} &\text{if } x \geq x_c, \text{ take action } A; \\ &\text{if } x < x_c, \text{ take action } B \end{aligned} \qquad (1)$$

Although simplistic, Equation 1 applies to many judgment/decision situations, for example: job hiring, promotion, admission to school, loan and credit granting, assignment to remedial programs, admission to social programs, journal article acceptance, grant awarding, etc. In these cases, a

---

[1] Much of this section is drawn from Einhorn and Hogarth (1978).

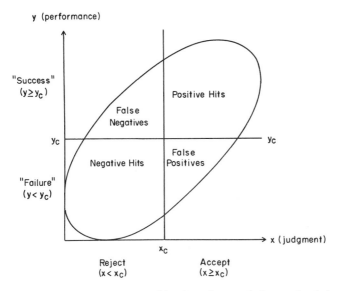

Figure 2. Action–outcome combinations that result from using judgment to make an accept–reject decision.

judgment of the degree of "deservedness" typically determines which action is to be taken, since the preferred action cannot be given to all.

In order to compare judgment with a standard, the existence of a criterion, denoted y, is assumed to serve as the basis for evaluating the accuracy of judgment. While the practical difficulties of finding and developing adequate criteria are enormous, the focus here is theoretical: The concept of a criterion is what is necessary for this analysis. To be consistent with the formulation of judgment, it is further assumed that the criterion has a cutoff point (y_c) such that $y \geq y_c$ and $y < y_c$ serve as the basis for evaluating the outcomes of judgment. Thus, as far as learning about judgment is concerned, representation of outcomes in memory is often of categorical form, that is, successes and failures (cf. Estes, 1976).

It is very important to note that the structure of the task is one in which judgments (predictions) lead to differential actions and that outcomes are then used as feedback for determining the accuracy of the predictions. The formal structure can be seen by considering the regression of y on x and the four quadrants that result from the intersection of x_c and y_c as illustrated in Figure 2. Denote the correct predictions as positive and negative hits and the two types of errors as false positives ($y < y_c | x \geq x_c$) and false negatives ($y \geq y_c | x < x_c$). To estimate the relationship between x and y (i.e., the correlation between x and y, ρ_{xy}) it is necessary to have information on *each* judgment–outcome combination. Assume first that such information becomes available over time (i.e., sequentially), and consider the experimental evidence concerned with learning the relationship between x and y in such circumstances. Research on the ability to judge the contingency between x and y from information in 2×2 tables (Jenkins & Ward, 1965; Smedslund, 1963; 1966; Ward & Jenkins, 1965) indicates that people judge the strength of relationships by the frequency of positive hits (in the terminology of Figure 2), while generally ignoring information in the three other cells. These results are extremely important, since they say that *even when* all of the relevant outcome information is available, people don't use it. This means that in laboratory studies that have outcome-relevant learning structures, people have transformed them into outcome-irrelevant learning structures. How can this be explained?

The explanation advanced here is that our experience in real-world tasks is such that we develop rules and methods that seem to "work" reasonably well. However, these rules may be quite poor and our awareness of their inadequacy is profound. This lack of awareness exists because positive outcome feedback can occur in spite of, rather than because of, our predictive ability. In order to illustrate, consider the study by Wason (1960) in which he presented subjects with a three-number sequence, for example: 2, 4, 6. Subjects were required to discover the rule to which the three numbers conformed (the rule being three ascending numbers). To discover the rule, they were permitted to generate sets of three numbers which the experimenter classified as conforming or not conforming to the rule. At any point, subjects could stop when they thought they had discovered the rule. The correct solution to this task should involve a search for disconfirming evidence rather than the accumulation of confirming evidence. For example, if someone believed that the rule had something to do with even numbers, this could only be tested by trying a sequence involving an odd number (i.e., accumulating vast amounts of confirming instances of even-number sequences would not lead to the rule). The fact that only 6 of 29 subjects found the correct rule the first time they thought they did, illustrates the dangers of induction by simple enumeration. As Wason (1960) points out, the solution to this task must involve "a willingness to attempt to falsify hypotheses, and thus to *test those intuitive ideas which so often carry the feeling of certitude*" (p. 139, italics added).

It is important to emphasize that in Wason's experiment, where actions were *not* involved, a search for disconfirming evidence is possible. However, when actions are based on judgment, learning based on disconfirming evidence becomes more difficult to achieve. Consider how one might erroneously learn an incorrect rule for making judgments and focus on the hypothetical case of a manager learning about his predictive ability concerning the "potential" of job candidates. The crucial factor here is that actions (e.g., accept/do not accept) are contingent on judgment. At a subsequent date the manager can only examine *accepted* candidates to see how many are "successful." If there are many successes, which is likely, these instances all confirm the rule. Indeed, the important point here is that it would be difficult to disconfirm the rule, even though it might be erroneous. One way in which the rule could be tested would be for the manager to accept a subset of those he judged to have low potential and then to observe their success rate. If their rate was as high as those judged to be of high potential, the rule would be disconfirmed. However, a systematic search for disconfirming evidence is rare and could be objected to on utilitarian and even ethical grounds, that is, one would have to withhold the preferred action from some of those judged most deserving and give it some judged least deserving. Therefore, utilitarian and/or ethical considerations may prevent one from even considering the collection of possibly disconfirming information. Note that the tendency not to test hypotheses by disconfirming instances is a direct consequence of the task structure in which actions are taken on the basis of judgment. Wason (1960) points out, "In real life there is no authority to pronounce judgment on inferences: the inferences can only be checked against the evidence" (p. 139). As a result, large amounts of positive feedback can lead to reinforcement of a non-valid rule.

Although outcomes contingent on the action-not-taken may not be sought, it is still the case that one can examine the number of positive hits and false positives as a way to check on the accuracy of one's predictions. Therefore, while such information is incomplete for accurately assessing the relationship between predictions and outcomes, such information is what most people have available. It is therefore important to consider the factors that affect these variables.

Factors affecting positive hits and false positives

Consider Figure 2 again and note that there are three factors that affect the rates of positive hits and false positives; the location of x_c, y_c, and the "tilt" of the ellipse (which is the correlation between x and y). For example, if x_c is moved to the right, holding y_c and ρ_{xy} constant, there is a point at which there will be no false positives. Of course, there will be a corresponding increase in false negatives. However, if one doesn't have information about these cases (as is generally the situation), one's experience of success can be quite convincing that judgmental quality is high. Therefore, when the criterion for giving the preferred action is raised (increasing x_c), the probability, $p(x \geq x_c)$ (also called the selection ratio, ϕ), is decreased and this leads to high positive hit and low false-positive rates. The second factor, y_c, obviously affects outcomes, since the level of y_c defines success and failure. Note that when y_c is lowered, the probability, $p(y \geq y_c)$ (also called the base rate, br), is raised and one's experience of successes may be high irrespective of judgmental ability; that is, if one *randomly* assigned people to the various actions, one would experience a success rate equal to $p(y \geq y_c)$. Therefore, to judge one's predictive ability, the comparison of the positive hit rate with $p(y \geq y_c)$ should be made and judgmental ability assessed on the marginal increase in successes. The third factor, ρ_{xy}, affects outcomes in a straightforward manner; namely, the larger ρ_{xy}, the greater the positive hit rate.

The effects of these three factors on the positive hit rate are well known. Taylor and Russell (1939), for example, have shown that one can increase the positive hit rate, for any given ρ_{xy} and base rate, by reducing the selection ratio (ϕ), that is, by giving the preferred action to a smaller percentage (assuming $\rho_{xy} \neq 0$). Thus, even if ρ_{xy} is low, it is possible to have a high positive hit rate depending on the values of ϕ and br. Taylor and Russell (1939) provide tables of positive hit rates for a wide range of values of ρ_{xy}, ϕ, and br. Examination of these tables shows that low correlations between judgments and criteria are not incompatible with large positive hit rates.

In addition to the three factors already mentioned, a fourth factor must be considered. This can be illustrated by imagining the following experiment. Assume that a series of judgments is made about some persons. Of those judged to be above x_c, *randomly* assign half to action A and half to action B. Similarly do the same for those judged below x_c. At some later point in time, measure performance and calculate the proportion of persons with $y \geq y_c$ in each cell (each person is assigned a 0 or 1 to indicate whether he or she is below or above the cutoff on y – the proportion above y_c being simply the mean of that cell). This is a 2×2 factorial design with one factor being "judgment" and the other "type of action." Note that because the criterion cannot be measured immediately before the decision (indeed, if it could, there would be no need for judgment), people receiving actions A and B have also received different experimental treatments. If this experiment were done, one could test for the main effect of judgment (which measures its accuracy); the main effect for the action, that is, whether receiving A or B in itself causes differences in performance; and the interaction between judgment and action. Observe that the advantage of the experiment is that it allows one to untangle the accuracy of judgment from the treatment effects of the action. However, such an experiment is rarely done, even conceptually, and especially not by people without extensive training in experimental design. Therefore, judgmental accuracy will almost always be confounded with possible treatment effects due to actions. Furthermore, and with reference to the earlier discussion, this experiment allows one to examine disconfirming information. In contrast to most real judgmental tasks, therefore, it would permit one to disconfirm the hypothesis of judgmental accuracy *as well as* to estimate any treatment effects due to the action.

An example of treatment effects is shown in Figure 3. The dotted ellipse is that shown in Figure 2 and represents the "true" relationship between judgements and outcomes. The shaded portion indicates those outcomes

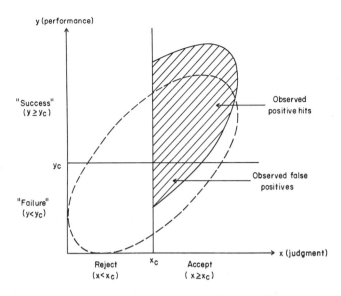

Figure 3. Effect of treatment on the observed positive hit rate.

that can be observed; hence only values for which $x \geq x_c$ are shown. The treatment effect occurs in that the outcomes (i.e., performance) of all those given action A are increased by a constant amount so that the number of positive hits is greater than would have been observed in the absence of treatment effects. From a psychological viewpoint, the key aspect of Figure 3 is that the nature of feedback to the judge is contaminated; the number of positive hits is inflated, and the number of false positives is reduced.

In order to quantify the effects of the four factors discussed above on the positive hit rate, Einhorn and Hogarth (1978) performed a simulation experiment in which various levels of treatment effects, selection ratios, base rates, and predictive abilities were varied in a factorial design. The dependent variable was the positive hit rate. The results of that simulation can be summarized as follows: (a) In general, the positive hit rate is greater than .50. When treatment effects exist, the positive hit rate can be high even when $\rho_{xy} = 0$; (b) when $\phi < br$, positive hit rates are particularly high. Furthermore, the positive hit rate is sensitive to treatment effects at low values of ρ_{xy}. This means that in highly selective situations, poor predictive ability is most likely to be reinforced by positive outcome feedback; (c) When $\phi > br$, positive hit rates are lowest. However, small treatment effects have a substantial impact on raising positive hit rates in these situations.

The simulation results demonstrate that positive feedback can exist when predictive ability is poor and that awareness of this is usually very low because of the failure to adequately understand the task structure. Therefore, although one might suppose that non-probabilistic judgments are made in an outcome-relevant learning structure, when judgments are made for the purpose of deciding between actions, outcome information may be irrelevant for providing self-correcting feedback.

Conclusion[2]

The basic theme of this chapter has been that outcome information, without knowledge of task structure, can be irrelevant for providing self-correcting feedback about poor heuristics. It has also been argued that knowledge of task structure is difficult to achieve because of the inductive way in which we learn from experience (cf. Hammond, 1978, on Galilean vs. Aristotelian modes of thought). These conclusions raise two issues that will be briefly discussed.

It may be the case that even with knowledge of task structure, one chooses to act in such a way that learning is precluded. For example, consider a waiter in a busy restaurant. Because he doesn't have time to give good service to all the customers at his station, he makes a prediction about which customers are likely to leave good or poor tips. Good or bad service is then given depending on the prediction. If the quality of service has a treatment effect on the size of the tip, the outcomes "confirm" the original predictions. Note that the waiter could perform an experiment to disentangle the treatment effects of quality of service from his predictions if he was aware of the task structure; that is, he could give poor service to some of those he judged to leave good tips and good service to some of those judged to leave poor tips. However, note that the waiter must be willing to risk the possible loss of income if his judgment is accurate, against learning that his judgment is poor. The latter information may have long-run benefits in that it could motivate the person to try to make better predictions or, if this is not possible, to use a strategy of giving good or poor service randomly, thus saving much mental effort. In organizational decisions, the long-run benefits from knowing about the accuracy of one's predictions could be substantial. For example, if selection interviews do not predict performance (independent of treatment effects), why spend money and time using them? Therefore, the costs and benefits of short-run strategies for action versus long-run strategies for learning need to be more fully investigated.

The second issue can be raised by stating the following question: If people learn and continue to use poor rules, does this not contradict the evolutionary concept of survival of the fittest? I take this question to mean that those who use bad rules should be less likely to survive than those who use better rules (they are more fit). However, the use of better rules

---

[2] I would like to thank J. E. R. Staddon for raising the points discussed in this section.

can still be quite removed from the use of optimal rules. The concept of most "fit" involves a relative ordering while optimality implies some absolute level. Therefore, the fact that suboptimal rules are maintained in the face of experience is not contradicted by Darwinian theory. Perhaps the most succinct way of putting this is to quote Erasmus: "In the land of the blind, the one-eyed man is king."[3]

---

[3] The intent of this quotation is to point out that *relative* advantages vis-à-vis one's environment are important. No slur is meant or intended toward blind people. Tom Wallsten has made the following comment, "In the land of the blind, the one-eyed man could only survive by closing his eye, since the environment would be arranged to rely on other senses." Although this is a fascinating comment, I disagree, because the one-eyed man would still have all of his other senses in addition to the seeing advantage.

Part VI
Overconfidence

20. Overconfidence in case-study judgments

Stuart Oskamp

It is a common phenomenon of clinical practice that as a psychologist accumulates case-study material about another human being, he comes to think that he knows that person pretty well. Consequently, sooner or later in the information-gathering process, the psychologist becomes confident enough to make diagnostic conclusions, describe the client's main dynamics, and perhaps even venture to predict his future behavior. Though the psychologist's conclusions may remain tentative, his increase in confidence from the time of first approaching the case to the time of writing his report is usually very marked.

This study investigated whether that increase in confidence is justified by a corresponding increase in accuracy of conclusions. Though the psychologist's confidence in his conclusions has often been mentioned as an important subject of scientific inquiry (Meehl, 1957), it has only rarely been studied intensively. Furthermore, when it has been studied, rather surprising findings have often resulted. For instance, L. R. Goldberg (1959) and Oskamp (1962) have shown that the diagnostic confidence of experienced psychologists is *less* than that of less experienced persons. The same studies and many others have also shown that professional psychologists are no better interpersonal judges, and sometimes are worse ones, than are untrained individuals (Taft, 1955).

Another rarely studied factor, which may provide a good index of the expertness of a judge, is the relationship between his level of confidence and his level of accuracy. This measure shows, for instance, whether the judge is overconfident or underconfident in making his decisions. On this measure, which may be termed appropriateness of confidence, experi-

This chapter originally appeared in *The Journal of Consulting Psychology*, 1965, 29, 261–265.

enced judges have been found to be far superior to inexperienced ones (Oskamp, 1962).

A number of studies (Hamlin, 1954; Hathaway, 1956; Kostlan, 1954; Soskin, 1954; Winch & More, 1956) have investigated the effects on clinical judgment of differing amounts of stimulus information. In the present experiment this factor was studied by giving each judge four sets of cumulatively increasing amounts of information as the basis for making his decisions, thus simulating the gradual buildup of information as a psychologist works his way through a typical case.

The hypotheses of the study were as follows:

1. Beyond some early point in the information-gathering process, predictive accuracy reaches a ceiling.

2. Nevertheless, confidence in one's decisions continues to climb steadily as more information is obtained.

3. Thus, toward the end of the information-gathering process, most judges are overconfident about their judgments.

Procedure

Since it was desired to simulate the usual clinical situation as closely as possible, an actual case study was chosen as the information to be given to the judges. The case finally chosen was selected because of its extensiveness, its description of many pertinent life incidents, and the fact that it involved a relatively normal individual (i.e. a case of adolescent maladjustment who had never been psychiatrically hospitalized). It was the case of Joseph Kidd, reported by White (1952) in his book, *Lives in Progress*.[1]

Historical background material from this case was summarized and organized into chronological sets of information which were presented to the judges in four successive stages. Stage 1 contained only the following brief demographic information about the case, in order to test for the "psychological chance" level of predictive accuracy (Patterson, 1955):

> Joseph Kidd (a pseudonym) is a 29 year old man. He is white, unmarried, and a veteran of World War II. He is a college graduate, and works as a business assistant in a floral decorating studio.

Stage 2 added 1½ single-spaced typed pages of material about Kidd's childhood, through age 12. Stage 3 (2 pages) covered his high school and college years, and Stage 4 (1⅓ pages) covered his army service and later activities up to age 29.

Case-study test

In order to have a basis for determining the accuracy of the judges, a multiple-choice case-study test was constructed, using a method similar to that of Soskin

[1] Use of this case had the disadvantage that a few judges remembered reading this material at some time during their training, but all but one reported that their earlier contact did not help them at all in the present study. Since their accuracy scores corroborated this impression, their results were retained in the data analysis.

Table 1. *Sample items from the case-study test*

---

5. During college, when Kidd was in a familiar and congenial social situation, he often:
   a. Tried to direct the group and impose his wishes on it.
   b. Stayed aloof and withdrawn from the group.
   c. Was quite unconcerned about how people reacted to him.
   d. Took an active part in the group but in a quiet and modest way.
   e. Acted the clown and showed off.[a]

10. Later during his Army service, as an officer and detachment commander, Kidd's attitude toward handing out punishment was:
    a. He was very disturbed by it because he preferred to be on the same level as other men, not over them.[a]
    b. He disliked it because he could never make a decision as to what to do.
    c. He avoided it as completely as possible because he felt that it was wrong to punish men no matter what they had done.
    d. He was happy because it gave him a chance to be in control of a situation and to be looked up to.
    e. He took a sadistic delight in disciplining others to make up for the times he had been punished.

15. Kidd's present attitude toward his mother is one of:
    a. Love and respect for her ideals.
    b. Affectionate tolerance for her foibles.
    c. Combined respect and resentment.[a]
    d. Rejection of her and all her beliefs.
    e. Dutiful but perfunctory affection.

20. In conversations with men, Kidd:
    a. Prefers to get them to talk about their work or experiences.[a]
    b. Likes to do most of the talking about subjects with which he is familiar.
    c. Prefers to debate with them about religion or their philosophy of life.
    d. Likes to brag about his Army days or college exploits.
    e. Confines his discussion mainly to sports, sex, and dirty jokes.

25. Kidd's attitude toward his life as a business assistant is shown by his recent decision to:
    a. Stay in his present position for at least a few more years.
    b. Expand the business by building another shop in a nearby town.
    c. Leave his job and open up his own flower shop.
    d. Make job applications to several larger companies in fields similar to his present line of work.
    e. Strike out on his own and find a different kind of job.[a]

---

[a] Correct answer.

(1954). Items dealt with Kidd's customary behavior patterns, attitudes, interests, and typical reactions to actual life events. Examples of some of these items are given in Table 1.

Items were constructed only where there was fairly objective criterion information presented in the case, either factual data or well-documented conclusions. The four incorrect alternatives for each item were made up with the help of sentence-completion responses to the item stems by psychology graduate students. They were constructed in such a way as to be clearly wrong, based on the published case material, but to be otherwise convincing and "seductive" alternatives. None of the items had its answer contained in the summarized case material; instead, judges were expected to follow the usual procedure in clinical judgment (C. McArthur, 1954) by forming a personality picture of Kidd from the material presented and then predicting his attitudes and typical actions from their personality picture of him.

Judges

Judges were drawn from three groups with varying amounts of psychological experience: (a) 8 clinical psychologists employed by a California state hospital, all of whom had several years of clinical experience, and 5 of whom had doctor's degrees;[2] (b) 18 psychology graduate students;[3] and (c) 6 advanced undergraduate students in a class in personality. None of the judges was in any way familiar with the hypotheses of the study.

Judges took part in the experiment in small groups ranging from four to nine in size, but each worked at his own individual pace with his own sheaf of materials. After reading each stage of the case, the judge answered all 25 questions of the case-study test before going on to read the next stage. In addition to answering the questions, the judge also indicated on each item how confident he was that his answer was correct.

Confidence judgments

The confidence judgments were made using a scale devised by Adams (1957) which defines confidence in terms of expected percentage of correct decisions. Since there were five alternatives for each test item, the scale began at 20% (representing a completely chance level of confidence) and extended to 100% (indicating absolute certainty of correctness). In addition to providing a clearly understood objective meaning for confidence, this scale has the great advantage of allowing a direct comparison between the level of accuracy and the level of confidence. Thus, for example, if a judge got 28% of the items correct and had an average confidence level of 43%, he could clearly be said to be overconfident.

Results

This judgment task proved to be a very difficult one, at least with the amount of case material provided. No judge ever reached 50% accuracy,

---

[2] One additional clinical psychologist was tested, but results had to be discarded due to failure to understand and follow the instructions. This problem did not occur with any of the students.

[3] About half of these graduate students had had some clinical or counseling experience, and one or two may possibly have been equivalent to the clinical psychologists in level of psychological experience.

Table 2. *Performance of 32 judges on the 25-item case-study test*

Measure	M score				F	p
	Stage 1	Stage 2	Stage 3	Stage 4		
Accuracy (%)	26.0	23.0	28.4	27.8	5.02	.01
Confidence (%)	33.2	39.2	46.0	52.8	36.06	.001
Number of changed answers	—	13.2	11.4	8.1	21.56	.001

and the average final accuracy was less than 28%, where chance was 20% (a nonsignificant difference). However, this low level of accuracy serves to provide an even more dramatic test of the hypotheses of the study.

A preliminary analysis was carried out to compare the scores of the three groups of judges, though no hypotheses had been formulated about their relative performance. These results clearly indicated that there were no significant differences among the three groups of judges either in accuracy, in confidence, or in total number of changed answers. The Stage 4 confidence scores were consistent with previous studies (Goldberg, 1959; Oskamp, 1962) in showing the more experienced judges to be *less* confident than the less experienced judges, but in this study these results did not approach signficance.

The main results of the study are shown in Table 2, where the successive columns show the judges' mean scores as they received successively greater amounts of information. As a result of the previous statistical tests, results for all 32 judges are combined in this table.

The first line of Table 2 shows that the fluctuation in accuracy over the four stages of the case was significant. However, a Duncan multiple-range test (A. E. Edwards, 1960, p. 136) showed that this significance was due primarily to the drop in accuracy at Stage 2. Comparing Stage 1 accuracy with Stage 4 accuracy showed no significant change ($t = 1.13$, $df = 31$). Thus, the first hypothesis concerning a ceiling on accuracy was not only supported, but in this experiment there was no significant increase in accuracy at all with increasing information!

Hypothesis 2 is tested in the second line of Table 2. There we see, as predicted, a striking and extremely significant rise in confidence from 33% at Stage 1 to 53% at Stage 4.

Finally, results of Hypothesis 3 are indicated by a comparison of the first and second lines of the table. At Stage 1 the average amount of overconfidence was 7 points; at Stage 4 it was 25 points, a difference significant far beyond the .001 level ($t = 5.14$, $df = 31$).

Sometimes group means may be significant but misleading because they may conceal individual subjects who perform contrary to prediction. That this was not the case here is clearly shown by the following figures for individual judges. Of the 32 judges, 14 increased in accuracy from Stage 1 to Stage 4, while 6 remained the same, and 12 decreased – a completely random result. By contrast, all judges except 2 increased in confidence, and most increased markedly.[4] At Stage 1 almost half of the judges (13 out of 32) were not overconfident; by Stage 4 only 2 remained underconfident – a highly significant change ($\chi^2 = 9.1, p < .01$).

Another interesting result of the study is contained in the last line of Table 2, which shows the average number of items on which the judges changed their answers at each stage of the case. This measure shows that as more information was presented, the number of changed answers *decreased* markedly and significantly. This finding suggests that the judges may frequently have formed stereotype conclusions rather firmly from the first fragmentary information and then been reluctant to change their conclusions as they received new information. At any rate, the final stage of information seems to have served mainly to confirm the judges' previous impressions rather than causing them to revamp their whole personality picture of Kidd.

Discussion

Careless generalization of these findings must certainly be avoided. There are three main factors about this study which might possibly limit the generality of the results. (a) The case may not be similar to the ones with which most psychologists are used to working. (b) The test items may not represent the sorts of behaviors which psychologists are used to predicting. (c) The judges may not have been good representatives of psychological decision makers. In answer to these possible objections it should be pointed out that the case, the test items, and the clinical judges were all chosen with the intention of approximating as closely as possible the situations found in actual psychological practice.

Even if these possible objections were to be granted though, some clear-cut conclusions can be drawn. Regardless of whether the task seemed strange or the case materials atypical, the judges' confidence ratings show that *they became convinced of their own increasing understanding of the case.* As they received more information, their confidence soared. Furthermore, their certainty about their own decisions became entirely out of proportion to the actual correctness of those decisions.

Thus, though this result may not hold for every psychologist and every

---

[4] One of the two judges who decreased in confidence, an undergraduate, later stated that he would normally have increased in confidence, but he had just been engaged in a computer research project in which the computer had repeatedly given incorrect results, to the point where he had completely lost his confidence even in computers.

type of decision, it can clearly be concluded that a psychologist's increasing feelings of confidence as he works through a case are *not* a sure sign of increasing accuracy for his conclusions. So-called clinical validation, based on the personal feelings of confidence of the clinician, is not adequate evidence for the validity of clinical judgment in diagnosing or predicting human behavior.

21. A progress report on the training of probability assessors

Marc Alpert and Howard Raiffa

In prescriptive analyses of decisions under uncertainty, decision makers and their expert advisors are often called upon to assess judgmental probability distributions of quantities whose values are unknown to them. This chapter discusses some empirical findings addressed to such questions as: How well can untrained individuals perform such assessments? Do they manifest certain recurrent biases? How can assessors be calibrated? How can they be taught to become better assessors?

This chapter deals only with assessments of uncertain quantities that can be thought of as taking on a continuum of possible values. Hence we shall work exclusively with univariate density functions and their cumulative distribution functions. Several different procedures are available for assessing probability distributions of continuous, univariate random variables, but we shall consider only one particular procedure that we and our colleagues have often used in practice. It is called the method of *direct fractile assessments*.

Procedure of direct fractile assessments

Let x^* be the true, objective value of some quantity and assume that x^* is unknown to the assessor. The assessor's kth judgmental fractile of x^* (for k in the interval from 0 to 1) is the number x_k such that the judgmental probability that he assigns to the event $\{x^* \leq x_k\}$ is k; in symbols, $P\{x^* \leq x_k\} = k$. The numbers $x_{.50}$, $x_{.25}$, and $x_{.75}$ will be referred to as the judgmental median, lower quartile, and upper quartile respectively. To find $x_{.50}$, the subject must think of a value, such that he believes it is just as likely that x^* is below $x_{.50}$ as above $x_{.50}$. Thus $x_{.50}$ divides the continuum into

This chapter was originally distributed in 1969 as an unpublished report. It has been revised specially for this book.

two judgmentally, equally likely intervals. The lower quartile, $x_{.25}$, divides the interval $(-\infty, x_{.50})$ into two judgmentally equally likely intervals; and the upper quartile, $x_{.75}$, divides the interval $(x_{.50}, \infty)$ into two judgmentally equally likely intervals. For each uncertain quantity, our experimental subjects were asked to assess their judgmental median and quartiles. Consistency (or "coherency," as some authors prefer) requires that the subject believe (a) that each of the four intervals

$$(-\infty, x_{.25}), (x_{.25}, x_{.50}), (x_{.50}, x_{.75}), (x_{.75}, \infty)$$

be just as likely to contain the true x^* value, and (b) that it is just likely as not that the true x^* value will be contained in the interval $(x_{.25}, x_{.75})$. Hereafter, we shall refer to the interval $(x_{.25}, x_{.75})$ as the judgmental, interquartile range. The subjects that participated in our training exercises were all taught to check these consistency requirements and were instructed, in cases of inconsistencies, to reevaluate their fractile assessments in order to achieve consistency.

In addition to the judgmental median and the two quartiles, the subjects were asked to assess various fractiles at the low end and high end of their distributions. More about this later. Once the assessor has determined several (x_k, k) points on his cumulative, left-tail, judgmental probability distribution, he then can use an eyeball, freehand process to "fair" in the remainder of his curve. In this chapter, however, we shall be concerned only with the directly assessed (x_k, k) points and not with the entire curve.

The possibility of external validation

If all we had from a given subject was one probability distribution for a single uncertain quantity, it would be meaningless for us to say that his distribution is "wrong." We might have hoped that our subject was more knowledgeable about the quantity in question, but his probability distribution is just a formal expression of what he knows – or doesn't know – about this quantity. We cannot say, for example, that his distribution is "too tight," or "too loose," or "too skewed to the right." But, in contrast to this case, suppose our subject gives us a thousand distributions of a thousand different uncertain quantities. If each of the actual true values were to fall either below his corresponding .01 fractile or above his .99 fractile, then we would be entitled to say that he is not externally calibrated, that his distributions tend to be too tight. Or, in contrast to this, if it happened that each of his assessed interquartile ranges were to contain the true value, then this would manifest his tendency to be too loose. Granted, these are extreme cases, but they establish the point that it is possible and relevant to talk about the external validation of a set of probability distributions.

The purposes of the exercises and the composition of the subject groups

Without going into any details, let us give you a brief orientation to what we have done. By means of a series of questionnaires we asked a large number of subjects (about a thousand) to record their judgmental fractiles for several quantities unknown to them at the time of the assessment. We then compared their assessments with the actual true values; we identified certain persistent biases; we investigated formal procedures for modifying their judgmental input data; we informed each subject about the quality of the group's responses and of his own particular set of responses; and finally, we suggested ways that each subject could take cognizance of his own past idiosyncrasies and thus modify his next set of assessments.

We conducted four separate but related exercises during the academic year 1968–1969, and for identification purposes, we list these now:

> *Group 1:* A total of 139 students enrolled in an elective course, Models for Planning under Uncertainty, in the second year of Harvard University's MBA program.
>
> *Group 2:* A total of 800 students, comprising the entire first-year student body in Harvard's MBA program.
>
> *Group 3:* A total of 67 "volunteers" from the Advanced Management Program at the Harvard Business School.
>
> *Group 4:* A total of 60 students enrolled in a course in decision analysis given in the Harvard Graduate School of Arts and Sciences. These students were from various departments at Harvard and the Massachusetts Institute of Technology: economics, statistics, engineering, mathematics, law, government, design, social relations, operations research.

All the subjects in these four groups had been exposed, prior to their participation in this training exercise, to the basic fundamentals of decision analysis: construction and analysis of decision trees, prior and posterior probability distributions, utility (or preference) theory, and value of information.

Group 1 served as a pilot study. Each student was required independently to assess distributions for 20 uncertain quantities. For this group we varied our instructions about tail probabilities; this is discussed later in the chapter. All 20 assessments were completed in one session with no feedback in between.

Groups 2, 3, and 4 were all treated alike. In the first session each subject was given 10 uncertain quantities to assess. The subjects were then briefed about the group's overall performance and their own particular performance. A second round of 10 different uncertain quantities was then administered.

The performances of Group 1 and of Groups 2, 3, and 4 in their first rounds were remarkably similar. The performances of Groups 2, 3, and 4 in their second rounds, after briefing and feedback sessions, were again remarkably similar; but marked improvements were noted between their first and second rounds. Because of the similarity of the behavior of all the groups we shall discuss and concentrate our remarks on the detailed performance of the largest of these groups.

The exercise and results before feedback

We reproduce here the instructions given to one-half of the first-year MBA class (Group 2). This half received what we called Form B; the other half received Form A, which was identical in content but which used different uncertain quantities.

Instructions: Form B

The purpose of this exercise is to see how well you as an individual and the class as a whole can assess probability distributions for Uncertain Quantities (uq's). We will list below 10 uq's and you will be asked to assess the median, the .25 fractile, the .75 fractile, and extreme values of each uq. (For your convenience brief definitions of these terms are given below.) Because of the type of uq used, you will have the opportunity to compare your assessments with the true values. You will thus be able to see if you tend to be "too tight," "too loose," or biased upwards or downwards on certain types of questions. Later you will be asked to repeat this exercise with other uq's. For this exercise you are to answer the questions independently without consulting any source materials although some simple calculations may be desirable for certain questions. Your knowledge is of interest to us no matter how vague it is or how uncomfortable you might feel.

  Definitions of fractiles . . . [Omitted]

  Below are 10 quantities which hopefully are uncertain quantities to you. You are to enter your assessment of these on each of the answer sheets provided. Fill out each question as best you can with your present knowledge but do not look up further information or discuss them with others even after turning in your answers. You will be expected to turn in one copy of the solution sheet before class tomorrow, keep the second copy so that you will have a record of your answers. [The students used their retained copy to score themselves. This will be described later.]

The values of some of the variables will be determined by the responses of first-year students to the following questions:

Questions

A. Do you prefer bourbon or scotch?
B. Do you favor draft deferments for all graduate students while in school regardless of field of concentration?
C. Would you accept a 50-50 gamble where you could lose $50 or win $100?

List of Uncertain Quantities

  1. The percentage of first-year students responding, excluding those who never drink, who prefer bourbon to scotch.

2. The percentage of first-year students responding who favor draft deferments for all graduate students while in school regardless of field of concentration.
3. The percentage of first-year students responding who would accept the gamble in question C above.
4. The percentage of respondents expressing an opinion to a July, 1968 Gallup Poll surveying a representative sample of adult Americans who felt that if a full-scale war were to start in the Middle East, the U.S. should send troops to help Israel.
5. The percentage of respondents expressing an opinion to a March, 1968 Gallup Poll surveying a representative sample of adult Americans who felt that public school teachers should be permitted to join unions.
6. The number of "Physicians and Surgeons" listed in the 1968 Yellow Pages of the phone directory for Boston and vicinity.
7. The total number of students currently enrolled in the Doctoral Program at the Harvard Business School.
8. The total egg production in millions in the U.S. in 1965.
9. The number of foreign automobiles imported into the U.S. in 1967 in thousands.
10. The toll collections of the Panama Canal in fiscal 1967 in millions of dollars.

[New page]

FORM B   (Sheet to be kept)

Section ___
Student Number ___
Please check one response for each of questions A, B, and C:
A. Beverage   Bourbon ___ (1)   Scotch ___ (2)   Never drink ___ (3)
B. Draft deferment   Favor ___ (1)   Oppose ___ (2)
C. 50-50 gamble   Accept ___ (1)   Reject ___ (2)

Please assess all 5 values for each of the 10 variables below. Notice that the highest number on each line is on the right. (Decimals are acceptable for answers. Where a percentage is requested answers should, however, be of the form 97.2 for 97.2%, not .972.)

Uncertain Quantity   *Fractiles*
                                                      (.01) (.25) (.50) (.75) (.99)
1. Bourbon (%)..

Feedback memorandum

About a week after the students completed Form B the following memorandum was distributed to the students. This memorandum was also discussed in class *before* the students were given Form A to complete.

The purpose of this memorandum is:
1. To describe the performance in aggregate of those completing Form B,
2. To indicate systematic biases in responses,
3. To enable you to calibrate yourself before you repeat this exercise once again with Form A.

Table 1. *Answers to questions in Form B*

Number	Title	True value
1	Bourbon	42.5
2	Draft deferment	65.5
3	50–50 gamble	55.2
4	Israel	10.4
5	Teacher's unions	63.5
6	Doctors listed	2,600
7	Doctoral students	235
8	Eggs produced (millions)	64,588
9	Cars imported (thousands)	697
10	Canal revenue (millions)	82.3

As you recall for each question you assessed five fractiles: .01, .25, .50, .75, .99. These fractiles divide the line interval into six categories:

Category 1: All numbers below the .01 fractile
2: All numbers between the .01 and .25 fractiles
3: All numbers between the .25 and .50 fractiles
4: All numbers between the .50 and .75 fractiles
5: All numbers between the .75 and .99 fractiles
6: All numbers above the .99 fractile.

For any of the ten questions, once you specify your five fractiles (or equivalently, once you specify the six categories) it is possible to indicate in which category the actual true value falls. For example, student John Doe gave the following fractiles for the bourbon–scotch question:

Assessment: $\underline{(.01)}$ $\underline{(.25)}$ $\underline{(.50)}$ $\underline{(.75)}$ $\underline{(.99)}$
                   5   15   30   40   45

The actual percentage favoring bourbon turned out to be 42.5; hence on this question Mr. Doe's answer falls in category 5.

Now before we discuss any further how well (or poorly) the class did on this exercise, please refer to *your* answer sheet and for each question mark which of your six categories contains the true value.

In Table 1 we list the true answers.

Analysis of the Interquartile Ranges

Let us first look at columns 3 and 4 of Table 2. For any particular question you should have chosen your .25, .50, .75 fractiles so that in *your* regard it would be just as likely that the true answer would fall into the .25 to .75 range (i.e., into categories 3 and 4) as would fall outside this range. In a totality of 1000 questions (100 × 10) we would then have a (mathematical) expectation of 500 responses in categories 3 and 4. We got only 334 such responses. Not too bad. This discrepancy could possibly be a statistical aberration but we doubt it. For example, a similar questionnaire was given out a few weeks ago to a large second-year MBA class – they answered 20 instead of 10 questions – and 33% of their responses fell into categories 3 and 4. We don't want to imply by any means that 33% is a "universal semi-constant" but it is a rather striking coincidence that bears watching. (The

Table 2. *Distribution of subjects' answers to Form B by category*

Number	Title	Below .01	.01 to .25	.25 to .50	.50 to .75	.75 to .99	Above .99	Total
1	Bourbon	3	16	20	40	11	10	100
2	Draft deferment	15	12	35	19	10	9	100
3	50–50 gamble	11	8	28	29	13	11	100
4	Israel	51	41	6	1	1	0	100
5	Teachers' union	1	1	13	28	29	28	100
6	Doctors listed	24	14	12	13	10	27	100
7	Doctoral students	1	3	11	9	15	61	100
8	Eggs produced	9	2	13	10	8	58	100
9	Cars imported	25	15	18	9	7	26	100
10	Canal revenue	18	8	8	12	16	38	100
Total		158	120	164	170	120	268	1,000
Expected frequency		10	240	250	250	240	10	1,000

corresponding percentage for those first completing Form A was 33%; the AMP's (Group 3) also yielded the 33% figure but the Arts and Sciences students (Group 4) registered a 36% response.)

In the aggregate, intervals from the .25 to the .75 fractiles were too tight. Just as many true values should have fallen outside the interquartile ranges (the .25 to .75 range) as fell inside, but as a matter of fact *twice* as many fell outside as inside. But it's not good enough for us to say, "Spread out your interquartile ranges" because there is a lot of variation from question to question and from individual to individual.

Let's compare questions 1 and 10. In question 1 you might feel you know quite a bit about the drinking preferences of your fellow classmates – at least quite a lot in comparison to what you know about canal revenues. You might feel that therefore there is a greater chance (ex ante) for you to capture in your interquartile range the true bourbon proportion than the true canal revenues. *But is this the way you should feel?* If you felt that way ex ante, you should have spread out your interquartile range for canal revenues. When you do Form A make sure that you feel, regardless of your state of information, that:

a. For any question it is just as likely that the true value will fall inside as outside your interquartile range; and

b. It is just as likely that the true value will fall in your interquartile range for a question you know a lot about as for a question you know little about.

(This last point about questions 1 and 10 was foolishly discussed with the Arts and Sciences students *before* rather than *after* they completed their first round of assessments. This might have accounted for the discrepancy between 33% and 36%. We will see a much more dramatic shift when we look at tail probabilities.)

Some of you were *really* too tight. For example, 13 out of 100 respondents only captured 0 or 1 true values in their 10 interquartile ranges. For each individual let his *interquartile score* be the number of times the true values fall in his interquartile ranges. Scores close to 0 imply the individual is "too tight"; scores close to 10 imply

Table 3. *Distribution of interquartile scores for Form B*

Interquartile score	Actual number of individuals	Expected number of individuals using $p = .33$
0	3	1.9
1	10	9.0
2	22	19.9
3	20	26.1
4	23	22.5
5	11	13.3
6	9	5.5
7	2	1.5
8	0	.3
9	0	.0
10	0	.0
Total	100	100.0

the individual is "too loose"; and scores near 5 imply he is "just about right." The distribution of scores is given in Table 3. In the third column of the table we list the expected number of respondents who would give any given interquartile score under the simplifying assumption that there is a .33 chance that any interquartile range includes the true value and that these dichotomous responses are independent from question to question. Be sure to get *your* interquartile score.

Analysis of Extremes

Presumably you set your .01 and .99 fractiles so that you would be "surprised" with a really low answer (category 1 response) and with a really high answer (category 6 response). In 1000 questions we should have "expected" a total of 20 surprises, 10 on the left and 10 on the right (see Table 2). *There were a total of 426 surprises!* That should not only surprise you but shock you! You can take some small comfort, however, that you are not as bad as that second-year (Group 1) class we referred to above. About 35 students were asked, just as you were, to list .01 and .99 fractiles for 20 questions. They recorded 46% surprises – a little worse than your 42.6%. Another 35 students were asked to record .001 and .999 fractiles and instead of an "expected" .2% surprises they recorded 40%. Another 35 were instructed in rather vague terms to list "minimum" and "maximum" values – we really don't know what that means – and they recorded 47% surprises. Finally another 35 were instructed to give "astonishingly low" and "astonishingly high" values and they recorded 38% surprises. Evidently "astonishingly low" is lower than "minimum."

For heaven's sake, *Spread Those Extreme Fractiles!* Be honest with yourselves! Admit what you don't know!

Let's look at question 6. There are 2600 medical doctors listed in the yellow pages of Boston and Vicinity. One-half of you were surprised at this result. Of this one-half, one-half were surprised at the low end and one-half at the high end. Fifty-eight percent of you were astonished at the fantastically *large* number of eggs

Table 4. *Distribution of surprise indices for Form B*

Surprise index	Actual number of individuals	Expected number of individuals using $p = .43$
0	1	.4
1	9	2.7
2	15	9.3
3	13	18.7
4	17	24.6
5	15	22.3
6	16	14.0
7	4	6.0
8	9	1.7
9	1	.3
10	0	.0
Total	100	100.0

produced – but still nine percent of you were equally astonished at the fantastically *small* number of eggs produced.

Let us define for each individual a *surprise index* which gives the number of times (out of 10) that he records a category 1 or 6 response. On the average over a lot of different, independent questions you should be surprised 1 out of 50 times. Surprise indices of 0 or 1 are what we would like to see and there is cause for concern if this surprise index hits 3 or more. The distribution of surprise indices is given in Table 4. In the third column of the table we list the expected number of respondents who would register given surprise indices under the simplifying assumption that there is a .43 chance at a surprise in each question and there is question-by-question independence. Forty-five (45) individuals were surprised on at least half of the ten questions!

For the typical uncertain quantity, we imagine that most of you want to assess a unimodal density curve (or equivalently an S-shaped left-tail cumulative distribution) where the highest point on the density curve (or the steepest portion of the S-shaped cumulative curve) occurs somewhere in the interval from your .25 to .75 fractiles. A good many of you, we imagine inadvertently, recorded bimodal curves. This would be the case if the length of your category 2 interval[1] is less than your category 3 interval and the length of your category 5 interval is less than the length of your category 4 interval. A case in point would be the following set of fractile assessments:

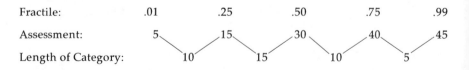

Fractile:	.01	.25	.50	.75	.99
Assessment:	5	15	30	40	45
Length of Category:	10	15	10	5	

---

[1] Let l_i designate the length of category 1. We would have bimodality if l_2 and l_5 are each less than $(l_3 + l_4)/2$.

Table 5. *Comparison of results on rounds 1 and 2*

	Form A		Form B	
	Round 1	Round 2	Round 1	Round 2
Values falling inside the inter-quartile ranges (%)	32.9	40.3	33.4	46.4
Values falling outside the .01 to .99 ranges (%)	38.8	24.9	42.6	22.2

Table 6. *Comparisons of results of rounds 1 and 2*

	Group 3		Group 4	
	Round 1	Round 2	Round 1	Round 2
Values falling inside the inter-quartile ranges (%)	33.4	44.8	35.6	42.5
Values falling outside the .01 to .99 ranges (%)	35.6	22.8	20.8	8.7

In the above illustration the ratio of the lengths of the .98 probability interval (from the .01 to the .99 fractiles) to the .50 probability interval (from the .25 to the .75 fractiles) is (45–5)/(40–15) or 1.6. This is much too small a number for a unimodal curve. For example, for the normal, bell-shaped curve this ratio is about 3.5. Ratios of 2.25 to 4.5 can serve as a rough guideline – but guidelines should be broken at times. Remember: Spread out those distributions!

Results after feedback

After discussing in class the feedback memorandum, we switched forms and repeated the exercise. After analyzing the responses, we distributed the following memorandum:

Memorandum number 2

Each of you has now participated in the following sequence:

a. (Round 1): You were given one of two Forms (A or B) and you gave fractile assessments for ten uncertain quantities;

b. (Feedback): You were then given the true values of these ten quartiles and were asked to score yourself on two factors: (1) how many of your answers fell *inside* your interquartile ranges, and (2) how many of your answers fell *outside* your .01 and .99 ranges. You were also informed about the aggregate performance of the class: about twice as many answers fell outside the interquartile ranges as fell inside, and there was a really shocking number of surprises – roughly 40% of the answers fell outside the .01 and .99 ranges.

c. (Round 2): You were then given the other Form and asked for fractile assessments.

Table 7. *Proportion of surprises for different interpretations of "low" and "high"*

Interpretation of "low"	Interpretation of "high"	Size of sample	Proportion of surprises
.01-fractile	.99-fractile	44	.46
.001-fractile	.999-fractile	25	.40
Minimum value	Maximum value	35	.47
Astonishingly low	Astonishingly high	35	.38

We have now calculated your answers for part (c) and are ready to comment on your aggregate performance. But first of all, we list the true values of the uncertain quantities so that you may calibrate yourself [a table presenting this information was shown in the memorandum].

How well did the class do as a whole? Did the feedback session help? It helped a bit but not as much as we hoped. Most of your distributions are much too tight. Table 5 summarizes the results.

If we aggregate Forms A and B, then the percentage of times the true values fell inside the interquartile ranges jumped from 33% to 43%. The direction of change is fine but we are still somewhat shy of that 50% we would have liked. The percentage of times the true values fell outside the extreme values (i.e., the .01 and .99 ranges) fell from a shocking 41% to a depressing 23%. This is a far cry from our goal of 2%. Something has to be done about those tails! We need another feedback session and a third round of practice; but unfortunately this is not administratively feasible. We propose to start experiments with other groups to get more realistic assessments of tail probabilities.

(For comparison purposes Table 6 exhibits the before-vs.-after performances of the AMP's [Group 3] and of the Arts and Sciences students [Group 4].)

More on the extreme tails

In the pilot study (Group 1) we varied the instructions concerning the extreme tails in order to see what effect it would have on the statistical distributions of responses. All of our subjects, however, were asked to give their judgmental medians and two quartiles. Our results are summarized in Tables 7 and 8, which we will explain in turn.

Of the 139 subjects, 44 were asked to give .01 and .99 fractiles and this subgroup registered 46% surprises (rather than 2%); 25 were asked to give .001 and .999 fractiles and this subgroup registered 40% surprises (rather than .2%). Thirty-five subjects were asked to give a "minimum value" and a "maximum value" and when some subjects asked for a clarification of what those terms meant, we shrugged them off with some noncommittal remark, such as, "Sure they are vague terms, but try to answer the questions anyway." We gave the same ambiguous advice to the remaining 35 subjects who were asked for "astonishingly low" and "astonishingly high"

Table 8. *Distribution of "high" assessments for question 10*

Points for winner	Interpretation of "high"			
	.99	.999	Maximum	Astonishingly high
< 29	8	1	6	2
29–35	15	6	7	6
6–42	10	5	7	11
43–49	2	6	5	4
50–56	7	3	8	7
57–63	2	0	2	4
64–70	0	4	0	1
Total	44	25	35	35

high" values. These last two groups registered 47% and 38% respectively. The different instructions had some effect but, as you see, not very much effect.

Another way of examining the effect of these four instructions about extremes is to look in detail at Table 8, which gives the distribution of responses to the "high" values for the following quantity: The number of points by the winning team in the next Harvard–Dartmouth football game. (This was asked a week before the game.) For example, of the 25 individuals who were told to give a .999 fractile, 1 recorded a score less than 29, 6 recorded scores between 29 and 35, 5 between 36 and 42, and so on. It looks as if the vague term "maximum" is interpreted as a .99-fractile and the vague term "astonishingly high" is interpreted as a .999-fractile.

We did not replicate these instructions about extreme values with Groups 2, 3, and 4; rather, we consistently asked those subjects for .01 and .99 fractiles.

22. Calibration of probabilities: The state of the art to 1980

Sarah Lichtenstein, Baruch Fischhoff, and Lawrence D. Phillips

From the subjectivist point of view (de Finetti, 1937/1964), a probability is a degree of belief in a proposition. It expresses a purely internal state; there is no "right," "correct," or "objective" probability residing somewhere "in reality" against which one's degree of belief can be compared. In many circumstances, however, it may become possible to verify the truth or falsity of the proposition to which a probability was attached. Today, one assesses the probability of the proposition "it will rain tomorrow." Tomorrow, one looks at the rain gauge to see whether or not it has rained. When possible, such verification can be used to determine the adequacy of probability assessments.

Winkler and Murphy (1968b) have identified two kinds of "goodness" in probability assessments: normative goodness, which reflects the degree to which assessments express the assessor's true beliefs and conform to the axioms of probability theory, and substantive goodness, which reflects the amount of knowledge of the topic area contained in the assessments. This chapter reviews the literature concerning yet another aspect of goodness, called calibration.

If a person assesses the probability of a proposition being true as .7 and later finds that the proposition is false, that in itself does not invalidate the assessment. However, if a judge assigns .7 to 10,000 independent propositions, only 25 of which subsequently are found to be true, there is something wrong with these assessments. The attribute that they lack is called calibration; it has also been called realism (Brown & Shuford, 1973), external validity (Brown & Shuford, 1973), realism of confidence (Adams & Adams, 1961), appropriateness of confidence (Oskamp, 1962), secondary validity (Murphy & Winkler, 1971), and reliability (Murphy,

This is a revised version of the paper that originally appeared in H. Jungermann and G. deZeeuw (Eds.), *Decision Making and Change in Human Affairs*. Dordrecht-Holland: D. Reidel Publishing Co., 1977. Reprinted by permission.

1973). Formally, a judge is calibrated if, over the long run, for all propositions assigned a given probability, the proportion that is true equals the probability assigned. Judges' calibration can be empirically evaluated by observing their probability assessments, verifying the associated propositions, and then observing the proportion true in each response category.

The experimental literature on the calibration of assessors making probability judgments about discrete propositions is reviewed in the first section of this chapter. The second section looks at the calibration of probability density functions assessed for uncertain numerical quantities. Although calibration is essentially a property of individuals, most of the studies reviewed here have reported data grouped across assessors in order to secure the large quantities of data needed for stable estimates of calibration.

Discrete propositions

Discrete propositions can be characterized according to the number of alternatives they offer:

> *No alternatives:* "What is absinthe?" The assessor provides an answer, and then gives the probability that the answer given is correct. The entire range of probability responses, from 0 to 1, is appropriate.
>
> *One alternative:* "Absinthe is a precious stone. What is the probability that this statement is true?" Again, the relevant range of the probability scale is 0 to 1.
>
> *Two alternatives:* "Absinthe is (a) a precious stone; (b) a liqueur." With the *half-range* method, the assessor first selects the more likely alternative and then states the probability ($\geq.5$) that this choice is correct. With the *full-range* method, the subject gives the probability (from 0 to 1) that the prespecified alternative is correct.
>
> *Three or more alternatives:* "Absinthe is (a) a precious stone; (b) a liqueur; (c) a Caribbean island; (d) ... " Two variations of this task may be used: (1) the assessor selects the single most likely alternative and states the probability that it is correct, using a response $\geq 1/k$ for k alternatives or (2) the assessor assigns probabilities to all alternatives, using the range 0 to 1.

For all these variations, calibration may be reported via a *calibration curve*. Such a curve is derived as follows:

1. Collect many probability assessments for items whose correct answer is known or will shortly be known to the experimenter.
2. Group similar assessments, usually within ranges (e.g., all assessments between .60 and .69 are placed in the same category).

3. Within each category, compute the proportion correct (i.e., the proportion of items for which the proposition is true or the alternative is correct).
4. For each category, plot the mean response (on the abscissa) against the proportion correct (on the ordinate).

Perfect calibration would be shown by all points falling on the identity line.

For half-range tasks, badly calibrated assessments can be either *overconfident*, whereby the proportions correct are less than the assessed probabilities, so that the calibration curve falls below the identity line, or *underconfident*, whereby the proportions correct are greater than the assessed probabilities and the calibration curve lies above the identity line.

For full-range tasks with zero or one alternative, overconfidence has two possible meanings. Assessors could be overconfident in the truth of the answer; such overconfidence would be indicated by a calibration curve falling always below the identity line. Alternatively, assessors could be overconfident in their ability to discriminate true from false propositions. Such overconfidence would be shown by a calibration curve below the identity line in the region above .5 and above the identity line in the region below .5.

Several numerical measures of calibration have been proposed. Murphy (1973) has explored the general case of k-alternative items, starting with the Brier score (1950), a general measure of overall goodness or probability assessments such that the smaller the score, the better. The Brier score for N items is:

$$B = \frac{1}{N} \sum_{i=1}^{N} (\mathbf{r}_i - \mathbf{c}_i)(\mathbf{r}_i - \mathbf{c}_i)'$$

where $\mathbf{r}_i$ is a vector of the assessed probabilities for the k alternatives of item i, $\mathbf{r}_i = (r_{1i}, \ldots r_{ki})$, $\mathbf{c}_i$ is the associated outcome vector, $\mathbf{c}_i = (c_{1i}, \ldots, c_{ji}, \ldots, c_{ki})$, where c_{ji} equals one for the true alternative and zero otherwise, and the prime (') denotes a column vector. Murphy showed that the Brier score can be partitioned into three additive parts. To do so, sort the N response vectors into T subcollections such that all the response vectors, $\mathbf{r}_t$, in subcollection t are identical. Let n_t be the number of responses in subcollection t, and let $\bar{\mathbf{c}}_t$ be the proportion-correct vector for subcollection t:

$$\bar{\mathbf{c}}_t = (\bar{c}_{1t}, \ldots, \bar{c}_{jt}, \ldots, \bar{c}_{kt}), \text{ where } \bar{c}_{jt} = \sum_{t=1}^{n_t} c_{jt}/n_t$$

Let $\bar{\mathbf{c}}$ be the proportion-correct vector across all responses,

$$\bar{\mathbf{c}} = (\bar{c}_1, \ldots, \bar{c}_j, \ldots, \bar{c}_k), \text{ where } \bar{c}_j = \frac{1}{N} \sum_{i=1}^{N} c_{ji}$$

Finally, let **u** be the unity vector, a row vector whose k elements are all one.

Then Murphy's partition of the Brier score is:

$$B = \bar{c}(u - \bar{c})' + \frac{1}{N}\sum_{t=1}^{T} n_t(r_t - \bar{c}_t)(r_t - \bar{c}_t)' - \frac{1}{N}\sum_{t=1}^{T} n_t(\bar{c}_t - \bar{c})(\bar{c}_t - \bar{c})'$$

The first term is not a function of the probability assessments; rather, it reflects the relative frequency of true events across the k alternatives. For example, suppose all the items being assessed had the same two alternatives, {rain, no rain}. Then the first term of the partition is a function of the base rate of rain across the N items (or days). If it always (or never) rained, this term would be zero. Its maximum value, $(k - 1)/k$, would indicate maximum uncertainty about the occurrence of rain. The second term is a measure of calibration, the weighted average of the squared difference between the responses in a category and the proportion correct for that category. The third term, called resolution, reflects the assessor's ability to sort the events into subcategories for which the proportion correct is different from the overall proportion correct.

Murphy's partition was designed for repeated predictions of the same set of events (e.g., rain vs. no rain). When the alternatives have no common meaning across items (e.g., in a multiple-choice examination), then all that the first term indicates is the extent to which the correct answer appears equally often as the first, second, etc., alternative.

When only one response per item is scored, Murphy's partition (Murphy, 1972) reduces to:

$$B' = \bar{c}(1 - \bar{c}) + \frac{1}{N}\sum_{t=1}^{T} n_t(r_t - \bar{c}_t)^2 - \frac{1}{N}\sum_{t=1}^{T} n_t(\bar{c}_t - \bar{c})^2,$$

where $\bar{c}$ is the overall proportion correct and $\bar{c}_t$ is the proportion correct in subcategory t. When the scored responses are the responses that are greater than or equal to .5 (as with the two-alternative, half-range task), the first term reflects the subject's ability to pick the correct alternative and thus might be called knowledge. As before, the second term measures calibration, and the third resolution.

Similar measures of calibration have been proposed by Adams and Adams (1961) and by Oskamp (1962). None of these measures of calibration discriminates between overconfidence and underconfidence. The sampling properties of these measures are not known.

Meteorological research

In 1906, W. Ernest Cooke, government astronomer for Western Australia, advocated that each meteorological prediction be accompanied by a single number that would "indicate, approximately, the weight or degree of probability which the forecaster himself attaches to that particular prediction." (Cooke, 1906b, p. 274). He reported (Cooke, 1906a, 1906b) results from 1,951 predictions. Of those to which he had assigned the highest degree of probability ("almost certain to be verified"), .985 were correct. For his middle degree of probability ("normal probability"), .938 were correct, while for his lowest degree of probability ("doubtful"), .787 were correct.

In 1951, Williams asked eight professional weather bureau forecasters in Salt Lake City to assess the probability of precipitation for each of 1095 12-hour forecasts, using one of the numbers 0, .2, .4., .6, .8, and 1.0. Throughout most of the range, the proportion of precipitation days was lower than the probability assigned. This might reflect a fairly natural form of hedging in public pronouncements. People are much more likely to criticize a weather forecast that leaves them without an umbrella when it rains than one that leads them to carry an umbrella on dry days.

Similar results emerged from a study by Murphy and Winkler (1974). Their forecasters assessed the probability of precipitation for the next day twice, before and after seeing output from a computerized weather prediction system (PEATMOS). The 7,188 assessments (before and after PEATMOS) showed the same overestimation of the probability of rain found by Williams.

Sanders (1958) collected 12,635 predictions, using the 11 responses 0, .1., ...9, 1.0, for a variety of dichotomized events: wind direction, wind speed, gusts, temperatures, cloud amount, ceiling, visibility, precipitation occurrence, precipitation type, and thunderstorm. These data revealed only a slight tendency for the forecasters' probability assessments to exceed the proportion of weather events that occurred.[1] Root (1962) reported a symmetric pattern of calibration of 4,138 precipitation forecasts: Assessed probabilities were too low in the low range and too high in the high range, relative to the observed frequencies.

Winkler and Murphy (1968a) reported calibration curves for an entire year of precipitation forecasts from Hartford, Connecticut. Each forecast was for either a 6-hour or a 12-hour time period, with a lead time varying from 5 to 44 hours. Unfortunately, it was unclear whether the forecasters had included "a trace of precipitation" (less than .01 inch) in their predictions. The data were analyzed twice, once assuming that "precipitation" included the occurrence of traces and again without traces. The inclusion or exclusion of traces had a substantial effect on calibration, as did the time period. Six-hour forecasts with traces included and 12-hour forecasts excluding traces exhibited excellent calibration. The calibration curve for 12-hour forecasts with traces lay above the identity line; the curve for 6-hour forecasts excluding traces lay well below it. Variations in lead time did not affect calibration.

[1] The references by Cooke (1906), Williams (1951), and Sanders (1958) were brought to our attention by Raiffa (1969).

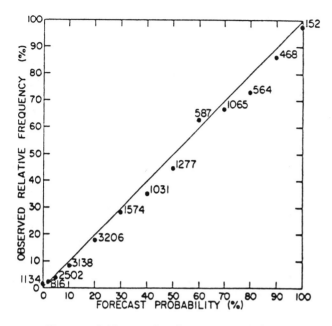

Figure 1. Calibration data for precipitation forecasts. The number of forecasts is shown for each point. (*Source:* Murphy & Winkler, 1977a.)

National Weather Service forecasters have been expressing their fore-casts of precipitation occurrence in probabilistic terms since 1965. The calibration for some parts of this massive data base has been published (Murphy & Winkler, 1977a; U.S. Weather Bureau, 1969). Over the years the calibration has improved. Figure 1 shows the calibration for 24,859 precip-itation forecasts made in Chicago during the four years ending June 1976. This shows remarkably good calibration; Murphy (1980) says the data for recent years are even better! He attributes this superior performance to the experience with probability assessment that the forecasters have gained over the years and to the fact that these data were gathered from real on-the-job performance.

Early laboratory research

In 1957, Adams reported the calibration of subjects who used an 11-point confidence scale: The subject was "instructed to express his confidence in terms of the percentage of responses, made at that particular level of confidence, that he expects to be correct. . . . Of those responses made with confidence p, about $p\%$ should be correct" (pp. 432–433).

In Adams's task, each of 40 words were presented tachistoscopically 10 times successively, with increasing illumination each time, to 10 subjects. After each exposure subjects wrote down the work they thought they saw and gave a confidence judgment. The resulting calibration curve showed that the proportions that were correct greatly exceeded the confidence ratings along the entire response scale (except for the responses of 100). Great caution must be taken in interpreting these data: Because each word was shown 10 times, the responses are highly interdependent. It is unknown what effect such interdependence has on calibration. Subjects may have chosen to "hold back" on early presentations, unwilling to give a high response when they knew that the same word would be presented several more times.

The following year, Adams and Adams (1958) reported a training experiment, using the same response scale but a new, three-alternative, single-response task: For each of 156 pairs of words per session, subjects were asked whether the words were antonyms, synonyms, or unrelated. The mean calibration scores (based on the absolute difference, $|r_t - \bar{c}_t|$) of 14 experimental subjects, who were shown calibration tallies and calibration curves after each of five sessions, decreased by 48% from the first session to the last. Six control subjects, whose only feedback was a tally of their unscored responses, showed a 36% mean increase in discrepancy scores.

Adams and Adams (1961) discussed many aspects of calibration (using the term *realism of confidence*), anticipating much of the work done by others in recent years, and presented more bits of data, including the grossly overconfident calibration curve of a schizophrenic who believed he was Jesus Christ. In a nonsense-syllable learning task, they found large overconfidence on the first trial and improvement after 16 trials. They also briefly described a transfer of training experiment: On day 1, subjects made 108 decisions about the percentage of blue dots in an array of blue and red dots. On days 2 and 4, the subjects decided on the truth or falsity of 250 general knowledge statements. On day 3, they lifted weights, blindfolded. On day 5, they made 256 decisions (synonym, antonym, or unrelated) about pairs of words. Eight experimental subjects, given calibration feedback after each of the first four days, showed on the fifth day a mean absolute discrepancy score significantly lower than that of 8 control (no feedback) subjects, suggesting some transfer of training. Finally, Adams and Adams reported that across 56 subjects taking a multiple-choice final examination in elementary psychology, poorer calibration was associated with greater fear of failure ($r = .36$). Neither knowledge nor overconfidence was related to fear of failure.

Oskamp (1962) presented subjects with 200 MMPI profiles[2] as stimuli. Half the profiles were from men admitted to a Veterans Administration (VA) hospital for psychiatric reasons; the others were from men admitted for purely medical reasons. The subjects' task was to decide, for each profile, whether the patient's status was psychiatric or medical and to state

[2] The MMPI (Minnesota Multiphasic Personality Inventory) is a personality inventory widely used for psychiatric diagnosis. A profile is a graph of 13 subscores from the inventory.

the probability that their decision was correct. Each profile had been independently categorized as hard (61 profiles), medium (88), or easy (51) on the basis of an actuarially derived classification system, which correctly identified 57%, 69%, and 92% on the hard, medium, and easy profiles, respectively.

All 200 profiles were judged by three groups of subjects: 28 undergraduate psychology majors, 23 clinical psychology trainees working at a VA hospital, and 21 experienced clinical psychologists. The 28 inexperienced judges were later split into two matched groups and given the same 200 profiles again. Half were trained during this second round to improve accuracy; the rest were trained to improve calibration.

Oskamp used three measures of subjects' performance: accuracy (percentage correct), confidence (mean probability response), and appropriateness of confidence (a calibration score):

$$\frac{1}{N} \sum_t n_t |r_t - \bar{c}_t|$$

All three groups tended to be overconfident, especially the undergraduates in their first session (accuracy 70%, confidence .78). However, all three groups were underconfident on the easy profiles (accuracy 87%, confidence .83).

The subjects trained for accuracy increased their accuracy from 67% to 73%, approaching their confidence level, .78, which did not change as a result of training.[3] The subjects trained for calibration lowered their confidence from .78 to .74, bringing it closer to their accuracy, 68%, which remained unchanged. As would be expected from these changes, the calibration score of both groups improved.

Signal detection research

In the early days of signal detection research, investigators looked into the possibility of using confidence ratings rather than yes–no responses in order to reduce the amounts of data required to determine stable receiver operating characteristic (ROC) curves. Swets, Tanner, and Birdsall (1961) asked four observers to indicate their confidence that they had heard signal plus noise rather than noise alone for each of 1,200 trials. Although three of the four subjects were terribly calibrated, the four calibration curves were widely different. One subject exhibited a severe tendency to assign too small probabilities (e.g., the signal was present over 70% of the times when that subject used the response category ".05–.19").

Clarke (1960) presented one of five different words, mixed with noise, to listeners through headphones. The listeners selected the word they

---

[3] MMPI buffs might note that with this minimal training the undergraduates showed as high an accuracy as either the best experts or the best actuarial prediction systems.

thought they heard and then rated their confidence by indicating one of five categories defined by slicing the probability scale into five ranges. After each of 12 practice tests of 75 items, listeners scored their own results and noted the percentage of correct identifications in each rating category, thus allowing them to change strategies on the next test. Clarke found that although all five listeners appeared well calibrated when data were averaged over the five stimulus words, analyses for individual words showed that the listeners tended to be overconfident for low-intelligibility words and underconfident for words of relatively high intelligibility.

Pollack and Decker (1958) used a verbally defined 6-point confidence rating scale that ranged from "Positive I received the message correctly" to "Positive I received the message incorrectly." With this rating scale it is impossible to determine whether an individual is well calibrated, but it is possible to see shifts in calibration across conditions. Calibration curves for easy words generally lay above those for difficult words, whatever the signal-to-noise ratio, and the curves for high signal-to-noise ratios lay above those for low signal-to-noise ratios, whatever the word difficulty.

In most of these studies, calibration was of secondary interest; the important question was whether confidence ratings would yield the same ROC curves as Yes–No procedures. By 1966, Green and Swets concluded that, in general, rating scales and Yes–No procedures yield almost identical ROC curves. Since then, studies of calibration have disappeared from the signal detection literature.

Recent laboratory research

Overconfidence. The most pervasive finding in recent research is that people are overconfident with general-knowledge items of moderate or extreme difficulty. Some typical results showing overconfidence are presented in Figure 2. Hazard and Peterson (1973) asked 40 armed forces personnel studying at the Defense Intelligence School to respond with probabilities or with odds to 50 two-alternative general-knowledge items (e.g., "Which magazine had the largest circulation in 1970, *Playboy* or *Time?*"). Lichtenstein (unpublished) found similar results, using the same items but only the probability response, with 19 Oregon Research Institute employees, as did Phillips and Wright (1977) with different items, using British undergraduate students as subjects.

Numerous other studies using general-knowledge questions have shown the same overconfidence (Fischhoff, Slovic, & Lichtenstein, 1977; Koriat, Lichtenstein, & Fischhoff, 1980; Lichtenstein & Fischhoff, 1977, 1980a, 1980b; Nickerson & McGoldrick, 1965). Cambridge and Shreckengost (1978) found overconfidence with Central Intelligence Agency analysts. Fischhoff and Slovic (1980) found severe overconfidence using a variety of impossible or nearly impossible tasks (e.g., predicting the

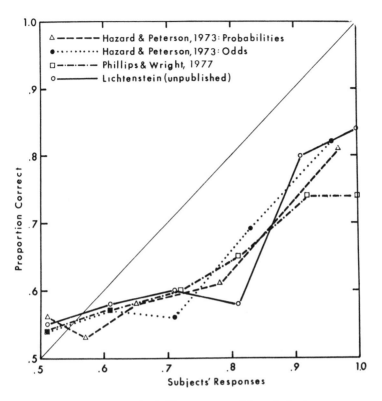

Figure 2. Calibration for half-range, general-knowledge items.

winners in 6-furlong horse races, diagnosing the malignancy of ulcers). Pitz (1974) reported overconfidence using a full-range method.

Fischhoff, Slovic, and Lichtenstein (1977) focused on the appropriateness of expressions of certainty. Using a variety of methods (no alternatives, one alternative, and two alternatives with half range and full range), they found that only 72% to 83% of the items to which responses of 1.0 were given were correct. In the full-range tasks, items assigned the other extreme response, zero, were correct 20% to 30% of the time. Using an odds response did not correct the overconfidence. Answers assigned odds of 1,000:1 of being correct were only 81% to 88% correct; for odds of 1,000,000:1 the correct alternative was chosen only 90% to 96% of the time. Subjects showed no reluctance to use extreme odds; in one of the experiments almost one-fourth of the responses were 1,000:1 or greater. Further analyses showed that extreme overconfidence was not confined to just a few subjects or a few items.

The effect of difficulty. Overconfidence is most extreme with tasks of great difficulty (Clarke, 1960; Nickerson & McGoldrick, 1965; Pitz, 1974). With essentially impossible tasks (discriminating between European and American handwriting, Asian and European children's drawings, and rising and falling stock prices) calibration curves did not rise at all; for all assessed probabilities, the proportion of correct alternatives chosen was close to .5 (Lichtenstein & Fischhoff, 1977). Subjects were not reluctant to use high probabilities in these tasks; 70% to 80% of all responses were greater than .5.

As tasks get easier, overconfidence is reduced. Lichtenstein and Fischhoff (1977) allowed one group of subjects in the handwriting discrimination task to study a correctly labeled set of sample stimuli before making its probability assessments. This experience made the task much easier (71% correct versus 51% for the no-study group) and the study group was only slightly overconfident. Lichtenstein and Fischhoff (1977) performed post hoc analyses of the effect of difficulty on calibration using two large collections of data from general-knowledge, two-alternative half-range tasks. They separated easy items (those for which most subjects chose the correct alternative) from hard items and knowledgeable subjects (those who selected the most correct alternatives) from less knowledgeable subjects. They found a systematic decrease in overconfidence as the percentage correct increased. Indeed, the most knowledgeable subjects responding to the easiest items were *under*confident (e.g., 90% correct when responding with a probability of .80). This finding was replicated with two new groups of subjects given sets of items chosen to be hard or easy on the basis of previous subjects' performance. The resulting calibration curves are shown in Figure 3, along with the corresponding calibration curves from the post hoc analyses.

In the research just cited, difficulty was defined on the basis of subjects' performance (Clarke, 1960; Lichtenstein & Fischhoff, 1977). More recently, Lichtenstein and Fischhoff (1980a), following the lead of Oskamp (1962), developed a set of 500 two-alternative general-knowledge items for which difficulty could be defined independently. The items were of three types: Which of two cities, states, countries, or continents is more populous (e.g., Las Vegas vs. Miami), which of two cities is farther in distance from a third city (e.g., "Is Melbourne farther from Rome or from Tokyo?"), and which historical event happened first (e.g., Magna Carta signed vs. Mohammed born). Thus, each item had associated with it two numbers (populations, distances, or elapsed time to the present). The ratio of the larger to the smaller of those numbers was taken as a measure of difficulty: The 250 items with the largest ratios were designated as *easy*; the remaining, as *hard*. This a priori classification was quite successful; over 35 subjects, the percentage correct was 81 for easy items and 58 for hard items. These results, too, showed overconfidence for hard items and underconfidence for easy items.

The hard–easy effect seems to arise from assessors' inability to appre-

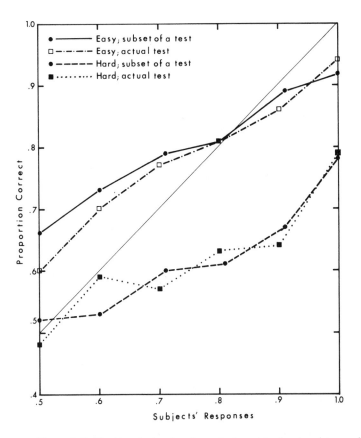

Figure 3. Calibration for hard and easy tests and for hard and easy subsets of a test.

ciate how difficult or easy a task is. Phillips and Chew (unpublished) found no correlation across subjects between percentage correct and the subjects' ratings on an 11-point scale of the difficulty of a set of just-completed items. However, subjects do give different distributions of responses for different tasks; Lichtenstein and Fischhoff (1977) reported a correlation of .91 between percentage correct and mean response across 16 different sets of data. But the differences in response distributions are less than they should be: Over those same 16 sets of data, the proportion correct varied from .43 to .92, while the mean response varied only from .65 to .86.

Ferrell and McGoey (1980) have recently developed a model for the calibration of discrete probability assessments that addresses the hard–easy effect. The model, based on signal detection theory, assumes that assessors transform their feelings of subjective uncertainty into a decision variable, X, which is partitioned into sections with cutoff values $\{x_i\}$. The assessor reports probability r_i whenever X lies between x_{i-1} and x_i. Ferrell and McGoey assume that, in the absence of feedback about calibration performance, the assessor will not change the set of cutoff values, $\{x_i\}$, as task difficulty changes. This assumption leads to a prediction of overconfidence with hard items and underconfidence with easy items. Application of the model to much of the data from Lichtenstein and Fischhoff (1977) showed a moderately good fit to both the calibration curves and the distribution of responses under the assumption that the cutoff values remained constant as difficulty changed. Thus the hard–easy effect is seen as an inability to change the cutoffs involved in the transformation from feelings of certainty to probabilistic responses.

Effect of base rates. One-alternative (true–false) tasks may be characterized by the proportion of true statements in the set of items. To be well calibrated on a particular set of items one must take this base-rate information into account. The signal detection model of Ferrell and McGoey (1980) assumes that calibration is affected independently by (a) the proportion of true statements and (b) the assessor's ability to discriminate true from false statements. Assuming that the cutoff values, $\{x_i\}$, are held constant, the model predicts quite different effects on calibration from changing the proportion of true statements (while holding discriminability constant) as opposed to changing discriminability (while holding the proportion of true statements constant). Ferrell and McGoey presented data supporting their model. Students in three engineering courses assessed the probability that the answers they wrote for their examinations would be judged correct by the grader. Post hoc analyses separating the subjects into four groups (high vs. low percentage of correct answers and high vs. low discriminability) revealed the calibration differences predicted by the model. Unpublished data collected by Fischhoff and Lichtenstein, shown in Figure 4, also suggest support for the model. Four groups of subjects received 25 one-alternative general-knowledge items (e.g., "The Aeneid was written by Homer") differing in the proportion of true statements: .08, .20, .50, and .71. The groups showed dramatically different calibration curves, of roughly the same shape as predicted by Ferrell and McGoey for their base-rate changing, discriminability constant case.

Individual differences. Unqualified statements that one person is better calibrated than another person are difficult to make, for two reasons. First, at least several hundred responses are needed in order to get a stable measure of calibration. Second, it appears that calibration strongly depends on the task, particularly on the difficulty of the task. Indeed, Lichtenstein and Fischhoff (1980a) have suggested that each person may have an "ideal" test (i.e., a test whose difficulty level leads to neither

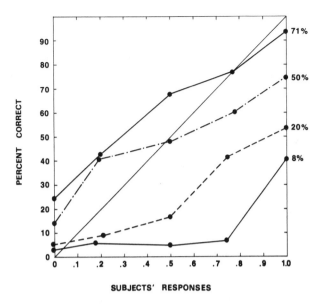

Figure 4. The effect on calibration due to changes in the percentage of true statements. (*Source:* Fischhoff & Lichtenstein, unpublished.)

overconfidence nor underconfidence, and thus the test on which the person will be best calibrated). However, the difficulty level of the "ideal" test may vary across people. Thus, even when one person is better than another on a particular set of items, the reverse may be true for a harder or easier set.

Comparisons between different groups of subjects have generally shown few differences when difficulty was controlled. Graduate students in psychology, who presumably are more intelligent than the usual subjects (undergraduates who answered an ad in the college newspaper), were no different in calibration (Lichtenstein & Fischhoff, 1977). Nor have we found differences in calibration or overconfidence between males and females (Lichtenstein & Fischhoff, 1981).

Wright and Phillips (1976) studied the relationships among several personality measures (authoritarianism, conservatism, dogmatism, and intolerance of ambiguity), verbal expressions of uncertainty (e.g., the number of words such as *unlikely* used in short written answers to 45 questions), and several measures of calibration. The only relationships they found between six personality scales and seven calibration measures were two modest correlations (.41 and .34) with the authoritarianism (F) scale. The calibration of certainty responses (i.e., responses of 1.0) was uncorrelated with the calibration of uncertainty (<1.0) responses. The measures of verbal uncertainty were uncorrelated with any of the numerical calibration measures. The authors concluded that probabilistic thinking is neither a single factor nor strongly related to individual differences on personality measures.

Wright et al. (1978) have studied cross-cultural differences in calibration. The calibration of their British sample was shown in Figure 2 (identified there as Phillips & Wright, 1977). Their other samples were Hong Kong, Indonesian, and Malay students. The Asian groups showed essentially flat calibration curves. The authors speculated that fate-oriented Asian philosophies might account for these differences.

Corrective efforts. Fischhoff and Slovic (1980) tried to ward off overconfidence on the task of discriminating Asian from European children's drawings by using explicitly discouraging instructions:

All drawings were taken from the Child Art Collection of Dr. Rhoda Kellogg, a leading proponent of the theory that children from different countries and cultures make very similar drawings. . . . Remember, it may well be impossible to make this sort of discrimination. Try to do the best you can. But if, in the extreme, you feel totally uncertain about the origin of all of these drawings, do not hesitate to respond with .5 for every one of them. (p. 792)

These instructions lowered the mean response by about .05, but substantial overconfidence was still found.

Will increased motivation improve calibration? Sieber (1974) compared the calibration of two groups of students on a course-related set of four-alternative items. One group was told that they were taking their mid-term examination. The other group was told that the test was not the mid-term but would be used to coach them for the mid-term. The two groups did not differ in the number of correct alternatives chosen, but the presumably more motivated group, whose performance would determine their grade, showed significantly *worse* calibration (greater overconfidence).

Training assessors by giving them feedback about their calibration has shown mixed results. As mentioned, Adams and Adams (1958) found modest improvement in calibration after five training sessions and, in a later study (1961), some generalization of training. Choo (1976), using only one training session with 75 two-alternative general-knowledge items, found little improvement and no generalization.

Lichtenstein and Fischhoff (1980b) trained two groups of subjects by giving extensive, personalized calibration feedback after each of either 2 or 10 sessions composed of 200 two-alternative general-knowledge items. They found appreciable improvement in calibration, all of which occurred between the first and the second session. Modest generalization occurred for tasks with different difficulty levels, content, and response mode (four rather than two alternatives), but no improvement was found with a fractile assessment task (described in the next section) or on the discrimination of European from American handwriting samples.

Another approach to improving calibration is to restructure the task in a way that discourages overconfidence. In a study by Koriat, Lichtenstein, and Fischhoff (1980), subjects first responded to 30 two-alternative general-knowledge items in the usual way. They then received 10 additional items. For each item they wrote down all the reasons they could think of that supported or contradicted either of the two possible answers, and then made the usual choice and probability assessments. This procedure significantly improved their calibration. An additional study helped to pinpoint the effective ingredient of this technique. After responding as usual to an initial set of 30 items, subjects were given 30 more items. For each, they first chose a preferred answer, then wrote (a) one reason supporting their chosen answer, (b) one reason contradicting their chosen answer, or (c) two reasons, one supporting and one contradicting. Then they assessed the probability that their chosen answer was correct. Only the group asked to write contradicting reasons showed improved calibration. This result, as well as correlational analyses on the data from the first study, suggests that an effective partial remedy for overconfidence is to search for reasons why one might be *wrong*.

Expertise. Students taking a college course are, presumably, experts, at least temporarily, in the topic material of the course. Sieber (1974) reported excellent calibration for students taking a practice mid-term examination (i.e., the group of students who were told that the test was *not* their mid-term). Over 98% of their 1.0 responses and only .5% of their 0 responses were correct. Pitz (1974) asked his students to predict their grade for his course; they also were well calibrated.

Would these subjects have been as well calibrated on items of equivalent difficulty that were not in their area of expertise? Lichtenstein and Fischhoff (1977) asked graduate students in psychology to respond to 50 two-alternative general-knowledge items and 50 items covering knowledge of psychology (e.g., "the Ishihara test is (a) a perceptual test, (b) a social anxiety test"). The two subtests were of equal difficulty, and the calibration was similar for the two tasks.

Christensen-Szalanski and Bushyhead (1981) reported nine physicians' assessments of the probability of pneumonia for 1,531 patients who were examined because of a cough. Their calibration was abysmal; the curve rose so slowly that for the highest confidence level (approximately .88), the proportion of patients actually having pneumonia was less than .20. Similar results have been reported for diagnoses of skull fracture and pneumonia by Lusted (1977) and for diagnoses of skull fracture by DeSmet, Fryback, and Thornbury (1979). The results of these field studies with physicians are in marked contrast with the superb calibration of weather forecasters' precipitation predictions. We suspect that several factors favor the weather forecasters. First, they have been making probabilistic forecasts for years. Second, the task is repetitive; the question to be answered (Will it rain?) is always the same. In contrast, a practicing physician is hour by hour considering a wide array of possibilities (Is it a skull fracture? Does she have strep? Does he need further hospitalization?). Finally, the outcome feedback for weather forecasters is well defined and promptly received. This is not always true for physicians; patients fail to return or are referred elsewhere, or diagnoses remain uncertain.

People who bet on or establish the odds for horse races might also be considered experts. Under the pari-mutuel (or totalizator) method, the final odds are determined by the amount of money bet on each horse, allowing a kind of group calibration curve to be computed. Such curves (Fabricand, 1965; Hoerl & Fallin, 1974) show excellent calibration, with only a slight tendency for people to bet too heavily on the long shots. However, such data are only inferentially related to probability assessment. More relevant are the calibration results reported by Dowie (1976), who studied the forecast prices printed daily by a sporting newspaper in Britain. These predictions, in the form of odds, are made by one person for all the horses in a given race; about eight people made the forecasts during the year studied. The calibration of the forecasts for 29,307 horses showed a modest underconfidence for probabilities greater than .4 and superb calibration for probabilities less than .4 (which comprised 98% of the data).

The burgeoning research on calibration has led to the development of a new kind of expertise: calibration experts, who know about the common errors people make in assessing probabilities. Lichtenstein and Fischhoff (1980a) compared the calibration of 8 such experts with 12 naive subjects and 15 subjects who had previously been trained to be well calibrated. The normative experts not only overcame the overconfidence typically shown by naive subjects but apparently overcompensated, for they were underconfident. The experts were also slightly more sensitive to item difficulty than the other two groups.

Future events. Wright and Wishudha (1979) have speculated that calibration for future events may be different from that for general-knowledge questions. If true, this would limit extrapolation from research with general-knowledge questions to the prediction of future events. Unfortunately, Wright and Wishudha's general-knowledge items were more difficult than their future events, which could account for the superior calibration of the latter.

Fischhoff and Beyth (1975) asked 150 Israeli students to assess the probability of 15 then-future events, possible outcomes of President

Nixon's much-publicized trips to China and Russia (e.g., "President Nixon will meet Mao at least once"). The resulting calibration curve was quite close to the identity line. However, Fischhoff and Lichtenstein (unpublished) have recently found that the calibration of future events showed the same severe overconfidence as was shown for general-knowledge items of comparable difficulty. Phillips and Chew (unpublished) obtained calibration curves for three sets of items: general knowledge, future events, and past events (e.g., "a jumbo jet crashed killing more than 100 people sometime in the past 30 days"). All three curves showed overconfidence. Calibration for future and past events was identical, and somewhat better than for the general-knowledge items. The difficulty levels of the three sets of items could not account for these results.

Jack Dowie and colleagues are now collecting calibration data at the Open University in Milton Keynes, England, from several hundred students in the course on risk, using course-related questions, general-knowledge questions, and future-event questions. The students received a general introduction to the concept of calibration and were given feedback about their performance and calibration. Preliminary results (Dowie, 1980) suggest that they were moderately overconfident. Calibration was best on general-knowledge items and worst on course-related items, but the significance and origins of these differences remain to be investigated.

Continuous propositions: Uncertain quantities

The fractile method

Uncertainty about the value of an uncertain continuous quantity (e.g., What proportion of students prefer Scotch to bourbon? What is the shortest distance from England to Australia?) may be expressed as a probability density function across the possible values of that quantity. However, assessors are not usually asked to draw the entire function. Instead, the elicitation procedure most commonly used is some variation of the fractile method. In this method, the assessor states values of the uncertain quantity that are associated with a small number of predetermined fractiles of the distribution. For the median or .50 fractile, for example, the assessor states a value of the quantity such that the true value is equally likely to fall above or below the stated value; the .01 fractile is a value such that there is only 1 chance in 100 that the true value is smaller than the stated value. Usually three or five fractiles, including the median, are assessed. In a variant called the *tertile* method, the assessor states two values (the .33 and .67 fractiles) such that the entire range is divided into three equally likely sections.

Two calibration measures are commonly reported. The *interquartile* index is the percentage of items for which the true value falls inside the interquartile range (i.e., between the .25 and the .75 fractiles). The perfectly calibrated person will, in the long run, have an interquartile index of 50. The *surprise index* is the percentage of true values that fall outside the most extreme fractiles assessed. When the most extreme fractiles assessed are .01 and .99, the perfectly calibrated person will have a surprise index of 2. A large surprise index shows that the assessor's confidence bounds have been too narrow to encompass enough of the true values and thus indicates overconfidence (or hyperprecision; Pitz, 1974). Underconfidence would be indicated by an interquartile index greater than 50 and a low surprise index; no such data have been reported in the literature.

The impetus for investigating the calibration of probability density functions came from a 1969 paper by Alpert and Raiffa (1969, **21**). Alpert and Raiffa worked with Harvard Business School students, all familiar with decision analysis. In group 1, all subjects assessed five fractiles, three of which were .25, .50, and .75. The extreme fractiles were, however, different for four subgroups; .01 and .99 (group A); .001 and .999 (group B); "the minimum possible value" and "the maximum possible value" (group C); and "astonishingly low" and "astonishingly high" (group D). The interquartile and surprise indices for these four subgroups are shown in Table 1. Discouraged by the enormous number of surprises, Alpert and Raiffa then ran three additional groups (2, 3, and 4) who, after assessing 10 uncertain quantities, received feedback in the form of an extended report and explanation of the results, along with perorations to "Spread Those Extreme Fractiles!" The subjects then responded to 10 new uncertain quantities. Results before and after feedback are shown in Table 1. The subjects improved, but still showed considerable overconfidence.

Hession and McCarthy (1974) collected data comparable to Alpert and Raiffa's first experiment, using 55 uncertain quantities and 36 graduate students as subjects. Their instructions urged subjects to make certain that the interval between the .25 fractile and the .75 fractile did indeed capture half of the probability. "Later discussion with individual subjects made it clear that this consistency check resulted in most cases in a readjustment, decreasing the interquartile range originally assessed" (p. 7) – thus making matters worse! This instructional emphasis, not used by Alpert and Raiffa, may explain why Hession and McCarthy's subjects were so badly calibrated, as shown in Table 1.

Hession and McCarthy also gave their subjects a number of individual difference measures: authoritarianism, dogmatism, rigidity, Pettigrew's Category-width Scale, and intelligence. The correlations of the subjects' test scores with their interquartile and surprise indices were mostly quite low, although the authoritarian scale correlated −.31 with the interquar-

Table 1. *Calibration summary for continuous items: Percentage of true values falling within interquartile range and outside the extreme fractiles*

	N	Observed interquartile index[a]	Surprise index Observed	Surprise index Ideal
Alpert & Raiffa (1969)				
Group 1-A (.01, .99)	880		46	2
Group 1-B (.001, .999)	500	33	40	.2
Group 1-C ("min" & "max")	700		47	?
Group 1-D ("astonishingly high/low")	700		38	?
Groups 2, 3, & 4				
before training	2,270	34	34	2
after training	2,270	44	19	2
Hession & McCarthy (1974)	2,035	25	47	2
Selvidge (1975)				
Five fractiles	400	56	10	2
Seven fractiles (incl. .1 & .9)	520	50	7	2
Moskowitz & Bullers (1978)				
Proportions				
Three fractiles	120	—	27	2
Five fractiles	145	32	42	2
Dow-Jones				
Three fractiles	210	—	38	2
Five fractiles	210	20	64	2
Pickhardt & Wallace (1974)				
Group 1,				
first round	?	39	32	2
fifth round	?	49	20	2
Group 2,				
first round	?	30	46	2
sixth round	?	45	24	2
T. A. Brown (1973)	414	29	42	2
Lichtenstein & Fischhoff (1980b)				
Pretest	924	32	41	2
Post-test	924	37	40	2
Seaver, von Winterfeldt, & Edwards (1978)				
Fractiles	160	42	34	2
Odds-fractiles	160	53	24	2
Probabilities	180	57	5	2
Odds	180	47	5	2
Log odds	140	31	20	2
Schaefer & Borcherding (1973)				
First day, fractiles	396	23	39	2
Fourth day, fractiles	396	38	12	2
First day, hypothetical sample	396	16	50	2
Fourth day, hypothetical sample	396	48	6	2

Table 1 *(cont.)*

	N	Observed interquartile index[a]	Surprise index	
			Observed	Ideal
Larson & Reenan (1979) "Reasonably Certain"	450	—	42	?
Pratt (1975) "Astonishingly high/low"	175	37	5	?
Murphy & Winkler (1974) Extremes were .125 & .875	132	45	27	25
Murphy & Winkler (1977b) Extremes were .125 & .875	432	54	21	25
Staël von Holstein (1971a)	1,269	27	30	2

Note: N = total number of assessed distributions.
[a] The ideal percentage of events falling within the interquartile range is 50, for all experiments except Brown (1973). He elicited the .30 and .70 fractiles, so the ideal is 40%.

tile score and $+.47$ with the surprise score ($N = 28$). This is consistent with Wright and Phillips's (1976) finding that authoritarianism was modestly related to calibration.

Selvidge (1975) extended Alpert and Raiffa's work by first asking subjects four questions about themselves (e.g., "Do you prefer Scotch or bourbon?"). Their responses determined the true answer for these *group-generated* proportions (e.g., what proportion of the subjects answering the questionnaire preferred Scotch to bourbon?). One group gave five fractiles, .01, .25, .5, .75, and .99. Another group gave those five plus two others: .1 and .9. As shown in Table 1, the seven-fractile group did a bit better. The five-fractile results are not as different from Alpert and Raiffa's results as they appear. Three of Alpert and Raiffa's uncertain quantities were group-generated proportions similar to Selvidge's items. On these three items, Alpert and Raiffa found 57% in the interquartile range and 20% surprises. Finally, for one of the items, half the subjects in the five-fractile group were asked to give .25, .5, and .75 first, and then to give .01 and .99, while the other half were instructed to assess the extremes first. Selvidge found fewer surprises for the former order (8%) than for the latter (16%).

Moskowitz and Bullers (1978) also used group-generated proportions, but found many more surprises than did Selvidge. One group gave the same five fractiles that Selvidge used (in the order .5, .25, .75, .01, .99). Another group was asked for only three assessments (the mode of the distribution and the .01 and .99 fractiles). Before making their assessments, the three-fractile group received a presentation and discussion of some typical reference events (e.g., "Consider a lottery in which 100 people are participating. Your chance of holding the winning ticket is 1 in 100") designed to give assessors a better understanding of the meaning of a .01 probability. As shown in Table 1, the three-fractile group had fewer surprises than the five-fractile group. In another experiment using the same two methods, Moskowitz and Bullers asked 44 undergraduate commerce students to assess the average value of the Dow-Jones industrial index for 1977, 1974, 1965, 1960, and 1950. Each subject gave assessments before and after engaging in three-person discussions. Since no systematic differences due to the discussions were found, the data have been combined in Table 1. Again, the three-fractile group (who had received the presentation on the meaning of .01) had fewer surprises than the five-fractile group. The performance of the five-fractile group was extremely bad.

Pickhardt and Wallace (1974) replicated Alpert and Raiffa's work with variations. Across several groups they reported 38% to 48% surprises before feedback and not less than 30% surprises after feedback. Two variations, using or not using course grade credit as a reward for good calibration and using or not using scoring rule feedback, made no difference in the number of surprises. Pickhardt and Wallace also studied the effects of extended training: Two groups of 18 and 30 subjects (number of uncertain quantities not reported) responded for five and six sessions with calibration feedback after every session. Modest improvement was found, as shown in Table 1.

Finally, Pickhardt and Wallace (1974) studied the effects of increasing knowledge on calibration in the context of a production simulation game called PROSIM. Thirty-two graduate students each made 51 assessments during a simulated 17 "days" of production scheduling. Each assessment concerned an event that would occur 1, 2, or 3 "days" hence. The closer the time of assessment to the time of the event, the more the subject knew about the event. Overconfidence decreased with this increased information: There were 32% surprises with 3-day lags, 24% with 2-day lags, and 7% with 1-day lags. No improvement was observed over the 17 "days" of the stimulation.

T.A. Brown (1973) asked 31 subjects to assess seven fractiles (.01, .10, .30, .50, .70, .90, .99) for 14 uncertain quantities. The results, shown in Table 1, are particularly discouraging, because each question was accompanied by extensive historical data (e.g., for "Where will the Consumer Price Index stand in December, 1970?" subjects were given the consumer price index for every quarter between March 1962 and June 1970). For 11 of the questions, had the subjects given the historical minimum as their .01 fractile and the historical maximum as their .99 fractile, they would have had no surprises at all. The other 3 questions showed strictly increasing or strictly decreasing histories, and the true value was close to any simple approximation of the historical trend. The subjects must have been relying heavily on their own erroneous knowledge to have given distributions so tight as to produce 42% surprises.

Lichtenstein and Fischhoff (1980b) elicited five fractiles (.01, .25, .5, .75, .99) from 12 subjects on 77 uncertain quantities both before and after the subjects received extensive calibration training on two-alternative discrete items. As shown in Table 1, the subjects did not significantly improve their calibration of uncertain quantities.

Other methods

Seaver, von Winterfeldt, and Edwards (1978) studied the effects of five different response modes on calibration. Two groups used the fractile method, either five fractiles (.01, .25, .50, .75, .99) or the odds equivalents of those fractiles (1:99, 1:3, 1:1, 3:1, 99:1). Three other groups responded with probabilities, odds, or odds on a log-odds scale to one-alternative questions that specified a particular value of the uncertain quantity (e.g., "What is the probability that the population of Canada in 1973 exceeded 25 million?"). Five such fixed values were given for each uncertain quantity, and from the responses the experimenters estimated the inter-quartile and surprise indices. For each method, seven to nine students responded to 20 uncertain quantities. As shown in Table 1, the groups giving probabilistic and odds responses had distinctly better surprise indices than those using the fractile method. It is unclear whether this superiority is due to the information communicated by the values chosen by the experimenter. The log-odds response mode did not work out well.

Schaefer and Borcherding (1973) asked 22 students to assess 18 group-generated proportions in each of four sessions. Each subject used two assessment techniques: (a) the fractile method (.01, .125, .25, .5, .75, .875, .99), and (b) the hypothetical sample method. In the latter method, the assessor states the size, n, and the number of successes, r, of a hypothetical sample that best reflects the assessor's knowledge about the uncertain quantity (i.e., I feel as certain about the true value of the proportion as I would feel were I to observe a sample of n cases with r successes). Larger values of n reflect greater certainty about the true value of the proportion. The ratio r/n reflects the mean of the probability density function. Subjects had great difficulty with this method, despite instructions that included examples of the beta distributions underlying this method. After every session, subjects were given extensive feedback, with emphasis on their own and the group's calibration. The results from the first and last sessions are shown in Table 1. Improvement was found for both methods. Results from the hypothetical sample method started out worse (50%

surprises and only 16% in the interquartile range) but ended up better (6% surprises and 48% in the interquartile range) than the fractile method.

Barclay and Peterson (1973) compared the tertile method (i.e., the fractiles .33 and .67) with a "point" method in which the assessor is asked to give the modal value of the uncertain quantity, and then two values, one above and one below the mode, each of which are half as likely to occur as is the modal value (i.e., points for which the probability density function is half as high as at the mode). Using 10 almanac questions as uncertain quantities and 70 students at the Defense Intelligence School in a within-subjects design, they found for the tertile method that 29% (rather than 33%) of the true answers fell in the central interval. For the point method, only 39% fell between the two half-probable points, whereas, for most distributions, approximately 75% of the density falls between these points.

Pitz (1974) reported several results using the tertile method. For 19 subjects estimating the populations of 23 countries, he found only 16% of the true values falling inside the central third of the distributions. In another experiment he varied the items according to the depth and richness of knowledge he presumed his subjects to have. With populations of countries (low knowledge) he found 23% of the true values in the central third; with heights of well-known buildings (middling knowledge), 27%; and with ages of famous people (high knowledge), 47%, the last being well above the expected 33%. In another study, he asked 6 subjects to assess tertiles and a few days later to choose among bets based on their own tertile values. He found a strong preference for bets involving the central region, just the reverse of what their too-tight intervals should lead them to.

Larson and Reenan's (1979) subjects first gave their best guess at the true answer (i.e., the mode) and then two more values that defined an interval within which they were "reasonably certain" the correct answer lay. Forty-two percent of the true values lay outside this region. Note how similar this surprise index is to the indices of Alpert and Raiffa's subjects given the verbal phrases "minimum/maximum" (47%) and "astonishingly high/low" (38%).

Real tasks with experts

Pratt (1975) asked a single expert to predict movie attendance for 175 movies or double features shown in two local theaters over a period of more than one year. The expert assessed the median, quartiles, and "astonishingly high" and "astonishingly low" values. As shown in Table 1, the interquartile range tended to be too small. Even though the expert received outcome feedback throughout the experiment, the only evidence of improvement in calibration over time came in the first few days.

Three experiments used weather forecasters for subjects. In two experiments, Murphy and Winkler (1974, 1977b) asked weather forecasters to give five fractiles (.125, .25, .5, .75, .875) for tomorrow's high temperature. The results, shown in Table 1, indicate excellent calibration. These subjects had fewer surprises in the extreme 25% of the distribution than did most of Alpert and Raiffa's subjects in the extreme 2%! Murphy and Winkler found that the five subjects in the two experiments who used the fractile method were better calibrated than four other subjects who used a fixed-width method. For the fixed-width method, the forecasters first assessed the median temperature (i.e., the high temperature for which they believed there was a .5 probability that it would be exceeded). Then they stated the probability that the temperature would fall with intervals of 5°F and of 9°F centered at the median. These forecasters were overconfident; the probability associated with the temperature falling inside the interval tended to be too large. The superiority of the fractile method over the fixed-width method stands in contrast to Seaver, von Winterfeldt, and Edwards's finding that fixed-value methods were superior, perhaps because the fixed intervals used by Murphy and Winkler (5°F and 9°F) were noninformative.

Staël von Holstein (1971a) used three fixed-value tasks: (a) average temperature tomorrow and the next day (dividing the entire response range into eight categories), (b) average temperature 4 and 5 days from now (eight categories), and (c) total amount of rain in the next 5 days (four categories). From each set of responses (four or eight probabilities summing to 1.0) he estimated the underlying cumulative density function. He then combined the 1,269 functions given by 28 participants. From the group cumulative density function shown in his article, we have estimated the surprise and interquartile indices (see Table 1). In contrast to other weather forecasters, these subjects were quite poorly calibrated, perhaps because the tasks were less familiar.

Summary of calibration with uncertain quantities

The overwhelming evidence from research using fractiles to assess uncertain quantites is that people's probability distributions tend to be too tight. The assessment of extreme fractiles is particularly prone to bias. Training improves calibration somewhat. Experts sometimes perform well (Murphy & Winkler, 1974, 1977b), sometimes not (Pratt, 1975; Staël von Holstein, 1971a). There is some evidence that difficulty is related to calibration for continuous propositions. Pitz (1974) and Larson and Reenan (1979) found such an effect, and Pickhardt and Wallace's (1974) finding that 1-day lags led to fewer surprises than 3-day lags in their simulation game is relevant here. Several studies (e.g., Barclay & Peterson, 1973; Murphy & Winkler, 1974) have reported a correlation between the spread of the assessed distribution and the absolute difference between the assessed median and the true answer, indicating that subjects do have a partial sensitivity to how much they do or don't know. This finding parallels the correlation between the percentage correct and the mean response with discrete propositions.

Discussion

Why be well calibrated?

Why should a probability assessor worry about being well calibrated? Von Winterfeldt and Edwards (1973) have shown that in most real-world decision problems with continuous decision options (e.g., invest X dollars) fairly large assessment errors make relatively little difference in the expected gain. However, several considerations argue against this reassuring view. First, in a two-alternative situation, the payoff function can be quite steep in the crucial region. Suppose your doctor must decide the probability that you have condition A, and should receive treatment A, versus having condition B and receiving treatment B. Suppose that the utilities are such that treatment A is better if the probability that you have condition A is greater than or equal to .4; otherwise treatment B is better. If the doctor assesses the probability that you have A as $p(A) = .45$ but is poorly calibrated, so that the appropriate probability is .25, then the doctor would use treatment A rather than treatment B and you would lose quite a chunk of expected utility. Real-life utility functions of just this type are shown by Fryback (1974).

Furthermore, when the payoffs are very large, when the errors are very large, or when such errors compound, the expected loss looms large. For instance, in the Reactor Safety Study (U.S. Nuclear Regulatory Commission, 1975) "at each level of the analysis a log-normal distribution of failure rate data was assumed with 5 and 95 percentile limits defined" (Weatherwax, 1975, p. 31). The research reviewed here suggests that distributions built from assessments of the .05 and .95 fractiles may be grossly biased. If such assessments are made at several levels of an analysis, with each assessed distribution being too narrow, the errors will not cancel each other but will compound. And because the costs of nuclear-power-plant failure are large, the expected loss from such errors could be enormous.

If good calibration is important, how can it be achieved? Cox (1958) recommended that one externally recalibrate people's assessments by fitting a model to a set of assessments for items with known answers. From then on, the model is used to correct or adjust responses given by the assessor. The technical difficulties confronting external recalibration are substantial. When eliciting the assessments to be modeled, one would have to be careful not to give the assessors any more feedback than they normally receive, for fear of their changing their calibration as it is being measured. As Savage (1971) pointed out, "You might discover with experience that your expert is optimistic or pessimistic in some respect and therefore temper his judgments. Should he suspect you of this, however, you and he may well be on the escalator to perdition" (p. 796). Furthermore, since research has shown that the type of miscalibration observed depends on a task's difficulty level, one would also have to believe that the future will match the difficulty of the events used for the recalibration.

The theoretical objections to external recalibration may be even more serious than the practical objections. The numbers produced by a recalibration process will not, in general, follow the axioms of probability theory (e.g., the numbers associated with mutually exclusive and exhaustive events will not always sum to one, nor will it be generally true that $P(A) \cdot P(B) = P(A,B)$ for independent events); hence, these new numbers cannot be called probabilities.

A more fruitful approach would be to train assessors to become well calibrated. Under what conditions might one expect that assessors could achieve this goal? One should not expect assessors to be well calibrated when the explicit or implicit rewards for their assessments do not motivate them to be honest in their assessments. As an extreme example, an assessor who is threatened with beheading should any event occur whose probability was assessed at $<.25$ will have good reason not to be well calibrated with assessments of .20. Although this example seems absurd, more subtle pressures such as "avoid being made to look the fool" or "impress your boss" might also provide strong incentives for bad calibration. Any rewards for either wishful thinking or denial could also bias the assessments.

Receiving outcome feedback after every assessment is the best condition for successful training. Dawid (in press) has shown that under such conditions assessors who are honest and coherent subjectivists will expect to be well calibrated regardless of the interdependence among the items being assessed. In contrast, Kadane (1980) has shown that in the absence of trial-by-trial outcome feedback, honest, coherent subjectivists will expect to be well calibrated if and only if all the items being assessed are independent. This theorem puts strong restrictions on the situations under which it would be reasonable to expect assessors to learn to be well calibrated. Even if the training process could be conducted using only events that assessors believed were independent, there may be good reason to doubt the independence of the real-life tasks to which the assessors would apply their training. Important future events may be interdependent either because they are influenced by a common underlying cause or because the assessor evaluates all of them by drawing on a common store of knowledge. In such circumstances, one would not want or expect to be well calibrated.

The possibility that people's biases vary as a function of the difficulty of the tasks poses a further obstacle to calibration training in the absence of immediate outcome feedback. The difficulty level of future tasks may be impossible to predict, thus rendering the training ineffective.

Calibration as cognitive psychology

Experiments on calibration can be used to learn how people think. Even if the immediate practical significance of each study is limited, it may still provide greater understanding of how people develop and express feelings of uncertainty and certainty. However, a striking aspect of much of the literature reviewed here is its "dust-bowl empiricism." Psychological theory is often absent, either as motivation for the research or as explanation of the results.

Not all authors have avoided theorizing. Slovic (1972a) and Tversky and Kahneman (1974, 1) argued that, as a result of limited information-processing abilities, people adopt simplifying rules or heuristics. Although generally quite useful, these heuristics can lead to severe and systematic errors. For example, the tendency of people to give unduly tight distributions when assessing uncertain quantities could reflect the heuristic called "anchoring and adjustment." When asked about an uncertain quantity, one naturally thinks first of a point estimate such as the median. This value then serves as an anchor. To give the 25th or 75th percentile, one adjusts downward or upward from the anchor. But the anchor has such a dominating influence that the adjustment is insufficient; hence the fractiles are too close together, yielding overconfidence.

Pitz (1974), too, accepted that people's information-processing capacity and working memory capacity are limited. He suggested that people tackle complex problems serially, working through a portion at a time. To reduce cognitive strain, people ignore the uncertainty in their solutions to the early portions of the problem in order to reduce the complexity of the calculations in later portions. This could lead to too-tight distributions and overconfidence. Pitz also suggested that one way people estimate their own uncertainty is by seeing how many different ways they can arrive at an answer, that is, how many different serial solutions they can construct. If many are found, people will recognize their own uncertainty; if few are found, they will not. The richer the knowledge base from which to build alternative structures, the less the tendency toward overconfidence.

Phillips and Wright (1977) presented a three-stage serial model. Their model distinguishes people who tend naturally to think about uncertainty in a probabilistic way from those who respond in a more black-and-white fashion. Their work on cultural and individual differences (Wright & Phillips, 1976, Wright et al., 1978) has attempted, with partial success, to identify distinct cognitive styles in processing this type of information.

Koriat et al. (1980) also took an information-processing approach. They discussed three stages for assessing probabilities. First one searches one's memory for relevant evidence. Next one assesses that evidence to arrive at a feeling of certainty or doubt. Finally, one translates the certainty feeling into a number. The manipulations used by Koriat et al. were designed to alter the first two stages, by forcing people to search for and attend to contradictory evidence, thereby lowering their confidence.

Ferrell and McGoey's (1980) model, on the other hand, deals entirely with the third stage, translation of feelings of certainty into numerical responses. By assuming that, without feedback, people are unable to alter their translation strategies as either the difficulty of the items or the base rate of the events changes, the model provides strong predictions that have received support from calibration data.

Structure and process theories of probability assessment are beginning to emerge; we hope that the further development of such theories will serve to integrate this rather specialized field into the broader field of cognitive psychology.

23. For those condemned to study the past: Heuristics and biases in hindsight

Baruch Fischhoff

Benson (1972) has identified four reasons for studying the past: to entertain, to create a group (or national) identity, to reveal the extent of human possibility, and to develop systematic knowledge about our world, knowledge that may eventually improve our ability to predict and control. On a conscious level, at least, we behavioral scientists restrict ourselves to the last motive. In its pursuit, we do case studies, program evaluations, and literature reviews. We even conduct experiments, creating artificial histories upon which we can perform our postmortems.

Three basic questions seem to arise in our retrospections: (a) Are there patterns upon which we can capitalize so as to make ourselves wiser in the future? (b) Are there instances of folly in which we can identify mistakes to avoid? (c) Are we really condemned to repeat the past if we do not study it? That is, do we really learn anything by looking backward?

Whatever the question we are asking, it is generally assumed that the past will readily reveal the answers it holds. Of hindsight and foresight, the latter appears as the troublesome perspective. One can explain and understand any old event if an appropriate effort is applied. Prediction, however, is acknowledged to be rather more tricky. The present essay investigates this presumption by taking a closer look at some archetypal attempts to tap the past. Perhaps its most general conclusion is that we should hold the past in a little more respect when we attempt to plumb its secrets. While the past entertains, ennobles, and expands quite readily, it enlightens only with delicate coaxing.

This is a revised version of the paper "For Those Condemned to Study the Past: Reflections on Historical Judgment," in R. A. Shweder and D. W. Fiske (Eds.), New Directions for Methodology of Behavioral Science: Fallible Judgment in Behavioral Research. San Francisco: Jossey-Bass, 1980. Reprinted by permission.

Looking for wisdom

Although the past never repeats itself in detail, it is often viewed as having repetitive elements. People make the same kinds of decisions, face the same kinds of challenges, and suffer the same kinds of misfortune often enough for behavioral scientists to believe that they can detect recurrent patterns. Such faith prompts psychometricians to study the diagnostic secrets of ace clinicians, clinicians to look for correlates of aberrant behavior, brokers to hunt for harbingers of price increases, and dictators to ponder revolutionary situations. Their search usually has a logic paralleling that of multiple regression or correlation. A set of relevant cases is collected and each member is characterized on a variety of dimensions. The resulting matrix is scoured for significant relationships that might aid us in predicting the future . . . .

Formal modeling

The *Daily Racing Form,* for example, offers the earnest handicapper some 100 pieces of information on each horse in any given race. The handicapper with a flair for data processing might commit to some computer's memory the contents of a bound volume of the *Form* and try to derive a formula predicting speed as a weighted sum of scores on various dimensions. For example:

$$\tilde{y} = b_1x_1 + b_2x_2 + b_3x_3 \tag{1}$$

where $\tilde{y}$ is our best guess at a horse's speed, x_1 is its percentage of victories in previous races, x_2 is its jockey's percentage of winning races, and x_3 is the weight it will carry in the present race. Assuming that standardized scores[1] are used, the weights (b_i) reflect the importance of the different factors. If $b_1 = 2b_2$, then a given change in the horse's percentage of wins affects our speed prediction twice as much as an equivalent change in the jockey's percentage of wins, because past performances have proved twice as sensitive to x_1 as x_2.

Sounds easy, but there are a thousand pitfalls. One emerges when the predictors (x_i) are correlated, as might (and in fact does) happen were winning horses to draw winning jockeys (or vice versa). In such cases of multicollinearity, each variable has some independent ability to explain past performance and the two have some shared ability. When the weights are determined, that shared explanatory capacity will somehow be split between the two. Typically, that split renders the (b_i) uninterpretable with any degree of precision. Thus the regression equation cannot be treated as a theory of horse racing, showing the importance of various factors.

---

[1] To standardize scores on a particular variable, one subtracts the mean of all scores from each score and then divides by the standard deviation. The result is a set of scores with a mean of 0 and a standard deviation of 1.

A more modest theoretical goal would simply be to determine which factors are and which factors are not important, on the basis of how much each adds to our understanding of y. The logic here is that of stepwise regression; additional variables are added to the equation as long as they add something to its overall predictive (or explanatory) power. Yet even this minimalistic strategy can run afoul of multicollinearity. If many reflections of a particular factor (e.g., different aspects of breeding) are included, their shared explanatory ability may be divided up into such small pieces that no one aspect makes a "significant" contribution.

Of course, these nuances may be of relatively little interest to handicappers as long as the formula works well enough to help them somewhat in beating the odds. We scientist types, however, want wisdom as well as efficacy from our techniques. It is hard for us to give up interpreting weights. Regression procedures not only express, but also produce, understanding (or, at least, results) in a mechanical, repeatable fashion. Small wonder then that they have been pursued doggedly despite their limitations. One of the best documented pursuits has been in the study of clinical judgment. Clinical judgment is exercised by a radiologist who sorts X rays of ulcers into "benign" and "malignant," by a personnel officer who chooses the best applicants from a set of candidates, or by a crisis-center counselor who decides which callers threatening suicide are serious. In each of these examples, the diagnosis involves making a decision on the basis of a set of cues or attributes. When, as in these examples, the decision is repetitive and all cases can be characterized by the same cues, it is possible to model the judge's decision-making policy statistically. One collects a set of cases for which the expert has made a summary judgment (e.g., benign, serious) and then derives a regression equation, like Equation 1, whose weights show the importance the judge has assigned to each cue.

Two decades of such policy-capturing studies persistently produced a disturbing pair of conclusions: (a) Simple linear models, using a weighted sum of the cues, did an excellent job of predicting judges' decisions, although (b) the judges claimed that they were using much more complicated strategies (L. R. Goldberg, 1968b, 1970; Slovic & Lichtenstein, 1971). A commonly asserted form of complexity is called configural judgment, in which the diagnostic meaning of one cue depends upon the meaning of other cues (e.g., "that tone of voice makes me think 'not suicidal' unless the call comes in the early hours of the morning").

Two reasons for the conflict between measured and reported judgment policies have emerged from subsequent research, each with negative implications for the usefulness of regression modeling for "capturing" the wisdom of past decisions. One was the growing realization that combining enormous amounts of information in one's head, as required by such formulas, overwhelms the computational capacity of anyone but an idiot savant. A judge trying to implement a complex strategy simply would not be able to do so with great consistency. Indeed, it is difficult to learn and use even a non-configural, weighted-sum, decision rule when there are many cues or unusual relationships between the cues and predicted variable (Slovic, 1974).

The second realization that has emerged from clinical judgment research is that simple linear models are extraordinarily powerful predictors (see Chap. 28). A simple substantive theory indicating what variables people care about when making decisions may be all one needs to make pretty good predictions of their behavior. If some signs encourage a diagnosis or decision and others discourage it, simply counting the number of encouraging and discouraging signs will provide a pretty good guess at the individual's behavior. The result, however, will be a more modest theory than one can derive by flashy regression modeling (Fischhoff, Goitein, & Shapira, in press). Thus, while the past seems to be right out there to be understood, our standard statistical procedures do not always tell us what we want to know. If not used carefully, they may mislead us, leaving us less wise than when we started. We are tempted to embrace highly complicated theories in their entirety, without realizing that their power comes from very simple underlying notions rather than from having captured the essence of the past.

Looking for folly

Focus on failure

Searching for wisdom in historic events requires an act of faith – a belief in the existence of recurrent patterns waiting to be discovered. Searching for wisdom in the behavior of historical characters requires a somewhat different act of faith – confidence that our predecessors knew things we do not know. The first of these faiths is grounded in philosophy; it distinguishes those who view history as a social science, not an ideographic study of unique events. The second of these faiths is grounded in charity and modesty. It distinguishes those who hope to see further by standing on the shoulders of those who came before from those satisfied with standing on their faces. Aphorisms like "those who do not study the past are condemned to repeat it" suggest that faith in the wisdom of our predecessors is relatively rare.

An active search for folly is, of course, not without merit. Not only do individuals for whom things do not go right often have a lot of explaining to do, but such explanations are crucial to learning from their experience. By seeing how things went wrong, we hope to make them go right in the future. The quest for misfortunes to account for is hardly difficult. The eye, journalist, and historian are all drawn to disorder. An accident-free drive to the store or a reign without wars, depressions, or earthquakes is for them uneventful.

Although it has legitimate goals, focus on failure is likely to mislead us by creating a distorted view of the prevalence of misfortune. The perceived likelihood of events is determined in part by the ease with which they are imagined and remembered (Tversky & Kahneman, 1973, 11). Belaboring failures should, therefore, disproportionately enhance their perceived frequency in the past (and perhaps future).

It is also likely to promote an unbalanced appraisal of our predecessors' performance. The muckracker in each of us is drawn to stories of welfare cheaters or the "over-regulation" of particular environmental hazards (e.g., the Occupational Safety and Health Administration's infamous standard for a workplace toilet-seat design). We tend to forget, though, that any fallible, but not diabolical, decision-making system produces errors of both kinds. For every cheater garnering undeserved benefits, there are one or several or a fraction of cheatees, denied their rights by the same imperfect system. In fact, the two error rates are tied in a somewhat unintuitive fashion dependent upon the accuracy of judgment and the total resources available, that is, the percentage of eligible indigent or hazards that can be treated (Einhorn, 1978). Before rushing to criticize the welfare system for allowing a few cheaters, we should consider whether or not there might not be too few horror stories of that type, given the ratio of errors of commission to errors of omission.

In general, there is a good chance of being misled when we examine in isolation decisions that only "work out" on a percentage basis.

What was the problem?

There are other contexts in which errors in the small may look different when some larger context is considered. For example, we are taught that scientific theories should roll over dead once any inconsistent evidence is present. As a result, we are quick to condemn the folly of scientists who persist in their theories despite having been "proved" wrong. Kuhn (1962), however, argued that such local folly might be consistent with more global wisdom in the search for scientific knowledge. Others (e.g., Feyerabend, 1975; Lakatos, 1970) have, in fact, extolled the role of disciplined anarchy in the growth of understanding and have doubted the possibility of wisdom's emerging from orderly adherence to any one favored research method. They argue that obstinate refusal to look at contrary evidence or to abandon apparently disconfirmed theories is often necessary to scientific progress.

The $125 million settlement levied against Ford Motor Company in the Pinto case made the company's decision to save a few dollars in the design of that car's fuel tank seem like folly. Yet in purely economic terms, a guaranteed saving of, say, $15 on each of 10 million Pintos makes the risk of a few large law suits seem like a more reasonable gamble. Since the judgment in this well-publicized suit was reduced to $6 million upon appeal, the company may actually be ahead in strict economic terms, despite having had worse come to worst. Where the company may be faulted is in seeing one larger context (the number of cars on which it would save money), but not another (the non-economic consequences of its decision). It seems not to have realized the impact that adverse publicity would have on Ford's image as a safety-conscious auto maker or on prices for used Pintos (although that price was borne by Pinto, owners not producers).

If reprobation is the name of the game, a mistake is a mistake. Yet, if one is interested in learning from the experience of others, it is important to determine what problem they were attempting to solve. Upon careful examination, many apparent errors prove to represent deft resolution of the wrong problem. For example, if it is to be criticized at all, Ford might be held guilty of tactical wisdom and strategic folly (or perhaps of putting institutional health over societal well-being).

This distinction is important, not only for evaluating the past, but also for knowing what corrective measures need to be taken in the future. Usually, tactical mistakes are easier to correct than strategic misunderstandings. Once we have properly characterized a situation, there may be a "book," recording conventional wisdom as accumulated through trial-and-error experience, or at least formulas for optimally combining the information at our disposal (Hexter, 1971). Baseball managers, for example, may either know that it has proven successful to have the batter sacrifice with a runner on first and no one out in a close game or else have the statistics needed to calculate how to "go with the percentages." These guides are, however, unhelpful or misleading if the real problem to be solved is maintaining morale (the runner has a chance to lead the league in stolen bases) or aiding the box office (the fans need to see some swinging). Studies of surprise attacks in international relations reveal that surprised nations have often done a good job of playing by their own book but have misidentified the arena in which they were playing (Ben Zvi, 1976; Lanir, 1978). In a sense, they were reading the wrong book; the better they read, the quicker they met their demise.

One reason for the difficulty posed by strategic problems is that they must be "thought through" analytically, without the benefit of cumulative (statistical) experience. A second limitation is that misconceptions are often widely shared within a decision-making group or community. One is consulted on decisions only after one has completed the catechism in the book. Recurrent pieces of advice for institutions interested in avoiding surprises are (a) set up several separate analytical bodies in order to provide multiple, independent looks at a problem or (b) appoint one member to serve as "devil's advocate" for unpopular points of view (Janis, 1972). In practice, the first strategy may fail because shared misconceptions make the groups very like one another, creating redundancy rather than pluralism (Chan, 1979). The second fails because advocates either bow to group pressure or are ostracized if they take their unpopular positions seriously, even when those "extreme" positions do not drastically challenge group preconceptions.

Failure to distinguish between tactical and strategic decisions can also create an undeserved illusion of wisdom. Banks and insurance companies are usually considered to be extremely rational and adroit in their decision-making processes. Yet a closer look reveals that this reputation comes from their success in making highly repetitive, tactical decisions in which they almost cannot lose. Home mortgages and life insurance policies are issued on the basis of conservative interpretations of statistical tables acquired and adjusted through massive trial-and-error experience. These institutions' ventures into more speculative decisions requiring analytical, strategic decisions suggest that they are no smarter than the rest of us. Commercial banks lost large sums of money in the 1960s through unwise investments in real estate investment trusts; a similarly minute percentage of their overall decisions in the 1970s has chained the U.S. economy to the future of semisolvent Third World countries to whom enormous ($60+ billion) loans have been made. (Although this linkage may be for the long-range good of humanity, that was not necessarily the problem the banks were solving.) The slow and erratic response of insurance companies to changes in the economics of casualty insurance and their almost haphazard, non-analytical methods for dealing with many non-routine risks should leave the rest of us feeling not so stupid when compared with these vaunted institutions.

Hindsight: Thinking backward?

If we know what has happened and what problem an individual was trying to solve, we should be in a position to exploit the wisdom of our own hindsight in explaining and evaluating his or her behavior. Upon closer examination, however, the advantages of knowing how things turned out may be oversold (Fischhoff, 1975). In hindsight, people consistently exaggerate what could have been anticipated in foresight. They not only tend to view what has happened as having been inevitable but also to view it as having appeared "relatively inevitable" before it happened. People believe that others should have been able to anticipate events much better than was actually the case. They even misremember their own predictions so as to exaggerate in hindsight what they knew in foresight (Fischhoff and Beyth, 1975).

As described by historian Georges Florovsky (1969):

The tendency toward determinism is somehow implied in the method of retrospection itself. In retrospect, we seem to perceive the logic of the events which unfold themselves in a regular or linear fashion according to a recognizable pattern with an alleged inner necessity. So that we get the impression that it really could not have happened otherwise. (p. 369)

An apt name for this tendency to view reported outcomes as having been relatively inevitable might be *creeping determinism*, in contrast with philosophical determinism, the conscious belief that whatever happens has to happen.

One corollary tendency is to telescope the rate of historical processes, exaggerating the speed with which "inevitable" changes are consummated (Fischer, 1970). For example, people may be able to point to the moment when the latifundia were doomed, without realizing that they took two and a half centuries to disappear. Another tendency is to remember people as having been much more like their current selves than was actually the case (Yarrow, Campbell, & Burton, 1970). A third may be seen in Barraclough's (1972) critique of the historiography of the ideological roots of Nazism. Looking back from the Third Reich, one can trace its roots to the writings of many authors from whose writings one could not have projected Nazism. A fourth is to imagine that the participants in a historical situation were fully aware of its eventual importance ("Dear Diary, The Hundred Years' War started today," Fischer, 1970). A fifth is the myth of the critical experiment, unequivocally resolving the conflict between two theories or establishing the validity of one. In fact, "the crucial experiment is seen as crucial only decades later. Theories don't just give up, since a few anomalies are always allowed. Indeed, it is very difficult to defeat a research programme supported by talented and imaginative scientists" (Lakatos, 1970, pp. 157–158).

In the short run, failure to ignore outcome knowledge holds substantial benefits. It is quite flattering to believe, or lead others to believe, that we would have known all along what we could only know with outcome knowledge, that is, that we possess hindsightful foresight. In the long run, however, undetected creeping determinism can seriously impair our ability to judge the past or learn from it.

Consider decision makers who have been caught unprepared by some turn of events and who try to see where they went wrong by re-creating their pre-outcome knowledge state of mind. If, in retrospect, the event appears to have seemed relatively likely, they can do little more than berate themselves for not taking the action that their knowledge seems to have dictated. They might be said to add the insult of regret to the injury inflicted by the event itself. When second-guessed by a hindsightful observer, their misfortune appears as incompetence, folly, or worse.

In situations where information is limited and indeterminate, occasional surprises and resulting failures are inevitable. It is both unfair and self-defeating to castigate decision makers who have erred in fallible systems, without admitting to that fallibility and doing something to improve the system. According to historian Roberta Wohlstetter (1962), the lesson to be learned from American surprise at Pearl Harbor is that we must "accept the fact of uncertainty and learn to live with it. Since no magic will provide certainty, our plans must work without it" (p. 401).

When we attempt to understand past events, we implicitly test the hypotheses or rules we use both to interpret and to anticipate the world around us. If, in hindsight, we systematically underestimate the surprises that the past held and holds for us, we are subjecting those hypotheses to inordinately weak tests and, presumably, finding little reason to change them. Thus, the very outcome knowledge which gives us the feeling that we understand what the past was all about may prevent us from learning anything from it.

Protecting ourselves against this bias requires some understanding of the psychological processes involved in its creation. It appears that when we receive outcome knowledge, we immediately make sense out of it by integrating it into what we already know about the subject. Having made this reinterpretation, the reported outcome now seems a more or less inevitable outgrowth of the reinterpreted situation. "Making sense" out of what we are told about the past is, in turn, so natural that we may be unaware that outcome knowledge has had any effect on us. Even if we are aware of there having been an effect, we may still be unaware of exactly what it was. In trying to reconstruct our foresightful state of mind, we will remain anchored in our hindsightful perspective, leaving the reported outcome too likely looking.

As a result, merely warning people about the dangers of hindsight bias has little effect (Fischhoff, 1977b). A more effective manipulation is to force oneself to argue against the inevitability of the reported outcomes, that is, try to convince oneself that it might have turned out otherwise. Questioning the validity of the reasons you have recruited to explain its inevitability might be a good place to start (Koriat, Lichtenstein, & Fischhoff, 1980; Slovic & Fischhoff, 1977). Since even this unusual step seems not entirely adequate, one might further try to track down some of the uncertainty surrounding past events in their original form. Are there transcripts of the information reaching the Pearl Harbor Command prior to 7 A.M. on December 7? Is there a notebook showing the stocks you considered before settling on Waltham Industries? Are there diaries capturing Chamberlain's view of Hitler in 1939? An interesting variant was Douglas Freeman's determination not to know about any subsequent events when working on any given period in his definitive biography of Robert E. Lee (Commager, 1965). Although admirable, this strategy does require some naive assumptions about the prevalence of knowledge regarding who surrendered at Appomattox.

Looking at all

Why look?

Study of the past is predicated on the belief that if we look, we will be able to discern some interpretable patterns. Considerable research suggests that this belief is well founded. People seem to have a remarkable ability to find some order or meaning in even randomly produced data. One of the most familiar examples is the gamblers' fallacy. Our feeling is that in flipping a fair coin, four successive "heads" will be followed by a "tail" (Lindman & Edwards, 1961). Thus in our minds, even random processes are constrained to have orderly internal properties. Kahneman and Tversky (1972b, 3) have suggested that of the 32 possible sequences of six binary events only 1 actually looks "random."

Although the gamblers' fallacy is usually cited in the context of piquant but trivial examples, it can also be found in more serious attempts to explain historical events. For example, after cleverly showing that Supreme Court vacancies appear more or less at random (according to a Poisson process), with the probability of at least one vacancy in any given year being .39, Morrison (1977) claimed that:

[President] Roosevelt announced his plan to pack the Court in February, 1937, shortly after the start of his fifth year in the White House. 1937 was also the year in which he made his first appointment to the Court. That he had this opportunity in 1937 should come as no surprise, because the probability that he would go five consecutive years without appointing one or more justices was but .08, or one chance in twelve. In other words, when Roosevelt decided to change the Court by creating additional seats, the odds were already *eleven to one in his favor* that he would be able to name one or more justices by traditional means that very year. (pp. 143–144)

However, if vacancies do appear at random, then this reasoning is wrong. It assumes that the probabilistic process creating vacancies, like that governing coin flips, has a memory and a sense of justice, as if it knows that it is moving into the fifth year of the Roosevelt presidency and that it "owes" FDR a vacancy. However, on January 1, 1937, the past four years were history, and the probability of at least one vacancy in the coming year was still .39 (Fischhoff, 1978).

Feller (1968) offers the following anecdote involving even higher stakes: Londoners during the blitz devoted considerable effort to interpreting the pattern of German bombing, developing elaborate theories of where the Germans were aiming (and when to take cover). However, when London was divided up into small, contiguous geographic areas, the frequency distribution of bomb-hits per area was almost a perfect approximation of the Poisson distribution. Kates (1962) suggests that natural disasters constitute another category of consequential events where (threatened) laypeople see order when experts see randomness.

One secret to maintaining such beliefs is failure to keep complete enough records to force ourselves to confront irregularities. Historians acknowledge the role of missing evidence in facilitating their explanations with comments like "the history of the Victorian Age will never be written. We know too much about it. For ignorance is the first requisite of the historian – ignorance which simplifies and clarifies, which selects and omits, with placid perfection unattainable by the highest art" (Strachey, 1918, preface).

Even where records are available and unavoidable, we seem to have a remarkable ability to explain or provide a causal interpretation for whatever we see. When events are produced by probabilistic processes with intuitive properties, random variation may not even occur to us as a potential hypothesis. For example, the fact that athletes chastised for poor performance tend to do better the next time out fits our naive theories of reward and punishment. This handy explanation blinds us to the possibility that the improvement is due instead to regression to those players' mean performance (Furby, 1973; Kahneman & Tversky, 1973, 4).

Fama (1965) has forcefully argued that the fluctuations of stock-market prices are best understood as reflecting a random walk process. Random walks, however, have even more unintuitive properties than the binary processes to which they are formally related (Carlsson, 1972). As a result, we find that market analysts have an explanation for every change in price, whether purposeful or not. Some explanations, like those shown in Figure 1, are inconsistent;[2] others seem to deny the possibility of any random component, for example, that ultimate fudge factor, the "technical adjustment."

The pseudopower of our explanations can be illustrated by analogy with regression analysis. Given a set of events and a sufficiently large or rich set of possible explanatory factors, one can always derive postdictions or explanations to any desired degree of tightness. In regression terms, by expanding the set of independent variables one can always find a set of predictors with any desired correlation with the independent variable. The price one pays for overfitting is, of course, shrinkage, failure of the derived rule to work on a new sample of cases. The frequency and vehemence of methodological warnings against overfitting suggest that correlational overkill is a bias that is quite resistant to even extended professional training (for references, see Fischhoff & Slovic, 1980).

An overfitted theory is like a suit tailored so precisely to one individual in one particular pose that it will not fit anyone else or even that same individual in the future or even in the present if new evidence about him comes to light (e.g., if he lets out his breath to reveal a potbelly). A historian who had built an airtight case accounting for all available evidence in explaining how the Bolsheviks won might be in a sad position were the USSR to release suppressed documents showing that the Mensheviks were more serious adversaries than had previously been thought. The price that investment analysts pay for overfitting is their long-run failure to predict any better than market averages (Dreman,

---

[2] One of my favorite contrasts is that when the market rises following good economic news, it is said to be responding to the news; if it falls, that is explained by saying that the good news had already been discounted.

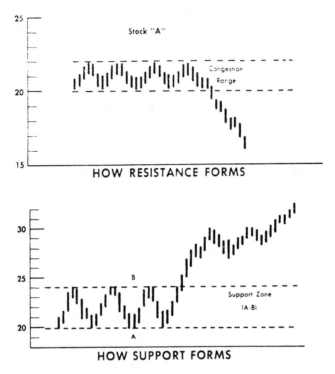

Figure 1. Two examples of cues used in identifying precursors of past shifts in stock prices: formation of resistance and formation of support. However, one might argue that prior to the dramatic shifts at their respective ends, these two patterns were essentially identical. In this light, an undulating pattern neither predicts nor explains anything in these data.

1979) – although the cynic might say that they actually make their living through the generation of hope (and commissions).[3]

Overfitting occurs because of capitalization on chance fluctuations. If measurement is sufficiently fine, two cases differing on one variable will also differ on almost any other variable one chooses to name. As a result, one can calculate a non-zero (actually, in this case, perfect) correlation between the two variables and derive an "interesting" substantive theory. Processes analogous to this two-dimensional case work with any m observations in the n-space defined by our set of possible explanatory concepts.

In these examples, the data are fixed and undeniable, while the set of possible explanations is relatively unbounded; one hunts until one finds an explanation that fits. Another popular form of capitalization on chance leaves the set of explanations fixed (usually at one candidate) and sifts

---

[3] A friend once took a course in reading form charts from a local brokerage. Each session involved the teaching of 10–12 new cues. When the course ended, five sessions and 57 cues later, the instructor was far from exhausting his supply.

through data until supporting evidence is found. Although the crasser forms of this procedure are well known, others are more subtle and even somewhat ambiguous in their characterization. For example, you run an experiment and fail to receive an anticipated result. Thinking about it, you note an element of your procedure that might have mitigated the effect of the manipulated variable. You correct that; again no result but, again, a possible problem. Finally, you (or your subjects) get it right and the anticipated effect is obtained. Now, is it right to perform your statistical test on that nth sample (for which it shows significance) or the whole lot of them? Had you done the right experiment first, the question would not even have arisen. Or, as a toxicologist, you are "certain" that exposure to chemical X is bad for one's health, so you compare workers who do and do not work with it in a particular plant for bladder cancer, but still no effect. So you try intestinal cancer, emphysema, dizziness, and so on, until you finally get a significant difference in skin cancer. Is that difference meaningful? Of course the way to test these explanations or theories is by replication on new samples. That step, unfortunately, is seldom taken and often is not possible for technical or ethical reasons (Tukey, 1977).

Related complications can arise even with fixed theories and data sets. Diaconis (1978) notes the difficulty of evaluating the amount of surprise in ESP results, even in the rare cases in which they have been obtained in moderately supervised settings, because the definition of the sought event keeps shifting. "A major key to B.D.'s success was that he did not specify in advance the result to be considered surprising. The odds against a coincidence *of some sort* are dramatically less than those against any prespecified *particular one* of them" (p. 132).[4]

Tufte and Sun (1975) discovered that the existence or non-existence of bellwether precincts depends upon the creativity and flexibility allowed in defining the event (for what office? in what elections? how good is good? are precincts that miss consistently to be included?). They are commonly believed to exist because we have an uncommonly good ability to find a signal even in total noise.

Have we seen enough?

Given that we are almost assured of finding something interpretable when we look at the past, our next question becomes, "Have we understood it?" The hindsight research described earlier suggests that we are not only quick to find order but also poised to feel that we knew it all along in some way or would have been able to predict the result had we been asked in time. Indeed, the ease with which we discount the informativeness of

---

[4] Diaconis continues, "To further complicate any analysis, several such ill-defined experiments were often conducted simultaneously, inter-acting with one another. The young performer electrified his audience. His frequently completely missed guesses were generally regarded with sympathy, rather than doubt; and for most observers they seemed only to confirm the reality of B.D.'s unusual powers."

anything we are told makes it surprising that we ever ask the past, or any other source, many questions. This tendency is aggravated by tendencies (a) not to realize how little we know or are told, leaving us unaware of what questions we should be asking in search of surprising answers (Fischhoff, Slovic, & Lichtenstein, 1977, 1978) and (b) to draw far-reaching conclusions from even small amounts of unreliable data (Kahneman & Tversky, 1973, 4; Tversky & Kahneman, 1971, 2).

Any propensity to look no further is encouraged by the norm of reporting history as a good story, with all the relevant details neatly accounted for and the uncertainty surrounding the event prior to its consummation summarily buried, along with any confusion the author may have felt (Gallie, 1964; Nowell-Smith, 1970). Just one of the secrets to doing this is revealed by Tawney (1961): "Historians give an appearance of inevitability to an existing order by dragging into prominence the forces which have triumphed and thrusting into the background those which they have swallowed up" (p. 177).[5]

Although an intuitively appealing goal, the construction of coherent narratives exposes the reader to some interesting biases. A completed narrative consists of a series of somewhat independent links, each fairly well established. The truth of the narrative depends upon the truth of the links. Generally, the more links there are and the more detail there is in each link, the less likely the story is to be correct in its entirety. However, Slovic, Fischhoff, and Lichtenstein (1976) have found that adding detail to an event description can increase its perceived probability of occurrence, evidently by increasing its thematic unity. Bar-Hillel (1973) found that people consistently exaggerate the probability of the conjunction of a series of likely events. For example, her subjects generally preferred a situation in which they would receive a prize if seven independent events each with a probability of .90 were to occur to a situation in which they would get the same prize if a fair coin fell on "heads." The probability of the compound event is less than .50, whereas the probability of the single event is .50. In other words, uncertainty seems to accumulate at much too slow a rate.

What happens if the sequence includes one or a few weak or unlikely links? The probability of its weakest link should set an upper limit on the probability of an entire narrative. Coherent judgments, however, may be compensatory, with the coherence of strong links "evening out" the incoherence of weak links. This effect is exploited by attorneys who bury the weakest link in their arguments near the beginning of their summations and finish with a flurry of convincing, uncontestable arguments.

Coles (1973) presents a delicious example of the overall coherence of a story obscuring the unlikelihood of its links: Freud's most serious attempt

---

[5] Such strategies may affect the spirit as well as the mind, by subjectively enhancing the strength and stability of the status quo and reducing its apparent capacity for change (Marković,1970).

at psychohistory was his biography of Leonardo da Vinci. For years, Freud had sought the secret to understanding Leonardo, whose childhood and youth were basically unknown. Finally, he discovered a reference by Leonardo to a recurrent memory of a vulture touching his lips while he was in the cradle. Noting the identity of the Egyptian hieroglyphs for "vulture" and "mother" and other circumstantial evidence, Freud went on to build an imposing and coherent analysis of Leonardo. While compiling the definitive edition of Freud's works, however, the editor discovered that the German translation of Leonardo's recollection (originally in Italian) that Freud had used was in error, and that it was a kite not a vulture that had stroked his lips. Despite having the key to Freud's analysis destroyed, the editors decided that the remaining edifice was strong enough to stand alone. As Hexter (1971) observed, "Partly because writing bad history is pretty easy, writing very good history is rare" (p. 59).

Conclusion

What general lessons can we learn about the study of the past, beyond the fact that understanding is more elusive than may often be acknowledged?

Presentism

Inevitably, we are all captives of our present personal perspective. We know things that those living in the past did not. We use analytical categories (e.g., feudalism, Hundred Years War) that are meaningful only in retrospect (E. A. R. Brown, 1974). We have our own points to prove when interpreting a past that is never sufficiently unambiguous to avoid the imposition of our ideological perspective (Degler, 1976). Historians do "play new tricks on the dead in every generation" (Becker, 1935).

There is no proven antidote to presentism. Some partial remedies can be generalized from the discussion of how to avoid hindsight bias when second-guessing the past. Others appear in almost any text devoted to the training of historians. Perhaps the most general messages seem to be (a) knowing ourselves and the present as well as possible; "the historian who is most conscious of his own situation is also most capable of transcending it" (Benedetto Croce, quoted in Carr, 1961, p. 44); and (b) being as charitable as possible to our predecessors; "the historian is not a judge, still less a hanging judge" (Knowles, quoted in Marwick, 1970, p. 101).

Methodism

In addition to the inescapable prison of our own time, we often further restrict our own perspective by voluntarily adopting the blinders that accompany strict adherence to a single scientific method. Even when used judiciously, no one method is adequate for answering many of the questions we put to the past. Each tells us something and misleads us somewhat. When we do not know how to get the right answer to a question, an alternative epistemology is needed: Use as broad a range of techniques or perspectives as possible, each of which enables us to avoid certain kinds of mistakes. This means a sort of interdisciplinary cooperation and respect different from that encountered in most attempts to commingle two approaches. Matches or mismatches like psychohistory too often are attempted by advocates insensitive to the pitfalls in their adopted fields (Fischhoff, in press-b). Hexter (1971) describes the historians involved in some such adventures as "rats jumping aboard intellectually sinking ships" (p. 110).

Learning

Returning to Benson (1972), if we want the past to serve the future, we cannot treat it in isolation. The rules we use to explain the past must also be those we use to predict the future. We must cumulate our experience with a careful eye to all relevant tests of our hypotheses. One aspect of doing this is compiling records that can be subjected to systematic statistical analysis: A second is keeping track of the deliberations preceding our own decisions, realizing that the present will soon be past and that a well-preserved record is the best remedy to hindsight bias: A third is making predictions that can be evaluated; one disturbing lesson from the Three Mile Island nuclear accident is that it is not entirely clear what that ostensibly diagnostic event told us about the validity of the Reactor Safety Study (U.S. Nuclear Regulatory Commission, 1975) that attempted to assess the risks from nuclear power: A fourth aspect is getting a better idea of the validity of our own feelings of confidence, insofar as confidence in present knowledge controls our pursuit of new information and interpretations (Fischhoff, Slovic, & Lichtenstein, 1977). Thus, we should structure our lives so as to facilitate learning.

Indeterminacy

In the end, though, there may be no answers to many of the questions we are posing. Some are ill-formed. Others just cannot be answered with existing or possible tools. As much as we would like to know "how the pros do it," there may be no way statistically to model experts' judgmental policies to the desired degree of precision with realistic stimuli. Our theories are often of "such complexity that no single quantitative work could even begin to test their validity" (O'Leary et al., 1974, p. 228). When groups we wish to compare on one variable also differ on another, there is no logically sound procedure for equating them on that nuisance variable

(Meehl, 1970). When we have tried many possible explanations on a fixed set of data, there is no iron-clad way of knowing just how many degrees of freedom we have used up, just how far we have capitalized on chance (Campbell, 1975). When we use multiple approaches, the knowledge they produce never converges neatly. In the end, we may have to adopt Trevelyan's philosophical perspective that "several imperfect readings of history are better than none at all" (cited in Marwick, 1970, p. 57).

Part VII

Multistage evaluation

24. Evaluation of compound probabilities in sequential choice

John Cohen, E. I. Chesnick, and D. Haran

Situations frequently occur in which a successful outcome depends on an individual making a correct choice at each of several more or less independent stages. The choice of mode of transport at various stages of a journey is one example. Comparable predicaments occur in professional, administrative, political and military life, and in communication networks generally. The temporal order of the several choices is not invariably a vital factor. Furthermore, the situation as a whole may have a stochastic character in that the probability of correct choice may vary from stage to stage.

We shall describe an experiment simulating this general type of situation, which clearly requires, for a successful outcome, the multiplication of probabilities. Studies of preference for locating a target in an $m \times n$ array, or in a display partitioned into concentric zones, indicate that the cells in the array or the concentric zones are not subjectively equiprobable as locations for the target (Cohen, Boyle, & Chesnick, 1969). Subjects do not seem to guess, at random, the unknown location of the target. Their strategy of search rather has the character of "divining" where the experimenter has hidden it, or of locating it where they would expect it to be. Other experiments (Cohen & Hansel, 1958) suggest that many people, when faced with a situation involving compound probabilities, tend to add, instead of multiply, the chances at the different stages.

We may accordingly predict that in an $m \times n$ array, with an unknown target in each of the m rows, the subject's estimate of his chance of guessing all targets correctly will be exaggerated, as judged by the compound probability, n^{-m}, of locating the target. Our experiment is designed to test this prediction, and to elucidate the phenomena which the situation will generate.

Table 1. *Psychological probabilities (Ψ) based on choice of lottery*

No. of alternatives per stage	No. of stages in array					
	2	3	4	5	8	M
2	0.45	0.51	0.36	0.38	0.37	0.41
3	0.41	0.21	0.21	0.21	0.17	0.24
4	0.31	0.23	0.21	0.12	0.11	0.19
5	0.30	0.22	0.17	0.18	0.08	0.19
8	0.07	0.16	0.11	0.13	0.05	0.11
M	0.31	0.27	0.21	0.20	0.16	

Note: Entries in the table represent means of ten observations.

The apparatus consisted of a board on which were set m rows each containing n receptacles, where m and n each took the values 2, 3, 4, 5 or 8. All the receptacles were empty except one in each row which contained a ticket. The number of separate stages therefore ranged from 2 to 8, with the chance of guessing correctly at each stage ranging from 2^{-1} to 2^{-3}.

The subjects were fifty grammar school boys aged 14–15 years whose "intelligence" may be assumed to be at least as good as that of the average adult. A subject was given to understand that in order to win a prize he had to guess the correct location of the ticket in each row, only one guess per row being allowed. His task was to equate what he thought was the chance of winning the prize with one of a set of lotteries.

There were fourteen lotteries in all. Ten of them had 100 tickets each, the chance of drawing a winning ticket, based on the number of winning tickets in the particular lottery, being 0.01, 0.1, 0.2, 0.3, ..., 0.9. The remaining four lotteries had 500, 1,000, 5,000 and 10,000 tickets respectively, with the corresponding chance of drawing a winning ticket, 0.002, 0.001, 0.0002 and 0.0001.

The range of values taken by the rows and the range of values of the receptacles allowed for twenty-five different situations. Each of the fifty subjects was assigned at random to five of these situations by means of randomized Latin squares. Ten subjects thus judged each $m \times n$ situation.

The amount of information actually required to locate the target is $m\log_2 n$ "bits," where m is the number of rows, which we will now call "stages," and n the number of receptacles, which will be designated "alternatives." The chance of drawing a winning ticket in the lottery chosen by the subject we shall treat as an indirect estimate of his psychological probability (Ψ) of winning a prize.

The results presented in Table 1 indicate that all values of Ψ are overestimates, as judged by the compound probabilities, p, thus confirming our prediction. The magnitude of the overestimation is indicated by the ratios of Ψ to p in Table 2, which suggests that the realism of the estimates is confounded by an apparent tendency to take less account of

Table 2. *Ratios, Ψ/p, of psychological to compound probabilities*

No. of alternatives per stage	No. of stages in array				
	2	3	4	5	8
2	1.8	4.0	5.7	12.2	95.0
3	3.8	5.9	17.8	53.2	10^3
4	4.9	14.8	54.0	118.0	7×10^3
5	7.5	27.8	106.0	563.0	3×10^4
8	4.3	82.4	465.0	4×10^3	9×10^5

the number of stages than of the number of alternatives per stage, although an analysis of variance shows that in relation to the residual variance, both the inter-stage and inter-alternative variances are significant ($P < 0.01$).

This differential effect becomes clear if we plot, as in Figure 1, the logarithm of relative overestimation, $\log_{10} \Psi/p$, against the amount of information in bits, $m \log_2 n$, required to locate the target. The relation is linear, and is given by the equation:

$$\log_{10} \Psi/p = 0.26 \, m \log_2 n - 0.31 \tag{1}$$

This may be re-written as:

$$\Psi/p = e^{(0.86 m \log_e n - 0.72)} \tag{2}$$

from which it follows that if we keep the number of stages constant, Ψ/p is directly proportional to a power of the number of alternatives per stage, whereas if we keep the number of alternatives constant, Ψ/p varies exponentially with the number of stages.

Given m and n, we can predict the mean value of Ψ because

$$p = n^{-m} \tag{3}$$

The compound probability p is obtained by multiplying the respective probabilities of guessing correctly at each of the m stages, each of these probabilities being equal to $1/n$.

Therefore, from (2)

$$\Psi = e^{-0.72} \, n^{-0.14m}$$
$$(e^{-0.72} = 0.49) \tag{4}$$

In the main, therefore, the relative overestimation of Ψ/p results from a subjective attenuation of the multiplicative factor, m, the number of stages. This attenuation is of the order of six-sevenths of the number of stages, within our experimental constraints. This leads us to infer that the multiplicative element in compound probability is far from being "primitive" or intuitive, which may help to explain the special difficulties which people encounter in the study of statistics.

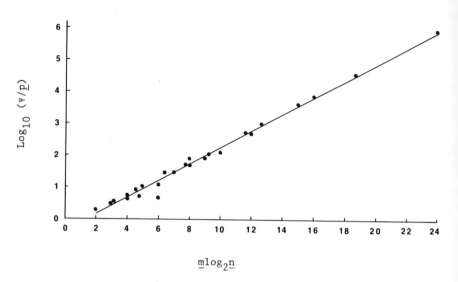

Figure 1. Log relative overestimation plotted against the number of bits ($\log_{10}(\Psi/p)$ against $m \log_2 n$). p = compound probabilities; m = number of stages; n = number of alternatives.

Our interpretation is supported by similar experiments with subjects aged 9+ and 10+ years, in which, apart from gross relative overestimation of Ψ, no trends are discernible with variations in the values of m and n. This too suggests that the multiplicative element is not primitive.

The method we have used involves an indirect evaluation of Ψ. A more direct evaluation could be obtained by asking the subject to choose between different types of array. The utility of the choice, however, might then become an important factor.

This experiment elucidates the apparent tendency, in a variety of multi-stage choice situations, for the decision maker to misjudge the likelihood of his success, and therefore to adopt an inappropriate strategy which he will later regret.

Of historical interest in this connection is the fact that the most subtle thinkers of ancient Greece, though greatly intrigued by the idea of the possible, especially in Stoic philosophy, never grasped combinatorial analysis, which had to wait until the sixteenth century for its development. Aristotle himself evidently had only a small appreciation of the concept of probability. Whatever intuition of the subject he and others might have had was submerged by long established habits of thought.

The relative overestimation of compound probabilities which the experiment has revealed may be a phenomenon of considerable generality in decision and choice. If so, it merits a special designation. We propose to name it the "inertial Ψ effect."

25. Conservatism in human information processing

Ward Edwards

. . . An abundance of research has shown that human beings are conservative processors of fallible information. Such experiments compare human behavior with the outputs of Bayes's theorem, the formally optimal rule about how opinions (that is, probabilities) should be revised on the basis of new information. It turns out that opinion change is very orderly, and usually proportional to numbers calculated from Bayes's theorem – but it is insufficient in amount. A convenient first approximation to the data would say that it takes anywhere from two to five observations to do one observation's worth of work in inducing a subject to change his opinions. A number of experiments have been aimed at an explanation for this phenomenon. They show that a major, probably the major, cause of conservatism is human misaggregation of the data. That is, men perceive each datum accurately and are well aware of its individual diagnostic meaning, but are unable to combine its diagnostic meaning well with the diagnostic meaning of other data when revising their opinions. . . .

Probabilities quantify uncertainty. A probability, according to Bayesians like ourselves, is simply a number between zero and one that represents the extent to which a somewhat idealized person believes a statement to be true. The reason the person is somewhat idealized is that the sum of his probabilities for two mutually exclusive events must equal his probability that either of the events will occur. The additivity property has such demanding consequences that few real persons are able to conform to all of them. Since such probabilities describe the person who holds the opinion more than the event the opinion is about, they are called personal probabilities (see Savage, 1954).

Bayes's theorem is a trivial consequence of the additivity property, uncontroversial and agreed to by all probabilists, Bayesian and other. One

Excerpts from a paper that appeared in B. Kleinmuntz (Ed.), *Formal Representation of Human Judgment*. New York: John Wiley and Sons, Inc., 1968. Reprinted by permission.

way of writing it is as follows. If $P(H_A|D)$ is the posterior probability that hypothesis A has after datum D has been observed, $P(H_A)$ is its prior probability before datum D is observed, $P(D|H_A)$ is the probability that datum D will be observed if H_A is true, and $P(D)$ is the unconditional probability of datum D, then

$$P(H_A|D) = \frac{P(D|H_A)\,P(H_A)}{P(D)} \tag{1}$$

$P(D)$ is best thought of as a normalizing constant, intended to make the posterior probabilities add up to one over the exhaustive set of mutually exclusive hypotheses being considered. If it must be calculated, it can be as follows:

$$P(D) = \sum_i P(D|H_i)\,P(H_i)$$

But more often $P(D)$ is eliminated rather than calculated. One convenient way of eliminating it is to transform Bayes's theorem into its odds-likelihood ratio form. Consider another hypothesis, H_B, mutually exclusive of H_A, and modify your opinion about it on the basis of the same datum that changed your opinion about H_A. Bayes's theorem says

$$P(H_B|D) = \frac{P(D|H_B)\,P(H_B)}{P(D)} \tag{2}$$

Now divide Equation 1 by Equation 2; the result is

$$\frac{P(H_A|D)}{P(H_B|D)} = \frac{P(D|H_A)}{P(D|H_B)} \cdot \frac{P(H_A)}{P(H_B)}$$

or

$$\Omega_1 = L \cdot \Omega_0, \tag{3}$$

where Ω_1 is the posterior odds in favor of H_A over H_B, Ω_0 is the prior odds, and L is a quantity familiar to statisticians as a likelihood ratio. Equation 3 is as appropriate a version of Bayes's theorem as Equation 1, and often considerably more useful especially for experiments involving two hypotheses.

Bayesian statisticians argue that Bayes's theorem is a formally optimal rule about how to revise opinions in the light of evidence, that revision of opinion in the light of evidence is exactly what statistical inference consists of, and that therefore statistical inference should be structured around Bayes's theorem – with many consequent differences from classical statistical practice. For an elementary exposition of these ideas written for experimenting psychologists, see Edwards, Lindman, and Savage (1963). But we are not statisticians, or at any rate none of us are wearing our statistician's dunce caps today. Instead, as psychologists, we are interested in comparing the ideal behavior specified by Bayes's theorem with actual human performance.

To give you some feeling for what follows, let us try an experiment with you as subject. This bookbag contains 1,000 poker chips. I started out with two such bags, one containing 700 red and 300 blue chips, the other containing 300 red and 700 blue. I flipped a fair coin to determine which one to use. Thus, if your opinions are like mine, your probability at the moment that this is the predominantly red bookbag is 0.5. Now, you sample, randomly, with replacement after each chip. In 12 samples, you get 8 reds and 4 blues. Now, on the basis of everything you know, what is the probability that this is the predominantly red bag? Clearly it is higher than 0.5. Please don't continue reading till you have written down your estimate.

If you are like a typical subject, your estimate fell in the range from 0.7 to 0.8 – though the statement frequently made in the preceding paragraphs that men are conservative information processors may have biased your answer upward. If we went through the appropriate calculation, though, the answer would be 0.97. Very seldom indeed does a person not previously exposed to the conservatism finding come up with an estimate that high, even if he is relatively familiar with Bayes's theorem.

In about 1960, William L. Hays, a graduate student named Lawrence D. Phillips, and I were interested in finding discrepancies between human performance and that specified by Bayes's theorem. The simple example of the previous paragraph didn't occur to us; instead we were sure that we would need to use a fairly complex situation in order to get non-Bayesian behavior. So we used a hypothetical computerized radar system. There were 12 possible observations, 4 possible hypotheses, and so subjects had to understand and use a display of 48 different values of $P(D|H)$. Subjects worked under two conditions. In one, the subject saw a single stimulus, a dot in a sector of a radar scope; he then revised his prior probabilities over the four hypotheses on the basis of the datum by setting four levers to his posterior probability estimates, then reset the levers to 0 in preparation for the next stimulus. The second stimulus consisted of the old dot plus a new one; the subject set his levers to report the cumulative impact of both dots. And so on, until 15 dots had accumulated. In the second condition, the stimuli were shuffled, and the subject in effect started afresh with each new stimulus. To the surprise of the experimenters the prediction of Bayes's theorem that this difference in conditions should make no difference to behavior was borne out. Moreover, there was yet another condition in which each new dot was displayed alone, but the subjects were allowed to preserve their estimates from one stimulus to the next rather than resetting levers to zero after each estimate. Again, the variation in conditions made little difference to behavior.

The positive findings of the Phillips-Hays-Edwards experiment were three in number. First, subjects were overwhelmingly conservative. Secondly, they were least conservative on the first dot, becoming more so with more dots. Finally, the sums of their probability estimates, which were not constrained, in general added up to more than 1, and increased as the subjects progressed through successive stimuli in an ordered sequence. Apparently the subjects found it easier to determine which hypothesis was favored by a stimulus, and so to increase the probability of that hypothesis, than to decide from which other hypotheses probability should be withdrawn in order to give it to the favored one.

We were notably dilatory in publishing this original conservatism experiment. Though the data were complete by 1962, the Phillips-Hays-Edwards paper didn't make it into print until 1966 (Phillips et al., 1966).

The magnitude and consistency of the conservatism finding startled us. It seemed appropriate to try much simpler tasks. So, without much faith, Phillips and I tried a pretest similar in character to the bookbag and poker chip example you tried above. To our surprise, it worked very well. Most of the current research comparing human behavior with Bayes's theorem can be traced to that pretest and the subsequent experiment.

If the proportion of red chips in the bookbag is p, then the probability of getting r red chips and $(n - r)$ blue chips in n samples with replacement in a particular order is $p^r(1 - p)^{n-r}$. So in a typical bookbag and poker chip experiment, if H_A is that the proportion of red chips is p_A and H_B is that that proportion is p_B, then the likelihood ratio is

$$L = \frac{p_A^r(1 - p_A)^{n-r}}{p_B^r(1 - p_B)^{n-r}} \tag{4}$$

Note that while Equation 4 was derived from considering the actual sequence of reds and blues in the sample, it could equally well have been derived from considering r reds and $(n - r)$ blues in any order; the binomial coefficient that represents the number of different ways one can obtain r reds in n draws appears in both numerator and denominator and thus cancels out of the likelihood ratio. This is an illustration of the likelihood principle of Bayesian statistics (see Edwards, Lindman, & Savage, 1963), which in effect says that a Bayesian need consider only the probability of the actual observation he has made, not the probabilities of other observations that he might have made but did not. This principle has sweeping impact on all statistical and nonstatistical applications of Bayes's theorem; it is the most important technical tool of Bayesian thinking.

In the special case in which $p_A = 1 - p_B$ (the symmetric binomial case), the likelihood ratio reduces to

$$L = \left(\frac{p_A}{1 - p_A}\right)^{2r-n} \tag{5}$$

Note that $2r - n = r - (n - r)$ is the difference between the number of reds and the number of blues in the sample; only that difference, and not the total number of observations, is relevant to inference in this symmetric case. Statistical tradition labels that difference successes minus failures, or $s - f$; $s - f$ is the usual independent variable of bookbag and poker chip experiments. To understand the rationale for the usual dependent variables, substitute Equation 5 into Equation 3, take logarithms and rearrange terms. The result is

$$\log L = (2r - n)\log \frac{p_A}{1 - p_A} = \log \Omega_1 - \log \Omega_0$$

If the subject is perfectly Bayesian, the log likelihood ratio that can be inferred by subtracting the log of the prior odds from the log of the posterior odds should be proportional to $s - f$, the independent variable. It is appropriate to plot the subject's inferred log likelihood ratio, thus calculated from his posterior odds (which in turn were calculated from his posterior probabilities if he was estimating probabilities) and the objectively appropriate prior odds, against $s - f$.

Most of the bookbag and poker chip experiments in the Michigan laboratory have used a display consisting of 48 numbered locations each containing a pushbutton, a red light, and a green light. When the button at a location is pushed, one of the lights goes on and stays on; subjects are told that this is equivalent to a sample with replacement of a chip of the corresponding color from the bookbag. The subjects are told that the program that controls the lights was prepared by sampling from a bookbag. Actually, for most experiments that program is rather carefully prepared so that the displayed sequence is appropriately representative of the bookbag, and in particular so that in each experiment samples of size n favor the untrue hypothesis appropriately often for the value of p_A being used, for all values of n.

Phillips and I (1966) investigated the effect of p_A, using sequences of 20 chips and p_A values of 0.55, 0.7, and 0.85. Subjects estimated posterior probabilities by distributing 100 white wooden discs over two troughs. Typical results of such experiments are presented in Figure 1, for the 0.7 bag with various prior probabilities. Three findings, illustrated in Figure 1, appeared for all subjects. First, the inferred log likelihood ratios were roughly proportional to $s - f$. Second, the prior probabilities were appropriately used; that is, the best fitting line through the data points passes through the origin. Third, subjects were conservative; the best fitting line was flatter than the line representing optimal Bayesian performance. The finding of near-linearity of inferred log likelihood ratios with $s - f$ (or, equivalently, with Bayesian log likelihood ratios) suggests yet another dependent variable: the ratio of the slope of the best-fitting line through the subject's estimates to the slope of the Bayesian line. Peterson, Schneider, and Miller (1965) have named that ratio the accuracy ratio; they also found it more or less constant with $s - f$.

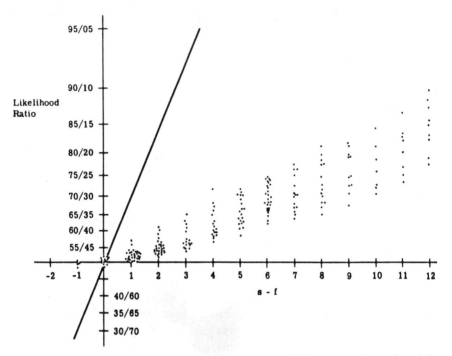

Figure 1. A single subject's estimates for p_A of 0.7, expressed in inferred log likelihood ratios as a function of the difference between the number of successes and the number of failures in the sample.

Figure 2 shows accuracy ratios for the Phillips-Edwards data for the three values of p_A. For the least diagnostic information, the subjects were more extreme than Bayes's theorem. (Dale has found the same thing; see W. Edwards, 1965.) But for information having reasonably high diagnostic value, subjects were conservative, and the accuracy ratio was nicely constant with $s - f$. Note that as diagnosticity increases, conservatism increases also. This is a standard finding of such experiments; any procedure that increases diagnosticity of the individual observation (of one chip or several) also increases conservatism. (See for example Peterson, Schneider, & Miller, 1965.)

Phillips and I, after obtaining these results, speculated that one reason for conservatism might be that subjects, knowing that the probability scale is bounded and observing that evidence might go on mounting up and up, were holding their estimates down. The obvious remedy, if so, is to use an unbounded response mode, like odds. So we ran a four-group study. The control group estimated probabilities by distributing 100 discs over two troughs, as before. The verbal odds group simply made verbal estimates of odds; we always take odds as numbers equal to or greater than one, and therefore always accompany odds statements by statements of which

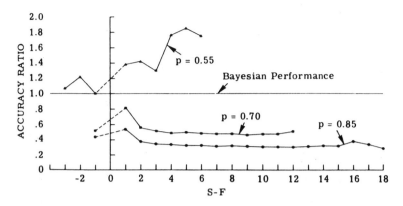

Figure 2. Accuracy ratios for three values of p_A over various sample compositions.

hypothesis is favored by the odds. The odds on a log scale group made their estimates by moving a pointer along an odds scale which contained four log cycles, so that odds anywhere from 1:1 to 10,000:1 could be estimated. The fourth group used the odds on a log scale device also, but the numbers entered opposite the scale markings were probabilities rather than odds (thus 0.5 rather than 1:1, 0.67 rather than 2:1, 0.80 rather than 4:1, etc.). It was called the probability on a log odds scale group. The findings were that all groups were quite conservative. The probability group was most so, probability on a log odds scale was next worst, and the two odds groups were about comparable, with odds on a log scale slightly superior.

This finding simply underlines a fact that has become increasingly clear in the course of Bayesian work. Probability is a rather poor measure of uncertainty, except in situations in which repartitioning or other direct use of the additivity property is necessary. Either odds or log odds is better. Odds is most intuitive for naive subjects, and can most easily be linked to simple acts (e.g., choices among bets); the fact that the gambling industry structures all its statements and displays around odds rather than probability is both recognition of and perhaps cause of the greater intuitive value of odds. Log odds, uniquely among the more-or-less common metrics for uncertainty, has the property that in that metric evidence is additive. If opinion is measured in log odds, the amount of change in opinion produced by a piece of evidence is independent of where the opinion was to start with. This elegant property makes log odds uniquely convenient for Bayesian experiments.

The Phillips-Edwards data can be well fit by a simple modification of Bayes's theorem:

$$\Omega_1 = L^c \, \Omega_0$$

The constant c, the power to which each likelihood ratio is raised before processing it by means of Bayes's theorem, is the accuracy ratio. Unfortunately, it is dependent on important independent variables, including diagnosticity of the data and response metric. Still, the fact that so simple a descriptive model fits so well must be explained by any theory of conservatism. . . .

. . . A Probabilistic Information Processing system, or *PIP*, . . . is an idea about how to design man–machine systems that must process information for the purpose of reaching a conclusion about what state the world is in. Examples of settings in which such information processing must be done include medical diagnosis, military command (in which a commander may need to determine whether or not he is under attack, and if so, what his opponent's plan is), and business management (for example, in the case of a businessman deciding whether or not to manufacture a new product). The idea of *PIP* is much too complicated to explain in detail here. For recent expositions of it, see Edwards, Lindman, and Phillips (1965), or W. Edwards (1966). The essence of it is that the task of diagnostic information processing can be divided into two classes of subtasks. One class of subtasks consists of the judgment of the diagnostic impact of an individual datum on a single hypothesis or pair of hypotheses. For the verbal, qualitative kinds of data and hypotheses that characterize many real diagnostic settings, this seems to be a task necessarily done by men, the more expert the better. But the second class of subtasks is the aggregation of these separate diagnostic impacts across data and across hypotheses into a picture of how all the hypotheses currently stand in the light of all available data. This aggregation task is readily mechanized by means of Bayes's theorem, if the diagnostic impacts of the individual data are judged in the form of $P(D|H)$ values or likelihood ratios. (In most situations, though not all, judgments of likelihood ratios are clearly preferable, for formal reasons, to judgment of $P(D|H)$.)

About fifteen collaborators and I were interested in finding out whether PIP works or not. So we designed an imaginary but elaborate world of 1975. In that world we listed six hypotheses that subjects were to consider, specified three data sources (the Ballistic Missile Early Warning System, a reconnaissance satellite system, and the intelligence system) that provided data bearing on these hypotheses, and designed four information processing systems to process the data. The four systems were named PIP, POP, PEP, and PUP. In PIP, the subjects estimated five likelihood ratios per datum. One of the six hypotheses was "Peace will continue to prevail" and the other five were various possible wars; the five pairings of a war with peace specified the five likelihood ratios to be estimated. The other three information processing systems all had in common that the subject estimated posterior odds or probabilities or similar posterior quantities; thus in PIP the computer aggregated the data by means of Bayes's theorem, while in all three other systems the subjects had to aggregate the data in their heads. To help them do this, the subjects in POP, PEP, and PUP had

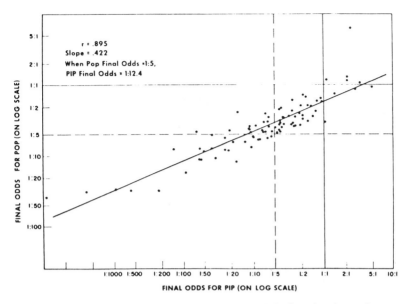

Figure 3. Final odds in favor of war for POP vs. PIP plotted on log scales.

their estimates after the *n*th datum available when they considered the (*n* + 1)th datum, so they only needed to modify those estimates affected by the datum.

There were a total of 18 scenarios, with 60 data items per scenario. All data items except for those from the Ballistic Missile Early Warning System were in the form of short paragraphs. The 34 subjects were exhaustively trained in the characteristics of the world, the hypotheses, the three data sources, and the information processing system each was to operate.

Since PIP was clearly best and POP was next best, I shall present only the comparison between them. (PUP was third best, and PEP, the nearest we could get to how such information processing is done now, was worst.) Figure 3 shows the final odds, after the 60th datum in each scenario, in favor of each war as compared with peace for PIP and for POP. The two most important things to note about the figure are that the two groups agree very well qualitatively (the correlation between them is 0.895), but they disagree quantitatively. PIP is much more sensitive to data than POP; the same scenario that will lead PIP to be very sure of peace or of some war will lead POP to be much less sure. To put it another way, PIP is much less conservative than POP – presumably because in POP, the subjects must aggregate the data, while in PIP, the subjects judge the diagnostic impact of each datum separately and Bayes's theorem does the aggregating.

You should note also that both axes on Figure 3 are logarithmically spaced. If you translate the difference in efficiency back into odds, the dramatic difference between PIP and POP becomes apparent. For example, calculating from the regression line, if a scenario led PIP to give 99:1 odds

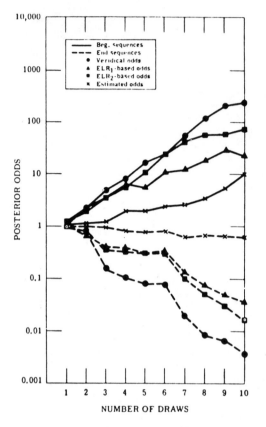

Figure 4. Median posterior odds, across subjects, in favor of the beginning bookbag as a function of number of draws.

in favor of some war over peace, POP would give only 4:1 odds in favor of that war over peace.

The misperception hypothesis cannot possibly explain this discrepancy between PIP and POP. The PIP subjects estimate the diagnostic impact of each datum separately; the POP subjects must aggregate in their heads – and do so quite conservatively. Since no model of the data-generating process is available, it is impossible to say what the right posterior odds are. But the difference between PIP and POP is clearly caused by a difference in the aggregation process.

Larry Phillips, one of the collaborators in this experiment, was concerned about the fact that no model of the data-generating process was available and so it was not possible to say with certainty whether PIP or POP was more nearly right. So for his Ph.D. thesis he compared PIP with POP in a situation in which a model of the data-generating process was available, it was meaningful to ask for a likelihood ratio estimate for a single datum, and the POP procedure produced conservative estimates.

His subjects were the editors of the University of Michigan student newspaper. He took each editor's editorials for a semester, counted the first two letters and the last two letters of each word of each editorial, and thus for each editor prepared a bookbag full of beginning bigrams and a bookbag full of ending bigrams. For the PIP task, he took certain bigrams, and asked an editor to estimate (for his own bookbags only) the likelihood ratio, taken with the beginning-bag hypothesis in the numerator and the ending-bag hypothesis in the denominator, associated with each bigram. For the POP task, he prepared a sequence of bigrams sampled from one of the bookbags, and asked the editor, as he worked through the sequence, to estimate the posterior odds that it was the beginning, not the ending, bag being sampled from. Much care was devoted to preliminary training of the editors, and likelihood ratio estimates were collected twice, once before and once after posterior odds estimates.

A problem in data analysis arose because all judgments, for both PIP and POP, were biased in favor of the beginning bag. This is probably because it is much easier, for example, to think of words that begin with *re* than to think of words that end in *re*, even though *re* is more common as an ending than as a beginning; we are accustomed to tagging words by their beginnings, not endings, when we, for example, look them up in a dictionary. However, it is possible to correct for such biases. Figure 4 shows the results after such a correction. The veridical odds, calculated from the actual bigram counts, are most extreme. Next come the odds calculated from the second set of likelihood ratio estimates. Next come the odds calculated from the first set of likelihood ratio estimates. And, closest to the middle and therefore most conservative, are the directly estimated posterior odds. If we believe these data (and I do), though PIP is considerably less conservative than POP, it is still too conservative – but PIP estimates improve with practice.

26. The best-guess hypothesis in multistage inference

Charles F. Gettys, Clinton Kelly III, and Cameron R. Peterson

Multistage inference consists of a series of single-stage inferences where the output of each previous stage becomes the input to the next stage. In a single-stage inference men reason from data or unambiguously observed evidence to a set of hypotheses. Multistage inference starts with the same unambiguous data or evidence in the first stage; however, the input for the next stage is the output of the previous stage. The next stage of inference is therefore based on the probabilities of events, rather than upon definite knowledge that a particular event is true (Gettys & Willke, 1969).

For example, suppose you wanted to predict the success or failure of a large garden party. Assume that the party is less likely to be successful if it is crowded indoors because of rain. Your datum is the presence of a dark cloud on the horizon. The first stage of inference would relate the dark cloud to the presence or absence of rain during the party. Suppose you estimated that the probability of rain was .70. This estimate would become the input to the next stage of inference. If you knew with certainty that it would rain, then you could infer the probability that the party would be a success. But you are not entirely sure that it will rain; the data that you have indicates rain with a probability of .70, so how should you proceed?

Modified Bayes Theorem (MBT) provides an optimal model for such multistage inferences (Dodson, 1961; Gettys & Willke, 1969). A number of studies have shown that intuitive performance in a multistage task results in *more* certainty being extracted from the data than is predicted by the MBT model. For example, in an odds estimation task the subjects' (Ss') odds are typically larger than those calculated by MBT. This result is quite surprising because evidence indicates human performance in a single-stage inference task is almost always conservative; i.e., humans extract less

This chapter originally appeared in *Organizational Behavior and Human Performance*, 1973, 10, 364–373. Copyright © 1973 by Academic Press, Inc. Reprinted by permission.

certainty than warranted by the data (e.g., W. Edwards, 1966). The paradox, of course, is that a multistage inference is a series of single-stage inferences. If people extract less certainty than the data warrant in single-stage inferences, then in the multistage situation one might expect the Ss to become more and more conservative with each succeeding stage since their departures from nonoptimality should accumulate from stage to stage. In fact the reverse is true; Ss are more certain at the end of two stages of inference than is warranted by the optimal model (MBT). This suggests that some process occurs at the "interface" of the single-stage tasks which is so excessive that any single-stage conservatism is overcome.

The single-stage inference task is always based upon data which are known with certainty. However, even though a multistage task starts with certain data, succeeding stages of inference deal with uncertain data. Several models have been formulated to explain how having to deal with the probabilities of data instead of certain data might create excessive certainty in multistage inference. One nonoptimal model having the property of predicting excessive certainty is the "As-If" model (Gettys and Willke, 1969; Howell, Gettys, and Martin, 1971). This model, designed for situations where people have the option to collect more data if they feel it is needed, assumes that data collection continues in the first stage of inference until the decision maker is sufficiently sure of the state of the world. Once his certainty exceeds some threshold value, he then proceeds to the next stage of inference, acting "as-if" he were entirely certain of the input to the next stage. To return to the garden party example, the decision maker, after seeing the dark cloud, might get a current weather report. Suppose a severe storm warning were forecast. His certainty for rain probably now would exceed his threshold value, and he would proceed to the second stage of inference acting "as-if" he were certain of rain. The result of the second stage of inference would be his estimate of the probabilities of success or failure based on his as-if assumption of rain. *His assessed probability for failure should now exceed the veridical (MBT) probability for failure because by making the as-if assumption of rain he is ignoring the possibility that it might not rain.* If, in fact, his as-if assumption is incorrect and it doesn't rain, then the party probably will be a success. The optimal model considers both possibilities, rain and no rain, in assigning probabilities to success or failure. The As-If model considers only the possibility of rain, and for this reason leads to excessive certainty that the party will be a failure.

How might a person behave if his certainty about the input to the second stage of inference were less than the threshold value required for an as-if assumption and there were no hope of increasing his certainty with more data? One possible hypothesis that is consistent with the excessive certainty found in previous studies is that he will first make an as-if assumption that is at best a guess. This model, termed the "Best-

Guess" model, is in effect a qualified As-If model and shares with the As-If model the idea that the decision maker will either ignore or tend to ignore the implications of the other less-likely events in the second stage of inference by concentrating almost exclusively on the most likely event. In terms of the example, if the only information you have is the dark cloud on the horizon, you might not be willing to make an *unqualified* as-if assumption, but you might first assume that it is going to rain and arrive at subjective odds for success based on this assumption. Then because you are not entirely certain that it will rain, you might reduce your subjective odds somewhat to take this into account. These subjective odds might well be different from those calculated with MBT, primarily because you have not explicitly considered the implications of no rain.

Snapper and Fryback (1971) reported results which are consistent with the above explanation in an experiment concerned with data reliability. However, their procedure did not permit a direct test of the Best-Guess model; that is the purpose of the present experiment.

Method

The goal of the experiment required at least three levels of variables constructed in such a manner that the intermediate level variable contained more than two events. It further required a manipulation of the probability distribution across all but the most likely of the intermediate events – a manipulation that would have a resulting impact on the magnitude of optimal probability revision at the upper level as the result of the occurrence of an event at the lower level.

Consequently, the three levels took the following form. The upper-level variable was comprised of two bags labeled I and II, respectively. Each bag served as a container that was filled with smaller containers which represented intermediate-level events. Specifically, each bag contained 18 small cans (35 mm. film cans) and each can was labeled with either *A, B, C,* or *D*. Finally, each can contained 100 small colored discs; each disc was either red, green, yellow or blue.

The composition of each container is described in Table 1. Part A of the table describes the bag composition with respect to cans and Part B of the table describes the can composition with respect to discs. For example, 8 cans labeled *A* are in Bag I whereas only 1 can labeled *A* is in Bag II. As shown in Part B, 80 discs are in Can *A*, 1 in Can *B*, 1 in Can *C*, and 18 in Can *D*.

The experiment proceeded as follows. One of the two bags was selected at random, a can was sampled at random from that bag, and a disc was sampled at random from that can. Thus, the draw of a red disc provides evidence in favor of Can *A*, which in turn provides evidence in favor of Bag I. Notice that it is only the bottom-level event, a disc, that is directly

Table 1. *Numerical composition of bookbag and film can components*

Film can letter	A. Bookbag composition	
	Bookbag I	Bookbag II
A	8	1
B	3	6
C	6	3
D	1	8

	B. Film can composition			
Disc color	Can A	Can B	Can C	Can D
Red	80	1	1	18
Green	1	80	18	1
Yellow	18	1	80	1
Blue	1	18	1	80

observed. That observation provides only partial evidence with regard to the intermediate-level event, the can, which in turn provides partial evidence about which upper-level event was selected. Thus, the first stage of inference relates disc color to can letter and the second stage of inference relates can letter to bag number.

The strategy of acting as if the most likely event is true at one level will lead to probability distributions that are extreme at the next higher level. Thus, this strategy is consistent with the empirical result that people revise upper-level probabilities excessively at a multistage task.

There is another testable hypothesis that can be derived from the best-guess strategy. If a person acts as if the most likely event is true at any intermediate level, he then ignores the probability distribution across all other events at this level. His probability revision at the upper level should therefore be insensitive to variations in the distribution of probabilities across all but the most likely event at the intermediate level. The present experiment was designed to test that hypothesis.

Experimental design

Three inference tasks of the type shown in Table 1 were constructed. The frequencies shown in Part A were used in all three tasks. The matrix shown in Part B was used in one task; in the other two tasks the value of 80 in the lower matrix was changed to either 70 or 90, and the value of 18 was changed to either 28 or 8, respectively. For purposes of later discussion these three tasks will be designated as the 70–28, the 80–18, or the 90–8 task. In all three tasks the Ss estimated the odds of the bags given the color of a single disc drawn from the can.

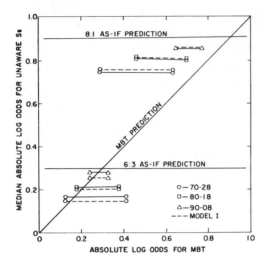

Figure 1. Best-Guess, As-If, and MBT models as predictors of performance of "unaware" Ss.

Subjects

The 25 Ss were University of Michigan students who had previously served in another multistage inference experiment lasting about two hours. In the previous experiment Ss had been trained in the response mode required, and had made an extensive series of odds estimates in a multistage inference task. However, the optimal model was never discussed, nor was any type of feedback used.

Instructions to Ss

The instructions were brief because of the previous experience of the Ss. The details of the task were explained. The Ss were asked to imagine that a bag had been randomly selected on the basis of a toss of a fair coin, that a can was then randomly drawn from the bag, and that a paper disc was randomly drawn from the can. Then they were asked to assume that a disc of a particular color was, in fact, drawn according to this random process, and were asked to estimate the odds of the bags on the basis of the color of the disc.

Procedure

Following the instructions, the Ss estimated the odds of the bags in all three tasks. Matrices like those in Table 1 were used to inform the Ss of the relative frequencies of the cans and the discs. The tasks were presented in a random order for each group of 4 to 6 Ss. Within each task each of the four possible colors was used in random order. The Ss estimated the odds of the bags for all possible colors before moving to the next task. When the Ss had completed the twelve estimates (4 colors per task × 3 tasks), the three tasks were then repeated using different random orders for a total of 24 judgments, two for each color in each task.

Results and discussion

An inspection of the data showed an extreme bimodality in the Ss' odds responses. For some Ss the theoretical difference between the blue and red dots, and the difference between the yellow and green dots, caused no difference in the odds estimates. Other Ss were more extreme in their odds estimates with a blue dot than they were with a red dot, and more extreme with a yellow dot than with a green dot. These latter Ss were consistent with MBT in at least an ordinal sense. It appeared that some subjects were "unaware" of the blue–red and the yellow–green differences, while other Ss were "aware" to the extent that they were responding in at least the right direction. With this thought in mind, all Ss who responded with at least one odds estimate for blue that was at least 2% greater than the odds estimate for red, or an estimate for yellow that was at least 2% greater than green, were classified as "aware" Ss. These Ss were at least marginally "aware" because for one or more judgments their odds estimates changed in the blue–red pair and the yellow–green pair in the direction that MBT dictates. Ten Ss of the 25 were classified as "aware" Ss by this conservative criterion.

The other 15 Ss, the "unaware" Ss, showed no tendency to respond differently to changes in the probabilities of the less likely events. They literally ignored the implications of the less likely cans. Their responses are consistent with an extreme form of the Best-Guess model. The medians of the responses of the "unaware" Ss are shown in Figure 1. Because the bag that the odds favor is formally irrelevant, the data are plotted on an absolute log odds scale. The median log odds responses to the red and the blue discs are connected by a solid line in the upper part of the figure for the three levels of data uncertainty, and the medians for yellow and green discs are similarly jointed in the lower part of the figure. Also shown in Figure 1 are predictions for MBT (the line on the positive diagonal), predictions for the As-If model (the two horizontal lines) and predictions for a version of the Best-Guess model, termed Model I in the figures.

The Model I predictions are obtained by multiplying the probability of the most likely event by the posterior odds obtained if that event were true. Suppose a red disc were drawn in the 80-18 task. The probability of Can A is .80 and the odds are 8:1 if in fact the dot came from A. The Model I prediction would then be $0.8 \times 8/1 = 6.4$ or odds of 6.4:1. The As-If model predicts odds of 8:1 for the blue and red discs and 6:3 for the yellow and green dots *provided that the threshold certainty for can type is exceeded.* For

MBT the optimal odds for a red dot are 2.86:1, and may be calculated according to the following formula for the posterior odds (adapted from formula 5 in Gettys & Willke, 1969):

$$\frac{P(\text{BI}\,|\,\text{color})}{P(\text{BII}\,|\,\text{color})} = \frac{P(\text{BI})}{P(\text{BII})} \times \frac{\displaystyle\sum_{i} P(\text{color}\,|\,\text{can}_i)P(\text{can}_i\,|\,\text{BI}_1)}{\displaystyle\sum_{i} P(\text{color}\,|\,\text{can}_i)P(\text{can}_i\,|\,\text{BII})} \tag{1}$$

where B stands for bag, and the other entries are calculated from conditional probabilities such as shown in Table 1.

The data in Figure 1 are clearly not fitted by either the as-if or the MBT predictions. The Ss responses are less extreme than the as-if predictions for the upper blue–red pairs, where the as-if prediction is 8:1 odds, and are similarly less extreme than the 6:3 odds prediction in the lower part of the figure. However, the extreme version of the Best-Guess model, Model I, fits the Figure 1 medians very well. The horizontal dashed lines in Figure 1 are the Model 1 predictions. For all tasks, the Model I predictions are to the right of the MBT diagonal for the yellow dots in the lower part of Figure 1. The As-If model and Model I do not necessarily predict odds estimates that are more extreme than MBT odds. These points arise, for example, in the 80-8 task when Can C is most likely (P = .80) and Can A (P = .18) is less likely. The most likely event gives 6:3 odds for Bag I if true and the less likely event gives odds of 8:1 for Bag I. In this case, any model which ignores the 8:1 ratio furnished by the less likely event will be conservative in respect to MBT.

If it is assumed Ss will not adopt a nonoptimal model if it deviates too much from their subjective feeling of certainty, then perhaps the important result is that Ss used Model I because they saw nothing wrong with it. The magnitude of their odds response was determined by Model I but in another situation they might use some other combination rule. More importantly, the fact that Model I predictions do fit the data suggests that Ss tended to concentrate on the most likely alternative, and ignored the implications of the less likely alternatives.

The data for the 10 "aware" Ss are presented in Figure 2. As in Figure 1, the predictions of the As-If and the MBT models are shown in the figure, but the Model I predictions are omitted because they clearly do not fit the data.

In general, the "aware" Ss seem to respond to the same variables as MBT, but the quantitative fit of the MBT model is poor. Ss are characteristically more certain than the MBT model, as has been found in previous research. Like MBT, the Ss are less certain than implied by the As-If model for the blue and the red discs. Also, as in MBT, their judgments to the yellow disc exceeds the as-if prediction. This, of course, occurs because the most likely event has odds of 6:3 and the less likely event has odds of 8:1. If the Ss are

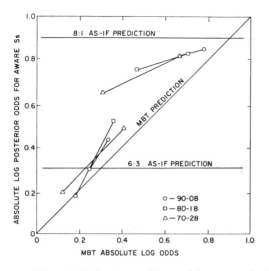

Figure 2. Performance of "aware" Ss compared with the predictions of the MBT and As-If models.

aware of the nuances of the multistage situation, they should realize that the odds must be greater than 6:3. The only exception to this general picture is the location of the 80-18 data for the yellow and green discs. The posterior based on yellow odds should increase as the probability of the most likely event decreases, while the odds based on green should decrease as the probability increases. The responses in the 80:18 condition do not follow this pattern. In general, the "aware" Ss seem to be using a combination rule that is somewhat like MBT, but which is somewhat excessive in respect to MBT.

The hypothesis of a Best-Guess tendency in multistage inference is clearly supported by the "unaware" Ss. Evidently, perhaps because of the complexity of the situation, some Ss tend to concentrate almost exclusively on the most likely event in subsequent stages in inference. The Best-Guess effect in multistage inference, like conservatism in single-stage inference (W. Edwards, 1966), seems to be another example of a general inability to combine complicated information. As much of human information processing is multistaged and probabilistic in nature, it would seem that the next appropriate step for application of Bayes' theorem is to find ways of preventing people from making the mistake of ignoring all but the most likely of the intermediate-level events.

27. Inferences of personal characteristics on the basis of information retrieved from one's memory

Yaacov Trope

Social judgment is frequently based on inaccurate recall of others' behavior. We are often called upon to make inferences about others' personal attributes even when we are unsure whether we can remember how they actually behaved. Under such circumstances, we have to base our attributions on uncertain behavioral evidence. The present study investigates whether and how people incorporate this source of uncertainty into their judgments about others. . . .

A Bayesian model for inferences from remembered behavior

In the present study, subjects inferred probabilities that actors possess certain attributes on the basis of their own unreliable retrieval of the actors' behaviors. In order to test the hypothesis that these subjective probabilities would be unjustifiably high and insufficiently sensitive to reliability, they were compared with optimal probabilities. The latter were derived from a Bayesian model which was developed by investigators of multiple-step probability inference (see Peterson, 1973). Beginning with a single-step inference from actual behavior B_j to a personal attribute A_i, Bayes' theorem has the following familiar form:

$$P(A_i/B_j) = P(A_i)P(B_j/A_i)/P(B_j) \qquad (1)$$

where $P(A_i/B_j)$ is the posterior probability of A_i given B_j; $P(A_i)$ is the prior probability of A_i; $P(B_j)$ is the total probability of B_j; and $P(B_j/A_i)$ is the conditional probability of B_j given A_i. The latter probability represents the behavior's *diagnostic value* with respect to the actor's attribute. A posterior

Excerpts from a paper that appeared in *The Journal of Personality and Social Psychology*, 1978, 36, 93–106. Copyright © 1978 by the American Psychological Association. Reprinted by permission.

probability $P(A_i/B_j)$ can be derived for each of the alternative behaviors that the actor might have chosen. Observers do not know, however, which behavior was actually chosen. They can only infer the probabilities of the behaviors from what they recall, B^*. With regard to this inferential step, Bayes' theorem states,

$$P(B_j/B^*) = P(B_j)P(B^*/B_j)/P(B^*) \tag{2}$$

where $P(B_j/B^*)$ is the posterior probability of an actual behavior B_j, given that B^* was recalled; $P(B_j)$ is the prior probability of B_j; $P(B^*)$ is the total probability of recalling B^*; and $P(B^*/B_j)$ is the conditional probability of recalling B^* given that the person's actual behavior was B_j. $P(B^*/B_j)$ reflects *reliability* – the higher the probability of retrieving a behavior that has actually occurred, the higher the reliability.

The Bayesian two-step inference model combines the $P(A_i/B_j)$ values, derived for each actual behavior via Equation 1, into a weighted average, with the posterior probabilities of each behavior, $P(B_j/B^*)$, derived via Equation 2, serving as weights. Thus, the posterior probability of an attribute given that a certain behavior was retrieved, $P(A_i/B^*)$, can be formulated as follows:

$$P(A_i/B^*) = \sum_j P(A_i/B_j)P(B_j/B^*) \tag{3}$$

Equation 3 expresses quantitatively the normative considerations discussed earlier. Specifically, since $P(A_i/B_j)$ is an increasing function of $P(B_j/A_i)$ (diagnosticity) and $P(B_j/B^*)$ is an increasing function of $P(B^*/B_j)$ (reliability), $P(A_i/B^*)$ should increase both with reliability and with diagnosticity, and the effect of one variable should depend on the level of the other. Stated in terms of Anderson's (1974) theory of information integration, each retrieved behavior has a certain weight in judgments of probabilities of attributes. This weight, in turn, is assumed to be a multiplicative function of the diagnosticity of the behavior and the reliability of its retrieval. The integration rule prescribed by Equation 3 can be applied both to optimal single-step inferences [i.e., the values of $P(A_i/B_j)$ and $P(B_j/B^*)$ obtained from Equations 1 and 2, respectively] and to *subjective* single-step inferences [i.e., subjects' own assessments of $P(A_i/B_j)$ and $P(B_j/B^*)$]. In the former case both the single-step inferences and their integration are optimal (i.e., Bayesian), whereas in the latter case only the integration is optimal. The present study compared observed probabilities with both kinds of predicted probabilities. Subjects made inferences about students' admission to graduate school and about students' political attitudes. The former inferences were based on subjects' memories of the students' grades, and the latter inferences were based on subjects' memories of the students' behavior.

Experiment 1

Method

Overview. Subjects were first presented with students' grades in an undergraduate course. Later, subjects had to retrieve the grades from memory and to assess the probabilities of each student's being accepted to the graduate school of business administration. This task involves two inferential steps: (a) from the retrieved grade, G^*, to the student's actual grade, G, and (b) from the actual grade to whether or not the student was accepted, A, to the graduate school. The uncertainty in the latter inferential step was manipulated by varying the diagnostic value of the grades with regard to admission to the school of business administration. Low-diagnosticity grades were final grades in "introduction to anthropology," whereas high-diagnosticity grades were final grades in "introduction to economics." Reliability of memory was manipulated by varying the number of students whose grades had to be retained.

Procedure. Subjects were informed that in a certain year 50% of the applicants to the school of business administration had been admitted. Thus, the prior probabilities of being accepted or rejected, $P(A_y)$ and $P(A_n)$, were .50. Subjects were told that they would assess probabilities of acceptance for randomly selected students. These judgments, subjects were told, would be based on whether each student's grade in a given undergraduate course was below 75 (G_l) or above 75 (G_h) on a 0–100 scale.

Manipulation of diagnostic value. Two probability distributions (each being presented by means of a bar diagram) related the grades to acceptance. One bar diagram displayed the proportions of accepted students who received G_l or G_h. These proportions represented the conditional probabilities $P(G_l/A_y)$ and $P(G_h/A_y)$. The other bar diagram displayed the proportions of rejected students who received these grades, that is $P(G_l/A_n)$ and $P(G_h/A_n)$. The bar diagrams for the high-diagnosticity grades (in the economics course) displayed the following proportions: $P(G_l/A_n) = P(G_h/A_y) = .85$ and $P(G_l/A_y) = P(G_h/A_n) = .15$. The bar diagrams for the low-diagnosticity grades (in the anthropology course) displayed the following proportions: $P(G_l/A_n) = P(G_h/A_y) = .55$ and $P(G_l/A_y) = P(G_h/A_n) = .45$. Each subject made judgments about two samples of students; for one sample the high-diagnosticity grades were presented, and for the other the low-diagnosticity grades were presented. The order of presentation of the samples was counterbalanced across subjects.

Manipulation of reliability. Extensive pretesting indicated that distinct levels of reliability can be obtained by varying the number of students whose grades had to be retained. Subjects were told that half of the sample received low grades and the other half received high grades and that they would be given a list of those students who received high grades. In order to minimize differences among items in this stimulus list, students were represented by two-digit identification numbers. The numbers were presented audibly by tape recorder at the rate of one per second. A high-pitched tone was presented to indicate the end of each stimulus list. Two seconds later a test list was presented by tape recorder. The test list consisted of eight two-digit identification numbers, of which four had appeared in the stimulus list (i.e., G_h numbers) and four had not appeared in the stimulus list (i.e., G_l numbers). The four G_h numbers in the test list were taken from the entire range of serial positions in the stimulus list. The order of G_h and G_l numbers was randomly determined for each of the test lists. The test numbers were presented at the rate of one every 10 seconds. During the intervals, subjects had to indicate whether the student's grade was more likely to be G_l or G_h and to assess the probability of the student's being accepted to the graduate school, $P(A_y/G^*)$, and the probability of not being accepted, $P(A_n/G^*)$. Pretesting showed that the 10-second time interval was sufficient for making these judgments.

Three list lengths were employed: 4-item lists, 7-item lists, and 14-item lists. Data from pretests indicated that percent of correct recognitions ranged from about 60% in the long lists (low-reliability condition) through about 75% in the medium lists (moderate-reliability condition) to about 90% in the short lists (high-reliability condition). Each subject responded to a high-diagnosticity list and a low-diagnosticity list. The sets of numbers in these lists were counterbalanced against diagnosticity. Twenty subjects were assigned to each of the three reliability conditions.

Perfect-reliability condition. In this single-step inference condition, a group of 46 subjects inferred probabilities of acceptance from grades that were known with certainty, $P(A_y/G)$ and $P(A_n/G)$. Subjects received a booklet which presented the bar diagrams (i.e., diagnosticity information) and the students' grades. After reading a student's grade, subjects indicated their probability judgments. Each subject made judgments about a student with a low-diagnosticity grade and about a student with a high-diagnosticity grade. For half of the subjects the student's grade was low and for the other half it was high.

Subjects. A total of 106 subjects (42 males and 64 females) from an introductory psychology course at the Hebrew University of Jerusalem participated individually in the experiment. Participation in the experiment constituted partial fulfillment of a course requirement.

Results and discussion

The proportions of correctly recognized low grades, $P(G^*_l/G_l)$, and high grades $P(G^*_h/G_h)$, served as measures of each subject's reliability. The means of $P(G^*_l/G_l)$ and $P(G^*_h/G_h)$ indicated near chance level performance in the low-reliability (14-item list) conditions ($M = .54$ and $.60$, respectively), excellent performance in the high-reliability (4-item list) conditions ($M = .93$ and $.89$, respectively), and intermediate performance in the moderate-reliability (7-item list) conditions ($M = .73$ and $.77$, respectively). Analysis of variance (Reliability $\times$ Diagnosticity) of these proportions revealed highly significant main effects of reliability, $F(2, 57) = 37.06$, $p < .001$, and $F(2, 57) = 20.17$, $p < .001$, on $P(G^*_l/G_l)$ and $P(G^*_h/G_h)$, respectively. No other source of variation was significant.

The data from the perfect-reliability condition revealed a clear effect of the diagnosticity manipulation on *single-step* inferences from grades known with certainty to probabilities of acceptance, $P(A/G)$. Subjects

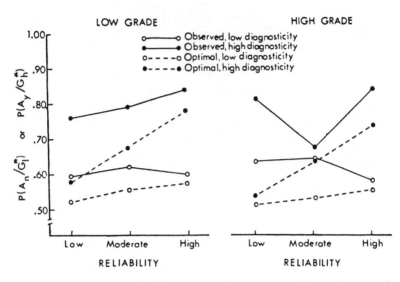

Figure 1. Observed and optimal $P(A_n/G_l^*)$ and $P(A_y/G_h^*)$ as a function of reliability and diagnosticity (Experiment 1).

inferred higher $P(A_n/G_l)$ and $P(A_y/G_h)$ from high-diagnosticity grades ($M = .81$ and $.78$, respectively) than from low-diagnosticity grades ($M = .57$ and $.55$, respectively); the difference was significant both for $P(A_n/G_l)$ and for $P(A_y/G_h)$, $t(22) = 8.08$, $p < .001$, and $t(22) = 8.59$, $p < .001$, respectively.

We now turn to the optimal posterior probabilities of acceptance given the retrieved grade, $P(A/G^*)$. These probabilities were determined for each subject by combining probabilities of actual grades given retrieved grades, $P(G/G^*)$, and probabilities of acceptance given actual grades, $P(A/G)$, according to Equation 3. $P(G/G^*)$ values were computed for each subject via Equation 2 from his own reliability in retrieving the grades, $P(G^*/G)$. The $P(A/G)$ values were the means of the judgments obtained in the perfect-reliability conditions. Thus, the optimal posterior probabilities of acceptance given the retrieved grades, $P(A/G^*)$, were based on a subjective single-step inference, from actual grades to probabilities of acceptance, and on an optimal single-step inference (Equation 2), from retrieved grades to actual grades. The dashed lines in the left-hand panel of Figure 1 represent means of $P(A_n/G^*_l)$, the optimal probability of the student's not being accepted given that his grade was recalled as being low; the dashed lines in the right-hand panel of Figure 1 represent means of $P(A_y/G^*_h)$, the optimal probability of the student's being accepted given that his grade was recalled as being high.[1] It is clear that the Bayesian model predicts these probabilities will increase both with reli-

[1] Another set of optimal $P(A/G^*)$ values was computed from optimal values of $P(A/G)$ derived via Equation 1. These probabilities are not discussed separately, since they were very close to the optimal $P(A/G^*)$ values derived from subjective estimates of $P(A/G)$.

ability and diagnosticity and that the effect of reliability will be more pronounced when diagnosticity is high than when it is low.

Two observed values were determined for each subject: The first was an average of the $P(A_n/G^*_1)$ values he assessed for students who, according to his memory, had low grades, and the second was an average of the $P(A_y/G^*_h)$ values he assessed for students who, according to memory, had high grades. The solid lines in Figure 1 show that these observed probabilities deviate qualitatively as well as quantitatively from the optimal probabilities. The diagnostic value of the true grade was the only factor that had a consistent effect on observed $P(A_n/G^*_1)$ and $P(A_y/G^*_h)$, $F(1, 57) = 96.97, p < .001$, and $F(1, 57) = 114.82, p < .001$, respectively. The higher diagnostic value of the true grade with regard to acceptance, the more extreme the posterior probabilities. The reliability with which the true grades were recognized had a very small and inconsistent effect on inferences ($F < 1$). Even the inferences in the two extreme levels of reliability within each level of diagnosticity did not differ significantly. In other words, inferences were no less extreme when the rate of correct recognition was near chance level than when it was nearly perfect. Subjects' inferences also failed to exhibit the Diagnosticity × Reliability interaction predicted by the Bayesian model. The effect of the true grades' diagnosticity was not attenuated as reliability decreased. The interactive effect of these variables was also tested at the level of inferences about individual students. Normatively, variation in confidence about different students' grades should produce a greater effect on inferences about their acceptance when the grades have a high diagnostic value than when they have a low diagnostic value. Hence, inferences about students within the high-diagnosticity list should be more variable than inferences about students within the low-diagnosticity list. The variance of $P(A/G^*)$ across the eight students within each of the two lists was computed for each subject. Contrary to the Bayesian model, these variances were not significantly different, $t(59) = 1.63$.

Figure 1 also shows that observed probabilities were more extreme than optimal probabilities. The overall difference between observed and optimal probabilities was highly significant both for $P(A_n/G^*_1)$ and for $P(A_y/G^*_h)$, $F(1, 57) = 33.38, p < .001$, and $F(1, 57) = 84.67, p < .001$, respectively. Finally, correlation coefficients were computed across subjects between optimal probabilities and observed probabilities within each of the six conditions. The correlations were very small and inconsistent, five correlations being positive and seven being negative. Two correlations were significant but negative [$r = -.50, p < .05$ and $r = -.55$, $p < .01$ for $P(A_n/G^*_1)$ and $P(A_y/G^*_h)$, respectively, in the low-reliability-high-diagnosticity condition].

These results suggest that subjects failed to integrate reliability considerations into their probability inferences. Subjects appeared to base their inferences only on the diagnostic value of the true grades. The probabilities inferred in the experimental conditions were somewhat lower than those inferred in the perfect-reliability condition, indicating that subjects did not fully adopt an "as if" strategy (i.e., making inferences as if the true grade were known with certainty). However, the reduction in confidence was very small and did not consistently vary with reliability. As a result, in comparison with Bayesian probabilities, subjects' inferences were unwarrantedly extreme. Note that this was not the case with single-step inferences from true grades to acceptance, $P(A/G)$. The probabilities inferred in the perfect-reliability condition were quite close to optimal probabilities derived from a Bayesian single-step inference model (Equation 1). This result suggests that the inoptimality (or overconfidence) in the two-step inference condition was due to the introduction of the additional source of uncertainty – the imperfect memory of the true grades. . . .

Experiment 4

Method

In this experiment, subjects inferred probabilities of male students' being in favor (A_p) or against (A_n) returning the West Bank (territory occupied by Israel in the 1967 war) to the Arabs. Voting for the Labor party (a relatively dovish party) or for the Likud party (a relatively hawkish party) served as high-diagnosticity information. The student's hair length, long versus short, served as low-diagnosticity information. Pretesting showed that short hair and voting for the Likud party (B_n) imply a negative attitude toward returning the West Bank, whereas long hair and voting for the Labor party (B_p) imply a positive attitude. The pretest also indicated that the student's voting is more diagnostic than his hair length.

The recognition memory task and other aspects of the design and procedure were the same as in Experiment 1. Twenty subjects were assigned to each of the three reliability conditions.

An additional group of 57 subjects was assigned to a perfect-reliability condition. In this condition, subjects knew with certainty the student's hair length or the party he voted for. Each subject inferred attitude probabilities from short hair, long hair, voting for the Likud party, and voting for the Labor party.

A total of 117 subjects (51 males and 66 females) from an introductory psychology course at the Hebrew University of Jerusalem took part in Experiment 4.

Results and discussion

The reliability manipulation had a strong effect on the rate of correct recognitions of both B_n (i.e., short hair or voting for the Likud party) and B_p (i.e., long hair or voting for the Labor party), $F(2, 57) = 55.45$, $p < .001$, and $F(2, 57) = 22.04$, $p < .001$, respectively. The means of $P(B^*_n/B_n)$ were .53, .76, and .96 for the low-, moderate- and high-reliability conditions, respectively; the corresponding means of $P(B^*_p/B_p)$ were .61, .82, and .91. The effects of diagnosticity and its interaction with reliability were insignificant.

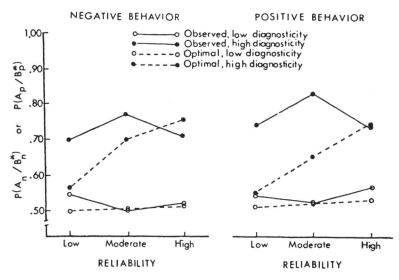

Figure 2. Observed and optimal $P(A_n/B_n^*)$ and $P(A_y/B_p^*)$ as a function of reliability and diagnosticity (Experiment 4).

As expected, the $P(A/B)$ values inferred by subjects in the perfect-reliability condition indicated that the subjective diagnostic value of voting was much greater than that of hair length. Thus, the attitude probabilities $P(A_n/B_n)$ inferred from the fact that the student voted for the Likud party ($M = .78$) were more extreme than those inferred from the fact that the student had short hair ($M = .52$), $t(56) = 13.61, p < .001$. Similarly, the attitude probabilities $P(A_p/B_p)$ inferred from the fact that the student voted for the Labor party ($M = .75$) were more extreme than those inferred from the fact that the student had long hair ($M = .53$), $t(56) = 9.89, p < .001$.

Optimal and observed probabilities are displayed in Figure 2. The former probabilities were derived from each subject via Equation 3 from $P(B/B^*)$ values [computed via Equation 2 from the subject's reliability in recognizing the students' behaviors, $P(B^*/B)$] and from the means of $P(A/B)$ obtained in the perfect-reliability condition. It can be seen that diagnosticity of the behaviors was the only consideration that guided inferences of attitude probabilities, $F(1, 57) = 68.94, p < .001$, and $F(1, 57) = 90.40, p < .001$, for $P(A_n/B^*_n)$ and $P(A_p/B^*_p)$, respectively.[2] In violation

---

[2] It might be noted that these results cannot be attributed to the fact that diagnosticity was manipulated as a within-subjects variable and reliability as a between-subjects variable. Analyses of variance were performed on inferences regarding the first list of students, whose behavior had low diagnostic value for half the subjects in each reliability condition and high diagnostic value for the other half. In these analyses, diagnosticity was of course a between-subjects factor. These analyses yielded highly significant effects of diagnosticity and insignificant effects of reliability and of Diagnosticity × Reliability. Such analyses of the data from the previous three experiments yielded similar results.

of the Bayesian model, the main effect of reliability and its interaction with diagnosticity were insignificant. Furthermore, the variances of observed probabilities within high-diagnosticity lists were no greater than the variances within low-diagnosticity lists, $t(59) = .59$. As in the previous experiments, observed probabilities were more extreme than optimal probabilities, $F(1, 57) = 5.68$, $p < .05$, and $F(1, 57) = 27.63$, $p < .001$, for $P(A_n/B^*_n)$ and $P(A_p/B^*_p)$, respectively. Finally, out of the 12 correlations across subjects within conditions between observed and optimal probabilities, 8 were positive but only 2 significant: $r = .436$, $p < .05$ for $P(A_n/B^*_n)$ in the high-diagnosticity–high-reliability condition, and $r = .402$, $p < .05$ for $P(A_p/B^*_p)$ in the low-diagnosticity–high-reliability condition.

Experiment 4 provides additional support for the generalizability of our findings. It shows that the biases observed in the previous experiments also affect inferences of attitudes from retrieved behavior. The diagnosticity of the actors' actual behavior was the sole determinant of inferences even when diagnosticity had to be based on subjects' own beliefs without externally provided actuarial evidence.

General discussion

The inferences our subjects drew from their own unreliable memories systematically violated normative rules of probability inference. Subjects tended to rely almost exclusively on diagnosticity of information, showing little sensitivity to reliability despite the fact that they were aware of the unreliability of their memory. In fact, comparisons between inferences from correctly recalled information (e.g., inferences from grades which were recalled as being low and which were, in fact, low) and inferences from incorrectly recalled information (e.g., inferences from grades which were recalled as being low and which were, in fact, high) indicated negligible, insignificant differences in all four experiments. That is, the latter probability inferences were no less extreme than the former. These results are consistent with the view that people tend to reduce the complexity of tasks by employing simple heuristic rules. The neglect of reliability information may reflect the use of one such judgmental heuristic–the representativeness heuristic (Kahneman & Tversky, 1973, 4). For instance, recalling the party for which the actor voted, subjects inferred the probability of being in favor of returning the West Bank to the Arabs according to the degree to which a vote for such a party is representative of the stereotype of an actor who holds such attitudes. An actor who votes for a dovish party embodies more features of this stereotype than an actor who grows long hair. (And in the first three experiments, a high grade in economics is more representative of students who are accepted to the school of business administration than is a high grade in anthropology.) A positive attitude toward returning the territories was, therefore, inferred with greater certainty in the former case. The accuracy of one's memory did not affect these probabilities because it did not affect the judged representativeness of the behavior retrieved.

In this respect, reliability of a report is comparable to considerations of sample size and base rates. The size of the sample on which the evidence is based and the base rate of the inferred attribute do not affect the similarity between the evidence itself and the attribute. The representativeness notion therefore suggests, and research has shown, that people are oblivious to these considerations in making inferences (Nisbett & Borgida, 1975; Tversky & Kahneman, 1974, 1). On the basis of this notion, one would expect that reliability will be taken into account in those cases in which it affects the representativeness of the report. Thus, with behavioral vignettes that are richer in detail than simple, binary events employed in the present study, poor memory (due to such factors as time lapse since the vignette was witnessed) is likely to affect the clarity, completeness, and vividness of the information retrieved. Such vague information may be less representative of the attribute in question and will, therefore, produce more regressive or more moderate probability judgments. . . .

Part VIII

Corrective procedures

28. The robust beauty of improper linear models in decision making

Robyn M. Dawes

Paul Meehl's (1954) book *Clinical Versus Statistical Prediction: A Theoretical Analysis and a Review of the Evidence* appeared 25 years ago. It reviewed studies indicating that the prediction of numerical criterion variables of psychological interest (e.g., faculty ratings of graduate students who had just obtained a Ph.D.) from numerical predictor variables (e.g., scores on the Graduate Record Examination, grade point averages, ratings of letters of recommendation) is better done by a proper linear model than by the clinical intuition of people presumably skilled in such prediction. The point of this article is to review evidence that even improper linear models may be superior to clinical predictions.

A *proper linear model* is one in which the weights given to the predictor variables are chosen in such a way as to optimize the relationship between the prediction and the criterion. Simple regression analysis is the most common example of a proper linear model; the predictor variables are weighted in such a way as to maximize the correlation between the subsequent weighted composite and the actual criterion. Discriminant function analysis is another example of a proper linear model; weights are given to the predictor variables in such a way that the resulting linear composites maximize the discrepancy between two or more groups. Ridge regression analysis, another example (Darlington, 1978, Marquardt & Snee, 1975), attempts to assign weights in such a way that the linear composites correlate maximally with the criterion of interest in a new set of data.

Thus, there are many types of proper linear models and they have been used in a variety of contexts. One example (Dawes, 1971) involved the prediction of faculty ratings of graduate students. All graduate students at the University of Oregon's Psychology Department who had been admit-

This chapter originally appeared in *American Psychologist*, 1979, *34*, 571–582. Copyright © 1979 by the American Psychological Association. Reprinted by permission.

ted between the fall of 1964 and the fall of 1967 – and who had not dropped out of the program for nonacademic reasons (e.g., psychosis or marriage) – were rated by the faculty in the spring of 1969; faculty members rated only students whom they felt comfortable rating. The following rating scale was used: 5, outstanding; 4, above average; 3, average; 2, below average; 1, dropped out of the program in academic difficulty. Such overall ratings constitute a psychologically interesting criterion because the subjective impressions of faculty members are the main determinants of the job (if any) a student obtains after leaving graduate school. A total of 111 students were in the sample; the number of faculty members rating each of these students ranged from 1 to 20, with the mean number being 5.67 and the median being 5. The ratings were reliable. (To determine the reliability, the ratings were subjected to a one-way analysis of variance in which each student being rated was regarded as a treatment. The resulting between-treatments variance ratio (n^2) was .67, and it was significant beyond the .001 level.) These faculty ratings were predicted from a proper linear model based on the student's Graduate Record Examination (GRE) score, the student's undergraduate grade point average (GPA), and a measure of the selectivity of the student's undergraduate institution.[1] The cross-validated multiple correlation between the faculty ratings and predictor variables was .38. Congruent with Meehl's results, the correlation of these latter faculty ratings with the average rating of the people on the admissions committee who selected the students was .19;[2] that is, it accounted for one fourth as much variance. This example is typical of those found in psychological research in this area in that (a) the correlation with the model's predictions is higher than the correlation with clinical prediction, but (b) both correlations are low. These characteristics often lead psychologists to interpret the findings as meaning that while the low correlation of the model indicates that linear modeling is deficient as a method, the even lower correlation of the judges indicates only that the wrong judges were used.

An *improper linear model* is one in which the weights are chosen by some nonoptimal method. They may be chosen to be equal, they may be chosen on the basis of the intuition of the person making the prediction, or they may be chosen at random. Nevertheless, improper models may have great utility. When, for example, the standardized GREs, GPAs, and selectivity indices in the previous example were weighted equally, the resulting linear composite correlated .48 with later faculty rating. Not only is the correlation of this linear composite higher than that with the clinical

---

[1] This index was based on Cass and Birnbaum's (1968) rating of selectivity given at the end of their book *Comparative Guide to American Colleges*. The verbal categories of selectivity were given numerical values according to the following rule: most selective, 6; highly selective, 5; very selective (+), 4; very selective, 3; selective, 2; not mentioned, 1.

[2] Unfortunately, only 23 of the 111 students could be used in this comparison because the rating scale the admissions committee used changed slightly from year to year.

judgment of the admissions committee (.19), it is also higher than that obtained upon cross-validating the weights obtained from half the sample.

An example of an improper model that might be of somewhat more interest – at least to the general public – was motivated by a physician who was on a panel with me concerning predictive systems. Afterward, at the bar with his wife and me, he said that my paper might be of some interest to my colleagues, but success in graduate school in psychology was not of much general interest: "Could you, for example, use one of your improper linear models to predict how well my wife and I get along together?" he asked. I realized that I could – or might. At that time, the Psychology Department at the University of Oregon was engaged in sex research, most of which was behavioristically oriented. So the subjects of this research monitored when they made love, when they had fights, when they had social engagements (e.g., with in-laws), and so on. These subjects also made subjective ratings about how happy they were in their marital or coupled situation. I immediately thought of an improper linear model to predict self-ratings of marital happiness: rate of lovemaking minus rate of fighting. My colleague John Howard had collected just such data on couples when he was an undergraduate at the University of Missouri – Kansas City, where he worked with Alexander (1971). After establishing the intercouple reliability of judgments of lovemaking and fighting, Alexander had one partner from each of 42 couples monitor these events. She allowed us to analyze her data, with the following results: "In the thirty happily married couples (as reported by the monitoring partner) only two argued more often than they had intercourse. All twelve of the unhappily married couples argued more often" (Howard & Dawes, 1976, p. 478). We then replicated this finding at the University of Oregon, where 27 monitors rated happiness on a 7-point scale, from "very unhappy" to "very happy," with a neutral midpoint. The correlation of rate of lovemaking minus rate of arguments with these ratings of marital happiness was .40 ($p < .05$); neither variable alone was significant. The findings were replicated in Missouri by Edwards and Edwards (1977) and in Texas by Thornton (1977a), who found a correlation of .81 ($p < .01$) between the sex–argument difference and self-rating of marital happiness among 28 new couples. (The reason for this much higher correlation might be that Thornton obtained the ratings of marital happiness after, rather than before, the subjects monitored their lovemaking and fighting; in fact, one subject decided to get a divorce after realizing that she was fighting more than loving; Thornton 1977b.) The conclusion is that if we love more than we hate, we are happy; if we hate more than we love, we are miserable. This conclusion is not very profound, psychologically or statistically. The point is that this very crude improper linear model predicts a very important variable: judgments about marital happiness.

The bulk (in fact, all) of the literature since the publication of Meehl's

(1954) book supports his generalization about proper models versus intuitive clinical judgment. Sawyer (1966) reviewed a plethora of these studies, and some of these studies were quite extensive (cf. L.R. Goldberg, 1965). Some 10 years after his book was published, Meehl (1965) was able to conclude, however, that there was only a single example showing clinical judgment to be superior, and this conclusion was immediately disputed by L.R. Goldberg (1968a) on the grounds that even the one example did not show such superiority. Holt (1970) criticized details of several studies, and he even suggested that prediction as opposed to understanding may not be a very important part of clinical judgment. But a search of the literature fails to reveal any studies in which clinical judgment has been shown to be superior to statistical prediction when both are based on the same codable input variables. And though most nonpositivists would agree that understanding is not synonymous with prediction, few would agree that it doesn't entail some ability to predict.

Why? Because people – especially the experts in a field – are much better at selecting and coding information than they are at integrating it.

But people *are* important. The statistical model may integrate the information in an optimal manner, but it is always the individual (judge, clinician, subject) who chooses variables. Moreover, it is the human judge who knows the directional relationship between the predictor variables and the criterion of interest or who can code the variables in such a way that they have clear directional relationships. And it is in precisely the situation where the predictor variables are good and where they have a conditionally monotone relationship with the criterion that proper linear models work well.[3]

The linear model cannot replace the expert in deciding such things as "what to look for," but it is precisely this knowledge of what to look for in reaching the decision that is the special expertise people have. Even in as complicated a judgment as making a chess move, it is the ability to code the board in an appropriate way to "see" the proper moves that distinguishes the grand master from the expert from the novice (deGroot, 1965; Simon & Chase, 1973). It is not in the ability to integrate information that people excell (Slovic, 1972b). Again, the chess grand master considers no more moves than does the expert; he just knows which ones to look at. The distinction between knowing what to look for and the ability to integrate information is perhaps best illustrated in a study by Einhorn (1972). Expert

---

[3] Relationships are conditionally monotone when variables can be scaled in such a way that higher values on each predict higher values on the criterion. This condition is the combination of two more fundamental measurement conditions: (a) independence (the relationship between each variable and the criterion is independent of the values on the remaining variables) and (b) monotonicity (the ordinal relationship is one that is monotone). (See Krantz, 1972; Krantz et al., 1971.) The true relationships need not be linear for linear models to work; they must merely be approximated by linear models. It is not true that "in order to compute a correlation coefficient between two variables the relationship between them must be linear" (advice found in one introductory statistics text). In the first place, it is always possible to compute something.

doctors coded biopsies of patients with Hodgkin's disease and then made an overall rating of the severity of the process. The overall rating did not predict survival time of the 193 patients, all of whom died. (The correlations of rating with survival time were all virtually 0, some in the wrong direction.) The variables that the doctors coded did, however, predict survival time when they were used in a multiple regression model.

In summary, proper linear models work for a very simple reason. People are good at picking out the right predictor variables and at coding them in such a way that they have a conditionally monotone relationship with the criterion. People are bad at integrating information from diverse and incomparable sources. Proper linear models are good at such integration when the predictions have a conditionally monotone relationship to the criterion.

Consider, for example, the problem of comparing one graduate applicant with GRE scores of 750 and an undergraduate GPA of 3.3 with another with GRE scores of 680 and an undergraduate GPA of 3.7. Most judges would agree that these indicators of aptitude and previous accomplishment should be combined in some compensatory fashion, but the question is how to compensate. Many judges attempting this feat have little knowledge of the distributional characteristics of GREs and GPAs, and most have no knowledge of studies indicating their validity as predictors of graduate success. Moreover, these numbers are inherently incomparable without such knowledge, GREs running from 500 to 800 for viable applicants, and GPAs from 3.0 to 4.0. Is it any wonder that a statistical weighting scheme does better than a human judge in these circumstances?

Suppose now that it is not possible to construct a proper linear model in some situation. One reason we may not be able to do so is that our sample size is inadequate. In multiple regression, for example, b weights are notoriously unstable; the ratio of observations to predictors should be as high as 15 or 20 to 1 before b weights, which are the optimal weights, do better on cross-validation than do simple unit weights. Schmidt (1971), L.R. Goldberg (1972), and Claudy (1972) have demonstrated this need empirically through computer simulation, and Einhorn and Hogarth (1975) and Srinivisan (1977) have attacked the problem analytically. The general solution depends on a number of parameters such as the multiple correlation in the population and the covariance pattern between predictor variables. But the applied implication is clear. Standard regression analysis cannot be used in situations where there is not a "decent" ratio of observations to predictors.

Another situation in which proper linear models cannot be used is that in which there are no measurable criterion variables. We might, nevertheless, have some idea about what the important predictor variables would be and the direction they would bear to the criterion *if* we were able to measure the criterion. For example, when deciding which students to admit to graduate school, we would like to predict some future long-term variable that might be termed "professional self-actualization." We have some idea what we mean by this concept, but no good, precise definition as yet. (Even if we had one, it would be impossible to conduct the study using records from current students, because that variable could not be assessed until at least 20 years after the students had completed their doctoral work.) We do, however, know that in all probability this criterion is positively related to intelligence, to past accomplishments, and to ability to snow one's colleagues. In our applicant's files, GRE scores assess the first variable; undergraduate GPA, the second; and letters of recommendation, the third. Might we not, then, wish to form some sort of linear combination of these variables in order to assess our applicants' potentials? Given that we cannot perform a standard regression analysis, is there nothing to do other than fall back on unaided intuitive integration of these variables when we assess our applicants?

One possible way of building an improper linear model is through the use of *bootstrapping* (Dawes & Corrigan, 1974; L.R. Goldberg, 1970). The process is to build a proper linear model of an expert's judgments about an outcome criterion and then to use that linear model in place of the judge. That such linear models can be accurate in predicting experts' judgments has been pointed out in the psychological literature by Hammond (1955) and Hoffman (1960). (This work was anticipated by 32 years by the late Henry Wallace, Vice-President under Roosevelt, in a 1923 agricultural article suggesting the use of linear models to analyze "what is on the corn judge's mind.") In his influential article, Hoffman termed the use of linear models a *paramorphic* representation of judges, by which he meant that the judges' psychological processes did not involve computing an implicit or explicit weighted average of input variables, but that it could be simulated by such a weighting. Paramorphic representations have been extremely successful (for reviews see Dawes & Corrigan, 1974; Slovic & Lichtenstein, 1971) in contexts in which predictor variables have conditionally monotone relationships to criterion variables.

The bootstrapping models make use of the weights derived from the judges; because these weights are not derived from the relationship between the predictor and criterion variables themselves, the resulting linear models are improper. Yet these paramorphic representations consistently do better than the judges from which they are derived (at least when the evaluation of goodness is in terms of the correlation between predicted and actual values).

Bootstrapping has turned out to be pervasive. For example, in a study conducted by Wiggins and Kohen (1971), psychology graduate students at the University of Illinois were presented with 10 background, aptitude, and personality measures describing other (real) Illinois graduate students in psychology and were asked to predict these students' first-year graduate GPAs. Linear models of every one of the University of Illinois judges did a better job than did the judges themselves in predicting actual grade point averages. This result was replicated in a study conducted in conjunction with Wiggins, Gregory, and Diller (cited in Dawes & Corrigan, 1974). L.R. Goldberg (1970) demonstrated it for 26 of 29 clinical psychology judges predicting psychiatric diagnosis of neurosis or psychosis from Minnesota Multiphasic Personality Inventory (MMPI) profiles, and Dawes (1971) found it in the evaluation of graduate applicants at the University of Oregon. The one published exception to the success of bootstrapping of which I am aware was a study conducted by Libby (1976). He asked 16 loan officers from relatively small banks (located in Champaign–Urbana, Illinois, with assets between $3 million and $56 million) and 27 loan officers from large banks (located in Philadelphia, with assets between $.6 billion and $4.4 billion) to judge which 30 of 60 firms would go bankrupt within three years after their financial statements. The loan officers requested five financial ratios on which to base their judgments (e.g., the ratio of present assets to total assets). On the average, the loan officers correctly categorized 44.4 businesses (74%) as either solvent or future bankruptcies, but on the average, the paramorphic representations of the loan officers could correctly classify only 43.3 (72%). This difference turned out to be statistically significant, and Libby concluded that he had an example of a situation where bootstrapping did not work – perhaps because his judges were highly skilled experts attempting to predict a highly reliable criterion. L.R. Goldberg (1976), however, noted that many of the ratios had highly skewed distributions, and he reanalyzed Libby's data, normalizing the ratios before building models of the loan officers. Libby found 77% of his officers to be superior to their paramorphic representations, but Goldberg, using his rescaled predictor variables, found the opposite; 72% of the models were superior to the judges from whom they were derived.[4]

Why does bootstrapping work? Bowman (1963), L.R. Goldberg (1970), and Dawes (1971) all maintained that its success arises from the fact that a linear model distills underlying policy (in the implicit weights) from otherwise variable behavior (e.g., judgments affected by context effects or extraneous variables).

Belief in the efficacy of bootstrapping was based on the composition of the validity of the linear model of the judge with the validity of his or her judgments themselves. This is only one of two logically possible comparisons. The other is the validity of the linear model of the judge versus the validity of linear models in general; that is, to demonstrate that bootstrapping works because the linear model catches the essence of the judge's valid expertise while eliminating unreliability, it is necessary to demon-

---

[4] It should be pointed out that a proper linear model does better than either loan officers or their paramorphic representations. Using the same task, Beaver (1966) and Deacon (1972) found that linear models predicted with about 78% accuracy on cross-validation. But I can't resist pointing out that the simplest possible improper model of them all does best. The ratio of assets to liabilities (!) correctly categorizes 48 (80%) of the cases studied by Libby.

strate that the weights obtained from an analysis of the judge's behavior are superior to those that might be obtained in other ways, for example, randomly. Because both the model of the judge and the model obtained randomly are perfectly reliable, a comparison of the random model with the judge's model permits an evaluation of the judge's underlying linear representation, or *policy*. If the random model does equally well, the judge would not be "following valid principles but following them poorly" (Dawes, 1971, p. 182), at least not principles any more valid than any others that weight variables in the appropriate direction.

Table 1 presents five studies summarized by Dawes and Corrigan (1974) in which validities (i.e., correlations) obtained by various methods were compared. In the first study, a pool of 861 psychiatric patients took the MMPI in various hospitals; they were later categorized as neurotic or psychotic on the basis of more extensive information. The MMPI profiles consist of 11 scores, each of which represents the degree to which the respondent answers questions in a manner similar to patients suffering from a well-defined form of psychopathology. A set of 11 scores is thus associated with each patient, and the problem is to predict whether a later diagnosis will be psychosis (coded 1) or neurosis (coded 0). Twenty-nine clinical psychologists "of varying experience and training" (L.R. Goldberg, 1970, p. 425) were asked to make this prediction on an 11-step forced-normal distribution. The second two studies concerned 90 first-year graduate students in the Psychology Department of the University of Illinois who were elevated on 10 variables that are predictive of academic success. These variables included aptitude test scores, college GPA, various peer ratings (e.g., extraversion), and various self-ratings (e.g., conscientiousness). A first-year GPA was computed for all these students. The problem was to predict the GPA from the 10 variables. In the second study this prediction was made by 80 (other) graduate students at the University of Illinois (Wiggins & Kohen, 1971), and in the third study this prediction was made by 41 graduate students at the University of Oregon. The details of the fourth study have already been covered; it is the one concerned with the prediction of later faculty ratings at Oregon. The final study (Yntema & Torgerson, 1961) was one in which experimenters assigned values to ellipses presented to the subjects, on the basis of figures' size, eccentricity, and grayness. The formula used was $ij + kj + ik$, where i, j, and k refer to values on the three dimensions just mentioned. Subjects in this experiment were asked to estimate the value of each ellipse and were presented with outcome feedback at the end of each trial. The problem was to predict the true (i.e., experimenter-assigned) value of each ellipse on the basis of its size, eccentricity, and grayness.

The first column of Table 1 presents the average validity of the judges in these studies, and the second presents the average validity of the paramorphic model of these judges. In all cases, bootstrapping worked. But then what Corrigan and I constructed were *random linear models*, that is,

Table 1. *Correlations between predictions and criterion values*

Example	Average validity of judge	Average validity of judge model	Average validity of random model	Validity of equal weighting model	Cross-validity of regression analysis	Validity of optimal linear model
Prediction of neurosis vs. psychosis	.28	.31	.30	.34	.46	.46
Illinois students' predictions of GPA	.33	.50	.51	.60	.57	.69
Oregon students' predictions of GPA	.37	.43	.51	.60	.57	.69
Prediction of later faculty ratings at Oregon	.19	.25	.39	.48	.38	.54
Yntema & Torgerson's (1961) experiment	.84	.89	.84	.97	—	.97

Note: GPA = grade point average.

models in which weights were randomly chosen except for sign and were then applied to standardized variables.[5]

The sign of each variable was determined on an a priori basis so that it would have a positive relationship to the criterion. Then a normal deviate was selected at random from a normal distribution with unit variance, and the absolute value of this deviate was used as a weight for the variable. Ten thousand such models were constructed for each example. (Dawes & Corrigan, 1974, p. 102)

On the average, these random linear models perform about as well as the paramorphic models of the judges; these averages are predicted in the third column of the table. Equal-weighting models, presented in the fourth column, do even better. (There is a mathematical reason why equal-weighting models must outperform the average random model.[6]) Finally, the last two columns present the cross-validated validity of the standard regression model and the validity of the optimal linear model.

Essentially the same results were obtained when the weights were selected from a rectangular distribution. Why? Because linear models are robust over deviations from optimal weighting. In other words, the bootstrapping finding, at least in these studies, has simply been a reaffirmation of the earlier finding that proper linear models are superior to human judgments – the weights derived from the judges' behavior being sufficiently close to the optimal weights that the outputs of the models are highly similar. The solution to the problem of obtaining optimal weights is one that – in terms of von Winterfeldt and Edwards (1973) – has a "flat maximum." Weights that are near to optimal level produce almost the same output as do optimal beta weights. Because the expert judge knows at least something about the direction of the variables, his or her judgments yield weights that are nearly optimal (but note that in all cases equal weighting is superior to models based on judges' behavior).

[5] Unfortunately, Dawes and Corrigan did not spell out in detail that these variables must first be standardized and that the result is a standardized dependent variable. Equal or random weighting of incomparable variables – for example, GRE score and GPA – without prior standardization would be nonsensical.

[6] Consider a set of standardized variables S_1, X_2, .X_m, each of which is positively correlated with a standardized variable Y. The correlation of the average of the Xs with the Y is equal to the correlation of the sum of the Xs with Y. The covariance of this sum with Y is equal to

$$\left(\frac{1}{n}\right) \sum_i y_i (x_{i1} + x_{i2} \ldots + x_{im})$$

$$= \left(\frac{1}{n}\right) \sum y_i x_{i1} + \left(\frac{1}{n}\right) \sum y_i x_{i2} \ldots + \left(\frac{1}{n}\right) \sum_i y_i x_{im}$$

$$= r_1 + r_2 \ldots + r_m \text{ (the sum of the correlations)}$$

The variance of y is 1, and the variance of the sum of the Xs is $M + M(M - 1)\bar{r}$, where $\bar{r}$ is the average inter-correlation between the Xs. Hence, the correlation of the average of the Xs with Y is $(\Sigma r_i)/(M + M(M - 1)\bar{r})^{1/2}$; this is greater than $(\Sigma r_i)/(M + M^2 - M)^{1/2}$ = average r_i. Because each of the random models is positively correlated with the criterion, the correlation of the average, which is the unit-weighted model, is higher than the average of the correlations.

The fact that different linear composites correlate highly with each other was first pointed out 40 years ago by Wilks (1938). He considered only situations in which there was positive correlation between predictors. This result seems to hold generally as long as these intercorrelations are not negative; for example, the correlation between $X + 2Y$ and $2X + Y$ is .80 when X and Y are uncorrelated. The ways in which outputs are relatively insensitive to changes in coefficients (provided changes in sign are not involved) have been investigated most recently by Green (1977), Wainer (1976), Wainer and Thissen (1976), W. Edwards (1978), and Gardiner and Edwards (1975).

Dawes and Corrigan (1974, p. 105) concluded that "the whole trick is to know what variables to look at and then know how to add." That principle is well illustrated in the following study, conducted since the Dawes and Corrigan article was published. In it, Hammond and Adelman (1976) both investigated and influenced the decision about what type of bullet should be used by the Denver City Police, a decision having much more obvious social impact than most of those discussed above. To quote Hammond and Adelman (1976):

In 1974, the Denver Police Department (DPD), as well as other police departments throughout the country, decided to change its handgun ammunition. The principle reason offered by the police was that the conventional round-nosed bullet provided insufficient "stopping effectiveness" (that is, the ability to incapacitate and thus to prevent the person shot from firing back at a police officer or others). The DPD chief recommended (as did other police chiefs) the conventional bullet be replaced by a hollow-point bullet. Such bullets, it was contended, flattened on impact, thus decreasing penetration, increasing stopping effectiveness, and decreasing ricochet potential. The suggested change was challenged by the American Civil Liberties Union, minority groups, and others. Opponents of the change claimed that the new bullets were nothing more than outlawed "dum-dum" bullets, that they created far more injury than the round-nosed bullet, and should, therefore, be barred from use. As is customary, judgments on this matter were formed privately and then defended publicly with enthusiasm and tenacity, and the usual public hearings were held. Both sides turned to ballistics experts for scientific information and support. (p. 392)

The disputants focused on evaluating the merits of specific bullets – confounding the physical effect of the bullets with the implications for social policy; that is, rather than separating questions of what it is the bullet should accomplish (the social policy question) from questions concerning ballistic characteristics of specific bullets, advocates merely argued for one bullet or another. Thus, as Hammond and Adelman pointed out, social policymakers inadvertently adopted the role of (poor) ballistics experts, and vice versa. What Hammond and Adelman did was to discover the important policy dimensions from the policymakers, and then they had the ballistics experts rate the bullets with respect to these dimensions. These dimensions turned out to be stopping effectiveness (the probability that someone hit in the torso could not return fire), probability of serious injury, and probability of harm to bystanders. When the ballistics experts rated the bullets with respect to these dimensions, it turned out that the last two were almost perfectly confounded, but they were not perfectly confounded with the first. Bullets do not vary along a single dimension that confounds effectiveness with lethalness. The probability of serious injury or harm to bystanders is highly related to the penetration of the bullet, whereas the probability of the bullet's effectively stopping someone from returning fire is highly related to the width of the entry wound. Since policymakers could not agree about the weights given to the three dimensions, Hammond and Adelman suggested that they be weighted equally. Combining the equal weights with the (independent) judgments of the ballistics experts, Hammond and Adelman discovered a bullet that "has greater stopping effectiveness and is less apt to cause injury (and is less apt to threaten bystanders) than the standard bullet then in use by the DPD" (Hammond & Adelman, 1976, p. 395). The bullet was also less apt to cause injury than was the bullet previously recommended by the DPD. That bullet was "accepted by the City Council and all other parties concerned, and is now being used by the DPD" (Hammond & Adelman, 1976, p. 395).[7] Once again, "the whole trick is to decide what variables to look at and then know how to add" (Dawes & Corrigan, 1974, p. 105).

So why don't people do it more often? I know of four universities (University of Illinois; New York University; University of Oregon; University of California, Santa Barbara – there may be more) that use a linear model for applicant selection, but even these use it as an initial screening device and substitute clinical judgment for the final selection of those above a cut score. L.R. Goldberg's (1965) actuarial formula for diagnosing neurosis or psychosis from MMPI profiles has proven superior to clinical judges attempting the same task (no one to my or Goldberg's knowledge has ever produced a judge who does better), yet my one experience with its use (at the Ann Arbor Veterans Administration Hospital) was that it was discontinued on the grounds that it made obvious errors (an interesting reason, discussed at length). In 1970, I suggested that our fellowship committee at the University of Oregon apportion cutbacks of National Science Foundation and National Defense Education Act fellowships to departments on the basis of a quasi-linear point system based on explicitly defined indices, departmental merit, and need; I was told "you can't systemize human judgment." It was only six months later, after our committee realized the political and ethical impossibility of

---

[7] It should be pointed out that there were only eight bullets on the *Pareto frontier*; that is, there were only eight that were not inferior to some particular other bullet in both stopping effectiveness and probability of harm (or inferior on one of the variables and equal on the other). Consequently, any weighting rule whatsoever would have chosen one of these eight.

cutting back fellowships on the basis of intuitive judgment, that such a system was adopted. And so on.

In the past three years, I have written and talked about the utility (and in my view, ethical superiority) of using linear models in socially important decisions. Many of the same objections have been raised repeatedly by different readers and audiences. I would like to conclude this article by cataloging these objections and answering them.

Objections to using linear models

These objections may be placed in three broad categories: technical, psychological, and ethical. Each category is discussed in turn.

Technical

The most common technical objection is to the use of the correlation coefficient; for example, Remus and Jenicke (1978) wrote:

It is clear that Dawes and Corrigan's choice of the correlation coefficient to establish the utility of random and unit rules is inappropriate [*sic*, inappropriate for what?]. A criterion function is also needed in the experiments cited by Dawes and Corrigan. Surely there is a cost function for misclassifying neurotics and psychotics or refusing qualified students admissions to graduate school while admitting marginal students. (p. 221)

Consider the graduate admission problem first. Most schools have k slots and N applicants. The problem is to get the best k (who are in turn willing to accept the school) out of N. What better way is there than to have an appropriate rank? None. Remus and Jenicke write as if the problem were not one of comparative choice but of absolute choice. Most social choices, however, involve selecting the better or best from a set of alternatives: the students that will be better, the bullet that will be best, a possible airport site that will be superior, and so on. The correlation coefficient, because it reflects ranks so well, is clearly appropriate for evaluating such choices.

The neurosis–psychosis problem is more subtle and even less supportive of their argument. "Surely," they state, "there is a cost function," but they don't specify any candidates. The implication is clear: If they could find it, clinical judgment would be found to be superior to linear models. Why? In the absence of such a discovery on their part, the argument amounts to nothing at all. But this argument from a vacuum can be very compelling to people (for example, to losing generals and losing football coaches, who know that "surely" their plans would work "if" – when the plans are in fact doomed to failure no matter what).

A second related technical objection is to the comparison of average correlation coefficients of judges with those of linear models. Perhaps by averaging, the performance of some really outstanding judges is obscured.

The data indicate otherwise. In the L.R. Goldberg (1970) study, for example, only 5 of 29 trained clinicians were better than the unit-weighted model, and none did better than the proper one. In the Wiggins and Kohen (1971) study, no judges were better than the unit-weighted model, and we replicated that effect at Oregon. In the Libby (1976) study, only 9 of 43 judges did better than the ratio of assets to liabilities at predicting bankruptcies (3 did equally well). While it is then conceded that clinicians should be able to predict diagnosis of neurosis or psychosis, that graduate students should be able to predict graduate success, and that bank loan officers should be able to predict bankruptcies, the possibility is raised that perhaps the experts used in the studies weren't the right ones. This again is arguing from a vacuum: If other experts were used, then the results would be different. And once again no such experts are produced, and once again the appropriate response is to ask for a reason why these hypothetical other people should be any different. (As one university vice-president told me, "Your research only proves that you used poor judges; we could surely do better by getting better judges" – apparently not from the psychology department.)

A final technical objection concerns the nature of the criterion variables. They are admittedly short-term and unprofound (e.g., GPAs, diagnoses); otherwise, most studies would be infeasible. The question is then raised of whether the findings would be different if a truly long-range important criterion were to be predicted. The answer is that of course the findings *could* be different, but we have no reason to suppose that they *would* be different. First, the distant future is in general less predictable than the immediate future, for the simple reason that more unforeseen, extraneous, or self-augmenting factors influence individual outcomes. (Note that we are not discussing aggregate outcomes, such as an unusually cold winter in the Midwest in general spread out over three months.) Since, then, clinical prediction is poorer than linear to begin with, the hypothesis would hold only if linear prediction got much worse over time than did clinical prediction. There is no a priori reason to believe that this differential deterioration in prediction would occur, and none has ever been suggested to me. There is certainly no evidence. Once again, the objection consists of an argument from a vacuum.

Particularly compelling is the fact that people who argue that different criteria or judges or variables or time frames would produce different results have had 25 years in which to produce examples, and they have failed to do so.

Psychological

One psychological resistance to using linear models lies in our selective memory about clinical prediction. Our belief in such prediction is reinforced by the availability (Tversky & Kahneman, 1974) of instances of successful clinical prediction – expecially those that are exceptions to some formula: "I knew someone once with ... who ..." (E.g., "I knew of someone with a tested IQ of only 130 who got an advanced degree in psychology.") As Nisbett, Borgida, Crandall, and Reed (1976, 7) showed, such single instances often have greater impact on judgment than do much more valid statistical compilations based on many instances. (A good prophylactic for clinical psychologists basing resistance to actuarial prediction on such instances would be to keep careful records of their own predictions about their own patients – prospective records not subject to hindsight. Such records could make all instances of successful and unsuccessful prediction equally available for impact; in addition, they could serve for another clinical versus statistical study using the best possible judge – the clinician himself or herself.)

Moreover, an illusion of good judgment may be reinforced due to selection (Einhorn & Hogarth, 1978) in those situations in which the prediction of a positive or negative outcome has a self-fulfilling effect. For example, admissions officers who judge that a candidate is particularly qualified for a graduate program may feel that their judgment is exonerated when that candidate does well, even though the candidate's success is in large part due to the positive effects of the program. (In contrast, a linear model of selection is evaluated by seeing how well it predicts performance *within* the set of applicants selected.) Or a waiter who believes that particular people at the table are poor tippers may be less attentive than usual and receive a smaller tip, thereby having his clinical judgment exonerated.[8]

A second psychological resistance to the use of linear models stems from their "proven" low validity. Here, there is an implicit (as opposed to explicit) argument from a vacuum because neither changes in evaluation procedures, nor in judges, nor in criteria, are proposed. Rather, the unstated assumption is that these criteria of psychological interest are in fact highly predictable, so it follows that if one method of prediction (a linear model) doesn't work too well, another might do better (reasonable), which is then translated into the belief that another *will* do better (which is not a reasonable inference) – once it is found. This resistance is best expressed by a dean considering the graduate admissions, who wrote, "The correlation of the linear composite with future faculty ratings is only .4, whereas that of the admissions committee's judgment correlates .2. Twice nothing is nothing." In 1976, I answered as follows (Dawes, 1976, pp. 6–7):

In response, I can only point out that 16% of the variance is better than 4% of the variance. To me, however, the fascinating part of this argument is the implicit assumption that that other 84% of the variance is predictable and that we can somehow predict it.

---

[8] This example was provided by Einhorn (1979).

Now what are we dealing with? We are dealing with personality and intellectual characteristics of [uniformly bright] people who are about 20 years old . . . . Why are we so convinced that this prediction can be made at all? Surely, it is not necessary to read *Ecclesiastes* every night to understand the role of chance. . . . Moreover, there are clearly positive feedback effects in professional development that exaggerate threshold phenomena. For example, once people are considered sufficiently "outstanding" that they are invited to outstanding institutions, they have outstanding colleagues with whom to interact – and excellence is exacerbated. This same problem occurs for those who do not quite reach such a threshold level. Not only do all these factors mitigate against successful long-range prediction, but studies of the success of such prediction are necessarily limited to those accepted, with the incumbent problems of restriction of range and a negative covariance structure between predictors (Dawes, 1975).

Finally, there are all sorts of nonintellectual factors in professional success that could not possibly be evaluated before admission to graduate school, for example, success at forming a satisfying or inspiring libidinal relationship, not yet evident genetic tendencies to drug or alcohol addiction, the misfortune to join a research group that "blows up," and so on, and so forth.

Intellectually, I find it somewhat remarkable that we are able to predict even 16% of the variance. But I believe that my own emotional response is indicative of those of my colleagues who simply assume that the future is more predictable. *I want it to be predictable, especially when the aspect of it that I want to predict is important to me.* This desire, I suggest, translates itself into an implicit assumption that the future is in fact highly predictable, and it would then logically follow that if something is not a very good predictor, something else might do better (although it is never correct to argue that it necessarily will).

Statistical prediction, because it includes the specification (usually a low correlation coefficient) of exactly how poorly we can predict, bluntly strikes us with the fact that life is not all that predictable. Unsystematic clinical prediction (or "postdiction"), in contrast, allows us the comforting illusion that life is in fact predictable and that we can predict it.

Ethical

When I was at the Los Angeles Renaissance Fair last summer, I overheard a young woman complain that it was "horribly unfair" that she had been rejected by the Psychology Department at the University of California, Santa Barbara, on the basis of mere numbers, without even an interview. "How can they possibly tell what I'm like?" The answer is that they can't. Nor could they with an interview (Kelly, 1954). Nevertheless, many people maintain that making a crucial social choice without an interview is dehumanizing. I think that the question of whether people are treated in a fair manner has more to do with the question of whether or not they have been dehumanized than does the question of whether the treatment is face to face. (Some of the worst doctors spend a great deal of time conversing with their patients, read no medical journals, order few or no tests, and grieve at the funerals.) A GPA represents $3\frac{1}{2}$ years of behavior on the part of the applicant. (Surely, not all the professors are biased against his or her particular form of creativity.) The GRE is a more carefully devised test. Do we really believe that we can do a better or a fairer job by a 10-minute folder evaluation or a half-hour interview than is done by these two mere numbers? Such cognitive conceit (Dawes, 1976, p. 7) is unethical, especially given the fact of no evidence whatsoever indicating that we do a better job than does the linear equation. (And even making exceptions must be done with extreme care if it is to be ethical, for if we admit someone with a low linear score on the basis that he or she has some special talent, we are automatically rejecting someone with a higher score, who might well have had an equally impressive talent had we taken the trouble to evaluate it.)

No matter how much we would like to see this or that aspect of one or another of the studies reviewed in this article changed, no matter how psychologically uncompelling or distasteful we may find their results to be, no matter how ethically uncomfortable we may feel at "reducing people to mere numbers," the fact remains that our clients are people who deserve to be treated in the best manner possible. If that means – as it appears at present – that selection, diagnosis, and prognosis should be based on nothing more than the addition of a few numbers representing values on important attributes, so be it. To do otherwise is to cheat the people we serve.

29. The vitality of mythical numbers

Max Singer

It is generally assumed that heroin addicts in New York City steal some two to five billion dollars worth of property a year, and commit approximately half of all the property crimes. Such estimates of addict crime are used by an organization like RAND, by a political figure like Howard Samuels, and even by the Attorney General of the United States. The estimate that half the property crimes are committed by addicts was originally attributed to a police official and has been used so often that it is now part of the common wisdom.

The amount of property stolen by addicts is usually estimated in something like the following manner:

There are 100,000 addicts with an average habit of $30.00 per day. This means addicts must have some $1.1 billion a year to pay for their heroin (100,000 × 365 × $30.00). Because the addict must sell the property he steals to a fence for only about a quarter of its value, or less, addicts must steal some $4 to $5 billion a year to pay for their heroin.

These calculations can be made with more or less sophistication. One can allow for the fact that the kind of addicts who make their living illegally typically spend upwards of a quarter of their time in jail, which would reduce the amount of crime by a quarter. (*The New York Times* recently reported on the death of William "Donkey" Reilly. A 74-year-old ex-addict who had been addicted for 54 years, he had spent 30 of those years in prison.) Some of what the addict steals is cash, none of which has to go to a fence. A large part of the cost of heroin is paid for by dealing in the heroin business, rather than stealing from society, and another large part by prostitution, including male addicts living off prostitutes. But no matter how carefully you slice it, if one tries to estimate the value of property stolen by addicts by assuming that there are 100,000 addicts and

This chapter originally appeared in *The Public Interest*, 1971, **23**, 3–9. Copyright © 1971 by National Affairs, Inc. Reprinted by permission.

estimating what is the minimum amount they would have to steal to support themselves and their habits (after making generous estimates for legal income), one comes up with a number in the neighborhood of $1 billion a year for New York City.

But what happens if you approach the question from the other side? Suppose we ask, "How much property is stolen – by addicts or anyone else?" Addict theft must be less than total theft. What is the value of property stolen in New York City in any year? Somewhat surprisingly to me when I first asked, this turned out to be a difficult question to answer, even approximately. No one had any estimates that they had even the faintest confidence in, and the question doesn't seem to have been much asked. The amount of officially reported theft in New York City is approximately $300 million a year, of which about $100 million is the value of automobile theft (a crime that is rarely committed by addicts). But it is clear that there is a very large volume of crime that is not reported; for example, shoplifting is not normally reported to the police. (Much property loss to thieves is not reported to insurance companies either, and the insurance industry had no good estimate for total theft.)

It turns out, however, that if one is only asking a question like, "Is it possible that addicts stole $1 billion worth of property in New York City last year?" it is relatively simple to estimate the amount of property stolen. It is clear that the two biggest components of addict theft are shoplifting and burglary. What *could* the value of property shoplifted by addicts be? All retail sales in New York City are on the order of $15 billion a year. This includes automobiles, carpets, diamond rings, and other items not usually available to shoplifters. A reasonable number for inventory loss to retail establishments is 2%. This number includes management embezzlements, stealing by clerks, shipping departments, truckers, etc. (Department stores, particularly, have reported a large increase in shoplifting in recent years, but they are among the most vulnerable of retail establishments and not important enough to bring the overall rate much above 2%.) It is generally agreed that substantially more than half of the property missing from retail establishments is taken by employees, the remainder being lost to outside shoplifters. But let us credit shoplifters with stealing 1% of all the property sold at retail in New York City – this would be about $150 million a year.

What about burglary? There are something like two and one-half million households in New York City. Suppose that on the average one out of five of them is robbed or burglarized every year. This takes into account that in some areas burglary is even more commonplace, and that some households are burglarized more than once a year. This would mean 500,000 burglaries a year. The average value of property taken in a burglary might be on the order of $200. In some burglaries, of course, much larger amounts of property are taken, but these higher value burglaries are much rarer, and often are committed by non-addict professional thieves. If we use the number of $200 × 500,000 burglaries, we get $100 million of property stolen from people's homes in a year in New York City.

Obviously, none of these estimated values is either sacred or substantiated. You can make your own estimate. The estimates here have the character that it would be very surprising if they were wrong by a factor of 10, and not very important for the conclusion if they were wrong by a factor of two. (This is a good position for an estimator to be in.)

Obviously not all addict theft is property taken from stores or from people's homes. One of the most feared types of addict crime is property taken from the persons of New Yorkers in muggings and other forms of robbery. We can estimate this, too. Suppose that on the average, one person in 10 has property taken from his person by muggers or robbers each year. That would be 800,000 such robberies, and if the average one produced $100 (which it is very unlikely to do), $8 million a year would be taken in this form of theft.

So we can see that if we credit addicts with *all* of the shoplifting, *all* of the theft from homes, and *all* of the theft from persons, total property stolen by addicts in a year in New York City amounts to some $330 million. You can throw in all the "fudge factors" you want, add all the other miscellaneous crimes that addicts commit, but no matter what you do, it is difficult to find a basis for estimating that addicts steal over a half billion dollars a year, and a quarter billion looks like a better estimate, although perhaps on the high side. After all, there must be some thieves who are not addicts.

Thus, I believe we have shown that whereas it is widely assumed that addicts steal from $2 billion to $5 billion a year in New York City, the actual number is *ten* times smaller, and that this can be demonstrated by five minutes of thought.[1] So what? A quarter billion dollars' worth of property is still a lot of property. It exceeds the amount of money spent annually on addict rehabilitation and other programs to prevent and control addiction. Furthermore, the value of the property stolen by addicts is a small part of the total cost to society of addict theft. A much larger cost is paid in fear, changed neighborhood atmosphere, the cost of precautions, and other echoing and re-echoing reactions to theft and its danger.

One point in this exercise in estimating the value of property stolen by addicts is to shed some light on people's attitudes toward numbers. People

---

[1] Mythical numbers may be more mythical and have more vitality in the area of crime than in most areas. In the early 1950s the Kefauver Committee published a $20 billion estimate for the annual "take" of gambling in the United States. The figure actually was "picked from a hat." One staff member said: "We had no real idea of the money spent. The California Crime Commission said $12 billion. Virgil Petersen of Chicago said $30 billion. We picked $20 billion as the balance of the two."

An unusual example of a mythical number that had a vigorous life – the assertion that 28 Black Panthers had been murdered by police – is given a careful biography by Edward Jay Epstein in the February 13, 1971, *New Yorker*. (It turned out that there were 19 Panthers killed, ten of them by the police, and eight of these in situations where it seems likely that the Panthers took the initiative.)

feel that there is a lot of addict crime, and that $2 billion is a large number, so they are inclined to believe that there is $2 billion worth of addict theft. But $250 million is a large number, too, and if our sense of perspective were not distorted by daily consciousness of federal expenditures, most people would be quite content to accept $250 million a year as a lot of theft.

Along the same lines, this exercise is another reminder that even responsible officials, responsible newspapers, and responsible research groups pick up and pass on as gospel numbers that have no real basis in fact. We are reminded by this experience that because an estimate has been used widely by a variety of people who should know what they are talking about, one cannot assume that the estimate is even approximately correct.

But there is a much more important implication of the fact that there cannot be nearly so much addict theft as people believe. This implication is that there probably cannot be as many addicts as many people believe. Most of the money paid for heroin bought at retail comes from stealing, and most addicts buy at retail. Therefore, the number of addicts is basically – although imprecisely – limited by the amount of theft. (The estimate developed in a Hudson Institute study was that close to half of the volume of heroin consumed is used by people in the heroin distribution system who do not buy at retail, and do not pay with stolen property but with their "services" in the distribution system.[2]) But while the people in the business (at lower levels) consume close to half the heroin, they are only some one-sixth or one-seventh of the total number of addicts. They are the ones who can afford big habits.

The most popular, informal estimate of addicts in New York City is 100,000-plus (usually with an emphasis on the "plus"). The federal register in Washington lists some 30,000 addicts in New York City, and the New York City Department of Health's register of addicts' names lists some 70,000. While all the people on those lists are not still active addicts – many of them are dead or in prison – most people believe that there are many addicts who are not on any list. It is common to regard the estimate of 100,000 addicts in New York City as a very conservative one. Dr. Judianne Densen-Gerber was widely quoted early in 1970 for her estimate that there would be over 100,000 teenage addicts by the end of the summer. And there are obviously many addicts of 20 years of age and more.[3]

In discussing the number of addicts in this article, we will be talking

---

[2] A parallel datum was developed in a later study by St. Luke's Hospital of 81 addicts – average age 34. More than one-half of the heroin consumed by these addicts, over a year, had been paid for by the sale of heroin. Incidentally, these 81 addicts had stolen an average of $9,000 worth of property in the previous year.

[3] Among other recent estimators we may note a Marxist, Sol Yurick, who gives us "500,000 junkies" (*Monthly Review*, December 1970), and William R. Corson, who contends, in the December 1970 *Penthouse*, that "today at least 2,500,000 black Americans are hooked on heroin."

about the kind of person one thinks of when the term "addict" is used.[4] A better term might be "street addict." This is a person who normally uses heroin every day. He is the kind of person who looks and acts like the normal picture of an addict. We exclude here the people in the medical profession who are frequent users of heroin or other opiates, or are addicted to them, students who use heroin occasionally, wealthy people who are addicted but do not need to steal and do not frequent the normal addict hangouts, etc. When we are addressing the "addict problem," it is much less important that we include these cases; while they are undoubtedly problems in varying degrees, they are a very different type of problem than that posed by the typical street addict.

The amount of property stolen by addicts suggests that the number of New York City street addicts may be more like 70,000 than 100,000, and almost certainly cannot be anything like the 200,000 number that is sometimes used. Several other simple ways of estimating the number of street addicts lead to a similar conclusion.

Experience with the addict population has led observers to estimate that the average street addict spends a quarter to a third of his time in prison. (Some students of the subject, such as Edward Preble and John J. Casey, Jr., believe the average to be over 40%.) This would imply that at any one time, one-quarter to one-third of the addict population is in prison, and that the total addict population can be estimated by multiplying the number of addicts who are in prison by three or four. Of course the number of addicts who are in prison is not a known quantity (and, in fact, as we have indicated above, not even a very precise concept). However, one can make reasonable estimates of the number of addicts in prison (and for this purpose we can include the addicts in various involuntary treatment centers). This number is approximately 14,000–17,000, which is quite compatible with an estimate of 70,000 total New York City street addicts.

Another way of estimating the total number of street addicts in New York City is to use the demographic information that is available about the addict population. For example, we can be reasonably certain that some 25% of the street addict population in New York City is Puerto Rican, and some 50% are blacks. We know that approximately five out of six street addicts are male, and that 50% of the street addicts are between the ages of

---

[4] There is an interesting anomaly about the word "addict." Most people, if pressed for a definition of an "addict," would say he is a person who regularly takes heroin (or some such drug) and who, if he fails to get his regular dose of heroin, will have unpleasant or painful withdrawal symptoms. But this definition would not apply to a large part of what is generally recognized as the "addict population." In fact, it would not apply to most certified addicts. An addict who has been detoxified or who has been imprisoned and kept away from drugs for a week or so would not fit the normal definition of "addict." He no longer has any physical symptoms resulting from not taking heroin. "Donkey" Reilly would certainly fulfill most people's ideas of an addict, but for 30 of the 54 years he was an "addict" he was in prison, and he was certainly not actively addicted to heroin during most of the time he spent in prison, which was more than half of his "addict" career (although a certain amount of drugs are available in prison).

16 and 25. This would mean that 20% of the total number of addicts are black males between the age of 16 and 25. If there were 70,000 addicts, this would mean that 14,000 blacks between the ages of 16 and 25 are addicts. But altogether there are only about 140,000 blacks between the ages of 16 and 25 in the city – perhaps half of them living in poverty areas. This means that if there are 70,000 addicts in the city, one in 10 black youths are addicts, and if there are 100,000 addicts, nearly one in six are, and if there are 200,000 addicts, one in three. You can decide for yourself which of these degrees of penetration of the young black male group is most believable, but it is rather clear that the number of 200,000 addicts is implausible. Similarly, the total of 70,000 street addicts would imply 7,000 young Puerto Rican males are addicted, and the total number of Puerto Rican boys between the ages of 16 and 25 in New York City is about 70,000.

None of the above calculations is meant in any way to downplay the importance of the problem of heroin addiction. Heroin is a terrible curse. When you think of the individual tragedy involved, 70,000 is an awfully large number of addicts. And if you have to work for a living, $250 million is an awful lot of money to have stolen from the citizens of the city to be transferred through the hands of addicts and fences into the pockets of those who import and distribute heroin, and those who take bribes or perform other services for the heroin industry.

The main point of this article may well be to illustrate how far one can go in bounding a problem by taking numbers seriously, seeing what they imply, checking various implications against each other and against general knowledge (such as the number of persons or households in the city). Small efforts in this direction can go a long way to help ordinary people and responsible officals to cope with experts of various kinds.

30. Intuitive prediction: Biases and corrective procedures

Daniel Kahneman and Amos Tversky

Introduction

Any significant activity of forecasting involves a large component of judgment, intuition, and educated guesswork. Indeed, the opinions of experts are the source of many technological, political, and social forecasts. Opinions and intuitions play an important part even where the forecasts are obtained by a mathematical model or a simulation. Intuitive judgments enter in the choice of the variables that are considered in such models, the impact factors that are assigned to them, and the initial values that are assumed to hold. The critical role of intuition in all varieties of forecasting calls for an analysis of the factors that limit the accuracy of expert judgments, and for the development of procedures designed to improve the quality of these judgments. . . .

Singular and distributional data

Experts are often required to provide a best guess, estimate, or prediction concerning an uncertain quantity such as the value of the Dow-Jones index on a particular day, the future sales of a product, or the outcome of an election. A distinction should be made between two types of information that are available to the forecaster: singular and distributional. Singular information, or case data, consists of evidence about the particular case under consideration. Distributional information, or base-rate data, consists of knowledge about the distribution of outcomes in similar situations. In predicting the sales of a new novel, for example, what one knows about the author, the style, and the plot is singular information,

This chapter is an abbreviated version of a paper that appeared in S. Makridakis and S. C. Wheelwright (Eds.), "Forecasting," *TIMS*, Studies in Management Science, 1979, *12*, 313–327. Copyright © 1979 by North-Holland Publishing Co. Reprinted by permission.

whereas what one knows about the sales of novels is distributional information. Similarly, in predicting the longevity of a patient, the singular information includes his age, state of health, and past medical history, whereas the distributional information consists of the relevant population statistics. The singular information describes the specific features of the problem that distinguish it from others, while the distributional information characterizes the outcomes that have been observed in cases of the same general class. The present concept of distributional data does not coincide with the Bayesian concept of a prior probability distribution. The former is defined by the nature of the data, whereas the latter is defined in terms of the sequence of information acquisition.

Many prediction problems are essentially unique in the sense that little, if any, relevant distributional information is available. Examples are the forecast of demand for nuclear energy in the year 2000, or of the date by which an effective cure for leukemia will be found. In such problems, the expert must rely exclusively on singular information. However, the evidence suggests that people are insufficiently sensitive to distributional data even when such data are available. Indeed, recent research suggests that people rely primarily on singular information, even when it is scanty and unreliable, and give insufficient weight to distributional information (Kahneman & Tversky, 1973, 4; Tversky & Kahneman, Chap. 10).

The context of planning provides many examples in which the distribution of outcomes in past experience is ignored. Scientists and writers, for example, are notoriously prone to underestimate the time required to complete a project, even when they have considerable experience of past failures to live up to planned schedules. A similar bias has been documented in engineers' estimates of the completion time for repairs of power stations (Kidd, 1970). Although this planning fallacy is sometimes attributable to motivational factors such as wishful thinking, it frequently occurs even when underestimation of duration or cost is actually penalized.

The planning fallacy is a consequence of the tendency to neglect distributional data and to adopt what may be termed an internal approach to prediction, in which one focuses on the constituents of the specific problem rather than on the distribution of outcomes in similar cases. The internal approach to the evaluation of plans is likely to produce underestimation. A building can only be completed on time, for example, if there are no delays in the delivery of materials, no strikes, no unusual weather conditions, and so on. Although each of these disturbances is unlikely, the probability that at least one of them will occur may be substantial. This combinatorial consideration, however, is not adequately represented in people's intuitions (Bar-Hillel, 1973). Attempts to combat this error by adding a slippage factor are rarely adequate, since the adjusted value tends to remain too close to the initial value that acts as an anchor (Tversky & Kahneman, 1974, 1). The adoption of an external approach that treats the specific problem as one of many could help overcome this bias. In this approach, one does not attempt to divine the specific manner in which a plan might fail. Rather, one relates the problem at hand to the distribution of completion time for similar projects. It is suggested that more reasonable estimates are likely to be obtained by asking the external question: how long do such projects usually last? and not merely the internal question: what are the specific factors and difficulties that operate in the particular problem?

The tendency to neglect distributional information and to rely mainly on singular information is enhanced by any factor that increases the perceived uniqueness of the problem. The relevance of distributional data can be masked by detailed acquaintance with the specific case or by intense involvement in it. The perceived uniqueness of a problem is also influenced by the formulation of the question that the expert is required to answer. For example, the question of how much the development of a new product will cost may induce an internal approach in which total costs are broken down into components. The equivalent question of the percentage by which costs will exceed the current budget is likely to call to mind the distribution of cost overruns for developments of the same general kind. Thus, a change of units – for example, from costs to overruns – could alter the manner in which the problem is viewed.

The prevalent tendency to underweigh or ignore distributional information is perhaps the major error of intuitive prediction. The consideration of distributional information, of course, does not guarantee the accuracy of forecasts. It does, however, provide some protection against completely unrealistic predictions. The analyst should therefore make every effort to frame the forecasting problem so as to facilitate utilizing all the distributional information that is available to the expert.

Regression and intuitive prediction

In most problems of prediction, the expert has both singular information about the specific case and distributional information about the outcomes in similar cases. Examples are the counselor who predicts the likely achievements of a student, the banker who assesses the earning potential of a small business, the publisher who estimates the sales of a textbook, or the economist who forecasts some index of economic growth.

How do people predict in such situations? Psychological research (Kahneman & Tversky, 1973, 4; Ross, 1977) suggests that intuitive predictions are generated according to a simple matching rule: the predicted value is selected so that the standing of the case in the distribution of outcomes matches its standing in the distribution of impressions. The following example illustrates this rule. An editor reviewed the manuscript of a novel and was favorably impressed. He said: "This book reads like a best-seller. Among the books of this type that were published in recent years, I would say that only one in twenty impressed me more." If the editor were now asked to estimate the sales of this novel, he would probably predict that it will be in the top 5 percent of the distribution of sales.

There is considerable evidence that people often predict by matching prediction to impression. However, this rule of prediction is unsound because it fails to take uncertainty into account. The editor of our example would surely admit that sales of books are highly unpredictable. In such a situation of high uncertainty, the best prediction of the sales of a book should fall somewhere between the value that matches one's impression and the average sales for books of its type.

One of the basic principles of statistical prediction, which is also one of the least intuitive, is that the extremeness of predictions must be moderated by considerations of predictability. Imagine, for example, that the publisher knows from past experience that the sales of books are quite unrelated to his initial impressions. Manuscripts that impressed him favorably and manuscripts that he disliked were equally likely to sell well or poorly. In such a case of zero predictability, the publisher's best guess about sales should be the same for all books – for example, the average of the relevant category – regardless of his personal impression of the individual book. Predictions are allowed to match impressions only in the case of perfect predictability. In intermediate situations, which are of course the most common, the prediction should be regressive; that is, it should fall between the class average and the value that best represents one's impression of the case at hand. The lower the predictability, the closer the prediction should be to the class average. Intuitive predictions are typically nonregressive: people often make extreme predictions on the basis of information whose reliability and predictive validity are known to be low. . . .

A corrective procedure for prediction

How can the expert be guided to produce properly regressive predictions? How can he be led to use the singular and distributional information that is available to him, in accordance with the principles of statistical prediction? In this section a five-step procedure that is designed to achieve these objectives is proposed.

Step 1: Selection of a reference class

The goal of this stage is to identify a class to which the case at hand can be referred meaningfully and for which the distribution of outcomes is known or can be assessed with reasonable confidence.

In the predictions of the sales of a book or of the gross earnings of a film, for example, the selection of a reference class is straightforward. It is relatively easy, in these cases, to define an appropriate class of books or films for which the distribution of sales or revenue is known.

There are prediction problems – for example, forecasting the cost of developing a novel product, or the time by which it will reach the market – for which a reference class is difficult to identify because the various instances appear to be so different from each other that they cannot be compared meaningfully. As was noted earlier, however, this problem can sometimes be overcome by redefining the quantity that is to be predicted. Development projects in different technologies, for example, may be easier to compare in terms of percentage of cost overruns than in terms of absolute costs. The prediction of costs calls the expert's attention to the unique characteristics of each project. The prediction of cost overruns, in contrast, highlights the determinants of realism in planning which are common to many different projects. Consequently, it may be easier to define a reference class in the latter formulation than in the former.

More often than not the expert will think of several classes to which the problem could be referred, and a choice among these alternatives will be necessary. For example, the reference class for the prediction of the sales of a book could consist of other books by the same author, of books on the same topic, or of books of the same general type, such as hardcover novels. The choice of a reference class often involves a trade-off between conflicting criteria. Thus, the most inclusive class may allow for the best estimate of the distribution of outcomes, but it may be too heterogeneous to permit a meaningful comparison to the book at hand. The class of books by the same author, on the other hand, may provide the most natural basis for comparison, but the book in question could well fall outside the range of previously observed outcomes. In this example, the class of books on the same topic could be the most appropriate.

Step 2: Assessment of the distribution for the reference class

For some problems – for example, sales of books – statistics regarding the distribution of outcomes are available. In other problems, the relevant distribution must be estimated on the basis of various sources of information. In particular, the expert should provide an estimate of the class average and some additional estimates that reflect the range of variability of outcomes. Sample questions are: how many copies are sold, on the average, for books in this category? What proportion of the books in that class sell more that 15,000 copies?

Many forecasting problems are characterized by the absence of directly relevant distributional data. That is always the case in long-term forecasting, where the relevant distribution pertains to outcomes in the distant future. Consider, for example, an attempt to predict England's share of the world market in personalized urban transportation systems in the year 2000. It may be useful to recast this problem as follows: "What is the likely distribution, over various domains of advanced technology, of England's share of the world market in the year 2000? How do you expect the particular case of transportation systems to compare to other technologies?" Note that the distribution of outcomes is not known in this problem. However, the required distribution could probably be estimated on the basis of the distribution of values for England's present share of the world market in different technologies, adjusted by an assessment of the long-term trend of England's changing position in world trade.

Step 3: Intuitive estimation

One part of the information the expert has about a problem is summarized by the distribution of outcomes in the reference class. In addition, the expert usually has a considerable amount of singular information about the particular case, which distinguishes it from other members of the class. The expert should now be asked to make an intuitive estimate on the basis of this singular information. As was noted above, this intuitive estimate is likely to be nonregressive. The objective of the next two steps of the procedure is to correct this bias and obtain a more adequate estimate.

Step 4: Assessment of predictability

The expert should now assess the degree to which the type of information that is available in this case permits accurate prediction of outcomes. In the context of linear prediction, the appropriate measure of predictability is ρ, the product–moment correlation between predictions and outcomes. Where records of past predictions and outcomes exist, the required value could be estimated from these records. In the absence of such data, one must rely on subjective assessments of predictability. A statistically sophisticated expert may be able to provide a direct estimate of ρ on the basis of his experience. When statistical sophistication is lacking, the analyst should resort to less direct procedures.

One such procedure requires the expert to compare the predictability of the variable with which he is concerned to the predictability of other variables. For example, the expert could be fairly confident that his ability to predict the sales of books exceeds the ability of sportscasters to predict point spread in football games, but is not as good as the ability of weather forecasters to predict temperature two days ahead of time. A skillful and diligent analyst could construct a rough scale of predictability based on computed correlations between predictions and outcomes for a set of phenomena that range from highly predictable – for example, temperature – to highly unpredictable – for example, stock prices. The analyst would then be in a position to ask the expert to locate the predictability of the target quantity on this scale, thereby providing a numerical estimate of ρ.

An alternative method for assessing predictability involves questions such as: If you were to consider two novels that you are about to publish, how often would you be right in predicting which of the two will sell more copies? An estimate of the ordinal correlation between predictions and outcomes can now be obtained as follows: If ρ is the estimated proportion of pairs in which the order of outcomes was correctly predicted, then $\tau = 2\rho - 1$ provides an index of predictive accuracy, which ranges from zero when predictions are at chance level to unity when predictions are perfectly accurate. In many situations τ can be used as a crude approximation for ρ.

Estimates of predictability are not easy to make, and they should be examined carefully. The expert could be subject to the hindsight fallacy (Fischhoff, 1975), which leads to an overestimate of the predictability of outcomes. The expert could also be subject to an availability bias (Tversky & Kahneman, 1973, 11) and might recall for the most part surprises, or memorable cases in which strong initial impressions were later confirmed.

Step 5: Correction of the intuitive estimate.

To correct for nonregressiveness, the intuitive estimate should be adjusted toward the average of the reference class. If the intuitive estimate was nonregressive, then under fairly general conditions the distance between the intuitive estimate and the average of the class should be reduced by a factor of ρ, where ρ is the correlation coefficient. This procedure provides an estimate of the quantity, which, one hopes, reduces the nonregressive error.

For example, suppose that the expert's intuitive prediction of the sales of a given book is 12,000 and that, on average, books in that category sell 4,000 copies. Suppose further that the expert believes that he would correctly order pairs of manuscripts by their future sales on 80 percent of comparisons. In this case, $\tau = 1.6 - 1 = 0.6$, and the regressed estimate of sales would be $4,000 + 0.6(12,000 - 4,000) = 8,800$.

The effect of this correction will be substantial when the intuitive estimate is relatively extreme and predictability is moderate or low. The rationale for the computation should be carefully explained to the expert, who will then decide whether to stand by his original prediction, adopt the computed estimate, or correct his assessment to some intermediate value.

The procedure that we have outlined is open to several objections that are likely to arise in the interaction between analyst and expert. First, the expert could question the assumption that his initial intuitive estimate was nonregressive. Fortunately, this assumption can be verified by asking the expert to estimate (1) the proportion of cases in the references class – for example, manuscripts – that would have made a stronger impression on him and (2) the proportion of cases in the reference class for which the outcome exceeds his intuitive prediction – for example, the proportion of books that sold more than 12,000 copies. If the two proportions are approximately the same, the prediction was surely nonregressive.

A more general objection may question the basic idea that predictions should be regressive. The expert could point out, correctly, that the present procedure will usually yield conservative predictions that are not far from the average of the class and is very unlikely to predict an exceptional outcome that lies beyond all previously observed values. The answer to this objection is that a fallible predictor can retain a chance to correctly predict a few exceptional outcomes only at the cost of erroneously identifying many other cases as exceptional. Nonregressive predictions over-predict: they are associated with a substantial probability that any high prediction is an overestimate and any low prediction is an underestimate. In most situations, this bias is costly, and should be eliminated. . . .

Concluding remarks

The approach presented here is based on the following general notions about forecasting. First, that most predictions and forecasts contain an irreducible intuitive component. Second, that the intuitive predictions of knowledgeable individuals contain much useful information. Third, that these intuitive judgments are often biased in a predictable manner. Hence, the problem is not whether to accept intuitive predictions at face value or to reject them, but rather how they can be debiased and improved.

The analysis of human judgment shows that many biases of intuition stem from the tendency to give little weight to certain types of information, for example, the base-rate frequency of outcomes and their predictability. The strategy of debiasing presented in this paper attempts to elicit from the expert relevant information that he would normally neglect, and to help him integrate this information with his intuitive impressions in a manner that respects basic principles of statistical prediction. . . .

31. Debiasing

Baruch Fischhoff

Once a behavioral phenomenon has been identified in some experimental context, it is appropriate to start questioning its robustness. A popular and often productive questioning strategy might be called destructive testing, after a kindred technique in engineering. A proposed design is subjected to conditions intended to push it to and beyond its limits of viability. Such controlled destruction can clarify where it is to be trusted and why it works when it does. Applied to a behavioral phenomenon, this philosophy would promote research attempting to circumscribe the conditions for its observation and the psychological processes that must be evoked or controlled in order to eliminate it. Where the phenomenon is a judgmental bias, destructive testing takes the form of debiasing efforts. Destructive testing shows where a design fails; when a bias fails, the result is improved judgment.

The study of heuristics and biases might itself be seen as the application of destructive testing to the earlier hypothesis that people are competent intuitive statisticians. Casual observation suggests that people's judgment is generally "good enough" to let them make it through life without getting into too much trouble. Early studies (Peterson & Beach, 1967) supported this belief, indicating that, to a first approximation, people might be described as veridical observers and normative judges. Subsequent studies, represented in this volume, tested the accuracy of this approximation by looking at the limits of people's apparent successes. Could better judgment have made them richer or healthier? Can the success they achieved be attributed to a lenient environment, which does not presume particularly knowledgeable behavior? Tragic mistakes provide important insight into the nature and quality of people's decision-

My thanks to Ruth Beyth-Marom, Don MacGregor, and Paul Slovic for their helpful comments on earlier drafts of this paper. This work was supported by the Office of Naval Research under Contract N00014-80-C-0150 to Perceptronics, Inc.

making processes; fortunately, they are rare enough that we have too small a data base to disentangle the factors that may have led people astray. Judgment research has used the destructive-testing strategy to generate biased judgments in moderately well-characterized situations. The theoretician hopes that a pattern of errors and successes will emerge that lends itself to few possible explanations. Thus, the study of biases clarifies the sources and limits of apparent wisdom, just as the study of debiasing clarifies the sources and limits of apparent folly. Both are essential to the study of judgment.

Although some judgment studies are primarily demonstrations that a particular bias can occur under some, perhaps contrived, conditions, many other studies have attempted to stack the deck against the observation of bias. Some of these are explicitly debiasing studies, conducted in the hope that procedures that prove effective in the laboratory will also improve performance in the field. Others had the more theoretical goal of clarifying the contexts that induce suboptimal judgments. The core of this chapter is a review of studies that can be construed as efforts to reduce two familiar biases, hindsight bias and overconfidence. It considers failures as well as successes in the belief that (a) failure helps clarify the virulence of a problem and the need for corrective or protective measures, and (b) the overall pattern of studies is the key to discovering the psychological dimensions that are important in characterizing real-life situations and anticipating the extent of biased performance in them.

The review attempts to be exhaustive, subject to the following three selection criteria:

1. Only studies published in sources with peer review are considered. Thus, responsibility for quality control is externalized.
2. Anecdotal evidence is (with a few exceptions) excluded. Although such reports are the primary source of information about some kinds of debiasing attempts (e.g., use of experts), they are subject to interpretive and selection biases that require special attention beyond the scope of this summary (see Chap. 23).
3. Some empirical evidence is offered. Excluded are suggestions that have yet to be tested and theoretical arguments (e.g., about the ecological validity of experiments) that cannot be tested.

Prior to that review, a framework for debiasing efforts will be offered, characterizing possible approaches and the assumptions underlying them. Such a framework might reveal recurrent patterns when applied to a variety of judgmental biases.

Debiasing methods

When there is a problem, it is natural to look for a culprit. Debiasing procedures may be most clearly categorized according to their implicit

Table 1. *Debiasing methods according to underlying assumption*

Assumption	Strategies
Faulty tasks	
Unfair tasks	Raise stakes
	Clarify instructions/stimuli
	Discourage second-guessing
	Use better response modes
	Ask fewer questions
Misunderstood tasks	Demonstrate alternative goal
	Demonstrate semantic disagreement
	Demonstrate impossibility of task
	Demonstrate overlooked distinction
Faulty judges	
Perfectible individuals	Warn of problem
	Describe problem
	Provide personalized feedback
	Train extensively
Incorrigible individuals	Replace them
	Recalibrate their responses
	Plan on error
Mismatch between judges and task	
Restructuring	Make knowledge explicit
	Search for discrepant information
	Decompose problem
	Consider alternative situations
	Offer alternative formulations
Education	Rely on substantive experts
	Educate from childhood

allegation of culpability. The most important distinction is whether responsibility for biases is laid at the doorstep of the judge, the task, or some mismatch between the two. Do the biases represent artifacts of incompetent experimentation and dubious interpretation, clear-cut cases of judgmental fallibility, or the unfortunate result of judges having, but misapplying, the requisite cognitive skills? As summarized in Table 1, and described below, each of these categories can be broken down further according to what might be called the depth of the problem. How fundamental is the difficulty? Are technical or structural changes needed? Strategies for developing debiasing techniques are quite different for the different causal categories.

Faulty tasks

Unfair tasks. Experimentalists have standard questions that they pose to their own and others' work. Studies are published only if they instill confidence (in reviewers and editors) that the more obvious artifacts have been eliminated. Since, however, it is impossible to control for everything and satisfy everyone in an initial study or series of studies, the identification of putative methodological artifacts is a first line of attack in attempting to discredit an effect. Among the claims that may be raised are: (a) Subjects did not care about the task – therefore one should raise the stakes accruing to good performance; (b) subjects were confused by the task – therefore use more careful instructions and more familiar stimuli; (c) subjects did not believe the experimenters' assertions about the nature of the task or perceived a payoff structure other than that intended by the experimenter – therefore assure them that their best guess at the right answer is all that is of interest and that they should respond as they see fit; (d) subjects were unable to express what they know – therefore use more familiar or pliable response modes; (e) subjects were asked too many questions and developed stereotypic response patterns to help them get through the task – therefore ask fewer questions (or define one's research interest as stereotypic responses).

Coping with such problems is part of good scientific hygiene. However, such efforts usually have little theoretical content. Since its goal is producing a better experimental environment, the study of artifacts may not even be very informative about the universe of contexts to which observed results can be safely generalized. "Successful" artifact studies provide primarily negative information, casting doubt on whether an effect has been observed in "fair" conditions. Whether life is "fair" in the same sense, when it poses questions, is a separate issue.

Misunderstood tasks. Artifact studies carry an implicit aspersion of experimental malpractice. The original investigator should have known better or should have been more careful. Such allegations are less appropriate with a second kind of task deficiency: the failure of the investigator to understand respondents' phenomenology or conceptual universe. Reformulation of the task to clarify what subjects were really doing has been used by critics of the heuristics-and-biases approach as well as by its promulgators. Among the ways one might try to show the wisdom of apparently biased behavior are: (a) demonstrating some alternative goal that is achieved by sacrificing optimality in the task at hand (e.g., learning about the properties of a system by making diagnostic mistakes); (b) demonstrating that respondents share a definition of key terms different from that held or presumed by the experimenter; (c) demonstrating that the task could not be done unless respondents chose to make some additional assumptions that would have to concur fortuitously with those made by the experimenter; (d) demonstrating that subjects make a reasonable distinction to which the experimenter was insensitive.

To make a contribution, such reformulations should include empirical demonstrations, not just claims about "what subjects might have been thinking." At their worst, such assertions can have a strong ad hoc flavor and defy falsification; indeed, contradictory versions may be used to explain away different biases. At their best, they can make strong theoretical statements about cognitive representations (Fischhoff, in press-a).

Faulty judges

Perfectible judges. If the task has been polished and the bias remains, the respondent must assume some responsibility. To eliminate an unwanted behavior, one might use an escalation design, with steps reflecting increasing pessimism about the ease of perfecting human performance: (a) warning about the possibility of bias without specifying its nature (this strategy differs from inspiring people to work harder by implying that the potential error is systematic and that respondents need instruction, not just a fair chance); (b) describing the direction (and perhaps extent) of the bias that is typically observed; (c) providing a dose of feedback, personalizing the implications of the warning; (d) offering an extended program of training with feedback, coaching, and whatever else it takes to afford the respondent cognitive mastery of the task.

Such steps fault the judge, not the task, by assuming that solutions will not emerge spontaneously or merely with careful question rephrasing. Although of great practical import, training exercises may have limited theoretical impact. The attempt to find something that works may create a grab bag of maneuvers whose effective elements are poorly defined. More systematic experimentation may then be needed to identify those elements. The ultimate goal is understanding how the artificial experience created by the training program differs from the natural experience that life offers. Why does one technique work to eliminate bias, while another does not?

Incorrigible judges. At some point, the would-be trainer may decide that success is impossible, or only attainable with procedures that coerce the subject to respond optimally. The "successes" that are obtained by essentially giving respondents the right answer or by creating unavoidable demand characteristics are bereft of both theoretical and practical interest. It is hardly news when people listen to what they are told; if they have to be told every time how to respond, who needs them?

Three options seem open in such situations: (a) replacing people with some superior answering device; (b) recalibrating fallible judgments to more appropriate values, assuming that the amount and direction of errors are predictable; (c) acknowledging the imprecision in people's judgments when planning actions based on them. The decision maker or decision analyst who has given up on people in any of these ways may still contribute to our understanding of judgment by assessing the size, prevalence, and resilience of such indelible biases. However, because improved judgment is not the intent of these corrective actions, they will be considered only cursorily here.

Mismatch between judge and task

Restructuring. Perhaps the most charitable, and psychological, viewpoint is to point no fingers and blame neither judge nor task. Instead, assume that the question is acceptably posed and that the judge has all requisite skills, but somehow these skills are not being used. In the spirit of human engineering, this approach argues that the proper unit of observation is the person-task system. Success lies in making them as compatible as possible. Just as a mechanically intact airplane needs good instrument design to become flyable, an honest (i.e., not misleading) judgment task may only become tractable when it has been restructured to a form that allows respondents to use their existing cognitive skills to best advantage.

Although such cognitive engineering tends to be task specific, a number of recurrent strategies emerge: (a) forcing respondents to express what they know explicitly rather than letting it remain "in the head"; (b) encouraging respondents to search for discrepant evidence, rather than collecting details corroborating a preferred answer; (c) offering ways to decompose an overwhelming problem to more tractable and familiar components; (d) suggesting that respondents consider the set of possible situations that they might have encountered in order to understand better the specific situation at hand; and (e) proposing alternative formulations of the presented problem (e.g., using different terms, concretizing, offering analogies).

Education. A variant on the people-task "systems" approach is to argue that people can do this task, but not these people. The alternatives are to use: (a) experts who, along with their substantive knowledge, have acquired some special capabilities in processing information under conditions of uncertainty; or (b) a new breed of individual, educated from some early age to think probabilistically. In a sense, this view holds that although people are not, in principle, incorrigible, most of those presently around are. Education differs from training (a previous category) in its focus on developing general capabilities rather than specific skills.

Hindsight bias: An example of debiasing efforts

A critical aspect of any responsible job is learning from experience. Once we know how something turned out, we try to understand why it happened and to evaluate how well we, or others, planned for it. Although such outcome knowledge is thought to confer the wisdom of hindsight on our judgments, its advantages may be oversold. In hindsight, people consistently exaggerate what could have been anticipated in foresight. They not only tend to view what has happened as having been inevitable, but also to view it as having appeared "relatively inevitable" before it happened. People believe that others should have been able to anticipate events much better than was actually the case. They even misremember their own predictions so as to exaggerate in hindsight what they knew in foresight (Fischhoff, 1975). Although it is flattering to believe that we would have known all along what we could only know in hindsight, that belief hardly affords us a fair appraisal of the extent to which surprises and failures are inevitable. It is both unfair and self-defeating to castigate decision makers who have erred in fallible systems, without admitting to that fallibility and doing something to improve the system. By encouraging us to exaggerate the extent of our knowledge, this bias can make us overconfident in our predictive ability. Perception of a surprise-free past may portend a surpriseful future.

Research on this bias has included investigations of most of the possible debiasing strategies included in the previous section. Few of these techniques have successfully reduced the hindsight bias; none has eliminated it. They are described below and summarized in Table 2.

Faulty tasks

Unfair tasks. In an initial experimental demonstration of hindsight bias (Fischhoff, 1975), subjects read paragraph-long descriptions of a historical event and assessed the probability that they would have assigned to each of its possible outcomes had they not been told what happened. Regardless of whether the reported outcome was true or false (i.e., whether it happened in reality), subjects believed that they would have assigned it a higher probability than was assigned by outcome-ignorant subjects. This study is listed among the debiasing attempts, since by concentrating on a few stories it answered the methodological criticism of "asking too many questions" that might be leveled against subsequent studies. Other studies that asked few questions without eliminating hindsight bias include Slovic and Fischhoff (1977), who had subjects analyze the likelihood of possible outcomes of several scientific experiments; Mitchell and Kalb (in press), who had nurses evaluate incidents taken from hospital settings; and Pennington, Rutter, McKenna, and Morley (1980), who had women assess their personal probability of receiving a positive result on a single pregnancy test (although the low power of this study renders its conclusion somewhat tentative).

Other attempts to demonstrate an artifactual source of hindsight bias that have been tried and failed include: substituting rating-scale judgments of "surprisingness" for probability assessments (Slovic & Fischhoff,

1977); using more homogeneous items to allow fuller evocation of one set of knowledge, rather than using general-knowledge questions scattered over a variety of content areas, none of which might be thought about very deeply (Fischhoff & Beyth, 1975); imploring subjects to work harder (Fischhoff, 1977b); trying to dispel doubts about the nature of the experiment (G. Wood, 1978); and using contemporary events that judges have considered in foresight prior to making their hindsight assessments (Fischhoff & Beyth, 1975).

Misunderstood tasks. One possible attraction of hindsight bias is that it may be quite flattering to represent oneself as having known all along what was going to happen. One pays a price for such undeserved self-flattery only if (a) one's foresight leads to an action that appears foolish in hindsight or (b) systematic exaggeration of what one *knew* leads to overconfidence in what one presently *knows*, possibly causing capricious actions or failure to seek needed information. Since these long-range consequences are not very relevant in the typical experiment, one might worry about subjects being tempted to paint themselves in a favorable light. Although most experiments have been posed as tests of subjects' ability to reconstruct a foresightful state of knowledge, rather than as tests of how extensive that knowledge was, temptations to exaggerate might still remain. If so, they would reflect a discrepancy between subjects' and experimenters' interpretations of the task. One manipulation designed to eliminate this possibility requires subjects first to answer questions and then to remember their own answers, with the acuity of their memory being at issue (Fischhoff, 1977b; Fischhoff & Beyth, 1975; Pennington et al., 1980; G. Wood, 1978). A second manipulation requires hindsight subjects to estimate the foresight responses of their peers, on the assumption that they have no reason to exaggerate what others knew (Fischhoff, 1975; G. Wood, 1978). Neither manipulation has proven successful. Subjects remembered themselves to have been more knowledgeable than was, in fact, the case. They were uncharitable second-guessers in the sense of exaggerating how much others would have (or should have) known in foresight.

Faulty judges

Learning to avoid the biases that arise from being a prisoner of one's present perspective constitutes a, or perhaps the, focus of historians' training (see Chap. 23). There have, however, been no empirical studies of the success of these efforts. The emphasis that historians place on primary sources, with their fossilized records of the perceptions of the past, may reflect a feeling that the human mind is sufficiently incorrigible to require that sort of discipline by document. Although it used a vastly less rigorous procedure, the one experimental training study offers no reason for optimism: Fischhoff (1977b) explicitly described the bias to subjects and asked them to avoid it in their judgments – to no avail.

Mismatch between judges and tasks

Restructuring. Three strategies have been adopted to restructure hindsight tasks, so as to make them more compatible with the cognitive skills and predispositions that judges bring to them. One such strategy separates subjects in time from the report of the event, in hopes of reducing its tendency to dominate their perceptual field (Fischhoff & Beyth, 1975; G. Wood, 1978); this strategy was not effective. With the second strategy, judges assess the likelihood of the reported event's recurring rather than the likelihood of its happening in the first place, in the hope that uncertainty would be more available in the forward-looking perspective (Mitchell & Kalb, in press; Slovic & Fischhoff, 1977); this, too, failed. The final strategy requires subjects to indicate how they could have explained the occurrence of the outcome that did *not* happen (Slovic & Fischhoff, 1977). Recruiting such negative evidence appreciably reduced the judged inevitability of the reported event. Such contradictory evidence was apparently available to subjects in memory or imagination but not accessible without a restructuring of the problem.

Education. There is little experimental evidence that hindsight bias is reduced by the sort of intense involvement with a topic that comes with a professional education. Detmer, Fryback, and Gassner (1978) found hindsight bias in the judgments of surgeons (both faculty and residents) appraising an episode involving a possible leaking abdominal aortic aneurism. Arkes, Wortmann, Saville, and Harkness (1981) demonstrated the bias with physicians considering clinical descriptions of a bartender with acute knee pain. Mitchell and Kalb (in press) found bias in nurses' appraisal of the outcome of acts performed by subordinates. If people judging events in their own lives are considered to be substantive experts, then the study by Pennington et al. (1980) of women judging the results of personal pregnancy tests might be considered a further example of bias in experts. In an even more limited sense of expertise, G. Wood (1978) found that with a task involving general-knowledge questions his most knowledgeable subjects were no less bias prone than less knowledgeable ones. The anecdotal evidence of experts falling prey to this bias is described briefly in Chapter 23 (this volume). It includes both casual observations and exhaustive studies, such as that of Wohlstetter (1962), who characterized the efforts of the highly motivated experts comprising the congressional investigatory committee following Pearl Harbor as 39 volumes of hindsight bias.

Summary

Although one of the lesser-studied judgmental problems, hindsight bias has produced enough research to allow some tentative general statements: It appears to be quite robust and widespread. Reducing it requires some understanding of and hypotheses about people's cognitive processes. One such hypothesis is that the manner in which people normally approach hindsight tasks does not use their knowledge or inferential skills to best advantage. Producing contrary evidence appeared to remedy that problem in part and to help them make better use of their own minds (Slovic & Fischhoff, 1977).

Before endorsing this solution, however, a number of empirical issues need to be addressed: (a) What additional steps are needed for the bias to be eliminated, not only reduced? (b) Will this procedure work with less clearly structured tasks? (c) Will practice in the procedure with a few exemplary tasks suffice to change behavior with other tasks, where no specific instruction is given? A debiasing procedure may be more trouble than it is worth if it increases people's faith in their judgmental abilities more than it improves the abilities themselves.

Overconfidence: Debiasing efforts

"Decision making under uncertainty" implies incomplete knowledge. As a result, one major component of making such decisions is appraising the quality of whatever knowledge is available. Although statistical methods may guide this appraisal, at some point or other judgment is needed to assess the confidence that can be placed in one's best guess at the state of the world. Because improper confidence assessment can lead to poor decisions, by inducing either undue or insufficient caution, a continuing focus of judgment research has been the identification of factors affecting confidence inappropriately. Receipt of outcome knowledge is one such factor, insofar as it leads people to exaggerate the completeness of their own knowledge. Although one suspects that outcome knowledge leaves people overconfident in their own knowledge, it is conceivable that people are subject to some sort of endemic underconfidence to which hindsight bias provides a useful counterbalance. Clarifying this possibility requires research evaluating the absolute validity of confidence judgments.

Because it is difficult to assess the absolute validity of any single confidence judgment, most research in this area has looked at the quality, or *calibration*, of sets of judgments, each representing the subjective probability that a statement of fact is correct (Chap. 22, this volume). For the perfectly calibrated individual, assessments of, say, .70 are associated with correct statements 70% of the time.

Overconfidence is by far the most commonly observed finding. A typical study might show probabilities of .75 to be associated with a "hit rate" of only 60% and expressions of certainty ($p = 1.00$) being correct only 85% of the time. When people assess how much they know about the values of numerical quantities (e.g., "I am .98 certain that the number of registered Republican voters in Lane County is between 12,000 and 30,000"), it is not uncommon to find true answers falling outside of their 98% confidence intervals 20% to 40% of the time. Such results are disturbing both to those who must rely on confidence assessments and to those accused (directly or indirectly) of exaggerating how much they know. The abundant research that has been produced to disprove, discredit, bolster, or bound the finding of overconfidence is characterized below from the perspective of debiasing efforts. This reanalysis of existing studies has been aided greatly by the availability of several comprehensive reviews of this literature, albeit conducted for somewhat different purposes. These include Henrion (1980), Hogarth (1975), Lichtenstein, Fischhoff, and Phillips (Chap. 22), and Wallsten and Budescu (1980). This reanalysis has been complicated by the fact that many of the studies cited also were conducted for somewhat different purposes. As a result, they do not always fall neatly into a single debiasing category. This mild mismatch may reflect limits on the present categorical scheme (for making unclear distinctions) or limits to the studies (for confounding debiasing manipulations).

Faulty tasks

Unfair tasks. The applied implications of overconfidence have spawned a large number of technical efforts at its eradication, almost all of which have proven unsuccessful. Many of these have involved response-mode manipulations, such as comparing probability and odds expressions of confidence (Ludke, Stauss, & Gustafson, 1977) or varying the confidence intervals assessed in creating subjective probability distributions (Selvidge, 1980). Freed of the necessity of generating and justifying their manipulations on the basis of some substantive theory, experimenters using such "engineering" approaches often show great ingenuity in the procedures they are willing to try. However, the absence of theory also makes it more difficult to know how to interpret or generalize their successes or failures. For example, Seaver, von Winterfeldt, and Edwards (1978) found less overconfidence when confidence intervals were elicited with a "fixed-value" method, in which the experimenter selected values and subjects assessed their likelihood, than with the "fixed-probability" method, in which the experimenter provides a probability and the respondent gives the associated value. This success may reflect some sort of greater compatibility between the fixed-value method and respondents' psychological processes, or it may reflect the information about the true value conveyed by the experimenter's choice of fixed values. A similar result by Tversky and Kahneman (1974, 1) is grounded on a hypothesized anchoring-and-adjustment heuristic, although it too may have informed fixed-value subjects.

In addition to the rather intense search for the right response mode for eliciting confidence, there have also been scattered attempts to eliminate the other threats to task fairness listed in the top section of Table 1. For example, the large number of responses elicited in many calibration studies so as to obtain statistically reliable individual results might be a matter of concern had not overconfidence been observed in studies with as few as 10 or even 1 question per subject (e.g., Hynes & Vanmarcke, 1976; Lichtenstein & Fischhoff, 1977). The brevity of the instructions used in some studies might be troublesome had not similar results been found with instructions that seem to be as long and detailed as subjects would tolerate (e.g., Chap. 21; Lichtenstein & Fischhoff, 1980b). The exhaustiveness, even pedantry, of such instructions might also be seen as an antidote to any temptation for subjects to second-guess the investigator. Regarding the clarity of the stimuli used, no change in overconfidence has been observed when diverse sets of general-knowledge questions are replaced with homogeneous items (e.g., Fischhoff & Slovic, 1980; Oskamp, 1962) or with non-verbal "perceptual" items (e.g., Dawes, 1980; Lichtenstein & Fischhoff, 1980b).

It would be reassuring to believe that overconfidence disappears when the stakes are raised and judges perform "for real" (i.e., not just for experiments). Unfortunately, however, the research strategies that might be used to study this hypothesis tend to encounter interpretive difficulties. Monitoring the confidence expressions of experts performing their customary tasks is one obvious approach. It is frustrated by the possibility that the experts' expressions are being evaluated on criteria that conflict with calibration; that is, there may be rewards for deliberately exuding undue confidence or for sounding overly cautious. For example, when physicians overestimate the likelihood of a malady (e.g., Christensen-Szalanski & Bushyhead, 1981; Lusted, 1977), it may be because they are out of touch with how much they know or because of malpractice worries, greed for the financial rewards that additional testing may bring, or other concerns irrelevant to the present purposes. Because of these complications, studies with experts are listed in the section devoted to them at the bottom of Table 2, rather than as attempts to raise the stakes.

A second strategy for raising the stakes is to append confidence assessments to inherently important tasks for which those assessments have no action implications. Sieber (1974) did so by soliciting students' confidence in their own test answers. The result was (the now-familiar) overconfidence, perhaps because calibration is insensitive to the stakes involved, perhaps because this method was not effective in raising them. The

Table 2. *Debiasing experience*

Strategies	Studies examining hindsight bias	Studies examining overconfidence
Faulty tasks		
Unfair tasks		
Raise stakes	4	1,30
Clarify instructions/stimuli	6	3,10,13,14,21
Discourage second guessing	11	13,21
Use better response modes	9	13,14,20,22,23,32,34,35?, 36,40?
Ask fewer questions	3,7,8,9	16
Misunderstood tasks		
Demonstrate alternative goal	3,4,6,8,9	14
Demonstrate semantic disagreement	—	3,14,19,30?
Demonstrate impossibility of task	—	13
Demonstrate overlooked distinction	—	15?
Faulty judges		
Perfectible individuals		
Warn of problem	—	13
Describe problem	4	**3**
Provide personalized feedback	—	**21**
Train extensively	5?	**1,2,4,17,21,26,27,31,34**
Incorrigible individuals		
Replace them	—	—
Recalibrate their responses	—	2,5,24
Plan on error	—	—
Mismatch between judges and task		
Restructuring		
Make knowledge explicit	—	18
Search for discrepant information	**9**	**18**
Decompose problem	6,11	—
Consider alternative situations	—	—
Offer alternative formulations	7,9	35?
Education		
Rely on substantive experts	1,2,7,8,10,11	**11,16,20,24,29,33,38,39**/ **8,9,23,28,31,32**[a]
Educate from childhood	—	6,7

Notes: Key to studies follows notes. Manipulations that have proven at least partially successful appear in boldface. Those that have yet to be subjected to empirical test or for which the evidence is unclear are marked by a question mark. [a]Entries before the slash are studies using experts who have not had calibration training; entries after the slash are studies using variable difficulty levels.

Key to studies

Hindsight
1. Arkes, Wortmann, Saville, & Harkness (1981)
2. Detmer, Fryback, & Gassner (1978)

3. Fischhoff (1975)
4. Fischhoff (1977b)
5. Fischhoff (1980)
6. Fischhoff & Beyth (1975)

Table 2. *(cont.)*

7. Mitchell & Kalb (in press)
8. Pennington, Rutter, McKenna, & Morley (1980)
9. Slovic & Fischhoff (1977)
10. Wohlstetter (1962)
11. G. Wood (1978)

Overconfidence
1. Adams & Adams (1958)
2. Adams & Adams (1961)
3. Alpert & Raiffa (1969, 21)
4. Armelius (1979)
5. Becker & Greenberg (1978)
6. Beyth-Marom & Dekel (in press)
7. Cavanaugh & Borkowski (1980)
8. Clarke (1960)
9. Cocozza & Steadman (1978)
10. Dawes (1980)
11. Dowie (1976)
12. Ferrell & McGoey (1980)
13. Fischhoff & Slovic (1980)
14. Fischhoff, Slovic, & Lichtenstein (1977)
15. Howell & Burnett (1978)
16. Hynes & Vanmarcke (1976)
17. King, Zechmeister, & Shaughnessy (in press)

18. Koriat, Lichtenstein, & Fischhoff (1980)
19. Larson & Reenan (1979)
20. Lichtenstein & Fischhoff (1977)
21. Lichtenstein & Fischhoff (1980b)
22. Lichtenstein, Fischhoff, & Phillips (Chap. 22)
23. Ludke, Stauss, & Gustafson (1977)
24. Moore (1977)
25. Morris (1974)
26. Murphy & Winkler (1974)
27. Murphy & Winkler (1977a)
28. Nickerson & McGoldrick (1965)
29. Oskamp (1962)
30. Phillips & Wright (1977)
31. Pickhardt & Wallace (1974)
32. Pitz (1974)
33. Root (1962)
34. Schaefer & Borcherding (1973)
35. Seaver, von Winterfeldt, & Edwards (1978)
36. Selvidge (1980)
37. Sieber (1974)
38. Staël von Holstein (1971a)
39. Staël von Holstein (1972)
40. Tversky & Kahneman (1974)

theoretically perfect strategy for manipulating stakes is to reward subjects with proper scoring rules, which penalize unfrank expressions of uncertainty. Such rules are, however, quite asymmetric, in the sense that they penalize overconfidence much more than underconfidence. As a result, subjects who understand the gist of those rules but who are uninterested in their particulars, might interpret scoring rules as roundabout instructions never to express great confidence. In that case, people might just mechanically reduce their confidence without improving understanding. All in all, perhaps the best way to get subjects to work hard is by exercising the experimentalists' standard techniques for increasing a task's intrinsic motivation and subjects' involvement in it.

Misunderstood tasks. However carefully one describes a task to respondents, some doubts may linger as to whether they really understood it and accepted its intended reward structure. A standard maneuver for checking whether a manipulation has "worked" is to see if participants will stand by the responses that they already have made when those responses are used in a new task with the reward structure intended for the old task.

Fischhoff, Slovic, and Lichtenstein (1977) adopted this strategy in asking people if they would be willing to accept a gamble based on confidence assessments they had just made. This gamble favored them if those assessments were frank or tended to underrate their confidence, but penalized them if, for whatever reason, they had exaggerated how much they knew. Deliberate exaggeration might, for example, serve the alternative goal of acting more knowledgeable than is actually the case. These subjects were quite eager to accept the gamble, despite being as overconfident as subjects observed elsewhere.

Another basis for claiming that subjects have understood the task differently from the way intended by the experimenter comes from the observation that "degrees of certainty are often used in everyday speech (as are references to temperature), but they are seldom expressed numerically, nor is the opportunity to validate them often available. . . . People's inability to assess appropriately a probability of .80 may be no more surprising than the difficulty they might have in estimating brightness in candles or temperature in degrees Fahrenheit" (Fischhoff et al., 1977, p. 553). One response to this possibility is restricting attention to the extremes of the probability scale in the belief that "being 100% certain that a statement is true is readily understood by most people and its appropriateness is readily evaluated" (Fischhoff et al., 1977, p. 553). A second response is providing verbal labels for numerical probabilities in order to make them more readily comprehensible (e.g., Chap. 21; Larson & Reenan, 1979). Neither manipulation has proven demonstrably effective. A deeper notion of semantic disagreement between experimenter and respondent may be found in claims that "uncertainty" itself may have a variety of interpretations, not all of which are meaningful to all individuals (Howell & Burnett, 1978; Phillips & Wright, 1977). Empirical debiasing efforts based on these concepts might prove fruitful.

Some of the most extreme overconfidence has been observed with tasks regarding which respondents have no knowledge whatsoever. Although experimenters typically attempt to give no hints as to how confident subjects should be, there still might be an implicit presumption that "the experimenter wouldn't give me a task that's impossible." If subjects had such expectations, having an appropriate level of confidence would then become impossible. Fischhoff and Slovic (1980) tested this possibility with a series of tasks whose content (e.g., diagnosing ulcers, forecasting the prices of obscure stocks) and instructions were designed to make them seem as impossible as they actually were. However, overconfidence was only reduced (and then but partially) when subjects were cautioned that "it may well be impossible to make this sort of discrimination. Try to do the best you can. But if, in the extreme you feel totally uncertain about [your answers], do not hesitate to respond with .5 [indicating a guess] for every one of them" (p. 752). Any stronger instructions might be suspected of having demand characteristics of their own.

Faulty judges

Perfectible individuals. With a modest change in interpretive assumptions, the last-mentioned study in the previous section might become the first-mentioned member of the present one. Assuring subjects that they could admit that every response was just a guess might be seen as a way to dispel any residual misunderstandings about the task or as a step toward correcting subjects who understand the task but not themselves. It carries an implicit warning that failure to admit to guessing may be a problem. This warning is made explicit in Alpert and Raiffa's (Chap. 21) instruction to subjects to "spread the tails" of their subjective probability distributions in order to avoid overconfidence. Whether the partial success of these manipulations reflects increased understanding or sensitivity to orders is unclear. Such ambiguity may explain the paucity of studies adopting these approaches.

These worries about demand characteristics disappear with deliberate training studies, where "experimenter effects" are the order of the day. As indicated by Table 2, a variety of training efforts have been undertaken with an admirable success rate – although one might worry that journals' lack of enthusiasm for negative results studies may have reduced the visibility of failures. Trainers' willingness to do whatever it takes to get an effect has tended to make training efforts rather complex manipulations whose effective elements are somewhat obscure. Some of the more necessary conditions for learning seem to be: receiving feedback on large samples of responses, being told about one's own performance (and not just about common problems), and having the opportunity to discuss the relationship between one's subjective feelings of uncertainty and the numerical probability responses. To their own surprise, Lichtenstein and Fischhoff (1980b) found that one round of training with intensive, personalized feedback was as effective as a long series of trials. It is unclear to what extent these various successes represent training, in the narrow sense of mastering a particular task (e.g., learning the distribution of responses the experimenter requires), or the acquisition of more general skills.

Incorrigible individuals. Impatience with training studies or skepticism about their generality has led a number of investigators to take fallible confidence assessments as inevitable and concentrate on helping decision makers to cope with them. Some suggest replacing individuals with groups of experts whose assessments are combined by direct interaction or a mechanical aggregation scheme (e.g., Becker & Greenberg, 1978; Morris, 1974); others call for liberal use of sensitivity analysis whenever confidence assessments arise in a decision analysis (e.g., Jennergren & Keeney, in press); still others propose to recalibrate assessments, using a correction factor that indicates how confident assessors should be as a function of how confident they are (Lichtenstein & Fischhoff, 1977). For example, the prevalence of overconfidence might suggest that when someone proclaims certainty, one might read it as a .85 chance of their being correct. Unfortunately for this strategy, when people are miscalibrated their degree of overconfidence depends upon the difficulty of the particular task facing them (Lichtenstein & Fischhoff, 1977). As a result, the needed amount of recalibration can be determined only if one knows the difficulty of the task at hand and can observe respondents' (over)confidence in a task of similar difficulty or at least surmise the relationship between observed and anticipated overconfidence (Ferrell & McGoey, 1980).

Mismatch between judges and task

Restructuring. The study of calibration, like some other topics in judgment, has remained relatively isolated from the mainstream of research in cognition, drawing more methodology than ideas from the psychological literature. Whether this lack of contact reflects the insularity of judgment researchers or the inadequate representations of confidence in current models of cognitive processes, it has likely hindered the development of methods to reduce overconfidence. Process models should both suggest more powerful manipulations and indicate why engineering approaches do or do not work (and how far their effects might generalize). Current research in eyewitness testimony, feeling of knowing, and metamemory might eventually provide points of contact (e.g., Gruneberg, Morris, & Sykes, 1978).

One possible direction for helping people use their existing cognitive skills in a way more compatible with the demands of confidence assessment may be seen in Koriat, Lichtenstein, and Fischhoff (1980), where overconfidence was reduced by having respondents list reasons why their preferred answer might be wrong. Listing reasons why one might be right or giving one reason for and one reason against one's chosen answer had no effect, indicating that the critical element is not just working harder or being explicit, but addressing one's memory differently from what is customary in confidence assessment tasks. Without the specific prompting to "consider why you might be wrong," people seem to be insufficiently critical or even intent on justifying their initial answer. Perhaps analogously, Markman (1979) found that 9- and 12-year-olds detected inconsistencies in textual material only when told to look for them.

Although it is advanced on practical rather than psychological grounds, Seaver et al.'s (1978) fixed-value technique might be seen as another way of restructuring respondents' approach to the task. Organizing one's knowledge around a set of values presumed to be incorrect may lead to a more complete appraisal of what one knows than the "traditional" fixed-probability method, in which attention may be focused on the respondents' best guess at the correct answer.

Education. Does overconfidence disappear as an indirect result of the substantive education that experts receive in their specialty? As mentioned earlier, the obvious way to explore this question, looking at the confidence expressions accompanying the performance of real tasks, is complicated by the possibility that real pressures restrict experts' candor. For example, one might find evidence of overconfidence in professions that make confident judgments with no demonstrated validity (e.g., predictions of stock price movements [Dreman, 1979; Slovic, 1972c], psychiatric diagnoses of dangerousness [Cocozza & Steadman, 1978]). Of course, if such "experts" are consulted (and paid) as a function of the confidence they inspire, they may be tempted to misrepresent how much they know.

Undoubtedly, the greatest efforts to ensure candor have been with weather forecasters, whose training often explicitly rewards them for good calibration. Their performance is superb (e.g., Murphy & Winkler, 1974, 1977a). Whether this success is due to calibration training or a by-product of their general professional education is unclear. A review of other studies with experts who have not had calibration training suggests that such training, and not just substantive education, is the effective element. Experiments that used problems drawn from their respective areas of expertise but isolated from real-world pressures have found overconfidence with psychology graduate students (Lichtenstein & Fischhoff, 1977), bankers (Staël von Holstein, 1972), clinical psychologists (Oskamp, 1962), executives (Moore, 1977), civil engineers (Hynes & Vanmarcke, 1976), and untrained professional weather forecasters (Root, 1962; Staël von Holstein, 1971a).

Dowie (1976) has found good calibration among the newspaper predictions of horse-racing columnists. Although these experts receive neither an explicit payoff function nor formal feedback, one might guess that they supply their own, monitoring their performance from day to day and rewarding themselves for good calibration. The idea that we should be trained from childhood for this kind of self-monitoring may be found in recent proposals to make judgment a part of the school curriculum (e.g., Beyth-Marom & Dekel, in press; Cavanaugh & Borkowski, 1980). The promise of these proposals remains to be tested.

Finally, there is a rather narrow form of expertise that has proven to be the most potent (and least interesting) method of reducing overconfidence. One reflection of people's insensitivity to how much they know is the fact that their mean confidence changes relatively slowly in response to changes in the difficulty of the tasks they face (Lichtenstein & Fischhoff, 1977). Typical pairs of proportions of correct answers and mean confidence are: .51, .65; .62, .74; .80, .78; and .92, .86. As accuracy ranges over .41, confidence changes only .23. The calibration curves corresponding to these summary statistics are in some senses about equally bad (or flat); however, their degree of overconfidence varies considerably. Whereas the first two of these pairs represent overconfidence, the third shows appropriate overall confidence and the fourth underconfidence. These examples are taken from Lichtenstein and Fischhoff (1977), but the same pattern has been revealed by Clarke (1960), Nickerson and McGoldrick (1965), Pickhardt and Wallace (1974), and Pitz (1974), among others. Indeed, any comparison of overconfidence across conditions must take into account the difficulty of the tasks used. In this light, the preponderance of overconfidence in the literature reflects, in part, the (perhaps natural) tendency not to present people with very easy questions.

Summary

Confidence assessments have been extracted from a variety of people in a variety of ways, almost always showing considerable insensitivity to the extent of their knowledge. Although the door need not be closed on methodological manipulations, they have so far proven relatively ineffective and their results difficult to generalize. What they have done is to show that overconfidence is relatively resistant to many forms of tinkering (other than changes in difficulty level). Greater reliance on psychological theory would seem to be the key to producing more powerful and predictable manipulations. The effectiveness of calibration training suggests that a careful analysis of what unique experiences are provided by that training but not by professional education could both guide debiasing and enrich psychological theory.

Discussion

Assuming that the studies reviewed here have been characterized accurately and that they exhaust (or at least fairly represent) the universe of relevant studies, their aggregate message would seem to be fairly reassuring to the cognitive psychologist. Both biases have proven moderately robust, resisting attempts to interpret them as artifacts and eliminate them by "mechanical" manipulations, such as making subjects work harder. Effective debiasing usually has involved changing the psychological nature of the task (and subjects' approach to it). In such cases, at least some of the credit must go to psychological theory. For example, a hypothesis about how people retrieve memory information prior to assessing confidence guided Koriat et al.'s (1980) manipulation of that retrieval process.

Even "throw everything at the subject" training programs have been based on well-tested and generally-applicable principles of learning.

Several conceptual caveats should accompany this summary (in addition to the methodological ones with which it opened). One is that the distinction between artifactual and psychological manipulations may be less clear than has been suggested here. For example, exhorting people to work harder would be an artifact manipulation when rooted in a claim that more casual instructions do not elicit "real behavior." However, if the investigator could advance substantive hypotheses about how different instructions affect judgmental processes, the artifact would become a main effect with separate predictions for real-world behavior in situations with and without explicit exhortations.

The second conceptual caveat is that questioning the reality of biases can reflect a limited and unproductive perspective on psychological research. To continue the example of the preceding paragraph, life has both casual and work-hard situations; neither one is inherently more "real" than the other. By like token, the relative validity of casual and work-hard laboratory experiments depends upon the real-world situations to which their results are to be extrapolated. Each has its place. Understanding the laboratory-world match requires good judgment in characterizing both contexts. For example, work-hard situations are not necessarily synonymous with important situations. People may not work hard on an important problem unless they realize both the centrality of a judgment to the problem's outcome and the potential fallibility of that judgment.

Using debiasing studies to discover the boundary conditions for observing biases leads to the third conceptual caveat. In this review, the summary tables and discussion implicitly afforded equal weight to the various studies, qualified perhaps by some notion of each study's definitiveness (as determined by competence, extensiveness, etc.). Such tallying of statistically significant and non-significant results is a dubious procedure on methodological grounds alone (e.g., Hedges & Olkin, 1980). It becomes conceptually questionable when one doubts that the universe of possible studies is being sampled adequately. In such cases, those data that are collected constitute conceptually dependent observations and need not be given equal weight. Any summary of how people behave needs a careful specification of the subuniverse of behavioral situations from which studies are being sampled. For example, some critics have charged that early studies of judgmental heuristics were "looking for trouble," in the sense of searching (grasping) for situations in which people would behave in an errant fashion. If this claim is true, then each demonstration of biased behavior need not be interpreted as a strike against people's overall judgmental ability; its relevance is limited to the kind of situations being studied (or overstudied) in those experiments. By focusing on the boundary conditions for assessing biases, more recent studies are subject to

Table 3. *A universe of discourse for biases and debiasing efforts*

---

1. *The underlying processes about which inferences are required are probabilistic.* That is, judgments are made under conditions of uncertainty, with biases arising from the confrontation between a deterministic mind and a probabilistic environment.
2. *Problems arise in the integration rather than discovery of evidence.* Although stimuli are complete and unambiguous as possible, they tell little about how the task might be structured. The subjects' task is interpreting and using those pieces of information that are provided
3. *The biases are non-substantive.* The operation of a cognitive process should be similar in any content area with a given informational structure. This eliminates "errors" due to misinformation and "misconceptions" due to deliberate deception.
4. *Some normative theory is available characterizing appropriate judgment.* This criterion rules out problems from the realm of preference (e.g., inconsistent attitudes), where no one response can be identified as optimal.
5. *No computational aids are offered or allowed (beyond pencil and paper).* This focus on intuitive judgment excludes such aids as dedicated hand calculators, statistical consultants, and interactive computers.
6. *No obvious inducements for suboptimal behavior are apparent.* That is, biases are cognitive, not motivational in nature. The "point" of bias research is, of course, that where people have no good reason to act suboptimally, errors suggest that they just do not know any better.

---

their own sampling bias, which needs to be considered in generalizing their results.

Further questions

Whether similar patterns will emerge with other biases requires analogous literature reviews. Table 3 offers a characterization of the domain of biases within which recurrent patterns might be sought, distinguishing the contents of this volume from other biases that have troubled psychologists.

A lingering metaquestion facing those reviews is, How good are people? Are they cognitive cripples or cognoscenti? Providing a single answer requires an answer to imponderable questions about the nature of life and the overall similarity of human experience to laboratory conditions. An elusive summary from the present review is that people's reservoir of judgmental skills is both half empty and half full. People are skilled enough to get through life, unskilled enough to make predictable and consequential mistakes; they are clever enough to devise broadly and easily applicable heuristics that often serve them in good stead, unsophisticated enough not to realize the limits to those heuristics. A more specific appraisal of people's ability can be given only in the context of a particular judgment task.

Such blanket statements (or evasions) about "people" reflect a common feature of most judgmental research – lack of interest in individual differences. Although this preference for group effects may be just a matter of taste, it might be justified theoretically by arguing that the main effects in judgment studies are so large and inadequately explored that individual differences can wait. The rather meager insight provided by studying groups with known characteristics provides some empirical support for this claim. Particularly striking was the lack of differences in experimental studies of the most consequential of known groups, experts making judgments in their fields of expertise. The anecdotal and case-study evidence collected by Dawes (1976), Eddy (Chap. **18**, this volume), Fischer (1970), and others also indicates that extensive training and high stakes are no guarantees of judgmental prowess. Nonetheless, further research is needed, both because of the firmness with which many believe that experts are better and the applied importance of using expert judgment to best advantage.

For the immediate practical goal of best deploying experts so as to avoid bias, it is sufficient to know whether they are better than lay people or at least better aware of their own judgmental limitations. For the eventual practical goal of debiasing all judges, it is important to know how the experts got where they did or why they got no further. The following is a list of conditions that are generally conducive to learning. For each, one can see ways in which experts might be at a particular advantage or disadvantage, depending upon the circumstances:

1. Abundant practice with a set of reasonably homogeneous tasks. Experts should have such experience. They may use it to hone their judgmental skills or they may develop situation-specific habitual solutions, freeing themselves from the need to analyze (and think).
2. Clear-cut criterion events. Although experts are often required to make their judgments quite explicit, the objects of those judgments are often components of such complex (natural, social, or biological) systems that it is hard to evaluate the judges' level of understanding. Off-target judgments may be due to unanticipated contingencies, whereas on-target judgments may have been right for the wrong reason.
3. Task-specific reinforcement. Experts are, in principle, paid for performance. However, even when the wisdom of their judgments can be discerned, they may be rewarded on other grounds (e.g., did they bring good news? did they disrupt plans? did things turn out for the best?).
4. Explicit admission of the need for learning. Entering an apprenticeship program that confers expertise is surely a sign of modesty.

Nonetheless, at every stage of that process and the professional life that follows it, certain advantages accrue to those who put on a good show and exude competence.

These are purely operant principles of learning, manipulating behavior without presuming any knowledge of underlying cognitive processes. Clarifying and exploiting those cognitive processes is obviously a major theoretical and practical task for debiasing research, especially when one considers that such manipulations seem to have a somewhat better track record than more mechanical efforts. Although the study of biases and debiasing has spanned a fair portion of the long path from basic research to field applications, it has yet to touch bases adequately at either end. It appears now that reaching one end will require reaching the other as well. Good practice will require better theory about how the mind works. Good theory will require better practice, clarifying and grappling with the conditions in which the mind actually works.

32. Improving inductive inference

Richard E. Nisbett, David H. Krantz,
Christopher Jepson, and Geoffrey T. Fong

In this chapter, we discuss the possibility of improving people's inferences in everyday life. Nisbett and Ross (1980) proposed that improvements could result from making the inferential tools of the scientist available to the layperson in the form of inferential maxims, such as "It's an empirical question," or "You can always explain away the exceptions." We shall refer to "statistical heuristics" for some of the most important of these informal guides to reasoning, such as "Think about evidence as if it were a sample, and reflect about sample size." We believe that such rough inferential guides, when embedded in a matrix of understanding of statistics and probability theory and when buttressed by experience in applying the heuristic to concrete problems, may prove to be of great value in reducing inferential error in daily life.

It is possible to be systematic in an examination of what could be accomplished by such a program and where difficulties are likely to be encountered. We believe that three such difficulties are clearly visible now, and we believe that attempts to solve each of the problems will pay dividends in terms of extending our understanding both of how people infer and of how they ought to infer.

1. It can be very difficult to establish that a given dubious inference is in fact erroneous. In most of the work by Kahneman and Tversky, the probabilistic models that are the basis for the prescribed inferences are standard statistical ones, and their application to the events in question is noncontroversial. As social-psychological work in the same vein has proceeded, however, it has become increasingly clear that it can be very difficult to know exactly what model for events is the correct one and thus to know what inferential procedures are called for.

The writing of this article and some of the research reported in it were supported in part by grant BNS 79-14094 from the National Science Foundation. We thank Lee Ross, Saul Sternberg, and Paul Thagard for comments on an earlier draft.

2. Even when it is possible to be fairly confident that an error has occurred, it can be very difficult to know *how* it occurred. It can be very hard to know whether the error is due to faulty reasoning, that is, to poor inferential procedures, or to incorrect models, that is, to wrong prior beliefs about the nature of the events in question.

3. Even when we can be fairly confident of appropriate models, we may lack clearly useful inferential guides. We currently have no clear idea about how to translate some of the most fundamental statistical considerations into guides for reasoning in everyday life. This seems especially clear in the instance of sample bias considerations. People are prone to pay too little attention to the possibility that evidence is biased, but it is far from clear what "statistical heuristics" would be appropriate to use for most real-world problems.

Models and heuristics in inductive reasoning

Let us start our discussion of faulty inductive reasoning by analyzing an example that is relatively free of the difficulties just alluded to. Many examples in this book would do, but the maternity-ward problem of Kahneman and Tversky (1972b, 3) is especially clear-cut and will help us to set out some definitions. Subjects were asked to judge whether a large hospital or a small one would have more days in a year on which over 60% of the babies born were male. The majority of subjects checked "about the same," and of the others, about half checked "large" and half checked "small." In other words, as a group, the subjects believed that such deviant days, with male births exceeding 60%, are equally likely at large and small hospitals.

Kahneman and Tversky theorized, on the basis of this and numerous other experiments, that the predominant mode of judgment leading to this result is the employment of the *representativeness heuristic*. A subject using this heuristic would focus on the dissimilarity of the deviant outcome (60%) from the presumed typical outcome (about 50%, in this case). Since the degree of similarity or "representativeness" is not influenced by the size of the hospital, the subject would judge the likelihood of the deviant outcome to be about the same for both hospitals.

In the correct approach to this problem, however, one regards the actual subset of "male" and "female" outcomes, on any given day at one hospital, as a random sample from an approximately 50–50 population. It then follows from the binomial formula or the law of large numbers that a deviant sample percentage is less likely with larger sample size. One concludes, following this application of a probabilistic model, that days with 60% or more male births are less likely at the large hospital.

In this example, reasoning guided by an *intuitive heuristic* (the representativeness heuristic) is contrasted with reasoning carried out within a mathematical *model*. We make a *normative* judgment, criticizing the intuitive conclusion as faulty, because a different conclusion is obtained from a model that we believe is an apt representation for sex of newborns. Our procedure here, in making a normative judgment on the basis of a model, illustrates a general principle: *Inductive reasoning must be justified in terms of the aptness of underlying models of the events in question.*

A mathematical model is only one sort of model, and at that, one rarely used in human reasoning: It requires mathematical training and plenty of time to think. But we shall use the term *model* to refer to any partial *representation* of some aspects of reality. We include physical models (for example, a model airplane, scaled down from the original), mathematical models (for example, equations describing air flow over the wings of an airplane), and, more generally, intuitive conceptual models. These are people's mental representations of airplanes or of air flow or of processes determining the sex of newborn babies or of any other aspect of reality. An extremely important distinction among models is between those that are purely *deterministic* (i.e., they contain no representation of unpredictability) and those models that are *probabilistic* (i.e., they include the assumption that the events are imperfectly predictable given standard conditions of information). Probabilistic models can be physical (shaking dice or drawing marbles out of an urn) or mathematical (random variables), but often they are less exact. For example, someone watching a long jump at a track meet may believe that the next competitor will jump about 8 m but that a somewhat longer or shorter jump would not be unusual and a jump of even 7.5 or 8.5 m would be possible. This person's mental representation of the long jump is an intuitive probabilistic model, involving a mental "typical distance" and a sort of "error distribution" that produces deviations from the typical.

The nature of one's model for events is of critical importance for the selection of the inferential tools to be used, including various heuristics. A *heuristic* is any guiding principle for transforming information to solve a problem or to form a judgment. Above, we spoke of the representativeness heuristic, but this really includes two different heuristics: one for constructing models (according to the representativeness heuristic, the underlying model should match closely the structural features of the observed data) and one for judging likelihood of outcomes (an outcome is more likely if its structure is more similar to that of the assumed underlying model). *Statistical heuristics* encourage one to think about information in terms of data properties, such as reliability and validity, and to manipulate information using probabilistic concepts, such as base rate. If one has an underlying probabilistic model for events of a particular type, then one is likely to employ statistical heuristics when thinking about those events.

Let us be more specific about how these concepts of model and heuristics apply in the maternity-ward problem. A completely satisfactory solution to that problem would use a mathematical model, that of random sampling from a 50–50 population. Most subjects probably employ too simple a model of newborn sex – a model that specifies a 50–50 division but does not include any relation between the randomness of the sampling process and the probable sampling error. Undoubtedly most subjects do know something about the relation between sample size and sampling error, but this knowledge is not incorporated into the intuitive model that they set up mentally to deal with the problem. Instead, the subjects supplement the simple 50–50 model with the representativeness heuristic, which leads them to the conclusion that 60% male births is somewhat unlikely but equally so in both hospitals. Note finally that subjects would not have to be statisticians to solve the problem in at least a qualitative way. If their model of the observed sex proportion included the intuitive notion of drawing a sample, then they might call to mind a statistical heuristic. In this case, the needed heuristic is the notion that large samples are more likely to have representative or typical structure than are small samples.

In short, reasoning is based on models. Depending on one's model, one may employ various algorithms or heuristics. A mathematician might deduce quantitative consequences from a mathematical model; someone with an intuitive sampling model might successfully use a statistical heuristic; and someone whose model is too simple might use the representativeness heuristic, and, in this problem at least, would be misled by it.

Application of probabilistic models in everyday inference

The failure to use probabilistic models or statistical heuristics does not cause errors merely in response to puzzles like the maternity-ward problem; it also affects people's inferences in everyday situations, especially in the social domain. Ross (1977) has suggested that people make a *fundamental attribution error:* They tend to overattribute other people's behavior to personal dispositions while overlooking situational causes or transient environmental influences on behavior. We shall give two examples of this error and shall indicate how consideration of probabilistic models helps us to define and to correct this kind of error.

Nisbett and Borgida (1975) showed that subjects often fail to utilize "consensus" information: They infer idiosyncratic, personal dispositions for a particular individual's behavior even when they are informed that most other people, in the same situation, behaved in the same way. For example, in one study, subjects rated "Greg R." as apathetic and cruel because he did not go to the aid of a "victim" who he believed was having a seizure. The tendency to give Greg R. such negative ratings was just as high in subjects who were given consensus information, namely, that *most* people in the identical situation failed to aid the victim, as in control subjects who were given no such consensus information and who therefore believed that most people would aid the victim.

How could people make use of the consensus information to moderate their inferences about personal traits or dispositions? It seems to us that some social scientists, who do emphasize the situational determinants of behavior, operate with an intuitive (and sometimes even formal) probabilistic model, in which some situations lead to a high probability of a certain behavior for nearly everyone, while some individuals may possess a high probability of the behavior in nearly every situation. In the framework provided by such a model, the consensus information is readily interpreted as evidence that the particular *situation* was of the high-probability sort, and therefore the occurrence of the behavior is not good evidence that the given *individual* possesses a high probability of such behavior across situations.

We think that probabilistic models of this sort are good representations of social behavior, and they provide the grounds for criticizing inferences that fail to make use of consensus information. Subjects in the Nisbett and Borgida study probably rely exclusively on the representativeness heuristic, constructing a model of the target person that matches the data: Greg R. is cruel and apathetic because his action seems cruel and apathetic.

In this example, as in the case of the maternity-ward problem, there is not too much temptation to defend the subjects' inferences. A pure trait model of social behavior, with *no* situational influence on probability, is not very reasonable, and the subjects themselves would most likely admit as much. Our second example of what *we* would hold to be an instance of the fundamental attribution error, however, leads to more of an argument.

Suppose that a candidate for an important administrative position has been offered an interview on the basis of very strong recommendations from former employers. The interview starts with a group lunch, at which the candidate exhibits nervous mannerisms. Later, several of the people who attended that lunch say that the candidate lacks the necessary interpersonal skills for the job.

A social psychologist might say that the employers' inference about "interpersonal skills" is dubious. A situational explanation of the offending behavior (involving the demands of the lunch-interview setting), or a probabilistic interpretation (he was having an off day) might be plausible, and indeed, in view of the recommendations from former employers, seem more plausible than the explanation in terms of the candidate's skills. But the employers might reply that anyone who cannot infallibly exhibit poise in the lunch-interview situation is extremely likely to fail in other job-related situations that are equally demanding of poise.

The argument is hard to win. The employers have justified their inference in terms of a model that postulates a high statistical association between failure in one kind of situation and failure in other situations that resemble the first on some variables, though not on others. It is hard to know whether the actual cognitive mechanism underlying the initial inference involved the use of such a model or instead simply relied on the representativeness heuristic (examining the fit between the candidate's lunch behavior and the prototypical lunch behavior of a stereotypic ideal candidate. And it is also hard to know for sure that the employers' proposed model is wrong. The social psychologist knows from experience that such correlations are usually very weak when tested empirically; but this particular one has not been tested directly, and to test it by applying existing psychological techniques would involve enormously detailed and prohibitively expensive exploration.

These examples illustrate two different ways in which inductive reasoning can be faulty, and they point to two different kinds of normative advice or education that may be required: (a) Sometimes the inferential procedures are faulty. Sometimes people may agree (upon reflection at least) on what model is reasonable, but may in practice use other, simpler models and correspondingly facile heuristics. Normative advice emphasizes avoidance of oversimplification and too-facile use of the representativeness heuristic. Educational goals include teaching models of broad usefulness such as the binomial sampling model, teaching concrete applications of these models, and emphasizing statistical heuristics that can sometimes take the place of rigorous deductive reasoning from models. (b) Sometimes the reasoning is correct given the model but the model is dubious or even demonstrably wrong. Normative advice stresses what is known (for example, about the weakness of certain types of behavioral correlations) that makes a particular model seem preferable.

This analysis also points to two very serious gaps in the availability of normative advice. In some cases, we may lack the knowledge needed to formulate adequate models. In other cases, we may lack sufficiently simple and usable statistical heuristics. The example of consensus information illustrates gaps in current social science models. We may criticize subjects who failed to use consensus information at all, but suppose the subjects reply, "Yes, you're right, situational factors are relevant; now tell us, how *much* should we correct our belief about Greg R.'s apathy, in view of the fact that most people behaved the same way?" To answer this would require a theory of trait/situation interactions that personality and social psychologists have not supplied thus far.

Demonstration of the fact that we lack certain essential statistical heuristics requires a section of its own.

Adjusting inference for sample bias: The need for statistical heuristics

Correct procedures for taking sample *size* into account in drawing inferences are well developed, for much of statistical theory is devoted to problems of that sort. Partly as a consequence, we do not anticipate great difficulty in teaching people to be more sensitive to considerations of sample size in the inferential problems presented in everyday life. When we consider questions of sample *bias,* however, matters are rather different. This is unfortunate because, as Nisbett and Ross (1980) have argued, inferential errors seem much more likely to result from bias than from small sample size.

In discussing the problems one encounters in trying to develop heuristics for dealing with sample bias, it will be helpful to distinguish two main kinds of information about a sample of observations: information about *sampling procedure* and information about *typicality of covarying features.* In the first kind of information, that is, about procedure, we shall distinguish rather grossly among haphazard samples, statistical samples, and illustrative samples. These terms rather quickly remove us from the domain of theoretical statistics – which is concerned with only one of the categories – and thrust us into the domain of incidental observations and communication of observed facts.

Haphazard samples are observations selected from among all possible ones in whatever way is feasible or most convenient. Most inferences, not only in everyday life but even in careful scientific work, are based on haphazard samples. For example, the subjects used in Kahneman and Tversky's studies were observed because they were available. *Statistical* samples involve a known probabilistic mechanism for selecting observations out of some universe of possible ones. They are the only kinds of samples for which rigorous statistical calculations are possible. In opinion polling or in quality-control testing, this kind of sampling is prevalent. A clever statistical modeler, however, may convert a haphazard sample into a statistical sample by formulating a reasonable population and a probabilistic selection model that might be satisfied by the actual selection procedure. Finally, an *illustrative* sample is a communication device, used to enhance the concreteness or vividness of a report based on a much larger body of data. Television reports and magazine articles sometimes illustrate what are supposed to be population characteristics by using vivid single cases. But even in science, much presentation of data is illustrative. In electrophysiology, for example, conclusions based on fragmentary observations of many nerve cells are often illustrated by sample records from cells that show the typical features well.

The other kind of information about a sample concerns the typicality of covarying features. Such information involves the values of variables other than the ones of chief interest, which may be correlates of the latter and which may be compared with known population values to assess the typicality of the sample. Consider an everyday life example where the variable of chief interest is income, but age and sex are also recorded for each individual. Suppose we want to know which group earns more, people who write poetry as a hobby or people who play musical instruments. We happen to have a friend, Jack, aged 50, who has many acquaintances (mostly middle-aged men) who write poetry, and we also have a friend, Jane, aged 25, who has many acquaintances, mostly young women, who play instruments. The income distribution for the poets is much higher than for the musicians. Everyone would agree that this proves nothing about the two populations in question: The samples are atypical of the populations on variables that correlate highly with income (at the present time). Clearly it matters a great deal both *how atypical* the features of the sample are and also *how useful* those features are for predicting the values of the target variable. Many of Kahneman and Tversky's experiments used Israeli high school students as subjects. Yet we and they draw much broader inferences from the results, because, though most adults are neither Israeli nor in high school, these features are judged to correlate poorly, if at all, with the target variables in their studies. Even in a carefully constructed statistical sample, it should be noted, atypicality must be considered: If a survey of the income of registered Democrats drew a small random sample with a preponderance of white, middle-aged males, we would not accept the standard sorts of inferences, based on random sampling, as valid.

To adjust for atypicality, a statistical modeler may attempt to formulate more precisely the relationships between the target variable and covariates and to correct the inference by using these relationships. For example, one might be able to guess or estimate the relationship between age, sex, and income and to compare adjusted incomes of the poets and the musicians. Such adjustments require experience, reflection, and often quantitative data and moderately large samples (for model testing and parameter estimation).

We have noted that haphazard sampling or atypical samples can sometimes be handled by sophisticated models, but it is unreasonable to expect non-experts to handle sample bias this way. What intuitive processes do laypeople use to correct for sample bias? And what recommendations, stemming from the statistician's rules of thumb, can we make to improve their inferences?

The question of how people adjust for sample bias was addressed in two studies by Hamill, Wilson, and Nisbett (1980). The overall conclusion was that people adjust very little: They show no systematic differences in the inferences made from haphazard samples versus typical samples and even draw the same sorts of inferences from samples specifically noted to be atypical (counterillustrative, as it were).

Some details of these studies may be valuable if the reader is to think seriously about what statistical heuristics people ought to use. In one study, subjects viewed a videotaped interview with a purported prison guard who appeared very humane for half the subjects and very cruel for the other half. Some subjects were led to believe that the single case presented was illustrative of a larger sample of prison guards. Other subjects were told that the single case was counterillustrative: They were told explicitly that the guard interviewed had been selected as one of the most extreme (one of the very most humane, for those who saw the humane guard, and one of the very least humane, for those who saw the cruel guard). A third group was given no information about illustrativeness, and in effect was presented a haphazard sample of size 1. In the other study, subjects read a magazine article with a vivid negative portrayal of a welfare recipient. Some of the subjects were led to believe that the case they read about was highly typical with regard to the length of stay on welfare: They were told (wrongly) that like most middle-aged welfare recipients the woman they read about had been on welfare for most of her adult life. Other subjects were told the truth about the woman's atypicality with regard to this feature: They were informed that most welfare recipients are on welfare for only a few years.

Attitudes about prison guards in general (in the first study) and about welfare recipients in general (in the second study) were evaluated with a variety of measures. Attitudes toward prison guards were much more favorable in the group exposed to the humane guard than in the group exposed to the cruel guard. This shows that inferences were drawn about guards in general from the single case. The attitudes toward welfare recipients of subjects who read the magazine article were much more negative than the attitudes of a control group, again showing that inferences were drawn about welfare recipients in general from the article about one recipient.

In the guard study, the subjects who were told the guard was typical drew inferences from the videotape not systematically different from those drawn by the subjects who had no sampling procedure information. Even the subjects who believed the guard was atypical made inferences in the same direction as the other groups, and in fact the differences between them and the other groups were not statistically reliable. Likewise, in the welfare recipient study, the "typical" and "atypical" groups drew similar inferences, and in fact the observed difference between their mean attitude scores was negligible.

It is important, for our later normative analysis, to speculate about how these results can be explained in terms of cognitive processes. The results are quite surprising if it is assumed that subjects have definite prior attitudes, shaped by past experience and information, toward welfare recipients or prison guards. For the subjects presented with an illustrative or typical case, a strong impact on such prior attitudes about the population might be reasonable, of course, since they properly believe that it is typical of a much larger group; but this justification is absent for subjects in the "haphazard" group. And why should the subjects presented with a counterillustrative or atypical case make any inference at all in the direction of the sample, rather than sticking to their original attitudes, or perhaps even moving somewhat in the direction opposite to the case presented?

Current theory of attitude formation and attitude change suggests some tentative explanations (Bem, 1967; Nisbett & Ross, 1980; Nisbett & Wilson,

1977). We may speculate that subjects, in responding to questions about their attitudes, do not *retrieve* attitudes from storage at all. Rather they *construct* them from materials at hand, including their current affective reactions to the object, their semantic associations to the object, and observations of their recent behavior toward the object. Much of the construction process is rapid and not accessible to consciousness. A vivid single case is likely to evoke affective reactions toward the entire class of objects it represents, despite countervailing but pallid assurances about typicality. (Affective reactions may be particularly likely to "fly the cognitive coop," as it were. No amount of assurances about the atypicality of the Parisian taxi driver who insulted us is likely to return us to our previous unwary attitude toward the class of Parisian taxi drivers.) The vivid single case may also serve as a prompting to recruit similar information from memory. Thus subjects may be reminded by the humane prison guard, quite involuntarily, of the kindly Nazi guards in "Hogan's Heroes" or of the sweet southern sheriff portrayed by Andy Griffith in the summer reruns of their childhood. When subjects come to construct their attitudes about prison guards in general, they may remind themselves to ignore the haphazard or counterillustrative evidence they just saw, and they might even be successful at that, but to no avail. The affective reactions and the now-biased contents of memory would be sufficient to produce an expressed attitude quite different from that of control subjects.

Bearing in mind the above notions about how subjects are influenced by the observed case, let us return to the normative question: How *should* people adjust their inferences in light of knowledge about sampling procedure and about typicality of the sample with respect to important covarying features? Formal theory and applied statistical practice offer us less than meets the eye and much less than we need.

One rule with a hardnosed and resolutely scientific flavor states that no conclusions about a population should be drawn except on the basis of properly randomized sampling, for otherwise the assumptions of statistical procedures are violated, and it is impossible to know what confidence to place in the conclusion. According to this austere rule, the subjects who received no information about the sampling procedure or typicality of the videotaped guard should have suspended all inferences, and thus their attitudes about prison guards should have been exactly the same whether they saw the humane or the cruel guard.

This rule can be rejected on three different grounds: epistemic, pragmatic, and logical.

1. The first argument derives from Goldman's observation that, ". . . epistemic advice or rules must be capable of being followed" (1978, p. 513). Our discussion of possible mechanisms of attitude construction suggests that "suspension of inferences" may not be a possible rule for everyday human cognition. A much more detailed rule, indicating how to debias the

contents of associative memory and how to compensate for affective reactions might be needed.

2. Even if we could apply the highly proscriptive rule, it would have the unfortunate effect of preventing us from learning most of the things that we do learn, both in everyday life and in science. In learning about college deans or traffic conditions on a freeway, one is pretty much stuck with one's haphazard samples, encountered personally or indirectly. And the scientific studies of human inference cited in this paper used subjects, materials, and settings that were not sampled statistically but were conveniently at hand or readily constructible.

3. Finally, randomness is not a directly observable or self-evident property of a sampling process: it is a property of mathematical models, which may or may not be good descriptions of real-world processes. A haphazard sample may be effectively "random" because we believe certain models to be good descriptions of the world, and, as we have pointed out, a clever statistical modeler may capture such intuitions in an adequate mathematical formulation.

How might we prescribe for the related problem of typicality of covarying features? On the surface, it might seem appealing to formulate a stricture against generalizing from a sample that differs substantially from the target population on features that conceivably are relevant. According to this rule, subjects who knew that the sample welfare case was atypical on one relevant feature (length of stay on welfare) should have suspended all inferences about other characteristics of welfare cases in general. But this rule is subject to the same sorts of criticisms as the one about randomness. The epistemic criticism is exactly the same: a correct rule must take account of the actual cognitive mechanisms used in drawing everyday inferences and must be capable of being followed. The pragmatic criticism is similar to the one for the previous rule. In most scientific studies one can find some features of the sample that are atypical and that conceivably are relevant. How much one believes in a model that asserts that such features are highly relevant matters a great deal. Finally, even if we know, or strongly suspect, that an atypical covarying feature is important, we may still be able to capture its importance in a model and introduce an appropriate correction. In the example of the income of amateur musicians and poets, we could try to get a rough estimate of the effects of age and sex and compare the adjusted means for the two groups. Of course, in that example, it would be almost inconceivable that we could draw inferences with any confidence – but that is precisely because we lack a good model for the effects of age and sex on income.

Are there perhaps softer and less forbidding principles that can be used? We might try, for example, "Knowledge is tentative." This is all right as far as it goes, but it seems too vague to be of much use. We need more detailed statistical heuristics. How *much* confidence should we place in generalizations drawn from haphazard samples? What kind of tentative inferences can one make from atypical samples? In part, these questions are addressed to statisticians and to philosophers. Is there any general approach to model building that can be a source of statistical heuristics for intuitive inference? But our discussion of mechanisms of attitude formation and of the unconscious processes affecting inference should make it clear that, as Goldman (1978) has urged, epistemic principles must pass tests of usability as well as of validity. And here we confront yet another issue. Part of the inferential process that we wish to modify is automatic and unconscious (Bem & McConnell, 1970; Goethals & Reckman, 1973; Nisbett & Wilson, 1977). At what cost is automaticity circumvented? Comprehension of instructions, stories, motives, etc., demands a flood of inferences in every waking hour. It is reasonable to suspect that automaticity may be found for these functions to nearly the same extent as for perception. Good statistical heuristics should be learnable to the point where they can be used easily, even automatically.

Can probabilistic models be used in everyday inference?

We envisage a program in which probabilistic models and statistical heuristics will eventually be incorporated into most people's everyday reasoning. We have discussed two major difficulties with such a program: ignorance about what models are correct and absence of convenient statistical heuristics in some important areas. A third, equally difficult question, which is of course logically prior, concerns human capacity for incorporating probabilistic models and heuristics into everyday thinking. Despite the difficulties there are grounds for optimism, and some questions may lend themselves to experimental research of a type we will sketch later.

One reason for optimism is that human reasoning changes with new cultural inventions. Genuine inferential advances appear to have occurred within recent historical times. The modern notion of probability is scarcely more than 300 years old (Hacking, 1975). And prior to about 1660, notions that were in *any* sense probabilistic were applied almost exclusively to the understanding of events generated by randomizing devices, such as dice and cards. Yet virtually every educated person today employs essentially statistical reasoning in some domains, for example, sports and weather, and has a statistical understanding of randomizing devices like cards and dice that is very different from premodern conceptions. (Hacking goes so far as to say that anyone playing at dice in ancient times with modern conceptions of probability would have owned the whole of Gaul in short order!)

In addition to purely statistical notions, a good many general inductive principles and guides are of quite recent vintage. The notion that correlation does not suffice to establish causation does not appear before Hume and does not receive a clear general statement until Bentham's (1824/1952) *Handbook of Political Fallacies*. A general indictment of the "resemblance criterion" (Nisbett & Ross, 1980) as a basis for inferring cause-and-effect relations does not appear until Mill's (1843/1974) *System of Logic*. Indeed, until the end of the eighteenth century the very opposite rule was followed by physicians, who were taught to reason in accordance with the "doctrine of signatures." This doctrine held that every natural curative agent could be expected to indicate, by a well-marked external property, the disease for which it was effective. Thus hard, gravelly objects were useful in treating gallstones, yellow objects were helpful in combating jaundice, and so on. Fortunately, physicians have proved capable of abandoning this inductive heuristic in favor of other, superior, ones.

A second reason for optimism is that good reasoning can sometimes be quicker and easier than faulty reasoning. We have said that errors sometimes come from oversimplification and that accurate models may be complex. But the opposite can be true as well. Errors may arise from overly complex causal reasoning, and the lack of a good simple approach to a problem may cause people to generate several complicated poor ones. In one of our current experiments, we are conducting telephone interviews about sports in which we have embedded some questions that lend themselves to probabilistic answers. Often we do get short, snappy (and in our view correct) probabilistic answers. Other interviewees, who do not think of a probabilistic approach, hesitantly offer several lengthy deterministic explanations, none of which seems to convince even the interviewees themselves that they are on the right track.

Both the historical and the anecdotal evidence reflect the same underlying point. Even the rapid and automatic processes of human inference draw on well-learned concepts and models. Human reasoning and preferred argument forms therefore change, not merely as a function of individual maturation, but also as a function of changes in language, culture, and education.

We have recently begun a program of research to examine how people reason, and how they learn to reason, about problems which ought, in our view, to be approached with a probabilistic slant. We have used problems with a variety of different structures and with content that tends, to a greater or lesser degree, to evoke probabilistic thinking. This is not the place to attempt even a preliminary report of results, but it may be helpful to illustrate the materials we are using in order to indicate the questions we feel are worth asking. To illustrate the materials, we offer the following problem.

College Choice

David L. was a senior in high school on the East Coast who was planning to go to college. He had completed an excellent record in high school and had been admitted to his two top choices: a small liberal arts college and an Ivy League university. The two schools were about equal in prestige and were equally costly. Both were located in attractive East Coast cities, about equally distant from his home town. David had several older friends who were attending the liberal arts college and several who were attending the Ivy League university. They were all excellent students like himself and had interests that were similar to his. His friends at the liberal arts college all reported that they liked the place very much and that they found it very stimulating. The friends at the Ivy League university reported that they had many complaints on both personal and social grounds and on educational grounds. David initially thought that he would go to the liberal arts college. However, he decided to visit both schools himself for a day. He did not like what he saw at the private liberal arts college: Several people whom he met seemed cold and unpleasant; a professor he met with briefly seemed abrupt and uninterested in him; and he did not like the "feel" of the campus. He did like what he saw at the Ivy League university: Several of the people he met seemed like vital, enthusiastic, pleasant people; he met with two different professors who took a personal interest in him; and he came away with a very pleasant feeling about the campus.

Which school should David L. choose, and why? Try to analyze the arguments on both sides, and explain which side is stronger.

This is a particularly difficult problem, because it contains two different probabilistic components: (a) a base-rate argument, to the effect that David L. is unlikely to come from the tail of a distribution (from his friends' reactions, he can guess that the modal response to the liberal arts college is very favorable and that the variability is low), and (b) a sample-size/ sample-bias argument concerning the adequacy of his one day's exposure. We guess, from pilot work, that each of these probabilistic components is blocked by a common set of beliefs, namely that the individual's profile of preferences and aversions is unique and is predictable only from that individual's experience and personality, and that the individual's feelings, however mysterious in origin, are at least reliable, with a little bit of information about an object being sufficient to produce a read-out of likes and dislikes that provides a confident guide to future reactions. Most of the open-ended responses to the problem reflect these beliefs (e.g., "He's got to choose for himself, not his friends"). But not all do. Here is one response from an undergraduate with no course work in probability or statistics:

I would say he should go to the liberal arts college. His negative experience there was a brief, very shallow contact with the school. His friends, all veritable clones of himself, have been there (presumably) for a while and know the place intimately, and like it, whereas the opposite statements are true of the Ivy League school. He would be justified, however, to go with his own feelings about the places. Often, this intuition is a higher perception that we can't analyze, and he may be right to go with it. I think, though, that the first choice I've mentioned is more reliable, for his experience is *too* limited with the 2 schools.

This response we regard as a fully satisfactory statistical one, though of course it is not phrased in the language of probability models.

We began these studies with the suspicion that in most cases where a formal probabilistic model can be usefully applied by a statistician there are analogs in the everyday world in which a similar intuitive use of probabilistic thinking occurs frequently in intelligent laypeople. For example, we noted earlier that people ordinarily fail to formulate a model in which an individual's behavior is viewed as a function of both situational variables and dispositional variables, and in which some situations give rise to a high probability of the behavior across most individuals. Yet we think that people do operate with something like that sort of model when the behavior is good performance on a test. The concept of an "easy test," where most people have a high probability of good performance, is widely known and used in our culture. We suspected that other kinds of probabilistic models, for other kinds of problems, would also be applied in everyday inference. Our experiments attempt to demonstrate this point, showing that people can do well with certain problems, while failing on others with similar formal structure, because their underlying models for the latter problems lack a probabilistic component.

If this suspicion is confirmed, we are led to a number of questions that we may try to answer experimentally. To what extent is good probabilistic reasoning due to application of an abstract or formal model of some sort? Why should a formal model be easily applied in some sorts of concrete problems and rarely in others? If successful reasoning is not the application of a content-free formal model, then how should it be described in theoretical terms? Other questions concern individual differences in modeling and use of rules. To what extent is the use of probabilistic reasoning a stable personal disposition? Correlated with intelligence? Related to educational background?

Finally, there are a set of important questions concerning the issues of teachability of probabilistic models. The basic question has already received an answer in our research: People can be taught, both by traditional statistics courses and by quicker methods, to answer at least many "word problems" of the above sort in a more probabilistic fashion. To what degree there is carryover to the actual judgments of everyday life, which teaching techniques are most effective, and, what the best inductive principles and methods to teach are – these are important questions we have only begun to ask. We hope that we will have help from many quarters.

Part IX

Risk perception

33.   Facts versus fears: Understanding perceived risk

Paul Slovic, Baruch Fischhoff, and Sarah Lichtenstein

People respond to the hazards they perceive. If their perceptions are faulty, efforts at personal, public, and environmental protection are likely to be misdirected. For some hazards, such as motor vehicle accidents, extensive statistical data are readily available. For other familiar activities, such as the consumption of alcohol and tobacco, assessment of risk requires complex epidemiological and experimental studies. However, even when statistical data are plentiful, the "hard" facts can only go so far toward developing policy. At some point, human judgment is needed to interpret the findings and determine their relevance.

Still other hazards, such as those associated with recombinant DNA research or nuclear power, are so new that risk assessment must be based on complex theoretical analyses such as fault trees (see Figure 1), rather than on direct experience. Despite an appearance of objectivity, these analyses, too, include a large component of judgment. Someone, relying on educated intuition, must determine the structure of the problem, the consequences to be considered, and the importance of the various branches of the fault tree. Once the analyses have been performed, they must be communicated to those who actually manage hazards, including industrialists, environmentalists, regulators, legislators, and voters. If these people do not understand or believe the data they are shown, then distrust, conflict, and ineffective hazard management are likely.

This chapter explores some psychological elements of the risk-assessment process. Its basic premises are that both the public and the experts

This is a revised version of a paper that originally appeared in R. Schwing and W. A. Albers Jr. (Eds.), *Societal Risk Assessment: How safe is safe enough?* New York: Plenum Press, 1980. Copyright © 1980 by Plenum Press. Reprinted by permission.

Support for this work was provided by the Technology Assessment and Risk Analysis Program of the National Science Foundation under Grant PRA79–11934 to Clark University under subcontract to Perceptronics, Inc.

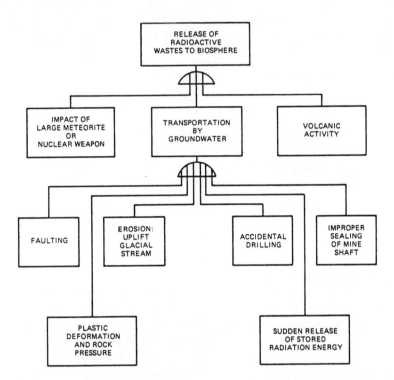

Figure 1. A fault tree indicating the various ways in which radioactive material might accidentally be released from nuclear wastes buried within a salt deposit. Each of the possible initiating events in the bottom two rows can lead to the transportation of radioactivity by groundwater. This transport can in turn release radioactivity to the biosphere. As indicated by the second level of boxes, release of radioactivity can also be produced directly (without the help of groundwater) through the impact of a large meteorite, a nuclear weapon, or a volcanic eruption. (*Source:* McGrath, 1974.)

are necessary participants in that process, that assessment is inherently subjective, and that understanding judgmental limitations is crucial to effective decision making.

Judgmental biases in risk perception

When laypeople are asked to evaluate risks, they seldom have statistical evidence on hand. In most cases, they must make inferences based on what they remember hearing or observing about the risk in question. Psychological research, much of which has been described earlier in this book, has identified a number of very general inferential rules that people seem to use in such situations. These judgmental rules, known as heuristics, are employed to reduce difficult mental tasks to simpler ones. Although they are valid in some circumstances, in others they lead to large and persistent biases with serious implications for decision making in areas as diverse as financial analysis (Slovic, 1972c) and the management of natural hazards (Slovic, Kunreuther, & White, 1974).

Availability

One heuristic that has special relevance for risk perception is called availability (Tversky & Kahneman, 1973, 11). People using this heuristic judge an event as likely or frequent if instances of it are easy to imagine or recall. Because frequently occurring events are generally easier to imagine and recall than are rare events, availability is often an appropriate cue. However, availability is also affected by numerous factors unrelated to frequency of occurrence. For example, a recent disaster or a vivid film, such as *Jaws* or *The China Syndrome*, could seriously distort risk judgments.

Availability bias helps explain people's misperceptions and faulty decisions with regard to certain natural hazards. For example, in discussing flood plain residents, Kates (1962) wrote:

A major limitation to human ability to use improved flood hazard information is a basic reliance on experience. Men on flood plains appear to be very much prisoners of their experience.... Recently experienced floods appear to set an upward bound to the size of loss with which managers believe they ought to be concerned. (p. 140)

Kates attributed much of the difficulty in improving flood control to the "inability of individuals to conceptualize floods that have never occurred" (Kates, 1962, p. 92). He observed that individuals forecasting flood potential "are strongly conditioned by their immediate past and limit their extrapolation to simplified constructs, seeing the future as a mirror of that past" (p. 88). Similarly, the purchase of earthquake insurance increases sharply after a quake and then decreases steadily as memories fade (Steinbrugge, McClure, & Snow, 1969).

One particularly important implication of the availability heuristic is that discussion of a low-probability hazard may increase its memorability and imaginability and hence its perceived riskiness, regardless of what the evidence indicates. For example, leaders in the field of recombinant DNA research quickly regretted ever bringing to public attention the remote risks of contamination by newly created organisms. Rosenberg (1978) summarized the reaction that followed the revelation of such hypothetical risks:

Initially, the response was one of praise for the . . . social responsibility shown by the scientists involved. . . . Gradually and predictably, however, the debate became heated. Speculation abounded and the scarier the scenario, the wider the publicity it received. Many of the discussions of the issue completely lost sight of the fact that the dangers were hypothetical in the first place and assumed that recombinant

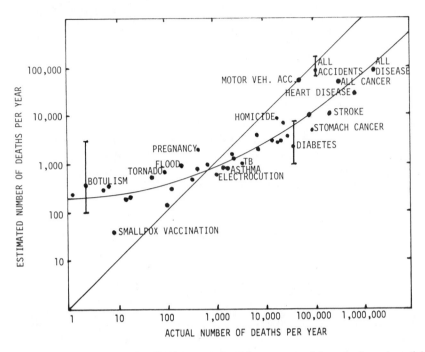

Figure 2. Relationship between judged frequency and the actual number of deaths per year for 41 causes of death. If judged and actual frequencies were equal, the data would fall on the straight line. The points, and the curved line fitted to them, represent the averaged responses of a large number of laypeople. As an index of the variability across individuals, vertical bars are drawn to depict the 25th and 75th percentiles of the judgments for botulism, diabetes, and all accidents. The range of responses for the other 37 causes of death was similar.

DNA laboratories were full of raging beasts. Ultimately, the very scientists whose self-restraint had set the whole process in motion were vilified. (p. 29)

Judged frequency of lethal events. Availability bias is illustrated by several studies in which college students and members of the League of Women Voters judged the frequency of 41 causes of death (Lichtenstein et al., 1978). In one study, these people were first told the annual death toll from 1 cause (motor vehicle accidents) in the United States (50,000) and then were asked to estimate the frequency of the other 40. In another study, participants were asked to judge which of 2 causes of death was more frequent. In both studies, judgments were moderately accurate in a global sense: People usually knew which were the most and least frequently lethal events. Within this global picture, however, people made serious misjudgments, many of which seemed to reflect the influence of availability.

Figure 2 compares the judged number of deaths per year with the number reported in public health statistics. If the frequency judgments were accurate, they would equal the statistical rates, with all data points

Table 1. *Bias in judged frequency of death*

Most overestimated	Most underestimated
All accidents	Smallpox vaccination
Motor vehicle accidents	Diabetes
Pregnancy, childbirth, and abortion	Stomach cancer
	Lightning
Tornadoes	Stroke
Flood	Tuberculosis
Botulism	Asthma
All cancer	Emphysema
Fire and flames	
Venomous bite or sting	
Homicide	

Source: Slovic, Fischhoff, & Lichtenstein (1979).

falling on the identity line. Although more likely hazards generally evoked higher estimates, the points seem scattered about a curved line that lies sometimes above and sometimes below the line of accurate judgment. In general, rare causes of death were overestimated and common causes of death were underestimated.

In addition to this general bias, sizable specific biases were evident. For example, accidents were judged to cause as many deaths as diseases, whereas diseases actually take about 16 times as many lives. Homicides were incorrectly judged more frequent than diabetes and stomach cancer deaths. Homicides were also judged to be about as frequent as death by stroke, although the latter actually claims about 11 times as many lives. Frequencies of death from botulism, tornadoes, and pregnancy (including childbirth and abortion) were also greatly overestimated. Table 1 lists the lethal events whose frequencies were most poorly judged in our various studies. In keeping with availability considerations, overestimated causes of death were dramatic and sensational, whereas underestimated causes tended to be unspectacular events, which claim one victim at a time and are common in nonfatal form.

Biased newspaper coverage and biased judgments. The availability heuristic highlights the vital role of experience as a determinant of perceived risk. If one's experiences are biased, one's perceptions are likely to be inaccurate. Unfortunately, much of the information to which people are exposed provides a distorted picture of the world of hazards. Consider author Richard Bach's observation about the fear shown by a couple taking their first airplane ride:

In all that wind and engineblast and earth tilting and going small below us, I watched my Wisconsin lad and his girl, to see them change. Despite their laughter, they had been afraid of the airplane. Their only knowledge of flight came from newspaper headlines, a knowledge of collisions and crashes and fatalities. They had never read a single report of a little airplane taking off, flying through the air and landing again safely. They could only believe that this must be possible, in spite of all the newspapers, and on that belief they staked their three dollars and their lives. (Bach, 1973, p. 37)

As a follow-up to the studies reported above, Combs and Slovic (1979) examined the reporting of causes of death in two newspapers on opposite coasts of the United States. Various indices of newspaper coverage were recorded for alternate months over a period of one year. The results indicated that both newspapers had similar biases in their coverage of life-threatening events. For example, examination of Table 2 reveals that many of the statistically frequent causes of death (e.g., diabetes, emphysema, various forms of cancer) were rarely reported by either paper during the period under study. In addition, violent, often catastrophic, events such as tornadoes, fires, drownings, homicides, motor vehicle accidents, and all accidents were reported much more frequently than less dramatic causes of death having similar (or even greater) statistical frequencies. For example, diseases take about 16 times as many lives as accidents, but there were more than 3 times as many articles about accidents, noting almost 7 times as many deaths. Among the more frequent events, homicides were the most heavily reported category in proportion to actual frequency. Although diseases claim almost 100 times as many lives as do homicides, there were about 3 times as many articles about homicides as about disease deaths. Furthermore, homicide articles tended to be more than twice as long as articles reporting disease and accident deaths.

Moreover, the biases in newspaper coverage and people's judgments were quite similar. The correlation between judged frequency of death and the number of deaths reported in the newspapers was about .70. This high correlation was not due to a common association of both judged and reported deaths with statistical frequency. When the latter was held constant, the partial correlations between people's judgments and the number of deaths reported were .89 and .85 for the two newspapers. Although it is tempting to conclude from these correlations that media coverage biases perceptions of risk, it might also be the case that people's opinions about what is important influence the media. The journalism literature is replete with instances in which influence has occurred in each direction (Brucker, 1973).

It won't happen to me. People's judgments of causes of death may be about as good as could be expected, given that they are neither specialists in the hazards considered nor exposed to a representative sample of information. Accurate perception of misleading samples of information might also be seen to underlie another apparent judgmental bias, people's predilection to view themselves as personally immune to hazards. The great majority of individuals believe themselves to be better than average drivers

Table 2. *Statistical frequency and newspaper coverage in the Eugene, Oregon,* Register Guard *and the New Bedford, Massachusetts,* Standard Times *for 41 causes of death*

Cause of death	Rate per 2.05×10^8 U.S. Res.	Subjects' estimates	Reported deaths R-G	Reported deaths S-T	Occurrences R-G	Occurrences S-T	Articles R-G	Articles S-T
1. Smallpox	0	57	0	0	0	0	0	0
2. Poisoning by vitamins	1	102	0	0	0	0	0	0
3. Botulism	2	183	0	0	0	0	0	0
4. Measles	5	168	0	0	0	0	0	0
5. Fireworks	6	160	0	0	0	0	0	0
6. Smallpox vaccination	8	23	0	0	0	0	0	0
7. Whooping cough	15	93	0	0	0	0	0	0
8. Polio	17	97	0	0	0	0	0	0
9. Venomous bite or sting	48	350	0	0	0	0	0	0
10. Tornado	90	564	36	25	10	6	14	7
11. Lightning	107	91	1	0	1	0	1	0
12. Non-venomous animal	129	174	4	2	4	2	4	2
13. Flood	205	736	4	10	2	2	2	2
14. Excess cold	334	314	0	0	0	0	0	0
15. Syphilis	410	492	0	0	0	0	0	0
16. Pregnancy, birth & abortion	451	1,344	0	0	0	0	0	0
17. Infectious hepatitis	677	545	0	0	0	0	0	0
18. Appendicitis	902	605	0	0	0	0	0	0
19. Electrocution	1,025	766	5	0	5	0	6	0
20. MV/train collision	1,517	689	0	1	0	1	0	1
21. Asthma	1,886	506	1	0	1	0	1	0
22. Firearm accident	2,255	1,345	8	1	8	1	9	1
23. Poison by solid/liquid	2,563	1,013	3	3	1	1	1	1
24. Tuberculosis	3,690	658	0	0	0	0	0	0
25. Fire and flames	7,380	3,336	94	46	33	9	38	10
26. Drowning	7,380	1,684	47	60	44	24	45	37
27. Leukemia	14,555	2,496	1	0	1	0	1	0
28. Accidental falls	17,425	2,675	15	7	15	6	16	9
29. Homicide	18,860	5,582	278	208	167	122	329	199
30. Emphysema	21,730	2,848	1	0	1	0	1	0
31. Suicide	24,600	4,679	29	19	28	18	36	20
32. Breast cancer	31,160	2,964	0	0	0	0	0	0
33. Diabetes	38,950	1,476	0	1	0	1	0	1
34. Motor vehicle accident	55,350	41,161	298	83	245	69	180	73
35. Lung cancer	75,850	9,764	3	2	3	2	4	2
36. Stomach cancer	95,120	3,283	0	1	0	1	0	1
37. All accidents	112,750	88,879	715	596	421	152	374	177
38. Stroke	209,100	7,109	12	4	12	4	13	4
39. All cancer	328,000	45,609	25	12	25	12	26	15
40. Heart disease	738,000	23,599	49	30	45	25	46	25
41. All disease	1,740,450	88,838	111	87	100	76	104	78
Total no. of reports (causes 10, 11, 13, 29, 31, 37 & 41)			1,174	945	729	376	860	483
Correlations (R-G vs. S-T)			$r = .97$		$r = .94$		$r = .98$	

Note: R-G = *Register Guard;* S-T = *Standard Times.*
Source: Combs & Slovic (1979).

(Näätänen & Summala, 1975; Svenson, 1981), more likely than average to live past 80 (Weinstein, 1980), less likely than average to be harmed by products they use (Rethans, 1979), and so on. Although such perceptions are obviously unrealistic, the risks look very small from the perspective of each individual's experience. Consider automobile driving: Despite driving too fast, tailgating, etc., poor drivers make trip after trip without mishap. This personal experience demonstrates to them their exceptional skill and safety. Moreover, their indirect experience via the news media shows them that when accidents happen, they happen to others. Given such misleading experiences, people may feel quite justified in refusing to take protective actions such as wearing seat belts (Slovic, Fischhoff, & Lichtenstein, 1978).

Out of sight, out of mind. In some situations, failure to appreciate the limits of "available" data may lull people into complacency. In a study by Fischhoff, Slovic, and Lichtenstein (1978), three groups of college student subjects were asked to evaluate the completeness of a fault tree showing the risks associated with starting a car (see Figure 3). One group saw the full tree. Each of the other two groups received a different pruned tree. In one version, the starting, ignition, and mischief branches were missing; the other version lacked branches detailing battery, fuel, and other engine problems.

Instructions for the task read as follows (numbers in brackets were given to people who saw the pruned trees):

Every day, across the United States, millions of drivers perform the act of getting into an automobile, inserting a key in the ignition switch, and attempting to start the engine. Sometimes the engine fails to start, and the trip is delayed. We'd like you to think about the various problems that might be serious enough to cause a car to fail to start so that the driver's trip is delayed for at least 1 minute.

The chart on the next page is intended to help you think about this problem. It shows six [three] major deficiencies that cause a car's engine to fail to start. These major categories probably don't cover all possibilities, so we've included a seventh [fourth] category, All Other Problems.

Please examine this diagram carefully and answer the following question:

For every 100 times that a trip is delayed due to "starting failure," estimate, on the average, how many of those delays are caused by each of the seven [four] factors. Make your estimates on the blank lines next to the factors named below. Your estimates should sum to 100.

If people who saw the pruned trees were properly sensitive to what had been omitted, the proportion of problems that they attributed to "other" would have equaled the sum of the proportions of problems attributed to the pruned branches and to "other" by those who saw the full tree. The results in Table 3 indicate that what was out of sight was effectively out of mind. For example, in pruned tree Group 1, "other" should have increased by a factor of six (from .078 to .468) to reflect the proportion of failures due

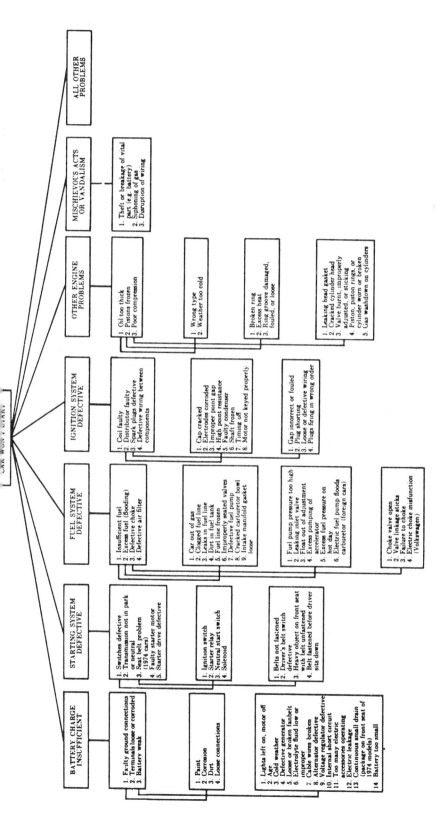

Figure 3. Fault tree indicating the ways in which a car might fail to start. It was used by the authors to study whether people are sensitive to the completeness of this type of presentation. Omission of large sections of the diagram was found to have little influence on the judged degree of completeness. In effect, what was out of sight was out of mind. Professional automobile mechanics did not do appreciably better on the test than did laypeople. (*Source:* Fischhoff, Slovic, and Lichtenstein (1978).)

Table 3. *Attribution of starting failures for pruned and unpruned trees*

| Group | n | M proportion of starting failures by type | | | | | | |
		Battery	Starting system	Fuel system	Ignition system	Engine	Mischief	Other
Unpruned tree	93	.264	.195	.193	.144	.076	.051	.078
Pruned tree 1	29	.432	—	.309	—	.116	—	.140[a]
Pruned tree 2	26	—	.357	—	.343	—	.073	.227[b]

Note: A dash indicates that the branch was deleted.
[a]Should be .468.
[b]Should be .611.
Source: Fischhoff, Slovic, and Lichtenstein (1978).

to starting and ignition problems and mischief, which had been omitted from the diagram. Instead, "other" was only doubled, whereas the importance of the three systems that were mentioned was substantially increased. A second study not only replicated these findings but showed that persons who observed pruned trees judged starting failure (due to all causes) to be less likely than did those who observed the unpruned tree.

Overconfidence

Knowing with certainty. A particularly pernicious aspect of heuristics is that people typically have great confidence in judgments based upon them. In another follow-up to the study on causes of death, people were asked to indicate the odds that they were correct in choosing the more frequent of two lethal events (Fischhoff, Slovic, & Lichtenstein, 1977). Table 4 shows the percentages of correct answers for each of the most frequently used odds categories. In Experiment 1, subjects were reasonably well calibrated when they gave odds of 1:1, 1.5:1, 2:1, and 3:1. That is, their percentage of correct answers was close to the appropriate percentage correct, given those odds. However, as odds increased from 3:1 to 100:1, there was little or no increase in accuracy. Only 73% of the answers assigned odds of 100:1 were correct (instead of 99.1%). Accuracy "jumped" to 81% at 1000:1 and to 87% at 10,000:1. For answers assigned odds of 1,000,000:1 or greater, accuracy was 90%; the appropriate degree of confidence would have been odds of 9:1. The 12% of responses that are not listed in Table 3 because they fell between the most common odds categories showed a similar pattern of overconfidence. In summary, subjects were frequently wrong at even the highest odds levels. Moreover, they gave many extreme odds responses. More than half of their judgments were greater than 50:1. Almost one-fourth were greater than 100:1.

A second experiment attempted to improve performance by giving subjects more instruction. The experimental session began with a 20-

Table 4. *Percentage of correct answers for major odds categories*

| Odds | Appropriate % correct[a] | Lethal events | | | | | | General-knowledge questions | | |
| | | Experiment 1[b] | | | Experiment 2[b] | | | Experiment 3[b] | | |
		N	%N	% correct	N	%N	% correct	N	%N	% correct
1:1	50	644	9	53	339	8	54	861	19	53
1.5:1	60	68	1	57	108	2.5	59	210	5	56
2:1	67	575	8	64	434	10	65	455	1	63
3:1	75	189	2	71	252	6	65	157	3.5	76
5:1	83	250	4	70	322	8	71	194	4	76
10:1	91	1,167	17	66	390	9	76	376	8	74
20:1	95	126	2	72	163	4	81	66	1.5	85
50:1	98	258	4	68	227	5	74	69	1.5	83
100:1	99	1,180	17	73	319	8	87	376	8	80
1,000:1	99.9	862	13	81	219	5	84	334	7	88
10,000:1	100	459	7	87	138	3	92	263	6	89
100,000:1	100	163	2	85	23	.5	96	134	3	92
1,000,000:1	100	157	2	90	47	1	96	360	8	94
Total		6,098	88		2,981	70		3,855	75	
Overall % correct				71.0			72.5			73.1

Note: % N refers to the percentage of odds judgments that fell in each of the major categories. There were 66 subjects in Experiment 1, 40 in Experiment 2, and 42 in Experiment 3.
[a]For well-calibrated subjects.
[b]Experiments 1, 2, and 3 were labeled Experiments 2, 3, and 4 in the original report.
Source: Fischhoff, Slovic, and Lichtenstein (1977).

minute lecture in which the concepts of probability and odds were carefully explained. The subtleties of expressing one's feelings of uncertainty as judgments of numerical odds were discussed, with special emphasis on how to use small odds (between 1:1 and 2:1) when one is quite uncertain about the correct answer. A chart was provided showing the relationship between various odds and the corresponding probabilities. Finally, subjects were taught the concept of calibration (Chap. **22**) and were urged to make odds judgments in a way that would lead them to be well calibrated. Although performance improved somewhat, subjects again exhibited unwarranted certainty (see Table 4). They assigned odds greater than or equal to 50:1 to approximately one-third of the items. Only 83% of the answers associated with these odds were correct.

In a third experiment, people proved to be just as overconfident when answering questions of general knowledge (e.g., Which magazine had the largest circulation in 1970? (a) *Playboy* or (b) *Time*) as when they answered questions about the frequency of lethal events (see Table 4). Additional studies by Fischhoff et. al. tested people's faith in their odds assessments by asking if they would stake money on them by playing the bet described below.

Instructions for "Trivia Question Hustling"

The experiment is over. You have just earned $2.50, which you will be able to collect soon. But before you take the money and leave, I'd like you to consider whether you would be willing to play a certain game in order to possibly increase your earnings. The rules of the game are as follows:

1. Look at your answer sheet. Find the questions where you estimated the odds of your being correct as 50:1 or greater than 50:1. How many such questions were there? ——— (write number).

2. I'll give you the correct answers to these "50:1 or greater" questions. We'll count how many times your answers to these questions were wrong. Since a wrong answer in the face of such high certainty would be surprising, we'll call these wrong answers "your surprises."

3. I have a bag of poker chips in front of me. There are 100 white chips and 2 red chips in the bag. If I reach in and randomly select a chip, the odds that I will select a white chip are 100:2 or 50:1, just like the odds that your "50:1" answers are correct.

4. For every "50:1 or greater" answer you gave, I'll draw a chip out of the bag. (If you wish, you can draw the chips for me.) I'll put the chip back in the bag before I draw again, so the odds won't change. The probability of my drawing a red chip is 1/51. Since drawing a red chip is unlikely, every red chip I draw can be considered "my surprise."

5. Every time you are surprised by a wrong answer to a "50:1 or greater" question, you pay me $1 (raised to $2.50 in some conditions). Every time I am surprised by drawing a red chip, I'll pay you $1.

6. If you are well calibrated, this game is advantageous to you. This is because I expect to lose $1 about once out of every 51 times I draw a chip, on the average. But since your odds are sometimes higher than 50:1, you expect to lose less often than that.

7. Would you play this game?

This bet is advantageous for perfectly calibrated and underconfident participants and disadvantageous to overconfident ones. Most participants in our study were eager to play the game. Because their confidence was unjustified, they suffered sizable monetary losses (which we returned to them after the experiment was over).

Although the psychological basis for unwarranted certainty is complex, a key element seems to be people's lack of awareness that their knowledge is based on assumptions that are often quite tenuous. For example, 30% of the respondents in Experiment 1 gave odds greater than 50:1 to the incorrect assertion that homicides are more frequent than suicides. These individuals may have been misled by the greater ease of recalling

Table 5. *Experts' insensitivity to omissions from the car-won't-start fault tree*

| Group | *n* | M proportion of starting failures by type | | | | | | |
		Battery	Starting system	Fuel system	Ignition system	Engine	Mischief	Other
Unpruned tree, ordinary subjects	93	.264	.195	.193	.144	.076	.051	.078
Unpruned tree, experts	13	.410	.108	.096	.248	.051	.025	.060
Pruned tree 1, experts	16	.483	—	.229	—	.073	—	.215[a]

[a]Should be .441.
Source: Fischhoff, Slovic, and Lichtenstein (1978).

instances of homicide, failing to appreciate that memorability is an imperfect basis for such an inference.

Hyperprecision. Overconfidence manifests itself in other ways as well. A typical task in estimating uncertain quantities such as failure rates is to set upper and lower bounds so that there is a 98% chance that the true value lies between them. Experiments with diverse groups of people making many different kinds of judgments have shown that, rather than 2% of true values falling outside the 98% confidence bounds, 20–50% do so (Chaps. 21 and 22). Thus people think that they can estimate such values with much greater precision than is actually the case. Tversky and Kahneman (1974, 1) have attributed such hyperprecision to reliance on the anchoring and adjustment heuristic.

Overconfident experts. Unfortunately, experts, once they are forced to go beyond their data and rely on judgment, may be as prone to overconfidence as laypeople. Fischhoff, Slovic, and Lichtenstein (1978) repeated their fault-tree study (Figure 3) with professional automobile mechanics (averaging about 15 years of experience) and found these experts to be almost as insensitive as laypersons to deletions from the tree (see Table 5). Hynes and Vanmarcke (1976) asked seven "internationally known" geotechnical engineers to predict the height of an embankment that would cause a clay foundation to fail and to specify confidence bounds around this estimate that were wide enough to have a 50% chance of enclosing the true failure height. None of the bounds specified by these individuals actually did enclose the true failure height. Figure 4 shows these results.

The multimillion dollar Reactor Safety Study (U.S. Nuclear Regulatory Commission, 1975), in assessing the probability of a core melt in a nuclear reactor, used the very procedure for setting confidence bounds that was

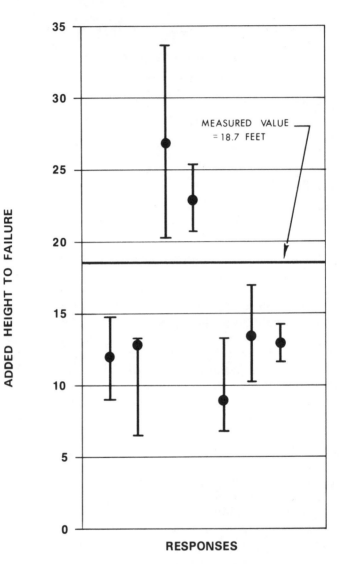

Figure 4. An example of overconfidence in expert judgment, as represented by the failure of error bars to contain the true value. The data represent estimates by seven "internationally known" geotechnical engineers of the height at which an embankment would fail. (*Source:* Hynes & Vanmarcke, 1976.)

shown in Chapters 21 and 22 to produce a high degree of overconfidence. In fact, the "Lewis Committee" concluded its review of the Reactor Safety Study by noting that despite the great advances made in that study "we are certain that the error bands are understated. We cannot say by how much. Reasons for this include an inadequate data base, a poor statistical treatment, [and] an inconsistent propagation of uncertainties throughout the calculation" (U.S. Nuclear Regulatory Commission, 1978, p. vi).

Further anecdotal evidence of overconfidence may be found in many other technical risk assessments (Fischhoff, 1977a). Some common ways in which experts may overlook or misjudge pathways to disaster are shown in the list below.

> *Failure to consider the ways in which human errors can affect technological systems.* Example: Because of inadequate training and control room design, operators at Three Mile Island repeatedly misdiagnosed the problems of the reactor and took inappropriate actions (Sheridan, 1980; President's Commission, 1979).
>
> *Overconfidence in current scientific knowledge.* Example: Use of DDT came into widespread and uncontrolled use before scientists had even considered the possibility of the side effects that today make it look like a mixed and irreversible blessing (Dunlap, 1978).
>
> *Failure to appreciate how technological systems function as a whole.* Example: The DC-10 failed in several early flights because its designers had not realized that decompression of the cargo compartment would destroy vital control systems (Hohenemser, 1975).
>
> *Slowness in detecting chronic, cumulative effects.* Example: Although accidents to coal miners have long been recognized as one cost of operating fossil-fueled plants, the effects of acid rains on ecosystems were slow to be discovered.
>
> *Failure to anticipate human response to safety measures.* Example: The partial protection afforded by dams and levees gives people a false sense of security and promotes development of the flood plain. Thus, although floods are rarer, damage per flood is so much greater that the average yearly dollar loss is larger than before the dams were built (Burton, Kates, & White, 1978).
>
> *Failure to anticipate "common-mode failures," which simultaneously afflict systems that are designed to be independent.* Example: Because electrical cables controlling the multiple safety systems of the reactor at Browns Ferry, Alabama, were not spatially separated, all five emergency core cooling systems were damaged by a single fire (U.S. House of Representatives, 1975; Jennergren & Keeney, in press).

The 1976 collapse of the Teton Dam provides another tragic example of expert overconfidence. The Committee on Government Operations attributed this disaster to the unwarranted confidence of engineers who were absolutely certain they had solved the many serious problems that arose during construction (Committee on Government Operations, 1976). Fail-

ure probabilities are typically not even calculated for new dams even
though about 1 in 300 fails when the reservoir is first filled.

Informing people about risks

Thinking clearly about risk is difficult. Unfortunately, it is also necessary.
Radiation hazards, medical side effects, occupational diseases, food
contaminants, toxic chemicals, and mechanical malfunctions increasingly
fill our newspapers and our thoughts. Since the management of these
hazards is vital to the well-being of individuals and society, people are
presently asserting their right to play an active role in the decision-
making process. As a result, the promoters and regulators of hazardous
enterprises face growing pressure to inform people about the risks they
face (see Figure 5). For example, in recent years:

> The Food and Drug Administration mandated patient information
> inserts for an increased number of prescription drugs.
> The Department of Housing and Urban Development began to
> require the sellers of homes built before 1950 to inform buyers
> about the presence of lead-based paints.
> The proposed federal products liability law placed increased
> weight on adequately informing consumers and workers about
> risks they are likely to encounter.
> The White House directed the Secretary of Health, Education, and
> Welfare to develop a public information program on the health
> effects of radiation exposure.

Despite these good intentions, creating effective informational
programs may be quite difficult. Doing an adequate job means finding
cogent ways of presenting complex, technical material that is often
clouded by uncertainty. Not only is the allotted time sometimes very
limited, but messages must confront the listeners' preconceptions (and
perhaps misconceptions) about the hazard in question and its consequences. For example, in some situations, misleading personal experiences
may promote a false sense of security, whereas in other circumstances,
mere discussion of possible adverse consequences may enhance their
apparent threat. Moreover, as Ross and Anderson (Chap. 9) have demonstrated, people's beliefs often change slowly and show extraordinary
persistence in the face of contrary evidence. What follows is a brief
overview of some additional challenges that information programs must
confront.

Presentation format is important

The precise manner in which risks are expressed can have a major impact
on perceptions and behavior. For example, an action increasing one's

Figure 5. Drawing by S. Harris; © 1979 *The New Yorker Magazine*.

annual chances of death from 1 in 10,000 to 1.3 in 10,000 would probably be seen as much more risky if it were described, instead, as producing a 30% increase in annual mortality risk. A sampling of format effects from the literature is presented below.

Fault trees. The designers of a fault tree like that in Figure 3 must make numerous discretionary decisions regarding how to organize and present the various sources of trouble. One such decision that apparently makes little difference is how much detail to offer; Fischhoff, Slovic, and Lichtenstein (1978) found similar perceptions with varying levels of detail. Merely mentioning a branch allowed people to estimate accurately how troublesome that branch would look when fully detailed. However, fusing branches (e.g., combining starting system and ignition system into one broader category) or splitting branches (e.g., separating ignition system into ignition system [coil faulty and spark plugs defective, see Figure 3] and distribution system [distributor faulty and wiring defective] did make a difference. A given set of problems was judged to account for about 30% more failures when it was presented as two branches than when it was presented as one.

Seat belts. A second demonstration of the importance of presentation format comes from a study of attitudes toward the use of automobile seat belts (Slovic, Fischhoff, & Lichtenstein, 1978). Drawing upon previous research demonstrating the critical importance of probability of harm in triggering protective action (Slovic, Fischhoff, Lichtenstein, Corrigan, & Combs, 1977), Slovic, Fischhoff, and Lichtenstein argued that people's reluctance to wear seat belts voluntarily might be due to the extremely small probability of incurring a fatal accident on a single automobile trip. Since a fatal accident occurs only about once in every 3.5 million person trips and a disabling injury only once in every 100,000 person trips, refusing to buckle one's seat belt may seem quite reasonable. It looks less reasonable, however, if one adopts a multiple-trip perspective and considers the substantial probability of an accident on some trip. Over 50 years of driving (about 40,000 trips), the probability of being killed rises to .01 and the probability of experiencing at least one disabling injury is .33. In a pilot study, Slovic, Fischhoff, and Lichtenstein showed that people asked to consider this lifetime perspective responded more favorably toward seat belts (and air bags) than did people asked to consider a trip-by-trip perspective. Whether the favorable attitudes toward seat belts induced by a lengthened time perspective would be maintained and translated into behavior remains to be seen.

Pseudocertainty. According to "prospect theory" (Kahneman & Tversky, 1979b), outcomes that are merely probable are underweighted in comparison with outcomes that are obtained with certainty. As a result, any protective action that reduces the probability of harm from, say, .01 to zero, will be valued more highly than an action reducing the probability of the same harm from .02 to .01.

Tversky and Kahneman (1981) note that mental representations of protective actions may be easily manipulated so as to vary the apparent certainty with which they prevent harm. For example, an insurance policy that covers fire but not flood could be presented either as full protection against the specific risk of fire or as a reduction in the overall probability of property loss. Prospect theory predicts that the policy will appear more attractive in the former perspective (labeled "pseudocertainty"), in which it offers unconditional protection against a restricted set of problems.

We have tested this conjecture in the context of one particular kind of protection, vaccination. Two forms of a "vaccination questionnaire" were created. Form I (probabilistic protection) described a disease expected to afflict 20% of the population and asked people whether they would volunteer to receive a vaccine that protects half of the people receiving it. According to Form II (pseudocertainty), there were two mutually exclusive and equiprobable strains of the disease, each likely to afflict 10% of the population; the vaccination was said to give complete protection against one strain and no protection against the other. The participants in this study were recruited by an advertisement in the University of Oregon student newspaper. Half received Form I; the other half received Form II. After reading the description, they rated the likelihood that they would get vaccinated in such a situation, using a scale ranging from 1 ("almost certainly would not get vaccinated") to 7 ("almost certainly would get vaccinated").

Although both forms indicated that vaccination reduced one's overall risk from 20% to 10%, we expected that vaccination would appear more attractive to those who received Form II (pseudocertainty) than to those who received Form I (probabilistic protection). The results confirmed this prediction: 57% of those who received From II indicated they would get vaccinated compared with 40% of those who received Form I.

The pseudocertainty effect highlights the contrast between the reduction and the elimination of risk. As Tversky and Kahneman have indicated, this distinction is difficult to justify on any normative grounds. Moreover, manipulations of certainty would seem to have important implications for the design and description of other forms of protection (e.g., medical treatments, insurance, flood- and earthquake-proofing activities).

Anchoring. One of the most general of presentation artifacts is the tendency of judgments to be anchored on initially presented values (Poulton, 1968; Tversky & Kahneman, 1974, 1). In another condition of the experiment presented in Figure 2, Lichtenstein et al. (1978) asked a second group of people to estimate the frequency of death in the United States from each of the 40 different causes. However, instead of being told that about 50,000 people die annually in motor vehicle accidents, these individuals were told about the 1,000 annual deaths from electrocution. Although both reports were accurate, provision of a smaller number reduced respondents' estimates of most frequencies. Such anchoring on the original number led the estimates of the two groups to differ by as much as a factor of 5 in some cases.

Fischhoff and MacGregor (1980) asked people to judge the lethality of various potential causes of death using one of four formally equivalent formats (e.g., For each afflicted person who dies, how many survive? For each 100,000 people afflicted, how many will die?). Table 6 expresses their judgments in a common format and reveals even more dramatic effects of question phrasing on expressed risk perceptions. For example, when

Table 6. *Lethality judgments with different response modes, geometric means*

Malady	Death rate per 100,000 afflicted				
	Estimated lethality rate	Estimated number that died	Estimated survival rate	Estimated number that sur-vived	Actual lethality rate
Influenza	393	6	26	511	1
Mumps	44	114	19	4	12
Asthma	155	12	14	599	33
Venereal disease	91	63	8	111	50
High blood pressure	535	89	17	538	76
Bronchitis	162	19	43	2,111	85
Pregnancy	67	24	13	787	250
Diabetes	487	101	52	5,666	800
Tuberculosis	852	1,783	188	8,520	1,535
Automobile accidents	6,195	3,272	31	6,813	2,500
Strokes	11,011	4,648	181	24,758	11,765
Heart attacks	13,011	3,666	131	27,477	16,250
Cancer	10,889	10,475	160	21,749	37,500

Note: The four experimental groups were given the following instructions:
   (a) Estimate lethality rate: For each 100,000 people afflicted, how many die?
   (b) Estimate number died: X people were afflicted, how many died?
   (c) Estimate survival rate: For each person who died, how many were afflicted but survived?
   (d) Estimate number survived: Y people died, how many were afflicted but did not die?
   Responses to questions (b), (c), and (d) were converted to deaths per 100,000 afflicted to facilitate comparisons.
Source: Fischhoff & MacGregor, 1980.

people estimated the lethality rate for influenza directly (column 1), their mean response was 393 deaths per 100,000 cases. When told that 80,000,000 people catch influenza in a normal year and asked to estimate the number who die (column 2), respondents' mean response was 4,800, representing a death rate of only 6 per 100,000 cases. This slight change in the question changed the estimated rate by a factor of more than 60. Similar discrepancies occurred with other questions and other hazards.

Other effects. Numerous other format effects have been documented in the literature on risk-taking behavior. For example, people have been found to evaluate gambles much differently when they consider them in pairs than when they judge them singly (Grether & Plott, 1979; Lichtenstein & Slovic, 1971; 1973). Fischhoff, Slovic, and Lichtenstein (1980), Hershey and Schoemaker (1980), and Schoemaker and Kunreuther (1979) have noted that decisions about whether to buy insurance are frequently reversed when the problem is portrayed as a choice between facing a gamble or accepting a loss of a smaller amount of money. The same risk options, described in terms of lives saved, may be evaluated much differently when framed in terms of lives lost (Tversky & Kahneman, 1981). Additional format and context effects can be found in Fischhoff, Slovic, and Lichtenstein (1980), Kahneman and Tversky (1979b), Slovic, Fischhoff, and Lichtenstein (in press-b), and Tversky and Kahneman (1981).

That subtle differences in how risks are presented can have marked effects on how they are perceived suggests that those responsible for information programs have considerable ability to manipulate perceptions. Moreover, since these effects are not widely known, people may inadvertently be manipulating their own perceptions by casual decisions they make about how to organize their knowledge.

Cross-hazard comparisons may be misleading

One of the most common approaches for deepening people's perspectives is to present quantified risk estimates for a variety of hazards. Presumably, the sophistication gleaned from examining such data will be useful for personal and societal decision making. Wilson (1979) observed that we should "try to measure our risks quantitatively.... Then we could compare risks and decide which to accept or reject" (p. 43). Lord Rothschild (1979) added, "There is no point in getting into a panic about the risks of life until you have compared the risks which worry you with those that don't, but perhaps should."

Typically, such exhortations are followed by elaborate tables and even "catalogs of risks" in which diverse indices of death or disability are displayed for a broad spectrum of life's hazards. Thus, Sowby (1965) provided extensive data on risks per hour of exposure, showing, for example, that an hour of riding a motorcycle is as risky as an hour of being 75 years old. Wilson (1979) developed a table of activities (e.g., flying 1,000 miles by jet, spending 3 hours in a coal mine), each of which is estimated to increase one's annual chance of death by 1 in 1 million. Wilson claimed that "these comparisons help me evaluate risks and I imagine that they may help others to do so, as well. But the most important use of these comparisons must be to help the decisions we make, as a nation, to improve our health and reduce our accident rate" (p. 45). Similarly, Cohen and Lee (1979) ranked many hazards in terms of their expected reduction in life expectancy on the assumption that "to some approximation, the ordering (in this table) should be society's order of priorities. However, we see several very major problems that have received very little attention . . . whereas some of the items near the bottom of the list, especially those involving radiation, receive a great deal of attention" (p. 720).

Properly speaking, comparing hazards is not a decision-making proce-dure. It does not require any particular conclusion to be drawn, say, from the contrast between the risks of motorcycling and advanced age (Fisch-hoff, Lichtenstein, Slovic, Derby, & Keeney, 1981). Moreover, even as aids to intuition, cross-hazards comparisons have a number of inherent limita-tions. For example, although some people feel enlightened upon learning that a single takeoff or landing in a commercial airliner reduces one's life expectancy by an average of 15 minutes, others find themselves completely bewildered by such information. On landing, one will either die prematurely (almost certainly by more than 15 minutes) or one will not. For many people, averages do not adequately capture the essence of such risks. Indeed, McNeil, Weichselbaum, and Pauker (1978) found that patients facing the prospect of surgery for lung cancer were as concerned with the possibility of imminent death during the operation as with its contribution to their life expectancy.

A further limitation is that summary statistics may mask important characteristics of risk. Where there is uncertainty or disagreement about the facts, presentation of point estimates may inspire undue confidence. Since people are particularly concerned about the potential for cata-strophic accidents (Slovic, Fischhoff, & Lichtenstein, 1980), some indica-tion of the probability and magnitude of extreme losses is needed. Other characteristics that affect people's attitude toward hazards, but are neglected in statistical summaries, are voluntariness, controllability, famil-iarity, immediacy of consequences, threat to future generations, the ease of reducing the risk and the degree to which benefits are distributed equita-bly to those who bear the risk (Slovic, Fischhoff, & Lichtenstein, in press-a). Although some faults, such as the omission of uncertainty bands, are easy to correct, determining how to weight catastrophic potential, equity, and other important characteristics, will require a serious research effort.

Conclusions

Informing people, whether by warning labels, package inserts, or exten-sive media programs, is but part of the larger problem of helping people cope with the risks and uncertainties of modern life. We believe that some of the responsibility lies with our schools. Public school curricula should include material designed to teach people that the world in which they live is probabilistic, not deterministic, and to help them learn judgment and decision strategies for dealing with that world (Beyth-Marom & Dekel, in press). These strategies are as necessary for navigating in a world of uncertain information as geometry and trigonometry are to navigating among physical objects.

Nuclear power: A case study of risk perception

Nowhere are issues of perceived risk more salient or the stakes higher than in the controversy over nuclear power. This section examines the controversy in light of the findings just discussed.

The general problem

Even before the accident at Three Mile Island, the nuclear industry was foundering on the shoals of adverse public opinion. A sizable and tenacious opposition movement had been responsible for costly delays in the licensing and construction of new power plants in the United States and for political turmoil in several European nations.

The errant reactor at Three Mile Island stimulated a predictable, immediate rise in antinuclear fervor. Any attempt to plan the role of nuclear power in the nation's energy future must consider the determinants of this opposition and anticipate its future course. One clue lies in recent research showing that the images of potential nuclear disasters that have been formed in the minds of the antinuclear public are remarkably different from the assessments put forth by many technical experts. We shall describe these images and speculate on their origins, permanence, and implications.

Basic perceptions

Questionnaire studies of people opposed to nuclear power show that they judge its benefits as quite low and its risks as unacceptably great (Fischhoff, Slovic, Lichtenstein, Read, & Combs, 1978). On the benefit side, these individuals do not see nuclear power as a vital link in meeting basic energy needs (Pokorny, 1977); rather, many view it as a supplement to other sources of energy that are themselves adequate (or could be made adequate by conservation). On the risk side, nuclear power evokes greater feelings of dread than almost any other technological activity (Fischhoff et al., 1978). Some have attributed this reaction to fear of radiation's invisible and irreversible contamination, threatening cancer and genetic damage. However, use of diagnostic X rays, a radiation technology that incurs similar risks, is not similarly dreaded. To the contrary, its risks are often underestimated (Slovic, Lichtenstein, & Fischhoff, 1979). The association of nuclear power with nuclear weaponry may account for these different perceptions. As a result of its violent origins, nuclear power is regarded as a technology whose risks are uncontrollable, lethal, and potentially catastrophic, characteristics that are not associated with the use of diagnostic X rays.

When people opposed to nuclear power describe their mental images of a nuclear accident and its consequences, they reveal the expectation that a serious reactor accident is likely within their lifetime and could result in hundreds of thousands, even millions, of deaths (Slovic, Fischhoff, & Lichtenstein, 1979; Slovic, Lichtenstein, & Fischhoff, 1979). Such an accident is also expected to cause irreparable environmental damage over a vast geographic area. These expectations contrast dramatically with the nuclear industry's view that multiple safety systems will limit the damage in the extremely unlikely event of a major accident.

One inevitable consequence of this "perception gap" is uncertainty and distrust on the part of a public suspecting that the risks are much greater than the experts' assessments (Kasper, 1979; Starr & Whipple, 1980). The experts, in turn, question the rationality of the public and decry the "emotionalism" stymying technological progress. Bitter and sometimes violent confrontations result.

Recognition of this perception gap has led some technical experts to claim that the public must be "educated" about the "real" risks from nuclear power. One public opinion analyst (Pokorny, 1977) put the matter as follows:

The biggest problem hindering a sophisticated judgment on this question is basic lack of knowledge and facts. Within this current attitudinal milieu, scare stories, confusion, and irrationality often triumph. Only through careful education of facts and knowledge can the people know what the real choices are. . . . (p. 12)

Our own view is that attempts designed to reduce the perception gap face major obstacles. This conclusion is based on two key aspects of the problem, one technical and one psychological.

Technical obstacles

The technical reality is that there are few "cut-and-dried facts" regarding the probabilities of serious reactor mishaps. The technology is so new and the probabilities in question are so small that accurate risk estimates cannot be based on empirical observation. Instead, such assessments must be derived from complex mathematical models and subjective judgments.

The difficulty of performing risk assessments has led many critics to question their validity (Bryan, 1974; Fischhoff, 1977a; Primack, 1975). One major concern is that important initiating events or pathways to failure may be omitted, causing risks to be underestimated. Another problem in assessing the reliability of reactor designs is the difficulty of taking proper account of "common-mode failures," in which ostensibly independent systems designed to back up one another fail because of the same unanticipated common cause. Nuclear critic John Holdren's skepticism regarding the defensibility of assessments of rare catastrophes summarizes the technical problem concisely:

The expert community is divided about the conceivable realism of probability estimates in the range of one in ten thousand to one in one billion per reactor year. I am among those who believe it to be impossible *in principle* to support numbers as small as these with convincing theoretical arguments. . . . The reason I hold this view is straightforward: nuclear power systems are so complex that the probability the safety analysis contains serious errors . . . is so big as to render meaningless the tiny computed probability of accident (Holdren, 1976, p. 21).

Psychological obstacles

Public fears of nuclear power should not be viewed as irrational. In part, they are fed by the realization that the facts are in dispute and that experts have been wrong in the past, as when they irradiated enlarged tonsils or permitted people to witness A-bomb tests at close range. What one may question is the extent to which people's fundamental ways of thinking (such as reliance on the availability heuristic) lead them to distorted views. Certainly the risks from nuclear power would seem to be a prime candidate for availability bias because of the extensive media coverage they receive and their association with the vivid, imaginable dangers of nuclear war.

As mentioned earlier, the availability heuristic implies that any discussion of nuclear accidents may increase their imaginability and hence their perceived risk. Consider an engineer arguing the safety of disposing of nuclear wastes in a salt bed by pointing out the improbability of the various ways radioactivity could be accidentally released (see Figure 1). Rather than reassuring the audience, the presentation might lead them to think, "I didn't realize there were that many things that could go wrong." In this way, reliance on memorability and imaginability may blur the distinction between what is remotely possible and what is probable. As one nuclear proponent lamented, "When laymen discuss what *might* happen, they sometimes don't even bother to include the 'might' " (B. L. Cohen, 1974, p. 36). Another analyst has elaborated a similar theme in the misinterpretation of "worst case" scenarios:

It often has made little difference how bizarre or improbable the assumption in such an analysis was, since one had only to show that some undesirable effect could occur at a probability level greater than zero. Opponents of a proposed operation could destroy it simply by exercising their imaginations to dream up a set of conditions which, although they might admittedly be extremely improbable, could lead to some undesirable results. With such attitudes prevalent, planning a given nuclear operation becomes . . . perilous. . . . (J. J. Cohen, 1972, p. 55)

Conclusion

Although the above discussion designated some possible sources of the perception gap between pronuclear and antinuclear individuals, it does not point unambiguously to one side or the other as having the most accurate appraisal of the overall risks from nuclear power. The effects of memorability and imaginability are capable both of enhancing public fears and obscuring experts' awareness of ways that a system could fail. Insofar as the actual risks may never be known with great precision and new information tends to be interpreted in a manner consistent with one's prior beliefs, the perception gap may be with us for a long time. Thus, for some people, Three Mile Island "proved" the possibility of a catastrophic meltdown, whereas for others, it confirmed their faith in the reliability of the multiple safety and containment systems.

Who shall decide?

The research described in this chapter demonstrates that judgment of risks is fallible. It also shows that the degree of fallibility is often surprisingly great and that faulty estimates may be held with great confidence. Since even well-informed laypeople have difficulty judging risks accurately, it is tempting to conclude that the public should be removed from society's risk assessment and decision-making processes. Such action would seem to be misguided on several counts. First, close examination shows that people do perceive some things quite well, although their perspective may often be quite different from that of technical experts. In situations where misunderstanding is rampant, people's errors can often be traced to biased experiences, which education may be able to counter. In some cases, people's strong fears and resistance to experts' reassurances can be traced to their sensitivity to the potential for catastrophic accidents, to their awareness of expert disagreement about the probability and magnitude of such accidents, and to their knowledge of serious mistakes made by experts in the past. Even in difficult cases, such as the conflict over nuclear power, an atmosphere of trust and a recognition that both experts and lay persons have something to contribute, may permit some exchange of information and deepening of perspectives.

Moreover, in many if not most cases, effective hazard management requires the cooperation of a large body of laypeople. These people must agree to do without some things and accept substitutes for others; they must vote sensibly on ballot measures and for legislators who will serve them as surrogate hazard managers; they must obey safety rules and use the legal system responsibly. Even if the experts were much better judges of risk than laypeople, giving experts an exclusive franchise for hazard management would mean substituting short-term efficiency for the long-term effort needed to create an informed citizenry.

For non-experts, the findings we have discussed pose an important series of challenges: to be better informed, to rely less on unexamined or unsupported judgments, to be aware of the factors that might bias risk judgments, and to be more open to new evidence; in short, to realize the potential of being educable.

For experts and policy makers, these findings pose what may be a more difficult challenge: to recognize and admit one's own cognitive limitations, to attempt to educate without propagandizing, to acknowledge the legitimacy of public concerns, and somehow to develop ways in which these concerns can find expression in societal decisions without, in the process, creating more heat than light.

Part X

Postscript

34. On the study of statistical intuitions

Daniel Kahneman and Amos Tversky

Much of the recent literature on judgment and inductive reasoning has been concerned with errors, biases, and fallacies in a variety of mental tasks (see, e.g., Einhorn & Hogarth, 1981; Hammond, McClelland, & Mumpower, 1980; Nisbett & Ross, 1980; Shweder, 1980; Slovic, Fischhoff, & Lichtenstein, 1977; Tversky & Kahneman, 1974, 1). The emphasis on the study of errors is characteristic of research in human judgment, but it is not unique to this domain: We use illusions to understand the principles of normal perception and we learn about memory by studying forgetting. Errors of reasoning, however, are unique among cognitive failures in two significant respects: They are somewhat embarrassing and they appear avoidable. We are not troubled by our susceptibility to the vertical–horizontal illusion or by our inability to remember a list of more than eight digits. In contrast, errors of reasoning are often disconcerting – either because the solution that we failed to find appears quite obvious in retrospect or because the error that we made remains attractive although we know it to be an error. Many current studies of judgment are concerned with problems that have one or the other of these characteristics.

The presence of an error of judgment is demonstrated by comparing people's responses either with an established fact (e.g., that the two lines are equal in length) or with an accepted rule of arithmetic, logic, or statistics. However, not every response that appears to contradict an established fact or an accepted rule is a judgmental error. The contradiction could also arise from the subject's misunderstanding of the question or from the investigator's misinterpretation of the answer. The description of a particular response as an error of judgment therefore involves assumptions about the communication between the experimenter and the subject. (We shall return to this issue later in the chapter.) The student of judgment should avoid overly strict interpretations, which treat reasonable answers as errors, as well as overly charitable interpretations, which attempt to rationalize every response.

Although errors of judgment are but a method by which some cognitive processes are studied, the method has become a significant part of the message. The accumulation of demonstrations in which intelligent people violate elementary rules of logic or statistics has raised doubts about the descriptive adequacy of rational models of judgment and decision making. In the two decades following World War II, several descriptive treatments of actual behavior were based on normative models: subjective expected utility theory in analyses of risky choice, the Bayesian calculus in investigations of changes of belief, and signal-detection theory in studies of psychophysical tasks. The theoretical analyses of these situations, and to a much lesser degree the experimental results, suggested an image of people as efficient, nearly optimal decision makers. On this background, observations of elementary violations of logical or statistical reasoning appeared surprising, and the surprise may have encouraged a view of the human intellect that some authors have criticized as unfairly negative (L. J. Cohen, 1979, 1981; W. Edwards, 1975; Einhorn & Hogarth, 1981).

There are three related reasons for the focus on systematic errors and inferential biases in the study of reasoning. First, they expose some of our intellectual limitations and suggest ways of improving the quality of our thinking. Second, errors and biases often reveal the psychological processes and the heuristic procedures that govern judgment and inference. Third, mistakes and fallacies help the mapping of human intuitions by indicating which principles of statistics or logic are non-intuitive or counter-intuitive.

The terms *intuition* and *intuitive* are used in three different senses. First, a judgment is called intuitive if it is reached by an informal and unstructured mode of reasoning, without the use of analytic methods or deliberate calculation. For example, most psychologists follow an intuitive procedure in deciding the size of their samples but adopt analytic procedures to test the statistical significance of their results. Second, a formal rule or a fact of nature is called intuitive if it is compatible with our lay model of the world. Thus, it is intuitively obvious that the probability of winning a lottery prize decreases with the number of tickets, but it is counter-intuitive that there is a better than even chance that a group of 23 people will include a pair of individuals with the same birthday. Third, a rule or a procedure is said to be part of our repertoire of intuitions when we apply the rule or follow the procedure in our normal conduct. The rules of grammar, for example, are part of the intuitions of a native speaker, and some (though not all) of the rules of plane geometry are incorporated into our spatial reasoning.

The present chapter addresses several methodological and conceptual problems that arise in attempts to map people's intuitions about chance and uncertainty. We begin by discussing different tests of statistical intuitions; we then turn to a critique of the question-answering paradigm in judgment research; and we conclude with a discussion of the non-intuitive character of some statistical laws.

Tests of statistical intuitions

Errors and biases in judgment under uncertainty are the major source of data for the mapping of the boundaries of people's statistical intuitions. In this context it is instructive to distinguish between errors of application and errors of comprehension. A failure in a particular problem is called an error of application if there is evidence that people know and accept a rule that they did not apply. A failure is called an error of comprehension if people do not recognize the validity of the rule that they violated.

An error of application is most convincingly demonstrated when a person, spontaneously or with minimal prompting, clutches his head and exclaims: "How could I have missed that?" Although many readers will recognize this experience, such displays of emotions cannot be counted on, and other procedures must be developed to demonstrate that people understand a rule that they have violated.

The understanding of a rule can be tested by (1) eliciting from subjects or (2) asking them to endorse a statement of (1) a general rule or (2) an argument for or against a particular conclusion. The combination of these features yields four procedures, which we shall now illustrate and discuss.

We begin with an informal example in which understanding of a rule is confirmed by the acceptance or endorsement of an argument. One of us has presented the following question to many squash players.

As you know, a game of squash can be played either to 9 or to 15 points. Holding all other rules of the game constant, if A is a better player than B, which scoring system will give A a better chance of winning?

Although all our informants had some knowledge of statistics, most of them said that the scoring system should not make any difference. They were then asked to consider the argument that the better player should prefer the longer game, because an atypical outcome is less likely to occur in a large sample than in a small one. With very few exceptions, the respondents immediately accepted the argument and admitted that their initial response had been a mistake. Evidently, our informants had some appreciation of the effect of sample size on sampling errors, but they failed to code the length of a squash game as an instance of sample size. The fact that the correct conclusion becomes compelling as soon as this connection is made indicates that the initial response was an error of application, not of comprehension.

A more systematic attempt to diagnose the nature of an error was made in a study of a phenomenon labeled the conjunction effect (see Chap. 6). Perhaps the most elementary principle of probability theory is the conjunction rule, which states that the probability of a conjunction (A & B) cannot exceed either the probability of A or the probability of B. As the following example shows, however, it is possible to construct tests in which most judges – even highly sophisticated ones – state that a conjunction of events is more probable than one of its components.

To induce the conjunction effect, we presented subjects with personality sketches of the type illustrated below:

Linda is 31 years old, single, outspoken, and very bright. She majored in philosophy. As a student, she was deeply concerned with issues of discrimination and social justice, and also participated in anti-nuclear demonstrations.

In one version of the problem, respondents were asked which of two statements about Linda was more probable: (A) Linda is a bank teller; (B) Linda is a bank teller who is active in the feminist movement. In a large sample of statistically naive undergraduates, 86% judged the second statement to be more probable. In a sample of psychology graduate students, only 50% committed this error. However, the difference between statistically naive and sophisticated respondents vanished when the two critical items were embedded in a list of eight comparable statements about Linda. Over 80% of both groups exhibited the conjunction effect. Similar results were obtained in a between-subjects design, in which the critical categories were compared indirectly (see Chap. 6).

Tests of rule-endorsement and argument-endorsement were used in an effort to determine whether people understand and accept the conjunction rule. First, we presented a group of statistically naive college students with several rule-like statements, which they were to classify as true or false. The statement: "The probability of X is always greater than the probability of X and Y" was endorsed by 81% of the respondents. In comparison, only 6% endorsed "If A is more probable than B, then they cannot both occur." These results indicate some understanding of the conjunction rule, although the endorsement is not unanimous, perhaps because of the abstract and unfamiliar formulation.

An argument-endorsement procedure was also employed, in which respondents were given the description of Linda, followed by the statements (A) and (B) and were asked to check which of the following arguments they considered correct:

(i) A is more probable than B because the probability that Linda is *both* a bank teller and an active feminist must be smaller than the probability that she is a bank teller.

(ii) B is more probable than A because Linda resembles a bank teller who is active in the feminist movement more than she resembles a bank teller.

Argument (i) favoring the conjunction rule was endorsed by 83% of the psychology graduate students but only by 43% of the statistically naive undergraduates. Extensive discussions with respondents confirmed this pattern. Statistically sophisticated respondents immediately recognized the validity of the conjunction rule. Naive respondents, on the other hand, were much less impressed by normative arguments, and many remained committed to their initial responses that were inconsistent with the conjunction rule.

Much to our surprise, naive subjects did not have a solid grasp of the conjunction rule; they tended to endorse it in the abstract but not when it conflicted with a strong impression of representativeness. On the other hand, statistically trained subjects recognized the validity of the rule, and were able to apply it in an especially transparent problem. Statistical sophistication, however, did not prevent the conjunction effect in less transparent versions of the same problem. In terms of the present treatment, the conjunction effect appears to be an error of application, at least for the more sophisticated subjects. For further discussion of this issue see Chapter 6.

In an attempt to describe the statistical intuitions of people at various levels of sophistication, Nisbett, Krantz, Jepson, and Fong (Chap. 32, this volume) used an elicitation procedure, in which respondents were required to evaluate and justify certain conclusions and inferences attributed to characters in brief stories. The investigators observed large individual differences in the comprehension of basic statistical principles, which were highly correlated with the level of statistical training. Naturally, statistical intuitions vary with intelligence, experience, and education. As in other forms of knowledge, what is intuitive for the expert is often non-intuitive for the novice (see e.g., Larkin, McDermott, Simon, & Simon, 1980). Nevertheless, some statistical results (e.g., the matching birthdays or the change of lead in a coin-tossing game) remain counterintuitive even for students of probability theory (Feller, 1968, p. 85). Furthermore, there is some evidence that errors (e.g., the gambler's fallacy) that are commonly committed by naive respondents can also be elicited from statistically sophisticated ones, with problems of greater subtlety (Tversky & Kahneman, 1971, 2).

The elicitation method was also used (Evans & Wason, 1976; Wason & Evans, 1975) in studies of logical intuitions in the well-known four-card problem (Wason, 1966). In the standard version of this problem, the experimenter displays four cards showing A, T, 4, and 7, and asks subjects to identify the cards that should be turned over to test the rule "If a card has a vowel on one side, it has an even number on the other." The correct response is that the cards showing A and 7 should be examined, because the observation of an odd number on the first card or a vowel on the second would refute the rule. In a striking failure of logical reasoning, most subjects elect to look at the hidden side of the cards showing A and 4. Wason and Evans investigated different versions of this problem, and required their subjects to give reasons or arguments for their decisions of whether or not to look at the hidden side of each of the four cards. The investigators concluded that the arguments by which subjects justified their responses were mere rationalizations, rather than statements of rules that actually guided their decisions.

Other evidence for people's inadequate understanding of the rules of verification was reported by Wason (1969) and by Wason and Johnson-Laird (1970). In order to provide "therapy," these investigators confronted subjects with the consequences of their judgments and called the subjects' attention to their inconsistent answers. This procedure had little effect on subsequent performance in the same task. Taken together, the results suggest that people's difficulties in the verification task reflect a failure of comprehension, not of application.

The examples that we have considered so far involved the endorsement of rules or arguments and the elicitation of arguments to justify a particular response. We have not discussed the procedure of asking respondents to state the relevant rule, because such a test is often unreasonably demanding: We may want to credit people with understanding of rules that they cannot articulate properly.

The preferred procedures for establishing an error of application require a comparison of people's responses to a particular case with their judgment about a relevant rule or argument (McClelland & Rohrbaugh, 1978; Slovic & Tversky, 1974). It is also possible to confirm an error of application in other research designs. For example, Hamill, Wilson, and Nisbett (1980) showed subjects a videotaped interview allegedly conducted with a prison guard. Half the subjects were told that the opinions of the guard (very humane or quite brutal) were typical of prison personnel, while the other subjects were told that the guard's attitudes were atypical and that he was either much more or much less humane than most of his colleagues. The subjects then estimated the typical attitudes of prison personnel on a variety of issues. The surprising result of the study was that the opinions expressed by an atypical guard had almost as much impact on generalizations as did opinions attributed to a typical member of the group. Something is obviously wrong in this pattern of judgments, although it is impossible to describe any particular judgment as erroneous, and it is unlikely that many subjects would realize that they had not been influenced by the information about the guard's typicality (Nisbett & Wilson, 1977). In this case and in other between-subjects studies, it appears reasonable to conclude that an error of application was made if the between-groups comparison yields a result that most people would consider untenable.

We have defined an error of application as a response that violates a valid rule that the individual understands and accepts. However, it is often difficult to determine the nature of an error, because different tests of the understanding and acceptance of a rule may yield different results.

Furthermore, the same rule may be violated in one problem context and not in another. The verification task provides a striking example: Subjects who did not correctly verify the rule "If a card has a vowel on one side, it has an even number on the other" had no difficulty in verifying a formally equivalent rule: "If a letter is sealed it has a five cent stamp" (see Johnson-Laird, Legrenzi, & Sonino-Legrenzi, 1972; Johnson-Laird & Wason, 1977; Wason & Shapiro, 1971).

These results illustrate a typical pattern in the study of reasoning. It appears that people do not possess a valid general rule for the verification of if-statements or else they would solve the card problem. On the other hand, they are not blind to the correct rule or else they would also fail the stamp problem. The statement that people do not possess the correct intuition is, strictly speaking, correct – if possession of a rule is taken to mean that it is always followed. On the other hand, this statement may be misleading, since it could suggest a more general deficit than is in fact observed.

Several conclusions of early studies of representativeness appear to have a similar status. It has been demonstrated that many adults do not have generally valid intuitions corresponding to the law of large numbers, the role of base rates in Bayesian inference, or the principles of regressive prediction. But it is simply not the case that every problem to which these rules are relevant will be answered incorrectly or that the rules cannot appear compelling in particular contexts.

The properties that make formally equivalent problems easy or hard to solve appear to be related to the mental models, or schemas, that the problems evoke (Rumelhart, 1979). For example, it seems easier to see the relevance of "not-q" to the implication "p implies q" in a quality-control schema (Did they forget to stamp the sealed letter?) than in a confirmation schema (Does the negation of the conclusion imply the negation of the hypothesis?) It appears that the actual reasoning process is schema-bound or content-bound so that different operations or inferential rules are available in different contexts (Hayes & Simon, 1977). Consequently, human reasoning cannot be adequately described in terms of content-independent formal rules.

The problem of mapping statistical or logical intuitions is further complicated by the possibility of reaching highly unexpected conclusions by a series of highly intuitive steps. It was this method that Socrates employed with great success to convince his naive disciples that they had always known truths, which he was only making them discover. Should any conclusions that can be reached by a series of intuitive steps be considered intuitive? Braine (1978) discussed this question in the context of deductive reasoning, and he proposed immediacy as a test: A statement is intuitive only if its truth is immediately compelling and if it is defended in a single step.

The issue of Socratic hints has not been explicitly treated in the context of judgment under uncertainty, and there are no rules that distinguish fair tests of intuitions from contrived riddles on the one hand and from Socratic instruction on the other. Imagine, for example, how Socrates might have taught a student to give the proper answer to the following question:

"Which hospital – a large or a small one – will more often record days on which over 60% of the babies born were boys?"

This is a difficult question for Stanford undergraduates (Kahneman & Tversky, 1972b, p. 441, 3), but a correct answer can be elicited in a series of easy steps, perhaps as follows:

"Would you not agree that the babies born in a particular hospital on a particular day can be viewed as a sample?"

"Quite right. And now, would you have the same confidence in the results of a large sample, or of a small one?"

"Indeed. And would you not agree that your confidence is greater in a sample that is less likely to be in error?"

"Of course you had always known that. Would you now tell me what is the proportion of boys in a collection of babies which you consider the closest to an ideal of truth?"

"We agree again. Does that not mean, then, that a day on which more than 60% of babies born are boys is a grave departure from that ideal?"

"And so, if you have great confidence in a sample, should you not expect that sample to reveal truth rather than error?" Etc.

The Socratic procedure is a heavy-handed way of leading the respondent to a desired response, but there are subtler ways of achieving the same goal. Fischhoff, Slovic, and Lichtenstein (1979) showed that subjects become sensitive to base rates and to the reliability of evidence when they encounter successive problems that vary only in these critical variables. Although these investigators did not obtain an effect of sample size even in a within-subjects design, such effects have been obtained by Evans and Dusoir (1977) and by Bar-Hillel (1979) with a more transparent formulation and more extreme sample outcomes.

The hint provided by parallel problems may lead subjects to assign weight to a variable that is actually irrelevant to the correct response: Fischhoff and Bar-Hillel (1980a) demonstrated that respondents were sensitive to irrelevant base-rate information if that was the only variable distinguishing a set of problems. Indeed, subjects are prone to believe that any feature of the data that is systematically varied is relevant to the correct response. Within-subjects designs are associated with significant problems of interpretation in several areas of psychological research (Poulton, 1975). In studies of intuitions, they are liable to induce the effect which they are intended to test.

On the limitations of the question-answering paradigm

In the preceding section we raised the possibility that within-subjects designs and Socratic hints could prompt the intuitions under study. The problem is actually much broader. Most research on judgment under uncertainty and on inductive inference has been conducted in a conversational paradigm in which the subject is exposed to information and is asked to answer questions or to estimate values, orally or in writing. In this section we discuss some difficulties and limitations associated with this question-answering paradigm.

The use of short questionnaires completed by casually motivated subjects is often criticized on the grounds that subjects would act differently if they took the situation more seriously. However, the evidence indicates that errors of reasoning and choice that were originally established with hypothetical questions are not eliminated by the introduction of substantial incentives (Grether, 1979; Grether & Plott, 1979; Lichtenstein & Slovic, 1971, 1973; Tversky & Kahneman, 1981). Hypothetical questions are appropriate when people are able to predict how they would respond in a more realistic setting, and when they have no incentive to lie about their responses. That is not to say that payoffs and incentives do not affect judgment. Rather, we maintain that errors of reasoning and choice do not disappear in the presence of payoffs. Neither the daily newspaper nor the study of past political and military decisions support the optimistic view that rationality prevails when the stakes are high (Janis, 1972; Janis & Mann, 1977; Jervis, 1975).

Perhaps a more serious concern regarding the question-answering paradigm is that we cannot safely assume that "experimental conversations" in which subjects receive messages and answer questions will simulate the inferences that people make in their normal interaction with the environment. Although some judgments in everyday life are made in response to explicit questions, many are not. Furthermore, conversational experiments differ in many ways from normal social interaction.

In interpreting the subjects' answers, experimenters are tempted to assume (i) that the questions merely elicit from subjects an overt expression of thoughts that would have occurred to them spontaneously and (ii) that all the information given to the subject is included in the experimental message. The situation is quite different from the subject's point of view. First, the question that the experimenter asks might not spontaneously arise in the situation that the experiment is meant to simulate. Second, the subject is normally concerned with many questions that the experimenter never thought of asking, such as: "Is there a correct answer to this question? Does the experimenter expect me to find it? Is an obvious answer at all likely to be correct? Does the question provide any hints about the expected answer? What determined the selection of the information that I was given? Is some of it irrelevant and included just to mislead, or is it all relevant?" The single overt answer that the experimenter observes is determined in part by the subject's answers to this cluster of tacit questions. And the experimental message is only one of the sources of information that subjects use to generate both the covert and the overt answers (Orne, 1973).

Following Grice's William James lectures in 1967 (Grice, 1975), a large body of literature in philosophy, linguistics, and psycholinguistics has dealt with the contribution of the cooperativeness principle to the meaning of utterances (for references, see Clark & Clark, 1977). By this principle, the listener in a conversation is entitled to assume that the speaker is trying to be "informative, truthful, relevant and clear" (Clark & Clark, 1977, p. 560). Grice listed several maxims that a cooperative speaker will normally follow. For example, the maxim of quantity prohibits the speaker from saying things that the listener already knows or could readily infer from the context or from the rest of the message. It is by this maxim that the statement "John tried to clean the house" conveys that the attempt was unsuccessful: The listener can assume that a successful attempt would have been described by the simpler sentence: "John cleaned the house."

Subjects come to the experiment with lifelong experience of cooperativeness in conversation. They will generally expect to encounter a cooperative experimenter, although this expectation is often wrong. The assumption of cooperativeness has many subtle effects on the subjects' interpretation of the information to which they are exposed. In particular, it makes it exceptionally difficult for the experimenter to study the effects of "irrelevant" information. Because the presentation of irrelevant information violates rules of conversation, subjects are likely to seek relevance in any experimental message. For example, Taylor and Crocker (1979a) commented on the fact that subjects' impressions of a person are affected by statements that are true of everybody, for example, "Mark is shy with his professors." But the subjects' inference that Mark is unusually shy could be justified by the belief that a cooperative experimenter would not include a wholly redundant statement in a personality description. Similar issues arise in other studies (e.g., Kahneman & Tversky, 1973, 4; Nisbett, Zukier, & Lemley, 1981), which investigated the impact of irrelevant or worthless information.

The role of presuppositions embedded in a question was illustrated in a study by Loftus and Palmer (1974), who showed that eyewitnesses give a higher estimate of the speed of a car when asked "How fast was the car going when it smashed the other car?" than when the question is "How fast was the car going when it hit the other car?" The use of the word *smash* in the question implies that the questioner, if sincere and cooperative, believes that the car was going fast.

The normative analysis of such an inference can be divided into two separate problems. (i) Should the witness be affected by the question in forming a private opinion of the speed of the car? (ii) Should the witness be affected by the question in formulating a public estimate? The answer to (i) must be positive if the question conveys new information. The answer to (ii) is less clear. On the one hand, it appears inappropriate for the reply to a question to echo information contained in the question. On the other hand, the cooperative witness is expected to give the best possible estimate in responding to a question about a quantity. What is the witness to do if that estimate has just been influenced by the question? Should the reply be: "Before you asked me, I would have thought . . ."? Whatever the normative merits of the case, the evidence indicates that people are often unable to isolate past opinions from current ones or to estimate the weight of factors that affected their views (Fischhoff, 1977b; Goethals & Reckman, 1973; Nisbett & Wilson, 1977; Ross & Lepper, 1980).

Our research on anchoring (Tversky & Kahneman, 1974, 1) further illustrates the potency of subtle suggestions. In one study we asked a group of subjects to assess the probability that the population of Turkey was greater than 5 million, and we asked another group to assess the probability that the population of Turkey was less than 65 million. Following this task, the two groups recorded their best guesses about the population of Turkey; the median estimates were 17 million and 35 million, respectively, for the groups exposed to the low and to the high anchors. These answers can also be rationalized by the assumption that the values that appear in the probability questions are not very far from the correct one.

We have argued that suggestion effects can sometimes be justified because there is no clear demarcation between suggestion and information. It is important to note, however, that people do not accept suggestions *because* it is appropriate to do so. In the first place, they usually do not know that they have been affected by a suggestion (Loftus, 1979; Nisbett & Wilson, 1977). Second, similar suggestion effects are observed even when respondents cannot reasonably believe that an anchor they are given conveys information. Subjects who were required to produce estimates of quantities by adjusting up or down from a randomly generated value showed strong evidence of anchoring effects (Tversky & Kahneman, 1974, 1). It is not suggestibility as such that is troublesome but the apparent inability to discard uninformative messages.

When subjects are required to indicate their response by choosing an answer from a list or by constructing a probability distribution over a given set of alternatives, the experimenter's choice of categories could be informative. Loftus (1979) has shown that respondents report many more headaches per week when the response scale is expressed as 1-5, 5-10, 10-15, etc., than when the scale is expressed as 1-3, 3-5, 5-7, etc. In this case, the scale could legitimately affect the boundaries of what is to be called a headache. Even when such reinterpretations are not possible, subjects may be expected to favor the middle of the range in their estimates of quantities and to produce subjective probability distributions in which each category is assigned a non-negligible probability (Olson, 1976; Parducci, 1965).

Suggestions implied by the questionnaire could also contribute to a result observed by Fischhoff, Slovic, and Lichtenstein (1978), who asked naive subjects and experienced garage mechanics to evaluate the probability of different malfunctions that could cause failure in starting a car. They found that the estimated probability of the category "all other problems" was quite insensitive to the completeness of the list and was hardly increased when a major factor (e.g., the entire electrical system) was deleted from that list.

Even subtle and indirect clues can be effective. In a recent study we gave subjects the following information: "Mr. A is Caucasian, age 33. He weighs 190 pounds." One group of subjects were asked to guess his height. Other subjects also guessed his height, after first guessing his waist size. The average estimate was significantly higher in the first group, by about one inch. We surmise that subjects who first guessed waist size attributed more of Mr. A's weight to his girth than did subjects who only guessed his height.

We conclude that the conversational aspect of judgment studies deserves more careful consideration than it has received in past research, our own included. We cannot always assume that people will or should make the same inferences from observing a fact and from being told the same fact, because the conversational rules that regulate communication between people do not apply to the information that is obtained by observing nature. It is often difficult to ask questions without giving (useful or misleading) clues regarding the correct answer and without conveying information about the expected response. A discussion of a related normative issue concerning the interpretation of evidence is included in Bar-Hillel and Falk (1980).

Naturally, the biasing factors that we have mentioned are likely to have most impact in situations of high uncertainty. Subjects' interpretations of the experimenter's conversational attitude will not be given much weight if they conflict with confident knowledge of the correct answer to a question. In the gray area where most judgment research is carried out, however, variations of conversational context can affect the reasoning process as well as the observed response.

Judgmental errors: Positive and negative analyses

It is often useful to distinguish between positive and negative accounts of judgmental errors. A positive analysis focuses on the factors that produced a particular incorrect response; a negative analysis explains why the correct response was not made. For example, the positive analysis of a child's failure in a Piagetian conservation task attempts to specify the factors that determine the child's response, such as, the relative height or surface area of the two containers. A negative analysis of the same behavior would focus on the obstacles that make it difficult for the child to acquire and to understand the conservation of volume. In the investigation of judgment under uncertainty, positive analyses are concerned with the heuristics that people use to make judgments, estimates, and predictions. Negative analyses are concerned with the difficulties of understanding and applying elementary rules of reasoning. In the case of an error of comprehension, the negative analysis focuses on the obstacles that prevent people from discovering the relevant rule on their own, or from accepting simple explanations of it. The negative analysis of an error of application seeks to identify the ways in which the coding of problems may mask the relevance of a rule that is known and accepted.

In general, a positive analysis of an error is most useful when the same heuristic explains judgments in a varied set of problems where different normative rules are violated. Correspondingly, a negative analysis is most illuminating when people consistently violate a rule in different problems but make errors that cannot be attributed to a single heuristic. It then becomes appropriate to ask why people failed to learn the rule if routine observations of everyday events offer sufficient opportunities for such learning. It also becomes appropriate to ask why people resist the rule if they are not convinced by simple valid arguments. The difficulties of learning statistical principles from everyday experience have been discussed by several authors, notably Einhorn and Hogarth (1978), L. R. Goldberg (1968b), and Nisbett and Ross (1980). Failures of learning are commonly traced to the inaccessibility of the necessary coding of relevant instances, or to the absence of corrective feedback for erroneous judgments. The resistance to the acceptance of a rule is normally attributed to its counter-intuitive nature. As an example, we turn now to the analysis of the reasons for the resistance to the principle of regressive prediction.

Studies of intuitive prediction have provided much evidence for the prevalence of the tendency to make predictions that are radical or insufficiently regressive. (For a recent review of this literature see Chap. 15.) In earlier articles we offered a positive analysis of this effect as a manifestation of the representativeness heuristic (Kahneman & Tversky, 1973, 4; 1979a, 30). However, as we shall see, there are reasons to turn to a negative analysis in order to provide a more comprehensive treatment.

A negative analysis is of special interest for errors of comprehension, in which people find the correct rule non-intuitive or even counter-intuitive. As most teachers of elementary statistics will attest, students find the concept of regression very difficult to understand and apply despite a lifetime of experience in which extreme predictions were most often too extreme. Sportscasters and teachers, for example, are familiar with manifestations of regression to mediocrity: Exceptional achievements are followed more often than not by disappointment, and failures are followed by improvement.

Furthermore, when the regression of a criterion variable on a predictor is actually linear, and when the conditional distributions of the criterion (for fixed values of the predictor) are symmetric, the rule of regressive prediction can be defended by a compelling argument: It is sensible to make the same prediction for all cases that share the same value of the predictor variable, and it is sensible to choose that prediction so that the mean and the median of the criterion value, for all cases that share the same predicted value Y, will be equal to Y. This rule, however, conflicts with other intuitions, some of which are discussed in the following paragraphs.

1. "An optimal rule of prediction should at least permit, if not guarantee, perfectly accurate predictions for the entire ensemble of cases." The principle of regressive prediction violates this seemingly reasonable requirement. It yields a set of predicted values that has less variance than the corresponding set of actual criterion values and thereby excludes the possibility of a set of precisely accurate predictions. Indeed, the regression rule guarantees that an error will be made on each pair of correlated observations: We can never find a son whose height was correctly predicted from his father's height and whose height also allowed an accurate prediction of the father's height, except when both values are at the mean of the height distribution. It appears odd that a prediction rule that guarantees error should turn out to be optimal.

2. "The relation between an observation and a prediction based on it should be symmetric." It seems reasonable to expect that if B is predicted from knowledge of A, then A should be the appropriate prediction when B is known. Regressive predictions violate this symmetry, of course, since the predictions of the two variables from each other are not governed by the same regression equation. A related asymmetry is encountered in comparing regressive predictions to the actual values of the criterion variable. Regressive predictions are unbiased, in the sense that the mean criterion value, over all cases for which a particular value Y was predicted, is expected to be Y. However, if we consider all the cases for which the criterion value was Y, it will be found that the mean of their predicted scores lies between Y and the group average. These asymmetries are puzzling and counter-intuitive for intelligent but statistically naive persons.

The asymmetries of regressive prediction are especially troubling when the initial observation and the criterion are generated by the same process and are not distinguishable a priori, as in the case of repeated sampling from the same population or in the case of parallel forms of the same test. The only mode of prediction that satisfies symmetry in such situations is an identity rule, where the score on the second form is predicted to be the same as the initial observation. The principle of regressive prediction introduces a distinction for which there is no obvious reason: How is it possible to predict the sign of the difference between two values drawn from the same population, as soon as one of these values is known?

3. "Any systematic effect must have a cause." The difference between initial observations and the corresponding criterion values is a fact, which can be observed in any scatterplot. However, it appears to be an effect without a cause. In a test–retest situation, for example, the knowledge that the first score was high entails the prediction that the second will be lower, but the first observation does not cause the second to be low. The appearance of an uncaused effect violates a powerful intuition. Indeed, the understanding of regression is severely hindered by the fact that any instance of regression on which one stumbles by accident is likely to be given a causal explanation. In the context of skilled performance, for example, regression from an initial test to a subsequent one is commonly attributed to intense striving after an initial failure and to overconfidence following an initial success. It is often difficult to realize that performers would regress even without knowledge of results, merely because of irreducible unreliability in their performance. The regression of the first performance on the second is also surprising because it cannot be given a simple causal explanation.

We have sketched a negative analysis of people's difficulties in understanding and applying the concept of regressive prediction. We propose that people have strong intuitions about statistical prediction and that some normatively correct principles are counter-intuitive precisely because they violate existing intuitions. In this view, the "principles" that people adopt represent significant beliefs, not mere rationalizations, and they play a substantial role in retarding the learning of the correct rules. These beliefs, however, are often contradictory and hence unrealizable. For example, it is impossible to construct a non-degenerate joint distribution of the height of fathers and (first) sons so that the mean height of a father will be an unbiased predictor of the height of his son and the height of a son will be an unbiased predictor of the height of his father.

In conclusion, we have proposed that some errors and biases in judgment under uncertainty call for a dual analysis: a positive account that explains the choice of a particular erroneous response in terms of heuristics and a negative account that explains why the correct rule has not been learned. Although the two analyses are not incompatible, they tend to highlight different aspects of the phenomenon under study. The attempt to integrate the positive and the negative accounts is likely to enrich the theoretical analysis of inductive reasoning.

Summary

We addressed in this chapter three clusters of methodological and conceptual problems in the domain of judgment under uncertainty. First, we distinguished between errors of application and errors of comprehension and discussed different methods for studying statistical intuitions. Second, we reviewed some limitations of the question-answering paradigm of judgment research and explored the effects of tacit suggestions, Socratic hints, and rules of conversation. Third, we discussed the role of positive and negative explanations of judgmental errors.

The considerations raised in this chapter complicate the empirical and the theoretical analysis of judgment under uncertainty; they also suggest new directions for future research. We hope that a deeper appreciation of the conceptual and the methodological problems associated with the study of statistical intuitions will lead to a better understanding of the complexities, the subtleties, and the limitations of human inductive reasoning.

35. Variants of uncertainty

Daniel Kahneman and Amos Tversky

Analyses of uncertainty in philosophy, statistics, and decision theory commonly treat all forms of uncertainty in terms of a single dimension of probability or degree of belief. Recent psychological studies of judgment under uncertainty have often followed this tradition and have focused on the correspondence of intuitive judgments to the standard logic of probability (Einhorn & Hogarth, 1981; Nisbett & Ross, 1980; Slovic, Fischhoff, & Lichtenstein, 1977; Chapter 34). A comprehensive psychological perspective on uncertainty, however, reveals a variety of processes and experiences, which include such basic mechanisms as habituation to repeated stimulation in a single neuron and such complex activities as the evaluation of scientific hypotheses.

In this chapter we sketch some extensions of the range of observations that are normally considered in psychological analyses of judgments under uncertainty. Two levels of responses to uncertainty are discussed. We first describe some basic processes of expectation and surprise in perception, which can be considered the precursors of subjective probability. We then turn to a phenomenological examination, in which we distinguish internal from external attributions of uncertainty and sketch four modes of judgment that people may adopt in assessing uncertainty.

Elementary forms of probability

Uncertainty is a fact with which all forms of life must be prepared to contend. At all levels of biological complexity there is uncertainty about the significance of signs or stimuli and about the possible consequences of actions. At all levels, action must be taken before the uncertainty is resolved, and a proper balance must be achieved between a high level of

This chapter originally appeared in *Cognition*, 1982, *11*, 143–157. Copyright © 1981 by Elsevier Sequoia. Reprinted by permission.

specific readiness for the events that are most likely to occur and a general ability to respond appropriately when the unexpected happens. Because the focus of the present treatment is on belief rather than on action, we shall not discuss the remarkable processes by which lower organisms distribute their response effort in accordance with probabilities of reinforcement (Herrnstein, 1970). Our principal concern in this section is with perceptual uncertainty.

Perceptual expectations

Before the event there are expectations. After the event there may be surprise. Surprise has been studied mainly by psychophysiological methods, and it has been measured by the various indicators of the orienting response (Lynn, 1966; Sokolov, 1969) and by the P300 component of event-related potentials (Duncan-Johnson & Donchin, 1977; Donchin, Ritter, & McCallum, 1978). Expectancies have been studied in many contexts and by a wide variety of methods.

Our discussion of perceptual expectancies will be organized around the scheme shown in Figure 1, which distinguishes three main types of expectations. The first major distinction separates active from passive expectations: An active expectation occupies consciousness and draws on the limited capacity of attention; in contrast, a passive expectation is automatic and effortless and is better described as a disposition than as an activity (Posner, 1978).

Some expectancies are relatively permanent. Long-lasting expectancies about covariations of attributes define the perceptual categories that we use to organize and encode experience (Broadbent, 1971). Specific expectations about objects, for example, that rooms and windows are likely to be rectangular, function as permanent assumptions that help determine the interpretation of ambiguous stimuli (Ittelson & Kilpatrick, 1951). We are chronically better prepared for some events than for others, as illustrated by the robust effect of past frequency on the recognition threshold for words (Broadbent, 1967; Morton, 1969). Indeed, expectations sometimes produce hallucinatory experiences that people cannot distinguish from real ones, as in the phonemic restoration effect. Thus, all the sensory information corresponding to the "s" in the word "legislature" can be removed from a recording of the word and be replaced by a cough or by some other natural sound. Subjects who are exposed to this recording are utterly convinced that they heard the phantom phoneme (Warren, 1970).

Passive and temporary expectancies mediate the large effects of context on recognition (Foss & Blank, 1980) and several variants of priming effects (Posner, 1978). For example, the inclusion of a letter in the warning signal that introduces a trial facilitates the response to that letter in a speeded matching task, even when the contingencies are so arranged that the warning signal conveys no valid information about the target. Posner

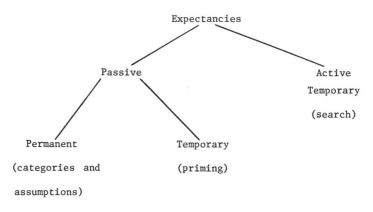

Figure 1. Perceptual expectancies.

(1978) has documented some important differences between the passive expectation that is set up by an uninformative warning signal and the active expectation produced when the target is in fact predictable, albeit imperfectly, from that signal. A passive expectation yields a benefit (i.e., a faster response) when it is confirmed, but it does not impede the response to targets that have not been primed. In contrast, a signal that causes the subject to prepare actively for a particular target also slows the response to unanticipated targets. In the language of probability theories, active expectations obey a principle of complementarity: A high degree of preparation for a particular event is achieved at the expense of a loss of preparation for other events. Passive priming is associated with a non-complementary pattern of benefit without cost.

Passive expectations and conscious anticipations can conflict, and there is evidence that the passive process exerts greater influence on the interpretation of ambiguous stimuli. Epstein and Rock (1960) pitted the two types of expectations against one another, using a picture in which a left-looking and a right-looking profile were joined to form a pattern of reversible figure-ground organization. Observers of the composite picture saw only one of the profiles, which appropriated the common contour. Having constructed two profiles that could be joined in this fashion, Epstein and Rock presented the profiles separately in regular alternation for a number of trials, creating a conscious expectation that each would always be followed by the other. The composite was then presented for the first time, and the face that the subjects saw in it was recorded. In accord with the priming effect, the observers almost always saw the profile that had been shown on the preceding trial rather than the one they consciously expected to occur.

A related demonstration of a conflict between different levels of expectation has been reported, in which the P300 component of the electroencephalogram (EEG) was the main dependent variable. The P300 is a positive deflection in the EEG, which occurs about 300 msec after the presentation of any stimulus that the observer treats as significant or relevant to the task. Many careful studies have demonstrated a close link between the prior probabilities of events and the magnitude of the P300 deflections they elicit (Donchin, Ritter, & McCallum, 1978). When a subject is exposed to a Bernoulli series, frequently repeated events elicit a smaller P300 than do rare ones. Furthermore, a run of repetitions of the same event is associated with a steadily decreasing P300, suggesting an increase in the subjective probability of further repetitions. In contrast, the conscious expectation of repetitions decreases consistently during a long run, by the familiar gambler's fallacy. Evidently, an observer can be prepared, or "primed" for one event while consciously expecting another – and can show physiological evidence of surprise at the occurrence of an event that was consciously predicted. Thus, there is a sense in which an individual can have conflicting probabilities for the same event at the same time. These observations suggest an image of the mind as a bureaucracy (Dennett, 1979) in which different parts have access to different data, assign them different weights, and hold different views of the situation.

Perception as a bet

Expectancies that have developed over a lifetime of visual experience have a profound effect on perception and are strikingly inaccessible to conscious knowledge or intention. The best-known demonstrations of these facts have been developed by the transactionalist students of perception (Ittelson & Kilpatrick, 1951; Kilpatrick, 1961). Observers of the famous distorted room and rotating window are led to have visual experiences that contradict both their general knowledge and their specific acquaintance with the objects of the illusions. Thus, one's friends may be seen as giants or midgets, who change size as they walk along the wall of the distorted room, and a paper napkin may appear to slice through the rotating window. These striking effects are produced by the dominant assumption that rooms and windows are rectangular. Although the observer knows quite well that the assumption is not applicable to the case at hand, this knowledge has no significant effect on conscious perception. Models of reality that have been built over the years cannot be revised on demand for a particular occasion. These observations again confirm that an observer can simultaneously hold conflicting views of the same event.

We have noted that perceptual expectancies determine what we "see" in an ambiguous stimulus. Indeed, the transactionalists have interpreted perception as a bet on reality (Kilpatrick, 1961). A significant aspect of such perceptual choices is the strong commitment to the chosen interpretation. Our experience contains no indication of the equivocation of stimuli, and even when perceptual interpretations fluctuate over time, as with the Necker cube, they tend to be quite definite at any particular moment. The suppression of uncertainty and equivocation in perception suggests that we may be biologically programmed to act on the perceptual best bet, as if this bet involved no risk of error. A significant difference between the conscious experiences of perception and thought is that the latter can represent doubt and uncertainty, whereas the former normally do not.

Although the suppression of uncertainty distinguishes perceptual bets from conscious judgments about uncertain events, the processing of uncertainty at the two levels may be similar in other respects. Two striking observations of transactionalist research suggest hypotheses that seem to apply to conscious beliefs. The first is that the reconstructed image of the environment tends to be coherent, reflecting the normal constraints and dependencies among the attributes of the scene and of the stimulus. Thus, when an object is presented under conditions that make both its size and its distance ambiguous, the chosen perceptual interpretation will select a size and a distance that relate to retinal size in the standard manner: If the object is perceived to be large, then it also appears to be farther away than if it is seen as small (Ittelson & Kilpatrick, 1951).

The second observation is that perceptual construction appears to be a hierarchical process, in which decisions about the global features of the scene constrain and dominate decisions about the objects contained in it. The distorted room provides the best example. What is seen is not a compromise between two extreme views: normal-sized people in a distorted room, or oddly sized people in a normal room. The latter view simply dominates the former, as if the shape of the room were computed before the processing of the people in it begins. Whether similar rules can be shown to operate, for example, in the construction of scenarios of future events is a problem that well deserves study.

The phenomenology of uncertainty

The preceding section sought to show that the rules that govern perceptual expectancies differ from the rules of probability theory. The present section extends this analysis to the experiences of doubt and uncertainty that judgments of subjective probability are assumed to reflect. As we shall see, the notion of probability refers in natural language to several distinct states of mind, to which the rules of the standard calculus of probability may not be equally applicable.

To appreciate the complexity of expectations, consider one of their manifestations: the surprise that we experience when an expectation is violated. Imagine that a coin is to be tossed 40 times. What number of "heads" would you expect? If you assume that the coin is fair, you would probably state that the 20–20 result is more likely than any other, yet you would be more surprised by this outcome than by a result of 22 "heads" and 18 "tails." Is the "true" subjective probability of the two events indicated by the considered judgment of their relative likelihood or by the involuntary reaction of surprise they would elicit?

One possible interpretation is that the example illustrates a conflict between two approaches to the judgment of probability: The judgment that the most likely outcome is 20–20 derives from knowledge of the rules of chances, but outcomes such as 22–18 or 17–23 are more probable at another level, where probability is determined by representativeness. A slightly uneven outcome represents both the fairness of the coin and the randomness of tossing, which is not at all represented by the exactly even result. In this view, the greater psychological reality of expectations based on representativeness manifests itself in the surprise reaction.

A slightly different interpretation, which focuses on the coding of the possible outcomes, is possible. As we shall see, it is frequently appropriate in conversation to extend the definition of an event X to "X or something like it." If the spontaneous coding of events follows similar rules, outcomes such as 22–18 or 17–23 will be spontaneously coded as "an approximately even split," while the outcome 20–20 will be assigned a distinctive code of "exactly even split." A person who attempts to judge the relative likelihood of the events will consider the explicit statement of the outcomes, and will note that 20–20 is more likely than, say, 22–18. But the reaction of surprise may be determined by the natural coding of events. The event 22–18 will then be relatively unsurprising because it is coded as an approximately even result, which is indeed more likely than a precisely even one.

The role of event coding is manifest in the interpretation of uncertain assertions, such as "I estimate that . . ." or sometimes "I think that . . ." Uncertain assertions are a class of speech acts, which are characterized by specific sincerity conditions and tests of validity. Consider, for example, the prediction: "I think that the price of gold will be higher by 50% in six months than it is today." Taken literally, this is a point prediction, which should be assigned a very small probability of confirmation. But the prediction is not intended to be taken literally. Point predictions are normally understood as comparative statements, or as statements of the range in which an outcome is expected to fall, for example, "I think the increase in the price of gold will be nearer to 50% than to X% or Y%." The speaker and the listener normally expect to agree on the tacitly implied values of X and Y. For example, the forecaster cited above will be considered remarkably accurate if the price of gold actually rises by 53% in the next six months, although the forecast was not strictly true. Thus, a speaker who asserts a numerical prediction is commited to a range rather than to a point. The speaker is also committed to the proposition that the value is about equally likely to be above the estimate as below it, except when the nature of the prediction makes this impossible. Thus, a person who says, "I think the price of gold will rise by 50% in the next six months," would be considered to be deliberately misleading if he or she also thought, but did not communicate, that the actual value was much more likely to be above the estimate than below it.

It is significant that the sincerity conditions associated with a prediction do not require that the predicted value (or range) of a variable be considered highly probable but only that it be considered more probable than comparable values (or ranges). For example, a man who asserts, "I think Billy John will win the gold medal for the high jump in the next Olympics," will not be considered a liar if he prefers to bet against this proposition rather than on it, but he is prohibited from adding, "and the chances of Jack Small are even better." Thus, natural language allows a privileged role to the best guess, and the identification of the favored guess conveys information about the alternatives to which it may fairly be compared. The mention of a favorite athlete indicates that he is to be compared to other individual athletes rather than to a disjunction of possible winners. One consequence of this rule is that it is sometimes possible to "predict" an event that is considered less probable than its complement if the complement is naturally coded as a disjunction.

A related restriction applies to expressions of confidence. A statement of confidence expresses one's uncertainty in a prediction, estimate, or inference to which one is already committed. Thus, it is natural to ask, "How confident are you that you are right?" but it is anomalous to ask, "How confident are you that you are wrong?" Confidence is the subjective probability or degree of belief associated with what we "think" will happen.

Common language also provides a large number of expressions to talk of events that may happen, although we do not necessarily "think" they will. Thus, people assess the chances of candidates, estimate the risks of different activities, give odds for football games, and understand forecasters' statements about the probability of rain. We now turn to a more detailed analysis of the states of uncertainty that such statements may express, following the scheme shown in Figure 2. The two levels of the figure, attributions of uncertainty and variants of uncertainty, are discussed in the following sections.

Attribution of uncertainty

The primary distinction shown in Figure 2 refers to two loci to which uncertainty can be attributed: the external world or our state of knowledge. For example, we attribute to causal systems in the real world the uncertainty associated with the tossing of a coin, the drawing of a hand of cards from a pack, the outcome of a football game, and the behavior of the St. Helens volcano. These causal systems have dispositions to produce different events, and we judge the probabilities of these events by assessing the relative strength of the competing dispositions. In contrast,

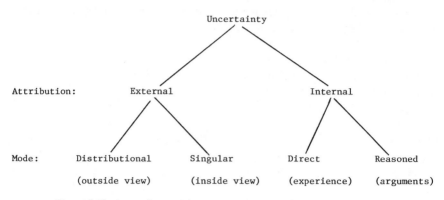

Figure 2. Variants of uncertainty.

such statements as, "I think Mont Blanc is the tallest mountain in Europe," or, "I hope I spelled her name correctly," reflect an uncertainty that is attributed to one's mind rather than to a mountain or a woman. (Howell & Burnett, 1978, have applied the terms *internal uncertainty* and *external uncertainty*, respectively, to events that the subjects can or cannot control.)

Our distinction between ignorance and external uncertainty is closely related to a more general distinction between internal and external attributions of experience. Color, size, and texture, for example, are normally experienced as properties that belong to external objects, but pains, feelings, and memories are attributed to the experiencing subject rather than to the eliciting object.

The attribution of uncertainty can sometimes be inferred from a simple linguistic test: Is it appropriate to describe the assessment of uncertainty as *"the* probability is . . . ?" Or should one say *"my* probability is . . . ?" In contrast to the Bayesian view, which treats all probabilities as subjective and personal, natural language marks the distinction between internal and external uncertainty. Thus it is legitimate to speak of "the best estimate of the probability of a change of regime in Saudi Arabia within the next year," but it is anomalous to say "the best estimate of the probability that the Nile is the largest river in the world is . . ." Best estimates of probability belong to the public domain. Expressions of private ignorance do not.

This test does not always distinguish internal from external uncertainty. For example, one may speak of *the* probability that Marlowe wrote *Hamlet*, although this uncertainty is attributed to our ignorance rather than to the strength of Marlowe's propensity to write plays. The use of *"the* probability" in this example is justified by the existence of a public body of knowledge, which reduces but does not eliminate the uncertainty about the authorship of *Hamlet*. Not everybody need have access to this knowledge, but the estimated probability refers to a reasonable or consensual inference from the available evidence. In the example of the Nile, however, the public body of evidence certainly includes the correct answer, and ignorance can only be private.

The attribution of uncertainty about an event to dispositions or to ignorance depends, among other things, on timing. Uncertainty about past events is likely to be experienced as ignorance, especially if the truth is known to someone else, whereas uncertainty about the future is more naturally attributed to the dispositions of the relevant system. Indeed, it has been noted that people exhibit different attitudes to the outcome of a coin toss, depending on whether or not the coin has already been tossed (Rothbart & Snyder, 1970).

Variants of uncertainty

The second level of Figure 2 distinguishes four prototypical variants of uncertainty, identified by the nature of the data that the judge might consider in evaluating probability. External uncertainty can be assessed in two ways: (i) a distributional mode, where the case in question is seen as an instance of a class of similar cases, for which the relative frequencies of outcomes are known or can be estimated; (ii) a singular mode, in which probabilities are assessed by the propensities of the particular case at hand. The two modes of judgment are illustrated by the following true story.

A team that was concerned with the development of a high school curriculum on thinking under uncertainty was conducting a planning session. The question was raised of the time that would be required to complete the first version of a textbook. The participants in the discussion were asked to estimate this value as realistically as possible; the seven estimates ranged from 18 months to 3 years. The team leader then turned to one of the participants, an educator with considerable expertise in the problems of curriculum development, with the following question: "What has been the experience of other teams that have tried to write a textbook and develop a curriculum in a new area, where no previous course of study existed? How long did it take them to complete a textbook, from a stage comparable to the present state of our project?" The chilling implications of the answer appeared to surprise the expert who gave it, much as they surprised the other participants: "Most teams I could think of failed and never completed a textbook. For those that succeeded, completion times have ranged from five to nine years, with a median of seven."

Subsequent probing revealed that all participants had produced their initial estimate in the singular mode, by constructing plans and scenarios, with some allowance of safety margins for unforeseen contingencies. Because of anchoring effects (Tversky & Kahneman, 1974, 1) an estimate obtained by adding safety margins to current plans is likely to be highly optimistic. A notable aspect of this anecdote is that the relevant distributional information was not spontaneously used, although it was available to one expert from personal knowledge and could have been estimated quite accurately by several other participants.

Our example illustrated the application of singular and distributional modes of reasoning to the prediction of a continuous variable: the time required to complete a project. The distributional information consisted in this case of knowledge about the relative frequencies of different completion times. Of course, a similar reasoning can be applied to assess the probability of a discrete outcome, such as the failure of the project. The relative frequency of that outcome in a relevant class provides the basis for a distributional assessment of probability, and other information about the particular case, used in the singular mode, may produce an impression of propensity to fail or to succeed. There are many instances in which the same question can be approached in either singular or distributional mode.

Compare the following examples:

1. "Chances are that you will find John at home if you call tomorrow morning. He said that he prefers to work at home."
2. "Chances are that you will find John at home if you call tomorrow morning. He has often been there when I called him."

Statement 1 allows only a singular judgment of the probability that John will be at home. Statement 2 could support both a distributional and a singular assessment. The relative frequency of similar mornings on which John has been at home provides a natural estimate of the probability of finding him there tomorrow, but the statement has also endowed John with a propensity to spend mornings at home, much as did statement 1.

We have conjectured (Kahneman & Tversky, 1979a, 30) that people generally prefer the singular mode, in which they take an "inside view" of the causal system that most immediately produces the outcome, over an "outside view," which relates the case at hand to a sampling schema. Our planning example illustrates this preference for the singular mode. It also illustrates another effect, which we suspect to be quite general: The distributional mode of judgment is more likely than the singular to yield accurate estimates of values and reasonable assessments of probability.

We now turn to a distinction between the modes of assessment of internal uncertainty, which are illustrated by the following examples:

3. "I believe New York is north of Rome, but I am not sure."
4. "I think her name is Doris, but I am not sure."

The uncertainty expressed in these statements is clearly internal: the statements reflect (partial) ignorance rather than dispositions of external objects. It is surely farfetched to speak of the propensity of New York to be north of Rome (incidentally, it is not) or of Linda to be remembered as Doris.

The two statements differ in the nature of the evidence on which they are based. Statement 3 could reflect a process of sifting and weighing of evidence and arguments (e.g., New York is much colder than Rome; Rome is in the middle of Italy, etc.). Statement 4 has a different character. The confidence that it expresses is based on an introspective judgment of the strength of an association. As often happens when we check the spelling of a word by examining whether it "looks right," confidence rests on an unanalyzed experience. In studies of psychophysics and of memory, the confidence associated with judgments is significantly correlated with accuracy: People are more likely to be confident when they are correct than when they are not, although their assessments of the probability that they are right are poorly calibrated (see Chap. 22).

As in the case of external uncertainty, the internal uncertainty associated with a given question can sometimes be assessed both in the reasoned and in the introspective modes. For example, a question concerning the age of a movie star can be approached introspectively by searching for an answer that sounds familiar or in a reasoned mode by trying to induce the answer from other knowledge.

We do not wish to suggest that any experience of uncertainty can be assigned to one of the four variants of Figure 2. There are undoubtedly many mixed and indeterminate cases. We have seen that the uncertainty in a given problem can be attributed to external dispositions, to one's ignorance, or to a combination of the two and that it may be assessed in a singular mode, in a distributional mode, or in a mixture of modes. The purpose of our treatment was to highlight some significant dimensions of variation in experiences of uncertainty, not to offer an exhaustive and mutually exclusive classification of these experiences. For an attempt to classify experimental operations in the measurement of subjective probability, see Howell and Burnett (1978).

Discussion

Although the language of probability can be used to express any form of uncertainty, the laws of probability theory do not apply to all variants of uncertainty with equal force. These laws are most likely to be accepted, and satisfied in intuitive judgments, when an external uncertainty is assessed in a distributional or frequentistic mode. For example, complementarity of subjective probability is very compelling when we consult weather statistics in order to assess the probability that it will rain next year on April 12: The relevant set of past April days is clearly separable into days on which there was rain and days on which there was not.

Complementarity is less compelling in other variants. When uncertainty is assessed in terms of propensities, arguments, or confidence, it is less obvious that the probabilities should add up to unity – even if it is known with certainty that one of the alternatives is correct. For example, one may question why the degree of belief in the assertion that New York is north of Rome and the degree of belief in the assertion that New York is south of Rome should sum to the same value as the degrees of belief for any other pair of complementary statements. Indeed, several authors (e.g., L. J. Cohen, 1977; Shafer, 1976) have proposed that complementarity should not apply to degree of belief. In particular, Shafer has argued against complementarity of belief on the grounds that there are situations in which two mutually exclusive and exhaustive hypotheses both have substantial support and other situations in which neither hypothesis has much support. Similar questions could be raised about the necessity of complementarity in impressions of confidence and in assessments of conflicting propensities.

The variants of uncertainty may differ in the confidence with which they are assessed. Imagine that a thumbtack has been tossed four times and has landed twice on its point and twice on its head. Given these data, most observers will assign a probability of .5 to the event that the thumbtack will land on its head on the next toss. They also assign a probability of .5 to the event that a tossed coin will show "heads," but they express much greater confidence in their judgment about the coin than about the tack. As this example illustrates, it is quite possible to assign different degrees of confidence to the same judgment of propensity. Confidence about probabilities is important because it controls decisions. There is evidence (Ellsberg, 1961; Raiffa, 1961) that people prefer to bet on events that have known probabilities, such as the toss of a coin, rather than on events that are associated with a combination of external uncertainty and ignorance, such as the toss of a thumbtack.

There are natural links between the conceptions of probability advanced by different schools of thought on this topic and the modes of uncertainty that we have discussed. Thus, the frequentistic or objective interpretation of probability restricts the concept to external uncertainty generated by a sampling process. In contrast, the Bayesian or personal school treats all uncertainty as ignorance. In the Bayesian school, preferences are the basis of beliefs, and probabilities are derived from preferences between bets. From a psychological point of view, however, this betting heuristic appears unrealistic. Controversy has often been sharp in this domain, because of the existence of intuitions that are individually compelling and mutually incompatible, and because there is no agreed' upon criterion for settling normative disputes when intuitions conflict. A psychological analysis could perhaps contribute to the normative discussion by providing an adequate description of the intuitions from which the various positions draw their appeal.

References

Abelson, R. P. Modes of resolution of belief dilemmas. *Journal of Conflict Resolution*, 1959, *3*, 343–352. (8)

Abelson, R. P., Aronson, E., McGuire, W. J., Newcomb, T. M., Rosenberg, M. J., & Tannenbaum, P. H. (Eds.). *Theories of cognitive consistency: A sourcebook*. Chicago: Rand-McNally, 1968. (15)

Adams, J. K. A confidence scale defined in terms of expected percentages. *American Journal of Psychology*, 1957, *70*, 432–436. (20, 22)

Adams, J. K., & Adams, P. A. Realism of confidence judgments. *Psychological Review*, 1961, *68*, 33–45. (22, 31)

Adams, P. A., & Adams, J. K. Training in confidence judgments. *American Journal of Psychology*, 1958, *71*, 747–751. (22, 31)

Adler, A. Individual psychology. In C. Murchinson (Ed.), *Psychologies of 1930*. Worcester, Mass.: Clark University Press, 1930. (16)

Adorno, T., Frenkel-Brunswik, E., Levinson, D., & Sanford, N. *The authoritarian personality*, New York: Harper, 1950. (15)

Ajzen, I. Intuitive theories of events and the effects of base-rate information on prediction. *Journal of Personality and Social Psychology*, 1977, *35*, 303–314. (10)

Alberoni, F. Contribution to the study of subjective probability, Part I. *Journal of General Psychology*, 1962, *66*, 241–264. (3)

Alexander, S. A. H. *Sex, arguments, and social engagements in marital and premarital relations*. Unpublished master's thesis, University of Missouri, Kansas City, 1971. (28)

Alker, H. A. Is personality situationally specific or intrapsychically consistent? *Journal of Personality*, 1972, *40*, 1–16. (15)

Allen, J. G. Breast surgery, principles and practice. In C. A. Moyer (Ed.), *Surgery: Principles and Practice*. Philadelphia: Lippincott, 1965. (18)

Allport, G. W. *The nature of prejudice*. Reading, Mass.: Addison-Wesley, 1954. (15)

Allport, G. W. Traits revisited. *American Psychologist*, 1966, *21*, 1–10. (15)

Alpert, W., & Raiffa, H. A progress report on the training of probability assessors. Unpublished manuscript, 1969. (1, 22, 33)

Anderson, C. A., Lepper, M. R., & Ross, L. The perseverance of social theories: The role of explanation in the persistence of discredited information. *Journal of Personality and Social Psychology*, 1980, *39*, 1037–1049. (9, 15)

Anderson, N. H. Information integration theory: A brief survey. In D. H. Krantz, R. C. Atkinson, R. D. Luce, and P. Suppes (Eds.), *Contemporary Developments in Mathematical Psychology* (Vol. 2). San Francisco: Freeman, 1974. (27)

Arkes, H. R., Wortmann, R. C., Saville, P. D., & Harkness, A. R. Hindsight bias among physicians weighing the likelihood of diagnoses. *Journal of Applied Psychology*, 1981, *66*, 252–254. (31)

Armelius, K. Task predictability and performance as determinants of confidence in multiple-cue judgments. *Scandinavian Journal of Psychology*, 1979, *20*, 19–25. (31)

Ashmore, R. D., & Collins, B. E. Studies in forced compliance X: Attitude change and commitment to maintain publicly a counter-attitudinal position. *Psychological Reports*, 1968, *22*, 1229–1234. (9)

Bach, R. Nothing by chance. *The American Way*, 1973, *6*, 32–38. (33)

Bacon, F. *The new organon and related writings.* New York: Liberal Arts Press, 1960. (Originally published in 1620.) (9)

Barclay, S., & Peterson, C. R. *Two methods for assessing probability distributions* (Tech. Rep. 73-1). McLean, Va.: Decisions and Designs, Inc., 1973. (22)

Bar-Hillel, M. On the subjective probability of compound events. *Organizational Behavior and Human Performance*, 1973, *9*, 396–406. (1, 23, 30)

Bar-Hillel, M. Similarity and probability. *Organizational Behavior and Human Performance*, 1974, *11*, 277–282. (5)

Bar-Hillel, M. The role of sample size in sample evaluation. *Organizational Behavior and Human Performance*, 1979, *24*, 245–257. (5, 34)

Bar-Hillel, M. The base-rate fallacy in probability judgments. *Acta Psychologica*, 1980, *44*, 211–233. (10, 34) (a)

Bar-Hillel, M. What features make samples seem representative? *Journal of Experimental Psychology: Human Perception and Performance*, 1980, *6*, 578–589. (5, 6) (b)

Bar-Hillel, M., & Falk, R. *Some teasers concerning conditional probabilities.* Unpublished manuscript, 1980. (34)

Bar-Hillel, M., & Fischhoff, B. When do base rates affect predictions? *Journal of Personality and Social Psychology*, 1981, *41*, 671–680. (10)

Barraclough, G. Mandarins and Nazis. *New York Review of Books*, 1972, *19*, 37–42. (23)

Bartlett, F. C. *Remembering.* Cambridge: Cambridge University Press, 1932. (12)

Beaver, W. H. Financial ratios as predictors of failure. In *Empirical research in accounting: Selected studies.* Chicago: University of Chicago, Graduate School of Business, Institute of Professional Accounting, 1966. (28)

Becker, B. W., & Greenberg, M. G. Probability estimates by respondents: Does weighting improve accuracy? *Journal of Marketing Research*, 1978, *15*, 482–486. (31)

Becker, C. Everyman his own historian. *American Historical Review*, 1935, *40*, 221–236. (23)

Beckman, L. Effects of students' performance on teachers' and observers' attributions of causality. *Journal of Educational Psychology*, 1970, *61*, 75–82. (9)

Bem, D. J. Self-perception: An alternative interpretation of cognitive dissonance phenomena. *Psychological Review*, 1967, *74*, 183–200. (7, 32)

Bem, D. J., & Allen, A. On predicting some of the people some of the time: The search for cross-situational consistencies in behavior. *Psychological Review*, 1974, *81*, 506–520. (15)

Bem, D. J., & Funder, D. C. Predicting more of the people more of the time: Assessing the personality of situations. *Psychological Review*, 1978, *85*, 485–501. (15)

Bem, D. J., & Lord, C. G. Template matching: A proposal for probing the ecological validity of experimental settings in social psychology. *Journal of Personality and Social Psychology*, 1979, *37*, 833–846. (15)

Bem, D. J., & McConnell, H. K. Testing the self-perception explanation of dissonance phenomena: On the salience of premanipulation attitudes. *Journal of Personality and Social Psychology*, 1970, *14*, 23–31. (32)

Benson, L. *Toward the scientific study of history: Selected essays.* Philadelphia; Lippincott, 1972. (23)

Bentham, J. *Handbook of political fallacies.* Baltimore: Johns Hopkins Press, 1952. (Originally published in 1824.) (32)

Ben Zvi, A. Hindsight and foresight: A conceptual framework for the analysis of surprise attacks. *World Politics*, 1976, *28*, 381–395. (23)

Beyth, R. *Man as an intuitive statistician: On erroneous intuitions concerning the description and prediction of events.* Unpublished master's thesis. The Hebrew University, Jerusalem, 1972. (In Hebrew) (4)

Beyth-Marom, R., & Dekel, S. *Thinking under uncertainty: A textbook for junior high school students.* In press. (In Hebrew) (31, 33)

Bierbrauer, G. *Effect of set, perspective, and temporal factors in attribution.* Unpublished doctoral dissertation, Stanford University, 1973. (9)

Block, M. A., & Reynolds, W. How vital is mammography in the diagnosis and management of breast carcinoma? *Archives of Surgery*, 1974, *108*, 588–591. (18)

Borgida, E. Scientific deduction–Evidence is not necessarily informative: A reply to Wells and Harvey. *Journal of Personality and Social Psychology*, 1978, *36*, 477–482. (10)

Borgida, E., & Brekke, N. The base-rate fallacy in attribution and prediction. In J. H. Harvey, W. J. Ickes, and R. F. Kidd (Eds.), *New Directions in Attribution Research* (Vol. 3). Hillsdale, N.J.: Erlbaum, 1981. (10)

Borgida, E., & Nisbett, R. The differential impact of abstract vs. concrete information on decisions. *Journal of Applied Social Psychology*, 1977, *7*, 258–271. (7)

Bousfield, W. A., & Sedgewick, C. H. An analysis of sequences of restricted associative responses. *Journal of General Psychology*, 1944, *30*, 149–165. (11)

Bowman, E. H. Consistency and optimality in managerial decision making. *Management Science*, 1963, *9*, 310–321. (28)

Bradley, G. W. Self-serving biases in the attribution process: A reexamination of the fact or fiction question. *Journal of Personality and Social Psychology*, 1978, *36*, 56–71. (9)

Braine, M. D. S. On the relation between the natural logic of reasoning and standard logic. *Psychological Review*, 1978, *85*, 1–21. (34)

Bransford, J. D., & Franks, J. J. The abstraction of linguistic ideas. *Cognitive Psychology*, 1971, *2*, 331–350. (6)

Brier, G. W. Verification of forecasts expressed in terms of probability. *Monthly Weather Review*, 1950, *75*, 1–3. (22)

Broadbent, D. E. Word-frequency effect and response bias. *Psychological Review*, 1967, *74*, 1–15. (35)

Broadbent, D. E. *Decision and Stress.* London: Academic Press, 1971. (35)

Brown, E. A. R. The tyranny of a construct: Feudalism and historians of medieval Europe. *American Historical Review,* 1974, *79,* 1063–1088. (23)

Brown, T. A. *An experiment in probabilistic forecasting* (Report R-944-ARPA). Santa Monica: The RAND Corp., 1973. (22)

Brown, T. A., & Shuford, E. H. *Quantifying uncertainty into numerical probabilities for the reporting of intelligence* (Report R-1185-ARPA). Santa Monica: The RAND Corp., 1973. (22)

Brucker, H. *Communication is power: Unchanging values in a changing journalism.* New York: Oxford University Press, 1973. (33)

Bruner, J. S. Going beyond the information given. In H. Gruber, et al. (Eds.), *Contemporary approaches to cognition.* Cambridge, Mass.: Harvard University Press, 1957. (15) (a)

Bruner, J. S. On perceptual readiness. *Psychological Review,* 1957, *64,* 123–152. (15) (b)

Bruner, J. S. The act of discovery. *Harvard Educational Review,* 1961, *31,* 21–32. (12)

Bruner, J. S., Postman, L., & Rodrigues, J. Expectations and the perception of color. *American Journal of Psychology,* 1951, *64,* 216–227. (15)

Bruner, J. S., & Potter, M. C. Interference in visual recognition. *Science,* 1964, *144,* 424–425. (11)

Brunswik, E. Organismic achievement and environmental probability. *Psychological Review,* 1943, *50,* 255–272. (19)

Bryan, W. B. Testimony before the Subcommittee on State Energy Policy, Committee on Planning, Land Use, and Energy, California State Assembly, February 1, 1974. (33)

Burton, I., Kates, R. W., & White, G. F. *The environment as hazard.* New York: Oxford University Press, 1978. (33)

Byrne, R. R. Correlation of thermography, xero-mammography and biopsy in a community hospital. *Wisconsin Medical Journal,* 1974, *73,* 35–37. (18)

Cambridge, R. M., & Shreckengost, R. C. *Are you sure? The subjective probability assessment test.* Unpublished manuscript. Langley, Va.: Office of Training, Central Intelligence Agency, 1978. (22)

Campbell, D. T. Blind variation and selective retention in creative thought as in other knowledge processes. *Psychological Review,* 1960, *67,* 380–400. (19)

Campbell, D. T. Reforms as experiments. *American Psychologist,* 1969, *24,* 409–429. (4)

Campbell, D. T. "Degrees of freedom" and the case study. *Comparative Political Studies,* 1975, *8,* 178–193. (23)

Carlsson, G. Random walk effects in behavioral data. *Behavioral Science,* 1972, *17,* 430–437. (23)

Carr, E. H. *What is history?* London: Macmillan, 1961. (23)

Carver, R. P. A critical review of mathagenic behaviors and the effect of questions upon the retention of prose materials. *Journal of Reading Behavior,* 1972, *4,* 93–119. (12)

Cass, J., & Birnbaum, M. *Comparative guide to American colleges.* New York: Harper & Row, 1968. (28)

Casscells, W., Schoenberger, A., & Grayboys, T. Interpretation by physicians of clinical laboratory results. *New England Journal of Medicine,* 1978, *299,* 999–1000. (10, 18)

Castellan, N. J., Jr. Decision making with multiple probabilistic cues. In N. J. Castellan, D. P. Pisoni, & G. R. Potts (Eds.), *Cognitive Theory*, 2. Hillsdale, N.J.: Erlbaum, 1977. (19)

Cavanaugh, J. C., & Borkowski, J. G. Searching for meta-memory–memory connections. *Developmental Psychology*, 1980, 16, 441–453. (31)

Chan, S. The intelligence of stupidity: Understanding failures in strategic warning. *American Political Science Review*, 1979, 73, 171–180. (23)

Chapman, L. J. Illusory correlation in observational report. *Journal of Verbal Learning and Verbal Behavior*, 1967, 6, 151–155. (15)

Chapman, L. J., & Chapman, J. P. Genesis of popular but erroneous psychodiagnostic observations. *Journal of Abnormal Psychology*, 1967, 73, 193–204. (15)

Chapman, L. J., & Chapman, J. P. Illusory correlation as an obstacle to the use of valid psychodiagnostic signs. *Journal of Abnormal Psychology*, 1969, 74, 271–280. (1, 15, 17)

Choo, G. T. G. Training and generalization in assessing probabilities for discrete events (Tech. Rep. 76–5). Uxbridge, England: Brunel Institute of Organizational and Social Studies, 1976. (22)

Christensen-Szalanski, J. J. J., & Bushyhead, J. B. Physicians' use of probabilistic information in a real clinical setting. *Journal of Experimental Psychology: Human Perception and Performance*, 1981, 7, 928–935. (22, 31)

Clark, H. H., & Clark, E. V. *Psychology and Language*. New York: Harcourt Brace Jovanovich, 1977. (34)

Clark, R. L., Copeland, M. M., Egan, R. L., Gallagher, H. S., Geller, H., Lindsay, J. P., Robbins, L. C., & White, E. C. Reproducibility of the technic of mammography (Egan) for cancer of the breast. *American Journal of Surgery*, 1965, 109, 127–133. (18)

Clark, R. L., & Robbins, L. C. Mammography (Egan) in cancer of the breast. *The American Journal of Surgery*, 1965, 109, 125–126. (18)

Clarke, F. R. Confidence ratings, second-choice responses, and confusion matrices in intelligibility tests. *Journal of the Acoustical Society of America*, 1960, 32, 35–46. (22, 31)

Claudy, J. G. A comparison of five variable weighting procedures. *Educational and Psychological Measurement*, 1972, 32, 311–322. (28)

Cocozza, J. J., & Steadman, H. J. Prediction in psychiatry: An example of misplaced confidence in experts. *Social Problems*, 1978, 25, 265–276. (31)

Cohen, B., & Lee, I. A catalog of risks. *Health Physics*, 1979, 36, 707–722. (33)

Cohen, B. L. Perspectives on the nuclear debate. *Bulletin of the Atomic Scientists*, 1974, 30, 25–39. (33)

Cohen, J. The statistical power of abnormal-social psychological research. *Journal of Abnormal and Social Psychology*, 1962, 65, 145–153. (2, 3)

Cohen, J. *Statistical power analysis in the behavioral sciences*. New York: Academic Press, 1969. (2)

Cohen, J., Boyle, L. E., & Chesnick, E. I. Patterns of preference in locating targets. *Occupational Psychology*, 1969, 43, 129–144. (24)

Cohen, J., Chesnick, E. I., & Haran, D. A confirmation of the inertial-ψ effect in sequential choice and decision. *British Journal of Psychology*, 1972, 63, 41–46. (1)

Cohen, J., & Hansel, C. E. M. *Risk and gambling*. New York: Philosophical Library, 1956. (3)

Cohen, J., & Hansel, C. E. M. The nature of decisions in gambling. *Acta Psychologica,* 1958, *13,* 357–370. (24)

Cohen, J. J. A case for benefit-risk analysis. In H. J. Otway (Ed.), *Risk vs. benefit: Solution or dream* (Report LA-4860-MS). Los Alamos Scientific Laboratory, February 1972. (Available from the National Technical Information Service.) (33)

Cohen, L. J. *The probable and the provable.* Oxford: Clarendon Press, 1977. (35)

Cohen, L. J. On the psychology of prediction: Whose is the fallacy? *Cognition,* 1979, *7,* 385–407. (34)

Cohen, L. J. Can human irrationality be experimentally demonstrated? *The Behavioral and Brain Sciences,* 1981, *4,* 317–331. (34)

Cohn, H. E. Mammography in its proper perspective. *Surgery, Gynecology and Obstetrics,* 1972, *134,* 97–98. (18)

Coles, R. Shrinking history. *New York Review of Books, Part I,* February 22, 1973, pp. 20, 15–21; *Part II,* March 8, 1973, pp. 20, 25–29. (23)

Collins, B. E., & Hoyt, M. F. Personal responsibility for consequences: An integration and extension of the forced-compliance literature. *Journal of Experimental Social Psychology,* 1972, *8,* 558–593. (9)

Combs, B., & Slovic, P. Causes of death: Biased newspaper coverage and biased judgments. *Journalism Quarterly,* 1979, *56,* 837–843, 849. (33)

Commager, H. S. *The nature and study of history.* Columbus, Ohio: Merrill, 1965. (23)

Committee on Government Operations. *Teton Dam Disaster.* Washington, D.C.: U.S. Government Printing Office, 1976. (33)

Cooke, W. E. Forecasts and verifications in Western Australia. *Monthly Weather Review,* 1906, *34,* 23–24. (22) (a)

Cooke, W. E. Weighting forecasts. *Monthly Weather Review,* 1906, *34,* 274–475. (22) (b)

Cox, D. R. Two further applications of a model for binary regression. *Biometrica,* 1958, *45,* 562–565. (22)

Cronbach, L. J. Beyond the two disciplines of scientific psychology. *American Psychologist,* 1975, *30,* 116–127. (19)

Crouse, T. *The boys on the bus.* New York: Random House, 1974. (7)

D'Andrade, R. G. Trait psychology and componential analysis. *American Anthropologist,* 1965, *67,* 215–228. (13)

Darley, J. M., & Latané, B. Bystander intervention in emergencies: Diffusion in responsibility. *Journal of Personality and Social Psychology,* 1968, *8,* 377–383. (7, 10)

Darlington, R. B. Reduced-variance regression. *Psychological Bulletin,* 1978, *85,* 1238–1255. (28)

Davis, W. L., & Davis, D. E. Internal-external control and attribution of responsibility for success and failure. *Journal of Personality,* 1972, *40,* 123–136. (9)

Dawes, R. M. A case study of graduate admissions: Application of three principles of human decision making. *American Psychologist,* 1971, *26,* 180–188. (28)

Dawes, R. M. Graduate admissions criteria and future success. *Science,* 1975, *187,* 721–723. (28) (a)

Dawes, R. M. The mind, the model, and the task. In F. Restle, R. M. Shiffrin, N. J. Castellan, H. R. Lindman & D. F. Pisoni (Eds.), *Cognitive theory,* Hillsdale, N.J.: Erlbaum, 1975. (19) (b)

Dawes, R. M. Shallow Psychology. In J. S. Carroll & J. W. Payne (Eds.), *Cognition and social behavior.* Hillsdale, N.J.: Erlbaum, 1976. (13, 28, 31)

Dawes, R. M. Confidence in intellectual judgments vs. confidence in perceptual judgments. In E. D. Lantermann & H. Feger (Eds.), *Similarity and Choice: Papers in honor of Clyde Coombs.* Bern: Hans Huber, 1980. (31)

Dawes, R. M., & Corrigan, B. Linear models in decision making. *Psychological Bulletin,* 1974, *81,* 95–106. (28)

Dawid, A. P. The well-calibrated Bayesian. *Journal of the American Statistical Association,* in press. (22)

Deacon, E. B. A discriminant analysis of predictors of business failure. *Journal of Accounting Research,* 1972, *10,* 167–179. (28)

DeCharms, R. C. *Personal causation: The internal affective determinants of behavior.* New York: Academic Press, 1968. (12, 16)

Deci, E. Effects of externally mediated rewards on intrinsic motivation. *Journal of Personality and Social Psychology,* 1971, *18,* 105–115. (9)

De Finetti, B. La prevision: Ses lois logiques, ses sources subjectives. *Annales de l'Institut Henri Poincaré,* 1937, *7,* 1–68. English translation in H. E. Kyburg, Jr., & H. E. Smokler (Eds.), *Studies in subjective probability.* New York: Wiley, 1964. (22)

De Finetti, B. Probability: Interpretations. In D. E. Sills (Ed.), *International Encyclopedia of the Social Sciences* (Vol. 12). New York: Macmillan, 1968. Pp. 496–504. (1)

Degler, C. N. Why historians change their minds. *Pacific Historical Review,* 1976, *48,* 167–189. (23)

DeGowin, E., & DeGowin, R. *Bedside diagnostic examination* (2nd ed.). New York: Macmillan, 1969. (18)

DeGroot, A. D. *Het denken van den schaker* [Thought and choice in chess]. The Hague, The Netherlands: Mouton, 1965. (28)

Del Regato, J. A. Diagnosis, treatment and prognosis. In L. V. Ackerman (Ed.), *Cancer* (4th Ed.) St. Louis: Mosby, 1970. (18)

DeLuca, J. T. A statistical comparison study of patients undergoing breast biopsy at a community hospital over a 16-year period. *Radiology,* 1974, *112,* 315–318. (18)

Dennett, D. C. *Brainstorms.* Hassocks, England: Harvester, 1979. (35)

DeSmet, A. A., Fryback, D. G., & Thornbury, J. R. A second look at the utility of radiographic skull examination for trauma. *American Journal of Radiology,* 1979, *132,* 95–99. (22)

Detmer, D. E., Fryback, D. G., & Gassner, K. Heuristics and biases in medical decision-making. *Journal of Medical Education,* 1978, *53,* 682–683. (31)

Diaconis, P. Statistical problems in ESP research. *Science,* 1978, *201,* 131–136. (23)

Dodson, J. D. *Simulation system design for a TEAS simulation research facility.* (Tech. Rep. No. AFCRL-1112, PRC R-194). Los Angeles: Planning Research Corporation, November, 1961. (26)

Donchin, E., Ritter, W., & McCallum, W. C. Cognitive psychophysiology: The endogenous components of the ERP. In E. Callaway, P. Teuting, & S. H. Koslow (Eds.), *Event-related brain potentials in man.* New York: Academic Press, 1978. (35)

Dowie, J. On the efficiency and equity of betting markets. *Economica,* 1976, *43,* 139–150. (22, 31)

Dowie, J. Personal communication. November 1980. (22)

Dreman, D. *Contrarian investment strategy.* New York: Random House, 1979. (23, 31)

Duncan-Johnson, C. C., & Donchin, E. On quantifying surprise: The variation of event-related potentials with subjective probability. *Psychophysiology,* 1977, *14,* 456–467. (35)

Dunlap, T. R. Science as a guide in regulating technology: The case of DDT in the United States. *Social Studies of Science*, 1978, *8*, 265–285. (33)

Duval, S., & Hensley, V. Extensions of objective self-awareness theory: The focus of attention-causal attribution hypothesis. In J. H. Harvey, W. L. Ickes, & R. F. Kidd (Eds.), *New directions in attribution research* (Vol. 1). Hillsdale, N.J.: Erlbaum, 1976. (9)

Duval, S., & Wicklund, R. A. *A theory of objective self-awareness.* New York: Academic Press, 1972. (9)

Edwards, A. E. *Experimental design in psychological research.* New York: Holt, Rinehart & Winston, 1960. (20)

Edwards, D. D., & Edwards, J. S. Marriage: Direct and continuous measurement. *Bulletin of the Psychonomic Society*, 1977, *10*, 187–188. (28)

Edwards, W. Optimal strategies for seeking information: Models for statistics, choice reaction times, and human information processing. *Journal of Mathematical Psychology*, 1965, *2*, 312–329. (25)

Edwards, W. *Nonconservative probabilistic information processing systems.* (Report ESD-TR-66-404). U.S. Air Force, AF Systems Command. Electronic Systems Division, Decision Sciences Laboratory, 1966. (25, 26)

Edwards, W. Conservatism in human information processing. In B. Kleinmuntz (Ed.), *Formal representation of human judgment.* New York: Wiley, 1968, 17–52. (1, 2, 3, 8)

Edwards, W. Bayesian and regression models of human information processing – a myopic perspective. *Organizational Behavior and Human Performance*, 1971, *6*, 639–648. (19)

Edwards, W. Comment. *Journal of the American Statistical Association*, 1975, *70*, 291–293. (34)

Edwards, W. Technology for director dubious: Evaluation and decision in public contexts. In K. R. Hammond (Ed.), *Judgment and decision in public policy formation.* Boulder, Colo.: Westview Press, 1978. (28)

Edwards, W., Lindman, H., & Phillips, L. D. Emerging technologies for making decisions. *New directions in psychology* (Vol. 2). New York: Holt, Rinehart & Winston, 1965. (25)

Edwards, W., Lindman, H., & Savage, L. J. Bayesian statistical inference for psychological research. *Psychological Review*, 1963, *70*, 193–242. (25)

Egan, R. L. Fundamentals of mammographic diagnoses of benign and malignant diseases. *Oncology*, 1969, *23*, 126–148. (18)

Egan, R. L. Contributions of mammography in the detection of early breast cancer. *Cancer*, 1971, *28*, 1555–1557. (18)

Egan, R. L. Mammography (2nd Ed.). Springfield, Ill.: Charles C. Thomas, 1972. (18)

Einhorn, H. J. Expert measurement and mechanical combination. *Organizational Behavior and Human Performance*, 1972, *7*, 86–106. (28)

Einhorn, H. J. Decision errors and fallible judgment: Implications for social policy. In K. R. Hammond (Ed.), *Judgment and decision in public policy formation.* Denver, Colo.: Westview Press, 1978. (23)

Einhorn, H. J. Personal communication, January 1979. (28)

Einhorn, H. J., & Hogarth, R. M. Unit weighting schemas for decision making. *Organizational Behavior and Human Performance*, 1975, *13*, 171–192. (28)

Einhorn, H. J., & Hogarth, R. M. Confidence in judgment: Persistence in the illusion of validity. *Psychological Review*, 1978, *85*, 395–416. (9, 19, 28, 34)

Einhorn, H. J., & Hogarth, R. M. Behavioral decision theory: Processes of judgment and choice. *Annual Review of Psychology*, 1981, *32*, 53–88. (34, 35)

Einhorn, H. J., Kleinmuntz, D. N., & Kleinmuntz, B. Linear regression and process tracing models of judgment. *Psychological Review*, 1979, *86*, 465–485. (19)

Ellis, R. J., & Holmes, J. G. *Focus of attention in social interaction: The impact on self evaluations.* Unpublished manuscript. Ontario, Canada: University of Waterloo, 1979. (9)

Ellsberg, D. Risk, ambiguity, and the Savage axioms. *Quarterly Journal of Economics*, 1961, *75*, 643–699. (35)

Epstein, W., & Rock, I. Perceptual set as an artifact of recency. *American Journal of Psychology*, 1960, *73*, 214–228. (35)

Erlick, D. E. Human estimates of statistical relatedness. *Psychonomic Science*, 1966, *5*, 365–366. (15)

Erlick, D. E., & Mills, R. G. Perceptual quantification of conditional dependency. *Journal of Experimental Psychology*, 1967, *73*, 9–14. (15)

Estes, W. K. Probability learning. In A. W. Melton (Ed.), *Categories of human learning*. New York: Academic Press, 1964. (2, 3)

Estes, W. K. The cognitive side of probability learning. *Psychological Review*, 1976, *83*, 37–64. (19)

Evans, J. St. B. T., & Dusoir, A. E. Proportionality and sample size as factors in intuitive statistical judgment. *Acta Psychologica*, 1977, *41*, 129–137. (34)

Evans, J. St. B. T., & Wason, P. C. Rationalization in a reasoning task. *British Journal of Psychology*, 1976, *67*, 486–497. (34)

Fabricand, B. P. *Horse sense.* New York: David McKay, 1965. (22)

Fama, E. F. Random walks in stock market prices. *Financial Analysts Journal*, 1965, *21*, 55–60. (23)

Feather, N. T. Attribution of responsibility and valence of success and failure in relation to initial confidence and task performance. *Journal of Personality and Social Psychology*, 1969, *13*, 129–144. (9)

Feller, W. *An introduction to probability theory and its applications* (3rd ed., Vol. 1). New York: Wiley, 1968. (3, 23, 34)

Ferrell, W. R., & McGoey, P. J. A model of calibration for subjective probabilities. *Organizational Behavior and Human Performance*, 1980, *26*, 32–53. (22, 31)

Festinger, L. *A theory of cognitive dissonance.* Stanford: Stanford University Press, 1957. (9, 15)

Festinger, L. *Conflict, decision and dissonance.* Stanford: Stanford University Press, 1964. (15)

Feyerabend, P. *Against method.* New York: NLB (Schocken), 1975. (23)

Fischer, D. H. *Historians' fallacies.* New York: Harper & Row, 1970. (23, 31)

Fischhoff, B. Hindsight ≠ foresight: The effect of outcome knowledge on judgment under uncertainty. *Journal of Experimental Psychology: Human Perception and Performance*, 1975, *1*, 288–299. (23, 30, 31)

Fischhoff, B. Attribution theory and judgment under uncertainty. In N. H. Harvey, W. J. Ickes, & R. F. Kidd (Eds.), *New directions in attribution research*. Hillsdale, N.J.: Erlbaum, 1976. (13)

Fischhoff, B. Cost-benefit analysis and the art of motorcycle maintenance. *Policy Sciences*, 1977, *8*, 177–202. (33) (a)

Fischhoff, B. Perceived informativeness of facts. *Journal of Experimental Psychology: Human Perception and Performance*, 1977, *3*, 349–358. (23, 31, 34) (b)

Fischhoff, B. Intuitive use of formal models. A comment on Morrison's "Quantitative Models in History." *History and Theory*, 1978, *17*, 207–210. (23)

Fischhoff, B. Latitude and platitudes. How much credit do people deserve? In G. Ungson & D. Braunstein (Eds.), *New directions in decision making*. New York: Kent, in press. (31) (a)

Fischhoff, B. No man is a discipline. In J. Harvey (Ed.), *Cognition, social behavior and the environment*. Hillsdale, N.J.: Erlbaum, in press. (23) (b)

Fischhoff, B., & Bar-Hillel, M. *Focusing techniques as aids to inference* (Decision Research Report 80-9). Eugene, Oreg.: Decision Research, 1980. (10, 34)

Fischhoff, B., & Beyth, R. "I knew it would happen" – Remembered probabilities of once-future things. *Organizational Behavior and Human Performance*, 1975, *13*, 1–16. (22, 23, 31)

Fischhoff, B., Goitein, B., & Shapira, Z. The experienced utility of expected utility approaches. In N. Feather (Ed.), *Expectancy, incentive and action*. Hillsdale, N.J.: Erlbaum, in press. (23)

Fischhoff, B., Lichtenstein, S., Slovic, P., Derby, S., & Keeney, R. *Acceptable risk*. New York: Cambridge University Press, 1981. (33)

Fischhoff, B., & MacGregor, D. Judged lethality (Decision Research Report 80-4). Eugene, Oreg.: Decision Research, 1980. (33)

Fischhoff, B., & Slovic, P. A little learning . . .: Confidence in multicue judgment. In R. Nickerson (Ed.), *Attention and Performance VIII*. Hillsdale, N.J.: Erlbaum, 1980. (22, 23, 31)

Fischhoff, B., Slovic, P., & Lichtenstein, S. Knowing with certainty: The appropriateness of extreme confidence. *Journal of Experimental Psychology: Human Perception and Performance*, 1977, *3*, 552–564. (22, 23, 31, 33)

Fischhoff, B., Slovic, P., & Lichtenstein, S. Fault trees: Sensitivity of estimated failure probabilities to problem representation. *Journal of Experimental Psychology: Human Perception and Performance*, 1978, *4*, 330–334. (19, 23, 33, 34)

Fischhoff, B., Slovic, P., & Lichtenstein, S. Subjective sensitivity analysis. *Organizational Behavior and Human Performance*, 1979, *23*, 339–359. (10, 34)

Fischhoff, B., Slovic, P., & Lichtenstein, S. Knowing what you want: Measuring labile values. In T. Wallsten (Ed.), *Cognitive processes in choice and decision behavior*. Hillsdale, N.J.: Erlbaum, 1980. (19, 33)

Fischhoff, B., Slovic, P., Lichtenstein, S., Read, S., & Combs, B. How safe is safe enough? A psychometric study of attitudes towards technological risks and benefits. *Policy Sciences*, 1978, *9*, 127–152. (33)

Fiske, S. T., Taylor, S. E., Etcoff, N., & Laufer, J. Imaging, empathy and causal attribution. *Journal of Experimental Social Psychology*, 1979, *15*, 356–377. (13)

Fitch, G. Effects of self-esteem, perceived performance, and chance on causal attributions. *Journal of Personality and Social Psychology*, 1970, *16*, 311–315. (9)

Florovsky, G. The study of the past. In R. H. Nash (Ed.), *Ideas of history* (Vol. 2). New York: Dutton, 1969. (23)

Forrester, J. W. *World dynamics*. Cambridge: Wright-Allen, 1971. (11)

Foss, D. J., & Blank, M. A. Identifying the speech codes. *Cognitive Psychology*, 1980, *12*, 1–31. (35)

Freize, I., & Weiner, B. Cue utilization and attributional judgments for success and failure. *Journal of Personality*, 1971, *39*, 591–606. (9)

Friedman, A. K., Ashovitz, S. I., Berger, S. M., Dodd, M. D., Fisher, M. S., Lapayowker, M. S., Moore, J. P., Parlee, D. E., Stein, G. N., & Pendergrass, E. P. A cooperative evaluation of mammography in seven teaching hospitals. *Radiology,* 1966, *86,* 886–891. (18)

Fryback, D. G. *Use of radiologists' subjective probability estimates in a medical decision making problem.* (Michigan Mathematical Psychology Program, Report No. 74-14). Ann Arbor: University of Michigan, 1974. (22)

Furby, L. Interpreting regression toward the mean in developmental research. *Developmental Psychology,* 1973, *8,* 172–179. (23)

Galbraith, R. C., & Underwood, B. J. Perceived frequency of concrete and abstract words. *Memory and Cognition,* 1973, *1,* 56–60. (1)

Gallie, W. B. *Philosophy and the historical understanding.* London: Chatto & Windus, 1964. (23)

Garcia, J., McGowan, B. K., & Greene, K. F. Sensory quality and integration: Constraints on conditioning. In A. H. Black & W. F. Prokasy (Eds.), *Classical conditioning II: Current research and theory.* New York: Appleton-Century-Crofts, 1972. (15)

Gardiner, P. C., & Edwards, W. Public values: Multi-attribute-utility measurement for social decision making. In M. F. Kaplan & S. Schwartz, (Eds.), *Human judgment and decision processes.* New York: Academic Press, 1975. (28)

Garner, W. R. Good patterns have few alternatives. *American Scientist,* 1970, *58*(1), 34–43. (3)

Gershon-Cohen, J., & Borden, A. G. G. Biopsy and mammography. *New York State Journal of Medicine,* 1964, 2751–2756. (18)

Gettys, C. F., & Willke, T. A. The application of Bayes' theorem when the true data state is uncertain. *Organizational Behavior and Human Performance,* 1969, *4,* 125–141. (26)

Ginosar, Z., & Trope, Y. The effects of base rates and individuating information on judgments about another person. *Journal of Experimental Social Psychology,* 1980, *16,* 228–242. (10)

Glanzer, M., & Clark, W. H. Accuracy of perceptual recall: An analysis of organization. *Journal of Verbal Learning and Verbal Behavior,* 1963, *1,* 289–299. (3)

Goethals, G. R., & Reckman, R. F. The perception of consistency in attitudes. *Journal of Experimental Social Psychology,* 1973, *9,* 491–501. (32, 34)

Goffman, E. *Interaction ritual.* New York: Anchor, 1967. (16)

Gold, R. H. The accuracy of mammography in the diagnosis of benign and malignant disease. *Oncology,* 1969, *23,* 159–163. (18)

Goldberg, L. R. The effectiveness of clinician's judgments: The diagnosis of organic brain damage from the Bender-Gestalt Test. *Journal of Consulting Psychology,* 1959, *23,* 25–33. (20)

Goldberg, L. R. Diagnosticians vs. diagnostic signs: The diagnosis of psychosis vs. neurosis from the MMPI. *Psychological Monographs,* 1965, *79.* (28)

Goldberg, L. R. Seer over sign: The first "good" example? *Journal of Experimental Research in Personality,* 1968, *3,* 168–171. (28) (a)

Goldberg, L. R. Simple models or simple processes? Some research on clinical judgments. *American Psychologist,* 1968, *23,* 483–496. (23, 34) (b)

Goldberg, L. R. Man vs. model of man: A rationale, plus some evidence, for a method of improving on clinical inferences. *Psychological Bulletin,* 1970, *73,* 422–432. (23, 28)

Goldberg, L. R. Parameters of personality inventory construction and utilization: A comparison of prediction strategies and tactics. *Multivariate Behavioral Research Monographs*, 1972, *72*, 1–59. (28)

Goldberg, L. R. Man vs. model of man: Just how conflicting is that evidence? *Organizational Behavior and Human Performance*, 1976, *16*, 13–22. (28)

Goldberg, P. Are women prejudiced against women? *Trans-Action*, April 1968, 28–30. (15)

Golding, S. L., & Rorer, L. G. Illusory correlation and the learning of clinical judgment. *Journal of Abnormal Psychology*, 1972, *80*, 249–260. (15)

Goldman, A. I. Epistemics: The regulative theory of cognition. *Journal of Philosophy*, 1978, *75*, 509–523. (32)

Goodfellow, L. D. A psychological interpretation of the results of the Zenith radio experiments in telepathy. *Journal of Experimental Psychology*, 1938, *23*, 601–632. (3)

Gray, C. W. Predicting with intuitive correlations. *Psychonomic Science*, 1968, *11*, 41–42. (4)

Green, B. F., Jr. Parameter sensitivity in multivariate methods. *Multivariate Behavioral Research*, 1977, *3*, 263. (28)

Green, D. M., & Swets, J. A. *Signal detection theory and psychophysics*. New York: Wiley, 1966. (22)

Greenwald, A. G. The totalitarian ego: Fabrication and revision of personal history. Unpublished manuscript, 1978. (12)

Greenwald, A. G., & Albert, R. D. Acceptance and recall of improvised arguments. *Journal of Personality and Social Psychology*, 1968, *8*, 31–34. (12)

Greenwald, A. G., & Sakumura, J. S. Attitude and selective learning: Where are the phenomena of yesteryear? *Journal of Personality and Social Psychology*, 1957, *7*, 387–397. (12)

Grether, D. M. Bayes' rule as a descriptive model: The representativeness heuristic (Social Science Working Paper No. 245). Pasadena: California Institute of Technology, 1979. (34)

Grether, D. M., & Plott, C. R. Economic theory of choice and the preference reversal phenomenon. *American Economic Review*, 1979, *69*, 623–638. (19, 33, 34)

Grice, H. P. Logic and conversation. In D. Davidson and G. Harman (Eds.), *The logic of grammar*. Encino: Dickenson, 1975. (34)

Gross, A. *Evaluation of the target person in a social influence situation*. Unpublished doctoral dissertation, Stanford University, 1966. (9)

Gruneberg, M. M., Morris, P. E., & Sykes, R. N. (Eds.), *Practical aspects of memory*. London: Academic Press, 1978. (31)

Guilford, J. P. *Psychometric methods*. New York: McGraw-Hill, 1954. (4)

Hacking, I. *The emergence of probability*. London: Cambridge University Press, 1975. (32)

Hamill, R., Wilson, T. D., & Nisbett, R. E. Insensitivity to sample bias: Generalizing from atypical cases. *Journal of Personality and Social Psychology*, 1980, *39*, 578–589. (9, 32, 34)

Hamilton, D. L. A cognitive attributional analysis of stereotyping. In L. Berkowitz (Ed.), *Advances in experimental social psychology* (Vol. 12). New York: Academic Press, 1979. (9)

Hamilton, D. L., & Rose, T. R. *Illusory correlation and the maintenance of stereotypic beliefs*. Unpublished manuscript, University of California at Santa Barbara, 1978. (13)

Hamlin, R. M. The clinician as judge: Implications of a series of studies. *Journal of Consulting Psychology*, 1954, *18*, 233–238. (20)

Hammerton, M. A case of radical probability estimation. *Journal of Experimental Psychology*, 1973, *101*, 252–254. (10)

Hammond, K. R. Probabilistic functioning and the clinical method. *Psychological Review*, 1955, *62*, 255-262. (28)

Hammond, K. R. Toward increasing competence of thought in public policy formation. In K. R. Hammond (Ed.), *Judgment and decision in public policy formation*. Boulder, Colo.: Westview Press, 1978. (19)

Hammond, K. R., & Adelman, L. Science, values, and human judgment. *Science*, 1976, *194*, 389–396. (28)

Hammond, K. R., McClelland, G. H., & Mumpower, J. *Human judgment and decision making: Theories, methods and procedures*. New York: Praeger, 1980. (34)

Hansen, R. D., & Donoghue, J. M. The power of consensus: Information derived from one's own and others' behavior. *Journal of Personality and Social Psychology*, 1977, *35*, 294–302. (10)

Hansen, R. D., & Lowe, C. A. Distinctiveness and consensus: The influence of behavioral information on actors' and observers' attributions. *Journal of Personality and Social Psychology*, 1976, *34*, 425–433. (10)

Hart, J. T. Memory and the memory-monitoring process. *Journal of Verbal Learning and Verbal Behavior*, 1967, *6*, 686–691. (11)

Hartshorne, H., & May, M. A. *Studies in the nature of character* (Vol. 1), Studies in deceit. New York: Macmillan, 1928. (15)

Hastie, R., & Kumar, P. A. Person memory: Personality traits as organizing principles in memory for behavior. *Journal of Personality and Social Psychology*, 1979, *37*, 25–38. (9)

Hathaway, S. R. Clinical intuition and inferential accuracy. *Journal of Personality*, 1956, *24*, 223–250. (20)

Hayes, J. R., & Simon, H. A. Psychological differences among problem isomorphs. In N. J. Castellan, Jr., D. B. Pisoni, & G. R. Potts (Eds.), *Cognitive theory*. Hillsdale, N.J.: Erlbaum, 1977. Vol. 2. (34)

Hazard, T. H., & Peterson, C. R. *Odds versus probabilities for categorical events* (Tech. Rep. (73-2). McLean, Va.: Decisions and Designs, Inc., 1973. (22)

Hedges, L. V., & Olkin, I. Vote counting methods on research synthesis. *Psychological Bulletin*, 1980, *88*, 359–369. (31)

Heider, F. Social perception and phenomenal causality. *Psychological Review*, 1944, *51*, 358–373. (9)

Heider, F. *The psychology of interpersonal relations*. New York: Wiley, 1958. (8, 9)

Hendrick, I. The discussion of the "Instinct to Master." *Psychoanalytic Quarterly*, 1943, *12*, 561–565. (16)

Henrion, M. *Assessing probabilities: A review*. Pittsburgh, Pa.: Carnegie-Mellon University, Department of Engineering and Public Policy, 1980. (31)

Henslin, J. M. Craps and magic. *American Journal of Sociology*, 1967, *73*, 316–330. (16)

Herrnstein, R. J. On the law of effect. *Journal of the Experimental Analysis of Behavior*, 1970, *13*, 243–266. (35)

Hershey, J. C., & Schoemaker, P. J. H. Risk taking and problem context in the domain of losses: An expected utility analysis. *Journal of Risk and Insurance.* 1980, 47, 111–132. (33)

Hession, E., & McCarthy, E. *Human performance in assessing subjective probability distributions.* Unpublished manuscript, September, 1974. (Available from Department of Business Administration, University College Dublin, Belfield, Dublin 4, Ireland.) (22)

Hexter, J. H. *The history primer.* New York: Basic Books, 1971. (23)

Hoerl, A. E., & Fallin, H. K. Reliability of subjective evaluations in a high incentive situation. *Journal of the Royal Statistical Society (Series A),* 1974, 137, 227–230. (22)

Hoffman, P. J. The paramorphic representation of clinical judgment. *Psychological Bulletin,* 1960, 57, 116–131. (23, 28)

Hogarth, R. M. Cognitive processes and the assessment of subjective probability distributions. *Journal of the American Statistical Association,* 1975, 70, 271–289. (19, 31)

Hohenemser, K. H. The failsafe risk. *Environment,* 1975, 17(1), 6–10. (33)

Holdren, J. P. The nuclear controversy and the limitations of decision making by experts. *Bulletin of the Atomic Scientists,* 1976, 32, 20–22. (33)

Holmes, D. S. Dimensions of projection. *Psychological Bulletin,* 1968, 69, 248–268. (9)

Holt, R. R. Yet another look at clinical and statistical prediction. *American Psychologist,* 1970, 25, 337–339. (28)

Horowitz, L. M., Norman, S. A., & Day, R. S. Availability and associative symmetry. *Psychological Review,* 1966, 73, 1–15. (11)

Hovland, C. I. Reconciling conflicting results derived from experimental and survey studies of attitude change. *American Psychologist,* 1959, 14, 8–17. (8)

Hovland, C. I., Mandell, W., Campbell, E. H., & Brock, T., Luchins, A. S., Cohen, A. R., McGuire, W. J., Janis, I. L., Feierabend, R. L., & Anderson, N. H. The effects of "commitment" on opinion change following communication. In C. I. Hovland et al., (Eds.), *The order of presentation in persuasion.* New Haven: Yale University Press, 1957. (9)

Howard, J. W., & Dawes, R. M. Linear prediction of marital happiness. *Personality and Social Psychology Bulletin,* 1976, 2, 478–480. (28)

Howell, W. C., & Burnett, S. A. Uncertainty measurement: A cognitive taxonomy. *Organizational Behavior and Human Performance,* 1978, 22, 45–68. (31, 35)

Howell, W. C., Gettys, C., & Martin, D. On the allocation of inference functions in decision systems. *Organizational Behavior and Human Performance,* 1971, 6, 132–149. (26)

Huntsberger, D. V. *Elements of statistics* (2nd ed.). Boston: Allyn & Bacon, 1967. (15)

Hynes, M., & Vanmarcke, E. Reliability of embankment performance predictions. *Proceedings of the ASCE Engineering Mechanics Division Specialty Conference.* Waterloo, Ontario, Canada: University of Waterloo Press, 1976. (31, 33)

Ittelson, W. H., & Kilpatrick, F. P. Experiments in perception. *Scientific American,* 1951, 185, 50–55. (35)

Janis, I. *Victims of groupthink.* Boston: Houghton Mifflin, 1972. (8, 23, 34)

Janis, I. L., & Mann, L. *Decision making.* New York: Free Press, 1977. (34)

Jenkins, H. M., & Ward, W. C. Judgment of contingency between responses and outcomes. *Psychological Monographs,* 1965, 79. (11, 15, 19)

Jennergren, L. P., & Keeney, R. L. Risk assessment. In *Handbook of applied systems analysis.* Laxenberg, Austria: IIASA, in press. (31, 33)

Jennings, D. L., Lepper, M. R., & Ross, L. *Persistence of impressions of personal persuasiveness: Perseverance of erroneous self assessments outside the debriefing paradigm.* Unpublished manuscript, Stanford University, 1980. (9, 15)

Jervis, R. *Perception and misperception in international relations.* Princeton: Princeton University Press, 1975. (8, 34)

Johnson, D. M. *Systematic introduction to the psychology of thinking.* New York: Harper & Row, 1972. (4)

Johnson, T. J., Feigenbaum, R., & Weiby, M. Some determinants and consequences of the teacher's perception of causation. *Journal of Experimental Psychology,* 1964, 55, 237–246. (9)

Johnson-Laird, P. N., Legrenzi, P., & Sonino–Legrenzi, M. Reasoning and a sense of reality. *British Journal of Psychology,* 1972, 63, 395–400. (6, 34)

Johnson-Laird, P. N., & Wason, P. C. A theoretical analysis of insight into a reasoning task. In P. N. Johnson-Laird and P. C. Wason (Eds.), *Thinking.* Cambridge: Cambridge University Press, 1977. (6, 34)

Jones, E. E., & Davis, K. E. From acts to dispositions: The attribution process in person perception. In L. Berkowitz (Ed.), *Advances in experimental social psychology* (Vol. 2). New York: Academic Press, 1965. (9, 13)

Jones, E. E., Davis, K. E., & Gergen, K. Role playing variations and their informational value for person perception. *Journal of Abnormal and Social Psychology,* 1961, 63, 302–310. (9)

Jones, E. E., & DeCharms, R. Changes in social perception as a function of the personal relevance of behavior. *Sociometry,* 1957, 20, 75–85. (9)

Jones, E. E., & Harris, V. A. The attribution of attitudes. *Journal of Experimental Social Psychology,* 1967, 3, 1–24. (9)

Jones, E. E., Kanouse, D. E., Kelley, H. H., Nisbett, R. E., Valins, S., & Weiner, B. *Attribution: Perceiving the causes of behavior.* Morristown, N.J.: General Learning Press, 1971. (8, 9, 15)

Jones, E. E., & Nisbett, R. E. The actor and the observer: Divergent perceptions of the causes of behavior. In E. E. Jones, D. Kanouse, H. H. Kelley, R. E. Nisbett, S. Valins, & B. Weiner, *Attribution: Perceiving the causes of behavior.* Morristown, N.J.: General Learning Press, 1971. (9, 11, 12)

Jones, J. M. *Prejudice and racism.* Reading, Mass.: Addison-Wesley, 1972. (15)

Jones, M. R. From probability learning to sequential processing: A critical review. *Psychological Bulletin,* 1971, 76, 153–185. (3)

Kadane, J. Personal communication, November 1980. (22)

Kahneman, D., & Tversky, A. On prediction and judgment. *ORI Research Monograph,* 1972, 12(4). (10) (a)

Kahneman, D., & Tversky, A. Subjective probability: A judgment of representativeness. *Cognitive Psychology,* 1972, 3, 430–454. (1, 4, 5, 6, 11, 23, 32, 34) (b)

Kahneman, D., & Tversky, A. On the psychology of prediction. *Psychological Review,* 1973, 80, 237–251. (1, 5, 6, 7, 8, 9, 10, 13, 15, 18, 23, 27, 30, 34)

Kahneman, D., & Tversky, A. Intuitive prediction: Biases and corrective procedures. *TIMS Studies in Management Science,* 1979, 12, 313–327. (8, 33, 34, 35) (a)

Kahneman, D., & Tversky, A. Prospect theory: An analysis of decisions under risk. *Econometrica,* 1979, 47, 263–291. (19, 33) (b)

Kasper, R. G. "Real" vs. perceived risk: Implications for policy. In G. T. Goodman & W. D. Rowe (Eds.), *Energy risk management.* London: Academic Press, 1979. (33)

Kassin, S. M. Base rates and prediction: The role of sample size. *Personality and Social Psychology Bulletin*, 1979, 5, 210–213. (10) (a)

Kassin, S. M. Consensus information, prediction, and causal attribution: A review of the literature and issues. *Journal of Personality and Social Psychology*, 1979, 37, 1966–1981. (10) (b)

Kates, R. W. *Hazard and choice perception in flood plain management* (Research Paper No. 78). Chicago: University of Chicago, Department of Geography, 1962. (23, 33)

Katz, D., & Allport, F. *Students' attitudes*. Syracuse: Craftsman Press, 1931. (9)

Kaufman, M. T. *The New York Times*, October 18, 1973. (7)

Kelley, H. H. Attribution theory in social psychology. In D. Levine (Ed.), *Nebraska Symposium on Motivation: 1967*. Lincoln: University of Nebraska Press, 1967, 192–241. (7, 9, 13, 15)

Kelley, H. H. Attribution in social interaction. In E. E. Jones, D. Kanouse, H. H. Kelley, R. E. Nisbett, S. Valins, & B. Weiner (Eds.), *Attribution: Perceiving the causes of behavior*. Morristown, N.J.: General Learning Press, 1971. (9, 15)

Kelley, H. H. The process of causal attribution. *American Psychologist*, 1973, 28, 107–128. (9, 15)

Kelley, H. H., & Stahelski, A. J. Social interaction basis of cooperators' and competitors' beliefs about others. *Journal of Personality and Social Psychology*, 1970, 16, 66–91. (9)

Kelly, L. Evaluation of the interview as a selection technique. In *Proceedings of the 1953 Invitational Conference on Testing Problems*. Princeton, N.J.: Educational Testing Service, 1954. (28)

Kelman, H. C. The human use of human subjects: The problem of deception in social psychological experiments. In A. G. Miller (Ed.), *The social psychology of psychological research*. New York: Macmillan, 1972. (9)

Kidd, J. B. The utilization of subjective probabilities in production planning. *Acta Psychologica*, 1970, 34, 338–347. (30)

Kilpatrick, F. P. *Explorations in transactional psychology*. New York: New York University Press, 1961. (35)

King, J. F., Zechmeister, E. B., & Shaughnessy, J. J. Judgment of knowing: The influence of retrieval practice. *American Journal of Psychology*, in press. (31)

Koltuv, B. Some characteristics of intrajudge trait intercorrelations. *Psychological Monographs*, 1962, 76. (15)

Koriat, A., Lichtenstein, S., & Fischhoff, B. Reasons for confidence. *Journal of Experimental Psychology: Human Learning and Memory*, 1980, 6, 107–118. (22, 23, 31)

Kostlan, A. A method for the empirical study of psychodiagnosis. *Journal of Consulting Psychology*, 1954, 18, 83–88. (20)

Krantz, D. H. Measurement structures and psychological laws. *Science*, 1972, 175, 1427–1435. (28)

Krantz, D. H., Luce, R. D., Suppes, P., & Tversky, A. *Foundations of measurement* (Vol. 1). New York: Academic Press, 1971. (28)

Kruskal, W., & Mosteller, F. Representative sampling I: Non-scientific literature. *International Statistical Review*, 1979, 47, 13–24. (6) (a)

Kruskal, W., & Mosteller, F. Representative sampling II: Scientific literature excluding statistics. *International Statistical Review*, 1979, 47, 111–127. (6) (b)

Kuhn, T. *The structure of scientific revolution*. Chicago: University of Chicago Press, 1962. (8, 23)

Kushner, R. Breast cancer–"The night I found out." *San Francisco Chronicle*, March 24, 1976. (18)

Lakatos, I. Falsification and scientific research programmes. In I. Lakatos & A. Musgrave (Eds.), *Criticism and the growth of scientific knowledge*. Cambridge: Cambridge University Press, 1970. (23)

Langer, E. J., Taylor, S. E., Fiske, S. T., & Chanowitz, B. Stigma, staring and discomfort: A novel stimulus hypothesis. *Journal of Experimental Social Psychology*, 1976, *12*, 451–463. (13)

Lanir, Z. *Critical reevaluation of the strategic intelligence methodology*. Tel Aviv: Center for Strategic Studies, Tel Aviv University, 1978. (23)

Larkin, J., McDermott, J., Simon, D. P., & Simon, H. A. Expert and novice performance in solving physics problems. *Science*, 1980, *208*, 1335–1342. (34)

Larson, J. R., & Reenan, A. M. The equivalence interval as a measure of uncertainty. *Organizational Behavior and Human Performance*, 1979, *23*, 49–55. (22, 31)

Lepper, M. R., & Greene, D. Turning play into work: Effects of adult surveillance and extrinsic rewards on children's intrinsic motivation. *Journal of Personality and Social Psychology*, 1975, *31*, 479–486. (9)

Lepper, M. R., & Greene, D. *The hidden costs of reward*. Hillsdale, N.J.: Erlbaum, 1978. (9)

Lepper, M. R., Greene, D., & Nisbett, R. E. Undermining children's intrinsic interest with extrinsic reward: A test of the overjustification hypothesis. *Journal of Personality and Social Psychology*, 1973, *28*, 129–137. (9)

Lepper, M. R., Ross, L., & Lau, R. *Persistence of inaccurate and discredited personal impressions: A field demonstration of attributional perseverance*. Unpublished manuscript, Stanford University, 1979. (9)

Lesnick, G. J. Mammography: A word of caution. *New York State Journal of Medicine*, 1966, 2005–2008. (18)

Libby, R. Man versus model of man: Some conflicting evidence. *Organizational Behavior and Human Performance*, 1976, *16*, 1–12. (28)

Lichtenstein, S., & Fischhoff, B. Do those who know more also know more about how much they know? The calibration of probability judgments. *Organizational Behavior and Human Performance*, 1977, *20*, 159–183. (22, 31)

Lichtenstein, S., & Fischhoff, B. *How well do probability experts assess probability?* (Decision Research Report 80–5). Eugene, Oreg.: Decision Research, 1980. (22) (a)

Lichtenstein, S., & Fischhoff, B. Training for calibration. *Organizational Behavior and Human Performance*, 1980, *26*, 149–171. (22, 31) (b)

Lichtenstein, S., & Fischhoff, B. The effects of gender and instructions on Calibration (Decision Research Report 81–5). Eugene, Oreg.: Decision Research 1981. (22)

Lichtenstein, S., Fischhoff, B., & Phillips, L. D. Calibration of probabilities: The state of the art. In H. Jungermann & G. deZeeuw (Eds.), *Decision making and change in human affairs*. Amsterdam: D. Reidel, 1977. (33)

Lichtenstein, S., & Slovic, P. Reversal of preferences between bids and choices in gambling decisions. *Journal of Experimental Psychology*, 1971, *89*, 46–55. (19, 33, 34)

Lichtenstein, S., & Slovic, P. Response-induced reversals of preference in gambling: An extended replication in Las Vegas. *Journal of Experimental Psychology*, 1973, *101*, 16–20. (33, 34)

Lichtenstein, S., Slovic, P., Fischhoff, B., Layman, M., & Combs, B. Judged frequency of lethal events. *Journal of Experimental Psychology: Human Learning and Memory*, 1978, *4*, 551–578. (33)

Lindman, H. G., & Edwards, W. Supplementary report: Learning the gambler's fallacy. *Journal of Experimental Psychology*, 1961, *62*, 630. (23)

Loftus, E. F. *Eyewitness testimony*. Cambridge, Mass.: Harvard University Press, 1979. (34)

Loftus, E. F., & Palmer, J. C. Reconstruction of automobile destruction: An example of the interaction between language and memory. *Journal of Verbal Learning and Verbal Behavior*, 1974, *16*, 585–589. (34)

Lord, C., Lepper, M. R., & Ross, L. Biased assimilation and attitude polarization: The effects of prior theories on subsequently considered evidence. *Journal of Personality and Social Psychology*, 1979, *37*, 2098–2110. (9, 15)

Ludke, R. L., Stauss, F. F., & Gustafson, D. H. Comparison of five methods for estimating subjective probability distributions. *Organizational Behavior and Human Performance*, 1977, *19*, 162–179. (31)

Lusted, L. B. *Introduction to medical decision making*. Springfield, Ill.: Charles C Thomas, 1968. (18)

Lusted, L. B. *A study of the efficacy of diagnostic radiologic procedures: Final report on diagnostic efficacy*. Chicago: Efficacy Study Committee of the American College of Radiology, 1977. (22, 31)

Lusted, L. B., Bell, R. S., Edwards, W., Roberts, H. V., & Wallace, D. L. Evaluating the efficacy of radiologic procedures by Bayesian methods: A progress report. In K. J. Snapper (Ed.). *Models in metrics for decision makers*. Washington, D.C.: Information Resources Press, 1977. (18)

Lynn, R. *Attention, arousal and the orientation reaction*. Oxford: Pergamon, 1966. (35)

Lyon, D., & Slovic, P. Dominance of accuracy information and neglect of base rates in probability estimation. *Acta Psychologica*, 1976, *40*, 287–298. (10, 18)

Lyons, A. S. Aids to the surgeon by mammography. *Mt. Sinai Journal of Medicine, New York*, 1975, *42*, 223–231. (18)

Machover, K. *Personality projection in the drawing of the human figure*. Springfield, Ill.: Charles C Thomas, 1949. (17)

Malpass, R. S. Effects of attitude on learning and memory. The influence of instruction-induced sets. *Journal of Experimental Social Psychology*, 1969, *5*, 441–453. (12)

Manis, M., Dovalina, I., Avis, N. E., & Cardoze, S. Base rates can affect individual predictions. *Journal of Personality and Social Psychology*, 1980, *38*, 231–248. (10)

Markman, E. M. Realizing that you don't understand: Elementary school children's awareness of inconsistencies. *Child Development*, 1979, *50*, 643–655. (31)

Marković, M. Social determinism and freedom. In H. E. Kiefer & M. K. Munitz, (Eds.), *Mind, science and history*. Albany, N.Y.: State University of New York Press, 1970. (23)

Marquardt, D. W., & Snee, R. D. Ridge regression in practice. *American Statistician*, 1975, *29*(1), 3–19. (28)

Marwick, A. *The nature of history*. London: Macmillan, 1970. (23)

Mayzner, M. S., & Tresselt, M. E. Tables of single-letter and bigram frequency counts for various word-length and letter-position combinations. *Psychonomic Monograph Supplements*, 1965, *1*, 13–32. (11)

McArthur, C. Analyzing the clinical process. *Journal of Counseling Psychology*, 1954, *1*, 203–207. (20)

McArthur, L. Z. The how and what of why: Some determinants and consequences of causal attribution. *Journal of Personality and Social Psychology*, 1972, *22*, 171–193. (7, 9)

McArthur, L. Z. The lesser influence of consensus than distinctiveness information on causal attributions: A test of the person-thing hypothesis. *Journal of Personality and Social Psychology*, 1976, *33*, 733–742. (9)

McArthur, L. Z., & Post, D. Figural emphasis and person perception. *Journal of Experimental Social Psychology*, 1977, *13*, 520–535. (9)

McArthur, L. Z., & Solomon, L. K. Perceptions of an aggressive encounter as a function of the victim's salience and the perceiver's arousal. *Journal of Personality and Social Psychology*, 1978, *36*, 1278–1290. (9)

McCauley, C., & Stitt, C. L. An individual and quantitative measure of stereotypes. *Journal of Personality and Social Psychology*, 1978, *36*, 929–940. (10)

McClelland, G., & Rohrbaugh, J. Who accepts the Pareto axiom? The role of utility and equity in arbitration decisions. *Behavioral Science*, 1978, *23*, 446–456. (34)

McClow, M. V., & Williams, A. C. Mammographic examinations (4030): Ten-year clinical experience in a community medical center. *Annals of Surgery*, 1973, *177*, 616–619. (18)

McGrath, P. E. *Radioactive waste management: Potentials and hazards from a risk point of view* (Report EURFNR 1204 [KFK 1992]). Karlsruhe, West Germany: U.S.-EURATOM Fast Reactor Exchange Programme, 1974. (33)

McNeil, B. J., Weichselbaum, R., & Pauker, S. G. Fallacy of the five-year survival in lung cancer. *New England Journal of Medicine*, 1978, *299*, 1397–1401. (33)

Meehl, P. E. *Clinical versus statistical prediction: A theoretical analysis and a review of the evidence*. Minneapolis: University of Minnesota Press, 1954. (28)

Meehl, P. E. When shall we use our heads instead of the formula? *Journal of Counseling Psychology*, 1957, *4*, 268–273. (20)

Meehl, P. E. Seer over sign: The first good example. *Journal of Experimental Research in Personality*, 1965, *1*, 27–32. (28)

Meehl, P. E. Nuisance variables and the ex post facto design. In M. Radner & S. Winokur (Eds.), *Minnesota studies in the philosophy of science*. Minneapolis: University of Minnesota Press, 1970. (23)

Meehl, P. E., & Rosen, A. Antecedent probability and the efficacy of psychometric signs, patterns or cutting scores. *Psychological Bulletin*, 1955, *52*, 194–216. (10)

Merton, R. K. The self-fulfilling prophecy. *Antioch Review*, 1948, *8*, 193–210. (15)

Mervis, C. B., & Rosch, E. Categorization of natural objects. *Annual Review of Psychology*, 1981, *32*, 89–115. (6)

Michotte, A. *The perception of causality*. New York: Basic Books, 1963. (19)

Milgram, S. Behavioral study of obedience. *Journal of Abnormal and Social Psychology*, 1963, *67*, 371–378. (7, 9)

Mill, J. S. *A system of logic, ratiocinative and inductive*. Toronto: University of Toronto Press, 1974 (Originally published in 1843). (32)

Miller, A. G. *The social psychology of psychological research*. New York: Macmillan, 1972. (9)

Miller, A. G., Gillen, B., Schenker, C., & Radlove, S. Perception of obedience to authority. *Proceedings of the 81st Annual Convention of the American Psychological Association*, 1973, 8, 127–128. (7)

Miller, D. T. What constitutes a self-serving attributional bias? *Journal of Personality and Social Psychology*, 1978, 36, 1221–1223. (9)

Miller, D. T., & Ross, M. Self-serving biases in the attribution of causality: Fact or fiction? *Psychological Bulletin*, 1975, 82, 213–225. (9)

Mischel, W. *Personality and assessment*. New York: Wiley, 1968. (4, 15)

Mischel, W. Continuity and change in personality. *American Psychologist*, 1969, 24, 1012–1018. (15)

Mischel, W. On the interface of cognition and personality: Beyond the person-situation debate. *American Psychologist*, 1979, 34, 740–754. (6)

Mischel, W., & Gilligan, C. Delay of gratification, motivation for the prohibited gratification, and responses to temptation. *Journal of Personality and Social Psychology*, 1964, 64, 411–417. (15)

Mitchell, T. R., & Kalb, L. S. Outcome knowledge and content as determinants of supervisor attributions and judgments of responsibility about a subordinate's poor performance. *Journal of Applied Psychology*, in press. (31)

Moore, P. G. The manager's struggle with uncertainty. *Journal of the Royal Statistical Society* (Series A), 1977, 140, 129–165. (31)

Morris, P. A. Decision analysis expert use. *Management Science*, 1974, 20, 1233–1241. (31)

Morrison, R. J. Franklin D. Roosevelt and the Supreme Court: An example of the use of probability theory in political history. *History and Theory*, 1977, 16, 137–146. (23)

Morton, J. Interaction of information in word recognition. *Psychological Review*, 1969, 76, 165–178. (35)

Moskowitz, H., & Bullers, W. I. *Modified PERT versus fractile assessment of subjective probability distributions* (Paper No. 675). Purdue University, 1978. (22)

Murphy, A. H. Scalar and vector partitions of the probability score (Part I). Two-state situation. *Journal of Applied Meteorology*, 1972, 11, 273–282. (22)

Murphy, A. H. A new vector partition of the probability score. *Journal of Applied Meteorology*, 1973, 12, 595–600. (22)

Murphy, A. H. Personal communication, August 1980. (22)

Murphy, A. H., & Winkler, R. L. Forecasters and probability forecasts: Some current problems. *Bulletin of the American Meteorological Society*, 1971, 52, 239–247. (22)

Murphy, A. H., & Winkler, R. L. Subjective probability forecasting experiments in meteorology: Some preliminary results. *Bulletin of the American Meteorological Society*, 1974, 55, 1206–1216. (22, 31)

Murphy, A. H., & Winkler, R. L. Can weather forecasters formulate reliable probability forecasts of precipitation and temperature? *National Weather Digest*, 1977, 2, 2–9. (22, 31) (a)

Murphy, A. H., & Winkler, R. L. The use of credible intervals in temperature forecasting: Some experimental results. In H. Jungermann & G. deZeeuw (Eds.), *Decision making and change in human affairs*. Amsterdam: D. Reidel, 1977. (22) (b)

Näätänen, R., & Summala, H. *Road-user behavior and traffic accidents*. Amsterdam: North-Holland, 1975. (33)

Nickerson, R. S., & McGoldrick, C. C., Jr. Confidence ratings and level of performance on a judgmental task. *Perceptual Motor Skills*, 1965, *20*, 311–316. (22, 31)

Nisbett, R. E., & Borgida, E. Attribution and the psychology of prediction. *Journal of Personality and Social Psychology*, 1975, *32*, 932–943. (7, 10, 27, 32)

Nisbett, R. E., Borgida, E., Crandall, R., & Reed, H. Popular induction: Information is not necessarily informative. In J. S. Carroll and J. W. Payne (Eds.), *Cognition and social behavior*. Hillsdale, N.J.: Erlbaum, 1976. (19, 28)

Nisbett, R. E., & Ross, L. *Human inference: Strategies and shortcomings of social judgment*. Englewood Cliffs, N.J.: Prentice-Hall, 1980. (6, 9, 10, 15, 32, 34, 35)

Nisbett, R. E., & Schachter, S. Cognitive manipulations of pain. *Journal of Experimental Social Psychology*, 1966, *2*, 227–236. (7)

Nisbett, R. E., & Wilson, T. D. Telling more than we can know: Verbal reports on mental processes. *Psychological Review*, 1977, *84*, 231–259. (19, 32, 34)

Nisbett, R. E., Zukier, H., & Lemley, R. E. The dilution effect: Nondiagnostic information weakens the implications of diagnostic information. *Cognitive Psychology*, 1981, *13*, 248–277. (34)

Norman, W. T., & Goldberg, L. R. Raters, ratees, and randomness in personality structure. *Journal of Personality and Social Psychology*, 1966, *4*, 681–691. (15)

Nowell-Smith, P. H. Historical explanation. In H. E. Kiefer & M. K. Munitz (Eds.), *Mind, science and history*. Albany, N.Y.: State University of New York Press, 1970, (23)

O'Leary, M. K., Coplin, W. D., Shapiro, H. B., & Dean, D. The quest for relevance. *International Studies Quarterly*, 1974, *18*, 211–237. (23)

Olson, C. L. Some apparent violations of the representativeness heuristic in human judgment. *Journal of Experimental Psychology: Human Perception and Performance*, 1976, *2*, 599–608. (5, 34)

Orne, M. T. Demand characteristics and their implications for real life: The importance of quasi-controls. In A. G. Miller (Ed.), *The social psychology of psychological research*. New York: Macmillan, 1972. (9)

Orne, M. T. Communication by the total experimental situation: Why it is important, how it is evaluated, and its significance for the ecological validity of findings. In P. Pliner, L. Krames, & T. Alloway (Eds.), *Communication and affect*. New York: Academic Press, 1973. (34)

Oskamp, S. The relationship of clinical experience and training methods to several criteria of clinical prediction. *Psychological Monographs*, 1962, *76*, (28, Whole No. 547). (20, 22, 31)

Overall, J. E. Classical statistical hypothesis testing within the context of Bayesian theory. *Psychological Bulletin*, 1969, *71*, 285–292. (2)

Parducci, A. Category judgment: A range-frequency model. *Psychological Review*, 1965, *72*, 407–418. (34)

Passini, F. T., & Norman, W. T. A universal conception of personality structure? *Journal of Personality and Social Psychology*, 1966, *4*, 44–49. (15)

Patterson, C. H. Diagnostic accuracy or diagnostic stereotypy? *Journal of Consulting Psychology*, 1955, *19*, 483–485. (20)

Payne, J. W. Information processing theory: Some concepts and methods applied to decision research. In T. Wallsten (Ed.), *Cognitive processes in choice and decision behavior*. Hillsdale, N.J.: Erlbaum, 1980. (19)

Pennington, D. C., Rutter, D. R., McKenna, K., & Morley, I. E. Estimating the outcome of a pregnancy test: Women's judgments in foresight and hindsight. *British Journal of Social and Clinical Psychology,* 1980, *79,* 317–323. (31)

Peterson, C. R. (Ed.). Special issue: Cascaded inference. *Organizational Behavior and Human Performance,* 1973, *10,* 315–432. (27)

Peterson, C. R., & Beach, L. R. Man as an intuitive statistician. *Psychological Bulletin,* 1967, *68*(1), 29–46. (3, 15, 31)

Peterson, C. R., DuCharme, W. M., & Edwards, W. Sampling distributions and probability revisions. *Journal of Experimental Psychology,* 1968, *76,* 236–243. (3)

Peterson, C. R., Schneider, R. J., & Miller, A. J. Sample size and the revision of subjective probabilities. *Journal of Experimental Psychology,* 1965, *69,* 522–527. (25)

Phillips, L. D. *Some components of probabilistic inference* (Tech. Rep. No. 1). Human Performance Center, University of Michigan, 1966. (11)

Phillips, L. D., & Edwards, W. Conservatism in simple probability inference tasks. *Journal of Experimental Psychology,* 1966, *72,* 346–357. (25)

Phillips, L. D., Hays, W. L., & Edwards, W. Conservatism in complex probabilistic inference. *IEEE Transactions on Human Factors in Electronics,* 1966, *HFE-7,* 7–18. (25)

Phillips, L. D., & Wright, G. N. Cultural differences in viewing uncertainty and assessing probabilities. In H. Jungermann & G. deZeeuw (Eds.), *Decision making and change in human affairs.* Amsterdam: D. Reidel, 1977. (22, 31)

Pickhardt, R. C., & Wallace, J. B. A study of the performance of subjective probability assessors. *Decision Sciences,* 1974, *5,* 347–363. (22, 31)

Pitz, G. F. Subjective probability distributions for imperfectly known quantities. In L. W. Gregg (Ed.), *Knowledge and cognition.* New York: Wiley, 1974. (22, 31)

Pitz, G. F., Downing, L., & Reinhold, H. Sequential effects in the revision of subjective probabilities. *Canadian Journal of Psychology,* 1967, *21,* 381–393. (3)

Pokorny, G. Energy development: Attitudes and beliefs at the regional/national levels. Cambridge, Mass.: Cambridge Reports, 1977. (33)

Polefka, J. *The perception and evaluation of responses to social influences.* Unpublished doctoral dissertation, Stanford University, 1965. (9)

Pollack, I., & Decker, L. R. Confidence ratings, message receptions, and the receiver operating characteristics. *Journal of the Acoustical Society of America,* 1958, *30,* 286–292. (22)

Posner, M. I. *Chronometric explorations of mind.* Hillsdale, N.J.: Erlbaum, 1978. (35)

Posner, M. I., & Keele, S. W. On the genesis of abstract ideas. *Journal of Experimental Psychology,* 1968, *77,* 353–363. (6)

Poulton, E. C. The new psychophysics: Six models for magnitude estimation. *Psychological Bulletin,* 1968, *69,* 1–19. (33)

Poulton, E. C. Range effects in experiments with people. *American Journal of Psychology,* 1975, *88,* 3–32. (34)

Pratt, J. W. Personal communication, October 1975. (22)

President's Commission on the Accident at Three Mile Island. *Report.* Washington, D.C.: U.S. Government Printing Office, 1979. (33)

Primack, J. Nuclear reactor safety: An introduction to the issues. *Bulletin of the Atomic Scientists,* 1975, *31,* 15–17. (33)

Pryor, J. B., & Kriss, M. The cognitive dynamics of salience in the attribution process. *Journal of Personality and Social Psychology,* 1977, *35,* 49–55. (13)

Raiffa, H. Risk, ambiguity and the Savage axioms: Comment. *Quarterly Journal of Economics*, 1961, *75*, 690–694. (35)

Raiffa, H. Assessments of probabilities. Unpublished manuscript, Harvard University, 1969. (22)

Rather, D., & Heskowitz, M. *The camera never blinks.* New York: Ballantine Books, 1977. (12)

Regan, D. T., & Totten, J. Empathy and attribution: Turning observers into actors. *Journal of Personality and Social Psychology*, 1975, *32*, 850–856. (9)

Remus, W. E., & Jenicke, L. O. Unit and random linear models in decision making. *Multivariate Behavioral Research*, 1978, *13*, 215–221. (28)

Rethans, A. *An investigation of consumer perceptions of product hazards.* Doctoral dissertation, University of Oregon, 1979. (33)

Rhoads, J. E. *Textbook of surgery.* Philadelphia: Lippincott, 1969. (18)

Rogers, T. B., Kuiper, N. A., & Kirker, W. S. Self-reference and the encoding of personal information. *Journal of Personality and Social Psychology*, 1977, *35*, 677–688. (12)

Root, H. E. Probability statements in weather forecasting. *Journal of Applied Meteorology*, 1962, *1*, 163–168. (22, 31)

Rosato, F., Thomas, J., & Rosato, E. Operative management of nonpalpable lesions detected by mammography. *Surgery, Gynecology, and Obstetrics*, 1973, *137*, 491–493. (18)

Rosch, E. Cognitive reference points. *Cognitive Psychology*, 1975, *7*, 532–547. (6, 8)

Rosch, E. Principles of categorization. In E. Rosch and B. B. Floyd (Eds.), *Cognition and categorization.* Hillsdale, N.J.: Erlbaum, 1978. (6)

Rosch, E., & Mervis, C. B. Family resemblances: Studies in the internal structure of categories. *Cognitive Psychology*, 1975, *7*, 573–605. (6)

Rosenberg, J. A question of ethics: The DNA controversy. *American Educator*, 1978, *2*, 27–30. (33)

Rosenhan, D. L. On being sane in insane places. *Science*, 1973, *179*, 250–258. (15)

Rosenthal, R., & Jacobson, L. *Pygmalion in the classroom: Teacher expectation and pupils' intellectual development.* New York: Holt, Rinehart & Winston, 1968. (9, 15)

Ross, L. The intuitive psychologist and his shortcomings: Distortions in the attribution process. In L. Berkowitz (Ed.), *Advances in experimental social psychology* (Vol. 10). New York: Academic Press, 1977, 174–177. (8, 9, 13, 15, 19, 30, 32)

Ross, L. Some afterthoughts on the intuitive psychologist. In L. Berkowitz (Ed.), *Cognitive theories in social psychology.* New York: Academic Press, 1978. (15)

Ross, L., Amabile, T. M., & Steinmetz, J. L. Social roles, social control, and biases in social perception processes. *Journal of Personality and Social Psychology*, 1977, *35*, 485–494. (9)

Ross, L., Bierbrauer, G., & Polly, S. Attribution of educational outcomes by professional and non-professional instructors. *Journal of Personality and Social Psychology*, 1974, *29*, 609–618. (9)

Ross, L., Greene, D., & House, P. The false consensus phenomenon: An attributional bias in self perception and social perception processes. *Journal of Experimental Social Psychology*, 1977, *13*, 279–301. (9)

Ross, L., & Lepper, M. R. The perseverance of beliefs: Empirical and normative considerations. In R. A. Shweder (Ed.), *New directions for methodology of behavioral sciences: Fallible judgment in behavioral research.* San Francisco: Jossey-Bass, 1980. (9, 34)

Ross, L., Lepper, M. R., & Hubbard, M. Perseverance in self perception and social perception: Biased attributional processes in the debriefing paradigm. *Journal of Personality and Social Psychology*, 1975, *32*, 880–892. (9, 15)

Ross, L., Lepper, M. R., Strack, F., & Steinmetz, J. L. Social explanation and social expectation: The effects of real and hypothetical explanations upon subjective likelihood. *Journal of Personality and Social Psychology*, 1977, *35*, 817–829. (9, 15)

Ross, M., & Sicoly, F. Egocentric biases in availability and attribution. *Journal of Personality and Social Psychology*, 1979, *37*, 322–336. (13)

Rothbart, M., Fulero, S., Jensen, C., Howard, J., & Birrell, P. From individual to group impressions: Availability heuristics in stereotype formation. *Journal of Experimental Social Psychology*, 1978, *14*, 237–255. (13)

Rothbart, M., & Snyder, M. Confidence in the prediction and postdiction of an uncertain event. *Canadian Journal of Behavioral Science*, 1970, *2*, 38–43. (35)

Rothschild, N. Coming to grips with risk. Address presented on BBC television, November 1978. (Reprinted in the *Wall Street Journal*, May 13, 1979.) (33)

Rumelhart, D. E. Schemata: The building blocks of cognition. In R. Spiro, B. Bruce, and W. Brewer (Eds.), *Theoretical issues in reading comprehension*. Hillsdale, N.J.: Erlbaum, 1979. (34)

Russell, B. *Philosophy*. New York: Norton, 1927. (7)

Russo, J. E. The value of unit price information. *Journal of Marketing Research*, 1977, *14*, 193–201. (19)

Sanders, F. *The evaluation of subjective probability forecasts* (Scientific Report No. 5). Cambridge: Massachusetts Institute of Technology, Department of Meteorology, 1958. (22)

Savage, L. J. *The foundations of statistics*. New York: Wiley, 1954. (1, 25)

Savage, L. J. Elicitation of personal probabilities and expectations. *Journal of the American Statistical Association*, 1971, *66*, 336, 783–801. (22)

Sawyer, J. Measurement *and* prediction, clinical *and* statistical. *Psychological Bulletin*, 1966, *66*, 178–200. (28)

Schachter, S., & Singer, J. E. Cognitive, social, and physiological determinants of emotional state. *Psychological Review*, 1962, *69*, 379–399. (7)

Schaefer, R. E., & Borcherding, K. The assessment of subjective probability distribution: A training experiment. *Acta Psychologica*, 1973, *37*, 117–129. (22, 31)

Schmidt, F. L. The relative efficiency of regression and simple unit predictor weights in applied differential psychology. *Educational and Psychological Measurement*, 1971, *31*, 669–714. (28)

Schoemaker, P. J. H., & Kunreuther, H. C. An experimental study of insurance decisions. *Journal of Risk and Insurance*, 1979, *46*, 603–618. (33)

Schum, D. Current developments in research and cascaded inference processes. In T. Wallsten (Ed.), *Cognitive processes in choice and decision behavior*. Hillsdale, N.J.: Erlbaum, 1980. (19)

Seaver, D. A., von Winterfeldt, D., & Edwards, W. Eliciting subjective probability distributions on continuous variables. *Organizational Behavior and Human Performance*, 1978, *21*, 379–391. (22, 31)

Selvidge, J. *Experimental comparison of different methods for assessing the extremes of probability distributions by the fractile method*. (Management Science Report Series, Report 75-13). Boulder, Colo. Graduate School of Business Administration, University of Colorado, 1975. (22)

Selvidge, J. Assessing the extremes of probability distributions by the fractile method. *Decision Sciences,* 1980, *11,* 493–502. (31)

Shafer, G. *A mathematical theory of evidence.* Princeton, N.J.: Princeton University Press, 1976. (6, 35)

Shapiro, S., Strax, P., & Venet, L. Periodic breast cancer screening. *Archives of Environmental Health,* 1967, *15,* 547–553. (18)

Shapiro, S., Strax, P., & Venet, L. Periodic breast cancer screening in reducing mortality from breast cancer. *Journal of American Medical Association,* 1971, *215,* 1777–1785. (18)

Sheridan, T. B. Human error in nuclear power plants. *Technology Review,* February 1980, 23–33. (33)

Shweder, R. A. (Ed.), *New directions for methodology of behavioral sciences: Fallible judgment in behavioral research.* San Francisco: Jossey-Bass, 1980. (34)

Shweder, R. A., & D'Andrade, R. G. The systematic distortion hypothesis. In R. A. Shweder (Ed.), *Fallible judgment in behavioral research.* San Francisco: Jossey-Bass, 1980. (6)

Sieber, J. E. Effects of decision importance on ability to generate warranted subjective uncertainty. *Journal of Personality and Social Psychology,* 1974, *30,* 688–694. (22, 31)

Siegel, S. *Nonparametric statistics for the behavioral sciences.* New York: McGraw-Hill, 1956. (5)

Siegler, R. S. The origins of scientific reasoning. In R. S. Siegler (Ed.), *Children's thinking: What develops?* Hillsdale, N.J.: Erlbaum, 1979. (19)

Silverman, I. *Motives underlying the behavior of the subject in the psychological experiment.* Paper presented at the meeting of the American Psychological Association, Chicago, September 1965. (9)

Simon, H. *Models of man: Social and rational.* New York: Wiley, 1957. (13)

Simon, H. A. Information-processing theory of human problem solving. In W. K. Estes (Ed.), *Handbook of learning and cognitive processes* (Vol. 5). Hillsdale, N.J.: Erlbaum, 1978. (19)

Simon, H. A., & Chase, W. G. Skill in chess. *American Scientist,* 1973, *61,* 394–403. (28)

Simon, H. A., & Hayes, J. R. The understanding process: Problem isomorphs. *Cognitive Psychology,* 1976, *8,* 165–190. (19)

Simon, H. A., & Newell, A. Human problem solving: The state of the theory in 1970. *American Psychologist,*1971, *26,* 145–159. (19)

Slovic, P. Cue consistency and cue utilization in judgment. *American Journal of Psychology,* 1966, *79,* 427–434. (4)

Slovic, P. From Shakespeare to Simon: Speculations – and some evidence – about man's ability to process information. *Oregon Research Institute Research Bulletin,* 1972, *12*(2). Available from Decision Research, Eugene, Oregon (8, 22) (a)

Slovic, P. Limitations of the mind of man: Implications for decision making in the nuclear age. In H. J. Otway (Ed.), *Risk vs. benefit: Solution or dream?* (Report LA 4860-MS). Los Alamos, N.M.: Los Alamos Scientific Laboratory, 1972. (Available from the National Technical Information Service). (28) (b)

Slovic, P. Psychological study of human judgment: Implications for investment decision making. *Journal of Finance,* 1972, *27,* 779–799. (31, 33) (c)

Slovic, P. Hypothesis testing in the learning of positive and negative linear functions. *Organizational Behavior and Human Performance*, 1974, *11*, 368–376. (23)

Slovic, P., & Fischhoff, B. On the psychology of experimental surprises. *Journal of Experimental Psychology: Human Perception and Performance*, 1977, *3*, 544–551. (23, 31)

Slovic, P., Fischhoff, B., & Lichtenstein, S. Cognitive processes and societal risk taking. In J. S. Carroll & J. W. Payne (Eds.), *Cognition and social behavior*. Hillsdale, N.J.: Erlbaum, 1976. (6, 19, 23)

Slovic, P., Fischhoff, B., & Lichtenstein, S. Behavioral decision theory. *Annual Review of Psychology*, 1977, *28*, 1–39. (8, 19, 34, 35)

Slovic, P., Fischhoff, B., & Lichtenstein, S. Accident probabilities and seat belt usage: A psychological perspective. *Accident Analysis and Prevention*, 1978, *10*, 281–285. (33)

Slovic, P., Fischhoff, B., & Lichtenstein, S. Rating the risks. *Environment*, 1979, *21*(3), 14–20, 36–39. (33)

Slovic, P., Fischhoff, B. & Lichtenstein, S. Facts vs. fears: Understanding perceived risk. In R. Schwing & W. A. Albers, Jr. (Eds.), *Societal risk assessment: How safe is safe enough?* New York: Plenum, 1980. (33)

Slovic, P., Fischhoff, B., & Lichtenstein, S. Characterizing perceived risk. In R. W. Kates & C. Hohenemser (Eds.), *Technological hazard management*. Cambridge, Mass.: Oelgeschlager, Gunn and Hain, in press. (33) (a)

Slovic, P., Fischhoff, B., & Lichtenstein, S. Response mode, framing, and information processing effects in risk assessment. In R. M. Hogarth (Ed.), *New directions for methodology of social and behavioral science: The framing of questions and the consistency of response*. San Francisco: Jossey-Bass, in press. (33) (b)

Slovic, P., Fischhoff, B., Lichtenstein, S., Corrigan, B., & Combs, B. Preference for insuring against probable small losses: Insurance implications. *Journal of Risk and Insurance*, 1977, *44*, 237–258. (33)

Slovic, P., Kunreuther, H., & White, G. F. Decision processes, rationality, and adjustment to natural hazards. In G. F. White (Ed.), *Natural hazards: Local, national, and global*. New York: Oxford University Press, 1974. (33)

Slovic, P., & Lichtenstein, S. Comparison of Bayesian and regression approaches to the study of information processing in judgment. *Organizational Behavior and Human Performance*, 1971, *6*, 649–744. (1, 3, 4, 23, 28)

Slovic, P., Lichtenstein, S., & Fischhoff, B. Images of disaster: Perception and acceptance of risks from nuclear power. In G. T. Goodman & W. D. Rowe (Eds.), *Energy risk management*. London: Academic Press, 1979. (33)

Slovic, P., & Tversky, A. Who accepts Savage's axiom? *Behavioral Science*, 1974, *19*, 368–373. (34)

Smedslund, J. The concept of correlation in adults. *Scandinavian Journal of Psychology*, 1963, *4*, 165–173. (15, 19)

Smedslund, J. Note on learning, contingency, and clinical experience. *Scandinavian Journal of Psychology*, 1966, *7*, 265–266. (11, 19)

Smith, E. E., Shoben, E. J., & Rips, L. J. Structure and process in semantic memory: A featural model for semantic decisions. *Psychological Review*, 1974, *81*, 214–241. (6)

Snapper, K. J., & Fryback, D. G. Inference based on unreliable reports. *Journal of Experimental Psychology*, 1974, *87*, 401–404. (26)

Snyder, M., & Swann, W. B., Jr. When actions reflect attitudes: The politics of impression management. *Journal of Personality and Social Psychology*, 1976, *34*, 1034–1042. (15)

Snyder, M., & Swann, W. B., Jr. Behavioral confirmation in social interaction: From social perception to social reality. *Journal of Experimental Psychology*, 1978, *14*, 148–162. (9) (a)

Snyder, M., & Swann, W. B., Jr. Hypothesis-testing processes in social interaction. *Journal of Personality and Social Psychology*, 1978, *36*, 1202–1212. (9) (b)

Snyder, M., Tanke, E. D., & Berscheid, E. Social perception and interpersonal behavior: On the self-fulfilling nature of social stereotypes. *Journal of Personality and Social Psychology*, 1977, *35*, 656–666. (9, 15)

Snyder, R. E. Mammography: Contributions and limitations in the management of cancer of the breast. *Clinical Obstetrics and Gynecology*, 1966, *9*, 207–220. (18)

Sokolov, E. N. The modeling properties of the nervous system. In I. Maltzman and K. Cole (Eds.), *Handbook of Contemporary Soviet Psychology*, New York: Basic Books, 1969. (35)

Soskin, W. F. Bias in postdiction from projective tests. *Journal of Abnormal and Social Psychology*, 1954, *49*, 69–74. (20)

Sowby, F. D. Radiation and other risks. *Health Physics*, 1965, *11*, 879–887. (33)

Srinivisan, V. *A theoretical comparison of the predictive power of the multiple regression and equal weighting procedures* (Research Paper No. 347). Stanford, Calif.: Stanford University, Graduate School of Business, 1977. (28)

Staddon, J. E. R., & Simmelhag, V. L. The "superstition" experiment: A reexamination of its implications for the principles of adaptive behavior. *Psychological Review*, 1971, *78*, 3–43. (19)

Staël von Holstein, C.-A. S. An experiment in probabilistic weather forecasting. *Journal of Applied Meteorology*, 1971, *10*, 635–645. (22, 31) (a)

Staël von Holstein, C.-A. S. Two techniques for assessment of subjective probability distributions–An experimental study. *Acta Psychologica*, 1971, *35*, 478–494. (1) (b)

Staël von Holstein, C.-A. S. Probabilistic forecasting: An experiment related to the stock market. *Organizational Behavior and Human Performance*, 1972, *8*, 139–158. (31)

Starr, B. J., & Katkin, E. S. The clinician as an aberrant actuary: Illusory correlation and the incomplete sentence blank. *Journal of Abnormal Psychology*, 1969, *74*, 670–675. (15)

Starr, C., & Whipple, C. Risks of risk decisions. *Science*, 1980, *208*, 1114–1119. (33)

Steinbrugge, K. V., McClure, F. E., & Snow, A. J. *Studies in seismicity and earthquake damage statistics* (Report [Appendix A] COM-71-00053). Washington, D.C.: U.S. Department of Commerce, 1969. (33)

Stevens, S. S., & Greenbaum, H. B. Regression effect in psychophysical judgment. *Perception and Psychophysics*, 1966, *1*, 439–446. (4)

Storms, M. D. Videotape and the attribution process: Reversing actors' and observers' points of view. *Journal of Personality and Social Psychology*, 1973, *27*, 165–175. (9, 12)

Storms, M. D., & Nisbett, R. E. Insomnia and the attribution process. *Journal of Personality and Social Psychology*, 1970, *16*, 319–328. (7)

Strachey, L. *Eminent Victorians*. New York: Putnam, 1918. (23)

Strickland, L. H. Surveillance and trust. *Journal of Personality*, 1958, *26*, 200–215. (9)

Strickland, L. H., Lewicki, R. J., & Katz, A. M. Temporal orientation and perceived control as determinants of risk-taking. *Journal of Experimental Social Psychology*, 1966, *2*, 143–151. (16)

Svenson, O. Are we all less risky and more skillful than our fellow drivers? *Acta Psychologica*, 1981, *47*, 143–148. (33)

Swets, J. A., Tanner, W. P., Jr., & Birdsall, T. Decision processes in perception. *Psychological Review*, 1961, *68*, 301–340. (22)

Taft, R. The ability to judge people. *Psychological Bulletin*, 1955, *52*, 1–23. (20)

Tawney, R. H. *The agrarian problems in the sixteenth century.* New York: Franklin, 1961. (23)

Taylor, H. C., & Russell, J. T. The relationship of validity coefficients to the practical effectiveness of tests in selection: Discussion and tables. *Journal of Applied Psychology*, 1939, *23*, 565–578, (19)

Taylor, S. E., & Crocker, J. *The processing of context information in person perception.* Unpublished manuscript, Harvard University, 1979. (34) (a)

Taylor, S. E., & Crocker, J. Schematic bases of social information processing. In E. T. Higgins, P. Herman, & M. P. Zanna (Eds.), *The Ontario Symposium on Personality and Social Psychology* (Vol. 1). Hillsdale, N.J.: Erlbaum, 1979. (13) (b)

Taylor, S. E., & Fiske, S. T. Point of view and perceptions of causality. *Journal of Personality and Social Psychology*, 1975, *32*, 439–445. (9, 12, 13)

Taylor, S. E., & Fiske, S. T. Salience, attention, and attribution: Top of the head phenomena. In L. Berkowitz (Ed.), *Advances in experimental social psychology* (Vol. 11). New York: Academic Press, 1978. (9)

Taylor, S. E., Fiske, S. T., Close, M., Anderson, D., & Ruderman, A. *Solo status as a psychological variable: The power of being distinctive.* Unpublished manuscript, Harvard University, 1976. (9, 13)

Taylor, S. E., Fiske, S. T., Etcoff, N., & Ruderman, A. The categorical and contextual bases of person memory and stereotyping. *Journal of Personality and Social Psychology*, 1978, *36*, 778–793. (13)

Taynor, J., & Deaux, K. When women are more deserving than men: Equity, attribution, and perceived sex differences. *Journal of Personality and Social Psychology*, 1973, *28*, 360–367. (15)

Testa, T. J. Causal relationships and the acquisition of avoidance responses. *Psychological Review*, 1974, *81*, 491–505. (15)

Thibaut, J. W., & Riecken, H. W. Some determinants and consequences of the perception of social causality. *Journal of Personality*, 1955, *24*, 113–133. (9)

Thornton, B. Linear prediction of marital happiness: A replication. *Personality and Social Psychology Bulletin*, 1977, *3*, 674–676. (28) (a)

Thornton, B. Personal communication, 1977. (28) (b)

Tufte, E. R., & Sun, R. A. Are there bellwether electoral districts? *Public Opinion Quarterly*, 1975, *39*, 1–18. (23)

Tukey, J. W. Some thoughts on clinical trials, especially problems of multiplicity. *Science*, 1977, *198*, 679–690. (23)

Tulving, E., & Pearlstone, Z. Availability versus accessibility of information in memory for words. *Journal of Verbal Learning and Verbal Behavior*, 1966, *5*, 381–391. (11)

Tune, G. S. Response preferences: A review of some relevant literature. *Psychological Bulletin*, 1964, *61*, 286–302. (2, 3)

Turoff, M. An alternative approach to cross-impact analysis. *Technological Forecasting and Social Change*, 1972, *3*, 309–339. (8)

Tversky, A. Intransitivity of preferences. *Psychological Review*, 1969, *76*, 31–48. (19)

Tversky, A. Features of similarity. *Psychological Review*, 1977, *84*, 327–352. (6, 8)

Tversky, A., & Kahneman, D. The belief in the "law of small numbers." *Psychological Bulletin*, 1971, *76*, 105–110. (1, 3, 4, 6, 7, 23, 34)

Tversky, A., & Kahneman, D. Availability: A heuristic for judging frequency and probability. *Cognitive Psychology*, 1973, *5*, 207–232. (1, 4, 9, 12, 13, 14, 23, 30, 33)

Tversky, A., & Kahneman, D. Judgment under uncertainty: Heuristics and biases. *Science*, 1974, *185*, 1124–1131. (6, 8, 13, 19, 22, 27, 28, 30, 31, 33, 34, 35)

Tversky, A., & Kahneman, D. Causal schemas in judgments under uncertainty. In M. Fishbein (Ed.), *Progress in social psychology*. Hillsdale, N.J.: Erlbaum, 1980. (6, 10, 19, 30)

Tversky, A., & Kahneman, D. The framing of decisions and the rationality of choice. *Science*, 1981, *211*, 453–458. (33, 34)

U.S. House of Representatives. *Browns Ferry nuclear plant fire: Hearing*. 94th Congress, 1st Session. Washington, D.C.: U.S. Government Printing Office, September 16, 1975. (33)

U.S. Nuclear Regulatory Commission. *Reactor safety study: An assessment of accident risks in U.S. commercial nuclear power plants* (WASH 1400 [NUREG-75/014]). Washington, D.C.: NRC, 1975. (22, 23, 33)

U.S. Nuclear Regulatory Commission. *Risk assessment review group report to the U.S. Nuclear Regulatory Commission* (NUREG/CR-0400). Washington, D.C.: NRC, 1978. (33)

U.S. Weather Bureau. *Report on weather bureau forecast performance 1967–8 and comparison with previous years* (Tech. Memorandum WBTM FCST, *11*), Silver Spring, Md.: Office of Meteorological Operations, Weather Analysis and Prediction Division, March 1969. (22)

Valins, S. Persistent effects of information about internal reactions: Ineffectiveness of debriefing. In H. London & R. E. Nisbett (Eds.), *Thought and feeling: Cognitive modification of feeling states*. Chicago: Aldine, 1974. (9)

Vitz, P. C., & Todd, D. C. A coded element model of the perceptual processing of sequential stimuli. *Psychological Review*, 1969, *76*, 433–449. (3)

Von Winterfeldt, D., & Edwards, W. *Flat maxima in linear optimization models* (Tech. Rep. 011313-4-T). Ann Arbor: University of Michigan, Engineering Psychology Laboratory, 1973. (22, 28)

Wagenaar, W. A. Subjective randomness and the capacity to generate information. In A. F. Sanders (Ed.), *Attention and Performance, III, Acta Psychologica*, 1970, *33*, 233–242. (3)

Wainer, H. Estimating coefficients in linear models: It don't make no nevermind. *Psychological Bulletin*, 1976, *83*, 312–317. (28)

Wainer, H., & Thissen, D. Three steps toward robust regression. *Psychometrika*, 1976, *41*, 9–34. (28)

Wallace, H. A. What is the corn judge's mind? *Journal of the American Society of Agronomy*, 1923, *15*, 300–304. (28)

Wallach, M. A., & Wing, C. W. Is risk a value? *Journal of Personality and Social Psychology*, 1968, *9*, 101–106. (16)

Wallis, W. A., & Roberts, H. V. *Statistics: A new approach*. New York: Free Press, 1956. (4)

Wallsten, T. Processes and models to describe choice and inference. In T. Wallsten (Ed.), *Cognitive processes in choice and behavior*. Hillsdale, N.J.: Erlbaum, 1980. (19)

Wallsten, T. S., & Budescu, D. F. *Encoding subjective probabilities: A psychological and psychometric review.* Research Triangle Park, N.C.: U.S. Environmental Protection Agency, Strategies and Air Standards Division, 1980. (31)

Walster, E., Berscheid, E., Abrahams, D., & Aronson, E. Effectiveness of debriefing following deception experiments. *Journal of Personality and Social Psychology,* 1967, *6,* 371–380. (9)

Ward, W. C., & Jenkins, H. M. The display of information and the judgment of contingency. *Canadian Journal of Psychology,* 1965, *19,* 231–241. (11, 15, 19)

Warren, R. M. Perceptual restoration of missing speech sounds. *Science,* 1970, *167,* 393–395. (35)

Wason, P. C. On the failure to eliminate hypotheses in a conceptual task. *Quarterly Journal of Experimental Psychology,* 1960, *12,* 129–140. (19)

Wason, P. C. Reasoning. In B. Foss (Ed.), *New horizons in psychology.* Middlesex, England: Penguin, 1966. (34)

Wason, P. C. Regression in reasoning? *British Journal of Psychology,* 1969, *60,* 471–480. (34)

Wason, P. C., & Evans, J. St. B. T. Dual processes in reasoning? *Cognition,* 1975, *3,* 141–154. (34)

Wason, P. C., & Johnson-Laird, P. N. A conflict between selecting and evaluating information in an inferential task. *British Journal of Psychology,* 1970, *61,* 509–515. (34)

Wason, P. C., & Johnson-Laird, P. N. *Psychology of reasoning: Structure and Content.* London: Batsford, 1972. (6, 9)

Wason P. C., & Shapiro, D. Natural and contrived experience in a reasoning problem. *Quarterly Journal of Experimental Psychology,* 1971, *23,* 63–71. (34)

Weatherwax, R. K. Virtues and limitations of risk analysis. *Bulletin of the Atomic Scientists,* 1975, *31,* 29–32. (22)

Weiner, B. *Achievement motivation and attribution theory.* Morristown, N.J.: General Learning Press, 1974. (9, 15)

Weiner, B., Frieze, I., Kukla, A., Reed, L., Rest, S., & Rosenbaum, R. *Perceiving the causes of success and failure.* Morristown, N.J.: General Learning Press, 1971. (7)

Weinstein, N. D. Unrealistic optimism about future life events. *Journal of Personality and Social Psychology,* 1980, *39,* 806–820. (33)

Wells, G. L., & Harvey, J. H. Do people use consensus information in making causal attributions? *Journal of Personality and Social Psychology,* 1977, *35,* 279–293. (10)

Wells, G. L., & Harvey, J. H. Naive attributors' attributions and predictions: What is informative and when is an effect an effect? *Journal of Personality and Social Psychology,* 1978, *36,* 483–490. (10)

Wessman, A. E., & Ricks, D. F. *Mood and personality.* New York: Holt, Rinehart & Winston, 1966. (7)

Wheeler, G., & Beach, L. R. Subjective sampling distributions and conservatism. *Organizational Behavior and Human Performance,* 1968, *3,* 36–46. (3)

Wheeler, W. M. An analysis of Rorschach indices of male homosexuality. *Rorschach Research Exchange,* 1949, *13,* 97–126. (17)

White, R. W. *Lives in progress: A study of the natural growth of personality.* New York: Dryden Press, 1952. (20)

White, R. W. Motivation reconsidered: The concept of competence. *Psychological Review,* 1959, *66,* 297–333. (12, 16)

Wicklund, R. A. Objective self-awareness. In L. Berkowitz (Ed.), *Advances in experimental social psychology* (Vol. 9). New York: Academic Press, 1975. (9)

Wiggins, N., & Kohen, E. S. Man vs. model of man revisited: The forecasting of graduate school success. *Journal of Personality and Social Psychology*, 1971, *19*, 100–106. (28)

Wilks, S. S. Weighting systems for linear functions of correlated variables when there is no dependent variable. *Psychometrika*, 1938, *8*, 23–40. (23, 28)

Williams, P. The use of confidence factors in forecasting. *Bulletin of the American Meteorological Society*, 1951, *32*, 279–281. (22)

Wilson, R. Analyzing the daily risks of life. *Technology Review*, 1979, *81*, 40–46. (33)

Winch, R. F., & More, D. M. Does TAT add information to interviews? Statistical analysis of the increment. *Journal of Clinical Psychology*, 1956, *12*, 316–321. (20)

Winkler, R. L. The assessment of prior distributions in Bayesian analysis. *Journal of the American Statistical Association*, 1967, *62*, 776–800. (31)

Winkler, R. L., & Murphy, A. H. Evaluation of subjective precipitation probability forecasts. In *Proceedings of the First National Conference on Statistical Meteorology, Hartford, Conn., May 27–29*. Boston: American Meteorological Society, 1968. (22) (a)

Winkler, R. L., & Murphy, A. H. "Good" probability assessors. *Journal of Applied Meteorology*, 1968, *7*, 751–758. (22) (b)

Wohlstetter, R. *Pearl Harbor: Warning and decision*. Stanford, Calif.: Stanford University Press, 1962. (23, 31)

Wolfe, J. N. Mammography: Report on its use in women with breasts abnormal and normal on physical examination. *Radiology*, 1964, *83*, 244–254. (18)

Wolfe, J. N. Mammography: Errors in diagnosis. *Radiology*, 1966, *87*, 214–219. (18)

Wolfe, J. N. *Mammography* (2nd ed.). Springfield, Ill.: Charles C Thomas, 1967. (18)

Wolosin, R. J., Sherman, S. J., & Till, A. Effects of cooperation and competition on responsibility attribution after success and failure. *Journal of Experimental Social Psychology*, 1973, *9*, 220–235. (9)

Wood, G. The knew-it-all-along effect. *Journal of Experimental Psychology: Human Perception and Performance*, 1978, *4*, 345–353. (31)

Woodworth, R. S. *Experimental psychology*. New York: Holt, 1938. (4)

Wright, G. N., & Phillips, L. D. *Personality and probabilistic thinking: An experimental study* (Tech. Rep. 76-3). Uxbridge, England: Brunel Institute of Organisational and Social Studies, 1976. (22)

Wright, G. N., Phillips, L. D., Whalley, P. C., Choo, G. T. G., Ng, K. O., Tan, I., & Wisudha, A. Cultural differences in probabilistic thinking. *Journal of Cross-cultural Psychology*, 1978, *9*, 285–299. (22)

Wright, G. N., & Wisudha, A. *Differences in calibration for past and future events*. Paper presented at the 7th Research Conference on Subjective Probability, Utility and Decision-Making, Göteborg, Sweden, August 1979. (22)

Yarrow, M., Campbell, J. D., & Burton, R. V. Recollections of childhood: A study of the retrospective method. *Monographs of the Society for Research in Child Development*, 1970, *35*(5). (23)

Yntema, D. B., & Torgerson, W. S. Man-computer cooperation in decisions requiring common sense. *IRE Transactions of the Professional Group on Human Factors in Electronics*, 1961, *2*(1), 20–26. (28)

Zadeh, L. A. Fuzzy sets as a basis for a theory of possibility. *Fuzzy Set and Systems I*, 1978, 3–28. (6)

Index